BIOGRAPHICAL DICTIONARY
OF BRITISH RADICALS IN THE SEVENTEENTH CENTURY
Volume III: P-Z

Biographical Dictionary of British Radicals in the Seventeenth Century

VOLUME III: P-Z

Edited by

RICHARD L. GREAVES

Professor of History, Florida State University

and

ROBERT ZALLER

Professor of History, University of Miami

THE HARVESTER PRESS

First published in Great Britain in 1984 by
THE HARVESTER PRESS LIMITED
Publisher: John Spiers
16 Ship Street, Brighton, Sussex

British Library Cataloguing in Publication Data

The Biographical dictionary of British radicals
   in the Seventeenth century
   Vol.3
   1. Radicals – Great Britain – Biography
   I. Greaves, Richard L.   II. Zaller, Robert
320.941'092'4   HN400.R3

   ISBN 0-7108-0486-5

Phototypeset in Great Britain by
C. Leggett & Son Ltd., Mitcham, Surrey
on Linotype-Paul VIP in 9pt Times
and printed by Whitstable Litho Ltd.,
Whitstable, Kent

CONTENTS

LIST OF CONTRIBUTORS

ANDERSON, GEORGE L.
University of Hawaii, Manoa
ANDRIETTE, EUGENE A.
University of Louisville
ASHCRAFT, RICHARD
University of California, Los Angeles
ASHTON, ROBERT
School of English and American Studies, University of East Anglia
BAN, JOSEPH D.
McMaster Divinity School
BARBOUR, HUGH
Earlham College
BARNARD, TOBY
Hertford College, Oxford
BARROWS, FLOYD D.
Michigan State University
BATTICK, JOHN F.
University of Maine, Orono
BERKOWITZ, DAVID S.
Brandeis University
BERLATSKY, JOEL
Wilkes College
BETTERIDGE, ALAN
British and Foreign Bible Society
BIDDLE, JOHN C.
Divinity School, Yale University
BIDWELL, WILLIAM B.
Center for Parliamentary History, Yale University
BITTLE, WILLIAM G.
Kent State University
BLEDSOE, WAYNE M.
University of Missouri, Rolla
BLETHEN, H. TYLER
Western Carolina University
BOYER, RICHARD E.
University of Toledo

BRACHLOW, STEPHEN J.
North American Baptist Seminary
BRAUER, JERALD C.
Divinity School, University of Chicago
BREWARD, IAN
Knox College, University of Otago, New Zealand
BROWN, JEROME F.
New Mexico State University
BROWN, MICHAEL J.
Agnes Scott College
BURG, B. RICHARD
Arizona State University
BURNS, NORMAN T.
State University of New York, Binghampton
BUSCH, ALLAN J.
Fort Hays Kansas State College
CAPP, BERNARD S.
University of Warwick
CARLTON, CHARLES H.
North Carolina State University
CARR, F. BENJAMIN
Addison, Maine, formerly of Mount Holyoke College
CARROLL, KENNETH
Southern Methodist University
CASADA, JAMES A.
Winthrop College
CHARLTON, KENNETH
King's College, University of London
CLARK, DAVID L.
Hope College
CLARK, PETER
University of Leicester
CLOUSE, ROBERT G.
Indiana State University
COAKLEY, THOMAS M.
Miami University, Ohio
COHEN, ALFRED
Trenton State College
COLE, MAIJA
Center for Parliamentary History, Yale University
COLLINS, NAOMI F.
Congressional Research Service, Library of Congress
COPE, ESTHER S.
University of Nebraska

CRAWFORD, PATRICIA
University of Western Australia
DANNER, DAN G.
University of Portland
DEBUS, ALLEN G.
Morris Fishbein Center for the Study of the History of Science and Medicine, University of Chicago
DICKINSON, W. CALVIN
Tennessee Technological University
DRAKE, GEORGE A.
Colorado College
EAVES, RICHARD G.
Auburn University
ELTON, GEOFFREY R.
Clare College, Cambridge
ENDY, MELVIN B., JR.
Hamilton College
ENGSTROM, HUGH R.
Bethany College
FIALA, ROBERT D.
Concordia College, Nebraska
FISK, WILLIAM L.
Muskingum College
FLEMION, JESSE S.
San Diego State University
FROST, J. WILLIAM
Friends Historical Library, Swarthmore College
GALGANO, MICHAEL J.
Marshall University
GIBSON, RICHARD M.
Department of Health, Education and Welfare, Akron, Ohio
GIMELFARB-BRACK, MARIE
Lausanne, Switzerland
GOLDWATER, ELLEN D.
Rowayton, Connecticut
GOTTDIENER, RUTH H.
Douglass College, Rutgers University
GREAVES, RICHARD L.
Florida State University
GREENBERG, JANELLE
University of Pittsburgh
GREENE, DOUGLAS G.
Old Dominion University
GRUENFELDER, JOHN K.
University of Wyoming

HALEY, K.H.D.
University of Sheffield
HANFT, SHELDON
Appalachian State University
HANNEN, ROBERT B., deceased
Central Baptist Theological Seminary
HARDACRE, PAUL H.
Vanderbilt University
HARRIS, BARBARA J.
Pace University
HARTMAN, MARILYN A.
Indiana University
HARVEY, RICHARD
Ohio University
HAWKINS, MICHAEL J.
School of English and American Studies,
University of Sussex
HAYES, T. WILSON
Baruch College, City University of New York
HILL, LAMAR M.
University of California, Irvine
HOLLIS, DANIEL W., III
Jacksonville State University
HOLSINGER, J. CALVIN
Evangel College
HOLZENBERG, PHYLLIS
Florida State University
HORLE, CRAIG W.
University of Maryland Overseas Program, and
Friends House Library, London
HOWELL, ROGER, JR.
Bowdoin College
JACOB, JAMES R.
John Jay College of Criminal Justice, City University of New York
JACOB, MARGARET C.
Baruch College, City University of New York
JOHNSON, WILLIAM
Southern Baptist Theological Seminary
JONES R. TUDUR
Coleg Bala-Bangor, Wales
JURETIC, GEORGE
Deparment of Education, State of Illinois
KAPLAN, LAWRENCE
City College, City University of New York

KNAFLA, LOUIS A.
University of Calgary
KYLE, RICHARD G.
Tabor College
LAMONT, WILLIAM M.
University of Sussex
LANDON, MICHAEL DE L.
University of Mississippi
LEE, PATRICIA-ANN
Skidmore College
LEHMBERG, STANFORD E.
University of Minnesota, Minneapolis
LEMOS, RAMON M.
University of Miami, Florida
LEVACK, BRIAN P.
University of Texas
LINDLEY, KEITH J.
New University of Ulster
LIU, TAI
University of Delaware
LUDLOW, DOROTHY
Indiana University
LUTAUD, OLIVIER
L'Université de Paris – Sorbonne
MACAULEY, JOHN S.
University of Kansas
MACCAFFREY, WALLACE T.
Harvard University
MACDONALD, WILLIAM W.
Lamar University
MCFARLAND, RONALD E.
University of Idaho
MCGEE, J. SEARS
University of California, Santa Barbara
MCGREGOR, J. FRANK
University of Adelaide
MACLEAR, JAMES F.
University of Minnesota, Duluth
MASEK, ROSEMARY
University of Nevada, Las Vegas
MAXWELL, MICHAEL P.
McGill University
MENDLE, MICHAEL J.
University of Alabama

MIKLOVICH, JAMES I.
University of West Florida
MOCK, DAVID
Florida State University
MOIR, THOMAS L.
Mankato State College
MORE, ELLEN
University of Rochester
MORGAN, IRVONWY
The London Committee, the Methodist Church
MORRILL, JOHN S.
Selwyn College, Cambridge
MORTON, A.L.
Clare, Suffolk
MULLETT, MICHAEL
Furness College, University of Lancaster
MULLIGAN, LOTTE
La Trobe University, Australia
NENNER, HOWARD A.
Smith College
NEVILLE, JOHN D.
Colonial Records Project, Virginia State Library
NEW, JOHN F.
University of Waterloo
PAGANO, ELISA R.
University of Missouri, Columbia
PAINTER, BORDEN W., JR.
Trinity College, Connecticut
PATTERSON, W. BROWN
University of the South
PAUL, ROBERT S.
Austin Presbyterian Theological Seminary
PECK, LINDA L.
Purdue University
PENNINGTON, DONALD H.
Balliol College, Oxford
POCOCK, J.G.A.
Johns Hopkins University
POLIZZOTTO, CAROLYN
University of Western Australia
POPOFSKY, LINDA
Mills College
PREST, WILFRID R.
University of Adelaide

RABB, THEODORE K.
Princeton University
REAY, BARRY G.
Adelaide, South Australia
ROOTS, IVAN A.
University of Exeter
RYNDER, CONSTANCE B.
University of Tampa
SACHSE, WILLIAM L.
University of Wisconsin, Madison
SCHLATTER, RICHARD
Rutgers University
SCHNUCKER, ROBERT V.
Northeast Missouri State University
SCHWARZ, MARC L.
University of New Hampshire
SEAVER, PAUL S.
Stanford University
SHARROCK, ROGER
King's College, University of London
SHIMP, ROBERT E.
Ohio Wesleyan University
SHIPPS, KENNETH W.
Trinity College, Illinois
SMITH, STEVEN R.
Savannah State College
SNOW, VERNON F.
University of Syracuse
SOLT, LEO F.
Indiana University
SOMMERVILLE, C. JOHN
University of Florida
SPALDING, JAMES C.
University of Iowa
SPRUNGER, KEITH L.
Bethel College, Kansas
SPUFFORD, MARGARET
University of Keele
SPURGEON, JONATHAN W.
University of Oklahoma
STEARNS, S.J.
College of Staten Island, City University of New York
TAFT, BARBARA
Washington, D.C.

TEMPLE, ROBERT K.G.
Sutton Mallet, Bridgwater, Somerset
TITTLER, ROBERT
Concordia University, Montreal
UNDERWOOD, TED L.
University of Minnesota, Morris
VANDERMOLEN, RONALD J.
California State College, Stanislaus
VOLKMAN, PAMELA
University of Rochester
WALLACE, DEWEY D., JR.
George Washington University
WEBER, BERNERD C.
University of Alabama
WESTON, CORINNE C.
Herbert H. Lehman College, City University of New York
WHITE, BARRINGTON R.
Regent's Park College, Oxford
WILLEN, DIANE
Georgia State University
WOOD, CURTIS W., JR.
Western Carolina University
WOODS, ROBERT
Pomona College
WOOLRYCH, AUSTIN H.
Furness College, University of Lancaster
YULE, GEORGE
King's College, University of Aberdeen
ZALLER, ROBERT
University of Miami, Florida

BIBLIOGRAPHY ABBREVIATIONS

Abbott	W.C. Abbott, ed., *The Writings and Speeches of Oliver Cromwell*, 4 vols. (1937-47)
Add. MSS	Additional Manuscripts, British Library
AHR	*American Historical Review*
Al. Cant.	J. Venn and J.A. Venn, comps., *Alumni Cantabrigienses*, 4 vols. (1922-27)
Al. Oxon.	J. Foster, ed., *Alumni Oxonienses*, 4 vols. (1891-92)
ARPB	B.R. White, ed., *Association Records of the Particular Baptists of England, Wales and Ireland to 1660*, 3 parts (1971-74)
Ashley, *CG*	M.P. Ashley, *Cromwell's Generals* (1954)
Ashley, *JW*	M.P. Ashley, *John Wildman* (1947)
Ath. Oxon.	A. Wood, *Athenae Oxonienses, an Exact History*, ed. P. Bliss, 4 vols. (1813-20)
Aubrey	J. Aubrey, *Brief Lives*, ed. A. Clark, 2 vols. (1898)
Aylmer, *Int.*	G.E. Aylmer, ed., *The Interregnum* (1972)
Aylmer, *KS*	G.E. Aylmer, *The King's Servants* (1961)
Aylmer, *SS*	G.E. Aylmer, *The State's Servants* (1973)
B. & P.	D. Brunton and D.H. Pennington, *Members of the Long Parliament* (1954)
Barnard	T. Barnard, *Cromwellian Ireland* (1975)
Barnes	T.G. Barnes, *Somerset, 1625-1640* (1961)
Barbour, *QPE*	H. Barbour, *The Quakers in Puritan England* (1964)
Bates Harbin	S.W. Bates Harbin, 'Members of Parliament for the County of Somerset,' *Somersetshire Archeological and Natural History Society Proceedings*, 83 (1939)
Bayley	A.R. Bayley, *The Great Civil War in Dorset, 1643-1660* (1910)
Bean	W.W. Bean, *The Parliamentary Representation of the Six Northern Counties of England* (1890)
Beaven	A.B. Beaven, *The Aldermen of the City of London*, 2 vols. (1908-13)
Besse	J. Besse, *A Collection of the Sufferings of the People Called Quakers*, 2 vols. (1753)
BIHR	*Bulletin of the Institute of Historical Research*
Bowyer	R. Bowyer, *The Parliamentary Diary of Robert Bowyer, 1606-1607*, ed. D.H. Willson (1931)
BQ	*Baptist Quarterly*
Brailsford	H.N. Brailsford, *The Levellers and the English Revolution*, ed. C. Hill (1961)

Braithwaite, *BQu*   W.C. Braithwaite, *The Beginnings of Quakerism*, 2nd ed., rev. by H.J. Cadbury (1955)

Braithwaite, *SP*   W.C. Braithwaite, *The Second Period of Quakerism*, 2nd ed., rev. by H.J. Cadbury (1961)

Brook   B. Brook, *The Lives of the Puritans*, 3 vols. (1813)

Brown   L.F. Brown, *The Political Activities of the Baptists and Fifth Monarchy Men in England During the Interregnum* (1912)

Burnet   G. Burnet, *History of My Own Time*, 6 vols. (1833)

Burrage   C. Burrage, *The Early English Dissenters in the Light of Recent Research (1550-1641)*, 2 vols. (1912)

Burton   J.T. Rutt, ed., *Diary of Thomas Burton, Esquire*, 4 vols. (1828)

Cadbury   H.J. Cadbury, *Narrative Papers of George Fox* (1972)

Calamy   E. Calamy, *Abridgement of Mr. Baxter's History of His Life and Times, with a Particular Account of the Ministers . . . Ejected after the Restauration*, 2 vols. (1713)

Calamy Revised   A.G. Matthews, *Calamy Revised* (1934)

Capp, *APP*   B.S. Capp, *Astrology and the Popular Press* (1979)

Capp, *FMM*   B.S. Capp, *The Fifth Monarchy Men* (1972)

Carlyle   T. Carlyle, ed., *Oliver Cromwell's Letters and Speeches*, rev. S.C. Lomas, 3 vols. (1904)

CCAM   M.A.E. Green, ed., *Calendar of the Proceedings of the Committee for Advance of Money*, 3 vols. (1888)

CCC   M.A.E. Green, ed., *Calendar of the Proceedings of the Committee for Compounding, 1643-60*, 5 vols. (1889-92)

CCSP   O. Ogle, W.H. Bliss and W.D. Macray, eds., *Calendar of the Clarendon State Papers*, 3 vols. (1869-76); F.J. Routledge, ed., vol. 4 (1932)

CD 1610   S.R. Gardiner, ed., *Parliamentary Debates in 1610 . . . from the Notes of the House of Commons*, Camden Society (1862)

CD 1621   W. Notestein, F. Relf, and H. Simpson, eds., *Commons Debates 1621*, 7 vols. (1935)

CD 1625   S.R. Gardiner, ed., *Debates in the House of Commons in 1625*, Camden Society, (1873)

CD 1628   R.C. Johnson, M.F. Keeler, M.J. Cole and W.B. Bidwell, *Commons Debates 1628* (1977)

CD 1629   W. Notestein and F. Relf, eds., *Commons' Debates for 1629* (1921)

CH   *Church History*

Chamberlain   N.E. McClure, ed., *The Letters of John Chamberlain*, 2 vols. (1939)

Chet. Soc., O.S.   *Chetham Society, Old Series. Remains Historical and Literary*

Christianson	P. Christianson, *Reformers and Babylon* (1978)
CJ	*Journals of the House of Commons 1547-1714*, 17 vols. (1742 ff.)
Clarendon	E. Hyde, Earl of Clarendon, *The History of the Rebellion and Civil Wars in England*, ed. W.D.Macray, 6 vols. (1888)
Clarke Papers	C.H. Firth, ed., *Clarke Papers*, 4 vols., Camden Society (1891-1901)
Cliffe	J. Cliffe, *The Yorkshire Gentry from the Reformation to the Eve of the Civil War* (1969)
CMHS	*Collections of the Massachusetts Historical Society*
Coate	M. Coate, *Cornwall in the Great Civil War and Interregnum, 1642-1660* (1933)
Cobbett	W. Cobbett, ed., *The Parliamentary History of England*, vols. 1-6 (1806-10; repr. 1966)
Cohn	N. Cohn, *The Pursuit of the Millennium* (1957)
Cokayne, *CB*	G.E. Cokayne, *Complete Baronetage*, 6 vols. (1900-9)
Cokayne, *CP*	G.E. Cokayne, *Complete Peerage of England, Scotland, Ireland, Great Britain and the United Kingdom*, rev. by V. Gibbs, H.A. Doubleday *et al.*, 14 vols. (1910-59)
Crosby	T. Crosby, ed., *The History of the English Baptists*, 4 vols. (1738-40)
CSPC	*Calendar of State Papers, Colonial Series* (America and the West Indies)
CSPD	*Calendar of State Papers, Domestic Series, 1603-1714*
CSPI	*Calendar of State Papers Relating to Ireland*
DAB	A. Johnson and D. Malone, eds., *Dictionary of American Biography*, 20 vols. (1928-36)
Davids	T.W. Davids, *Annals of Evangelical Nonconformity in the County of Essex* (1863)
Davies, *RC*	G. Davies, *The Restoration of Charles II, 1658-1660* (1955)
D'Ewes, *Jour.* (C)	W.H. Coates, ed., *The Journal of Sir Simonds D'Ewes* (1942)
D'Ewes, *Jour.* (N)	W. Notestein, ed., *The Journal of Sir Simonds D'Ewes* (1923)
DNB	L. Stephen and S. Lee, eds., *Dictionary of National Biography*, 63 vols. (1885-1900)
Dodd	A.H. Dodd, *Studies in Stuart Wales* (1971)
Dow	F.D. Dow, *Cromwellian Scotland* (1979)
DQB	W.B. Evans, ed., 'Dictionary of Quaker Biography,' Haverford College Library and Friends House, London
Dunlop	R. Dunlop, *Ireland Under the Commonwealth*, 2 vols. (1913)
DWB	J.E. Lloyd and R.T. Jenkins, eds., *The Dictionary of Welsh Biography* (1959)

Earle	P. Earle, *Monmouth's Rebels* (1977)
Eg. MSS	Egerton Manuscripts, British Library
EHR	*English Historical Review*
Ellis	P.B. Ellis, *Hell or Connaught!* (1975)
EQL	G.F. Nuttall, ed., *Early Quaker Letters from the Swarthmore MSS. to 1660* (1952)
EQW	H. Barbour and A.O. Roberts, *Early Quaker Writings 1650-1700* (1973)
Everitt	A.M. Everitt, *The Community of Kent and the Great Rebellion* (1966)
Fairfax Corr.	G.W. Johnson, ed., *The Fairfax Correspondence* (1848)
Fasti Oxon.	A. Wood, *Fasti Oxonienses, ad. cal. Athenae Oxonienses*, ed. P. Bliss, 4 vols. (1813-20)
Firth & Davies	C.H. Firth and G. Davies, *The Regimental History of Cromwell's Army*, 2 vols. (1940)
Firth & Rait	C.H. Firth and R.S. Rait, eds., *Acts and Ordinances of the Interregnum 1642-1660*, 3 vols. (1911)
Firth, *LYP*	C.H. Firth, *The Last Years of the Protectorate*, 2 vols. (1909)
Fletcher	A. Fletcher, *A County Community in Peace and War: Sussex 1600-1660* (1975)
Fortescue	G.K. Fortescue, ed., *Catalogue of the Pamphlets . . . Collected by George Thomason, 1640-1661*, 2 vols. (1908)
Foster	S. Foster, *Notes from the Caroline Underground* (1978)
Fox, *CJ*	N. Penney, ed., *The Journal of George Fox,* 2 vols. (1911)
Fox, *SJ*	N. Penney, ed., *Short Journal and Itinerary Journals of George Fox* (1925)
FPT	N. Penney, ed., '*The First Publishers of Truth*' (1907)
Frank	J. Frank, *The Levellers* (1955)
Gangraena	T. Edwards, *Gangraena or a Catalogue and Discovery of Many of the Errours, Heresies, Blasphemies and Pernicious Practices*, 3 parts in 1 vol. (1646)
Gardiner2, *FDW*	S.R. Gardiner and C.T. Atkinson, *Letters and Papers Relating to the First Dutch War, 1652-1654*, 5 vols. (1898-1912); vol. 6, ed. Atkinson (1930)
Gardiner, *GCW*	S.R. Gardiner, *History of the Great Civil War, 1642-9*, rev. ed., 4 vols. (1893)
Gardiner, *HCP*	S.R. Gardiner, *History of the Commonwealth and Protectorate*, rev. ed., 4 vols. (1903)
Gardiner, *HE*	S.R. Gardiner, *History of England from the Accession of James I to the Outbreak of the Civil War, 1603-42*, rev. ed., 10 vols. (1883-84)
Glass	H.A. Glass, *The Barebone Parliament and the*

	Religious Movements of the Seventeenth Century (1899)
Godwin	G.N. Godwin, *The Civil War in Hampshire,* 2nd ed. (1904)
Gooder	A. Gooder, *The Parliamentary Representation of the County of York, Yorkshire Archaeological Society Record Series*, 96 (1937)
Greaves, *PRET*	R.L. Greaves, *The Puritan Revolution and Educational Thought* (1969)
Grey's Debates	*Debates of the House of Commons from the Year 1667 to the Year 1694*, comp. by A. Grey, 10 vols. (1763)
Haley, *FES*	K.H.D. Haley, *The First Earl of Shaftesbury* (1968)
Haley, *WOEO*	K.H.D. Haley, *William of Orange and the English Opposition, 1672-4* (1953)
Haller, *LRPR*	W. Haller, *Liberty and Reformation in the Puritan Revolution* (1955)
Haller, *RP*	W. Haller, *The Rise of Puritanism* (1938; repr. 1957)
Haller, *Tr.*	W. Haller, *Tracts on Liberty in the Puritan Revolution*, 3 vols. (1933)
Harg. MSS	Hargrave Manuscripts, British Library
Harl. Misc.	T. Park, ed., *Harleian Miscellany: or a Collection of Scarce . . . Tracts*, 10 vols. (1808-13)
Harl. MSS	Harleian Manuscripts, British Library
Harl. Soc.	*Harleian Society Publications*
Hayden, *RCCB*	R. Hayden, ed., *The Records of a Church of Christ in Bristol, 1640-1687, Bristol Record Society Publications*, 27 (1974)
Hetherington	W.M. Hetherington, *History of the Westminster Assembly of Divines* (1843)
Hexter	J.H. Hexter, *The Reign of King Pym* (1941; repr. 1960)
Hill, *C. & C.*	C. Hill, *Change and Continuity in Seventeenth-Century England* (1975)
Hill, *IOER*	C. Hill, *Intellectual Origins of the English Revolution* (1965)
Hill, *MER*	C. Hill, *Milton and the English Revolution* (1977)
Hill, *P & R.*	C. Hill, *Puritanism and Revolution* (1958; repr. 1964)
Hill, *S. & P.*	C. Hill, *Society and Puritanism in Pre-Revolutionary England*, 2nd ed. (1967)
Hill, *WTUD*	C. Hill, *The World Turned Upside Down* (1972)
Hirst	D. Hirst, *The Representative of the People?* (1975)
HJ	*Historical Journal*
HLQ	*Huntington Library Quarterly*
HMC	*Historical Manuscripts Commission, Reports*
Holmes	C. Holmes, *The Eastern Association in the English Civil War* (1974)
Howell, *NPR*	R. Howell, *Newcastle upon Tyne and the Puritan Revolution* (1967)

Hull, *RQA*	W.I. Hull, *The Rise of Quakerism in Amsterdam* (1938)
Hutchinson	C.H. Firth, ed., *Memoirs of the Life of Colonel Hutchinson* (1906)
James	M. James, *Social Problems and Policy During the Puritan Revolution, 1640-1660* (1930)
JEH	*Journal of Ecclesiastical History*
JFHS	*Journal of the Friends Historical Society*
JHI	*Journal of the History of Ideas*
JMH	*Journal of Modern History*
Jones, *AM*	R.F. Jones, *Ancients and Moderns*, 2nd ed. (1961)
Jones, *FW*	J.R. Jones, *The First Whigs* (1961)
Jones, *QAC*	R.M. Jones, *The Quakers in the American Colonies*, 2nd ed. (1966)
Jones, *SMR*	R.M. Jones, *Studies in Mystical Religion* (1909)
Jordan	W.K. Jordan, *The Development of Religious Toleration in England*, 4 vols. (1932-40)
Judson, *TPR*	M. Judson, *From Tradition to Political Reality* (1980)
JURCHS	*Journal of the United Reformed Church History Society*
Keeler	M.F. Keeler, *The Long Parliament, 1640-1641* (1954)
Keeton	G.W. Keeton, *Lord Chancellor Jeffreys and the Stuart Cause* (1965)
Kishlansky	M.A. Kishlansky, *The Rise of the New Model Army* (1979)
Lacey	D.R. Lacey, *Dissent and Parliamentary Politics in England, 1661-1689* (1969)
Lamont, *GR*	W.M. Lamont, *Godly Rule: Politics and Religion, 1603-60* (1969)
Lamont, *RBM*	W.M. Lamont, *Richard Baxter and the Millennium* (1979)
Lans. MSS	Lansdowne Manuscripts, British Library
Lev. Man.	D.M. Wolfe, ed., *Leveller Manifestoes of the Puritan Revolution* (1944; repr. 1967)
Lev. Tr.	W. Haller and G. Davies, eds., *The Leveller Tracts, 1647-1653* (1944)
Liu	T. Liu, *Discord in Zion* (1973)
LJ	*Journals of the House of Lords 1578-1714*, vols. 2-19 (1767 ff.)
Ludlow	C.H. Firth, ed., *Memoirs of Edmund Ludlow*, 2 vols. (1894)
Lumpkin	W.L. Lumpkin, *Baptist Confessions of Faith* (1959)
Luttrell	N. Luttrell, *A Brief Relation of State Affairs from September 1678 to April 1714*, 6 vols. (1857)
MacCormack	J.R. MacCormack, *Revolutionary Politics in the Long Parliament* (1973)
McGee	J.S. McGee, *The Godly Man in Stuart England* (1976)
McLachlan, *SSCE*	H.J. McLachlan, *Socinianism in Seventeenth Century England* (1951)

Manning, *EPER*	B. Manning, *The English People and the English Revolution* (1976)
Masson	D. Masson, *The Life of John Milton*, 7 vols. (1859-94; repr. 1946)
MCR	J.C. Jeaffreson, ed., *Middlesex County Records*, vols. 1-4 (1886-92)
Moir	T.L. Moir, *The Addled Parliament of 1614* (1958)
Morley	I. Morley, *A Thousand Lives* (1954)
Morrill	J.S. Morrill, *Cheshire 1630-1660* (1974)
Morton	A.L. Morton, *The World of the Ranters* (1970)
MPHC	M. Noble, *Memoirs of the Protectoral-House of Cromwell* (1787)
N. & Q.	*Notes and Queries*
Neal	D. Neal, *The History of the Puritans or Protestant Nonconformists*, 2 vols. (1843)
Newton	A.P. Newton, *The Colonizing Activities of the English Puritans* (1914)
Nickolls	J. Nickolls, ed., *Original Letters and Papers of State Addressed to Oliver Cromwell* (1743)
Noble	M. Noble, *The Lives of the English Regicides*, 2 vols. (1798)
Notestein, *WIHC*	W. Notestein, *The Winning of the Initiative by the House of Commons* (1924; repr. 1949)
Nuttall, *HSPFE*	G.F. Nuttall, *The Holy Spirit in Puritan Faith and Experience* (1946)
Nuttall, *VS*	G.F. Nuttall, *Visible Saints* (1957)
Nuttall, *WS*	G.F. Nuttall, *The Welsh Saints* (1957)
Nuttall, *Yorks.*	W.L.F. Nuttall, 'The Yorkshire Commissioners for the Trial of King Charles the First,' *Yorkshire Archaeological Journal*, 43:147-57
P. & P.	*Past and Present*
Palmer	S. Palmer, ed., *The Nonconformists' Memorial*, 3 vols. (1802-3), a revision of Calamy
PBHRS	*Publications of the Bedfordshire Historical Records Society*
PCC, Wills	Prerogative Court of Canterbury, Wills
Pearl	V. Pearl, *London on the Outbreak of the Puritan Revolution* (1961)
Pepys	R. Latham and W. Matthews, *The Diary of Samuel Pepys*, 11 vols. (1970 ff.)
Pink MSS	W.D. Pink's Manuscripts, John Rylands Library, Manchester
Plomer, *DBP*	H.R. Plomer, *A Dictionary of the Booksellers and Printers . . . from 1641 to 1667* (1907)
Plomer, *DPB*	H.R. Plomer, *A Dictionary of the Printers and Booksellers . . . from 1668 to 1725* (1922)
PP 1610	E.R. Foster, ed., *Proceedings in Parliament 1610*, 2 vols. (1966)

Prall	S.E. Prall, *The Agitation for Law Reform During the Puritan Revolution* (1966)
PSP 1640	E.S. Cope and W.H. Coates, eds., *Proceedings of the Short Parliament of 1640*, Camden Society, 19 (1977)
QH	*Quaker History*
Rawl. MSS	Rawlinson Manuscripts, Bodleian Library
Rel. Bax.	M. Sylvester, ed., *Reliquiae Baxterianae* (1696)
Richards	T. Richards, *The Puritan Movement in Wales, 1639-1653* (1920)
Rogers	P.G. Rogers, *The Fifth Monarchy Men* (1966)
Ruigh	R.E. Ruigh, *The Parliament of 1624* (1971)
Rushworth	J. Rushworth, *Historical Collections of Private Passages of State*, 7 vols. (1659-1701)
Russell, *PEP*	C. Russell, *Parliaments and English Politics, 1621-1629* (1979)
Sachse	W.L. Sachse, 'England's "Black Tribunal": An Analysis of the Regicide Court,' *Journal of British Studies*, 12 (May 1973): 69-85
Seaver	P.S. Seaver, *The Puritan Lectureships* (1970)
Shaw	W.A. Shaw, *A History of the English Church During the Civil Wars and Under the Commonwealth 1640-1660, 2 vols. (1900)*
Smith, *Cat.*	J. Smith, *A Descriptive Catalogue of Friends' Books*, 2 vols. (1867)
Solt	L.F. Solt, *Saints in Arms* (1959)
Somers Tracts	W. Scott, ed., *Collection of Scarce and Valuable Tracts . . . of the late Lord Somers*, 13 vols. (1809-15)
Spufford	M. Spufford, *Contrasting Communities* (1974)
ST	W. Cobbett, T.B. Howell, *et al.*, *Cobbett's Complete Collection of State Trials and Proceedings*, 34 vols. (1809-28)
TBHS	*Transactions of the Baptist Historical Society*
TCHS	*Transactions of the Congregational Historical Society*
Thomas	K. Thomas, *Religion and the Decline of Magic* (1971)
Thurloe, *SP*	T. Birch, ed., *A Collection of State Papers of John Thurloe*, 7 vols. (1742)
Tolmie	M. Tolmie, *The Triumph of the Saints* (1977)
Trench	C.C. Trench, *The Western Rising* (1969)
TRHS	*Transactions of the Royal Historical Society*
Turnbull	G.H. Turnbull, ed., *Hartlib, Dury, and Comenius* (1947)
Turner	G.L. Turner, ed., *Original Records of Early Nonconformity*, 3 vols. (1911-14)
Underdown, *PP*	D. Underdown, *Pride's Purge* (1971)
Underdown, *SCWI*	D. Underdown, *Somerset in the Civil War and Interregnum* (1973)
Underhill, *RCCF*	E.B. Underhill, ed., *Records of the Churches of Christ Gathered at Fenstanton, Warboys, and Hexham, 1644-1720, Hanserd Knollys Society Publications*, 9 (1854)

Underwood	A.C. Underwood, *A History of the English Baptists* (1947)
Vann	R.T. Vann, *The Social Development of English Quakerism 1655-1755* (1969)
VCH	*The Victoria History of the Counties of England*
Veall	D. Veall, *The Popular Movement for Law Reform* (1970)
Waters	H.F. Waters, *Genealogical Gleanings in England and Wales* (1901)
Watts	M.R. Watts, *The Dissenters*, 1 (1978)
Webster, *GI*	C. Webster, *The Great Instauration* (1975)
Webster, *SHAL*	C. Webster, ed., *Samuel Hartlib and the Advancement of Learning* (1970)
Wedgwood, *CKC*	C.V. Wedgwood, *A Coffin for King Charles* (1964); published in England as *The Trial of Charles I* (1964)
White	B.R. White, *The English Separatist Tradition* (1971)
Whitelocke, *Lib. Fam.*	J. Bruce, ed., *Liber Famelicus of Sir James Whitelocke*, Camden Society (1858)
Whitelocke, *Memorials*	B. Whitelocke, *Memorials of English Affairs (1625-60)*, 4 vols. (1853)
Whiting	C.E. Whiting, *Studies in English Puritanism from the Restoration to the Revolution, 1660-1688* (1931; repr. 1968)
Whitley, *BL*	W.T. Whitley, *The Baptists of London 1612-1928* [1928]
Whitley, *Minutes*	W.T. Whitley, ed., *Minutes of the General Assembly of the General Baptist Churches in England*, vol. 1 (1909)
Wilbur	E.M. Wilbur, *A History of Unitarianism*, 2 vols. (1945, 1952)
Williams, *Wales*	W.R. Williams, *The Parliamentary History of the Principality of Wales* (1895)
Williams, *Worcester*	W.R. Williams, *The Parliamentary History of the County of Worcester* (1897)
Wilson, *HADC*	W. Wilson, *The History and Antiquities of Dissenting Churches and Meeting Houses, in London, Westminster, and Southwark*, 4 vols. (1808-14)
Wilson, *PP*	J.F. Wilson, *Pulpit in Parliament* (1969)
Wing	D.G. Wing, *Short-Title Catalogue of Books . . . 1641-1700*, 3 vols. (1945-51; 2nd ed., 1972 ff.)
Woodhouse	A.S.P. Woodhouse, ed., *Puritanism and Liberty* (1938)
Woolrych	A. Woolrych, *Commonwealth to Protectorate* (1982)
Worden	B. Worden, *The Rump Parliament, 1648-1653* (1974)
Yule	G. Yule, *The Independents in the English Civil War* (1958)
Zagorin, *CC*	P. Zagorin, *The Court and the Country* (1969)
Zagorin, *HPT*	P. Zagorin, *A History of Political Thought in the English Revolution* (1954)
Zaller	R. Zaller, *The Parliament of 1621* (1971)

ABBREVIATIONS: MANUSCRIPT DEPOSITORIES

AN	National Library of Wales, Aberystwyth
BC	Birmingham Central Reference Library
BM	Bristol Museum
BQ	Queen's University, Belfast
BRO	Berkshire Record Office
C	Cambridge University Library
CCA	Gonville and Caius College, Cambridge
CCRO	Chester City Record Office
CE	Emmanuel College, Cambridge
CH	Henry E. Huntington Library, San Marino, Calif.
CK	King's College, Cambridge
CORO	Cornwall Record Office
CRO	Cheshire Record Office
CS	St. John's College, Cambridge
CT	Trinity College, Cambridge
DFHL	Friends' Historical Library, Dublin
DPR	Public Record Office, Dublin
DT	Trinity College, Dublin
E	Edinburgh University
EN	National Library of Scotland (Advocates'), Edinburgh
ERO	Essex Record Office
EXRO	Exeter Record Office
HARO	Hampshire Record Office
HRO	Hereford Record Office
KAO	Kent Archives Office
KS	Southern Baptist Theological Seminary, Louisville, Kentucky
KU	Spencer Research Library, University of Kansas
L	British Library, London
LC	Library of Congress, Washington, D.C.
LCL	Congregational Library, London
LERO	Leicestershire Record Office
LF	Friends Library, London
LG	Guildhall, London
LGA	Gemeente Archief, Leiden
LI	Inner Temple, London
LIRO	Liverpool Record Office
LIU	Liverpool University
LJRO	Lichfield Joint Record Office

LL	Lincoln's Inn, London
LLP	Lambeth Palace, London
LPR	Public Record Office, London
LRO	Lincolnshire Record Office
LSH	Somerset House, London
LW	Dr. Williams' Library, London
MHS	Massachusetts Historical Society, Boston
MMO	Osler Library, McGill University, Montreal
MR	John Rylands Library, Manchester
MRO	Middlesex Record Office
MSL	Massachusetts State Library, Boston
MWA	American Antiquarian Society, Worcester, Mass.
NOT	Nottingham University
NOTPL	Nottingham Public Library
NOTRO	Nottingham Record Office
NRO	Northamptonshire Record Office
O	Bodleian Library, Oxford
OAS	All Souls' College, Oxford
OCC	Corpus Christi College, Oxford
OE	Exeter College, Oxford
OJ	Jesus College, Oxford
ON	New College, Oxford
OQ	Queen's College, Oxford
ORP	Regent's Park College, Oxford
OS	St. John's College, Oxford
OU	University College, Oxford
OW	Worcester College, Oxford
PH	Haverford College, Haverford, Pa.
PHS	Historical Society of Pennsylvania, Philadelphia
SCL	Sheffield City Library
SRO	Somerset Record Office
SS	William Salt Library, Stafford
SUL	Sheffield University Library
VNL	National Library, Vienna
WF	Folger Library, Washington, D.C.
Y	Yale University, New Haven, Conn.

Asterisks are used to indicate separate entries for the radicals so indicated; no asterisks are used for the frequent references to Oliver Cromwell.

P

PACKER, William (fl. 1644-1662)

Army radical, served in Cromwell's original horse troop early in the Civil War and may have been a native of Huntingdonshire. He was a lieutenant in the Ironsides by 1644 when he was arrested by the Presbyterian Maj.-Gen. Crawford for professing Particular Baptist doctrines. Cromwell strongly defended him as a godly man and secured his release. He was promoted to captain in 1646 and as the senior officer of that rank led Cromwell's regiment at the battle of Dunbar in Sept. 1650. He became major and effective commander of the regiment, on a colonel's pay, in 1652. The same year he was a radical representative on the Hales* law reform commission and in 1653 was appointed to a number of minor committees by the Council of State after the suppression of the Commonwealth.

Packer attended the army debates of 1647-48 but had no sympathy for the Levellers. By 1652 he was allied with the London Fifth Monarchy preachers demanding the dissolution of Parliament and the calling of a godly representative. He favored junior officers of his own religious persuasion and they bought and subdivided, as a group, the royal manor of Theobalds in Hertfordshire, constituting themselves a Baptist congregation. It was a unique experiment – a religious syndicate of improving farmers which aroused the hostility of the local population. During the Protectorate Packer acquired considerable political influence in the region. He was made JP for Hertfordshire and deputy to Fleetwood* as major-general for Hertfordshire, Buckinghamshire and Oxfordshire in 1656. He was elected MP for Woodstock in 1658 and for Hertford in Richard Cromwell's* Parliament of 1659 but was unseated on a disputed return.

Packer parted company with the Fifth Monarchy party and most of the senior Baptist officers when he failed to express his opposition to the dissolution of the Barebones. In a parliamentary speech attacking the powers of the Protector in Feb. 1659, he frankly admitted that fear and hope of preferment, as well as trusting regard for Cromwell, had led him to suppress his dissatisfaction. Under pressure from his Theobalds captains he finally took his stand in Feb. 1658 against the restoration of an Upper House. In several interviews with the Protector they professed their personal loyalty to him but not to the Protectorate. Cromwell reacted with angry surprise to the discontent in his own regiment. In physical and mental decline, he was no longer swayed by nostalgic affection for old comrades, and peremptorily dismissed Packer and five of his captains. The fall of the Protectorate saw Packer recover command of his regiment with the rank of colonel. A leading supporter of Lambert,* he was a member of the military junto which restored the Rump Parliament in May 1659 and forcibly suppressed it five months later when it revoked their commissions. The grandees enjoyed two or more months of power until Parliament, revived and assured of Monck's support, ended Packer's military career. He was ordered to quit London in Jan. 1660 and was arrested in April when Lambert temporarily escaped from custody. At the Restoration he lost Theobalds and was imprisoned in the Gate House early in 1661 and again on suspicion of plotting in October. He was probably transported in Sept. 1662.

As Packer confessed in 1659, his radical idealism was always tempered by the attraction of appropriated estates and generous military pay. The sincerity of his protestations of godliness was questioned by those such as George Fox,* John Lilburne* and William Erbery* who encountered his narrow Calvinist intolerance. He remained, however, consistently faithful to the body which had given him power, status and wealth. The army's interest was Packer's.

Burton, 3:158-69; 4:249-53; D. Underdown, 'Cromwell and the Officers, February 1658,' *EHR*, 83:101-7; Capp, *FMM*; I. Gentles, 'The Management of the Crown Lands, 1649-60,' *Agricultural History Review*, 19:35-37; *DNB*.

J.F. McGregor

PALMER, Anthony (1616-1679)

Independent minister and Fifth Monarchist, was christened on 27 Oct. 1616, the son of Anthony Palmer of Great Comberton, Worcs. He matriculated at Balliol Coll., Oxf. on 5 Dec. 1634, and graduated B.A. (7 Apr. 1638) and M.A. (16 Dec. 1641). From 1640 to 1649 he was a fellow of Balliol, during which time he subscribed to the Solemn League and Covenant (1643) and accepted the Rectory of Bourton-on-the-Water, Glos. In the 1640s he was apparently a Presbyterian, for he signed the Gloucestershire Ministers' Testimony professing adherence to the Solemn League and Covenant and presbyterian polity. He took the Engagement in 1650 and four years later served as an assistant to the Gloucestershire Commission. Sometime during this period he adopted Independent views and became particularly warm toward the Baptists, though he continued to hope for a reconciliation of Independents and Presbyterians. According to Anthony Wood he was 'anabaptistically inclined, and a great favorer of those of that persuasion and their tenets. 'He was especially concerned with the problem of unworthy communicants at the Lord's Supper, a subject to which he devoted *A Scripture-Rale to the Lords Table* (1654). The same year he was the signatory of the nominating letter from the Bourton church for the Saintes' Parliament. Palmer's republicanism was manifested by his signing the remonstrance of the Gloucestershire churhes in 1656 urging Cromwell not to become king. He attended the Savoy Conference in 1658.

Palmer's religious views provoked the ire of the local gentry, who in Mar. 1660 drove him out of his rectory, followed shortly thereafter by his curate. Apparently provoked by this experience, he adopted Fifth Moanrchy views in London, perhaps building on earlier millenarian principles so common among the Independents. He preached at various places in London, including Allhallows the Great, sometimes in association with John Simpson,* as well as in the counties. He and Carnsew Helme* were accounted 'violent projecting men,' and in 1661 his sermons reportedly attacked the Restoration court and predicted divine retribution. The following year he was alleged, without evidence, to be a part of the plot of Ens. Thomas Tong* and others to restore the republic. Palmer was living at Little Moorfields in 1663, associating with Helme, Thomas Palmer* and Lawrence Wise,* and preaching in the house of a sailmaker at Tower Wharf. A warrant for Palmer's arrest was issued on 25 Feb. 1664, ordering that he be taken before Sir Henry Bennet, Secretary of State. Imprisonment probably followed, for he does not appear in the records again until 1669, when he was preaching at Mill Lane, Southwark, and in Windsor. About the same time he became pastor of a mixed congregation of Baptists and Congregationalists at Pinners' Hall, London, where his assistant was the Baptist George Fownes.* In May 1670 Palmer was fined £20 for illegally preaching at the Poultry in London. One of the City's most influential Nonconformists, he was one of those to whom the magistrates and ministers of Massachusetts wrote on 21 Aug. 1671 regarding the affairs of Harvard College, and he was also a signatory of the response on 5 Feb. 1672. Palmer was a friend of John Bunyan,* and his church was one of the places where Bedford people could transfer their membership when they moved to the City. On 19 Apr. 1672 Palmer was licensed as a Congregationalist to preach at a house on London Bridge. The Declaration of Indulgence prompted him to join

John Owen* and George Griffith* in thanking Charles II personally on 28 Mar. There is no evidence that Palmer maintained his Fifth Monarchist views after 1663. He died on 26 Jan. 1679. His wife was the widow of the Puritan John Smith of Clavering, Essex, author of *An Exposition of the Creed*, which Palmer had published. Palmer's successor at Pinners' Hall was Richard Wavel.* His most influential works were evangelical in tone: *The Tempestuous Soul Calmed* (1653) and *The Gospel New-Creature* (1658). Palmer is not to be confused with Anthony Palmer (1613-1693), son of William Palmer of Barnstaple, who was Rector of Bratton Fleming, Devon, from about 1650 until his ejection in 1662, and who was licensed as a Presbyterian at Barnstaple in 1672.

CSPD, Chas. II, 3:494; 10:221; 12 *passim*; *Calamy Revised*; Capp, *FMM*; *DNB*; R.L. Greaves, 'John Bunyan's "Holy War" and London Nonconformity,' *BQ*, 26:158-68; Nuttall, *VS*.

R.L. Greaves

PALMER, Herbert (1601-1647)

Puritan minister, was born at Wingham, Kent, the younger son of Sir Thomas Palmer. He became a fellow-commoner of St. John's Coll., Camb. in 1616, graduated B.A. (1619), M.A. (1622) and B.D. (1631), was elected fellow of Queens' College (1623), and showed a precocious interest in religion. 'Gracious and learned little Palmer,' as Robert Baillie called him, was ordained in 1624 and licensed for a lectureship at St. Alphage's, Canterbury, but was relieved of his fellowship about 1630 for overzealously catechizing students. In 1632 he became University Preacher at Cambridge and in the same year his social connections secured him the Rectory of Ashwell, Herts., but in 1633 he refused to read the Book of Sports and began to protest against Laudian policy. Palmer was an original member of the Westminster Assembly (1643) and later

became one of its Assessors. He represented the more moderate Puritanism that eventually became reconciled to Presbyterianism. Palmer was particularly active in preparing the Directory and the Shorter Catechism, but died prior to 28 Sept. 1647, before this work was complete. Palmer preached before the House of Commons and was one of the seven morning lecturers at Westminster Abbey. In 1644 he was appointed Master of Queens' Coll., Camb., by the Earl of Manchester. Laud refused his ministrations at the scaffold. A bachelor of diminutive appearance and frail, he was universally respected and used his personal wealth in charitable works, particularly to help needy students. Baillie regarded him as the best catechist in England.

S. Clarke, *The Lives of Thirty-Two English Divines* (1677); Hetherington; *DNB*; Neal; D. Laing, ed., *Letters and Journals of Robert Baillie* (1842); J. Lightfoot, *Journal of the Assembly of Divines, Works* (1824), 13; Hill, *S. & P.*

R.S. Paul

PALMER (*alias* Vaulx), John (1609?-1660)

Parliamentary radical, MP LP 1646, 1659 (Taunton). The son of an apothecary of Taunton, Som., Palmer matriculated at Queen's Coll., Oxf. He was a physician by profession and fought on the side of Parliament during the Civil War. Elected as a recruiter in 1646 to represent his home borough, he was a political Independent although Presbyterian in religious persuasion. Palmer was absent from the House at Pride's purge and took no part in the trial of the King. On 5 Feb. 1649 he dissented to the 5 Dec. vote and remained a member of the Rump. He served on the Somerset County Committee, was a JP, and was promoted to the quorum in Apr. 1649 where he remained until purged from the Commission of the Peace in Mar. 1657. He was again elected for Taunton in a disputed election for the Parliament called by Richard Cromwell.* On 13 Apr. 1647 Palmer was imposed as Warden on All Souls Coll., Oxf. by the Chancellor and visitors sent by Parliament. He is referred to as a 'Parliamento Pseudo-Custos Constituitur' in the college records. He was friendly with Oliver Cromwell who stayed at his lodgings while visiting Oxford in 1649. Palmer presided over the purging of the college to remove royalist and Episcopalian sympathizers and to introduce those of parliamentary and Puritan persuasion. In addition, he made rigorous efforts to improve the moral and academic fiber of the college. Palmer died on 4 Mar. 1660.

Yule; *Al. Oxon.*; Underdown, *SCWI* and *PP*; C.G. Robertson, *All Souls College* (1899).

E.A. Andriette

PALMER, Thomas (b.c. 1612)

New Model chaplain and Fifth Monarchist, was born in Shepshed, Leics., the son of Robert Palmer, a minister. Palmer matriculated at St. Edmund Hall, Oxf. on 1 July 1631 and received the B.A. in 1635. He may have joined the parliamentary army and by 1644 was chaplain to Maj.-Gen. Skippon's* regiment, and was reported to have become a major in the army. Palmer married Joyce Powell of St. Albans, who gave birth to a daughter Martha at Navestock, Essex on 7 Sept. 1646. He was Curate of St. Lawrence Pountney, London from 24 Nov. 1644 to 22 Apr. 1646 and in Apr. 1646 became Rector of Aston-on-Trent, Derby. This living he retained until removed in 1660, although he also referred to himself as pastor of the Congregational church at Skegby, Notts. in 1659. Palmer was responsible for communicating to the churches of Derbyshire and Nottinghamshire the decisions of the Congregational ministers at Oxford in 1658. That year he was prosecuted at the Lincoln Assizes for refusing to administer the sacrament to parishioners, who were advised by Judge Wyndham to withhold tithes. After being turned out in 1660, he itinerated as a preacher in Derbyshire, Nottinghamshire and London, and was arrested and imprisoned for preaching at Egerton, Kent in 1662 and at Nottingham in 1663.

Palmer was a millenarian by the time he published *The Saints Support in These Sad Times* in 1644 and had become a Fifth Monarchist by 1654. During the 1650s he traveled and worked for the Fifth Monarchists in addition to carrying on his ministerial activities, especially in Nottinghamshire and London. After the Restoration he increased his Fifth Monarchist activity and became a prominent leader of the movement. In 1662 he was arrested at Egerton, Kent, barely escaping a summary execution, and he was imprisoned in Nottinghamshire as a leading organizer of the Farnley Wood plot of 1663. Palmer was active in similar work, especially around London, in the mid-1660s and went to Ireland with Col. Thomas Blood* in 1666 to organize for the Fifth Monarchists. In 1667 he published a defense of the recent rebellion entitled *The Saints Freedom from Tyranny Vindicated*. In it he denied the allegedly biblical statement that all governing powers – including anti-Christian kings – are ordained of God, and argued that it was the right and duty of saints to overthrow the anti-Christian Stuart monarchy. Not surprisingly, he was not licensed in 1672.

Additional publications include *A Little View of This Old World* (1659) and, according to Wood, a sermon on 1 Cor. 3:22-23 (1647).

CSPD, Comm., 12:195; *Chas. II*, 2-3 *passim*; 5:159; 6:64, 297; 11:335; Capp, *FMM*; *Ath. Oxon.*; *Calamy Revised*; *DNB*.

M.B. Endy

PAPILLON, Thomas (1623-1702)

Parliamentary radical, MP 1674, 1679,

1680, 1681, 1689, 1690, 1695, 1698 (Dover). Papillon was born on 6 Sept. 1623 at Roehampton, Surrey, the fifth (but second surviving) son of David Papillon, builder, and his second wife, Anne Marie, daughter of Jean Calendrine of Putney. Papillon attended school at Drayton, Northants., and was articled in 1637 to Thomas Chambrelan, a London merchant. In 1638 he was apprenticed to the Mercers' Company, whose freedom he received in 1646. After taking part in the Presbyterian demonstrations of 26 July 1647 he fled to France to escape arrest, but returned in November and was committed briefly to Newgate in Feb. 1648. Papillon took no further part in public affairs until the Restoration, devoting his energies to business, serving as a deacon in the Huguenot church, and joining the revamped East India Company in 1657. In 1661 he joined the Eastland Company, and served four times as Master of the Mercers' Company, in 1673-74, 1682-83, 1692-93 and 1698-99. From 1668 to 1672 he was a Trade Commissioner, in 1672-73 sat on the Common Council, served as Auditor of the Navy in 1672-74, 1675-77 and 1680-82, and was an Assessment Commissioner for Kent (1673-80) and London (1677-80). In 1673 he was Sheriff of London.

Papillon was returned to the Cavalier Parliament in a disputed election, taking his seat on 16 Jan. 1674. He immediately assumed a leading role in the opposition, serving on 65 committees and making twenty recorded speeches. In 1675 he supported Danby's impeachment, urged the House to refuse supply until assurance about the King's foreign commitments were provided, and took an active part in investigations of the Popish plot. Charles II retaliated by vetoing his election as Deputy Governor of the East India Company in 1678, though he held the position in 1680-82.

Named on both returns for Dover in the Parliament of 1679, Papillon sat on 33 committees, including those for the Habeas Corpus Bill and for security against Popery, and made three recorded speeches. He supported exclusion and helped draw up the address for the removal of Lauderdale. Overwhelmingly returned again in 1680, his 25 committees included those on abhorring, the Irish plot and the impeachment of Seymour, and he delivered six speeches. In the Oxford Parliament, he served on the Committee for Privileges, as a manager for the impeachment of Fitzharris, and in the conference to consider the disappearance of the bill to repeal the penal laws against Dissenters. At the same time, Papillon was active in the City. As Deputy Governor, he fought against the Tory interest represented by Sir Josiah Child in the East India Company, and for the expanded trade policy spelled out in his treatises, *The East-India-Trade a Most Profitable Trade* (1677) and *A Treatise Concerning the East India Trade* (1680, republished 1696). In Nov. 1681 he was selected to the grand jury considering the indictment of the Earl of Shaftesbury,* a long-standing business and political associate, and helped secure the verdict of *ignoramus*. The following year he stood again for sheriff. In Apr. 1683 he caused the arrest of Sir William Pritchard and the Tory aldermen of London for failing to answer a writ of *mandamus*. Pritchard was awarded £10,000 in a suit for false imprisonment, and in Jan. 1685 Papillon fled to Holland to avoid payment.

Returning to England with William of Orange, Papillon was immediately elected to Parliament for his Dover constituency and within the year resumed a variety of functions: JP for Kent, Assessment Commissioner for Kent, London and Dover, Alderman for Portsoken Ward, London, and Commissioner for Victualing the Navy, which last position he held until his resignation on 26 May 1699. In Parliament, Papillon was a Court Whig. He was particularly active in the Convention Parliament, serving on 58 committees, delivering nine reports, and making sixteen speeches. Papillon died in London on 5 May 1702 and was buried at Acrise, Kent, where he had bought an estate in 1666. On 30 Oct. 1651 he married Jane (d. 1698), daughter of Thomas Broadnax of Godmersham, Kent; their issue included Philip

(1660-1736), MP for Dover (1701-20), and Elizabeth (b. 1658), wife of Edward Ward, later Chief Baron of the Exchequer.

DNB; A.F.W. Papillon, *Memoirs of Thomas Papillon* (1887); *Grey's Debates*; Lacey; *ST*, 8:759-821; 10:319-72; *Proceedings of the Huguenot Society*; History of Parliament draft biography; Beaven.

R. Zaller

PARKE (or Park, Parkes), James (1636-1696)

Quaker, lived as a young man in the area of Wrexham, Denb., or Welshpool, Mont. These were places where the Independents, led by Vavasor Powell* and Morgan Llwyd,* were strong, and Parke was under their influence until he adopted Quaker views no later than 1663. In March of that year he went on a preaching foray in Wales, perhaps at the instigation of Margaret Fell.* By the summer of 1664 he was in London urging the Friends to stand fast in refusing to obey laws contrary to conscience. Parke took the Quaker message the following December and January to Surrey, Middlesex, Berkshire, Buckinghamshire, Oxfordshire and Bristol, and in 1666-67 preached in the eastern counties. An account of his debate with Col. John Wigan* at Lancaster appears in Wigan's *Antichrists Strongest Hold Overturned* (1665). In May 1666 Parke was a signatory of Richard Farnsworth's* letter calling for a Quaker board of censorship. Parke was imprisoned at Harwich in 1667 for attending a Quaker conventicle, probably in the course of his travels to and from Holland. He knew Dutch and published several sermons in that language. With George Whitehead* and others he later (1683) advised the Dutch Friends on notifying magistrates of Quaker marriages. About 1667 Parke moved to Horsleydown, Southwark, where Quakers had met since about 1655, but his itinerant preaching continued. He was in Cornwall in 1670-71

and Hampshire in 1683. A Quaker petition to Charles II and Parliament in 1675 protesting mandatory oaths and opposing penalties for matters of conscience was signed by Parke, Ellis Hookes and John Grove. In Aug. 1683 Parke was fined £12 for not attending church in the parish of St. Olave's, Southwark. Fox* visited him at Horsleydown in 1685 and 1686, and the following year he traveled with the Quaker leader. Parke was a signatory in 1689 of the epistle, 'Corruptions Creeping in about Marriages,' and four years later he endorsed Whitehead's *Christian Doctrine*. Parke, who had spoken at Fox's funeral in Jan. 1691, died in St. Olave's parish on 11 or 12 Nov. 1696, aged sixty. His wife, the former Frances Ceele (c. 1634-1696), widow of Horsleydown, whom he had married in 1667, died shortly before he did. His numerous works include several published epistles to Friends and general warnings of impending judgment.

Fox, *CJ*; *DNB*; Besse, 1:119, 202, 484, 705; *CSPD, Chas. II*, 17:90; *FPT*; Braithwaite, *SP*; *EQW*. Papers: LF.

R.L. Greaves

PARKE, Robert (1600-1668)

Independent minister, was born in Bolton, Lancs., the son of John Parke. He matriculated at age fifteen at Emmanuel Coll., Camb., receiving his B.A. in 1619 and his M.A. in 1622. Between 1625 and 1630 Parke was Vicar of Bolton, having been curate previously. In 1630 he fled to Rotterdam where he became pastor of a Congregational church until his return to Bolton in 1644. Calamy describes Parke as 'much beloved' of the people, 'a man of incomparable parts, learning and piety, and a very exact preacher,' noted for his keen wit. Ejected in 1662, Parke refused to conform, and he held private meetings in Bolton until he was expelled by the Five Mile Act in 1665. He returned soon after and preached at Bolton until his death.

DNB; Calamy, 2 (1713); 402; *Calamy Revised*.

R.E. McFarland

PARKER, Alexander (1628-1689)

Quaker, was born at Chipping, near Bowland, Yorks. Well-educated and for a time a merchant in London, his letters are full of shrewd observations. He became a Quaker at Lancaster, one of George Fox's* close friends, and a lifelong traveling companion. His affectionate letters to Margaret Fell* illustrate the depth of sympathy between men and women which was one of Quakerism's most remarkable features. Parker traveled widely in the Midlands, East Anglia, Norfolk and Suffolk in 1654-55. By 1657 he was traveling in the West Country, as well as journeying through the north with Fox, a trip which took them into Scotland as well. They had some success among the English garrisons there, but the Scots were very unresponsive and handled Parker roughly when he attempted to speak in Glasgow Cathedral. Although Parker was not a prolific writer, he expounded Quaker doctrines clearly in works like *A Testimony to the Light Within* (1657) and engaged in controversy in *A Testimony of God* (1656). Parker played an important part in Quaker organization and finances, which enabled the movement to survive an increasingly hostile environment. His broad sympathy with differing views enabled him to mediate in the Nayler* affair, as well as in the divisions caused by Perrot,* Wilkinson* and Story.* Although he attempted to win concessions for the Quakers from Henry Vane* and the Rump in May and June 1659 and later from Charles II in Aug. 1683, he increasingly came to see the importance of internal consolidation and lower-key witness. Imprisoned several times himself, he played an important role in adapting the movement to conditions under the later Stuarts. The Minute and Epistle which he helped to draft at the General Meeting of May 1672 exemplify the change in emphasis. There were stern warnings against controversy, on the need for the young to keep their place and stress on caution in speaking of doctrines like perfection. Parker's belief in the importance of authority being given to the experienced was shaped by his efforts at mediation and was reflected in the weight given to the counsel of the traveling ministers or overseers. Spreading responsibility for collections on behalf of overseas workers and financing publicity were other important changes. Parker's friendship with Penn* and his journey to Holland with Fox in 1684 attest his continuing interest in spreading Quaker doctrine. That they alone of the radical movements of the period still survive is a tribute to the insights of Parker and his colleagues who showed that their radicalism was a source of strength to English society.

Braithwaite, *BQu* and *SP*; Besse; *DNB*; A.R. Barclay, ed., *Letters of Early Friends* (1847); L.V. Hodgkin, *Quaker Saint of Cornwall* (1927). Papers: LF.

I. Breward

PARKER, Henry (1604-1652)

Pamphleteer and political theorist, was the fourth son of Sir Nicholas Parker of Ratton, Sussex, by his third wife, Catherine, daughter of Sir John Temple of Stowe, Bucks. He matriculated at St. Edmund's Hall in 1625, receiving his B.A. in 1625 and his M.A. in 1628. Parker was called to the bar of Lincoln's Inn in 1637. He married Jane Cannon, probably in 1634. Parker's eldest brother, Sir Thomas Parker, sat for Seaford in the Long Parliament; his uncle was Lord Saye and Sele.*

Family connections notwithstanding, Parker's means were slight; his political activities and pamphleteering were professional rather than occasional, with pecuniary concerns often evident. This is clear enough in the case of the pamphlets Parker wrote for the Vintners, the Stationers, the

Merchant Adventurers, and the engineer William Wheeler, but in *The Altar Dispute* (1641) Parker styles himself in a dedication as Saye's "allies-man.' Further literary and documentary evidence suggests that Parker may well have been writing in the Fiennes interest, at least intermittently, from his two earliest pamphlets, *The Case of Shipmoney* and *A Discourse Concerning Puritans* (late 1640 or early 1641), through his decisive statements of bicameral parliamentary sovereignty, the important but unattributed broadsheet *A Question Answered* (Apr. 1642), *Some Few Observations* (May 1642), and the famous *Observations upon Some of His Majesties Late Answers and Expresses* (July 1642). D'Ewes openly suggested a connection between the *Observations* and a contemporaneous declaration issuing from a Commons committee headed by Nathaniel Fiennes;* the severity of the reaction from Fiennes, Denzil Holles,* Henry Marten* and William Strode* to this points to acute sensitivity over the charge (L: Harl. MS 163, ff. 288v, 291v). However, Parker's strong anticlericalism was even in 1640-41 at least as hostile to Presbyterianism as to Episcopacy; in this he spoke only for himself.

From his appointment as secretary to the army under Essex* (12 July 1642) Parker's fortunes and talents were openly yoked to the parliamentary cause. He may also have been secretary to the Committee of Safety in 1642-43. His petition to the Commons for the registrarship of the prerogative office (Nov. 1643) was rejected in favor of the appointment of Michael Oldsworth,* though in 1649 Parker and Oldsworth were jointly appointed. In June 1645 Parker and John Sadler* were appointed secretaries to the Commons; along with Thomas May they prepared the anonymous, all-but-official edition of the King's papers captured at Naseby, *The King's Cabinet Opened*. For his labors Parker received a parliamentary grant of £100 in Jan. 1646, with £50 following in February for his report of the fall of Chester. In the same year Parker went to Hamburg as secretary to the Merchant Adventurers, while maintaining his political connections, now to the Council of State, and continuing his pamphleteering activities. After the King's execution, he returned to England, busying himself with several appointments and commissions, culminating in his appointment as secretary to Cromwell's army in Ireland, where he remained from Aug. 1649 to his death in late 1652; his widow, Jane, secured his arrears from the Council of State on 18 Jan. 1653, and in October she was appointed to the joint tenure of the registrarship of the prerogative office with Oldsworth.

Parker's theory of bicameral parliamentary sovereignty in 1642 was based upon a repudiation of divine right and a clear-sighted enunciation of popular sovereignty. 'Power,' he declared, 'is originally inherent in the people,' and in 1644 he wrote, 'Princes were created by the people, for the people's sake and so limited by express laws as that they might not violate the people's liberty.' Parker asserted that kingship had been established by the people in Parliament, or at least 'by such bodies of men, as our parliaments now are.' Thus while in normal times King and Parliament ruled together, in times of crisis Parliament could exercise sovereignty alone by virtue of its position as the ultimate repository of the people's liberty.

Parker's clear understanding that a final locus of power must be determined in the state and his appeal to popular consent was a sharp break with tradition. It was the first effective reply to the royalist assertion that Parliament was in a state of rebellion against legitimate authority, and as such of inestimable value. As the first exponent of parliamentary legitimacy, Parker commands pride of place among the radical political theorists of the period. Yet Parker permitted no appeal beyond Parliament; having vested ultimate authority in their representative, the people could not recall it. To do so, he said, would be truly to 'proclaim civil war' and dissolve the bonds of society. Parker thus found himself overtaken by the subsequent complaints against a self-perpetuating Parliament and by Leveller demands for an enlarged franchise and a responsible legislature. His religious ideas were uncompromisingly secularist and anticlerical; he adhered to them despite his many services to largely Presbyterian mercantile interests and the Puritan commonwealth.

W.K. Jordan, *Men of Substance* (1942); M.A. Judson, 'Henry Parker and the Theory of Parliamentary Sovereignty,' in *Essays in History and Political Theory in Honor of Charles Howard McIlwain* (1936); M.A. Judson, *The Crisis of the Constitution 1603-1649* (1949); Haller, *Tr.*; Aylmer, *SS*; *DNB*; Judson, *TPR*.

M.J. Mendle and R. Zaller

PARKER, Robert (c. 1564-1614)

Puritan minister, was born probably in Wilton, Wilts. and received his B.A. in 1582 and M.A. in 1587 from Magdalen Coll., Oxf., where he was fellow (1585-93). Parker's growing nonconformity in these years is apparent: the Vice President's Register records his failure to wear proper vestments in church; with others he opposed the Queen's choice for president of the College; he obtained ordination by 1589 without subscription; he denounced the calling of ministers by bishops. Following his eventual subscription in 1591, and with the patronage of Henry Herbert, second Earl of Pembroke, to whom he had become chaplain, Parker became Rector of Patney, Master of the Hospital of St. Nicholas, Salisbury (1591-93), and Prebendary of Stanton St. Bernard (1594-1607). Publication of his *Scholastical Discourse Against Symbolizing with Antichrist in Ceremonies: Especially in the Sign of the Cross* (Amsterdam, 1607), along with charges of Brownism or Separatism which he vehemently denied, led to his deprivation and escape to Holland in that year. By 1610 he was boarding with the semi-Separatists Henry Jacob* and William Ames* in Leiden. In person and later by letter Parker, with Ames, did much to moderate the early rigid Separatism of the Pilgrim pastor, John Robinson.* In the next years he preached frequently and moved to Amsterdam where he failed in efforts to become a minister of the English Presbyterian church there. In 1613 he became preacher to the English garrison in Doesburg, Gelderland, where he died the following year. His wife Dorothy survived as did at least three children: Sarah (b. 1593), whose son Benjamin Woodbridge was first graduate of Harvard College; Thomas (b. 1593), first minister of the Newbury church, Massachusetts Bay Colony; and Elizabeth, later a Quaker.

Besides his 1607 book Parker completed *De descensu Domini nostri Jesu Christi ad Infernos*, begun by Hugh Sanford before his premature death and printed by Giles Thorp (1611). Incomplete at Parker's own death was his major work, *De politeia ecclesiastica Christi, et hierarchica opposita*, published posthumously in 1616 in Frankfurt and republished in 1638 (probably in Amsterdam) without Book 3, which contained Parker's positive views of the church. Very possibly the 'Admonition to Readers' in the 1616 edition was written by John Robinson. A fourth book, *An Exposition of the Pouring Out of the Fourth Vial; Mentioned in the Sixteenth of the Revelation*, was published in 1650 and republished a year later with an altered title and some additions.

Parker belongs in the mainstream of English Puritanism. His affirmation of the primacy of the particular church wherein authority and ecclesiastical jurisdiction lay 'essentially, properly, primarily and immediately' (*De politeia*, III, 14) shows that he was not a Presbyterian. Rather, apart from allowing synods to exercise limited authority beyond advice and counsel, Parker belongs with those who would be called Congregationalists. His significance lay in his moderate semi-separatism held at an early date; in the influence he and Ames wielded on John Robinson; and most especially in his influence on men better known than he. Both Thomas Hooker* and John Davenport,* when interrogated in Holland, appealed to Parker for justification of their positions. John Cotton* wrote that he learned about the church and its ministry from Parker, and Richard Mather* attributed his conversion to Congregationalism in part to Parker's writing. Such attestations establish Parker as a prominent and respected leader of that generation preceding the first Massachusetts settlements.

DNB (to be used with caution on Parker's benefices); P. Miller, *Orthodoxy in Massachusetts* (1959); Nuttall, *VS*; F.B. Carr, 'The Thought of Robert Parker . . . and His Influence on Puritanism before 1650' (Ph.D. thesis, Univ. of London, 1964).

F.B. Carr

PARNELL (or Parnel), James (1636-1656)

Quaker. The main facts of Parnell's short life are told in his *Fruits of a Fast* (1655) and his friends' posthumous *Lamb's Defence against Lyes* (1656). Born in East Retford, Notts., his small and weak physique earned him the nickname 'quaking boy' while he still explored gathered churches in villages near home. Probably included was the Aldam*-Killam*-Farnworth* circle around Balby, which perhaps inspired him to travel to Carlisle in 1653 to visit Fox* in jail. Convinced, in 1654 Parnell went with Fox to debate 'Priest Stephen' at Fenny Drayton. After receiving an inward call to preach himself, he was led to Cambridge, where he was jailed three months for placards condemning ministers and magistrates. The jury would find only that he had written them. Parnell's first tract, *A Trial of Faith* (1654), was his most reprinted. In 1655 he wrote the tracts *Christ Exalted; The Stone which the Builders Have Rejected; The Trumpet of the Lord Blowne, or a Blast against Pride*, an attack on the titles, luxury and pleasures of the gentry; *A Shield of Truth*,

a concise and able defense of Quaker beliefs on baptism, communion, prayer, ministry, magistracy, courtesy and perfectionism; and *A Watcher*, detailing his debates with Baptists at Fenstanton, Cambridge and Littleport, Ely.

In the first half of 1655 Parnell also preached and debated intensively, stirring up a Ranter whose nakedness shocked the Justices, though Alderman James Blackley at Cambridge set Parnell free from another jailing. In June he carried his message into Essex. After stops in five small Puritan towns, at Colchester he held four major meetings in one Sunday, convincing Stephen Crisp* and John Furly. A week later, on 12 July 1655, he returned to Coggeshall for a fast-day called by Independent pastors from three Essex towns, and tried to speak following the sermon. He was followed out of the church by a crowd, and arrested in the street by Dionysius Wakering, MP. Parnell was imprisoned for the remaining nine months of his life in the Norman castle of Colchester, except for a march in chains to and from the Assizes at Chelmsford. He was refused yard exercise, his food was taken by or given to other prisoners, and his many visitors were turned away or charged high fees. He was placed in an alcove, 'the Hole,' reached only by a six-foot ladder and a rope, from which he fell and was badly injured. Parnell was then put in an airless cubicle, 'the Oven.' His death on 10 Apr. 1656 led to inquest and controversy. Thomas Shortland, who spent his last night with him, admitted he had just ended a ten-day fast and could hardly eat, though healed of outward injuries, but rejected the jury's claim that he had starved himself to death. All the testimonies to him prefacing the *Collection of Several Writings [of] James Parnell* retell his death and his last words, 'Here I die innocently.'

Braithwaite, *BQu*; *DNB*; *DQB*; *EQW*; C.F. Smith, *The Life of James Parnell* (1906). Papers: LF (A.R. Barclay MSS #58).

H. Barbour

PARR (or Parre), John (c. 1633-c. 1716)

Ejected minister, was admitted sizar at Trinity Coll., Camb. on 24 May 1659 and took a B.A. in 1662. He preached at Preston, Lancs., and at Walton, Yorks., having been ejected from Farrington, Lancs. in 1662. He was, according to Matthew Henry, a most effective preacher. After the Declaration of Indulgence in 1672 he ministered at Darwen, Lancs. On two occasions during Charles II's reign, he was brought to court or fined for nonconformity. During the Monmouth rebellion he was imprisoned for six weeks at Warrington and then at Chester without any charges being brought against him. Parr became a member of the United Brethren in Lancashire, an association of Presbyterians and Independents with antecedents in London. He represented the northern district from 6 Aug. 1695 onwards. In 1700 he became the annual moderator of the group. He apparently had a call to Liverpool, a matter discussed by the Brethren. He died after 1713; the Preston and Walton churches elected John Turner as their minister in 1714, suggesting that Parr was either in ill health or deceased.

R. Halley, *Nonconformity in Lancashire* (1869); W. Shaw, ed., *Minutes of the Manchester Classis* (1891); *Calamy Revised*.

R. Masek

PARTRIDGE, John (1644-1715)

Whig astrologer and journalist, was born on 18 Jan. 1644 at East Sheen, Mortlake, Surrey, the son of John Partridge, a waterman. He was apprenticed to a shoemaker and practiced the trade for many years in Covent Garden. As a young man he taught himself Latin and medicine, and some Greek and Hebrew, and began to practice as an astrologer and physician. In 1678 he began a long series of annual almanacs, which soon became violently Whig in tone, attacking Catholics and demanding exclusion. He was later accused of complicity in the Rye House conspiracy, and of predicting a glorious destiny for Monmouth on the basis of the Duke's nativity. Partridge fled to the Netherlands in James' reign, and in 1687 published there an anonymous almanac predicting the King's downfall and championing republicanism. The following year he prophesied that James would die in the autumn of 1688. He accompanied William's invasion fleet, and claimed that his prophecy had been substantially fulfilled. With this triumph Partridge became the foremost almanac-maker of the 1690s, heaping praise on William and threatening destruction to the Jacobites and Louis XIV. He lived at the Blue Ball, Salisbury Street, in the Strand, where he had a large medical practice and issued pills, which were widely distributed. He claimed to be a royal physician to Charles II and William and Mary, though such titles meant little, and to be a medical doctor of Leiden, which has not been substantiated.

Under Anne, Partridge continued to attack Tories and professional rivals. His notoriety led Jonathan Swift to make him the target of a celebrated jest, by posing as an astrologer and predicting that Partridge would die on 29 Mar. 1708, and subsequently publishing a spurious account of his victim's end. Partridge's almanacs failed to appear in 1710-13, but this was a result of his quarrel with the Stationers over royalties, not of Swift's attack, and they were resumed in time for him to celebrate the Hanoverian succession.

Partridge married Jane Kirkman, a widow, in 1694. In his will, dated 3 Dec. 1714, he called himself a gentleman and left over £2000 in cash, £700 to his widow. There were no children. His books and papers were bequeathed to his patron, Francis Bennett, a Dorset gentleman. Partridge died in London on 24 June 1715, and was buried at Mortlake six days later.

His widow survived for many years, and was still selling his pills from the same address in 1741.

G. Mayhew, 'The Early Life of John Partridge,' *Studies in English Literature*, 1:31-42; *Dr. Partridge's Last Will and Testament* (1716); Capp, *APP*.

B.S. Capp

PATIENT (or Patience), Thomas (d. 1666)

Particular Baptist, seems to have been in New England during the 1630s. While there he came to the conclusion that infant baptism was wrong, and with his wife and at least one child had to leave. In 1644 he signed the Calvinistic Baptist *Confession* in London as a representative, with William Kiffin,* of one of the congregations whose views it proclaimed. He was noticed as with Kiffin by Thomas Edwards in 1646 and signed the new edition of the 1644 *Confession* that year. Probably about this time he baptized Lawrence Clarkson.* In Feb. 1647 Patient was reported to have been ordained in a house in Bell Alley, Coleman Street, London. On 2 Apr. 1649 he joined with other London Baptist leaders in a petition to the House of Commons aimed at dissociating themselves from the Levellers, *The Humble Petition and Representation*. He joined the same circle to sign *Heart-bleedings for Professors Abominations*, warning against the Ranters and Quakers in 1650. The same year he joined Kiffin, John Spilsbury* and John Pearson in commending Daniel King's* *A Way to Sion*.

The earliest evidence of Patient's presence in Ireland is a letter dated from Kilkenny and addressed to Cromwell on 15 Apr. 1650. Identified as he had been with those who insisted on closed communion (no church membership without believer's baptism) Patient naturally shared responsibility for a letter dated 14 Jan. 1652 from Waterford where he seemed to be leading a congregation of some Baptists in membership with John Rogers'* Independent

congregation in Dublin. The approach seems to have been effective and the group separated from Rogers to form their own congregation. Among others baptized by Patient in Ireland was Jerome Sankey.* Patient evidently had considerable influence with officials there. He converted the Governors of Waterford and Kilkenny, Richard Lawrence* and Daniel Axtell,* and in Dec. 1652 he was one of those appointed to preach in turn in Dublin Cathedral. On 1 June 1653 a letter signed by Patient and other Baptists in Ireland to London leaders made proposals for strengthening the links between the various Calvinistic Baptist communities in the British Isles.

When Cromwell became Lord Protector the Irish Baptists there showed some hostility but a letter from three London leaders calmed them. There was a report that Patient's congregation was dwindling but he continued to act as one of those appointed to examine ministers of religion who applied for positions in Ireland. During 1655-56 there seems to have been a coolness between Henry Cromwell,* commander of the troops in Ireland, and the Baptists because he believed them to be disloyal. He did not attend the funeral conducted by Thomas Patient for the wife of Adj.-Gen. William Allen.* But in Oct. 1656, just before the radical officers' breach with Henry, Patient visited him to express his support, and in 1657 Patient and his friends cemented relationships with the authorities by a loyal address to Cromwell when he refused to accept the English throne.

After the Restoration Patient returned to England and for a time served the closed-membership Calvinistic Baptist church at the Pithay, Bristol. He was imprisoned for a period in 1663-64, apparently for illegal preaching. By 28 June 1666 Patient was back in membership with Kiffin's congregation which on that day elected him to be joint-elder with Kiffin. He died on 29 July 1666.

The *DNB* article is unreliable. T. Patient, *The Doctrine of Baptism*

(1654); Hayden, *RCCB*; B.R. White, 'Thomas Patient in England and Ireland,' *Irish Baptist Historical Society Journal*, 2:36-48; Tolmie.

B.R. White

PATSHALL (or Pachell, Packtell), John (fl. 1661-1683)

Fifth Monarchist, was captured, along with Thomas Venner* and some twenty other Fifth Monarchy Men, after the attempted rising in London in Jan. 1661. He could not, however, be convicted of treason as there was only one witness against him. Patshall was apprehended again in 1665, this time for his alleged connection with the Yorkshire rising of 1663. He is known to have been in prison for sedition, at the Gatehouse, Westminster, from about Feb. 1665 to May 1666, when he escaped. Between 1678 and 1683 Patshall was twice implicated in assassination plots. In July 1678 he was reported by Thomas Blood* to have been active with other Fifth Monarchists in contriving the assassination of unspecified persons; and in 1683 he was accused of complicity in the Rye House plot. A warrant was issued for Patshall and a search made for him between July and Dec. 1683, but without apparent success. Patshall, at the time of his 1666 imprisonment, was known to have had a wife, Elizabeth, and, in 1683 he was reported to be a brewer's clerk in Southwark. He is referred to in 1683 as 'grown decrepit and will never be sound again, but as vile as ever' (*CSPD, Chas. II*, 24:184).

CSPD, Chas. II, 4:293; 5:400, 404, 416; 20:290; 24:66, 104, 184; 25:4, 77; L. Echard, *The History of England*, 3 (1718); Capp, *FMM*.

H.A. Nenner

PAUL, Thomas (fl. 1673-1674)

Particular Baptist, was active in London where he was associated with such prominent Baptists as William Kiffin,* Hanserd Knollys* and Daniel Dyke.* He was probably a member of the Devonshire Square Church which Kiffin served as pastor for nearly sixty years. Paul is notable for his participation in two controversies, one in opposition to John Bunyan* and the other against the Quakers. The first was precipitated by the publication of Bunyan's *Confession of My Faith, and a Reason of My Practice* (1672), which advocated the principle of open church membership. That principle was then criticized in printed works by Paul, Kiffin, John Denne* and Henry Danvers,* all of whom held that believers' baptism was a prerequisite for membership and communion. Paul's *Some Serious Reflections on That Part of Mr. Bunion's Confession of Faith, Touching Church Communion with Unbaptized Believers* was published in 1673 and included an epistle to the reader by Kiffin. Whereas Bunyan held that an attitude of love should prevail over differing opinions on this issue, Paul argued that judgment rather than affection should be paramount and pointed out that 'want of light' did not excuse persons from baptism any more than it excused them from almsgiving, partaking of the Lord's Supper or any other of God's commands. Bunyan responded in *Differences in Judgment About Water-Baptism, No Bar to Communion* (1673) and *Peaceable Principles and True* (1674).

The second controversy began with a public debate in Sept. 1672 between the Baptist Thomas Hicks* and the Quaker George Whitehead.* Hicks then published *A Dialogue Between a Christian and a Quaker* (1672) which elicited Quaker charges of forgery in his representations of Quaker writings and doctrines. Kiffin and Knollys arranged for a second debate to be held on 28 Aug. 1674 at a Baptist hall in Paul's Alley, Barbican. Paul, Kiffin, Knollys and others signed a letter inviting William Penn* to participate, but neither Penn nor Whitehead was in London at the time. Nevertheless, the meeting was held and Paul was one of 22 persons who attested to the accuracy of Hicks' quotations from Quaker tracts. The meeting was described in Hicks' *The Quakers Appeal Answered* (1674), and Paul was among those who signed the epistle to the reader.

J. Brown, *John Bunyan*, rev. F.M. Harrison (1928); Crosby; R.L. Greaves, *John Bunyan* (1969); Whitley, *BL*.

T.L. Underwood

PEARD, George (1594-1644)

Parliamentary radical and law reformer, SP, LP 1640 (Barnstaple), was the eldest son of the barrister John Peard and his wife Gillian Beaple of Barnstaple, Devon. The Peard family had been one of the borough's leading families for several generations, serving as aldermen, mayors, borough legal counsel and MPs. The family was also an early Protestant one, and George Peard was a Puritan with a strong belief in predestination. The family owned and leased land, houses and shops in and around Barnstaple, and had considerable wealth. Peard, however, did little to augment these holdings, devoting his life to the law and to the divisive religious, political and constitutional issues of his day.

Peard matriculated to the Middle Temple on 23 June 1613, and was admitted to the bar on 30 June 1620. He spent several years in London on behalf of Barnstaple clients, becoming the corporation's legal counsel in 1628, Deputy Recorder in 1637 and Recorder in 1641. Practicing before the common law and the bill courts, he took chambers in Kellaway's buildings in 1623 and Humphrey Lowe's in 1626. He frequently assisted the sons of Devon and Dorset merchants and gentry in matriculating to the Temple, and became close friends with fellow Templars George Beare and John Northcote. Peard did not become involved in politics until the late years of the 1630s, when he protested against the policies of Charles' government. Elected for his borough to the Short and Long Parliaments, the whole of his parliamentary career occurred in the last four years of his life, 1640-44.

Peard spoke out strongly against the imposition of ship money, which his mother had defaulted on, as an 'abomination' in the Short Parliament. In the Long Parliament he attacked prerogative government in church and state, and was active in promoting impeachments against Strafford, Laud and Finch. He sat on, and was an important member of the committees for the bill of attainder against Strafford, the reform of recusant laws and church polity, and the reform of the courts of justice. As chairman of the Committee on Monopoly he secured the expulsion of a number of monopolists from the House. He was a Presbyterian ally in the Commons of his fellow Middle Templars Simonds D'Ewes, Sir John Northcote and Sir John Maynard*, all of whom came from or had connections in Devon and Dorset, and was close to John Pym* and Sir Edward Dering. Serving often as a contact between Parliament and the judges, he acted personally to release men who had been imprisoned by Charles' government.

Peard had an unswerving belief in the supremacy of law. Neither Parliament nor the King, he asserted, could command obedience. Office-holders were bound to the law, and not to the person who employed them. If the King commanded a person to do an 'unjust' act, he committed treason and his life was forfeit. Peard also believed in the principles of a decentralized state. Local communities should be strong; concentrated regal power was inevitably tyrannical. Peard supported the parliamentary cause physically and financially. He gave £100 to the Commons in 1642, plus £50 p.a. for the Civil War and £50 p.a. for the defense of Barnstaple. He helped to construct the 'Great Fort' above the town, organized the ordnance, and sat on the local council of war. When the war turned badly in the southwest he tried to get his townsmen to fight to the end. When Barnstaple was taken in July 1643, the Royalists plundered Peard's residence and half hung him. Sent to prison in Exeter, he never recovered.

C.T. Martin, ed., *Middle Temple Record: Minutes of Parliament* (1901), 2; D'Ewes, *Jour.* (C); Keeler; R.W. Cotton, *Barnstaple and the Northern Part of Devonshire During the Great Civil War 1642-1646* (1889); *DNB*; B. & P.; *PSP 1640*. Papers: L (Add. MSS); O (Rawl. MSS; Barnstaple MSS).

L.A. Knafla

PEARSON, Anthony (c. 1626-1666)

Quaker, was born at Cartmel Fell, Lancs., the son of Edward Pearson, probably late in Dec. 1626, for he was baptized on 7 Jan. 1627. He had at least one brother, John (later to become postmaster for Cumberland and Westmorland). Nothing is known about his education, but he may have received some legal training in London, although he does not appear in the records of the Inns of Court. In 1648 Pearson became a clerk in Newcastle to Sir Arthur Haselrig,* Governor for the North. In 1649 he was appointed judge advocate at Newcastle for the trial of non-commissioned officers and soldiers of the northern garrisons for offenses not extending to life or limb. In the same year he was appointed clerk and registrar of the Committee for Compounding, probably by Haselrig's influence. In 1650 he went into Durham to look after Haselrig's estates, one of which was the manor of Bishop Auckland, and probably at that time purchased Ramshaw Hall, five miles from Bishop Auckland, which became his permanent residence. On 10 Feb. 1652 the Committee for Compounding appointed him Sequestration Commissioner for county Durham. Acquisitive as well as ambitious, Pearson purchased several manors in Cumberland (May 1650) on the sale of bishops' lands, as well as Marrow-lee, N'land (Mar. 1653), and other delinquents' estates belonging to Sir Thomas Riddell and the Marquis of Newcastle. Prior to 1652 he married Grace, daughter of Thomas Lamplough, of Ribton Hall, Cumb.

In Mar. 1652 Pearson was appointed JP for Cumberland and Westmorland, and in Jan. 1653 was on the bench, along with Gervase Benson (a Quaker) and others, at the trial for blasphemy of James Nayler* at Appleby Sessions, W'land. As a result of Nayler's impassioned though fruitless defense, Pearson was attracted to Quakerism, and soon after visited Swarthmore Hall, the home of Judge Thomas Fell* and his wife Margaret,* a Quaker convert. There he met George Fox,* who greatly impressed him. Realizing the importance of this potential convert, Friends kept up the pressure, with Francis Howgill* and Margaret Fell both writing encouraging letters to Pearson, and James Nayler visiting him at Ramshaw Hall in July 1653. By that time Pearson was probably fully convinced, for meetings were being held at his home.

In Aug. and Sept. 1653 Pearson used his influence to secure the release of George Fox from his imprisonment at Carlisle. In Oct. 1653 he wrote a paper to the Barebones Parliament (*To the Parliament of the Common-wealth of England, Christian Friends*) defending Quaker principles, attacking the 'ignorant' zeal of judges and justices and including a list of Friends who were then in prison. By 1654 Ramshaw Hall was the center of a growing Quaker community in Durham and with Fox's visit there in March, a Men's Monthly meeting was established for Durham with Pearson as one of the representatives. In July 1654 he was in London to see Oliver Cromwell, to whom he made an unsuccessful appeal for complete religious toleration. At that time Pearson also wrote *A Few Words to All Judges*, which had strong Antinomian overtones. He ministered in London before returning to Durham in August.

Pearson attended the meetings organized by John Wildman* in Sept. 1654, but there is little indication of any active sympathy by Pearson for Wildman's plot. In October Pearson returned to London, met with Cromwell and managed to secure a discharge for Thomas Aldam,* a Friend imprisoned at York. By 1655 Pearson was acting as one of the Quaker treasurers in the north. In Apr. 1655 he and Aldam wrote a paper to the magistrates of Cheshire which denounced their treatment of Quakers, and the following month they were in London aiding Friends who were to appear in court for refusing to pay tithes, as well as meeting with Cromwell on behalf of imprisoned Friends.

For the next two years Pearson spent much of his time gathering information for his pamphlet, *The Great Case of Tythes Truly Stated* (1657). Although in part historically confused and theologically speculative, this was the most concise Quaker tract against tithes and went through three editions in three years, with four more in the eighteenth century. From 1657 to 1660 Pearson played a leading role in the development of Quaker business meetings in the north and the expansion of that concept to the rest of England. Early in Oct. 1658 Pearson with nineteen other Friends sent a lengthy paper to the Council defending Quaker principles and including a list of 115 Quaker prisoners in England. In 1659 he and fifteen other Friends wrote *A Declaration of the People of God* which, among other things, stated the willingness of Friends to hold public office, and in conjunction with this the Quakers sent in lists of potential JPs, which included Pearson (recommended for Westmorland and Cumberland, from which Commissioners he had been removed prior to 1657). On 27 June 1659 Pearson was one of twenty Quakers who presented a petition with 15,000 signatures to the Rump Parliament calling for the suppression of tithes.

Yet Pearson was controversial. In May 1656 he was reproached by William Caton* for his failure to aid Scottish Friends in their unsuccessful efforts to purchase a meeting-house in Edinburgh. In July 1656 Lancelot Wardell complained that Pearson and two other Durham Friends had refused to allow the printing of a paper concerning the persecution of some Durham Quakers. Wardell and Pearson also had a protracted dispute over money the former claimed to have given Pearson as a Quaker treasurer. In May 1657 John Lilburne,* the Leveller turned Quaker, bitterly denounced Pear-

son for conveying land which Lilburne claimed as his own to his wife. Early in 1658 Pearson unsuccessfully attempted to establish a rapport between George Fox and two of Pearson's former colleagues on the Committee for Compounding, Sir Henry Vane* and Thomas Ledgard.

In Aug. 1659 Pearson was appointed a Commissioner for the Militia in the north, disarmed Cavaliers and their sympathizers, stockpiled the arms in Ramshaw Hall and would have raised the northern counties against Booth's rising but for the reluctance of local JPs and his fellow Commissioners. Francis Howgill and Thomas Aldam each expressed concern at this time over Pearson's apparent efforts to promote his own status within the Quaker movement. Significantly, Pearson did not attend the important General Meeting of Friends at Skipton in Apr. 1660. In that year both Margaret Fox (Fell) and George Fox wrote warnings to Pearson against his un-Quakerly activities. Although still a Quaker as late as Apr. 1661 Pearson's relationship with men like Vane and Haselrig, as well as his behavior in 1659, put his freedom in jeopardy. In June 1660 the House of Lords investigated a report that Pearson was continuing to stockpile arms at Ramshaw Hall, but the matter was dropped. In Dec. 1661 Pearson was arrested in London for being there contrary to the proclamation of 28 Nov. 1661 against officers and soldiers of the late armies from coming within 20 miles of London. On examination Pearson denied charges that he had been a colonel under Lambert* during Booth's rising, professed his loyalty and disingenuously claimed that he had acted in 1659 as a JP (rather than as a Commissioner for the Militia). On 16 Jan. 1662 he was released from any further restraint and on 2 Mar. 1663 was appointed Under-sheriff of Durham by Bishop Cosin. Pearson died on 23 Jan. 1666, probably from plague, and was buried the following day at Little St. Mary's, Durham, having proclaimed himself an Anglican on his deathbed.

A. Wallis, 'Anthony Pearson 1626-1666', *JFHS*, 51:77-95; *CCC*; *DQB*;

DNB. Papers: LF; LPR (Docquet Book).

   C.W. Horle

Corp. MSS; L (Stowe MSS).

   M.J. Brown

PELHAM, Peregrine (1602-1650)

Regicide and parliamentary radical, MP LP 1641 (Hull). Pelham was the grandson of Sir William Pelham, Lord Justice of Ireland under Queen Elizabeth, and son of Peregrine Pelham of Wickham, Lincs. Pelham was twice married: first to the daughter of a family named Bowes and later to Dame Jacoba Van Lore, the widow of a wealthy merchant and money-lender. He spent most of his life at Hull and was closely associated with the affairs of the town. Pelham was apprenticed to a local merchant, Thomas Aslaby, and was admitted to the freedom of the city in Aug. 1626. He exported lead and imported French wines. His public career began in 1630 when he was elected chamberlain at Hull; then he became successively sheriff (1636), alderman (after 1640) and mayor (1649). To accept this last post, Pelham had to seek the permission of the House of Commons where, in Jan. 1641, he had been chosen to assume the seat recently made vacant by the death of Sir John Lister. When the war started the city of Hull was of great strategic importance; accordingly Pelham himself assumed a role of some prominence in the House. He served on several important committees, especially those that dealt with naval affairs. Staunchly radical, Pelham was impatient of any attempt to negotiate with the King and he approved of the execution of traitors to the parliamentary cause. He was a strong admirer of Cromwell, a committed Puritan and, in the argot of the time, a 'fiery spirit.' Pelham accepted appointment to the High Court and, unlike many others, performed his duty with enthusiasm and did not shrink from signing the death warrant. He sat in the Rump but died late in 1650.

   Keeler; Noble; Nuttall, *Yorks*.; Underdown, *PP*; Yule; A. Collins, *History of the Family of Pelham* (1755). Papers: Hull

PELHAM, Sir Thomas, Bt. (1597-1654)

Parliamentary radical, MP 1621 (East Grinstead), 1624, 1625, SP LP 1640 (Sussex). Pelham was the only son of Sir Thomas Pelham, Bt., of Laughton, Sussex, and Mary, daughter of Sir Thomas Walsingham of Scadbury, Kent. The family owned the entire rape of Hastings and three hundreds as well as nearly twenty manors and other smaller properties, and ran a highly profitable ironworks as well. Pelham matriculated at Emmanuel Coll., Camb. in 1615 and subsequently entered Gray's Inn. He succeeded his father in 1624 and became a JP and DL. In 1627 and again in 1639 he resisted loans. Pelham was thrice married, first to Mary, daughter of Sir Roger Wilbraham, Master of Requests, who died in 1635; secondly in 1637 to Judith, widow of John Shurley of Lewes, who died in 1638; and in 1640 to Margaret, daughter of Sir Henry Vane, Sr.* Pelham was active in the Long Parliament, where he led a radical Sussex contingent that included Herbert Morley,* Anthony Stapley* and James Rivers.* His Puritan sympathies led to appointments on committees for London Catholics and for a preaching ministry. In Feb. 1641 he and Stapley presented the Root and Branch petition for Sussex. Pelham offered his bond for £1000 for the loan in 1640, and in Sept. 1642 promised £200 more. He was appointed to help provide for the defense of Sussex, and in the summer of 1641 assisted in disarming recusants there. Throughout the Civil War he was active on the county committee, where he exerted great influence. Pelham's zeal was questioned in the House in 1643 and 1644, but this was in part based on local rivalry. Still hoping for a settlement based on monarchy, he was secluded in 1648 and retired to his estates, where after several years of declining health he died in Aug. 1654.

Keeler; Fletcher; Underdown, *PP*; *Al. Cant.*; *CJ*, 2 *passim*; Rushworth, 3:914. Papers: L (Add. MSS 5697; 33,058; 33,084; 33,137; 33,143-49; 33,154-55; 33,171-85; 33,188).

M.J. Brown

PELL, John (1611-1685)

Mathematician and reformer, was born on 1 Mar. 1611 at Southwick, Sussex, the younger son of John Pell (d. 1616), a minister, and Mary (née Holland, d. 1617), of Halden, Kent. After attending the free school at Steyning, Sussex, he matriculated as a sizar from Trinity Coll., Camb. in 1624, receiving his B.A. in 1629 and M.A. in 1630. His correspondence with Henry Briggs in 1628 regarding logarithms provided a foretaste of mathematical interests, and he also wrote on the quadrant and sundials. By the time he was incorporated at Oxford in 1631, he had gone to Chichester to teach in Samuel Hartlib's* academy, but when that failed he established his own school in Sussex. He left for London at Hartlib's bidding. Preferring to devote his time to mathematical and educational pursuits, he refused Bishop John Williams' tender of a benefice.

Between 1630 and 1634 Pell formulated a Baconian scheme for a 'Natural History of Mathematics.' At the heart of his proposal was a mathematical library to collect books and instruments, prepare abstracts and research reports, facilitate the interchange of information, provide public references, maintain a register of mathematicians, and serve as an employment agency for them. Pell himself proposed to write a guide to mathematical study, a summary of mathematical knowledge, a pocket book of mathematical tables and a manual for teaching oneself mathematics. The program was published by Hartlib in 1638 as *An Idea of Mathematics*, circulated abroad by Hartlib and Theodore Haak,* and reprinted as an appendix to John Dury's* *The Reformed School* in 1651 and by the Royal Society in 1679. It set the tone for the reform tracts of the Hartlib school and influenced Hartlib's proposal for an Office of Addresses. When Hartlib considered establishing a universal college in 1639, he thought Pell was qualified to formulate 'a perfect enumeration of all things.'

Pell's interests extended beyond mathematics. In 1639 he expressed regret that the recommendations for timber conservation in Arthur Standish's *The Commons Complaint* (1611) had not been effected, and he was a friend of Sir Richard Weston, who was noted for his experiments in husbandry and interest in enclosure. Through his correspondence with Sir Charles Cavendish he kept abreast of scientific developments on the Continent and probably espoused the new science in England. He was an admirer of Joachim Jungius, a German authority on plant morphology, and in 1634 personally wrote an 'Eclipse Prognosticator.' He also worked with Henry Gellibrand, whose interests included astronomy as well as mathematics.

The hopes of the Hartlib circle were high in Sept. 1641 when Comenius arrived in England and was greeted by Pell and others. In 1642 Pell, Hartlib, Dury, Comenius and Joachim Hübner proposed to develop fifteen graded texts to serve educational needs from infancy to adolescence, but the onset of the Civil War dashed this scheme as well as their broader dreams for reform. Pell followed Comenius and Dury to the Continent, accepting, with the encouragement of Haak and Sir William Boswell, a professorship of mathematics at Amsterdam in 1643. William Petty* began corresponding with him in 1645, the year before the Prince of Orange lured him to Breda as a professor of mathematics and philosophy. He returned to England in 1652 when war with the Dutch was imminent. In response to his petition, the Council of State appointed a committee consisting of Cromwell, Bulstrode Whitelocke* and Oliver St. John* which recommended that he receive £200 p.a. to enable him to lecture on mathematics. Apparently the Council hoped to establish a mathematics lectureship at Cambridge, but this did not materialize. Nor did the Wardenship of Merton Coll., Oxf., which Haak thought Pell might have if Jonathan Goddard left. For his part Hartlib hoped in 1653 to establish a 'Council for Schooling' on which Pell would serve with Dury, John Milton,* Marchamont Nedham,* Ezerel Tong and others. Ultimately Haak could do no better than persuade the government to send Pell to Zurich in 1654 as a diplomat. While in Switzerland he and Samuel Morland were given authority in Nov. 1655 to distribute £7000 for the relief of Protestants in the Piedmont. The following February the Council voted him an allowance of £800 p.a. to commence 'from his arrival at Geneva.' In Switzerland he maintained his scholarly interests through correspondence with Hartlib, Petty, William Brereton and others.

The difficulties encountered by Pell gradually dimmed his reforming ardor. In Mar. 1655 he wrote to John Thurloe* about the general disillusionment of 'men variously impoverished by the long troubles, full of discontents, and tired by long expectation of amendment, [who] must needs have great propensions to hearken to those that proclaim times of refreshing – a golden age – at hand. . . .' Recalled to England, he arrived in London in Aug. 1658, and in November met with a group of mathematicians which included Goddard, Paul Neile, Laurence Rooke and Christopher Wren; this was the nucleus of the future Royal Society. An admirer of Milton and a friend of James Harrington,* Pell may have been involved in the discussions of the Rota Club in 1659-60. In the same period Hartlib interested him in a scheme – the Antilian project – to establish a colony of religious idealists from which a world reformation could be launched. It was also in 1659 that he produced, at Robert Boyle's suggestion, an English translation of Yonker de Bill's *Tract Touching the Skill of . . . Anatomy*.

At the Restoration Pell yielded to the new regime and overcame his long-standing reluctance to accept preferment in the church. Ordained deacon (31 Mar. 1661) and priest (June 1661), he was appointed Rector of Fobbing, Essex on 16 June 1661, and on 23 July 1663 Bishop Sheldon made him Vicar of Laindon, Essex; he held both positions until his death. On 20 May 1663 he became one of the original fellows of the Royal Society, but was not active. Some interest in reform remained. With William Sancroft's support he submitted a proposal for reforming the calendar to the upper house of Convocation on 5 Dec. 1661, and in 1664 his letter to Haak favoring such reform was published as *Easter Not Mistimed*. When Sheldon became Archbishop of Canterbury, Pell was appointed his chaplain, and on 7 Oct. 1663 received the D.D. degree at Lambeth. William Lord Brereton was his patron for some years, enabling him to live at Brereton Hall, Ches., but generally his intellectual activities disappointed others. An incompetent manager of finances, he was imprisoned twice in the King's Bench prison for debt. From Mar. 1682 until June 1684 he lived in the College of Physicians, moving finally to Westminster due to ill health. He died there on 12 Dec. 1685 and was buried in the church of St. Giles-in-the-Fields.

Pell married Ithumaria, daughter of Henry Reginolles (or Reginalds) of London, on 3 July 1632, and by her had four sons and four daughters. She died on 11 Sept. 1661, and he remarried prior to 1669. His sister, Bathsua Makin (or Makins), was an admirer of Comenius, concerned with the reform of female education, and the author of an *Essay to Revive the Ancient Education of Gentlewomen* (1673).

Webster, *GI* and *SHAL*; *DNB*; Aubrey; *CSPD, Comm.*, 4:461, 494-95; 5:437; 6:311, 345, 422, 457; 7:50; 9:13, 190; P.J. Wallis, 'An Early Mathematical Manifesto – John Pell's Idea of Mathematics,' *Durham Research Review*, 18:139-48. Papers: L (Birch MSS; Harl. MSS; Lans. MSS; Sloane MSS).

R.L. Greaves

PEMBROKE, third Earl of. *See* Herbert, William.

PEMBROKE, fourth Earl of. *See* Herbert, Philip

PENDARVES (or Pendarvis), John (c. 1623-1656)

Particular Baptist and Fifth Monarchist, matriculated from Exeter Coll., Oxf. on 9 Feb. 1638 as from Crowan, Corn. He graduated B.A. on 3 Mar. 1642. Probably after Abingdon, Berks. fell into the hands of Parliament in May 1644 he became Vicar of St. Helen's parish church. Pendarves' stipend was augmented with some difficulty and without complete success by the Committee for Plundered Ministers. By Dec. 1649 he had been replaced at St. Helen's and in Jan. 1650 was being paid as minister of the parish church at Wantage some twelve miles away. On 18 Jan. 1650 he signed the Engagement to be faithful to the republic as established without 'a King or House of Lords.' From 1648 to 1656 he was a weekly lecturer in the village of Marcham during the summer and at St. Helen's during the winter, paid for by a legacy from Richard Wrigglesworth. While Pendarves may not have founded the Abingdon Baptist church it was in being and he was apparently its pastor as early as 1650. Pendarves married Thomasina Newcomen of Dartmouth, daughter of a leading supporter of the parliamentary cause there and sister of Elias who was to be father of Thomas Newcomen (1663-1729), the famous engineer and pastor of the Dartmouth Baptists. The Council of State gave Pendarves permission to preach in St. Saviour's Church, Dartmouth in 1652 and Robert Steed, probably from Abingdon, was Baptist pastor in the town in 1656. In Feb. 1654 the Kilmington, Devon church invited Pendarves to become its pastor, but although he continued to be linked with the west country he

evidently refused. Two months later he was present at the ordination of Thomas Collier* at Bridgwater and attended other Western Association meetings during the next two years. The last to which he went was that at Wells in Apr. 1656 where he expected to meet Robert Bennet* from Hexworthy, Corn.

During the early 1650s Pendarves and his friends were also active in the villages around Abingdon and Wantage, and as a result several new congregations were founded in such villages as Watlington, Bledlow and Kingston Blount. During 1652-53 his own church at Abingdon was a founding member of the association which was to grow far beyond the borders of the Thames Valley where it began. This work saw Pendarves closely associated with Benjamin Cox.* Through Cox he was linked with the Particular Baptist leaders in London, and especially with the church meeting in Petty France. In the 1650s Pendarves was also involved with moderate Fifth Monarchist leaders. He seems to have shared in Henry Jessey's* program for the reform of the calendar and in a letter to Robert Bennet he expressed cautious sympathy with the views of John Tillinghast.* On 15 Feb. 1655 Pendarves was present at an examination of Fifth Monarchist leaders by Cromwell. Pendarves himself denied the legitimacy of the Protectorate and claimed that arms could be taken up against it without sin, and though he himself was never apparently involved in plots, his funeral in Sept. 1656 was the occasion for a great Fifth Monarchist rally at which the question 'whether God's people must be a bloody people' was put and carried with enthusiasm. The rally was itself thereupon dispersed by force.

The pamphlet which Pendarves published with other west country Calvinistic Baptists in 1656 entitled *Sighs for Sion* expressed an expectation of a near approach of a crisis in God's dealings with his church in England. Pendarves in particular seems to have seen the reformation of the outward structures of the church away from enforced conformity towards the fellowship of believers as part of the duty required in preparation for the crisis. He joined with Christopher Feake* in writing a preface to the tract *The Prophets Malachy and Isaiah* and preached a sermon to the Petty France congregation which was published in 1657 after his death: both stressed the need for reform. Pendarves died of the plague in London. In 1672 the surviving members of his congregation applied for a license under the Declaration of Indulgence.

E.A. Payne, *The Baptists of Berkshire* (1951); Capp *FMM*; *DNB*; *Ath. Oxon.*; B.R. White, 'John Pendarves, the Calvinistic Baptists and the Fifth Monarchy,' *BQ*, 25:251-71.

B.R. White

PENINGTON (or Pennington), Isaac (c. 1587-1661)

Parliamentary radical, MP SP, LP 1640 (London). Penington was the eldest son of the London fishmonger Robert Penington and his wife Judith, daughter of Isaac Shetterden of London. His eldest son by his first wife, Abigail, daughter of the London merchant John Allen, was the Quaker Isaac Penington.* The elder Penington was the second cousin of the admiral, Sir John Penington of Muncaster. In the early 1630s Penington was interested in the cloth trade and the affairs of the East India Company (in which his father had been engaged), and jointly owned a brewery in Whitefriars. Between 1640 and 1642 he was Prime Warden of the Fishmongers' Company, and in Feb. 1644 he became the Governor of the Levant Company. Penington was elected Sheriff of London in 1638 and alderman the following year, when he and 23 other aldermen refused a Privy Council demand to raise £30,000 to loan the government. He was one of seven aldermen who refused to submit a list of the richest men in his ward preparatory to a forced loan.

As a member of the Long Parliament one of Penington's first actions was to read a petition expressing citizens' concerns regarding religious innovations. He subsequently presented a number of petitions to the Commons dealing with ecclesiastical reform, the chief of these being the Root and Branch Petition on 11 Dec. 1640. An opponent of episcopal government, he made his presence felt on various committees concerned with church reform. The key to his power in the Commons was his leadership of the City radicals whose financial backing was essential to the parliamentary cause. He played a major role in raising a loan in the City late in 1640 which enabled John Pym* to succeed in keeping the Scottish army in the north. As treasurer for the loan, Penington was the conduit of City money to the parliamentary leaders. More extreme than Pym, his principal allies in the Commons in 1641 were Sir Walter Erle,* William Strode,* Sir Henry Vane* and Capt. John Venn.* Penington was unsuccessful in his attempt to ensure Strafford's execution by holding up the Subsidies Bill in 1641, but he was instrumental in persuading the Commons to order (in August) that communion rails be removed, and (in September) that weekly lectures be approved in the churches. In the aftermath of the attempt to seize the five MPs, Penington served on the Commons' committee to prepare the City's defense, and may have been personally responsible for hiding the offending members. One of the six regiments of the trained bands was placed under his command. In Sept. 1642 he was appointed to the Militia Committee, and the same year was responsible for raising £1000 for the Irish venture, approximately half of which was his own money. Elected Lord Mayor in 1642 and 1643 with the support of City Puritans, he used his power to denounce three royalist clergy to the Committee for Scandalous Ministers, resulting in their ejection. Penington was a vigorous war supporter and sometimes proved troublesome to Pym. In Aug. 1643 he planned a coup whose object was the arrest of Holles* and other members of the peace party. In July he became Lieutenant of the Tower, but relinquished the post in 1645 in accord with the Self-Denying Ordinance. Penington strongly supported the establishment of a militia subcommittee at Salters' Hall, the chief meeting place of City radicals, but the attempt to free the subcommittee from the main Militia Committee failed, and on 27 Apr. 1647 Penington lost his own place on the committee. Penington and Thomas Andrewes* were the only two London aldermen who actually sat on the High Court, but he declined to sign the death warrant. Penington subsequently became an active member of the Council of State, serving on numerous committees, but withdrew from politics after 1655 when he sustained severe financial losses, and was discharged as an alderman in 1657.

Penington's religious views were staunchly Puritan. The efforts of John Davenport,* William Gouge, Richard Sibbes* and Thomas Taylor* to establish a public fund to relieve Protestants in the Palatinate received his backing. His concern with able preaching led to service as a Feoffee of Impropriations and an attempt to establish a lectureship at Chalfont St. Peter, Bucks., where he owned a country residence. The local vicar condemned him for his opposition to Laud and Arminianism. As a member of the vestry of St. Stephen's, Coleman Street, London, Penington was one of those responsible for the selection of John Goodwin* as vicar, but in 1645 he helped oust Goodwin and replace him with the Presbyterian William Taylor. In 1642 Penington persuaded the House of Commons that the Paul's Cross preachers should be appointed by the lord mayor and aldermen. When Laud was condemned, it was Penington who took him the news in the Tower and subsequently accompanied him to the scaffold on Tower Hill on 10 Jan. 1645. During Penington's mayoralty his chaplain was the influential Puritan Thomas Case, and he was a friend of John Milton.* Puritan leaders who visited London found hospitality in Penington's home, thanks especially to the religious convictions of his second wife, Mary, daughter of the brewer Matthew Young. As a key figure in the

parliamentary cause, he was imprisoned in the Tower at the Restoration and died there in Dec. 1661.

Keeler; Beaven; Pearl; R. Ashton, *The City and the Court* (1979); *DNB*; *CSPD, Chas. I*, 11:311-12; 17:560; 18:237, 342; 21:470; 23:651; *Comm.*, 1-2, 4 *passim*; Tolmie. Papers: LPR; L (Add. MSS).

R.L. Greaves

PENINGTON, Isaac (the younger) (1616-1679)

Quaker, was the son of Sir Isaac Penington,* a merchant and alderman in London. Educated at Cambridge, Penington early began a spiritual quest which led him first into Puritanism and later Quakerism. In 1654 he married Lady Springett,* only daughter and heiress of Sir John Proude and widow of Sir William Springett, and settled near London. Before his conversion to Quakerism in 1658, Penington wrote pamphlets on both political and religious subjects. His political theory, expressed between 1651 and 1653, was based on the thesis that even good men in high places often have difficulty in seeing justice done to their inferiors because unchecked power dulls the moral sense. Kingly government, Penington felt, had become corrupt and Parliament was headed the same way. The only check against parliamentary abuse was frequent and free elections. The people should choose those of their own rank to sit in Parliament. Penington's attitude toward Parliament was similar to that adopted in the Instrument of Government. Parliament was not an executive, and its role was to meet for short periods to pass laws against abuses. The powers of Parliament were limited to the secular sphere; political authority had no concern in spiritual matters.

In *A Voyce Out of Thick Darkness* (1650) Penington hoped for a speedy outpouring of the Holy Spirit to cure the nation's spiritual malaise. The kind of worship Penington wanted was not formal; rather, knowledge of God could come through the self-disclosure of the indwelling God. Although Penington's ideas were very similar to those of Friends, his first encounter with Quaker tracts made no impression. In 1656 he began attending Quaker meetings and in 1657 heard George Fox* preach. Soon after, he and his wife publicly joined the Friends.

Penington's rank in society and gift for expressing mystical insight as well as formal doctrine made him an important Friend. Along with William Penn* and Robert Barclay,* he remains a prime example of the intellectual sophistication of the second generation of Quaker converts.

Like other Friends, Penington drew a stark contrast between the religion made by man and that discovered by the Light of God. Man, he wrote, is naturally corrupt and has no faculty to reach God; even reason used in religious matters leads astray. By contrast, the Christian must silence his own will and listen to the seed of God in his conscience. Penington argued that since true religion is purely spiritual, any forced worship or coercion of conscience bears the mark of the Antichrist. Christ, who always operates by spiritual means, requires no earthly powers and has his own ways of punishing error. The church, he asserted, must remain free from the magistrate because the power of law extends only to the physical realm. These doctrines were not novel, but Penington expressed them with cogency and force.

Penington strongly attacked the persecution of Quakers in Massachusetts Bay in 1660, rebuked the army in 1659 for betraying liberty of conscience, and denounced the Cavaliers after the Restoration for their abuse of Friends. In 1661 he defined the Quakers' political program: universal freedom of worship, no laws contrary to equity and righteousness, no party exalted over another, and no plotting. He insisted that Quakers must never use outward weapons, though he never denounced the use of force by the army. Unlike the works of George Bishop,*

Edward Burrough* and William Penn, very few of Penington's writings are specifically political in content. Far more characteristic are his paeans to the joy of experiencing Christ and his clear defense of Quaker beliefs about the nature of the Trinity, the person of Christ, the role of Scripture, tithes, oaths and perfection.

As a wealthy and prominent Friend, Penington attracted persecution and spent six periods in jail between 1661 and 1671. Prison life undermined his already delicate health and after a period of weakness followed by a short illness, he died on 8 Oct. 1679.

Smith, *Cat.*; Wing; Fox, *CJ*; *EQL*; Braithwaite, *BQu*; *DNB*; *DQB*; *FPT*. Papers: LF.

J.W. Frost

PENINGTON, Mary Springett (c. 1625-1682)

Quaker, was the daughter and heiress of Sir John Proude of Goodnestone Court, Kent, an officer in the service of the United Provinces. Orphaned in 1628, Mary Penington joined the household of her uncle, Sir Edward Partridge, where she met her first husband, Partridge's nephew William Springett, whom she married in Jan. 1642. Sir William Springett, a DL of Kent, was commissioned by Parliament as colonel of foot under the Earl of Essex.* Following Springett's death in Feb. 1644 from an illness contracted at the capture of Arundel Castle, Sussex, Mary lived with her mother-in-law and her children by Springett, John and Gulielma Maria. On 13 May 1654, she married Isaac Penington the younger,* eldest son of Alderman Sir Isaac Penington,* at St. Margaret's, Westminster.

Mary Penington's autobiography, *A Brief Account of My Exercises from Childhood*, written between 1668 and 1680, describes a life marked by spiritual unrest and religious experimentation. The Puritan sympathies of her childhood led her through Springett to Independency, but she ultimately rejected what she perceived as its residual impurity and its inability to satisfy her need for assurance of salvation. During a period of 'wearied seeking and not finding' she met and married Isaac Penington, whose spiritual state was analogous to her own. Both Peningtons were convinced about 1656 through the joint efforts of Thomas Curtis and William Simpson, and were affilitated with the Quakers by 1658. The Peningtons' home, the Grange, Chalfont St. Peter, Bucks., housed the local Quaker meeting and Mary Penington wrote of her first experiences of 'worship in the full assurance of acceptation' during the first meeting at the Grange.

Penington was acutely conscious of the social disabilities of radical religion. When she refused to have Springett's posthumous daughter baptized she became a by-word and a hissing amongst the people of my own rank in the world.' She was reluctant to join the Quakers after her convincement as she feared the loss of her honor and reputation, 'the place and rank I stood outwardly in.' But when she publicly identified herself with the Quakers, she noted that she 'received strength against many things that I once thought it not possible to deny.' Conforming to the Quaker plain style in dress and language, she rejected the things 'of the world,' the customs and prerogatives of her birth.

During Isaac Penington's second imprisonment in Aylesbury jail in 1666-68, the Peningtons were evicted from the Grange, which had been confiscated with Alderman Penington's estates. Mary lost much of her own land by her testimony against oaths, which prohibited her from swearing to the validity of her claim against a relative's suit in Chancery. A strong desire to continue with the Chalfont meeting kept the family from removing to her remaining estate in Kent. With the remainder of her funds Mary arranged to purchase and rebuild Woodside, near Amersham, Bucks., where the Peningtons moved in 1669. Isaac, weakened by intermittent imprisonment, died on 8 Oct. 1679 while the Peningtons were visiting Goodnestone Court. Mary survived him by

three years, dying on 18 July 1682 while on a visit to her daughter Gulielma Maria, wife of William Penn,* at Worminghurst, Sussex. By 1680, Mary had discharged her debts and left 'handsome provision' for Gulielma Maria and her children John, Edward, William and Mary by Isaac Penington.

J.G. Bevan, *Memoirs of the Life of Isaac Penington* (1807); T. Ellwood, *The History of the Life of Thomas Ellwood* (1906); J. Penington, *Complaint Against William Rogers* (1681); *DNB*; M. Webb, *The Penns and Peningtons in the Seventeenth Century* (1867).

P.B. Volkman

PENN, William (1644-1718)

Quaker, was the key personality in early Quakerism after George Fox.* Penn's high social status was unique in the movement. He was born on 14 Oct. 1644. His father, Capt. (soon Admiral) William Penn, had gained successes in the parliamentary fleet's Irish Sea campaign. The elder Penn lived on Tower Hill, London, with his wife, Margaret Jaspers Vanderschuren, widow of a Dutch merchant in Ireland and perhaps daughter of another. Briefly arrested in 1646 for suspected royalist sympathies in the second Civil War, Admiral Penn retired to Wanstead, Essex. There the boy William, having survived small-pox, attended the school at Chigwell (1650-56) where he learned the Latin classics and some Greek moralists in Latin. The Admiral had meanwhile undertaken a Mediterranean expedition, a first campaign against the Dutch, and the capture of Jamaica. But disgraced again, and suspect for contacts with Prince Charles in Holland, Penn retired to his recently awarded Irish estates at Macroom, later exchanged for Shangarry, near Cork. There young William was impressed by a Quaker visitor, Thomas Loe.*

In 1659 the Admiral had already turned from the Rump Parliament to Charles, whom he carried home on his flagship at the Restoration. He became staff chief and secretary to the Duke of York. Young William enrolled at Christ Church, Oxf. in Oct. 1660 under a strict Anglican, Dr. Fell. He attended unofficial lectures of John Owen,* the displaced Vice-Chancellor, but did not absorb his Calvinism. Expelled in Mar. 1662, Penn was sent by his father to France, where he studied at the Protestant College at Saumur and lived in the home of its head, Moise Amyraut, until the latter's death in Jan. 1664. He completed his education with a tour of Italy, the Rhineland and Holland, and a year of law at Lincoln's Inn. Penn's father sent him to manage their Irish estates in Jan. 1666. He remained until Dec. 1667, except for a trip home to attend his sister's wedding. Penn's religious character now emerged after a winter of soul-searching following another encounter with Thomas Loe, an imprisonment alongside Quakers at Cork, and an appeal to Lord Broghill-Orrery, who wrote to his friend the Admiral. Penn was recalled to face his father. Despite gentler moments at Isaac Penington's* home, Thomas Loe's deathbed, and missions to ask the Duke of Buckingham and Sir Henry Berwick to intercede against the Clarendon Code, Penn remained sternly radical. His writings of 1668 (*Truth Exalted* and *The Guide Mistaken* against the conformer Jonathan Clapham), his 1669 letter against Vice-Chancellor Mews of Oxford, and his twin tracts, *A Trumpet Sounded* against Dutch pride (printed 1671) and 'God's Controversy' against England (1670, unpublished), all proclaiming God's purposes in history, were climaxed by a final conversion to Quakerism.

In debate with three Puritan pastors, Penn and George Whitehead* tried to prove the Quaker tenets that atonement alone was insufficient for salvation, and that the name 'Trinity' was unscriptural. Penn repeated the arguments in *The Sandy Foundation Shaken* (Nov. 1668), and was promptly imprisoned in the Tower of London on a charge of Unitarianism. Penn had indeed quoted from tracts by John Biddle* and other English Socinians, whom he admitted admiring for their moral earnestness. The Admiral persuaded the Privy Council to send a royal chaplain, Edward Stillingfleet, to persuade Penn to deny any rejection of Christ's divinity. Penn's *Innocency* (1669) secured his release. In his nine prison months he had written the first version of *No Cross, No Crown* (1669), a call to moral absolutism. *A Letter of Love* to Quakers appeared while he was again in Ireland (Nov. 1669 to Aug. 1670). There he wrote the first drafts of *The People's Ancient and Just Liberties* and *A Seasonable Caveat against Popery* (both 1670) and held another, more fruitful interchange of letters and interviews with Broghill and other administrators about hailed Irish Quakers. Returning to London after the Second Conventicle Act, Penn tested it by speaking in an open-air Quaker meeting in front of the padlocked Grace-Church Street Meetinghouse, and was arrested for inciting to riot. The resulting Penn-Meade* trial before Sir John Howell at the Old Bailey (see *Great Case of Liberty*, 1670) established on appeal the right of the jury, headed by Edward Bushel, to a verdict independent of the judges'. Penn's fine was paid by his dying father, with whom he was reconciled. In Feb. 1671 Penn was arrested at a meeting in Wheeler Street, and spent six months in Newgate. That autumn he made his first trip to Holland, traveling as far eastward as Emden and Danish Friedrichstadt, and returning via Herford in Westphalia to visit the Labadists, who rejected him, and the King's cousin, Princess Elizabeth of the Palatinate. After a pastoral visit to East Anglian Quakers, he returned in midwinter 1672 to marry Gulielma Springett, daughter by her first marriage of Mary Penington of Amersham, Bucks. They lived nearby at Rickmansworth, and after 1676 at Worminghurst, Sussex, losing in infancy five of their eight children.

In the next seven years Penn published 43 books and tracts in English and four in Dutch, besides writing seven epistles later printed in his *Works* (2 vols., 1726). Both longest and most in number were the tract debates. Penn challenged the 'heavenly witnesses,' Reeve* and Muggleton* (*New Witnesses*, 1672) and the similarly inspired Labadie (*Plain Dealing and Advice*, 1672) and William Mucklow (*Spirit of Alexander the Coppersmith* and *Judas and the Jews*, both 1673), as well as the Socinians (*Spirit of Truth*, 1672). The keenest fight was against the Baptists, both before and after the Declaration of Indulgence allowed the public Barbican debates in 1672. Penn wrote against John Morse (*Plain Dealing with a Traducing Anabaptist*, 1672), John Faldo (*Quakerism a New Nickname*, 1672; *Invalidity of John Faldo's Vindication*, 1673; *William Penn's Return*, 1674), and against Thomas Hicks* and Jeremiah Ives* (*Reason against Railing*, 1673; *Counterfeit Christian*, *Naked Truth Needs no Shift*, and *Jeremy Ives' Sober Request*, all 1674). Each salvo was returned in kind. In these tracts Penn matured and refined his theology. In particular, *The Christian Quaker* (against Hicks, 1673 and 1674) forced Penn to explore the deeper implications of Quaker belief in the universality and transforming power of the Light of Christ within men. Here his humanism and radicalism finally fused. He had quoted classical authors abundantly in tracts for toleration and in *No Cross, No Crown*. Penn now quoted both the pagans and Scripture to prove that classical philosophers lived saving truth and knew it. Penn's responsiveness to truths already experienced by non-Quaker hearers became the cornerstone of his liberalism in theory and practice. He appealed to persecutors' consciences, but also increasingly to their common sense, in his tracts for toleration (*The Proposed Comprehension*, 1672; *England's Present Interest* and *The Continued Cry*, 1675; *An Address to Protestants*, 1678 and 1679; *A Brief Examination and State of Liberty Spiritual*, 1681; *Reasons Why the Oaths*, 1683; *A Perswasive to Moderation* and *A Defense of the Duke of Buckingham's Book*, 1685; *Good Advice to the Church of England*, 1687). In these tracts Penn appealed increasingly to legal and pragmatic motives, began to identify the divine

Light with reason, private judgment and even natural interest, and was ever more willing to co-opt any ally for toleration, even the libertine Duke of Buckingham.

Penn's move into the political world showed the same character. In 1677 he went with George Fox, Robert Barclay* and George Keith* for a final major mission, twice around the circuit from Holland to Herford to Mulheim, adding Bremen, Cassel, Worms, Mannheim, Mainz, and pursuing the Labadists to Leeuwarden. Already in 1673 he spent a year invoking legal technicalities to free Fox from Worcester jail, and in 1679 he became deeply involved with Whig election politics (*England's Great Interest*), and campaigned for his friend Algernon Sidney* as member for Guildford or Bramber. The disastrous failure of the Whigs, culminating in Monmouth's rebellion (1685), shaped Penn's politics thereafter.

The West New Jersey territory, taken from the Dutch in 1665 and assigned by James to Berkeley, fell into Penn's hands when he saw that land development there could be used to rescue Edward Billing, a Quaker brewer bankrupted by fines and debts. As a trustee for Billing, working with him on land allotment and the settler's charter of *Concessions and Agreements* in 1675, Penn saw visions of American colonies as a 'holy experiment' as well as a refuge from persecution. He persuaded Robert Barclay and others to buy out Carteret's claim to East Jersey. Meanwhile a bigger project opened, perhaps from the King's shrewd willingness to ship troublesome Quakers overseas: the west bank of the Delaware became Pennsylvania in settlement of an old naval debt to the Admiral. The successive drafts of its *Frame of Government* owed changes to the Quaker Benjamin Furly* as well as the Whig Henry Sidney, and perhaps some ideas to Harrington* and Locke,* but moved steadily towards paternalism. Power was to center in a council of rich Friends, partly appointed by Penn, and overlap the oligarchical Society of Free Traders. Nevertheless, laws inviolable even by the feudal proprietor protected religious liberty, jury trial, free elections, and legal if not political equality for all citizens and Indians. Learning by Jersey's experience, Penn sailed for America only in Aug. 1682, after his Deputy Gov. William Markham and many colonists. Penn's relations with the Delaware Indians were cordial, but with his colonists, who had paid him for land and shipping and had no cash remaining, he fought from the start over taxes and quitrents. In Pennsylvania the popularly elected Assembly tried from the start to wrest the right to initiate legislation, and Penn experimented with a succession of deputy governors in hopes of satisfying both them and the Crown, especially over military defense. A boundary dispute with Lord Baltimore also necessitated a return to England in Aug. 1684.

English events now swept Penn along. James II sent Penn on a mission to Holland to sound out William of Orange on his proposed toleration of Dissenters and Catholics, and later to conciliate Baptists. Penn also played the 'weighty Friend' in meetings around London and on a trip among Quakers in western England, and he published a pair of pamphlets against the Test Acts for public office, the Whigs' key balking point. Yet his friendship for James already made him suspect. On this relationship Penn's critics since Burnet and Macaulay, and his supporters from Sewel* and Dixon to Buranelli have argued, each ultimately falling back on an analysis of the two men's motives. Penn was indeed troubled by James' efforts to pack Catholics into the Council, modify Parliament and replace or imprison bishops. Whether for the sake of English toleration or of Pennsylvanian autonomy, he acquiesced. Having turned to the King rather than the Whigs for toleration after 1680, Penn was left isolated when the Whigs brought William and Mary to rule in 1688. The next ten years are obscure. He cleared himself of treason charges in June 1689 and July 1690, only to be hopelessly entangled by the false charges of an informer, William Fuller, and the perhaps valid ones of his friends John Ashton and Viscount Preston. Penn spent 1691 in hiding at Hoddesdon, Herts., or with William Popple,* while his Irish lands were sequestered and Pennsylvania placed under Gov. Fletcher of New York. In November he was cleared, but in Feb. 1692 another blow fell; Gulielma Springett Penn died.

Penn returned to theology and meditation. He wrote *Some Fruits of Solitude* (1693), eventually his best-loved book, repaying with wit his debt to the Stoics, and a preface to Fox's *Journal*, promptly printed separately as *A Brief Account of the Rise and Progress of the People Called Quakers* (1694, etc.). He tried to revive the early Quakers' zeal in *Primitive Christianity Revived* (1696). He returned to theology in *A Key Opening a Way* (1692, re-edited in 1694, as was the *Christian Quaker*). He also defended Quakerism against outsiders in *New Athenians* (1693) and against George Keith's schism in tracts of 1696 and 1698. More creative in retrospect was his *Essay Towards the Present and Future Peace of Europe* (1693), combining ideas from the old Holy Roman Empire with others foreshadowing the United Nations. After an increasingly ardent courtship through 1695, he married Hannah Callowhill in Friars Meetinghouse, Bristol, in Mar. 1696, though his beloved son Springett died in April from a lung infection. Penn returned to Ireland in 1698 to reclaim his lands.

Penn also recovered title to Pennsylvania, and finally in Dec. 1699, after publishing two farewells to English Friends, sailed again for his colony with Hannah and their children (seven more, in the end). They stayed at Penn Manor until Oct. 1701, mediating political disputes. As he sailed home Penn signed a new Charter of Privileges and Bill of Property, acknowledging the power the Assembly had gained during his absence, and the cession of Delaware. He meant thereby to guard the colony's autonomy against new threats. King William's War had begun against the French, and Penn's sketch of a 'Plan of Union of the Colonies' (1697) was an inadequate response to the military and financial pressures upon the pacifist Pennsylvanians. Penn also had to sail home to face a court proceeding by an angry Admiralty officer, Robert Quary, and his own financial agent, Philip Ford, whose padded bills and statements of indebtedness Penn had earlier signed carelessly, placing his lands as collateral. In Jan. 1708 Penn was in debtor's prison in London, until popular support forced Ford's widow to accept a reasonable settlement. Penn's *More Fruits of Solitude* (1702) and the posthumously printed *Fruits of a Father's Love*, written under these pressures, emphasize faith as much as virtue. Penn's heir, William Penn, Jr., was an immature spendthrift who had failed as a deputy governor. Penn was in the process of negotiating a transfer of Pennsylvania to the royal Board of Trade when his plans were cancelled by a stroke on 4 Oct. 1712, which left him in a state of dotage until his death on 20 July 1718. He was buried beside Guli Penn and their children at Jordans.

W. Penn, *Works*, 2 vols. (1726; repr. AMS Press); *The Papers of William Penn*, ed. R.S. and M.M. Dunn (1981-); E. Bronner, *William Penn's 'Holy Experiment'* (1962); M.M. Dunn, *William Penn: Politics and Conscience* (1967); M.B. Endy, Jr., *William Penn and Early Quakerism* (1973); J.E. Illick, *William Penn the Politician* (1965); C.O. Peare, *William Penn* (1956); *DNB*. Papers: PHS (microfilm and photocopies of all Penn's documents and his Letter-Book); LF; O; L (Add. MSS; Harl. MSS; Sloane MSS; Stowe MSS).

H. Barbour

PENNOYER, William (d. 1671)

City radical, was a goldsmith and clothworker and a close associate of Maurice Thompson.* Pennoyer subscribed to the Irish adventure in June 1642 and was a major provisioner for the army in Ireland, supplying both clothing and arms. He served again as a commissioner to raise money for Ireland in 1648. Pennoyer shared interests with Thompson both in the Americas, where he owned sugar plantations in Barbados and land in Virginia, and in Africa, and Asia, where he participated in Thompson's saltpeter trade and his venture in Assada. He worked with Thompson to gain control of the East India Company and in Sept. 1647 joined him in refusing to take the traditional Company oath of allegiance to the King. He also served with the Militia Committee of Tower Hamlets, one of the suburban committees that contested the power of the London Presbyterians. On 16 Jan. 1649 Pennoyer was appointed a Commissioner of the Navy and Customs, and served as a Trade Commissioner as well. On 11 Aug. 1651 he was appointed to the Committee of Safety set up in the wake of the Presbyterian plot and the Scots' invasion. Pennoyer signed the petition of 20 May 1653 to reinstate the Long Parliament, but like Thompson and others was ultimately reconciled to the Protectorate. On the recommendation of Isaac Penington* and others he was elected Alderman of Billingsgate Ward on 6 Aug. 1657, but he declined to serve and was discharged five days later on payment of a £420 fine. Pennoyer was host to meetings of a Fifth Monarchist group that included Henry Danvers* and John Vernon* in 1664. His will was dated 25 May 1670 and proved on 13 Feb. 1671. He left £20 each to the Independent ministers William Bridge* and William Greenhill,* £10 p.a. from the income of his estate in Norfolk to the Corporation for the Propagation of the Gospel in New England and the remainder to endow two fellows and two scholars at Harvard College, and £100 to the poor of Great St. Helens, London. Pennoyer was married to Martha (d. 1674), daughter of John Joycelyn of Hyde Hall in Sawbridgeworth, Herts. They had no children. A brother, Samuel, died in 1654.

Beaven; Capp, *FMM*; Waters; R.P. Brenner, 'The Civil War Politics of London's Merchant Community,' *P. & P.*, 58:53-107; idem., 'Commercial

Change and Political Conflict: The Merchant Community in Civil War London' (Ph.D. diss., Princeton Univ., 1970); J.E. Farnell, 'The Navigation Act of 1651,' *Economic History Review*, 2nd ser., 16:439-54; idem., 'The Usurpation of Honest London Householders,' *EHR*, 82:24-46; Firth & Rait; *CSPD, Chas. I*, 18:327; 19:229, 232, 254, 273; 22:432; 23:643, 657, 670, 704; *Comm.*, 1, 3-8 *passim*.

R. Zaller ·

PERROT (or Perrott), Sir James (1571-1637)

Parliamentary radical, MP 1597, 1604, 1614, 1621 (Haverfordwest), 1624 (Pemb.), 1626 [?], 1628 (Haverfordwest). Of Harroldston, Pemb., Perrot was the leading Welsh Puritan and 'reform' MP in the early seventeenth century. An illegitimate son of Sir John Perrot, former Lord Deputy of Ireland, he attended Jesus Coll., Oxf., and the Middle Temple and also traveled on the Continent before returning to Pembrokeshire to launch an apparent career as a country gentleman and author. He took an increasingly active role in county government, was knighted in 1603 and served in seven Parliaments. His constituency for the Parliament of 1626 is unknown.

Perrot's interest in religious questions was constant throughout his parliamentary service and he was, unlike most Welsh members, an active parliamentarian, serving on over forty committees in James' first Parliament. In 1614 his outspoken attacks on impositions, Bishop Neile and the undertakers brought him chastisement by the Privy Council. In 1621 Perrot took a leading role; he criticized royal religious policy, repeatedly urged the Commons to defend the Protestant cause in the Palatinate, favored war with Spain, and vociferously opposed the Spanish match. It was Perrot who on 4 June introduced the Commons' Declaration of support on behalf of the Palatinate. His reward was temporary banishment; after the session he was sent by James as a commissioner to Ireland. In the Parliament of 1624 Perrot continued to act as a defender of parliamentary privileges and urged the appointment of a parliamentary committee to investigate the 'state of the King and kingdom.' He served in the Parliament of 1626 and, in his last appearance at Westminster, in 1628, made Bishop William Laud the target of his wrath. Always alert to the encroachments of Catholicism, he repeatedly urged in Parliament that all members be required to receive communion as a test for admission. His frequent admonitions on the dangers of a house divided gained special poignancy from the fact that his wife, Mary, the daughter of Robert Ashfield of Chesham, Bucks., was a Recusant and reputed Papist.

Perrot was a power in Pembrokeshire, a lessee of the county's royal mines and a substantial property owner, and he served as a deputy vice-admiral. He was a member of the Virginia Company. Some years before his death on 4 Feb. 1637 at Harroldston, he published a religious treatise on the Lord's Prayer and the Ten Commandments. He also wrote a chronicle of Ireland as well as two philosophical works.

DNB; H.A. Lloyd, *The Gentry of South West Wales* (1968); Zaller; *CD 1621*; P.W. Hasler, *The History of Parliament: The Commons 1558-1603* (1982); *CJ*. Papers: L (Add. MSS).

J. Gruenfelder

PERROT, John (d.c. 1671)

Quaker, was born in Waterford, Ireland, and was a Baptist until converted by Edward Burrough.* In 1656 he was preaching in Limerick, from which he and John Luffe (or Love) embarked on a mission to convert the Pope. Reaching Leghorn, the pair visited a Jewish synagogue. Examined and dismissed by the Inquisition, Perrot and his allies sailed for Jerusalem. After parting from them at Zante, Perrot crossed the Morea. The English consul discouraged them from their plan to convert the Turkish Sultan and started them on their way home. Reaching Venice in 1658, Perrot and Luffe visited the Doge, but in Rome they were imprisoned. Luffe was hanged and Perrot committed to a madhouse from which he occasionally corresponded with English Quakers. Released in 1661 through the efforts of Charles Bayley* and Jane Stokes, Perrot again set out for England, but in France was temporarily incarcerated for speaking to priests who bowed to images. In England Quaker leaders received him coolly and George Fox* condemned his activities and publications because, while imprisoned in Rome, Perrot led a schism among Quakers over his opposition to the removal of hats during prayer. He continued to attract large audiences. Imprisoned in 1661 and 1662, Perrot in the latter year emigrated to Barbados where he became a clerk to the magistrates. Deeply in debt, he died in Jamaica sometime before Oct. 1671.

Braithwaite, *BQu*; *DNB*; Fox, *CJ*; Thurloe, *SP*, 7:32, 287; K. Carroll, *John Perrot, Early Quaker Schismatic* (*JFHS*, supp. 33, 1971); *DQB*; *EQW*; Besse. Papers: LF.

J.D. Neville

PERROTT, Robert (d. 1685)

Fifth Monarchist, was a silk-dyer in London who served as a lieutenant in Thomas Harrison's* regiment. His convictions undampened by the Restoration, he was active in the radical underground and was imprisoned in Surrey in 1662 for his Fifth Monarchist activities. With John Tirret and the locksmith Thomas Fletcher he was arrested at a Fifth Monarchist conventicle in 1663 and on 24 Nov. had to provide a recognizance of £40. The following year he was presented at an episcopal visitation, and in 1666 he schemed with Thomas Blood,* Henry Danvers,* Jeremiah Marsden,* Edward Cary* and John Lockyer.* With Blood and Richard Halliwell,* he was involved in the audacious 1671 plot to steal the crown and sceptre from the Tower. On 9 May a warrant was issued to Sir John Robinson to take Perrott and Blood into custody; at that time Perrott was described as a teacher in a Baptist church (which was the London congregation associated with Henry Danvers). Like Blood, Perrott may have informed on other radicals, for a warrant for his release was issued in July 1671 and he was pardoned on 2 Jan. 1672. (A Thomas Perrot, presumably a relative, was pardoned on 31 Aug. 1671.) It was probably in 1671 that Margaret Swan pressed Lord Arlington to examine Perrott to ascertain the whereabouts of William Goffe,* whom she had been unsuccessfuly tracking. Perrot was still in touch with Blood in July 1678, when he was seen visiting Blood's London house.

In 1682 Perrott and his followers were associated with other Fifth Monarchists and members of the Green Ribbon Club in plots against the government. In 1685 he fought with Monmouth at Sedgemoor, serving in the Yellow Regiment under Col. Edward Matthews, was wounded and captured, and died on the scaffold at Taunton, Som.

Capp, *FMM*; *CSPD, Chas. II*, 11:225, 247, 385, 460; 12:57, 65; 20:320; *MCR*, 3:328-29; Morley; Earle.

R.L. Greaves

PETER (or Peters), Hugh (1598-1660)

Independent minister and army chaplain, was born at Fowey, Corn. in June 1598, the son of Thomas Dickwoode and Martha, daughter of John Treffry of Treffry, Corn. The Dickwoodes were sixteenth-century Flemish refugees from Antwerp. In England they adopted the name of Peter, and Hugh always used this surname though contemporaries often referred to him as 'Peters.' He was educated at Trinity Coll., Camb. (B.A. 1617-18, M.A. 1622). His religiosity was deepened through esposure to the preaching of such well-known London ministers as Richard Sibbes,* Thomas Hooker,* William Gouge and John Davenport,* but Peter attributed his actual conversion to a sermon by an unidentified preacher at St. Paul's. He was ordained in 1623, and took his first pastorate as curate at Rayleigh, Essex. He moved to London and gained prominence as lecturer at St. Sepulchre's church, and was also active in the work of the Puritan Feoffees.

His nonconformity put him in danger, and in 1628, his preaching license having been suspended, he fled to the Netherlands. For a few months (1628-29) he had a temporary position as disciplinarian of the student burse at the University of Franeker, where William Ames,* whom he much admired, was Professor of Theology. He next was called to become minister of the English Reformed Church of Rotterdam (1629-35). By this time Peter was well on the road to Independency. Under his leadership the church in 1633 was remodeled on Independent lines with a covenant, strict discipline, and stringent membership requirements. Peter himself took a new ordination at the covenanting. Ames was briefly co-pastor with him in 1633, having come 'because of my church's Independency.' In 1635 John Davenport was also co-pastor or 'lecturer.' Peter was one of the active workers of the English Synod, headed by John Forbes,* which was the focal point of the Laudian opposition abroad in the early 1630s.

In 1635 Peter emigrated to New England and succeeded Roger Williams* as pastor of the congregation at Salem, Mass., where his preaching was popular. Through his marriage to Elizabeth Read, he had connections with the Winthrop family. Active in political affairs, he attended the trial of Anne Hutchinson.* In 1641 he was sent back to England as a colony agent. Soon caught up in the revolution, he never returned to the New World. Peter wrote, preached and took to the battlefield with the army on behalf of the parliamentary cause. He took service as army chaplain in

Lord Forbes' expedition to Ireland in 1642 and thereafter in many campaigns with the Earl of Warwick,* Lt.-Gen. Fairfax* and the New Model Army. His army sermons were famous, even notorious, for their revolutionary zeal. At the battle of Naseby he first preached and then during the fight 'rode from rank to rank with a Bible in one hand and a pistol in the other exhorting the men to do their duty.' He was so often called upon to carry reports from the army to Parliament that he was referred to as Cromwell's 'secretary' and he was invited to preach before Parliament several times. One of these sermons, *God's Doings, and Man's Duty* (1646) was printed. In appreciation for his services the House of Commons in Apr. 1645 voted to grant him lands worth £200 p.a. from the lands of the Earl of Worcester. Peter retained his close links to the army, and in *Mr Peters Last Report of the English Wars* (1646) he reflected the army's own attitude of pragmatic toleration. Peter also remained close to Cromwell. In 1649 Peter joined his army in Ireland, arriving after the capture of Drogheda but in time for the storming of Wexford. 'I bless the Lord for what I see,' he wrote. 'God is with our general certainly, however he deal with him.'

Peter initially supported the Revolution on all fronts. In 1643 Parliament sent him to the Netherlands for 'special services' to raise money and counteract royalist activity. His sermons were popular in Parliament. As the parties of the Revolution splintered, Peter took his stand with the Independents. He had practiced Independency since his Rotterdam pastorate and saw no reason to compromise. In 1643 he published *Church-Government and Church-Covenant Discussed*, a pro-Independent book written by Richard Mather* with a general introduction by himself. His zealous advocacy of Independency brought him into conflict with Presbyterians. Thomas Edwards taunted him in *Gangraena* as 'solicitor-general for the sectaries'; Peter in turn called Edwards 'a knave and stinking fellow.' Because the Parliament refused to advance the revolution at Peter's pace, he turned increasingly to the army to lead it. He vigorously supported Pride's purge, the ensuing execution of the King, and the establishment of a republican regime.

Although not an official member of the High Court, Peter attended its sessions, which he blessed as 'glorious' work, and incited the judges to give the death penalty. He preached to them from Psalm 149: 'To bind the kings with chains and their nobles with fetters of iron.' When Charles stood condemned he attempted to force his ministrations on him; some even accused him of playing the King's executioner in false wig and beard.

During the Commonwealth and Protectorate Peter continued as a firm supporter of Cromwell. In 1651 he published *Good Work for a Good Magistrate*, a book of advice for Christian rulers. He advocated various social reforms, including reform of the universities, trade, poor relief, banking and other affairs, though he supported neither the Levellers nor the Fifth Monarchists. He was named one of the Commission of Triers in 1654. When Oliver Cromwell died in 1658, Peter preached a melancholy sermon on the text, 'Moses my servant is dead.'

Peter was a marked man at the Restoration. Parliament added his name to the list of persons excluded from the royal pardon. He was arrested and charged with treason for 'compassing and imagining the death of the King.' His well-remembered exultation at the King's death precluded any mercy. 'I wish I had never been vain in a vain world,' he told his daughter in *A Dying Fathers Last Legacy* (1660), written as he awaited execution. Peter met his end with dignity on 16 Oct. 1660. His head was exhibited on London Bridge. 'I confess I did what I did strenuously,' he wrote. Neither the most fanatic nor the most vindictive of the saints, he was always the most militant. It cost him his life.

R.P. Stearns, *The Strenuous Puritan* (1954); Stearns, 'Letters and Documents by or Relating to Hugh Peter,' *Essex Institute Historical Collections*, 71:303-18; 72:43-72; M.J. Patrick, *Hugh Peters*

(1946); P. Miller, *Orthodoxy in Massachusetts* (1933); Wilson, *PP*; Hill, *WTUD* and *C. & C.*; Solt; R.W. Pacy, 'Spiritual Combat: The Life and Personality of Hugh Peters' (Ph.D. diss., State Univ. of New York at Buffalo, 1978); *ST*, 5:1125-30. Papers: L (Add. MSS; Lans. MSS).

K.L. Sprunger

PETER (or Peters), Thomas (c. 1596-1654)

Independent minister, was the elder brother of Hugh Peter.* Thomas matriculated from Brasenose Coll., Oxf. in 1610, and graduated B.A. in 1614 and M.A. in 1625. He returned to his native Cornwall as Vicar of Mylor. Sometime after 1638 he left for New England, perhaps in 1643 when royalist troops overran Cornwall. He was living in Saybrook, Conn. by 1645 and was appointed the first minister in New London in May 1646. He returned to Mylor in Dec. 1646, resuming his ministry, and died there in 1654. Peter was close to the Winthrop family while in Connecticut, and is said to have married a sister of John Winthrop* before going to New England. She does not appear to have accompanied him to New England. Peter published a sermon given before the judges at Launceston Assizes on 17 Mar. 1652, under the title *A Remedie Against Ruine* (1652).

DNB; R.P. Stearns, *The Strenuous Puritan* (1954).

C.J. Sommerville

PETTO (or Pettaugh), Samuel (c. 1624-1711)

Congregational minister, may have been the son of Sir Edward Petto (d. 24 Sept. 1658) of Warwickshire by his wife Elizabeth, daughter of Sir Greville Verney. Petto was admitted as a sizar to St. Catharine's Hall, Camb. on 15 June 1644, matriculated on 19 Mar. 1645, and graduated M.A. In 1648 he became Rector of Sandcroft, South Elmham, Suff. His first works appeared in 1654: *The Voice of the Spirit*, published for Livewell Chapman* with a commendatory preface by Samuel Habergham, Vicar of Syleham, Suff., and Edward Barker, probably Vicar of Eye, Suff.; and *Roses from Sharon*, a spiritual anthology, published with John Martin, Rector of Edgefield, Norf., and Frederick Woodall,* lecturer at Woodbridge, Suff. In the latter work Petto discussed the significance attributed by sectaries to religious experience: 'It seemeth to be one work of this generation to declare God's works. Many opportunities and advantages are afforded, for the drawing out [of] experiences, which for many years have been denied.' With John Manning, minister at Rendham-cum-Swefling, Suff., Petto edited the *Six Severall Treatises* of John Tillinghast* in 1657. The following year he and Habergham edited Tillinghast's *Elijah's Mantle*, and on 4 May of that year the Council of State recommended to the Trustees for the Maintenance of Ministers that Petto receive an augmentation of £50 p.a.

It was also in 1658 that Petto, Martin and Woodall entered the lists in the debate over the right of the unordained to preach in *The Preacher Sent*, published by Chapman with a preface almost certainly by Morgan Llwyd.* In it Petto, Martin and Woodall defended lay preaching and the gathered church. There is no universal church, they argued, for the true church 'is a particular company of saints in mutual union for mutual fellowship in the means of worship appointed by Christ . . .' In response to their assertion of the right of gifted persons to preach despite the absence of a formal office, Matthew Poole retorted in *Quo warranto; or a Moderate Enquiry* (1658) that this practice led to confusion in the state and church; it 'opened the gap unto all that crew . . . which hath been the unhappy occasion of involving this poor church and nation in those crowds of errors and confusion which are now too rife amongst us.' But Petto and Woodall remained

unconvinced, defending their theses in *A Vindication of the Preacher Sent* (1659), published by Chapman.

At the Restoration Petto was ejected from his living at Sandcroft, which was vacant on 15 Jan. 1662. Moving to Wortwell, Norf., he preached there and at Harleston and Alburgh. In May 1672 he was licensed as a Congregationalist to preach in his house at Wortwell-cum-Alburgh and in the house of John Wesgate at Redenhall-cum-Harleston, Norf. His ministerial concerns are reflected in his *Two Scripture Catechisms* (1672). He subsequently helped minister to the Congregational church at Denton, Norf., and by 1675 had moved to Sudbury, Suff., where he became pastor of the Congregational church. He wrote one of the standard works on covenant theology, *The Difference between the Old and New Covenant Stated and Explained*, published by Elizabeth Calvert* in 1674, which defended the strict Calvinist position. From this time Petty became one of the dominant leaders of East Anglian Congregationalism. With Francis Holcroft* and Joseph Oddy* he was at Bury St. Edmunds in 1674 for the ordination of Thomas Milway, and in 1678 he was with Milway, Woodall and others for the ordination of Edmund Whincop at Wattisfield, Suff. Also in 1678 he helped edit the *Sermons* of Timothy Armitage,* and in 1681 his life of Ellen Asty, mother of Robert Asty, a teacher at the Norwich Congregational church, was prefixed to Owen Stockton's sermon, *Consolation in Life and Death*, which Petto edited. In 1686 Petto was at Ipswich with Milway and others for the induction of John Langston.*

Petto's attention now turned to the defense of paedobaptism, which he espoused in *Infant Baptism of Christ's Appointment* (1687) and, against Thomas Grantham,* *Infant-Baptism Vindicated* (1691). In 1693 he drew up a form of dismission for Milway from the Bury St. Edmunds church and published *A Faithful Narrative of the Wonderful and Extraordinary Fits* of Thomas Spatchet, former pastor of the Dunwich Congregational church, which were attributed to witch-craft and had been personally observed by Petto. The same year he published *The Revelation Unvailed*. In 1696 he was at Wattisfield, Suff., for the ordination of Thomas Wickes, and in 1700 he preached the funeral sermon for Wickes' father-in-law, Samual Baker. The parhelia which he observed in Suffolk on 28 Aug. 1698 were reported to the Royal Society. He preached the ordination sermon for John Beart, Milway's successor at Bury, in 1701. After an active career in ministerial leadership and writing, Petto died in 1711 and was buried at All Saints', Sudbury, on 21 Sept. 1711. The vitality of Congrega-tionalism in East Anglia owed much to his work.

Nuttall, *VS*; *Calamy Revised*; *DNB*; *Al. Cant.*; *CSPD, Chas. II*, 12:411, 502; 13:140, 196.

R.L. Greaves

PETTY (or Pettus, Pettie; originally Le Petite), Maximilian (b. 1617, d. after 1660)

Leveller, was descended from an ancient family of Oxfordshire gentry. One of his uncles, another Maximilian, was MP for Westbury in 1628, and several Pettys were educated at Oxford. Maximilian was bap-tized at Tetsworth on 3 June 1617, the second son of John Petty of Stoke-Talmage and of his second wife, Anne Webley (née Johnson), but at the age of five he was orphaned. He wed Mary, daughter of his uncle Leonard of Thame, and they had a daughter, Mary.

In May 1634 Petty was apprenticed in the Grocers' Company of London, where he met Edward Sexby,* apprenticed in 1632. Petty was probably among the radical apprentices who were John Lil-burne's* early followers. Although he apparently never signed any tract, he was an important figure in the Leveller move-ment, and his name is closely connected with the first two *Agreements of the People*, which he helped write and defend.

On 22 Oct. 1647 Petty and John Wildman* were chosen to be civilian spokesmen at the Putney debates. In the first two debates on 28 and 29 Oct., Petty showed his grasp of the Levellers' (and especially Over-ton's*) position, helping to clarify points of the first *Agreement* concerning property and the extension of the electoral fran-chise, as well as calling unequivocally for the disestablishment of the monarchy and the House of Lords. His name, however, does not appear after 29 Oct. in the records of the debates. According to Lilburne (*Legal Fundamental Liberties*, 8 June 1649), Petty was one of the five civilian authors (with Lilburne himself, Wildman, William Walwyn* and the MP Henry Marten*) of the second *Agreement of the People* (1648). Again he was not present when this document was discussed at the general Whitehall debates in December. In July 1649, when Lilburne, Walwyn, Over-ton and Thomas Prince* were kept close prisoners in the Tower of London, Petty was contacted by Thomas Scott* as one of the chief Levellers still at large. His career under the Protectorate is obscure, but between Sept. 1659 and Feb. 1660 he was an active member of the Rota, Harring-ton's* republican club. The place and date of his death are unknown.

G. Aylmer, 'Gentlemen Levellers?' *P. & P.*, 49:120-25; *Ath. Oxon.*; *Al. Oxon.*; *Lev. Tr.*; C.H. Firth, 'Thomas Scot's Account,' *EHR*, 12:116-26; *Clarke Papers*; C. Thompson, 'Maximilian Petty and the Putney Debate on the Franchise,' *P. & P.*, 88:63-69; Frank. Also cf. Anne Petty's will, proved 3 Oct. 1622, MS Wills Oxon. 51/1/23.

M. Gimelfarb-Brack

PETTY, Sir William (1623-1687)

Scientist and social and educational reformer, was born in Romsey, Hants., the eldest surviving son of a 'poor' clothier. Petty showed precocious interest in improving cloth-making techniques, in navigation and boat-building. Having gone to sea and been shipwrecked, he enrolled in 1637 in the Jesuit College at Caen, where he received advanced mathematical and geographical training. After another spell at sea, his education continued in Holland after 1643. At Leiden he encountered Harvey's ideas, clinical training and dissection. He met the mathematician John Pell,* who introduced him to Merin Mersenne, Samuel Hartlib* and Sir Charles Cavendish. Holland also offered him a model – which he later used – of efficient social and economic organization. In 1645 Petty, now in Paris, came to Hobbes'* notice, helped the latter prepare a discourse on optics for the press, and imbibed the latest work in mathematics, mechanics, theoretical physics and dynamics. Back in England by 1646, he supported himself by medical practice, and sketched designs for diffusing, adding to and collating useful knowledge, for extending and improving education, for reducing poverty and unemployment, and for reforming medical training and care on the model of clinical centers such as that of Padua, which won him Hartlib's, Robert Boyle's and Benjamin Worsley's* praise. Official recognition came with his appointment to a fellowship at Brasenose Coll., Oxf. in 1650, and, in 1651, to the Oxford Professorship of Public Anatomy and the Gresham College Professorship of Music. In Oxford he joined informal groups experimenting and planning scientific regeneration, and won notoriety by resuscitating the body of a hanged woman, Ann Green.

Petty went to Ireland in 1652 as physician to the Lord Deputy (at £365 p.a.), and soon supplanted the official Surveyor-General in surveying two and a half million acres of confiscated land, work essential to Ireland's resettlement. This survey, rapidly and successfully completed, proved the utility of Petty's skills and his organizational capacity, and stimulated an interest in better assessing and using Ireland's resources. The survey earned Petty £9000 and appointment as clerk to the Irish Council and secretary to Ireland's effective ruler, Henry Cromwell.* After 1656 he quarreled with Worsley over the appropriation of funds for implementing Hartlib's schemes in Ireland. An unsuccessful attempt to impeach Petty was made in the 1659 Parliament, to which he had been elected for Irish and Cornish seats, by radical enemies of Henry Cromwell's *politique* regime, of which Petty was a valuable prop. In his religious and political attitudes Petty was flexible to the verge of indifference, although in 1659 he associated with the republican Rota Club.

Petty easily weathered the Restoration, being knighted, sitting in the 1661 Irish Parliament and having his lands confirmed. However, his past affiliations and his habitual arrogance and litigiousness denied him high public office, even though he cultivated James II and Tyrconnell. The range of Petty's interests, in addition to the necessity of dividing his time between England and Ireland, hampered him. He developed his Kerry estates, introducing iron-making and fisheries, but those projects ultimately failed. Unable to persuade the Irish government to establish land registries or to instruct the tax collectors to gather demographic and cadastral information, he culled figures from his own surveys, from the poll-tax and hearth-money returns and from the bills of mortality, in order to estimate and predict population and wealth, and to propose how both might be augmented, as he did in his *Political Arithmetick* (1690) and *Political Anatomy of Ireland* (1691). In 1685 he published highly accurate and technically proficient maps of Ireland. Although he could not persuade the Royal Society (of which he was a charter member) in the 1670s or the Dublin Philosophical Society in 1683 to inaugurate a systematic program of utilitarian experiments, by cogent writing and persistent lobbying he diffused new scientific ideas and thereby contributed to both institutions' foundation. Most important, his analysis and publication of socio-economic information in mathematical form, expressing all 'in number, weight and measure,' pioneered statistical and population studies. Petty died in London on 16 Dec. 1687. He married Elizabeth, widow of Sir Maurice Fenton and daughter of Sir Hardress Waller,* who was created Baroness Shelburne by James II in exile. She died in 1708, leaving two sons and a daughter.

E. Fitzmaurice, *The Life of Sir William Petty* (1895); *DNB*; Y. Goblet, *La Transformation de la Géographie Politique de l'Irlande*, 2 vols. (1930); C. Hull, ed., *The Economic Writings of . . . Petty*, 2 vols. (1899); L. Sharp, 'Sir William Petty and Some Aspects of Seventeenth-Century Natural Philosophy' (D.Phil. thesis, Oxford Univ., 1976); Greaves, *PRET*; E. Strauss, *Sir William Petty* (1954); Webster, *GI*; Pepys. Papers: Bowood House; DT; L (Add. MSS; Harl. MSS; Lans. MSS; Royal MSS; Sloane MSS; Stowe MSS); MMO; O; OQ.

T.C. Barnard

PETYT, William (1636-1707)

Whig lawyer and antiquarian. Petyt was born in Skipton, Yorks., and was at one time employed by the Royalist Fabian Philipps. He matriculated at Christ's Coll., Camb. in 1660, and in 1670 was made a barrister of the Inner Temple, apparently for services to his Inn, while his brother Sylvester followed a career at Barnard's Inn. They took out a patent of gentility in 1676 which changed the spelling of their name from 'Petty.' During the same year William began to collect materials for a reply to the contention, made in Sir William Dugdale's *Baronage of England* (1675) and Sir Henry Spelman's *Glossarium archaiologium* (edited by Dugdale in 1664), that the House of Commons had originated as late as 1265 (49 Henry III). He published nothing until 1680, when *Miscellanea Parliamentaria* and *The Antient Right of the Commons of England Asserted* vindicated the antiquity of the Commons against 'several great and learned authors of our age,' also including Sir Robert Filmer's *The Freeholder's Grand Inquest* and *Patriarcha*, which had

been republished in 1679-80. Petyt's writings are among the first responses to Filmer, and had been begun when James Tyrrell* urged him to undertake the reply. He was also aware of William Prynne's* writings on the subject, and of James Howell's *Some Sober Inspections Made into the Carriage and Consults of the Late Long Parliament* (1656), which is partly transcribed from the *Freeholder's Inquest*. *The Antient Right* is dedicated to Arthur Capel, Earl of Essex.*

Petyt's work was attacked by Robert Brady, but he left the ensuing controversy to William Atwood,* publishing only a little-noticed and now rare pamphlet, *The Pillars of Parliament Struck at by the Hands of a Cambridge Doctor*. Petyt seems to have been a collector and researcher rather than a controversial writer. He assisted Gilbert Burnet with the first volume of *The History of the Reformation* (1679) and left large manuscript collections on legal and ecclesiastical history to the Inner Temple at his death. In Jan. 1689 he was one of the legal counsel who advised the House of Lords in the Convention Parliament, where he argued that the original contract was to be found in the Coronation Oath. In March he was appointed Keeper of the Records in the Tower of London, displacing Robert Brady. Some of his books were bequeathed to found a library at Skipton by his brother Sylvester. A posthumous collection, *Jus Parliamentarium*, was published in 1739.

DNB; *A Catalogue of the Petyt Library at Skipton* (1964); J.G.A. Pocock, *The Ancient Constitution and the Feudal Law* (1957); C. Weston and J. Greenberg, *Subjects and Sovereigns* (1981); C.C. Weston, 'Legal Sovereignty in the Brady Controversy,' *HJ*, 15:409-31. Papers: L (Add. MSS; Harl. MSS; Harg. MSS; Lans. MSS).

J.G.A. Pocock

PHAIRE (or Phayre), Robert (c. 1619-1682)

Army radical and sectary, was probably

the son of Emanuel Phaire, Vicar of Kilshannig, co. Cork from 1612. Phaire was reported to be 35 years of age on 24 Mar. 1654. He may have joined William Jephson's troop of horse in Ireland in Nov. 1641 and was lieutenant-colonel in Richard Townshend's regiment in Sept. 1646. In Feb. 1648 he was made prisoner with three other officers for refusing to join Lord Inchiquin's royalist rising. Phaire was exchanged on 4 Oct. for Inchiquin's son, and returned to Bristol with Admiral Penn in December. He was given command of the halberdiers who guarded the High Court during the King's trial, was one of the three officers to whom the warrant for execution was addressed, and was present on the scaffold. In Apr. 1649 he was commissioned to raise a regiment in Kent for service in Ireland. It landed at Youghal in November and surprised Cork, whose governor Phaire became. He was also appointed a commissioner for settling Munster. On 10 Apr. 1650 Phaire took part in the victory of Macroom, and in August he marched to Kerry to prevent Inchiquin from raising forces there.

Phaire staunchly supported republican and sectarian elements in the army and opposed the Instrument of Government. He permitted Quakers to proselytize his regiment, attended their meetings, and was said to have preached in the open air at or near the Lough of Cork. According to Henry Cromwell,* he took part in discussions which asserted 'that God is nothing, that heaven is not local, that the Scriptures . . . are not the work of God.' Phaire's first wife, whose name is unknown, is mentioned in a letter of 29 July 1653 from Col. John Jones.* She may have been a sister or daughter of Onesiphorus Houghton of Ballingarry, co. Cork. On 16 Aug. 1658 he married Elizabeth, daughter of Sir Thomas Herbert, later Baronet of Tintern. Herbert, the last person to attend Charles I and the author of the *Threnodia Carolina*, had made his peace with the Cromwellian regime, and it was to this connection that Phaire probably owed the leniency of his treatment at the Restoration. On 8 July 1659 he was commissioned a colonel of foot by the Committee of Safety, and in December he joined Ludlow* in vainly resisting the parliamentary coup in Dublin. Arrested in Cork on 18 May 1660, he was conveyed to Dublin in June and thence to the Tower. After testifying in the trial of Francis Hacker,* he petitioned on 2 Nov. for the release of his sequestered estate. This was not granted, but in December he was given the liberty of the Tower, and on 3 July 1661 he was released for one month in his father-in-law's custody on payment of a £2000 bond. On 19 July he was granted a further month to go into the country. On 28 Feb. 1662 he was furloughed for three months to Herbert's home in Petty France, Westminster, and was finally discharged on 22 June.

Phaire was held again in Limerick in June 1663 where he was suspected of participating in the conspiracy which resulted in the executions of Cols. Alexander Jephson and Edward Warren,* but no evidence was produced. According to Ludlow, the assassin who slew the Regicide John Lisle* in 1664 mistook him for Phaire. Phaire was again suspected of conspiracy in 1666, and in 1668 was accused of heading an intended insurrection in Munster. His latter years were chiefly occupied with his ironworks near Enniscorthy, which occasioned numerous lawsuits. Shortly after the Restoration he became a disciple of Lodowick Muggleton,* who also converted his wife and elder daughters. Phaire's will was dated 13 Sept. 1682 and was proved on 10 Nov. In it he left £1000 apiece to each of his eight children in addition to lands, chiefly in Cork, Wexford and co. Tipperary. By his first wife Phaire had a son, Onesiphorus, whose wife Elizabeth died in 1702, and two daughters, Elizabeth, who married Richard Farmer, and Mary, who married George Gamble. By his second wife he had three sons, Thomas (d. 1716), Alexander Herbert (d. 1752), and John, in addition to three daughters.

DNB; Firth & Davies; Thurloe, *SP*; Ludlow; Barnard; W.H. Weply, 'Col. Robert Phaire . . .,' *N. & Q.*, 12th ser.,

12:123-25, 143-46, 164-67, 185-87, 376; J.C., 'Col. Phaire, the Regicide,' *Journal of the Cork Historical and Archaeological Society*, 2nd ser., 20:146-50, 199-203; 21:46-49; *CSPD, Comm.* and *Chas. II*, *CSPI*, *passim*; J. Reeve and L. Muggleton, *Spiritual Epistles* (1755). Papers: LF.

R. Zaller

PHELIPS, Sir Robert (c. 1586-1638)

Parliamentary radical, MP 1604 (East Looe), 1614 (Saltash), 1621, 1624, 1625, 1628 (Somerset). Phelips was the eldest son of Sir Edward Phelips, Attorney General, Master of the Rolls, and Speaker of the House of Commons, by his first wife Margaret, daughter of Robert Newdegate of Newdigate, Surrey. A brilliant career seemed assured him from birth. He held the reversion to the clerkship of the Petty Bag, and was knighted in 1603. In 1613 he traveled in France, and in 1615 accompanied Lord Digby to Madrid at the inception of negotiations for the Spanish match. As heir to one of the two richest estates in Somerset, he assumed naturally the prerequisites of local authority: JP from at least 1613, DL from 1624. Yet a statesman's career, though it more than once beckoned, was not to be his. Phelips found his place instead as one of the prime leaders of the parliamentary opposition to prerogative government under the first two Stuarts.

Phelips' first active Parliament was that of 1614. When Bishop Neile of Durham launched an attack on the privileges of the Commons, Phelips was the first in the Lower House to cite him by name, and later suggested a 'forbearance' of all business until the matter was settled. This tactic was ultimately adopted, and led shortly thereafter to an abrupt dissolution by the King. Phelips' conduct in 1614, says the historian of this Parliament, 'broke his father's heart.' Certainly it was in marked contrast to Sir Edward's sedulously royalist behavior as Speaker in the Parliament of

1604. The elder Phelips did not long survive his disgrace, dying in September.

By 1621, Phelips had assumed a position in the front rank of the Commons' leadership. At the outset of this Parliament he defined its principal concerns: freedom of speech, control of Recusants at home and support of Protestants abroad, the abuse of power by royal patentees. The investigation of patents led him to the chair of the Committee for Courts of Justice just as it was about to receive allegations of bribery against Lord Chancellor Bacon. It was Phelips himself who helped draft and then presented the indictment against Bacon in the Lords, leading to the Chancellor's fall and the revival of a parliamentary impeachment power that had lain dormant for nearly 200 years. Phelips rightly regarded this as a cardinal achievement; when Van Dyck painted his portrait it was with Bacon's indictment in his hand.

At the end of the first session of Parliament in June, it was Phelips again who spoke for the Commons in declining to hear the commission for adjournment read as an infringement of parliamentary privilege. During the second session, he spoke out against the Spanish match and, decrying the King's 'soul-killing' rejection of the Commons' petition against it, moved as he had in 1614 for a sitdown strike against royal policy. With dissolution again imminent, he successfully moved a protestation which went far beyond any previous statement of the inherent nature of Parliament's privileges and its responsibility for the general welfare.

As a result of these activities, Phelips was arrested at the breakup of Parliament and kept close prisoner for the first eight months of 1622. This treatment had its effect; he repaired his relations at Court, even accompanying the Prince of Wales on his ill-fated trip to Madrid in 1623. Phelips' rapprochement with the Duke of Buckingham, now curiously documented by a manuscript 'Dialogue betweene a Counsellor of State and a Country gentleman . . .' (Phelips MSS 227/16), was shown in his strong support for a Spanish war and for the impeachment of Sir Lionel Cranfield in the Parliament of 1624. But this was a temporary coincidence of interest and not an abandonment of political independence. With the Parliament of 1625 Phelips returned to opposition. This was the noontide of his influence: if in 1624, as T.G. Barnes puts it, he had stood 'on the threshold of unshared leadership of the Commons,' in 1625 he emerged as 'the premier spokesman of the opposition' (Barnes), assuming 'that unacknowledged leadership which was all that the traditions of Parliament at that time permitted' (S.R. Gardiner). It was Phelips who demanded an accounting of the Subsidy Act of 1624 (whose provisions he had drafted) before voting further supply and who suggested that Tonnage and Poundage be granted not for life but 'for a limited time of years' only, who questioned the French marriage treaty and moved to send for the Arminian cleric Richard Montague, and who led the attack on Buckingham in the Oxford session, demanding his impeachment. If Phelips had come full circle, so, he felt, had the situation in the country: 'the privileges of this House have been so broken,' he declared, '[and] such burdens laid upon the people, that no time can come into comparison with this.' 'We are the last monarchy in Christendom that retains our original rights and constitutions,' he observed in his speech against Buckingham on 10 Aug. The implication was clear: if the Duke were not removed, arbitrary taxation ceased and Recusants curtailed, the last major representative institution in Europe would go the way of others extinguished or rendered impotent by Continental absolutism.

Phelips was not imprisoned this time. But he was removed from the commission of the peace, suspended from his lieutenantship and pricked for sheriff to disable him from sitting in Parliament. Returned as usual for the county, he attempted to take his seat despite the shrievalty, but was barred. Phelips stood firm with others against the forced loan, but it was not until the Parliament of 1628 that he returned to the national stage. If the outlook had seemed gloomy three years before, it was now positively Tartarean: 'I am sure no man can think this state ever stood in more danger' (20 Mar.); 'We now little differ from the course in Turkey, where the Janissary sets his halberd there he is master without resistance' (22 Mar.). Phelips was no longer the dominating figure he had been in 1625, in part because of the rise of other leaders like Eliot,* in part to the necessity for legal expertise from men like Selden* in drafting the Petition of Right. But he was still, with Digges, Eliot and Wentworth, one of the key political strategists in the House, and still, with Sir Benjamin Rudyard,* its most eloquent and respected orator. Phelips' speeches are hyperbolic for modern taste, but no man expressed the temper of Parliament in the 1620s more acutely and evocatively than he.

After the session of 1629, in which Phelips protested breaches of the Petition of Right and again attacked his old *bête noire*, Bishop Neile, he returned to tend county politics, where, despite the sycophantic efforts of his archrival John Lord Poulett and his cool relations with the Lord Lieutenant, Pembroke,* he remained supreme. Though he no longer dreamed of a Court-Country alliance or angled for favor, as he had in 1624 when he sought the ambassadorship to Holland, Phelips was not a man to burn bridges behind him: even after attacking Buckingham in 1625 he sought to patch up relations with him. By 1629 he had been restored to the deputyship and the commission of the peace, and his assistance in suppressing a grain riot at Langport in April had not gone unnoticed. Charles himself wrote Phelips in August, urging him to 'rather use your best endeavors and care for the preservation and increase of our . . . inheritance than for the favor of the multitude, and doubt not but what benefit we shall receive by your service we shall thankfully accept.' As always, Phelips kept his own counsel. If his behavior in the early 1630s was indistinguishable from any other local magnate, he galvanized resistance to ship money from the first writ. This was Phelips' last battle, fought far from Westminster but with the political skill of a lifetime. In the three years until his death at Montacute on 13 Apr. 1638, he stymied ship money assessments in Somerset, effectively halted the equally hated operations of the saltpetre men in the eastern part of the county, and successfully resisted attempts to force compliance with government edicts on his fellow JPs. Ironically, his eldest sons Edward and Robert (by Bridget, daughter of Sir Thomas Gorges of Longford, Wilts.), were both prominent Royalists in the Civil War. There can be no doubt where his own choice would have lain.

Barnes; *DNB*; Moir; Zaller; Ruigh; *CD 1621*; *CD 1625*; *CD 1628*; *CD 1629*; Russell, *PEP*; S.D. White, *Sir Edward Coke and 'The Grievances of the Commonwealth,' 1621-1628* (1979); K. Sharpe, ed., *Faction and Parliament* (1978); E. Farnham, 'The Somerset Election of 1614,' *EHR*, 46:579-99; K.S. van Eerde, 'The Spanish Match through an English Protestant's Eyes,' *HLQ*, 32:59-75; T.G. Barnes, 'County Politics and a Puritan Cause Célèbre: Somerset Churchales, 1633,' *TRHS*, 5th ser., 9:103-22. Papers: SRO (Phelips MSS); L (Add. MSS; Harl. MSS; Lans. MSS; Sloane MSS; Stowe MSS).

R. Zaller

PHILLIPS, George (d. 1662), plotter. *See* TONG, Thomas.

PHILLIPS, John (fl. 1626-1648)

Enclosure resister, was a tanner of Gillingham, Dorset. He was born about 1578, giving his age as sixty in 1638. About 1630 he held a cottage with a small garden and tanning house at an annual rent of 3d. Phillips was a leader in the riots against disafforestation and enclosure which erupted sporadically in Gillingham from at least June 1626 to Dec. 1628 and involved sizable bands of armed rebels. In 1630 he was fined £200 in Star Chamber and bound to good behavior for two years. The fine remained unexecuted but continued to hang over his head. In 1631 he was again apprehended for pulling down fences. On examination before William Whitaker, JP, Phillips defended his action as an attempt to try his right and title to common land. He refused to be bound over to the assizes and was committed, but another justice bailed him. On 13 June the Privy Council, fearing that Phillips and a fellow rebel, Henry Hoskins, were coordinating riots in Wiltshire and Dorset, ordered their arrest. Hoskins escaped, but Phillips was confined in the Fleet, from which he petitioned for release in September and October. He may have been freed soon after, presumably bound again to good behavior, but the date of his release is not known. In 1638 he appeared as a witness in the action between another enclosure resister, John Wolridge, and the Earl of Elgin.

Phillips was again active in the renewed anti-enclosure resistance around Gillingham and Mere, Wilts., between 1643 and 1645. By 1644 he had replaced the linen-weaver Richard Butler as leader of the movement. A streak of anarchic individualism ran through his behavior; in January of that year he urged the men of Mere to beat down their enclosures, insisting that he would do it alone if they did not join him, while in July he rode a horse through the gaps in the fence of a close in Gillingham Manor, telling its tenant 'that if he made up his hedges any more he would come and bring some others with him and pull it down again before his face.' On yet another occasion Phillips rode about saying, 'I ride in and I ride out of these grounds at my pleasure, and I take and will keep possession of them.'

In June 1645 Phillips was once more breaking enclosures. In 1646 he was imprisoned by the Sheriff of Dorset, and in November of that year was presented before the Barons of the Exchequer to answer for his old Star Chamber fine. Still undaunted, he was one of five men seized for the destruction of enclosures in June

1648. The House of Lords released them on 7 Aug. with an admonition, but they remained bound in default of £170 in fees owed to the Clerk of the Lords and others. Phillips' subsequent fate is unclear. His case nicely illustrates what might be called the continuity of oppression under both royal and parliamentary regimes; the resurrection of Star Chamber fines under the revolutionary government (apparently the suggestion of John Maynard*) clearly prefigures the double standard which the Levellers and the Agitators were to discover at Putney.

B. Sharp, *In Contempt of All Authority* (1980); D.G.C. Allan, 'The Rising in the West, 1628-1631,' *Economic History Review*, 2nd ser., 5:76-85; E. Kerridge, 'The Revolts in Wiltshire against Charles I,' *William and Mary Quarterly*, 57:64-75; *Acts of the Privy Council*, 33:382; *LJ*, 10:421. Papers: LPR; MR (Nicholas MSS).

R. Zaller

PICKERING, Sir Gilbert, Bt. (1611-1668)

Parliamentary radical, MP SP, LP 1640, 1653, 1654, 1656 (Northants.). Pickering, the son and heir of Sir John Pickering (d. 1628) of Titchmarsh, Northants., by Susannah, daughter of Sir Erasmus Dryden, was baptized at Titchmarsh on 10 Mar. 1611. Pickering was admitted to Emmanuel Coll., Camb. in 1625, graduated B.A. in 1629, and entered Gray's Inn the same year. He was created a Baronet of Nova Scotia in 1638, and about 1640 he married Elizabeth, daughter of Sir Sidney Montagu of Hinchingbrooke, Hunts. His second wife was Elizabeth, daughter of John Pepys. A man of considerable wealth, he owned land in Huntingdonshire as well as Northamptonshire.

Early in the Long Parliament Pickering criticized Secretary Windebank and Robert Read for seizing the books of a schoolmaster from the Palatinate. A strong opponent of episcopacy, he presented a petition for the reformation of religion from the ministers of the diocese of Peterborough. After the Civil War began he played an active role in raising troops and money for the parliamentary cause in his county, and he gained a reputation for his zeal in ejecting ministers from their benefices. Although accused of having traveled the full route from Presbyterianism to Anabaptism, he is best regarded as an Independent. In 1644 he joined Oliver St. John,* Isaac Penington* and others in commending Roger Williams* to John Winthrop* and his associates in Massachusetts.

Pickering's activities in 1644 identified him with the most radical members of Parliament, and he remained at least on the fringe of that group during the next four years. He made very few appearances in the House during the months immediately preceding Pride's purge. He did not, however, dissent from the resolution of 5 Dec. 1648 until 12 Feb. 1649. Although he was appointed one of the judges to try Charles I, he attended only two sessions of the High Court, did not sign the death warrant, and refused to give retrospective approval to the trial and execution. Pickering was nevertheless included as a member of the Council of State of the Commonwealth, and he cooperated with Cromwell, a close friend and distant kinsman, in his attempts to achieve social and religious reform in the Rump Parliament. He served on a committee to consider the petition of army officers for a new parliament and law reform. He argued for leniency in the treatment of the Presbyterian minister Christopher Love, not only because he hoped to heal the wounds of the parliamentary party, but because of his commitment to religious toleration.

In the Barebones Parliament Pickering allied himself with the moderates and was later accused by Fifth Monarchists of collaborating with Cromwell in packing the House. He opposed the bill declaring Barebones to be a parliament, and he modified the radical position he had previously taken on the question of tithes. He was instrumental in the self-dissolution of

Dec. 1653. During the Protectorate Pickering continued to serve as a member of the Council of State, receiving an annual income of £1000. In 1655 he was appointed Lord Chamberlain and in 1656 Lord High Steward of Westminster. In Parliament he joined other members of the Council in defending James Nayler,* and in that context he called for a debate on the judicial powers of Parliament. He supported the attempt to make both the decimation tax and the authority of the major-generals permanent. In 1657 he was appointed to Cromwell's Upper House.

Pickering was one of seven civilians to serve on Richard Cromwell's* Council of State, although his loyalty to Richard was never very strong. He was not included in the new Council created by Parliament in May 1659, and in August of that year he obtained a leave of absence from the restored Rump. After the army seized power in Oct. 1659 he was appointed to the Council of Safety and designated one of the Conservators of Liberty. At the Restoration Pickering was pardoned and left out of the exemptions to the Act of Indemnity.

DNB; Underdown, *PP*; Worden; Liu; J. Winthrop, *The History of New England*, ed. J. Savage (1853); Woolrych; Keeler. Papers: L (Add. MSS; Stowe MSS).

B.P. Levack

PIERREPONT (or Pierpoint), William (c. 1607-1678)

Parliamentary radical, MP SP 1640 (Shropshire), LP 1640 (Much Wenlock), 1656 (Notts., declined), 1660 (Notts.). Pierrepont, the second son of Robert, first Earl of Kingston, matriculated at Emmanuel Coll., Camb. in 1624 and entered Lincoln's Inn in 1627. Pierrepont was given Thoresby, Notts. by his father and received Tong Castle, Shrops., through marriage. He was Sheriff of Shropshire in 1638 when, encountering resistance to ship money, he petitioned for its reduction. Pierrepont's family divided over the Civil War; his eldest brother was a Royalist, while his younger brother supported the parliamentary cause.

From his first entry into Parliament, 'Wise William' was a factional leader. He was initially a moderate who was considered a possible mediator with the King. His competence and rhetorical skill were much admired, and he served on both the committee appointed during the adjournment of the Commons following the attempt on the Five Members and on the Committee of Safety. In 1643 he served as a parliamentary negotiator at Oxford, again winning commendation. By 1644, however, Pierrepont participated vigorously on behalf of the war effort as a member of the Committee of Both Kingdoms. His group of Independents allied with the radicals to rid England of the Scots, to frustrate an intolerant Presbyterian settlement and to preserve the army until Charles I could be forced to accept the parliamentary program of 1641. Pierrepont managed the peace propositions in Commons during the first Civil War, but, following the collapse of the Independent coalition and the invasion of the House by the City apprentices in 1647, he fled to the army. Prior to Pride's purge, Pierrepont led the moderates, drafting the declaration against the King of 11 Feb. 1648 and supporting the Vote of No Addresses. Yet in Mar. 1648 Pierrepont joined a caucus of parliamentary radicals who determined that negotiations should continue in hopes of winning the King away from a Scottish alliance. Faced with a possible Scottish invasion, radicals joined the moderates in April in a vote declaring that mixed monarchy would be preserved. Pierrepont opposed the radicals' proposed oath which would bind MPs to all acts and measures taken by the Long Parliament. He was of the joint committee of Parliament which considered the terms of a proposed treaty with the King and he was a Parliamentary Commissioner in the negotiations at Newport. Pierrepont's attempt to mediate between Parliament and an increasingly suspicious army was however to no avail.

Following the purge, Pierrepont refused to resume his seat but he was not immediately secluded. A prominent abstainer, he was not voted out of the House until 1651, and though non-Rumpers were ordered out of committees Pierrepont remained on the Army Committee as late as Mar. 1649. Though much courted, he remained aloof from the new regime. He remained in touch with Cromwell and St. John* through the Interregnum and in 1656 was returned for Nottinghamshire, but he refused the seat and later refused a place in Cromwell's Upper House. On Richard Cromwell's* succession Pierrepont counselled the new Protector privately but he stayed out of active politics until the restoration of the secluded members in 1660. Pierrepont received the greatest number of votes when the reconvened Long Parliament elected the new Council of State on 23 Feb. He used his position to join in forming a 'junto' to force the terms of the Treaty of Newport on Charles II. The effort failed and Royalists alleged that Pierrepont was among those trying to bargain for office under the restored monarchy. Returned to the Convention Parliament, Pierrepont went into opposition under Lord Wharton's management. Pierrepont helped to foil the Royalists by securing the Speakership for his old Presbyterian colleague, Sir Harbottle Grimston, Bart.* He also intervened on behalf of such radicals as Lambert,* Vane* and his old friend Col. John Hutchinson.* Pierrepont might be described as a parliamentary legitimist. Though not a republican, he was on friendly terms with many who were. He believed the legitimate authority of the Long Parliament had ended with Pride's purge, and looked with contempt on the Rump and its Cromwellian successors. Under Richard Cromwell he apparently hoped for a restoration of constitutional rule, and at the return of the original Long Parliament showed he was once again prepared to play an active role. Defeated for the Cavalier Parliament, Pierrepont retired from politics and moved to the country, where he died in the summer of 1678. By his wife Elizabeth, daughter and coheiress of Sir Thomas Harris, Bt., he had five sons and five daughters.

G.F.T. Jones, *Saw-Pit Wharton* (1967); *DNB*; MacCormack; V. Pearl, 'The "Royal" Independents in the English Civil War,' *TRHS*, 5th ser., 13:69-96; Underdown, *PP*; Worden; Keeler. Papers: L (Stowe MSS).

L.M. Hill

PILKINGTON, Sir Thomas (d. 1691)

Parliamentary radical, MP 1679, 1681, 1689 (London), was the son of Thomas Pilkington of Northampton and his wife, Anne Mercer. Pilkington became a public figure late in life and almost nothing is known about his early years. Apparently he went to London while quite young. He met and married Hannah Bromwich, by whom he had two sons. Prospering in business, Pilkington became a staunch Whig and stood for Parliament in 1679. The election came in the wake of the Popish plot and in London Pilkington and three other 'implacable Whigs' were easily elected. He demanded in the Commons that the Duke of York should return from exile in Brussels 'that we may impeach him of high treason.' Pilkington enthusiastically supported the Exclusion Bill offered by his fellow London MP, Sir Thomas Player.* The chief focus of Pilkington's activities now turned to City affairs, where he vigorously opposed the Crown's attempt to destroy the independent government of London. Pilkington was prominent in City affairs by this time. A leading member of the Skinners' Company, he was elected alderman in 1680, and in 1681, despite strong opposition from Court candidates, he and Shute were chosen sheriffs. The election was disorderly and it was alleged that there had been serious irregularities. As sheriff, Pilkington selected the jury which threw out an indictment of treason against the Earl of Shaftesbury.* He was charged by the mayor with having rigged it and was rebuked by the judge. In 1682 the vendetta intensified. Pilkington was tried for libel, found guilty and fined £800. He appealed the amount, but the House of Lords upheld the judgment. After the riotous shrievalty elections of 1682, Pilkington and Shute were sent to the Tower and tried together with other prominent Whigs in Feb. 1683. Pilkington was again found guilty and fined £500. At the same time, his term as sheriff came to an end. The Duke of York now brought against him an action of 'scandalum magnatum.' This asserted that Pilkington, as sheriff, had refused to accompany the mayor and aldermen to greet the Duke on his return from Scotland and had charged that, having been responsible for burning the City in 1666, he was now coming to cut the citizens' throats. Burnet's description of Pilkington as 'an honest but an indiscreet man, that gave himself great liberties in discourse' seems to have been merited. The jury awarded the Duke the fantastic sum of £50,000. Pilkington resigned his office as alderman and was imprisoned until June 1686. His fortunes rebounded dramatically after the flight of James II. Within two months he was elected alderman again; chosen as one of the City's representatives to Parliament; elected, upon the death of the lord mayor, to fill the remainder of the term; and finally, on 10 Apr. 1689, knighted by the King. In the autumn he was elected lord mayor for a full term and entertained the King and Queen at his installation banquet. In 1690 he was elected mayor for the third time. He served out the term and died on 1 Dec. 1691.

Jones, *FW*; Beaven; J. Levin, *The Charter Controversy in the City of London* (1969); R. North, *Examen* (1740); *DNB*.

M.J. Brown

PINNELL (or Pinnel), Henry (b.c. 1613)

New Model chaplain and reformer, was born in Brinkworth, Wilts., the son of Henry Pinnell. He matriculated at Hart Hall, Oxf. on 13 Apr. 1632 and received the B.A. from St. Mary Hall on 22 Apr. 1634. He became chaplain to Col. John Pickering's regiment of the New Model Army and served until Dec. 1647 or Jan. 1648, when he, following the lead of chaplains John Saltmarsh* and William Sedgwick,* became disenchanted with the 'carnal' ways of Cromwell and the army officers. In an interview with Cromwell at Windsor in Dec. 1647, Pinnell praised him for not disbanding the army and for enjoining it to relieve oppression but also reproved the Lieutenant-General, the army and Parliament for their dissimulation to Gen. Fairfax,* and their failure to keep many of their political and religious promises. The result of this 'recidination,' Pinnell told Cromwell, was that the kingdom was as oppressed as before (*A Word of Prophecy Concerning the Parliament, Generall and the Army* [1648], 4, 5, 8; *Nil Novi. This Year Fruit, from the Last Years Root* [1655], 34-36). Although his account of his separation from the army, as well as his Antinomian sentiments, in *A Word of Prophecy*, alienated Pinnell from some army factions, he reported in *Nil Novi* that Cromwell and several army officers had wanted him to return. He refused both because he no longer believed in 'carnal' means of bringing in the kingdom of God and because he had become increasingly convinced that the army leaders had been corrupted by worldly ambitions (*Nil Novi*, 37-38). Pinnell confessed in *A Word of Prophecy* that he had not been immune to such temptation himself. 'Sometimes,' he admitted, 'the flesh would put me forward with motives of pride, vainglory, singularity, popular applause, getting a name, becoming famous, eminent, and be[ing] taken notice of, as Mr. Sedgwick, [and] Mr. Saltmarsh were. . . .'

Pinnell was apparently unable to acquire a ministerial position after leaving the army. Having retired to Brinkworth, he was selected as pastor by the congregation at Christian-Malford, with the approval of its dying minister, one Master Dolman, but the congregation's petition and visitation to the Office of Requests were ignored, and

Col. Goffe* appointed a Master Goffe (no relation) instead of Pinnell. On losing the appointment he took a 'less public place' in the parish and claimed that although he was not a parson, vicar or curate, the people in four places had 'some expectation' of him (*Nil Novi*, 50).

Probably more significant than his New Model chaplaincy were Pinnell's activities as a publicist for the religious position shared by such men as Saltmarsh, Dell,* Erbery,* Sprigge,* Cradock* and Crisp,* which has been variously termed radical Puritanism, Antinomianism and Spiritualism. In *A Word of Prophecy* Pinnell described his obviously heterodox visionary experience of 'full assurance and consolation' of fourteen years earlier. In *Nil Novi* he undertook to defend himself not only in the Christian-Malford affair but also against the charge that he was 'too seraphical and allegorical' and that he spiritualized away the resurrection. He also defended the position that it is not deifying man to hold that the Spirit indwells the true Christian personally and substantially and argued that perfect obedience is demanded of Christians. In addition to these publications, he collaborated with John Maddocks on *Gangraenachrestum, or, a Plaister to Allay the Tumor* (1646) against Thomas Edwards' criticism of their doctrine of Christ's person and work, and wrote a preface to the 1646 edition of Tobias Crisp's sermons entitled *Christ Alone Exalted*.

After settling at Brinkworth, Pinnell became attracted, as others had been, to the link between Paracelsian medicine and the theology of free grace. In 1652 he published *Five Treatises of the Philosophers Stone*, a compilation derived mainly from pre-Paracelsian alchemical authors. In 1657 he produced his major work in this vein, *Philosophy Reformed & Improved in Four Profound Tractates*, a translation mainly composed of the lengthy preface to Oswald Croll's *Dasilica chymica* and Paracelsus' *Philosophia ad Athenienses* with numerous annotations by Pinnell, who described Paracelsianism as a 'theological philosophy wherefore the new

birth is first to be sought for, and then all other natural things will be added without much labor.' This emphasis on the harmony between 'nature, grace, physick and divinity,' as Pinnell put it, allied him with other radical critics such as John Webster.* He praised as well the doctrines of Jacob Boehme then becoming current in England. Pinnell was a vigorous critic of university education, especially in *This Year's Fruit, from the Last Years Root* (1655).

Al. Oxon.; Hill, *WTUD*; G. Huehns, *Antinomianism in English History* (1951); Solt; Webster, *GI*; Thomas.

M.B. Endy

PLATTES (or Platt), Gabriel (fl. 1639-1644/45)

Agricultural reformer, may have worked with the inventor and drainage engineer William Engelbert, to whom he dedicated his first works. Plattes was probably in his forties and claimed 24 years' practical experience in agriculture and mining when he published *A Discovery of Infinite Treasure* and *A Discovery of Subterraneall Treasure*, both in 1639. In the former he proposed the establishment of a 'college for inventors in husbandry,' an idea later taken up by Cressy Dymock.* Plattes' approach was boldly empiricist. He judged 'no knowledge perfect' until confirmed by experiment, and declared it his intention 'to turn plow-men into philosophers.' Plattes' writing attracted the attention of Samuel Hartlib,* who promoted and encouraged him. In 1641 he produced *A Description of the Famous Kingdome of Macaria*, issued to coincide with the opening of the Long Parliament and designed to interest its members in a comprehensive state-sponsored program of economic planning and improvement. General supervision of reform was to be vested in five councils of Parliament concerned with husbandry, fishing, trade by land, trade by sea and new plantations.

Plattes repeated his call for a college of husbandry and coupled this with a proposal for a 'college of experience' for innovations in medicine. He argued that the solution of poverty was not in more almshouses but the improvement of land. Implicit in this was not only the practical idea of turning a social burden into an asset but the ideal of a productive and self-reliant peasantry. Failure to properly exploit the resources of the kingdom for the benefit of all, he warned, could only sow the seeds of civil strife.

Macaria was one of the key texts of the revolutionary period, and the first of the many utopias it produced. The college of experience was a feature in the reform proposals brought forward by the Hartlib group between 1647 and 1657. Novel also was the suggestion for government patronage of scientific endeavor and the free dissemination of technological innovation which, as Nicholas Culpepper* pointed out, was bound to be resisted by the guilds and monopolies. In both *Macaria* and *The Profitable Intelligencer* (1644), however, Plattes alluded to a major work, 'The Treasure House of Nature Unlocked,' which, he insisted, would not be published until promised parliamentary support. The work has not survived. Plattes himself, who was destitute, fell dead in the street one day in the winter of 1644-45 while on his way to visit Hartlib.

Plattes' work is repetitive, a common failing of the era, but his ideas are set out with vigor and clarity. His interests were wide-ranging and he wrote from a fund of broad personal experience. His insistence on experiment, his intuition of the critical importance of chemistry and his call for public sponsorship of scientific research all anticipated developments of a later date, while his abhorrence of idle land and labor and his faith in a technological solution to the problem of poverty combined both traditional Puritan attitudes and the new scientific temper.

Webster, *GI*; *DNB*; C. Webster, 'The Authorship and Significance of Macaria,' *P. & P.*, 56:34-48; R.E. Prothero, *English Farming Past and Present* (1917); S. Hartlib, *Samuel Hartlib His Legacy of Husbandry* (1655); C. Webster, *Utopian Planning and the Puritan Revolution* (1979); J.C. Davis, *Utopia and the Ideal Society* (1981).

R. Zaller

PLAYER, John (c. 1595-1660)

Puritan minister, was born in St. Andrew's parish, Cambridge, the son of Robert Player of Canterbury. Player went from the King's School, Canterbury, to Clare Coll., Camb., matriculating as a sizar at Easter 1612. He graduated B.A. (1616) and M.A. (1619), was incorporated at Oxford in 1619, and was ordained deacon (31 May 1618) and priest (21 Feb. 1619) in London. On 26 May 1620 Player was appointed Vicar of Kennington, Kent. When he refused to read the Book of Sports in 1633, he was suspended and had his annual income reduced by £20. In the elections to the Long Parliament he actively supported his friend, Sir Edward Dering. Although Player was supposed to testify against Laud, he was prevented by illness, but did send written testimony for Richard Culmer* to use on his behalf. On 1 July 1646 Player was appointed lecturer at St. Alphege's, Canterbury, and in Feb. 1647 he helped establish a new Congregational church in the town. He was named lecturer at St. George's, Canterbury in 1650, assistant to the Kent Commission in 1654, and preacher at Canterbury Cathedral on 23 May 1656. In Sept. 1658 he expressed interest in the representatives to the Savoy Conference from the Congregational churches in Kent. Player was buried in Canterbury Cathedral on 6 Dec. 1660. He had married Elizabeth, daughter of William Masters, in the Cathedral on 7 Dec. 1619. Player's brother, Sir Thomas (1608-1672), was Chamberlain of London.

CSPD, Chas. 1, 17:453; 18:545; 19:15, 217; *Comm.*, 6:201; 7:433; *Calamy*

Revised; Everitt; *Al. Cant.* Papers: KAO; LPR.

R.L. Greaves

PLAYER, Sir Thomas (d. 1686)

City and parliamentary radical, MP 1679, 1680, 1681 (London). Player was the oldest son of Thomas Player, a hosier of Mare Street, Hackney, who served as a captain in the trained bands, was sent to the relief of Gloucester in 1643 and was Chamberlain of London from 1651 until his death in 1672, and his wife Rebecca. The younger Player was married in 1641 to Joyce, daughter of William Kendall, Merchant Taylor of London, and in 1659 became a member of the Haberdashers' Company. He was knighted with his father on 5 Aug. 1660, in the same year becoming colonel of the White auxiliary regiment of militia and a JP for Middlesex, and in 1661 Assessment Commissioner for Middlesex. Leader of the Honorable Artillery Company from 1669 to 1677, he also served as colonel of the Orange regiment (1674-77), and in 1672 succeeded his father as chamberlain and joined the Common Council.

Player soon emerged as an active and influential opposition figure on the Council. In 1673 he joined Thomas Pilkington* in promoting an address of grievances, and was closely involved with the Dissenting bankers Thompson and Nelthorpe. By 1677 the Court was making strenuous efforts to remove him from the Council, but he was re-elected by a huge majority. The Duke of York succeeded in ousting him as leader of the Artillery Company by the expedient of abolishing the post. By now Player was closely associated with the Earl of Shaftesbury,* and was instrumental in blocking a City loan in 1678.

Elected to Parliament in 1679, Player served on 34 committees, including those for elections and privileges and for the Bill of Habeas Corpus, and made eleven recorded speeches. On 27 Apr. he prophesied that under a popish successor 'we shall not have the honor of ancient martyrdom in flames, but die like dogs and have our throats cut,' and on 11 May moved the first bill to exclude the Duke of York from the throne. After the dissolution of Parliament, he and Pilkington organized citizen petitions to call another in a revival of the prerevolutionary tactics of 1641, and accompanied by several hundred prominent citizens he urged the Court of Aldermen to double the City guards against the return of the Duke of York.

Player was removed from the commission of assessment and the commission of the peace in 1680. He remained in the forefront of opposition in the Parliament of that year, serving on 38 committees and delivering thirteen speeches. Once again he called for the exclusion of the Duke of York as well as the impeachment of Seymour, and demanded the removal of George Jeffreys as Recorder of London for threatening the withdrawal of the City charter. In the Oxford Parliament he demanded the impeachment of Fitzharris as well. After the abrupt dissolution of that body he held meetings at his home in Guildhall with Pilkington, Sir Robert Clayton,* Patience Ward* and others to concert tactics. On 28 Apr. 1681 he presented a petition for a new parliament to the Court of Aldermen, which was approved on 13 May despite Court efforts to block it. Evidence was then presented accusing Player of being treasurer of a Whig fund to maintain witnesses in the Popish plot, but he was not prosecuted, perhaps because the shrievalty was in Pilkington's hands. Player was active in the defense of London's charter against the writ of *quo warranto* in 1682 as well as in the shrievalty election. But in December he was defeated in the Common Council elections, and in Feb. 1683 he was fined 500 marks for promoting electoral riots. In a further judgment, his estate was distrained until a deficiency of £3246 found in funds paid to him as a disbandment commissioner were made up. In September, Player declined to stand again for chamberlain, and sued for pardon from the Court.

With this, his career came to an end. He died on 14 Jan. 1686, and was buried in Hackney. Player is the 'railing Rabsheka' of Dryden's *Absalom and Achitopel*, and his lechery was a frequent target of satire.

Beaven; Haley, *FES*; *Grey's Debates*; Luttrell; *ST*; *CSPD, Chas. II, passim.*; *HMC, Ormond*; History of Parliament, draft biography. Papers: O (Carte MSS).

R. Zaller

POLWHELE, Theophilus (c. 1628-d. 1689)

Ejected minister, was a native of Cornwall who married the daughter of William Benn of Dorchester. Polwhele was voted £10 by the residents of that town at the time of the wedding. His second wife Maria died in 1671 and he took a third wife Johannah. Polwhele had a son, Isaac, an Anglican cleric, and three daughters: Elizabeth, who married Stephen Lobb, Susanna and Johannah. Polwhele was educated at Emmanuel Coll., Camb. (B.A. 1648, M.A. 1651). Rector of Langston, Long Blandford in Dorset in 1649, Polwhele became lecturer at St. Mary's and St. Cuthbert's, Carlisle in 1651. He stayed at Carlisle until 1655, assisting the Commission to Eject Scandalous Ministers for the Northern Counties in 1654. His salary for his two parishes in 1652 was £12. He removed to become Vicar of Tiverton, Devon in 1655 and assisted the Devon Commission in 1657. After his ejection Polwhele was accused of seditious conventicles in 1665 and in 1669 he confessed such activities, for which he was fined at the Devon Assizes. In 1672 he was licensed as a Congregationalist at Tiverton. Polwhele continued to serve the Independents at Tiverton and after James II's indulgence a meeting-house was built in 1687. From 1658 to 1674 he published several volumes of sermons, the best known being *Choice Directions How to Serve God Every Working Day and Every Lords Day* (1667). Polwhele was buried at St. Peter's churchyard, Tiverton.

Calamy Revised; *CSPD, Chas. II*, 12; B. Nightingale, *The Ejected of 1662 in Cumberland and Westmorland* (1911); PCC, Wills (8 June 1689).

J.A. Berlatsky

POMFRET, Samuel (1650-1722)

Puritan minister, was born at Coventry and educated at local grammar schools there and at Islington. After his mother's death about 1669, he became pious. He was chaplain to Sir William Dyer of Tottenham and served for two years as chaplain aboard a Mediterranean trading ship. Upon his return to England, he preached at Lincoln's Inn Fields before he accepted a parish in Sandwich, Kent. There he was arrested for nonconformity, but escaped on the way to Dover Castle. During the following years in London Pomfret became an immensely popular preacher. About 1685, as he was conducting services in the crowded upper room of a house in Winchester Street, the floor collapsed and several people were injured. Pomfret's enemies saw the incident as one of divine retribution, but the publicity made him even more famous. A church with a capacity of 1500 was built for him in Gravel Lane, Houndsditch. It was often filled, and Pomfret served as many as 800 communicants. As he grew older his health failed and he was unable to walk, but he had himself carried to his pulpit in a chair. After Pomfret's death on 11 Jan. 1722, Thomas Reynolds, a Presbyterian minister, preached the funeral sermon. The published text is the main source of information about Pomfret's life. Pomfret himself published only two sermons, one in 1697 and another in 1701. His *Directory for Youth* was published posthumously.

DNB; T. Reynolds, *Watch and Remember* (1722); Wilson, *HADC*.

T.W. Hayes

PONDER, Nathaniel (1640-1699)

Bookseller, was the son of John Ponder, a Puritan mercer of Rothwell, Northants. He was bound apprentice on 5 June 1656 to Robert Gibbs, bookseller, of Chancery Lane, and on 4 July 1663 he was made free of the Stationers' Company. In 1666 he married Mary Guy of Itham, Northants., whose father was described as a gentleman. He established himself as a bookseller at the Sign of the Peacock in Chancery Lane where he became known as a publisher of Nonconformist writings. He was imprisoned briefly (1-26 May 1676) for publishing Andrew Marvell's* *Rehearsal Transpros'd*, and he later published Sir Bulstrode Whitelocke's* *Memorials* (1682). His major achievement was as publisher of *The Pilgrim's Progress*, and his name appears on the title-pages of the first eleven editions (1678-88). His profits, however, were consumed by litigation against printers who issued pirated editions, and he was imprisoned in 1688 for debt. He was buried in St. Gregory-by-Paul on 22 June 1699.

F.M. Harrison, 'Nathaniel Ponder: the Publisher of *The Pilgrim's Progress*,' *The Library*, 4th ser., 15:257-94; Plomer, *DPB*; J.B. Wharey and R. Sharrock, eds., *The Pilgrim's Progress* (1960); H.R. Plomer, 'A Lawsuit as to an Early Edition of the "Pilgrim's Progress",' *The Library*, 3rd ser., 5:60-69.

H.T. Blethen

POOLE, Elizabeth (fl. 1648-1649)

Sectarian visionary, appeared before the General Council of the Army on 29 Dec. 1648 and 4 Jan. 1649. She was probably the daughter of Robert Poole, who castigated William Kiffin* in 1645 for seducing Poole's children and servants into Particular Baptist errors. Elizabeth's first Council appearance was simply to encourage the members with news of an allegorical vision which she had, recognizing and justifying the *de facto* transfer of power from King to Parliament and thence to the army. On her second visit, however, she also discussed the disposal of Charles I, insisting it was God's will that his life be spared. Four days later she published a tract describing the two encounters with the Council. Shortly thereafter she was disowned by Kiffin and his congregation, who testified against her to the Council. In June 1649 a second edition of her tract appeared, endorsed by a Baptist friend, who was probably Thomasina Pendarves, wife of the evangelist John Pendarves,* then at Abingdon. Elizabeth also published another tract in which she expressed her sorrow over the King's death, her views of the Regicides, and her fears for England as a consequence of the shedding of royal blood. Modern interpretations of the Council visits differ, but Elizabeth was probably introduced by Cromwell and Ireton* to reinforce resistance to Leveller demands. Surprised by her espousal of clemency towards the King, they later repudiated her through Kiffin's group.

W. Kiffin, *A Brief Remonstrance* (1645); E. Poole, *A Vision* (1649); *An Alarm of War* (1649); *Another Alarm of War* (1649); *Clarke Papers*, 2; D. Ludlow, ' "Arise and Be Doing" ' (Ph.D. diss., Indiana Univ., 1978).

D.P. Ludlow

POOLEY (or Powley), Christopher (b.c. 1620)

Fifth Monarchist, Seventh Day Baptist and millenarian. Pooley matriculated as a pensioner from King's Coll., Camb. in Michaelmas term, 1639, and graduated B.A. (1642-43) and M.A. (1647). Ordained a deacon at age 23 in Norwich on 28 May 1643, he became Curate of Thwaite, Suff. the same year. He may have served in the army from 1647 to 1651. In 1653 the church at Wymondham, Norf., with which he was now associated, nominated members for the Barebones Parliament. With other

Fifth Monarchists he became disillusioned with Cromwell when the Barebones was dismissed, and in 1656, as one of the leading Fifth Monarchists in Norfolk, he, Thomas Buttevant* and Thomas Rudduck were contemplating a rising. The same year he adopted Baptist principles, and at North Walsham, Norf., he and Richard Breviter,* 'being both dipped,' argued against messengers of various Independent churches for adult baptism by immersion.

By 1660 Pooley had become a disciple of Thomas Tillam,* and in that year wrote a commendatory epistle to Tillam's *The Temple of Lively Stones* (1660). Convinced that God was about to destroy England for its iniquity, Pooley and Tillam left for the Continent where they hoped to found a godly community of 200 families. On 31 July 1661 Pooley, now working closely with Lieut. Love in this scheme, returned from the Netherlands to Lowestoft, Suff., and became the pastor of a Seventh Day Baptist church at Norwich, where he was known as 'a grand dipper in Norfolk.' Arrested the same year, as was Tillam, Pooley subsequently returned to the Continent to further their millenarian community. Writing from Rotterdam on 11 Nov. 1664, John Pigeon warned Pooley's wife in England that her husband had taken another wife, debunked his reports of plenty and comfort (which he had espoused on a recruiting mission that year), and urged her not to join him. The same year John Cowell hurled charges of communism, polygamy and concubinage against the Tillam-Pooley community in *Divine Oracles*.

In June 1666 Pooley returned to England at Tillam's behest to proselytize, telling of the favors received from the Palgrave and their hopes to restore the kingdom of Christ in the Palatinate. His companion this time was John Foxey, but a government agent did not believe they were intent on fomenting rebellion. Although Pooley and Foxey were reluctant to give copies of their 'solemn covenant' to any but subscribers, the government acquired one. In it the millenarians renounced all powers and rulers contrary to Christ and his government, insisting they could accept no ruler not in communion with them, nor even their coinage. Separation from everything associated with false religion was a *sine qua non*, and they demanded strict adherence to divine law, especially on the sabbath and marriage (no union with 'strangers'). Oaths and bearing arms for unchristian rulers were forbidden, and Christ alone was recognized as king. Communal or private property was allowed according to the dictates of each individual conscience. Convinced they must live where they could be a distinct people, these millenarians insisted on an annual renewal of the covenant.

After traveling through Northumberland, Yorkshire and Nottinghamshire, Pooley was apprehended at Ipswich in 1667. Although he briefly escaped, he was recaptured and placed in the custody of Lord Arlington in June 1667. The Recorder and Bailiffs of Ipswich informed the Duke of Albemarle that Pooley 'is of dangerous principles, and refuses to take the oath of obedience, or acknowledge himself a subject of the King.' By Jan. 1668 he was once again recruiting in the north, visiting Raby Castle, where the Baptist Henry Blackett was preaching. He achieved some success, for in Mar. 1668 more emigrants sailed from Harwich to join their community. It adopted Jewish rites, including sacrifices, ceremonial laws and circumcision, and it hoped to rebuild the Temple. Cowell renewed his attack on the community in 1673 in *The Snare Broken*. Probably discouraged by Tillam's death, by 1677 Pooley had apparently returned to England to espouse Seventh Day Baptist views.

CSPD, Chas. II, 2:79; 4:101-2; 6:346, 495; 7:229, 235; 8:154; Capp, *FMM*; *Al. Cant.*; Nuttall, *VS*; E.A. Payne, 'Thomas Tillam,' *BQ*, 17:61-66; Thurloe, *SP*, 5:188, 219-20, 372.

R.L. Greaves

POPHAM, Alexander (1605-1669)

Civil War officer, was the second son and

heir of Sir Francis Popham of Littlecote, Wilts. Popham studied at Oxford and the Middle Temple and amassed debts at the latter, thanks in part to the extravagance of his older brother. These marked the beginning of financial problems which continued to plague him for the remainder of his life. After seeing service with the army in the north in 1639 he was elected to the Short Parliament for Minehead and Bath, choosing to sit for the latter. He also served for Bath in the Long Parliament, and at the outbreak of war was among the minority of the Somerset gentry supporting the parliamentary cause. He was a DL for the shire and active in raising men for parliament, and although he won no notable military honors (unlike his younger brother, Edward,* who became an important figure in the navy) rose to the rank of colonel. Popham was a Presbyterian elder for a time but continued to sit as one of the more conservative Rumpers after 1648. He was relatively inactive in the Rump, and this fact, together with his moderate outlook, doubtless explains his early selection as a member of Cromwell's Council of State in 1649. Popham remained a staunch Cromwellian and in 1657 was among those elevated to the Upper House. He sensed that political change was in the air after the Protector's death, and he was among those approached by adherents of Charles. Popham remained noncommittal, but his adroitness in retaining his position both in national affairs and among the Somerset gentry is evidenced by his success in weathering the changes wrought by the Restoration. He raised a troop of horse to pay homage to the restored monarch, and this action evidently had the desired effect. His influence was such that he was able to take the remains of his brother, whose naval activity had gained him considerable renown, away from Westminster Abbey rather than have the family exposed to public disgrace. He was well to the top of the poll of those elected for a new Council of State in 1660, and he sat in the Cavalier Parliament.

T.L. Auffenberg, 'Cromwell's Other House' (M.A. thesis, Vanderbilt Univ., 1972); Bates Harbin; Keeler; Underdown, *PP*. Papers: SRO; L (Add. MSS).

J.A. Casada

POPHAM, Edward (c. 1610-1651)

Civil War officer and General at Sea, was the fifth and youngest son of Sir Francis Popham (d. 1644) of Littlecote, Wilts. and Wellington, Som., MP for Minehead in the Long Parliament, and Anne, daughter of John Dudley of Stoke Newington. Among his brothers was the Civil War officer and MP for Bath, Alexander Popham.* In 1627 an Edward and Alexander Popham were outlawed for debt. The *DNB* suggests that these were different parties, but Keeler regards their identity with our subjects as probable. An elder brother, John, was rumored to have left £38,000 in debts at his death in 1638. Popham attended the Middle Temple before going to sea. In 1636 he was commissioned a lieutenant on the 'Henrietta Maria' in the fleet commanded by the Earl of Northumberland. In Mar. 1637 he became captain of the 'Fifth Whelp,' which went down off the Dutch coast with an unseaworthy bottom on 28 June 1637. Seventeen lives were lost, the survivors being rescued by a passing English ship which conveyed them to Rotterdam. In 1639 Popham commanded a ship in the Downs under Sir John Penington, possibly the 'Rainbow'.

The Pophams all declared for Parliament at the outbreak of the Civil War, one of the few families of stature in the west country to do so. Edward, Alexander and another brother, Hugh, all raised forces in Somerset, where Alexander was a DL. Edward was forced to abandon Taunton to royalist forces in June 1643, but it was probably he who, commanding 'a good strength of horse and foot,' relieved Dorchester that same year. In 1644 Edward and Alexander again raised troops in Somerset, passing through enemy lines with a body of 200 horse. On 11 June 1645 Edward was ordered to take command of forces at Romsey to lift the siege of Taunton, where his lieutenant-colonel, Robert Blake,* had held out for eight months. He probably fought at Ilminster, Langport and Bridgwater in the ensuing campaign. Popham was active on the Somerset County Committee, and succeeded his father as MP for Minehead in 1646.

Popham resumed his naval career during the second Civil War. On 17 June 1648 he was ordered to sea against the Prince of Wales' fleet, though this was countermanded three days later, Walter Strickland* sailing in his stead. In the reorganization of the naval command in Feb. 1649 following the Earl of Warwick's* resignation, Popham was named General at Sea together with Blake and Richard Deane,* though he had taken his dissent in Parliament only days earlier. Of the three he had most experience as a sailor, though his seniority in command was determined not by this but by the priority of his regimental commission. Chosen by lot to oppose a squadron under Prince Rupert lying in the mouth of the Channel, he captured two frigates, forcing Rupert to withdraw to Kinsale. For most of the rest of the year he kept station in the Downs and the North Sea against privateers with letters of marque from the Prince of Wales to prey on English shipping. In Apr. 1650 Popham was ordered to join Blake's blockade of Rupert off Lisbon with a force of eight ships. He arrived on 26 May and remained until early September, though no action resulted. The following year he resumed his station in the Downs. In July he was ordered to blockade the Duke of Lorraine off Ostend and Dunkirk, but he died suddenly of a fever at Dover on 19 Aug. Popham was given a state funeral and a parliamentary delegation was sent to condole his widow, who received a year of his salary (£1095). She was Anne, daughter of William Carr, a groom of the bedchamber, by whom Popham had two children, Letitia and Alexander. Popham was disinterred from Westminster Abbey with his two fellow Generals at the Restoration, but while their remains were thrown into a pit,

his were privately removed in deference to his brother Alexander, now a Cavalier, and buried in the chapel of St. John the Baptist. Popham lacked Blake's genius, but he was a conscientious and dedicated officer, and in the words of a contemporary 'a gallant man, [who] steers as right at sea, and marches as fair at land as any man I know.' A portrait of Popham exists, reproduced by Underdown, but its present ownership is unknown.

DNB; Barnes; Underdown, *SCWI*; Ludlow; Thurloe, *SP*; Keeler, s.v. Alexander Popham; C.E. Lucas Phillips, *Cromwell's Captains* (1972); *HMC Portland MSS*; *CSPD, Chas. I*, 2:104; 10:485; 11:136, 143, 283; 14:93, 274; 15:26; 20:585-87; 22:195, 201, 207; *Comm.*, vols. 1-3 *passim*; Underdown, *PP*; Ashley, *CG*.

R. Zaller

POPPLE, William (1638-1708)

Deist and toleration advocate, was born in Hull on 4 Feb. 1638, the son of the city's sheriff, Edmund Popple, and his wife Catherine, daughter of the Rev. Andrew Marvell and sister of the poet. Nothing is known of his education, but he acquired facility in Latin and a taste for literature and philosophy. By 1661 he was engaged in the London office of his family's wine importing business. About 1664 Popple married Mary Alured, daughter of John,* the Cromwellian colonel. He took his wife and three children to Bordeaux in 1670, acting as agent for the family business. While there he enjoyed the company of French intellectuals, and he maintained a correspondence with his uncle, the poet Andrew Marvell.* When religious toleration ended in 1685 Popple was trapped in France. Having been naturalized earlier, he was obliged to convert to the Catholic Church. Anxious to leave France, Popple used contacts in the English and French governments to secure permission to emigrate and even to take his goods with him. In 1688 he moved back to England, settling in London.

The Quaker publisher, Andrew Sowle,* issued Popple's *A Rational Catechism* in 1687. It develops a natural theology by means of a Socratic dialogue, and argues the historical trustworthiness of the Gospels. Once back in England Popple published *Three Letters Tending to Demonstrate How the Security of This Nation Against all Future Persecution for Religion, Lys in the Abolishment of the Present Penal Laws* (1688), sometimes attributed to William Penn.* In it Popple advocated a constitutional law forbidding any interference with freedom of conscience, to be secured by binding oaths on magistrates, MPs and the monarch. Popple's *A Letter to Mr. Penn*, dated 20 Oct. 1688, absolves his friend from rumors that his support of James II's Indulgence stemmed from Catholic sympathies. In 1689 Popple published his translation of John Locke's* *A Letter Concerning Toleration*, adding a preface advocating 'absolute liberty' of conscience in preference to the policies of comprehension and toleration then being debated. With Henry Neville* and others, Locke and Popple formed the Dry Club to discuss religious liberty. Locke was probably instrumental in Popple's appointment as secretary to the Board of Trade and Plantations in 1696. In 1707 he retired in favor of his son, William, and he died the next year. Popple anonymously published *Two Treatises of Rational Religion* in 1692 which consisted of the second edition of the *Rational Catechism* and a short poem, 'Advice to a Son.'

C. Robbins, 'Absolute Liberty: the Life and Thought of William Popple,' *William and Mary Quarterly*, 24:190-223; *HMC*, *14th Report*; H.M. Margoliouth, *The Poems and Letters of Andrew Marvell* (1971). Papers: L (Add. MSS 8888; 34, 515, f. 43); LPR (C6/526/178); O (Lovelace Collection, MS Locke, c. 17).

C.J. Sommerville

PORDAGE, John (1607-1681)

Religious radical, was christened on 21 Apr. 1607 at St. Dionis Backchurch, London, the eldest son of the grocer Samuel Pordage and his wife Elizabeth (née Taylor). He was admitted as a pensioner at Pembroke Coll., Camb. on 21 Apr. 1623, and graduated B.A. in 1626 and M.D. in 1640 (incorporated from Leiden). In 1644 he was appointed Curate of St. Lawrence, Reading, but by 1647 he had become Rector of Bradfield, Berks. As a result of his mystical and astrological beliefs, he was charged with nine articles of heresy but acquitted in Mar. 1651. He and his wife, the former Mary Lane Freeman of Tenbury, Worcs., organized a group to study the writings of Boehme in 1652. The Berkshire Commission was sufficiently concerned with his activities in Sept. 1654 to order his appearance the following month, particularly due to the instigation of John Tickel, the Presbyterian Vicar of St. Helen's, Abingdon. A record of the proceedings, entitled *Daemonium Meridianum. Satan at Noon* (1655), was provided by Christopher Fowler, Vicar of St. Mary's, Reading. The charges involved heresy and immorality, but were largely without foundation. Pordage admitted that as early as 1654 he had had visions and communion with angels, and his testimony of 'the fiery Deity burning in the center of the soul' unsettled his traditional critics. Perhaps more serious was Pordage's known association with William Erbery,* (William?) Everard* and Thomas Tany,* 'who styled himself King of the Jews,' and his public defense of Abiezer Coppe* and approbation of a book of Richard Coppin.* Pordage was accused of asserting that there would shortly be no parliament, governor or magistrate in England, and that saints should seize the estates of the wicked and enslave their persons. His wife was a proponent of communal ownership and may have been a Digger. Not surprisingly, Pordage was ejected on 8 Dec. 1654. He subsequently published his defense as *Innocencie Appearing* (1655).

Pordage was restored to his rectory in 1660, but appears to have encountered further difficulties, for in 1669 he is reported as the head of a conventicle of tradesmen at Reading. He met and influenced Jane Leade* in 1663, and worked closely as well with another mystic, Edward Hooker. In Leade's judgment Pordage was 'another Moses in some sort' and a Seeker who pursued 'an internal contemplative life.' Baxter regarded him as the leader of the 'sect of Behmenists,' and Boehme's influence is clearly revealed in Pordage's *Theologia mystica* (1683), which explores the divine essence but steers clear of social and political matters. After the death of his first wife in 1668, he married Elizabeth, widow of Thomas Faldo of London. Pordage's son Samuel went to Lincoln's Inn, and his brother Francis (M.A., St. Catharine's, Camb., 1651) was Rector of Stanford-Dingley, Berks. Pordage was buried at St. Andrew's, Holborn, London, on 11 Dec. 1681.

Al. Cant.; C. Fowler, *Daemonium Meridianum* (1655); *DNB*; D. Hirst, 'The Riddle of John Pordage,' *Boehme Society Quarterly,* 1 (1953-54); *Hidden Riches* (1964); Hill, *MER* and *WTUD*.

R.L. Greaves

PORTMAN, John (fl. 1652-1667)

Fifth Monarchist, first appears as Deputy Treasurer of the Fleet and Secretary to the Generals at Sea in 1652, which posts he held to the end of the first Anglo-Dutch War in 1654. By that time he was the leader of the Fifth Monarchist faction which seceded from John Simpson's* congregation at Allhallows the Great, London in 1656. Portman took part in the negotiations with Commonwealth officers in the winter of 1656. He was arrested and dismissed from office the following summer for these activities. In September he attended the massive Fifth Monarchist rally in Abingdon on the death of John Pendarves.* He was arrested in 1657 on suspicion of complicity in Venner's* plot, and again in Feb. 1658 for harboring seditious books. He remained in the Tower until his escape

in December, and was formally discharged by Richard Cromwell's* Parliament in Feb. 1659. Portman subscribed to the *Essay towards Settlement* in September, and was condemned for his part in Venner's rising in Jan. 1661. Reprieved, he led a prison riot in Newgate in April, and a few days later called publicly for revenge for the execution of Thomas Harrison.* Portman is last recorded as a prisoner in 1667. His brother Edmund (fl. 1652-57) was also a Fifth Monarchist. He served as a clerk to the Treasurer of the Navy in the Anglo-Dutch War, was a member of Simpson's congregation, and had negotiations with John Venner in 1657.

Capp, *FMM*; *ST*, 6:117; Gardiner, *FDW*; *CSPD, Comm.,* 5-6, 10 *passim*; *Chas. II*, 15:259, 271; Thurloe, *SP*, 6:163, 185, 775; 7:599, 619-20, 623.

J.W. Spurgeon

POSTLETHWAITE, Walter (d. 1672)

Independent minister and Fifth Monarchist, was born about 1627, the son of John Postlethwaite, Rector of Kingston Bowsey, Sussex. He was admitted as a sizar to Emmanuel Coll., Camb., on 18 June 1643, and graduated B.A. in 1646. Hugh Peter* converted him to the Independent cause. From 1646 until his ejection in 1660, he was Rector of St. Michael's, Lewes, Suff. By 1655 he had adopted moderate Fifth Monarchist views and was pressing for the release of imprisoned saints. When Lewes sectaries, including Baptists, petitioned Cromwell in the fall of 1655 for the abolition of tithes and Chancery and the disbandment of the army, Postlethwaite's congregation refused to sign on the grounds that such actions recognized the legitimacy of the Protectorate government. In *A Voice from Heaven*, published the same year, he warned that England was in danger of losing the anticipated reign of Christ to America and the East Indies. In 1661 he subscribed to the Oaths of Allegiance and Supremacy at the Lewes

Quarter Sessions. He served as pastor of an Independent conventicle in All Saints parish, Lewes, in the 1660s, but apparently relinquished his Fifth Monarchy views. He was buried at St. Michael's on 11 Jan. 1672; his will, dated 1 Jan. 1672, does not mention a wife or children. His successor as pastor of the Lewes congregation was Joseph Whiston, former chaplain of Maj.-Gen. Harrison.*

Calamy Revised; Capp, *FMM*; Thurloe, *SP*, 4:151; *Al. Cant.*

R.L. Greaves

POTTER, Vincent (1614-1661?)

Regicide, was born in Warwickshire in 1614. A Puritan, he emigrated to Boston, Mass. in 1635 where the following year he was employed as a soldier at the fort on Castle Island at a salary of £10 p.a. Potter returned to England in 1639, joined the parliamentary army, and served as a captain of horse in the Warwickshire militia during the first Civil War. On 14 July 1645 he succeeded his brother, Capt. John Potter, who was slain at Naseby, as a commissioner in the army. Potter subsequently became the only New Englander to sit on the High Court which tried King Charles and to sign the death warrant. On 6 Mar. 1649 he also signed the death warrant for the royalist commanders Capel, Hamilton, Holland and Goring. By June 1649 Potter had risen to the rank of colonel, and during the Interregnum continued his duties as an Army Commissioner, coordinating the receipt and issuance of provisions for Cromwell's campaigns in Ireland and Scotland, and ultimately being appointed a Parliamentary Commissioner for both countries. At the Restoration Potter was tried as a Regicide (16 Oct. 1660), found guilty and condemned to death. The sentence was never carried out, and he spent the remainder of his life in prison.

Abbott; *CSPD, Comm.*, 1-4 *passim*; *Chas. II*, 1:153; W.L. Sachse, 'Migration of New Englanders to England, 1640-1660,' *AHR*, 53:251-78; R. Temple, unpublished manuscript material (1978).

C.B. Rynder

POWELL, Vavasor (1617-1670)

Fifth Monarchist, was born at Cnwcglas (Knucklas), a hamlet in the parish of Heyop, Powys, Wales, the son of Richard Powell, a freeholder, and his wife Penelope, a descendant of the Vavasors of Spalding, Yorks. Powell was educated at Christ's Coll., Brecon, but his inclusion in *Ath. Oxon.* as a student of Jesus College is not otherwise attested. There is no proof that he was episcopally ordained but he served as curate to his maternal uncle, Erasmus Powell, at Clun, Shrops., and kept school at Llanfairwaterdine from 1634 to 1642. As a consequence of his religious conversion, under the influence of Walter Cradock* and others, he initiated a vigorous preaching mission in his home neighborhood and was arrested on two occasions.

Powell withdrew to England at the outbreak of war and was in London by Aug. 1642. He was Vicar of Dartford, Kent, from 1644 to 1646. On 11 Sept. 1646 he was granted a certificate by the Westminster Assembly and in June 1648 took up his duties as a preacher in north Wales. He was injured during Gen. Thomas Mytton's attack on Beaumaris in Sept. 1648. Powell supported the King's trial, and justified his execution on the grounds that he had broken all Ten Commandments. By this time he had gained public attention. He preached before the Lord Mayor of London on 2 Dec. 1649, and on 31 Dec. engaged in public debate with John Goodwin.* On 28 Feb. 1650 he preached before the House of Commons, precisely a week after the Act for the Propagation of the Gospel in Wales had been passed. Maj.-Gen. Harrison* was head of the Commission to implement the act, and Powell along with other Welsh ministers accompanied him to Scotland in 1651 with troops raised from their own congregations. Powell was named as an Approver under the Act and soon became a key figure in its administration. The plan of replacing ejected Anglican ministers with itinerant preachers serving large areas was said to be his. His enthusiasm provoked virulent opposition, expressed in *The Petition of the Six Counties of South-Wales* presented to the Commons on 10 Mar. 1652, and unofficially, after the expiration of the Act, by Alexander Griffith (d. 1676) in *Strena Vavasoriensis* (1654), to which Powell's admirers made reply in *Vavasoris examen et purgamen* (1654). Powell, together with the other Propagators, was blamed for treating Anglican incumbents harshly, as well as for using force to intimidate his opponents and misappropriating church funds to his own advantage.

Powell saw the Propagation Act as part of the preparation for the second coming of Christ to reign personally as the Fifth Monarch. When the Act lapsed at the end of three years, he was bitterly disappointed. On 17 Mar. 1653 he was preaching violently at Charterhouse, London, and on 8 Apr. one of 'Vavasor Powell's party' caused a riot at Smithfield. In May there were rumors that he was recruiting men in the Welsh marches to support by force his Fifth Monarchy campaign. His disappointment was assuaged with the calling of the Barebones Parliament, for the nominees for north Wales were largely his. His bitterness returned when that Parliament was dissolved and he saw the assumption of the title of Protector by Cromwell as a blasphemous defiance of 'King Jesus.' On 18 Dec. 1653 he joined Christopher Feake* at Christ Church in attacking the new Protector in unmeasured terms and repeated his attack at Blackfriars on the following day. On 20 Dec. he was arrested and examined by the Council of State but he was released and immediately resumed his public attacks at Christ Church on 9 Jan. Yet his message to his followers was to abandon political action.

This was a decisive break with the Cromwellian establishment. Threatened with arrest, Powell retired to Wales and launched a vigorous campaign in Feb. 1654 against the government. It took the form of promoting a petition, *A Word for God*. The campaign was a disappointment, for only 322 people signed it. In any case, Powell betrayed his deepest allegiance by showing vigorous support for the government during the royalist unrest of 1655. He raised a force from his parishioners and was wounded leading a successful engagement. However, he found no employment under the Protectorate and, apart from controversy with Quakers in 1657-58, lived in comparative retirement at his house, Goetre in Ceri, Powys. He was said to have presided over a suspicious meeting of 400 people from seven or eight counties in June 1656, but specifically denied having any part in Thomas Venner's* Fifth Monarchy plot of 1657. Powell was invited to the Savoy Conference in Sept. 1658 but did not attend, partly, no doubt, because he had adopted the Baptist position in 1655.

At the Restoration Powell was a marked man. He was arrested on 23 Apr. 1660 and held at Shrewsbury until the end of June. His period of freedom was a brief one for he was arrested on the basis of an Order in Council on 18 July. On 3 May 1661 the Privy Council excepted him from among those who were to receive pardon for acts committed during the Interregnum, and so by Sept. 1661 he was in the Fleet Prison and a year later was transferred to Southsea. He continued in prison until the fall of Clarendon and tasted freedom again in Nov. 1667. He immediately resumed his preaching and about Sept. 1668 was arrested for preaching illegally at Merthyr Tydfil. After a series of cross-examinations by local magistrates at Cowbridge and Cardiff, he was transferred in May 1669 by a writ of *habeas corpus* to be tried at the Court of Common Pleas in London. The proceedings against him were quashed but he continued to be held in custody in the Fleet. He died after a short illness on 27 Oct. 1670, aged 53, and was buried at Bunhill Fields where his memorial contained a fulsome epitaph composed by his biographer, Edward Bagshaw.

Powell was twice married, first to Joan Quarrel, widow of Paul Quarrel of Presteign, and second to Katherine, the fifth daughter of Gilbert Gerard of Crewood, Chester. Powell had no children.

Powell was the most vigorous protagonist of Fifth Monarchy views in Wales and maintained his faith in the imminent Second Coming of Christ to the day of his death. His firm adherence to his convictions made him a determined, even a rash, opponent of Cromwell and cost him the friendship of such close friends as Walter Cradock and Morgan Llwyd.*

He published *The Scriptures Concord* (1646), *God the Father Glorified* (1649), *Christ and Moses Excellency* (1650), *Saving Faith* (1651), *Christ Exalted* (1651), *Three Hymns* (1650), *Common-Prayer-Book No Divine Service* (1660), *The Bird in the Cage Chirping* (1661), *The Sufferers-Catechism* (1664), and *A New and Useful Concordance* (1671). John Conniers also collected *The Golden Sayings . . . of Mr. Vavasor Powell* (n.d.). *Divine Love* was published in 1677. National Library of Wales MS. 1961A is a collection of Powell's prayers and MS 366A a collection of his poetry.

E. Bagshaw, *The Life and Death of Mr. Vavasor Powell* (1671); D. Davies, *Vavasor Powell* (1896); R.T. Jones, *Vavasor Powell* (in Welsh, 1971); Jones, 'The Sufferings of Vavasor Powell,' *Welsh Baptist Studies*, ed. M. John (1976), 77-91; Nuttall, *WS*; Hill, *C. & C.*; R.T. Jones, 'The Life, Work, and Thought of Vavasor Powell, 1617-1670' (D.Phil. thesis, Oxford Univ., 1947); Capp, *FMM*; Woolrych; *DNB*;*DWB*. Papers: AN.

R.T. Jones

POWLE, Henry (1630-1692)

Parliamentary radical, MP 1671, 1679, 1680 (Cirencester), 1681 (East Grinstead), 1689 (New Windsor). Powle was born at Shottesbrook, the second son of Henry Powle of Shottesbrook, Berks., by Katherine, daughter of Matthew Herbert of Monmouth. Matriculating from Christ Church, Oxf. on 16 Dec. 1646, he entered Lincoln's Inn on 11 May 1647, and became a barrister in 1654 and a bencher in 1659. Not long after entering the Cavalier House of Commons he became prominent in the rising Country party and by 1677 was listed as 'worthy' by Shaftesbury* in assessing the House. A critic of Charles II's Declaration of Indulgence (1672), Powle took the chair of the Committee of the Whole House that examined the King's action. He then served as chairman of two committees that prepared two addresses hostile to the Declaration, which the House of Commons approved on 14 Feb. and 26 Feb. respectively. In the second address appeared the much-quoted statement on the dispensing power that 'if it should be admitted, [it] might tend to the interrupting of the free course of the laws, and altering the legislative power, which hath always been acknowledged to reside in your majesty, and your two Houses of Parliament.' This public assertion of a legal sovereignty in King, Lords and Commons was the view of the constitution that would shape the Bill of Rights, the centerpiece of the Revolution Settlement.

Powle entered the Privy Council in 1678, at a time when Charles II was wooing his political enemies. Resigning from the Council on 17 Apr. 1679 on the advice of Shaftesbury, he was appointed to the Sacheverell committee of the House of Commons, which was active in the Danby impeachment. That committee prepared an influential public pronouncement on the government known as the *Narrative and Reasons* (1679), in which the Answer to the Nineteen Propositions – an important statement of the constitution made public during the Civil War – was invoked against Charles II. Although the law-making power was not at issue, it is of much interest that the Answer, which was closely associated with the theory of a legal sovereignty in King, Lords and Commons, should have been called so dramatically to public attention a decade before the Glorious Revolution. Many members of the

Sacheverell committee were subsequently appointed to the committee of the Convention House of Commons that in 1689 wrote the Bill of Rights. Powle was also foremost in the ranks of those opposed to Charles II's maintenance of a standing army, and he pressed the attack on the King's foreign policy. Like other members of the Country party, he accepted a pension from Louis XIV. At the time of the Exclusion Crisis, he drew back, fearful of civil war once more and apparently uncertain whether the legislative power could determine the succession to the crown. At the time of the first Exclusion Bill he was still a member of the Privy Council, but even after leaving it he did not take up exclusion.

Powle's reservations were gone by the time of the Revolution. In the months before it he was in correspondence with William Bentinck (later Duke of Portland), William of Orange's leading advisor. After the Prince arrived in England, Powle entered into communication with him and played a leading role in the events that led to summoning the Convention Parliament. Elected Speaker of the Parliament, though not without a hot contest from the Tory, Sir Edward Seymour, Powle worked closely with another Whig, Richard Hampden,* in managing the House of Commons during the debates of 28 and 29 Jan. when the critical decision was made to draw up the Bill of Rights. Powle presented William and Mary with the completed document on 16 Dec. 1689. William had relied on Powle for advice throughout the Convention Parliament, and he was named to the King's first Privy Council and made Master of the Rolls. He died on 21 Nov. 1692. Powle was twice married: to Elizabeth, daughter of the first Lord Newport of High Ercall (d. 1672), and to Frances, daughter of Lionel Cranfield, first Earl of Middlesex, and widow of Richard Sackville, Earl of Dorset. His daughter Katherine (by Elizabeth) married Henry Ireton, son of the Regicide.*

B. Henning, ed., 'Draft Biographies for the History of Parliament, 1660-90;' L.G. Schwoerer, *'No Standing Armies!'*

(1974); Schwoerer, ed., 'Jornall of the Convention at Westminster Begun the 22 of January 1688/89,' *BIHR*, 49:242-63; *DNB*; C.C. Weston, *English Constitutional Theory and the House of Lords* (1965).

C.C. Weston

PRESTON, John (1587-1628)

Puritan minister, was born in Upper Heyford, Northants. He was educated at the Northampton Free School, King's Coll., Camb. (1604) and Queens' College. He became a fellow of Queens' in 1609 and Prebendary of Lincoln Cathedral in 1610. Preston was converted by a sermon preached in St. Mary's Church, Cambridge, by John Cotton,* who migrated to Boston, Mass., in 1633. After studying divinity, Preston was ordained a deacon and priest in the Diocese of Peterborough in 1614. Thomas Fuller calls Preston a 'perfect politician' whose enemies likened him to Aquaviva, the General of the Jesuits. In 1614 he showed his capacity in this direction on the death of Dr. Tyndale, Master of Queens' College. Preston was interested in promoting his own candidate, Dr. John Davenant, Lady Margaret Professor of Divinity, against Dr. George Mountain, Dean of Westminster, as the master. He kept a horse and carriage waiting and on hearing of Dr. Tyndale's death he rode to court, got permission for a free election and promptly persuaded the fellows to elect Dr. Davenant. In the same year (1614) he caught the eye of the Court when King James came to Cambridge. Preston was chosen one of the disputants in the Philosophy Act, a semi-serious debate before the King where wit was appreciated as much as learning. The subject was 'Can dogs make syllogisms?' Preston was persuaded to give up his position as first opponent in favor of Dr. Matthew Wren, the future Bishop of Ely, so he had to argue that dogs could reason. He did this so well that the King publicly commended him, and Sir Fulke Greville gave him a pension of £50 p.a. Later when preaching at St. Botolph's Church Preston was accused of nonconformity for some remarks on 'free prayer' and had to preach a recantation. This was reported to the King who always held it against him. James refused to make him one of his chaplains, though requested to by the Marquis of Hamilton. However, Ralph Freeman, Master of Requests at Court, and John Packer, the Duke of Buckingham's secretary, persuaded the Duke that he could win support in Parliament by making Preston chaplain to Prince Charles in 1621.

Thomas Ball asserts that Preston anonymously drafted a letter to Buckingham, pressing him to use his influence to frustrate the Spanish match. This letter was copied by Thomas Alured, a dependent of Greville's, and taken to the Duke. Alured was jailed for presumption and the real author never known. About 1621 Preston made a journey in disguise and visited James' daughter, Elizabeth, and her husband the Elector Frederick, in exile in the Hague. Such information as he gathered about Spanish intentions may have been for Buckingham, whose reward was his support for Preston's election as Master of Emmanuel College. The Duke's favor brought other rewards. In 1622 Preston was elected to follow John Donne as preacher at Lincoln's Inn, and in 1623 he received a D.D. degree from Cambridge. The following year he won the appointment of Town Preacher of Cambridge despite the opposition of the King and the Arminian faction at court. He refused the Bishopric of Gloucester as an alternative appointment. Ball connects Preston to the oppositionist leaders Lord Saye* and Sir Richard Knightley* of Fawsley Hall, where a Marprelate tract, *The Epitome*, had been printed. They joined with Preston in supporting Buckingham until the York House Conference where the Duke refused to condemn the Arminian theologians and rejected the proposal of Saye and the Earl of Warwick* to approve the resolutions of the Synod of Dort as definitive in interpreting the Articles of the Church of England. Preston was thereupon disaffected from his patron, though he retained his court chaplaincy and preached before the King in his turn. He used these occasions to urge the King to root out 'Popish and Arminian' errors from the church. He appealed for support from the Continental Protestants and prophesied disaster for Buckingham's expedition to the Isle of Rhé. Preston died in July 1628 at Fawsley Hall one month before the murder of the Duke, whom he once had thought of as one of the saints.

Preston was one of the most eloquent and influential Puritan spokesmen of his day. He was also one of the very few to penetrate the inner court circle under James and Charles. His career demonstrates the continuing Puritan hope of reform from within the church which was finally crushed by Laud. A dexterous politician but never a sycophant, Preston also upheld the Elizabethan tradition of plain speaking to the magistrates. With his passing, Charles was effectively isolated from all protest within the church.

I. Morgan, *Prince Charles's Puritan Chaplain* (1957); *DNB*; Hill, *P. & R.*; McGee; Haller, *RP*; Seaver. Papers: L (Sloane MSS).

I. Morgan

PRICE, John (fl. 1638-1673)

Separatist, Independent pamphleteer, and London radical, was a leading figure in the Arminian congregation of John Goodwin* and a proponent of religious toleration. Price's family included his brothers William, Lewis and Capt. Richard Price as well as an uncle, also named Richard Price. They appear to have had roots in Wales; Capt. Price was named Treasurer to the Committee for Compounding Delinquents' Estates in North Wales. Whatever his provenance, John Price spent his adult life as a London haberdasher, and lived at least until 1655 in Goodwin's parish of St. Stephen's, Coleman Street. Between 1638 and 1645 Price helped found Goodwin's gathered church while also maintaining an active role in parish affairs. In 1645 he sat on the parish committee to arbitrate the dispute between the parishioners and Goodwin. When Goodwin was ejected from the living later that year, Price withdrew with him. He became one of Goodwin's staunchest supporters and probably acted as a lay preacher to Goodwin's gathered church. Price signed the congregation's defense of Goodwin, *An Apologeticall Account of Some Brethren* (1647), and their 1652 declaration of Arminianism, *The Agreement and Distance of Brethren*. Most of his close friends, including Daniel Taylor,* the radical printer Henry Overton, Alderman Mark Hildesley, Alderman Robert Tichborne,* and the Baptist merchant William Kiffin,* were intimates of the circle around Goodwin.

Price's political career began in the early 1640s. Like Goodwin's, his earliest political tracts (*A Spirituall Snapsacke for the Parliament Souldiers* [1643]; *Honey out of the Rock* [1644]; *Unity our Duty* [1645]), urged general support for the parliamentary army on the basis of a theory of parliamentary sovereignty. By the middle of the decade he had shifted his ground and focused on the problem of religious toleration. In the face of a Presbyterian threat to religious liberty, Price and other members of Goodwin's church resorted to a pragmatic, if intermittent, alliance with the Levellers. In 1646 Price published *The City Remonstrance Remonstrated*, rebuking the Common Council for demanding an immediate peace treaty with the King and the institution of a Presbyterian polity. In Mar. 1647, with Parliament considering dissolution of the army, Price and others met with Cromwell to plead the necessity of Cromwell's siding with the army. From this date forward Price identified himself with the goals and policies of the army Independents. His pamphlets took on a much more strident tone in 1648 when he accused the Presbyterian clergy of Sion College of fomenting the second Civil War and trying to wreck all chance for an Independent church settlement. Although Price helped organize the first meetings between the Levellers, the army, and the Independents in the fall of that year, he and William Walwyn* were excluded from them because of their mutual antipathy. Price was present at the next round held at Windsor at which the *Second Agreement of the People* was drafted. By 1649 all the Goodwin circle, including Price, had broken completely with the Levellers and thrown their support behind the army. Price and Kiffin were probably the principal authors of *Walwyn's Wiles*, a warning to 'Gentleman Soldiers' not to be taken in by Walwyn's seductive rhetoric.

Price subsequently focused his efforts on London municipal politics. In 1650 he presented a petition to the Common Council demanding that London freemen be assured their rightful part in electing the mayor. He and the former Leveller John Wildman* debated the matter before the Common Council soon after. The following year Price was himself elected to the Common Council, a position he retained until 1653. In 1654 he published a 'loyalist' defense of the Protectorate, *Tyrants and Protectors Set Forth*, his last political act. He died in 1673, survived by his wife and three brothers.

He is not to be confused with the minister, Dr. John Price, whose *Some Few and Short Considerations* (1642) advocated an early settlement with the King.

E.S. More, 'The New Arminians: John Goodwin and His Coleman Street Congregation' (Ph.D. diss., Univ. of Rochester, 1980); Tolmie; Beaven; *Lev. Tr.*; *Gangraena*; J.E. Farnell, 'The Usurpation of Honest London Householders; Barebone's Parliament,' *EHR*, 82: 24-46.

E.S. More

PRICE, Richard (fl. 1645-d. 1675)

Fifth Monarchist, belonged to a family of Welsh gentry settled at Gunley, Mont. since the fifteenth century. He was the son of Edward Price (d. 1643) and his wife Bridget, daughter of John ap Richard. Price was an early and active Parliamentarian. Cromwell later commended him to Parliament as the only man in his county to be declared a rebel and have his estates seized by the King. He was commissioned lieutenant in 1645 and fought at Denbigh in 1646; he was a captain by 1647, and was serving with that rank in the North Wales militia in 1650. Price was active from 1647 on the Assessment Committee for Montgomeryshire, and in 1649 was added to the committees for Anglesey and Caernarvon. He was also prominent as a sequestrator, serving as treasurer to the Sequestrations Committee which in 1649 was given authority over six counties in North Wales. Price became one of the Commissioners for the Propagation of the Gospel in Wales, appointed by Parliament in 1650. He was a JP for Montgomery by 1650 and served as sheriff of the county in 1650-51, with his brother Edward as deputy.

In religious terms Price was a close disciple of Vavasor Powell,* whom, with his colleague John Williams,* he fetched from Dartford in Kent to head the Radnor church in 1645. He was probably the Capt. Price who, with his wife, Morgan Llwyd* and other Welsh saints, visited the celebrated Sarah Wight in London in 1647. In 1653 Price sat as one of the six Welsh members of the Barebones Parliament. He shared Powell's hostility to the Protectorate, signed Powell's remonstrance, *A Word for God*, in 1655 and handed a copy of it to Cromwell in person. He was appointed to the Committee for Ejecting Scandalous Ministers in North Wales in 1654, and to the Montgomery Assessment Committee in 1657, but it is not clear whether he served in these roles. Price attained a new prominence in 1659. He was on the Militia Committees for the six North Welsh counties (26 July 1659), and was appointed by the Council of State to command all the militia forces in North Wales, with the rank of colonel (10 Aug. 1659). In this capacity he was energetic in suppressing George Booth's supporters. In September he was among the signatories

of the *Essay Towards Settlement*, a Fifth Monarchy/Baptist declaration which commended Barebones as a model for government, and called for sweeping legal reforms along Mosaic lines. After the Restoration Price remained an active Nonconformist. He was reported in 1669 as a preacher at his own house, and in 1672 was licensed to preach there as a Congregationalist. In 1675 Henry Maurice noted that Price, an 'elder and pillar' of Powell's former church, was lately dead.

In 1640 Price married Mary, daughter of John Trotman of Peers Court, Stinchcombe, Glos., and then, after her death, Rosamond, whose family is unknown. There were no surviving children. His will, drawn up in 1671 and amended in 1675, left the Gunley estate to Rosamond for life, with reversion thereafter to Richard, son of his brother Edward. A brother John and two sisters were also mentioned, and Price's mother was still alive when the will was written in 1671. It was proved in Feb. 1676.

Capp, *FMM*; W.V. Lloyd, 'The Sheriffs of Montgomeryshire,' *Collections Historical . . . Relating to Montgomery*, 27:175-81; *CCC*; E.B. Underhill, ed., *The Records of a Church of Christ . . . Broadmead, Bristol* (1847); PCC, Wills, Bence 109; Woolrych; Williams, *Wales*.

B.S. Capp

PRIDE, Thomas (d. 1658)

Army radical and Regicide, was born at Ashcott near Glastonbury, Som. He is reported to have been a brewer's drayman in his youth. He entered the parliamentary army as a captain, rose to the rank of major by 1644 after serving with Essex,* and became a lieutenant-colonel in Harley's regiment of foot in the New Model. In Harley's absence Pride did an outstanding job of commanding the regiment in 1645 at Naseby, Bridgwater, Bristol and Dartmouth. Active in supporting soldiers' rights in the quarrel between the army and

Parliament in the spring of 1647, Pride was summoned to answer for his actions at the bar of the House. On 7 Apr. he was a signatory of the vindication of the officers, helped prepare the charge against the eleven MPs impeached by the army on 15 June, and was given command of Harley's regiment before it occupied Southwark on 4 Aug. In 1648 his regiment saw service under Cromwell in South Wales, in northern England, and at Preston. Together with Richard Deane's* regiment, his soldiers presented a petition to the Army General Council in Nov. 1648 urging the punishment of the King and the removal of the 'contrary minded' from positions of prominence. His troops joined in the occupation of London in December. He may have been one of the committee that drew up the list of MPs to be excluded, and on 6 Dec. he commanded the guard which surrounded Parliament. Politely but firmly he secluded or arrested almost a hundred MPs, using force where necessary, as in the case of Prynne.* He was appointed to the High Court for the trial of the King in Jan. 1649, attended almost every session and signed the death warrant.

Throughout 1649 and the spring of 1650 Pride's regiment remained at St. James to protect Parliament and the Council of State. On 16 Aug. 1649 Pride carried to the Rump an army petition asking for the end of laws requiring religious conformity. That October he was appointed by the Council to raise and bring 2000 recruits to Ireland. On 21 Dec. he was elected a member of the London Common Council. He appears also to have maintained his interest in Somerset politics by providing support to the Pyne* faction of the County Committee. In the spring of 1650 he went to Scotland with Cromwell, commanded a brigade at Dunbar, and served at the battle of Worcester. On 30 Nov. 1650 he joined with a group that contracted to supply provisions to the navy, an arrangement which continued until Oct. 1654. On 14 May 1652 he was rewarded for his services to the state with a grant of Scottish lands worth £500 p.a., though Parliament refused to appoint him a commissioner to protect

Royalists. In October Pride signed the conciliatory army pamphlet which, while attacking religious Presbyterians, also professed loyalty to the Rump. In the final phase of the Rump he was one of its severest critics and supported Harrison's* efforts to bring about a dissolution.

Pride's social involvement in London was demonstrated in various ways, but especially in his efforts, along with Samuel Chidley,* to bring relief to the government's poorer creditors. On 26 Dec. 1651 he was present at the door of the House while the Rump debated the question of law reform and moved to establish the Hale Commission. Pride supported law reform. His antipathy to the legal profession was indicated in his professed desire to see the lawyers' gowns hanging next to the Scots' colors in Westminster Hall. In 1652 he was placed on the Commission of the Peace for Somerset, notwithstanding his tenuous connection with that county. In the spring of 1653 he was appointed with others to look into the possible use of Ely House and the Savoy as hospitals. From 15 Oct. 1652 Pride and three others were authorized to provide services at the church of Bartholomew the Less in London. He was also appointed to suppress cock-fighting and bull and bear-baiting in the London area (5 May 1653).

Pride played no major role in the politics of the Protectorate, although he served in the Parliament of 1656 for Reigate. His advanced republican views were said to have resulted in his being kept in England in 1654 when his regiment was again sent to Scotland, but it is possible that his business affairs caused him to stay behind. By this time he was sufficiently prosperous to purchase Nonsuch Park and house in Surrey, and in 1655-56 he became sheriff of that county. On 17 Jan. 1656 Pride was knighted by Cromwell and on 25 Mar. made a commissioner for securing the peace in London. He was active among the officers opposed to Cromwell becoming king and was involved in the army petition which finally caused the Protector to refuse the crown. He did, however, accept promotion to the Cromwellian Upper

House. He supported Richard Cromwell's* accession and in Apr. 1658 was one of those selected to supervise the hospitals. Pride died a rich man on 23 Oct. 1658 and was buried on 2 Nov. at Nonsuch. On 15 May 1660 the Convention Parliament attainted him and later ordered his body to be exhumed and defiled. While his corpse was not dragged to Tyburn and reburied as intended, his estates were confiscated and returned to the Crown. Pride had married Elizabeth, daughter of Thomas Monck, and fathered a son and two daughters.

DNB; Underdown, *PP*; Worden; Firth & Davies; Kishlansky; Tolmie. Papers: L (Add. MSS).

E.A. Andriette

PRIDEAUX, Edmund (1601-1659)

Legal reformer and parliamentary radical, MP SP, LP 1640, 1653, 1654, 1656, 1659 (Lyme Regis). The second surviving son of the eminent lawyer, Sir Edmund Prideaux, Bt., of Netherton, Corn., by his second wife Katherine, daughter of Piers Edgecombe of Mount Edgecombe, Devon, Prideaux was admitted to the Inner Temple in 1615 and called to the bar in 1623, though attending neither university. He married twice, first, a daughter of a gentleman named Collins of Ottery, St. Mary, Devon, and second, Mary, a daughter of a gentleman named Every of Cottey, Som. During the 1630s Prideaux resided in Devon and served as a JP and a Sewer Commissioner; he entered national politics with his return to the Short Parliament in the spring of 1640.

An active partisan of the parliamentary cause throughout the 1640s and 1650s, Prideaux became linked with Oliver Cromwell as early as June 1642 when the two men were charged with managing a joint House committee to secure military forces for suppressing the Irish revolt. With the outbreak of the Civil War, Prideaux obtained appointments as Chairman of the Committee of the West in 1643, Postmaster-General in 1644, and a Commissioner of the Great Sea! in 1643. Each of these positions he utilized to further the radical party's cause, especially after the failure of the parliamentary commission, of which he was a member, to treat for peace with the King at Uxbridge in 1645. Prideaux was the principal electoral manager of the war or Independent party in the recruiter elections of 1645 and 1646, elections which sought the return of MPs committed to victory at all costs. Election writs were delivered at timely moments by the Commissioners of the Great Seal and local patronage was carefully dispensed by the chairman of the Committee of the West. In some cases collusion between the Post Office and the army brought the interception of letters promoting the peace or Presbyterian party candidates. The success of these election tactics intensified the animosity arising between the two major parliamentary factions by 1647.

Prideaux built up a lucrative legal practice in Chancery during the 1640s; he served as Recorder for Exeter (1643-48) and for Bristol (1647-50), and in Oct. 1648 he was appointed Solicitor General. Although supporting the breach of negotiations with the King in December, he resigned this latter office early in Jan. 1649 when Charles I's trial became imminent. The resignation must not have damaged his image in the Rump, however, for in April he was appointed Attorney General, a position he continued to hold until his death ten years later. Prideaux also served on the Council of State in 1651 and 1652. As Attorney General, Prideaux promoted legal reform and prosecuted opponents of the Commonwealth and the Protectorate. He served on numerous parliamentary committees for legal reform, including a committee for the reform of Chancery which produced a manual of the court's procedures in 1649. His assistance in drafting the Treason Act of 1649 later forced him to prosecute John Lilburne,* the Leveller leader, for writing pamphlets that asserted the Rump Parliament was tyrannical, usurped and unlawful. Despite Prideaux's forensic skill, Lilburne's passive resistance and emotional appeal to the jury brought a verdict of not guilty. Prideaux was more successful in prosecuting Col. Penruddock and his co-conspirators in the Western Rising of 1655; they were executed for their opposition to the Cromwellian regime.

Controversy continuously surrounded Prideaux's Postmaster-Generalship from 1644 to 1653. Nonetheless, despite political rivalry and the Civil War Prideaux succeeded in establishing weekly services throughout England by 1649. He resigned after the dissolution of the Rump as criticism rose over his methods of handling the post and his reputed income of £15,000 p.a. from this office. Rumor or no, Prideaux did construct a fine country house at Ford Abbey, Dorset, and completed his social elevation with a baronetcy in May 1658. He died on 19 Aug. 1659.

Keeler; *DNB*; H. Robinson, *The British Post Office, A History* (1948); D. Underdown, 'Party Management in the Recruiter Elections, 1645-48,' *EHR*, 83:235-64; Worden. Papers: L (Add. MSS).

R.E. Shimp

PRINCE, Mary (fl. 1656-1657)

Quaker, was from the Bristol region and undertook her first missionary work as a traveling companion of Sarah Bennett. Her pronounced admiration for George Fox* is revealed in a letter written about July 1656, in which the Quaker leader is depicted as 'thou that killest and makest alive, thou that woundest and makest whole, thou that art joined to the Lord and art made one with thy eternal God.' After visiting London in 1656, Prince went with Dorothy Waugh,* Sarah Gibbons,* Mary Wetherhead, Christopher Holder, Thomas Thurston,* William Brend and John Copeland to America, where they arrived at Boston on 7 Aug., only to be detained, examined and expelled after an imprisonment of some eleven weeks. The following year she joined with Mary Fisher,* Beatrice Beckly, John Perrot,* John Luffe and John Buckley on a missionary campaign to the Turks. Arriving at Leghorn on 29 July, they witnessed for approximately two weeks to mostly hostile listeners, though they claimed some success after visiting the Jewish synagogue. The journey to Jerusalem was resumed on 20 Aug. 1657. While Perrot and Buckley left the party at Zante to take a separate route, Prince, Fisher and the others continued via Candia to Smyrna, arriving on 18 Nov. There the English consul pressed them to return to England. Prince was not with Fisher and Beckly when they obtained an audience with Mohammed IV at Adrianople, for she remained for several weeks in Smyrna before returning to England via Venice. Her overseas campaigns underscore the missionary determination and fortitude of Friends of both sexes.

EQL; Besse; *EQW*; Braithwaite, *BQu*; Jones, *QAC*. Papers: LF (Swarthmore MSS).

R.L. Greaves

PRINCE, Thomas (fl. 1640-1653)

Leveller, was a well-to-do cheese merchant who helped supply the army in Ireland in the early 1640s and also kept his own shop. In 1642 he delivered £1000 worth of butter and cheese, for which he remained unpaid seven years later. When Gloucester was besieged by Royalists in the summer of 1643, Prince raised one of the first trained bands for its relief and was himself severely wounded at Newbury. By 1647 he was active in the Levellers' London organization. In November the House of Commons briefly imprisoned him with four others for presenting the 'humble petition of many free-born people' calling on Parliament to debate the *Agreement of the People*. Prince became co-treasurer of the Levellers with Samuel Chidley* in Jan. 1648, overseeing a network of agents who collected not only thousands of signatures for their petitions but weekly contributions ranging from two pence to half a crown. In Mar. 1649 he was charged with high treason along with Lilburne,* Overton* and Walwyn* by the Council of State for publishing the second part of *England's New Chains Discovered*, which attacked the leaders of the new Commonwealth. Interrogated at Whitehall, Prince refused to answer, insisting that law protected the citizen from arbitrary arrest and self-incrimination and denying the Council of State's authority.

Although imprisoned in the Tower, the four Levellers published *A Picture of the Council of State, A Manifestation*, and the third *Agreement of the People*. On behalf of seven Independent ministers, former allies of Lilburne and Prince, John Price wrote *Walwyn's Wiles*, attacking Walwyn as the author of *A Manifestation*. Like some recent historians who have distinguished between moderate and radical Levellers, Price argued that Lilburne and Prince were devout and public spirits deceived by cunning imposters. Yet in the only pamphlet which Prince wrote, *The Silken Independents' Snare Broken* (20 June 1649), Prince challenged Price's analysis and attacked the ministers for 'a New England design that under pretense of religion, our laws, our liberties and many men's lives should all lie at your mercy. . . .' Prince's tract combines Walwyn's emphasis on toleration and Lilburne's on law with the fundamental Leveller belief in the people as the fount of all political power. Released with the others from the Tower in Nov. 1649, Prince apparently took the Engagement to support the new regime. He did not participate in politics except to join Lilburne on the latter's return from the Netherlands in 1653. He may have been the Thomas Prince granted a privateer's commission in 1653, and the dry-salter whose will, proved in 1665, described him as resident in St. Mildred Breadstreet, a ward inhabited by wealthy merchants.

Brailsford; Woodhouse; Tolmie; *CSPD, Chas. I*, 17; *Comm.*, 1, 5; *Lev. Man.*;

G.E. Aylmer, 'Gentlemen Levellers?', in *The Intellectual Revolution of the Seventeenth Century*, ed. C. Webster (1974).

L.L. Peck

PRYNNE, William (1600-1669)

Pamphleteer, MP 1648 (Newport, Corn.), sec. 1648, 1660 (Bath), was born in Swainswick near Bath, the son of Thomas Prynne and Marie Sherston. He was educated at Bath Grammar School and Oriel Coll., Oxf.; he obtained his B.A. in 1621 and became a barrister at Lincoln's Inn in 1628. The years 1628 to 1640 were occupied with intensive pamphleteering against Arminian clergy which resulted in his prosecution in Star Chamber twice in 1634 and 1637, the mutilation of his ears, imprisonment in the Tower of London, and exile in the Channel Isles (1637-40). The violence of Prynne's language obscured the moderation of his message, both to contemporaries and to later historians. His bitterness was localized in its application to the Laudian minority whom he believed to be infiltrating the Church of England. He appealed against them to older Elizabethan traditions of non-separatism, respect for the civil magistrate, Calvinistic doctrine and ceremonial simplicity. These principles were honored in the writings of Foxe and Jewel, but no less, in Prynne's mind, by contemporary bishops such as Williams, Hall and Davenant, who had themselves been ousted by the Laudian clique. Prynne's radicalism in the pre-Civil War period was thus largely spurious. He rejected Brownism, sided with Archbishop Whitgift against Cartwright when he reviewed earlier doctrinal struggles, attacked Court patronage of plays in his *Histriomastix* (1632) but not the Crown itself, and – apart from one anonymous protest against ship money in 1637 which was not published until 1641 – held himself aloof from the conventional constitutional criticisms of monarchical power in the decade before the Civil War.

The watershed in Prynne's career is 1641, but even then his new-found radicalism took an ecclesiastical rather than constitutional form. The title of his testament of conversion, *The Antipathie of the English Lordly Prelacie, Both to Regall Monarchy and Civill Unity*, published in July 1641, is itself significant. Prynne had not changed his mind about monarchy, but about the claims of the Church of England to be its defender. This pamphlet reversed his previous conviction that non-Laudian bishops can defend Crown against Pope; its commitment to the 'root and branch' thesis owes something to a disillusionment with bishops like Hall and Williams but even more to the influence of millenarian writers like Thomas Brightman. Prynne's disillusionment with the Crown post-dates the outbreak of Civil War. Ecclesiastical radicalism was compatible with political conservatism: heady visions of a New Jerusalem with a sober rescue of the Crown from evil counsellors. Although commissioned by Parliament to produce its official apology, which he did in 1643 under the title, *The Soveraigne Power of Parliaments*, Prynne was not even at that date the architect of radical political solutions. Although Prynne was familiar with the writings of Bodin he did not see parliamentary sovereignty as the answer to constitutional deadlock; in this sense the title of his pamphlet was a misnomer. Like Philip Hunton,* he viewed it as a transient expedient until trust in the King could be restored to make the balanced polity workable once more. Such trust was further eroded in 1643, with the interception of Charles I's correspondence with Irish Papists, and 1643-45 marked the only period in Prynne's life (to be used against him by regicide opponents in 1649) when he countenanced resistance theories, and even depicted Charles I in one pamphlet under the title, *The Popish Royall Favourite*.

His prosecution of Laud in these years, culminating with the Archbishop's execution in 1645, was similarly inspired by his fear of a 'Popish plot.' In *Canterburies Doome* (1646) – his belated account of Laud's trial – can now be seen as a deliberate attempt to doctor the record of the proceedings in order to make them appear as a crusade against popery, rather than the commentary on the relative powers of Crown and Parliament that they were. Developments between 1645 and 1649 encouraged Prynne to revert to his earlier constitutional moderation. The influence of London Presbyterian ministers waned with their inability to satisfy unrealistic millenarian hopes. The Commons proved unable to control an egalitarian army because, Prynne argued in 1648, their political philosophy was rotten: many MPs believed in the sovereignty of the Commons, but Prynne used the antiquarian researches of Sir Robert Filmer to shatter the historical foundations of this belief. He did so, not in order to support Filmer's royalism, but to argue for a revival of the balanced polity in which the House of Lords was seen as the senior partner. The death of Charles I removed the last doubts about the fidelity of the monarchy to such an arrangement; the author of *Eikon Basilike* had expiated former faults by his martyrdom at the hands of Papists. Thus pen and sword (evidence of actual conspiracy, although circumstantial, is strong) were offered by Prynne in the service of the exiled Charles II during the Interregnum. Imprisonment (1650-53) did not silence his advocacy of the case of those MPs who had been secluded by Pride's purge. He opposed the Commonwealth as a constitutional impropriety, no less remarkable for its moral laxity. Thus attempts to revive the Good Old Cause of 1642-49 were combined with efforts to halt the slide into indiscipline. Prynne deplored the religious toleration of the Cromwellian period. He opposed the readmission of the Jews into England with arguments of a naked crudity; attacked Quakers as masked Jesuits; defended tithes and sought to stem the sectarian drift by advocacy of free admission to communion.

Prynne was appointed Keeper of the Records in the Tower of London in 1661 as a mark of Charles II's respect for the contribution which he had made to the Restoration. But his support of the Restoration settlement, never unconditional, was short-lived; in 1661 he was forced to retract his attack on the Corporation Bill by a formal rebuke in the Commons. From then until his death on 24 Oct. 1669, his principles had to find covert expression for the most part in a number of valuable antiquarian studies. It was fashionable, both then and later, to dismiss Prynne's principles as little more than a paranoid rejection of authority under any guise. Research of recent years has led to a more sympathetic view of his position. The key to his actions is to be found in an old-fashioned, sentimental (but not insincere) attachment to Tudor imperial ideas of a strong Crown and a deferential church. It was a warning against the revival of a Laudian church supremacy, and of the Commons' assertions of sovereignty, which inspired his attack on the Corporation Bill in 1661. It was only because he recognized in Charles II (unlike Cromwell) the legitimate imperial authority, and that Sheldon was not quite Laud, that resistance in the last years of his life was not again pushed to the extremes of his earlier career.

Christianson; W. Haller, *Foxe's Book of Martyrs and the Elect Nation* (1963); C. Hill, *Antichrist in Seventeenth Century England* (1971); W.M. Lamont, *Marginal Prynne* (1963) and *GR*; Foster; C. Weston and J. Greenberg, *Subjects and Sovereigns* (1981); J.G.A. Pocock, *The Ancient Constitution and the Feudal Law* (1957); N. Tyacke, 'Puritanism, Arminianism and Counter-Revolution,' in *The Origins of the English Civil War*, ed. C. Russell (1973). Papers: C; CS; O; OAS; EN; DT; L (Add. MSS; Harg. MSS; Harl. MSS; Lans. MSS; Sloane MSS; Stowe MSS).

W.M. Lamont

PUREFOY, William (1580?-1659)

Regicide, of Caldecote, Warks., was descended from an old and established family of that county and Lincolnshire, and was a man of some means and education. He may have spent some time at Emmanuel Coll., Camb., studied at Gray's Inn and possibly took his B.A. at Pembroke College. He traveled on the Continent and visited Geneva, an experience which apparently made a lasting impression on his religious and political views. In the late 1620s and 1630s Purefoy fulfilled many of the obligations expected of the members of a county elite. He was a JP in Warwickshire and served on numerous county commissions. In 1627, as a commissioner for the forced loan, Purefoy was summoned before the Privy Council for his refusal to lend and general opposition to the scheme. He was Sheriff for Warwickshire in 1635 and again opposed the Crown, criticizing the ship money rates levied on Coventry.

Purefoy was first elected to Parliament for Coventry in 1628, thanks to a bitter local quarrel between the town's governing corporation and its freemen. Coventry's politics had long been unsettled by its declining economy and the increasing conflict between its oligarchy and the freemen who backed Purefoy in the election. In both 1640 elections, Purefoy, now clearly identified as a 'popular' or 'reform' candidate, was returned for Warwick where he enjoyed the powerful support of a close friend and fellow reformer, Lord Brooke.* Brooke also backed Purefoy in his unsuccessful bid for a county seat in the autumn elections. Purefoy stood against a royalist candidate supported by the Earl of Northampton whose ally, the sheriff, saw to Purefoy's defeat. Purefoy would, however, serve for Warwickshire in Cromwell's first Parliament in 1654 and won election at Coventry in the second Parliament of that year and again in 1656.

Purefoy was in arms for Parliament as early as Aug. 1642 and played a leading role in the struggle in Warwickshire and its adjoining counties through 1644. He participated in the defense of Coventry and led the capture of Compton in 1644. He found time to attend meetings of the Committee of Both Kingdoms at Derby House as well. He was one of the King's judges and signed the death warrant; it is indicative of his rising political reputation that he was among the first members selected for the Council of State and served on it from 1649 to 1653. Although ill and of great age, he again took up arms to save Warwickshire and Coventry for Parliament during Booth's rising in 1659.

Purefoy was a consistent opponent of any negotiations with Charles and, as late as 1652, opposed any Act of Oblivion. However, he also opposed Pride's purge and the abolition of the House of Lords, and was an adamant foe of the Levellers. A staunch Presbyterian, he voted consistently to maintain tithes and hoped for the establishment of a national church, condemning toleration as a vehicle of social and political upheaval. Purefoy died in 1659, but his estate was exempted from the Act of Indemnity at the Restoration; his goods reverted to the Crown.

Keeler; *DNB*; Underdown, *PP*; Noble; Worden; *CSPD, Chas. I*, 8:437; 18-23 *passim*; *Comm.*, 1-5 *passim*; 9:100; 13:12. Papers: LPR; L (Add. MSS).

J. Gruenfelder

PUREFOY, William (fl. 1644-1661)

Army radical, MP 1654 (Limerick and Kilmallock). Purefoy was the second son of Edward Purefoy of Kent and a kinsman of the Regicide of the same name.* He and his elder brother George described the repulse of a royalist attack at Compton House in 1644. In 1646 the younger Purefoy was commissioned a major in Col. James Castle's regiment of foot bound for Ireland. After distinguishing himself at Balliston, Purefoy became a lieutenant-colonel after the siege of Drogheda in 1649. He was a member of the Irish delegation to the first Protectorate Parliament in 1654. Election was tantamount to nomination by the military regime headed by Maj.-Gen. Charles Fleetwood.* Lack of sympathy

with Henry Cromwell's* more moderate regime probably accounts for Purefoy's failure to obtain the nomination again in 1656, for he was succeeded by Walter Waller, son of an old associate of the Lord Protector. Purefoy retained his regiment in 1659 when the Irish army was remodeled by the republican regime and was included in 1661 among the '30 fanatics' whom the Irish Parliament wished excluded from the Act of Indemnity. This proposal was not enacted and the descendants of Purefoy were established on an estate in Tipperary in the mid-nineteenth century.

Harl. Soc., 2: *Visitation of Leicester, 1619* (1870); Firth & Davies; E.D. Goldwater, 'Two Cromwellian Parliaments' (Ph.D. diss., City Univ. of New York, 1973); J. Burke, *A Genealogical and Heraldic Dictionary of the Landed Gentry*.

E.D. Goldwater

PURY, Thomas (c. 1590-1666)

Parliamentary radical, MP LP 1640, 1654, 1659 (Gloucester). Although attacked by the Royalists for his lowly origins as a 'weaver' and an 'ignorant attorney,' Pury was connected by birth to Gloucester's ruling oligarchy. His paternal grandfather and namesake (d. 1579) had been an alderman and mayor in 1550 and Pury counted among his ancestors and kin other mayors and aldermen, like the Machens. His father, Walter Pury, was not a weaver but a clothier, i.e. a merchant. After his father's death in 1606 Pury was apprenticed to Lawrence Wilshire, another clothier of the city. By 1618 Pury had prospered sufficiently to marry Mary Ayle of Tewkesbury, and a son, Thomas, was born the following year. Pury's local political career also began to flourish. He became Common Councillor of Gloucester (1618-38), Steward (1619-20), Sheriff and Bailiff (1636) and JP and Alderman from 1638 on. By 1630 he had begun to practice law and represented Gloucester in the local courts and at Westminster. In 1632 he was formally appointed solicitor for part of the sheriff's business.

Pury was a staunch Puritan throughout the 1630s, and as a lawyer he led the city's resistance to the Court of High Commission in several major cases. When the Commission removed a Nonconformist minister from his lectureship, Gloucester voted him a stipend. The Commission declined to accept this circumvention of its will. Pury defended the city in the ensuing action, though unsuccessfully, and in a similar struggle over the city's hospital. In 1639-41 he succeeded in putting a Nonconformist minister into Christ School, in spite of royal support for the incumbent. He was also a leading opponent of ship money in the county. Although he was defeated when he stood as a member for the city in the election for the Short Parliament, he was returned for the Long Parliament, a stunning victory for the Puritan party. In the House he was a vigorous critic of episcopacy, speaking out for the Root and Branch Bill. Later he had a hand in the impeachment of Laud, providing damaging testimony concerning their disputes in the 1630s. During the Civil War Pury was the principal liaison between Parliament and Gloucester and was energetic in overseeing the military preparedness of the city. During the siege of the city (Aug.-Sept. 1643), although nominally only a militia captain in Col. Henry Stephens' regiment, Pury had a substantial role in organizing its defense, despite a bitter quarrel with Col. Massey, the military governor. By the end of the Civil War he was a figure of some influence in national politics. His son was returned as a recruiter MP for neighboring Monmouth and both father and son were identified as Independents. Pury was not excluded at Pride's purge, but he did not sit in the House until after the King's trial and execution had been completed. Thereafter he followed a cautious course and for a time exercised a moderating influence. As a lawyer and placeholder (he had recently secured a Clerkship of the Petty Bag) Pury was particularly resistant to reform of the legal system. After Jan. 1652 he rarely sat

in the Rump. In 1653 he was elected Mayor of Gloucester and in 1654 was returned to the first Protectorate Parliament. He sat again in the restored Rump, and in Aug. 1659 had the short-lived satisfaction of capturing his old antagonist, Col. Massey, who led an abortive royalist attempt on Gloucester. Although Pury supported Monck and probably accepted the inevitability of the Restoration, the change of regime was costly for him. He was forced to sell the estates he had accumulated in his time of power, and he died unmolested in obscurity.

B. & P.; *CSPD, Chas. I*, 15:582; 18-22 *passim*; *Comm.*, 1-4, 13 *passim*; Keeler; W.R. Williams, *The Parliamentary History of Gloucester* (1898); Worden. Papers: LPR.

S.J. Stearns

PYE, Sir Robert (d. 1701)

Army officer and parliamentary radical, MP 1654, 1658, 1660 (Berks.), was the eldest son of Sir Robert Pye, MP for Woodstock in the Long Parliament, and his wife, Mary (née Croker) of Gloucestershire. The younger Pye married Anne, daughter of John Hampden.* After an active military career as a colonel of horse in Essex's* service and a commander in the New Model, Pye left the army in 1647 when he and a small troop of his men upheld the parliamentary cause against the rest of the army. Parliament voted him money and thanks, hoping that his moderation would be followed by others, but Pye found it expedient to leave the country on 3 Aug. with a pass from Fairfax.* The reallocation of parliamentary seats in 1653 ensured the return of men favorable to the Protectorate, among them Pye. His premature presentation of a petition early in 1660 for the return of secluded members, and his determined stand against military intervention in politics led to his imprisonment in the Tower, but he was released upon suing out a writ of *habeas corpus* and the charge expunged from the records when the secluded members were readmitted. As a recognition of his loyalty to the restored monarchy, Charles II created him a baronet in 1662; he succeeded to his father's manor of Farringdon in the following year. His loyalty to the monarchy was again attested in 1670, when he was in government service. In 1688 he accompanied William or Orange, and in 1700 he was a DL for Berkshire. He died in 1701, leaving two sons by his wife Anne.

CSPD, Chas. I, 20-21 *passim*; *Comm.*, 11; *Chas. II*, 2, 10; Kishlansky; *Wm. III*, 11; Brailsford; Davies, *RC*; Firth & Davies; V.F. Snow, 'Parliamentary Reapportionment Proposals in the Puritan Revolution,' *EHR*, 74:409-42. Papers: L (Add. MSS; Harl. MSS).

M.A. Mullett

PYM, John (1584-1643)

Parliamentary radical, MP 1621 (Colne), 1624, 1625, 1626, 1628, SP, LP 1640 (Tavistock). Pym was in many ways England's first Prime Minister. Although he had no organized 'party' and was often defeated in the House of Commons, he became by 1641 an accepted leader and policy-maker. By patient day-to-day maneuver rather than spectacular domination he held together men with a wide variety of political and religious views. His aims were a stable parliamentary monarchy and a firmly Protestant church. Both, he came to believe, required the forcible destruction of a royalism that was tainted by Popery. In the first year of the Civil War he headed a system of government by MPs and peers more active and effective than any previous central regime. When he died no one else could preserve the unity of the cause.

Pym's background was undistinguished. He did not belong to a prominent county family and took little part in local judicial and administrative affairs. The Pym estate at Brymore, Som., was small. His father, Alexander, died when John was about four years old, and his mother Philippa married a richer second husband, Anthony Rous of Halton St. Dominick, Corn. This gave Pym a connection decisive in his career; for besides being linked to many of the leading gentry in the southwest, Rous managed the estates in Devon and Cornwall of the Russells, already a leading aristocratic family. There is little information about Pym's early life. He studied at Broadgates Hall, Oxf. and, like several of his later allies, at the Middle Temple. His one experience of royal office came when he acquired the reversion of the receivership of crown revenues in Hampshire (the home of his wife Anne Hooke), Wiltshire and Gloucestershire. In the later parliaments of James I he became an active and widely respected member. Many of his speeches reiterated the conventional political ideas on maintaining kingship as the keystone of the social structure. He insisted that Parliament must be strengthened as a part of the machinery of government, and that when it advocated policies it must provide money to pay for them. Pym was soon recognized as an expert on finance; but the one subject that aroused his passions was the danger from Catholicism. This is the greatest puzzle of his career; hard-headed politican though he was, he appeared to believe firmly, and on little evidence, in the existence of an insidious conspiracy to destroy English Protestantism and the stable propertied society that went with it.

In the early parliaments of Charles I Pym's devotion to the existing constitution was shaken, largely by his growing knowledge of the Court and of the trends in the church. He quickly won prominence as a leading spokesman and organizer on religious questions, but also as an advocate of caution in confronting the royal government. He was now sitting for Tavistock, the recently enfranchised family borough of the Russells. Francis Russell, fourth Earl of Bedford,* had become a closer political associate as well as patron, though Pym was never a mere mouthpiece for the Earl. In the impeachment of Buckingham and in the debates on the Petition of Right,

Pym's stature as a politician grew. He was increasingly concerned with a problem he never completely solved: how could Parliament uphold royal authority as the essential basis of the state and at the same time reject the King's policies and ministers? He was attracted by the claims of Sir Edward Coke* that the common law, or an ancient constitution, could somehow be set not above but alongside the kingly power. He began to hint at a distinction between royal sovereignty and that of Charles I in person, but it was still unthinkable to him that parliament should exercise the functions of the King. Its aim must be to win him over, and avoid 'distractions betwixt King and people.'

Pym did not join the group of MPs who refused to pay or collect the forced loan of 1627; nor did he take an active part in the token defiance of royal authority at the dissolution of Parliament in 1629 that led to the imprisonment of Eliot* and his allies. Nevertheless, by 1640 there was no doubt that he had become the accepted leader of opposition to the Laudian regime. It is not obvious how this came about. A multiplicity of personal contacts was an essential basis. One valuable link lay in the trading and colonizing schemes initiated by some of the peers and gentry at the center of Puritan politics. Pym was one of the patentees of Saybrook, the scheme for a settlement in Connecticut, and in 1630 was chosen as treasurer of the Providence Island Company, a project for a Puritan community in the West Indies that would also be a profitable commercial venture. But while Hampden* became a popular hero for his resistance to ship money, Pym remained the inconspicuous planner and manager.

The election in the spring of 1640 produced a House of Commons dominated by opponents of Crown policies. How far Pym had been at the center of anything like a national campaign is still doubtful; but the two-hour speech, restrained and unrhetorical, in which he drew together the major grievances against the personal rule established him as the outstanding spokesman of the House. When the Long Parliament met in November the outlook of Pym's inner circle of allies had changed. Faced with evidence that Charles, supported by Catholic courtiers and officers, intended to use the armies in the north to enforce a 'design to alter law and religion,' they planned a direct attack on the King's ministers, which was precipitated by reports that the parliamentary leaders themselves were to be accused of treason. In the prolonged trial of Strafford, and in the charges against Laud, Finch and other councillors, Pym's guidance was crucial. At the same time he played a large part in the work of the succession of committees that began gradually to insert themselves into the process of government, though he was skilful in picking other members who became experts in their own fields. The demolition of the administrative and legal machinery of the personal rule had wide support. The church was more difficult. Despite his deep Calvinist beliefs, Pym was not eager to uphold the demand for a 'root-and-branch' abolition of episcopacy, which would inevitably produce bitter divisions. Exclusion of the bishops from Parliament was for the moment all that political realism allowed. Pym's devices to keep Parliament united were manifold. The Protestation, unspecific in its commitment to Protestantism, King and Parliament, collected mass support in the country as well as the two Houses. Reports of the army plots were presented to the Commons in well-chosen sequence to build up the fear of conspiracy.

Another uncertainty in Pym's career is his attitude to the various hints that he and other opposition leaders might be given high offices in the royal government. It could reasonably be assumed that this was the ambition of men who denounced the Crown's ministers but sought to win the ear of the King. It would not necessarily have meant abandoning Pym's principles or his authority in the Commons. A scheme for Bedford to become Lord Treasurer and Pym Chancellor of the Exchequer was certainly canvassed at Court, but the death of Bedford and Charles' unpredictable attitudes made such a role impossible. Pym's alternative government was to arise from Parliament alone. There, despite all his successes, his position was seldom secure for long. When the short recess began in September he presided over the newly-devised 'recess committee' with extensive powers of action. His report to the Commons on their return was unimpressive, and momentarily he seemed to have lost the initiative. Then, in November, the Irish rebellion broke out.

All Pym's assertions about a vast popish conspiracy seemed to be confirmed by the Irish rising. At the same time, it gave Charles an unassailable reason for raising a national army. This, inescapably, was the moment when Parliament was obliged to go further in demanding power over the state and its forces. After some uncharacteristic fumbling, Pym proposed an instruction to the commissioners who were closely watching the King to threaten that unless he would employ ministers approved by Parliament it would provide for Ireland without him. This demand for an administration completely controlled by the legislature was one of the controversial clauses in the Grand Remonstrance, the long-discussed survey of Parliament's policies and the sins of the King's advisors, which was put to the vote on 22 Nov. 1641. On its religious proposals especially, Pym agreed to compromises with the less radical members. But the Commons accepted the Remonstrance by only eleven votes, and Pym's hopes of keeping up an appearance of unity were finally abandoned. Many firm opponents of Strafford and Laud found the King's apparently conciliatory replies preferable to the appeal for mass support implicit in the decision to publish the Remonstrance. In the tense 'December Days' Pym welcomed, even if he did not initiate, the mob demonstrations in London that built up a feeling of irrevocable confrontation. Charles' attempt to arrest Pym and four of his colleagues in a dramatic show of strength in the House itself turned into a humiliating fiasco that helped to re-establish 'King Pym,' as royalist pamphleteers began to call him, at the head of the Commons. His enemies saw him too readily as the greatest of the 'fiery spirits' who were openly preparing for war; but in working to establish what soon became a system of government by MPs and peers he moved nearer to the militant radicals than his theories appeared to justify.

There were many sources of power on which such a government could draw. The City of London, where Pym's friends were now in control, put its wealth more readily than ever before at the disposal of the Commons; the Committee of Safety, an entirely new parliamentary institution, acted under his guidance as a rival to the King's Council, though repeatedly attacked by the militants for its caution; local officials increasingly took orders from Parliament. It was through the existing county institution of the militia and the Lords Lieutenant that Parliament in March took the power to recruit and control armies, abandoning the principle that the King was an essential part of the legislative process. Pym resolved that the Earl of Essex,* a courtier but a friend of leading Puritans, should be commander in chief. When fighting began in August, Essex was soon denounced by the advocates of uncompromisingly energetic war as slow-moving and unenthusiastic. Pym rarely wavered in his support, and Essex in return refused to join wholeheartedly in moves for peace on the King's terms.

The last year of Pym's life saw disaster for the parliamentary armies and triumph for his political and administrative skill. The ultimate victory was made possible above all by the financial system he created. Ruthless direct taxation, loans, penalties and the excise involved amounts and methods that made the hated impositions of the 1630s look trivial. The elaborate ordinances that Pym drove through an often reluctant Parliament were a framework constantly modified by local demands and practices. The conception of a new civil and military machinery of county committees linked in regional 'associations' was never as comprehensive as it looked on paper. Here too successes came through adaptation to the changing realities of power. Nothing worked smoothly. Parliamentary committees maneuvered against each other; factions in the counties, the armies, and in Lords and Commons had ceaselessly to be placated; every defeat produced bitter recriminations. But Pym's mastery of parliamentary tactics was now complete. Its final test came in his achievement of the alliance with Scotland, when conflicting aims and suspicions were reconciled by some devious verbal contrivances. By the time the Solemn League and Covenant was signed Pym's powers were giving way to the cancer from which he died on 8 Dec. 1643. He could not then have been sure that military victory would be won; still less could he foresee the brief triumph of a revolutionary spirit he would have found hard to tolerate.

S.R. Brett, *John Pym 1583-1643* (1941); Hexter; Newton; *CD 1625*; L. Glow, 'Pym in Parliament: the Methods of Moderation,' *JMH*, 36:373-97; K. Sharpe, ed., *Faction and Parliament* (1977); C. Russell, 'Parliament and the King's Finances,' in *The Origins of the English Civil War*, ed. C. Russell (1973); Keeler; Zaller; *DNB*; *PSP 1640*; D. Pennington, 'The Making of the War, 1640-1642,' in *Puritans and Revolutionaries*, ed. Pennington and K. Thomas (1978); P. Christianson, 'The Peers, the People, and Parliamentary Management in the First Six Months of the Long Parliament,' *JMH*, 49:575-99; C. Roberts, 'The Earl of Bedford and the Coming of the English Revolution,' *JMH*, 49:600-16; M. Kishlansky, 'The Emergence of Adversary Politics in the Long Parliament,' *JMH*, 49:617-39; C. Thompson, 'The Origins of the Politics of the Parliamentary Middle Group,' *TRHS*, 5th ser., 22:71-86; Russell, *PEP*; D. Pennington, 'The Parliamentary Career of John Pym, 1621-9,' in *The English Commonwealth, 1647-1640*, ed. P. Clark *et al.* (1979).

D. Pennington

PYNE (or Pine), Hugh (fl. 1596-d.1628)

Lawyer, was born at Curry Malet, Som., the second son of John Pyne (d. 1609), lawyer and JP. Hugh married Maybelle (Mabel) Staverton sometime before 1606. Pyne was a member of Lincoln's Inn where he was called to the bar in June 1596 and to the bench in Oct. 1613. He apparently divided his time between his practice in London and residence in Somerset, principally at Cathanger. By 1614 he was a JP in Somerset and subsequently deputy *custos rotulorum*. He was also a member of the Commission of the Peace in Dorset and sometime Recorder of Weymouth and Melcombe Regis. In 1626 he was removed from the Somerset Commission because of a scathing attack on royal policy which he delivered at the Ilchester Quarter Sessions. His local rival, Lord Poulett, was doubtless instrumental in bringing Pyne's criticism of Charles and Buckingham to the attention of the Court. In Nov. 1627 Pyne was cited to answer for slanderous and treasonous speech against the King. His remarks, supposedly derived from private conversations, described Charles I as an unwise King, who had no more political competence than a village simpleton. Pyne escaped an indictment for treason when the judges resolved that the statute of Edward III did not encompass treason by words. Nevertheless he was briefly imprisoned and, according to his petition, deprived of his legal practice. Apparently the case against him was still pending when he died in Nov. 1628.

CSPD, Chas. I, 1-2 *passim*; G. Croke, *Reports* (1893); T. Birch, ed., *The Court and Times of Charles the First* (1848); Barnes.

E.R. Pagano

PYNE, John (1600-1678)

Parliamentary radical, MP 1625, 1626, 1628, SP, LP 1640 (Poole). Pyne was born on 26 Mar. 1600, the son of Thomas Pyne of Merriott, Som. and his wife Amy, daughter of Thomas Hanham of Wimborne Minster, Dorset. In 1612, after study at Hart Hall, Oxf., Pyne received a B.A. degree. Seven years later he entered the Middle Temple, where he kept a chamber until 1637. In 1629 he was called to the bar. Soon afterwards he eloped with his cousin, Eleanor Hanham, daughter and heiress of Sir John Hanham of London and Dorset.

Pyne began his parliamentary career in 1625. Both his mother's relatives and his uncle, Hugh Pyne,* a lawyer and JP in Dorset and Somerset who was imprisoned for opposition to the forced loan, probably assisted him. Little more is known about Pyne's early experience in politics. By 1636 he was serving as a JP, had acquired other responsibilities in local government, and was opposing ship money. In the Long Parliament Pyne participated in the prosecution of the Bishop of Bath and Wells and gave his support to other measures for religious reform. He also took part in promoting the war. Closely allied with his parliamentary activities were those he undertook in Somerset. Pyne was first and foremost a local politician. On 31 Mar. 1642 he was appointed a DL to organize the parliamentary militia. Later he helped raise troops in the western division. Although not a soldier, he served in June 1643 in the Earl of Stamford's army in Devon. From 1645 until 1653 he was probably the major figure in Somerset. He outmaneuvered the moderates in the County Committee in 1645, ran the Committee for Sequestration of Estates, and kept counter-revolutionaries under control. Part of his success derived from his sensitivity to local feeling. He recognized that supporting the war was burdensome to his countrymen. In 1648 he actively sought their support for Pride's purge. His own politics were Independent, while his religious preference was Presbyterian. In 1648 he was appointed a lay elder. He was nevertheless not intolerant, and may have had a Baptist chaplain at Poole in 1645.

Pyne was not appointed to the High Court, though he sponsored the Somerset petition for the King's trial composed by Thomas Collier.* Pyne dissented from the Rump's proceedings on 1 Feb. 1649 but worked for the regime until 1653, vigorously opposing Levellers and supporting the Engagement. Thereafter he retired from political activity, though in 1659 he admitted that 'my soul still panteth' for the Good Old Cause. Arrested at the Restoration, he escaped the execution he feared. He lived in relative obscurity until his death in 1678.

HMC, 9th Report, App., 493-96; Keeler; Underdown, *PP* and *SCWI*; Worden; Woolrych; B. & P. Papers: SRO; L (Sloane MSS).

E.S. Cope

PYOTT (or Piotte, Piatt), Edward (d. 1670)

Quaker, was from the Bristol area and served as a captain, probably in the parliamentary army. He was a man of some substance. No later than 1655 he was involved in the Quaker cause, one of his activities that year being attendance at the trial of John Audland's* wife in Banbury. The same year he was with George Fox,* Thomas Aldam,* Richard Farnsworth,* Edward Burrough,* Francis Howgill* and Audland for a Quaker meeting at Swannington, Leics. Late in 1655 Pyott left with Fox on a trip to the southwest, visiting such places as Poole, Dorchester, Southampton, Weymouth, Totnes and Bodmin. Threatened at one point by Col. William Goffe,* who accused them of being in league with the devil, they were summoned before constables at Marazion, but because the constables lacked a warrant, Pyott took the occasion to preach to them. Joined now by William Salt, the Quaker party was taken into custody at St. Ives on 18 Jan. 1656, and imprisoned at Launceston for eight months commencing on 22 Jan. When Cromwell offered (through John Desborough*) to free the prisoners if they would return home and cease preaching, Pyott retorted that Englishmen had liberty to travel throughout the nation, 'it being as the Englishman's house by the law.' He unsuccessfully petitioned Justice Glyn for his release on 14 July, but he was nevertheless set free on 13 Sept. 1656, and continued his westward trek to such places as Tregony. During this year he also was a joint author of *The Cry of Blood*, recounting the persecution of the Friends in Bristol.

It was approximately Mar. 1657 when Pyott and Fox obtained an audience at Whitehall with Cromwell in the presence of John Owen,* though nothing seems to have come of it. The two Quakers subsequently took their message to Buckinghamshire. About 1657 Pyott warned Cromwell not to assume the crown. Pyott had returned home by 1659, for the Quakers were meeting at his house outside Bristol, and the same year he was one of seven Friends appointed militia commissioners due to the threat posed by Booth's rising. In 1660 Pyott was one of several persons asked by Fox to intercede with the Bristol authorities in the hope of leaving the Quakers unmolested. At a meeting at Pyott's house on 7 Feb., at which William Dewsbury* was present, a mob attacked the Quakers. Pyott's estate achieved some fame as a Quaker center, for Fox recounts how a meeting he had at Pyott's house drew thousands. Subsequent to that meeting Pyott and Fox went on a mission to Gloucester, and Fox again met at Pyott's house in 1662. In the spring of the previous year Pyott, with Fox, Hubberthorn,* Burrough and George Whitehead,* spoke at the bar of the House of Commons in opposition to the bill against the Quakers.

On 28 Nov. 1663 Pyott was arrested for participation in an illegal assembly, for refusing the Oath of Allegiance, and for refusing to provide surety; he was committed to the Newgate prison in Bristol, but released in a week. Arrested again on 13 Dec. 1663, he was sent to Bridewell prison for attending an illegal meeting and refusing the Oath. On this occasion he was fined £50 and imprisoned approximately two weeks until it was paid. In his 1667 tract, *The Quakers Vindicated*, he asserted that the Friends obey magistrates in all lawful matters, though magistrates have no authority to coerce people to attend church. He insisted it was contrary to love and equity to impose matters of religion on others when those matters were antithetical to the dictates of their consciences. In 1669 he signed the Fell*-Fox wedding certificate, but he died the next year in London.

Braithwaite, *BQu* and *SP*; Fox, *CJ*; *FPT*; *EQL*. Papers: LF.

R.L. Greaves

R

RADMAN, John (fl. 1647-1649)

Mutineer, was a private in Richard Ingoldsby's* regiment of foot. Radman was elected Agitator for the regiment in June 1647 and represented it at the Army Council. He circulated John Lilburne's* pamphlet, *An Outcry of the Young Men and Apprentices of London Addressed to the Private Soldiers of the Army*, published in Aug. 1649, among the soldiers of Ingoldsby's regiment, then stationed at Oxford where Col. Ayres* was a prisoner. Radman led a mutiny in September, demanding re-establishment of the Army Council and immediate realization of the Leveller program. Many of Col. Tomlinson's* regiment of horse also went over. On 8 Sept. the magazine at New College was seized, and Ingoldsby captured on his arrival from London. More forces were dispatched but Ingoldsby, who had not been disarmed, broke free and was able to suppress the mutiny two days later. Two men were shot, but Radman himself escaped, and was next (and apparently last) heard of robbing the post office at Newbury.

Firth & Davies; *Clarke Papers*; *The Moderate*, 7-14 Aug., 11-18 Sept. 1649; *Proceedings of the Oxford Archaeological and Historical Society* (1884).

R. Zaller

RADNOR, first Earl of. *See* Robartes, John.

RAINSBOROUGH (or Rainborow, Rainborowe), Thomas (d. 1648)

Leveller and Civil War officer, was the son of Capt. William Rainsborough, a naval officer in the King's service. The family had close affinities with emigrants to New England; one sister married Gov. John Winthrop* and another his fourth son.

Rainsborough, following the example of his father, was a seaman, and though little is known of his career prior to the Civil War, there is some evidence to suggest that he had gained a reputation as a serviceable mariner before 1640. In the war itself he served with distinction both at sea and on land. His initial service was with the navy in guarding the Irish Sea in order to prevent Irish volunteers from joining the King's army in northern England. In Oct. 1643 he assisted Fairfax* in the defense of Hull, and at this time switched from the naval service to a command in the army; the petition of his wife asking that he be exchanged after being captured in the fighting at Hull refers to him as a colonel. Once re-entered on army service after the exchange, he raised a regiment in Manchester's army which was notable for the number of key officers who were returned emigrants from New England. His best known achievement in this phase of the war was the recapturing of Crowland Abbey, an event rather exaggerated at the time but not without significance. If nothing else, it placed him among the prominent parliamentary commanders and helped to assure his appointment as colonel of a newly formed infantry regiment in the New Model Army. As an officer in the New Model, Rainsborough fought with distinction in various engagements including Naseby, the sieges of Bristol and Sherborne, the blockade of Oxford and the siege of Worcester. At the conclusion of the latter action, Fairfax recommended him to Parliament as the Governor of Worcester.

In 1646 Rainsborough was elected MP as a recruiter for Droitwich; it was not, however, in Parliament but the army that he continued to play a leading role. In 1647 Rainsborough sided fully with the army radicals, and by allying with the Levellers became the one key officer to take up consistently the popular cause. His own regiment had been designated in Apr. 1647 to take part in the reduction of Jersey, but at the end of May the regiment mutinied and marched from Hampshire back to Abingdon, thus joining the bulk of the army in protesting against parliamentary policy. Rainsborough's personal role in these events is not wholly clear, since he was at the time in London in his capacity as MP. He was accused by Holles* of having withheld from Parliament information about the intentions of his regiment in order to give them the opportunity to mutiny. Whatever his initial relationship with the mutineers had been, he was soon at one with his men, and in the summer and fall of 1647 he emerged as one of the most outspoken and active radical leaders and commanded the forces which occupied Southwark when the army marched on London.

It was in the discussions within the Council of the Army, and especially during the Putney debates, that Rainsborough's radicalism was most openly revealed. That he sympathized both with the practical grievances of the rank and file and with the broader political program being put forward on their behalf is manifest. Indeed, he appears to have gone well beyond the Leveller position on suffrage. While many Levellers argued for a modest extension of the suffrage to a non-servant franchise, Rainsborough seems to have argued consistently for the far more radical proposal of manhood suffrage. Asserting that 'every man that is to live under a government ought first by his own consent to put himself under that government,' he declared that 'the poorest man in England is not bound in a strict sense to that government that he hath not had a voice to put himself under.'

Rainsborough's radical politics severely strained his relations with Parliament and his fellow officers. On 27 Sept. 1647 he had been appointed vice-admiral of the fleet, but his political stance stood in the way of his active employment on this duty; on 10 Dec. the House of Commons voted against sending him to sea, while a month earlier Cromwell had expressed the opinion that 'a speedy course' needed to be found to oust Rainsborough from both the House and the army. The situation was considerably modified, however, by the overwhelming need of the army to close ranks and preserve unity. In the general reconciliation that followed the 22 Dec. prayer meeting at Windsor, Cromwell and Rainsborough came to terms, Rainsborough agreeing henceforth to be 'conformable to the judgment and direction' of Cromwell and Ireton.* On 24 Dec. the House reversed its previous vote on his going to sea and on 1 Jan. 1648 he received orders to take up his command. Rainsborough's five month period as vice-admiral amounted to a tumultuous fiasco. His appointment was extremely unpopular with the navy on a number of grounds. He was accused of 'insufferable pride, ignorance and insolency' as well as being distrusted as one who had left the fleet for land service. His replacement of the popular William Batten was much resented, as were his affiliations with the Independents and the Levellers. In May the squadron in the Downs revolted in favor of the King; the appointment by Parliament of the Earl of Warwick* as Lord High Admiral superseded Rainsborough's command, and he returned to army service. He was one of the leading commanders at the siege of Colchester; his regiment was the first to enter the town after its surrender, and he presided over the execution of the royalist leaders Lucas and Lisle with a studied defiance of the rules of war. In Oct. 1648 he was sent to take command of the siege of Pontefract Castle. The incumbent commander Sir Henry Cholmley refused to relinquish his command, and Rainsborough withdrew to Doncaster while the matter was being settled. On 29 Oct. a royalist raiding party attempted to kidnap him with the apparent intention of exchanging him for the Royalist Sir Marmaduke Langdale; in the struggle Rainsborough was killed. His funeral was turned into an extensive public demonstration by the Levellers, some 50 coaches and 1500 horse accompanying his body to the grave. His death removed a leader of considerable potential from the Leveller ranks. A man of action rather than a theorist, he had raised the possibility of the widespread conversion of the army to a more radical stance. His death weakened Leveller influence in the army, and must be reckoned a significant factor in the failure of the Leveller risings in the spring of 1649.

DNB; E. Peacock, 'Notes on the Life of Thomas Rainborowe,' *Archaeologia*, 46:9-64; R.W. Stent, 'Thomas Rainsborough and the Army Levellers' (M.Phil. thesis, Univ. of London, 1975); D.E. Kennedy, 'The English Naval Revolt of 1648,' *EHR*, 77:242-56; H.R. Williamson, *Four Stuart Portraits* (1949); Frank; Brailsford. Papers: O, OW; L (Add. MSS).

R. Howell

RAINSBOROUGH (or Rainborow, Rainborowe), William (fl. 1638-1673)

Civil War officer and Ranter, was the son of Capt. William Rainsborough (d. 1642) and the younger brother of the Leveller Col. Thomas Rainsborough.* Like his older brother, William was apparently a seaman with definite interests in New England, where he purchased a house at Watertown, Mass. in Dec. 1640. He was part of the expeditionary force against Galway commanded by his brother in 1642, with Hugh Peter* as chaplain. He subsequently served as a captain in James or Thomas Sheffield's regiment of horse in the west. When Sheffield declared for Parliament at Saffron Walden on 15 May 1647 he was flatly opposed by Rainsborough, who presented the grievances of his troop. Sheffield and his adherents left the regiment in early June, and he was replaced by Thomas Harrison,* while Rainsborough as senior captain was promoted major. Like his brother he embraced Leveller tenets, and in the Putney debates (1647) asserted that the chief end of government was to preserve persons as well as estates. He adhered to his brother

in the fall of 1648 and marched at his funeral. After his brother's death he embraced Ranter principles, which may have been the reason for his dismissal as major of horse by Cromwell in 1649. In the aftermath of the passage of the Act for the Punishment of Atheistical, Blasphemous and Execrable Opinions (9 Aug. 1650) he was cited in the Commons on 27 Sept. for countenancing Lawrence Clarkson's* book, *The Single Eye*, discharged from his office as JP of Middlesex, and barred from henceforth holding such an office in England and Wales. His home, variously at Fulham and Ilford, was a meeting place for Ranters, including Clarkson.

On 19 July 1659 Rainsborough petitioned the Commons on behalf of the sheriffs, JPs and gentry of Northamptonshire, and was made a Militia Commissioner for that county the same day. On 9 Aug. 1659 the restored Rump made him colonel of a regiment of horse in the county. A warrant was issued for his arrest on grounds of treason on 17 Dec. 1660, at which time he was living at Mile End Green, Stepney, and he was confined in the Gatehouse the next day. The same month his wife Margery petitioned for his examination, and on 7 Feb. 1661 a bond of £500 was posted for his release. Sometime thereafter he returned to New England, where he was apparently living in Boston in 1673 with his nephew of the same name. His sister Martha had married Gov. John Winthrop* and his sister Judith was married to Winthrop's fourth son, Col. Stephen Winthrop.*

CJ, 6:474-75; 7:723, 753; *CSPD, Chas. II*, 1:416, 450, 505; *New England Historical and Genealogical Register*, 40:161, 168-70; Morton; Woodhouse; Firth & Davies.

R.L. Greaves

RAINTON, Sir Nicholas (1569-1646)

City radical and Puritan patron, was the third son of Robert Rainton by his wife Margaret, and was baptized at Heighington, Lincs. on 10 June 1569. Rainton set up as a mercer in Lombard Street, London, and prospered as an importer of satin, taffeta, and velvet from Florence and Genoa. Inigo Jones built him a mansion in Enfield called Forty Hall. Rainton was sheriff in 1621-22, an alderman from 1621, twice Master of the Haberdashers' Company, and Lord Mayor in 1632-33. Charles I knighted him in May 1633. Rainton was elected chairman of the Feoffees of Impropriations in 1632, and served until Laud dissolved the organization the following year. While Lord Mayor, Rainton also quarreled with the Bishop of London over his right to carry the ceremonial sword into St. Paul's Cathedral. In 1639 he refused to lend to the King, and in May 1640 he was imprisoned with his fellow aldermen Thomas Atkins,* John Gayre and Thomas Soame* for refusing to provide a list of wealthy citizens in his ward, Cornhill. Rainton was the only senior alderman to support Parliament in its breach with the King, and the only one elected in Jan. 1642 to the Committee of Safety, though he declined to serve. Rainton was inactive after 1642. He was assessed £2000 by the Committee for the Advance of Money on 21 Aug. 1646, two days after his death. In 1602 Rainton married Rebecca, sister of Sir Thomas Moulson, his successor as Lord Mayor in 1633-34. She predeceased him in 1640. His portrait is preserved in St. Bartholomew's Hospital, of which he was President from 1634 until his death, and which he benefited in his will.

DNB; Pearl; I.M. Calder, *Activities of the Puritan Faction of the Church of England* (1957). Papers: LSH (Twisse 129).

R. Zaller

RAM, Robert (c. 1595-1657)

New Model chaplain and Puritan minister, was the son of Thomas Ram (1564-1634), Bishop of Ferns and Leighton. Ram was educated at the University of Dublin, receiving the M.A. in 1614 and becoming a fellow in 1615. The degree was incorporated from Dublin by Cambridge and granted by the latter University in 1615. While a student at Dublin, Ram was made Prebendary of Crosspatrick, Ferns and held this position for three or four years. On 5 Sept. 1639 he married Anne, daughter of Tyringham Norwood. He became minister of Spalding, Lincs., in 1642 and probably remained in the living at least until 1655, although he was also nominated by Parliament to officiate at Barrowby Lincs., in place of Dr. Hurst on 6 Mar. 1646. Ram supported the parliamentary cause and on 31 Jan. 1643 wrote to the people of Croyland arguing against their support of the Crown. Croyland attacked Spalding in March and took Ram prisoner until the Croylanders surrendered to Cromwell on 25 Apr. He was the chaplain to Col. Edward Rossiter's regiment of the New Model Army and in this capacity preached to committees of both Houses of Parliament and to the army on the day of humiliation, 27 Mar. 1646. The sermon was published the same year.

Ram's most prominent accomplishment was the publication of *The Souldiers Catechism, Composed for the Parliaments Army* in 1644. The work was republished seven times by the end of 1645, and John Turner, who published another edition in 1684 along with his refutation of its justification of the Revolution, claimed for it almost official status during the rebellion. It provides a general justification for Christian participation in war – mainly from the Bible – and proceeds to enumerate the criteria of *jus ad bellum*, including just cause, right intention, reasonable hope of success, and last resort, and then justifies the revolution in terms of these criteria. It continues with discussions of the glories and virtues of the military profession and the characteristics of a good soldier and justifies the New Model's destruction of crosses, images and books of prayer as legitimate opposition to idolatry and superstition, if not divinely inspired acts. At least as significant as the work's justification for the war and its guidelines for military behavior is its fervid, crusading religious ideology. Readers were told in strident and inflammatory language that the struggle was one between the forces of the Gospel and the minions of Antichrist with salvation the reward for those who died as martyrs for Christ.

Ram also published *Paedo-Baptisme: or, the Baptizing of Infants Justified* (1645), an anthology of Christian authors on the subject. He was still active as minister of Spalding when he published his last work, *The Countrymans Catechism*, in 1655. Ram was buried there on 4 May 1657.

DNB; C.H. Firth, *Cromwell's Army* (3rd ed., 1921); Shaw; Solt; *Al. Cant*.

M.B. Endy

RANDALL, Giles (b.c. 1608)

Sectary, the son of Edward Randall of Chipping Wycombe, Bucks., matriculated at Lincoln Coll., Oxf. on 30 Apr. 1624, and graduated B.A. on 13 Feb. 1626. He was apparently the nephew of John Randall, the Puritan lecturer at St. Andrew Hubbard, London, from 1600 to 1622. As Vicar of Easton, Hunts., Giles Randall preached on 23 Nov. 1636 that the forced loan and ship money brought divine wrath on England. Such exactions were irreligious and unjust, for the forced loan violated the eighth commandment and the unequal levying of ship money cast the burden 'from rich men's shoulders' and placed it 'on poor men's necks.' Without restitution there could be no salvation. In Star Chamber Randall was charged with scandalous and seditious words. On 18 June 1640 the High Commission licensed him to depart and appear by proctor. In 1643 Randall was charged in Star Chamber with Anabaptism, Antinomianism and Familism for a sermon preached at St. Martin Orgar. Although ejected from the ministry, he continued to preach, prompting an attack against him in the Commons by Stephen Marshall* on 9 Aug. 1644. According to Marshall, Randall believed that a wicked woman married to a godly husband was sanctified by the marriage. The Commons resolved that Randall be taken into custody, examined by the Committee for Plundered Ministers and if necessary imprisoned. Randall subsequently wrote prefaces to, and may have translated, the anonymous mystical works *A Bright Starre* (1646) and *Theologica Germanica* (1648), as well as Nicholas of Cusa's *Single Eye* (1646). Randall is sometimes identified as the author of *Divinity and Philosophy Dissected* (Amsterdam, 1644), which claims to have been written by a 'mad man.' An Antinomian and an advocate of religious toleration, Randall was attacked in print by Thomas Edwards, John Etherington and Samuel Rutherford.

Al. Oxon.; *CSPD, Chas. I*, 11 *passim*; 16:424; *CJ*, 3:584-85; R.M. Jones, *Spiritual Reformers* (1928), 253-63; Hill, *MER*. Papers: LPR.

R.L. Greaves

RATHBONE, John (d. 1666)

Fifth Monarchist and army radical, was reputedly a member of the gentry, but little is known about him. He served in the parliamentary army, having joined by 1646, and attained the rank of colonel. After John Rogers* stated his case against tithes to the parliamentary committee considering that subject in the Barebones Parliament on 16 Sept. 1653, Rathbone supported Rogers' views and was physically assaulted by a London mob. Rogers himself remarked on the attack in his *Sagrir*, published the same year. After the Restoration Rathbone became part of the underground network of dissidents opposed to the Stuart regime. In 1665 he was implicated in a plot with Henry Danvers* and others to seize the Tower of London, assassinate the King, establish a republic and redistribute property. As a consequence he was arrested with seven other Commonwealth officers and executed on 30 Apr. 1666.

Capp, *FMM*; Ludlow, 2:489; *MCR*, 3:376; W.C. Abbott, 'English Conspiracy and Dissent,' *AHR*, 14:699-700; Liu.

S.R. Smith and R.L. Greaves

RAWLINSON, Thomas (d. 1689)

Quaker, was a gentleman of Graythwaite, Furness, Lancs. After Rawlinson, a Separatist, was convinced as a Quaker in 1652, he was disowned by his family. He carried the Quaker message to much of England, including Cumberland, Durham and the Midlands. In July 1656 he was imprisoned at Exeter with James Nayler* and other Friends, and he subsequently traveled with George Fox* on his southern tour, which took them in 1657 to Kent, Surrey, Sussex, Exeter, Bristol, Reading and London. Rawlinson also visited Cromwell after Nayler's trial and was a correspondent of Martha Fell's.* Rawlinson's tract, *Light Sown*, was published in 1657 for Thomas Simmons. By his wife Dorothy, Rawlinson had a daughter, Lydia Lancaster (1684-1761), who was very active in the Society of Friends.

EQL; *EQW*; Braithwaite, *BQu* and *SP*; *FPT*; Fox, *CJ*. Papers: LF (Swarthmore MSS).

R.L. Greaves

REDE (or Reade, Reid), John (fl. 1647-1665)

Leveller and army radical, was a Wiltshire man. In 1647 he was appointed Governor of Poole and Brownsea Castle; however in 1650 opponents petitioned for his removal because of his sympathy with the Levellers, his attempts to impose a Baptist as pastor and lecturer at Poole, and his cashiering of men who supported Cromwell. During the conflict Rede disarmed the garrison and arrested the Mayor of Poole, and, when George Skutt arrived with a commission as his replacement, filed counter-charges against Skutt. Rede was MP for Wiltshire and served on committees dealing with Wiltshire from 1647 to 1652, and in 1657, 1659 and 1660. In 1653 he was a judge concerning prisons and prisoners. In 1659 when the Committee for Nomination of Officers removed from their commands officers believed to be Cromwellians rather than republicans, Rede was probably the lieutenant-colonel and major in Henry Cromwell's* regiment. In 1661 Rede was imprisoned in the Tower for alleged involvement in a plot. In 1665 he denied involvement in plots and contact with such men as Pleadwell and Col. Booth. He also said that, although some members of conventicles did stir up trouble, most of them did not; however they could not in good conscience attend the parish churches and could not be compelled to do so by persecution.

Bayley; Firth & Rait, 1: 977, 1095; 2 *passim*; Firth & Davies; Underdown, *PP*; *CSPD, Chas. II*, 4:545, 551.

J.D. Neville

REEVE, John (1608-1658)

Sectary, was co-founder with his cousin Lodowick Muggleton* of the Muggletonians. Reeve was born in Wiltshire in 1608, the son of Walter Reeve, who was later described by Muggleton as a clerk to a Deputy of Ireland. Although Muggleton said that he and Reeve never read any books but the Bible, it is likely that Reeve, as befitted the son of a clerk, received some education. His theological works indicate some acquaintance with mystical books, especially those of Jacob Boehme. In the 1620s, when his father seems to have had financial difficulties, Reeve was apprenticed in London as a tailor. Muggleton, who knew him during these years, detected no signs of religious enthusiasm: 'He was of an honest, just nature, and harmless; but a man of no great natural wit or widsom. No subtlety or policy was in him, nor no great store of religion he had but what was traditional. . . .' The ferment of the 1640s, however, made Reeve question such traditional attitudes. It seems that he was on the fringes of political radicalism, for in 1653 he criticized the Rump Parliament for having broken its engagements with the free-born people of England.

Toward the end of the 1640s Reeve became a Ranter and believed that all men were saved even if they lived unrighteous lives. By 1650, however, he withdrew from this universalism and joined the followers of John Robins,* who proclaimed himself to be God Almighty. Robins' belief that the saved and the damned were determined by those who supported and those who opposed him, and his cursing anyone who denied his preaching, had great influence on Reeve. Not content to be a disciple of Robins, Reeve desired to receive revelations directly from God. In Jan. 1652 Reeve told Muggleton that he understood portions of the Scripture 'in large measure.' Thus prepared, on 3, 4 and 5 Feb. 1652 he heard Jesus speak directly to him. This was the crucial point in the beginning of Muggletonianism; although the sect was eventually identified with Muggleton's name, it was based on Reeve's revelations and on his extraordinary book which was published in 1652, *A Transcendent Spiritual Treatise*.

Reeve's theology was in part a reaction to the Ranter emphases on universal salvation, the spirituality of God and his existence within all creatures. The Muggletonians were rigidly predestinarian, asserting that God ordained the Seed of Adam (or faith) to salvation and the Seed of Cain (or reason) to damnation. Reeve wrote that Cain was the son of the Devil, not of Adam; at Cain's conception the Devil became flesh and therefore he exists only in reprobate men. Reeve and Muggleton received a commission from God to curse the Seed of Cain, beginning with Robins and John Tany,* a sectary who had proclaimed himself to be the Lord's High Priest. Cursing those who despised Muggletonian teachings became a characteristic of the sect.

Unlike the Ranters and the Quakers who spoke of an Inner Light of God within men, Reeve said that God dwells apart from this world and that he has a body in the form of a man, for God made Adam in his image. There is only one God, the man Jesus, who when he entered Mary's womb left heaven; Elijah ruled heaven in his absence. At the ascension Jesus returned to heaven, and he is not in any physical or spiritual sense within men.

A Transcendent Spiritual Treatise was, however, not merely a reaction to the Ranters. Probably influenced by the writings of Boehme (and thus indirectly by the twelfth-century mystic Joachim of Fiore) Reeve posited a threefold scheme of revelation or commissions: water (Moses and the Old Testament prophets), blood (the apostles) and Spirit (Reeve and Muggleton, the witnesses of the Spirit prophesied in Revelation 11). The third commission superseded the other two, and thus in this age of the Spirit the Scripture written by previous prophets and apostles was no longer a guide to faith and conduct. The Commission of the Spirit allowed no formal worship or ecclesiastical organization.

Reeve quickly attempted to gain converts to his beliefs. During 1653 he had letters printed to Presbyterian and Independent ministers, to the Recorder of London, to the Lord Mayor, and to Cromwell, Parliament and the Council of State. Although these letters were signed by both Reeve and Muggleton, the latter admitted in his autobiography that Reeve had written them. Reeve also engaged in correspondence with other sectaries including the Quakers, but primarily attempted to gain converts from the Ranters. Reeve and Muggleton attended Ranter meetings in the Minories at which Reeve was physically attacked. Several Muggletonian leaders, nevertheless, including Jeremiah Mount, Capt. Clark and Lawrence Clarkson,* were former Ranters, and the sect spread to Cambridge and Kent through the influence of Ranters who had been convinced by Reeve's writings.

In 1653 Reeve's teachings came to the

attention of the London authorities, and the two witnesses of the Spirit were imprisoned in Newgate to await trial for blasphemy. When their case was heard, Reeve said that the Lord Mayor was damned and therefore could not speak at the trial. Such words were unlikely to improve the witnesses' chances to avoid further imprisonment. They were convicted and sent to Bridewell until Apr. 1654.

That experience may have discouraged Reeve from engaging in further public disputes, and the Muggletonians later claimed that they were uninterested in proselytizing. Reeve, however, wrote a letter in 1654 'discovering the dark light of the Quakers,' and he asked its recipient to show it to Quakers. In addition, he wrote a list of fifteen queries aimed against those who believed in a non-material God. The Quaker Edward Burrough* published a vehement answer, but Reeve did not continue the debate. During his last four years Reeve wrote two theological books, *A Divine Looking-Glass* (1656) and *Joyfull News from Heaven* (1658); he engaged in correspondence with his followers; and he accepted gifts from the faithful. He died in July 1658. His letters were later published in *Sacred Remains* (1706), *Verae fidei floria est corona vitae, a Volume of Spiritual Epistles* (1755), *A Stream from the Tree of Life* (1758), and *A Supplement to the Book of Letters* (1831).

After Reeve's death, Muggleton became the leader of the sect, but through the seventeenth and eighteenth centuries various groups, calling themselves Reevites, broke from the main Muggletonian congregation. The Muggletonians numbered between three and four hundred in the nineteenth century before dwindling in the twentieth. Regular meetings ceased in the 1920s or the 1930s but the sect is not quite extinct today.

L. Muggleton, *The Acts of the Witnesses of the Spirit* (1699); A. Gordon, *The Origin of the Muggletonians* (1869); Gordon, *Ancient and Modern Muggletonians* (1870); J. Smith, *Bibliotheca Anti-*

Quakeriana (1873); Morton; Hill, *WTUD* and *MER*; B. Reay, 'The Muggletonians: A Study in Seventeenth-Century English Sectarianism,' *Journal of Religious History*, 9:32-49.

D.G. Greene

REYNER (or Reiner), Edward (1600-1660)

Puritan minister, was born at Morley, near Leeds, Yorks. Influenced early by Puritan preaching, he matriculated at St. John's Coll., Camb., commencing B.A. in 1620 and M.A. in 1624. He taught school at Asterby, Lincs. until the Countess of Warwick provided another school at Market Rasen and, after four years, the lectureship at Welton. In Aug. 1626 Reyner was appointed to the lectureship of St. Benedict's, Lincoln, and in the following March to the Rectory of St. Peter at Arches. Although known as a Nonconformist, he accepted a benefice from the Bishop of Lincoln, John Williams, and was collated to St. Botolph's prebend on 10 Sept. 1635, but had resigned by 15 Sept. 1636. In 1639 Reyner refused an offer made by Philip Nye* and Thomas Goodwin* to be the pastor of the English church in Arnhem, Gelderland. Had the Civil War not begun, he would certainly have been disciplined for nonconformity. During the war years he preached and lectured at Boston, Kings Lynn, Norwich and Yarmouth, settling at Norwich for two years (1643-45), after which he returned to Lincoln. Ejected in 1662, he remained in Lincoln until his death in 1668. His published works include *Precepts for Christian Practice* (1645; thirteen eds. by 1668); *Orders from the Lord of Hostes* (1646); *Rules for the Government of the Tongue* (1656); *Considerations Concerning Marriage* (1657); *A Treatise of the Necessitie of Humane Learning for a Gospell-preacher* (1663); *The Properties of the Righteous Described* (1668); and *The Being and Wellbeing of a Christian* (1669).

Nuttall, *VS*; *Calamy Revised*; Calamy; E. Hanbury, *Historical Memorials* (1839); Wing.

R. Masek

REYNOLDS (or Rainolds), John (1549-1607)

Puritan educator, was born at Pinhoe, near Exeter, 'about Michaelmas day,' 1549, the fifth son of Richard Reynolds. The Reynolds family had long been associated both with the Church and with Oxford; Reynolds' brothers preceded him in the university (William subsequently becoming a Catholic priest and Professor of Divinity and Hebrew at the English College in Rheims); an uncle, Thomas Reynolds, was Warden of Merton College and Dean of Exeter. Reynolds appears to have entered Merton originally, but on 29 Apr. 1563 he was elected to a scholarship at Corpus Christi where two other brothers, Hierome and Edmond, were already fellows. On 11 Oct. 1566 he became a probationary fellow and two years later a full fellow, graduating B.A. on 15 Oct. 1568. He received his M.A. on 14 June 1572 and a B.D. on 24 June 1579, and in June 1585 was awarded the D.D. Reynolds was assigned as a tutor to Richard Hooker, and from 1572 to 1578 was Greek Reader in the College. Here he made a considerable reputation both for the matter and manner of his lectures on Aristotle, helping to spread Ramist ideas in England and popularizing what later came to be called the Euphuistic style. In 1576 Reynolds led the fight against the admission of the minister of the Spanish church in London, Anthony Corrano, to Corpus Christi, and two years later he was embroiled in controversy over the choice of his successor in the readership. These and other differences with the College led to the resignation of his fellowship in 1586, when he moved to Queen's College to assume a temporary lectureship for the refutation of Catholic doctrine endowed by Sir Francis Walsingham.

Reynolds was heavily involved in the Presbyterian movement which reached its climax in the late 1580s, and in 1587 was host of a conference on discipline at Oxford whose participants included Walter Travers and William Chark. With the collapse of the movement, Reynolds urged prudence and retrenchment, and in 1590 he counseled Edward Fleetwood not to abandon the ministry over the issue of wearing the surplice. Nonetheless Queen Elizabeth rebuked him in 1592 'for his obstinate preciseness, willing him to follow her laws and not run before them.'

On 10 Dec. 1593 Reynolds became Dean of Lincoln, a position he found even more controversial than his old one at Corpus Christi. Almost exactly five years later, on 11 Dec. 1598, he succeeded the unpopular William Cole as President of Corpus Christi, where he remained until his death on 21 May 1607. During the 1590s Reynolds was also involved in a prolonged dispute with the Oxford playwright William Gager, which culminated in Reynolds' *The Overthrow of Stage-Playes* (1599), a work heavily mined by later Puritan opponents of the theatre.

As the most learned and eloquent Puritan controversialist of his generation as well as a leading supporter of James I's accession, Reynolds was a natural choice as spokesman for the reformers at the Hampton Court conference in Jan. 1604. Evaluations of his performance have varied. Reynolds emphasized points of doctrine and citations of authority rather than symbolic grievances such as the surplice, and more impatient heads felt that his argument for Presbyterian reform – ill-received as it was – did not go far enough. Yet the Puritans emerged from the conference as an acknowledged voice in the Church for the first time since the days of Grindal. Once considered a debâcle, Hampton Court is now seen as a first step back from the wilderness of Elizabeth's last decade. Reynolds had in fact gauged his royal patron shrewdly, engaging him on shared points of interest rather than the lost battles of the previous age. His leadership bore quiet fruit in the still largely-unexplored development of Jacobean Puritanism, and proved its ultimate worth in the resistance to Arminianism in the 1620s.

Among the most precious of Reynolds' victories was the approval of a new translation of the Bible, which Archbishop Bancroft had stoutly resisted. Reynolds was the guiding spirit of the project until his death, continuing to hold weekly meetings in his chambers even though gravely weakened by consumption, and the translation of the prophets in the King James version is particularly indebted to him. At the same time he held out against the Canons of 1604, to which he conformed but refused to subscribe. Threatened with expulsion from Oxford, he wrote to Salisbury denying any promise to subscribe at Hampton Court, and to Bancroft that to affirm the article which declared there to be nothing in the Book of Common Prayer contrary to the word of God would be to assert 'a known untruth.'

Reynolds died unmarried, as James' famous gibe at the Hampton Court conference reminds us, and was buried in the chapel of Corpus Christi. His works include *Sex theses de Sacra Scriptura et ecclesia* (1580, revised 1602), *The Summe of the Conference betwene John Rainolds and John Hart Touching the Head and Faith of the Church* (1584), and *De Romanae Ecclesiae idolatria* (1596). His Greek lectures were published in 1587. In 1641 Reynolds' attack on Bancroft's concept of episcopacy was published as part of the Root and Branch campaign, and the *Sermons on the Prophecies of Haggai* were printed in 1648 as 'very useful for these times.' Perhaps Reynolds' most lasting contribution is summed up by his insistence in *Advice on Study of Divinitie* that the Scriptures must be read 'out of the very well-spring, not out of the brooks of translations,' and that the student must 'travail painfully' in Calvin's *Institutes*. A generation after his death, textual scholarship and predestinarian doctrine were to provide the twin pillars of resistance to the Laudian regime.

DNB; *Ath. Oxon.*; C.E. Mallet, *A History of the University of Oxford* (1924); M.H. Curtis, *Oxford and Cambridge in Transition, 1558-1642* (1965); P. Collinson, *The Elizabethan Puritan Movement* (1967); R.G. Usher, *The Reconstruction of the English Church* (1910); S.B. Babbage, *Puritanism and Richard Bancroft* (1962); M.H. Curtis, 'Hampton Court Conference and its Aftermath,' *History*, 46:1-16. Papers: O.

R. Zaller

REYNOLDS, Sir John (1625-1657)

Civil War officer, was born on 10 Mar. 1625 in Castle Camps, Cambs., the third son of Sir James Reynolds. He pursued legal studies before entering the parliamentary army, where he rose to prominence after the founding of the New Model. Reynolds strongly opposed disbanding the army in 1647 and at that time enjoyed considerable popularity with radical elements among the common soldiers. Many of the men serving under him participated in the Leveller mutiny in the spring of 1649, but he remained faithful to Cromwell and was instrumental in suppressing the revolt. His loyalty was rewarded during the Commonwealth, when he played a prominent role in Irish affairs. His regiment took part in the important victory over Ormond at Rathmines on 2 Aug. 1649 and in November of the following year he captured and successfully defended Carrick. These and other endeavors earned him the post of Commissary-General of the Horse in Ireland and resulted in his obtaining a grant of lands from a grateful Parliament, and through shrewd investments he parlayed his holdings into a vast Irish estate. He sat for Galway and Mayo in 1654 and for Waterford and Tipperary in 1656 as one of the Irish MPs provided for by the Instrument of Government, but was not particularly active. He had considerable political influence thanks to his sympathies for the Cromwellian regime and through his marriage to Sarah, the daughter of Sir Francis Russell* of Chippenham and the sister-in-law of Henry Cromwell.* In 1657 Reynolds left Ireland to assume the post of Commander-in-Chief of the English forces fighting with the French army in Flanders. He was paid the munificent sum of £5 per diem for his services, but disease, lack of cooperation from the French, and the rigors of the campaign took a heavy toll of both his own energies and the forces under him. Discouraged by the turn of events and concerned with rumors that he had lost favor with the Protector, he sailed for England late in 1657. The ship carrying him wrecked on Goodwin Sands on 5 Dec. and Reynolds drowned. He had no heir and by his will his lands were divided between his brother, Robert,* and his brother-in-law, James Calthorpe. In 1660 his widow married Lord Thomond.

Ashley, *CG*; *DNB*; *MPHC*. Papers: L (Lans. MSS).

J.A. Casada

REYNOLDS, Robert (c. 1601-1661)

Parliamentary radical, MP LP 1640 (Hindon), 1659 (Whitchurch). Reybolds was born about 1601 in Castle Camps, Cambs., the son of Sir James Reynolds and Margaret Melbourne of Dunmow, Essex. He studied at Queens' Coll., Camb. before entering the Middle Temple in 1620, and was called to the bar in 1628.

Reynolds married twice, first, in 1635, to Mary, daughter of Nathaniel Deards of Dunmow, Essex, and second, in 1646, to Priscilla, daughter of Sir Hugh Wyndham of Pillesdon, Dorset. Returned for Hindon, Wilts. in the Long Parliament, probably through the influence of the Earl of Pembroke,* Reynolds sat on 53 committees before July 1642. Shortly after the outbreak of the Civil War he was sent by the House of Commons to Dublin as one of two commissioners charged with winning over the Irish Privy Council to the parliamentary cause. The commissioners

avoided arrest as demanded by Charles I, but failed to secure Irish support. Returning to England in 1643, Reynolds labored for moderate religious and political reform both in the Westminster Assembly of Divines and in Parliament. A Presbyterian elder, he opposed the exaggerated claims of the Assembly and worked in Parliament with the middle group who sought reconciliation. In Nov. 1644, as the chief critic of those who were profiting from a prolongation of the war, Reynolds was appointed chairman of a Commons' committee to investigate the offices and benefits of all parliamentary appointments. The war party outmaneuvered Reynolds' committee with the Self-Denying Ordinance which halted the investigation and eliminated generals not committed to victory at all costs. Reynolds was concerned with the mounting power of the military in the years following the defeat of the royalist forces and from 1646 to 1648 he spoke out in support of the sequestration and compounding of royalist estates, and served on the parliamentary commission at Goldsmith's Hall established to deal with delinquents. He argued that money raised through sequestration and compounding could be used to pay the army's arrears and thus permit its disbanding. In 1648 Reynolds moved slowly over to the Independent position and not only survived Pride's purge, but was named to the High Court. A pragmatist who opposed the purge and the King's trial, Reynolds avoided the Commons and the Court, reluctantly returning to Parliament after Charles' death in Feb. 1649. He and his fellow lawyers brought a moderating force to the actions of the Rump and in 1650 he was appointed Solicitor General for the Commonwealth. It was Reynolds who revealed in the 1659 Parliament that the Rump, having prepared for new elections, had actually voted to dissolve itself prior to its dissolution. Reynolds retired from national politics after the dissolution of the Rump until the accession of Richard Cromwell,* at which time he was returned for Whitchurch. He opposed the recognition of Richard's Protectorate because it lacked constitutional guarantees. The restoration of the Rump Parliament in May 1659 thrust Reynolds back into prominence as a member of the Council of State. Here he supported Gen. Monck's appointment as commander-in-chief of all forces in England and Scotland with the power to destroy any forces hostile to Parliament. Having paved the way for the restoration of the monarchy, Reynolds received a royal pardon and a knighthood from Charles II and died shortly thereafter in retirement.

Davies, *RC*; Keeler; Burton; *DNB*; Worden; MacCormack. Papers: L (Add. MSS).

R.E. Shimp

RICH, Sir Nathaniel (1585-1636)

Parliamentary radical and colonizer, MP 1614 (Totnes), 1621 (East Retford), 1624 (Harwich), 1625 (Newport, Isle of Wight), 1626, 1628 (Harwich). Rich was perhaps born at Ash, Essex, and was probably the eldest son of Richard Rich and a daughter of John Machell, a London sheriff and alderman. He acquired legal training and was admitted to Gray's Inn on 2 Feb. 1610; he was knighted at Hatton House on 8 Nov. 1617. Rich was an original member of the Bermuda Company, chartered in June 1615, and served that company as well as the Virginia Company as a business and legal advisor. As a close ally of his cousin, Robert Rich,* the second Earl of Warwick, he played a prominent role in the series of confrontations with Sir Edwin Sandys* over the tobacco monopoly and the leadership of the Virginia Company. He was the leading opponent of the Sandys' party when the Virginia dispute came before Parliament in 1624, and was a member of the Virginia commission when the colony passed into royal hands in July. Rich had displeased the Crown by opposition in 1621, and had been put on the Irish commission as punishment after the breakup of Parlia-

ment. The failure of the Spanish match and the breach with Spain in 1623 brought the Warwick faction closer to Charles and the Duke of Buckingham. This was short-lived, and Rich played a prominent role in the parliamentary estrangement from Charles I. A major speech on 6 Aug. 1625, setting forth five conditions which had to be fulfilled before the supply was granted, strained relations with Buckingham, and in May 1626 the Commons chose Rich to carry their request for the imprisonment of Buckingham to the House of Lords. Rich was prominent in the Parliament of 1628 where he was closely allied with his friend and fellow colonizer John Pym,* served on a number of important committees, and played a leading role in the debates on the Petition of Right. Among the earliest and most vocal opponents of Arminianism, Rich and Pym were the leaders of those who saw in Arminianism the chief threat to the state and the subject in the session of 1629.

Rich was one of the most prominent oppositionist MPs of the 1620s, and his proposals were frequently daring. It was Rich who first moved the Monopoly Bill in the Parliament of 1621, and in the foreign policy debate in Nov. 1621 he made the extraordinary suggestion that the King's alliances should be subject to confirmation by Act of Parliament. Similarly, his demand that the King appoint 'grave counsellors' in 1625 was one of the earliest suggestions of ministerial responsibility. At the same time, Rich was one of those who most clearly saw that only a reform of royal finances could get to the root of the continuing confrontation between King and Parliament. After the violent dissolution of 1629, Rich and others of the godly party threw their energies into colonizing activities. Rich played an important role in the negotiations which led to the granting of the charter to the Massachusetts Bay Company in 1629. He invested £275 in an expedition to Providence Island (Santa Catalina) in 1629, and he was instrumental in the formation of the Providence Company in late 1630. Rich saw the Providence Island expedition in particular as a model

Puritan community and a base for war against the Spaniards. He also took a strong interest in crop development and administration so it would be a profitable investment. Rich served as deputy governor in 1635 and although he never visited the New World, he continued his active support of colonial affairs to the end of his life. He died in 1636 and was buried at Stondon. He left that manor to his nephew, Nathaniel, and divided his company holdings among his friends and relatives, and for the purpose of founding a school in Bermuda. Rich was among those who saw the colonial ventures as logical corollaries to their struggles at Westminster; they hoped to establish havens for Puritan theology and civil liberty during a period of political crisis at home.

N. & Q. 5th ser., 10:31; *N. & Q.* 8th ser., 1:66-67; W.F. Craven, *Dissolution of the Virginia Company* (1932); Newton; *CD 1621*; *CD 1625*; *CD 1628*; Russell, *PEP*; *DNB*. Papers: LPR (Manchester Papers); L (Add. MSS).

R.D. Fiala

RICH, Nathaniel (d. 1701)

Civil War officer, was the eldest son of Robert Rich and his wife Elizabeth, the daughter of Sir Thomas Dutton. He was admitted to Gray's Inn in 1639 and continued his studies at the Inns of Court until the outbreak of the Civil War. He entered service in the Earl of Essex's* lifeguards, was commissioned captain in 1643 and, after raising a troop of horse in Essex, joined the army under Manchester. He was soon promoted to lieutenant-colonel and became a full colonel of a regiment of horse after the establishment of the New Model Army. Rich distinguished himself in various engagements and was very much to the forefront in the army's differences with Parliament. He opposed disbanding, was instrumental in formulating the Heads of the Proposals of the Army, and spoke regularly in the army debates in 1647 and 1648. He was essentially republican in outlook and tended toward Fifth Monarchist views in religion. He did evince reservations on matters such as the King's execution, universal manhood suffrage, and direct petitioning by the army's rank-and-file. Early in 1649 Rich took a seat in Parliament for Cirencester (having been elected earlier but excluded because of a double return), and in 1650 suppressed a rising of Norfolk Royalists. He apparently experienced some doubts about the political direction of the Commonwealth, and in 1655, with the death of his first wife, Elizabeth, the sister of John Hampden,* perhaps as a catalyst, he voiced open opposition to Cromwell. This led to loss of his command and a summoning before the Council of State on charges of disaffection. Adamant in his views, Rich was in and out of prison during the final years of the Protectorate. With the return of the Long Parliament in 1659, he regained his command and managed to retain it until immediately prior to the Restoration. He supported the restoration of Parliament after Lambert* had disbanded it in Oct. 1659, and when he was ordered to lay siege to the Parliament's commissioners at Portsmouth in Dec. 1659, he convinced his entire regiment to join the parliamentary cause. They united with the forces in Portsmouth and joined them in the march to London, but a few months later Rich broke with Monck when he determined that Monck's policy would result in the restoration of monarchy. Monck removed him from his post, and at the order of the Council of State he was again imprisoned for several days.

Rich was included in the Act of Indemnity, but owing to his republican views he remained suspect and was once more arrested at the time of Venner's* plot. In 1663, while still a prisoner but under rather relaxed confinement, Rich married Elizabeth Kerr, the daughter of Lord Ancrum. The connections resulting from this marriage and the good offices of Lord Falmouth resulted in Rich's release in 1665, and he lived the remainder of his long life quietly, in striking contrast to his previous career. He had two sons by his first marriage, and both – Nathaniel and Robert – survived him.

Capp, *FMM*; *Clarke Papers*; Ludlow; *DNB*; Kishlansky; p. Morant, *History and Antiquities of the County of Essex*, 2 vols. (1768); Woodhouse. Papers: L (Add. MSS; Stowe MSS).

J.A. Casada

RICH, Robert, second Earl of Warwick (1587-1658)

Colonizer, Puritan patron and Civil War officer, was born about June 1587, the eldest son of Robert Lord Rich (first Earl of Warwick as of 2 Aug. 1618) and Penelope (née Devereux). Of the seven children in the Rich family only Robert and his younger brother Henry, who became the Earl of Holland, rose to prominence among radicals. Rich was admitted to Emmanuel Coll., Camb. on 4 June 1603, where he studied for a year. Unlike many young aristocrats, he remained in touch with his college and eventually worked to support its Puritan leadership. Rich completed his education at the Inner Temple, though his stay was so short that he probably acquired only a basic familiarity with legal business. His cousin, Sir Nathaniel Rich,* and other close associates had more training in law and handled many of the Earl's legal affairs. Rich was at first a courtier. He was created a Knight of the Bath on 24 July 1603, played in Ben Jonson's *Masque of Beauty* in 1608-9, and performed well in tiltings. Soon though, he turned his attention away from Court affairs. He sat as an MP for Maldon, Essex in 1610 and 1614. In 1614 he also became one of the charter members for the Somers or Bermudas Company. From that point on he was preoccupied with colonial and country matters.

With his new-found interests, Rich created adversaries at Court and had such frequent associations with Puritans and other anti-Court groups that he became identified with the Country opposition. Rich also began privateering ventures that disturbed the East India Company in 1616. In Apr. 1618 he sent a ship to Virginia and the West Indies which interfered with the interests of the Virginia Company. He was a charter member of the Guinea Company (Nov. 1618), and in Nov. 1620 he obtained a seat on the council of the New England Company. In the late 1620s he helped to procure the patent for the Massachusetts Bay Company. During the 1620s he and his Puritan associates in the Providence Island Company (patent granted on 4 Dec. 1630) met as much to discuss reforms and resistance to Court policies as to take care of company business. Indeed Rich, who in 1619 succeeded to his father's title of Earl of Warwick and Baron of Leighs, Essex, now emerged as a prominent opposition leader to the policies of Charles I.

Even though alliances with Puritans such as Sir Francis Barrington* had begun with real estate and county matters in the early 1620s, the Earl took his first clear anti-Court stand with the Puritan opposition in 1626. He agitated for a conference on Arminianism, and in the ensuing York House debates sponsored by the Duke of Buckingham, he supported the position of John Preston.* As early as 1624 Preston was working with the Parliamentarians associated with the Rich circle. Preston was able to make the Court cleric Richard Montague admit that his writings contained at least two conditions to predestination, but he evaded censure by promising to modify his position at an undeclared future date. In Parliament, meanwhile, associates of Warwick in the House of Commons (John Pym,* Sir Nathaniel Rich) continued the attack with a subcommittee to investigate Montague's opinions. More instances of opposition occurred late in 1626. During the fall Warwick brought Hugh Peter* from the Earl's advowson at Rayleigh, Essex to preach in London. Peter aimed his blasts directly at the Court. By Warwick's charge, Peter preached at a private fast in Christ's Church, London on St. Andrew's Day (30 Nov.). He closed with a prayer that asked that the new

French Catholic Queen 'would forsake the idolatry and superstition wherein she was and needs perish if she continued in the same.' Someone reported the key phrases of the prayer to the Bishop of London, who notified the Duke of Buckingham. Buckingham required Warwick to attend the Bishop. Diplomatically, Warwick defended his preacher against accusations that Peter was 'never guilty of,' but also warned Peter to 'give mild answers and let me hear what is done.' Peter was able temporarily to satisfy the listless Bishop, and he also was able to keep up new Puritan activities that he had begun during his short stay: participation in the Feoffees of Impropriations, the collection of money for Palatine refugees, and companies planning for overseas immigration. Warwick does not seem to have had much if any direct role in these ventures, though it is likely that Peter acted as the Earl's intermediary on New England affairs. Certainly he tried to help Peter out in 1628 when the latter had prayed again 'for the Queen,' but he had used such seditious language that he ended up in New Prison. Warwick tried in vain to obtain Peter's immediate release, but was finally able to post bail. Once free, Peter fled to Rotterdam with Warwick's help, and by 1636 he succeeded Roger Williams* at Salem, Mass. Peter returned to England in the early 1640s and in 1644 he accompanied Warwick and acted as chaplain.

Warwick's interest in Puritans was soon to become renowned, but so was his alliance with the parliamentary opposition. In Nov. 1626, along with about twenty lords and scores of parliamentary gentlemen, the Earl refused to subscribe to the forced loan. He refused another similar request in 1628. In 1628 Warwick's candidates for Parliament allegedly received votes given by poor men temporarily 'sold' enough property by the Earl to qualify as electors. Warwick and his clients were among the most prominent opposition leaders in this Parliament, and on 21 Apr. 1628 Warwick himself gave a vehement speech against the King's claim of prerogative to imprison without showing cause.

The Petition of Right owed much to men under his sponsorship.

In 1630 Warwick and others, including Lord Saye,* Lord Brooke* and Oliver St. John,* acquired a patent for a company to settle the island of Providence. With Pym as its treasurer, the Providence Island Company included key critics of Charles I in the 1630s and early 1640s. The most famous incident involving this coalition was the opposition to ship money payments, culminating in the trial of John Hampden,* who was defended by St. John. Warwick, who had taken the lead as early as 1635, staunchly refused to aid the ship money collection. When called before Charles to explain his behavior, Warwick lectured the King on unjust taxation and requested that he call a parliament as a proper means for raising revenue. After the dissolution of the Short Parliament the King ordered a search of Warwick, Saye, Brooke, Pym and others.

Another element of Warwick's resistance to royal policy was his patronage of Puritans. Through nominating Puritan clerics to parishes by advowson and through other informal kinds of patronage, Warwick by 1640 deservedly earned the reputation as 'temporal head of the Puritans.' He did not directly support a large number of radical clerics, but no other prominent lord supported as many. Yet some of his clients turned against the Puritans, and one, Samuel Hoard, converted to Arminianism. Warwick, however, won great favor among Puritans for his widespread and consistent support. Much of Warwick's personal patronage resulted from his landed wealth, largely centered in Essex. This wealth gave him *jus patronatus* or advowson rights acquired with land to nominate a clergyman for a parish and *patrocinium* or the general influence which he could use on behalf of his clients. Warwick presented at least forty clerics to his own advowsons between 1620 and 1641. During this time, over half of Warwick's clerics had to defend themselves in an ecclesiastical court and most of these received admonitions or fines for nonconformity. Thirteen clerics presented during the 1630s came under episcopal censure for offenses such as not wearing the surplice or seditious, extemporaneous prayer. Of the Earl's twenty-three advowsons, evidence of Puritan sympathies appeared in nineteen. Six incumbents of Warwick's livings signed a petition endorsing the conformity of Thomas Hooker* in 1629. In 1632 the Earl moved John Beadle from Little Leighs, the Earl's home parish, to the more lucrative advowson of Barnston. After the bishop, William Laud, allowed the move, he had to charge the young student of Hooker with flagrant nonconformity. Another Nonconformist who found refuge in a Warwick benefice was Edmund Calamy,* who was in trouble with Bishop Wren in the diocese of Norwich when Warwick offered him a benefice at Rochford, Essex. Calamy was ill and miserable in Rochford, and when he became Rector of St. Mary Aldermanbury, Warwick obtained a pew in the church. With more moderate Puritan clerics, Calamy pushed for Presbyterian reforms during the 1640s, while remaining a legal trustee, political ally and personal confidant of the Earl.

More evidence of Warwick's support of the most vehement Puritans is manifested in the *patrocinium* or general influence which he used for clients. The Earl supported three ministers besides Hugh Peter who later became famous New England divines: John Wilson, Thomas Hooker and Nathaniel Ward. For Wilson, who was lecturer at Sudbury, Suff. and a close friend of Sir Francis Barrington, Warwick obtained a release from prison and a relaxation of his suspension. For Thomas Hooker, whom he had heard preach many times, the Earl made a supreme effort. When Hooker's conformity was challenged, ministers in the Earl's benefices took the first step with a petition to Laud in support of Hooker's conformity. Warwick then sought to avert Hooker's suspension. When the Court of High Commission wanted to question the cleric, Warwick tried to prevent Hooker's appearance. When that failed, one of Warwick's tenants put up Hooker's bail.

Finally, the Earl provided for Hooker's family while the divine found a position in Holland. Hooker's colleague Nathaniel Ward, who had signed a parliamentary petition against the King's chaplain in 1624, received the presentment of Sir Nathaniel Rich (Warwick's half-brother) to Stondon Massey, Essex. On several occasions when Ward was in England he relied on highly placed friends, such as Warwick, to intervene in support of the Puritan cause. Besides Ward, Hooker and Wilson, it is possible to link Warwick with numerous other zealous Puritans. These included Richard Sibbes,* Stephen Marshall,* William Twisse, Nicholas Beard, William Munnings, John Sym, John Owen,* Obadiah Sedgwick,* Calybute Downing* and Samuel Clark.

In 1637 Warwick aided Jeremiah Burroughs,* later one of the five Dissenting Brethren of the Westminster Assembly. Burroughs, a protegé of Hooker, received aid against the church hierarchy from the Warwick circle in early 1637 when he faced deprivation of his benefice in the diocese of Norwich. After the deprivation was decreed, he became a chaplain to the Warwick circle. In the fall of 1637 he made a brief trip to Holland and returned in 'disguised habits' smuggling seditious books, such as Bastwick's* *Letany*, to be distributed at Yarmouth by 'barme' or heady conventiclers. By the summer of 1638 Burroughs was living with Warwick at Leighs, Essex, and according to the cleric, 'I found [as] much undeserved love and respect . . . as a man deprived, and under the Bishop's rage, could expect.' That fall Burroughs got in trouble for supporting the Scottish Covenant. Among the Earl's intimates he also advocated republican government and armed resistance to the King, singular positions in prerevolutionary days. When the High Commission heard of these opinions, they drew up formal accusations against Burroughs, prompting Warwick to intervene and ask Burroughs to explain. Burroughs eventually persuaded everyone except the Bishop of London that the accusers had mistaken his meaning. In Dec. 1638 while in London attending the ailing Earl, Burroughs learned that the Court was going to pursue his opinions further, and he left England to join William Bridge* in Rotterdam.

Warwick thus clearly exerted broad influence for the Puritan cause. The Earl's patronage reflected the broad spectrum of Puritan thought. He himself probably did not agree with many of the radicals that he aided, though many in his circle were zealots. But his openness to diversity encouraged debate at a time when religious options in England had drastically narrowed.

After the breakup of the Short Parliament, Warwick was one of the dozen peers who called for a new parliament in Aug. 1640. When the Long Parliament met it was a Warwick client, Sir John Clotworthy, who delivered the first attack on the Earl of Strafford, and Warwick firmly supported the subsequent impeachments both of Strafford and of Laud. Warwick joined the Privy Council in Feb. 1641 but his position remained unswayed, as both the Earl's own conduct and the continued support of the parliamentary cause in his home county of Essex showed.

With the outbreak of the Civil War, Warwick took up arms for Parliament. He was primarily a naval commander, but at times he had responsibilities for land forces. As early as Feb. 1642 he executed the Militia Ordinance for Essex, and on 2 Oct. 1642 he was given command of a second army that Parliament intended to raise. When that army did not materialize, Warwick resigned his commission. From then on he concentrated on being Admiral of the Fleet. Warwick's reputation as a successful privateer and sea commander soon won Parliament control of the entire fleet. When in the summer of 1642 there was a conflict over who should command it, Warwick immediately won the loyalty of most junior commanders and sailors. One group of Warwick's supporters seized two recalcitrant royalist captains and brought them before the bar of the House of Lords. Warwick's success at taking control of the fleet meant that the Royalists had problems in obtaining arms and beleaguered coastal

cities could be aided. In 1642 Warwick took valuable magazines from the King's grasp at Hull. In 1643 his fleet helped Exeter and in May 1644 he relieved Lyme Regis. Weymouth was won over through his assistance, as was Pembrokeshire. Throughout, Charles I protested that Warwick was guilty of treason.

Even as Warwick was managing naval operations, he frequently came to London for sessions of Parliament. He obtained a parliamentary resolution to clear his name of treason. He also worked on committees, especially those concerned with religion. He participated on the committee for a fast day ordinance as well as those for scandalous ministers and sequestrations of papist and royalist estates. On 2 Nov. 1643 Parliament named Warwick as head of a commission to oversee English colonies. Throughout Warwick used his influence for religious freedom within the colonies. In 1644 he with other commissioners granted a patent to Roger Williams* incorporating Rhode Island with freedom of worship and liberty of conscience, and in 1645 he issued a declaration freeing worship in the Bermudas from Anglican restrictions. As divisions among the Puritans grew, Warwick stood with Calamy and other Presbyterians.

In 1647 Parliament employed Warwick to disband the army, but a year later asked him to resume command of the fleet, which had been decimated by those who had defected to the King. By assuming command of the fleet and restoring its power, Warwick again showed his loyalty to the Parliament. By June 1648 he had restored to service over half of those who had shirked their duty. He also raised contingents for a new fleet, and by the end of August his restored fleet neutralized the Prince's armada. For a while he blockaded it near Holland and recovered at least four ships belonging to Parliament. Warwick's loyalty to the unpurged Parliament finally forced an end to his military career in 1649. In Feb. 1649 Parliament rescinded the Earl's command and vested it in three commissioners. He had continued to attend meetings of the Navy Committee throughout the King's trial, and feelers continued to be put out to him despite the execution of his royalist brother in Mar. 1649. On 1 Nov. 1649 Warwick attended a thanksgiving sermon in the Commons for recent successes in Ireland preached by his client Stephen Marshall.

Warwick took no active role in public affairs thereafter. He did help invest Cromwell as Lord Protector in June 1654 however. Before his death on 19 Apr. 1658, he wrote Cromwell, praising his 'prudent, heroic and honorable management' of state affairs, and admonished him to 'go on happily, to love religion, to exemplify it.' The Earl concluded with the hope that Cromwell would remain 'an instrument of use, a pattern of virtue, and a precedent of glory.' These phrases were not unlike those penned by Calamy for Warwick's own funeral sermon, *A Pattern for All, Especially for Noble Persons* (1658).

Warwick was thrice married: on 24 Feb. 1605 to Frances (d. 1634), daughter of Sir William Hatton; to Susan (d. 1646), daughter of Sir Rowe Rowe, Lord Mayor of London in 1607 and widow of William Haliday, alderman; and on 30 Mar. 1646 to Eleanor, daughter of Sir Edward Wortley and Dowager Countess of Sussex. Warwick had four sons, of whom the first two, Robert and Charles, succeeded to his title, as well as three daughters.

J.L. Beatty, *Warwick and Holland* (1965); K.S. Shipps, 'Lay Patronage of East Anglian Puritan Clerics in Pre-revolutionary England' (Ph.D. diss., Yale Univ., 1971); B. Donagan, 'The Clerical Patronage of Robert Rich, Second Earl of Warwick, 1619-1642,' *Proceedings of the Amer. Phil. Soc.*, 120:388-419; C. Thompson, 'The Origins of the Politics of the Parliamentary Middle Group, 1625-1629,' *TRHS*, 5th ser., 22:71-86; Newton; W.F. Craven, 'The Earl of Warwick, a Speculator in Piracy,' *Hispanic Amer. Hist. Rev.*, 10:457-79; *DNB*; Worden; V. Snow, *Essex the Rebel* (1970); Zagorin, *CC*; Holmes. Papers: O; C; L (Add. MSS; Harl. MSS; Lans. MSS; Sloane MSS; Stowe MSS).

K. W. Shipps

RICHARDSON, Christopher (1619-1698)

Nonconformist minister, was christened on 17 Jan. 1619 at St. Mary Bishophill Junior, York, the son of Thomas and Frances Richardson. He matriculated at Cambridge as a sizar from Trinity College in 1633, and graduated B.A. in 1637 and M.A. in 1640. In 1646 he was appointed Rector of Kirkheaton, Yorks. At this time he was a Presbyterian, for he appears as a signatory on 6 Apr. 1648 of the *Vindiciae veritatis* with other ministers of the West Riding, calling for adherence to the Solemn League and Covenant, opposing religious toleration, supporting the work of the Westminster Assembly, and condemning Independency and Erastianism. Following his ejection in 1662 he preached at his country estate, Lassell(s) Hall, Kirkheaton, where the Presbyterian minister and diarist Oliver Heywood frequently visited him. In 1672 he applied under the Declaration of Indulgence for a license to preach as a Congregationalist, but the license listed him as a Presbyterian. His house (then at Layton) was an approved meeting place, and he was also licensed to preach at the home of William Cotton of Denby Grange, Penistone, to whom he served as chaplain until 1687. In that year he moved to Liverpool, where his own Nonconformist chapel was opened in 1689 and where he was reported to have a congregation of 400 in 1690. He also preached at Sheffield and Norton, Derby. According to Calamy, 'his preaching to the last was very neat and accurate, but plain and popular.' On 5 Dec. 1698 he was buried in the church at St. Nicholas, Liverpool. His first wife, Elizabeth, had died in 1668, and on 23 Jan. 1683 he married Hepzibah, daughter of Edward Prime, a Presbyterian minister at Sheffield.

Calamy Revised; Calamy; *DNB*; *Al. Cant.*

R.L. Greaves

RICHARDSON, Samuel (fl. 1637-1658)

Particular Baptist, was a substantial London merchant from Northamptonshire and a leading member of John Spilsbury's* congregation. He was one of 21 persons named in a 1637 indictment filed by the Attorney General in Star Chamber accusing them of distributing John Bastwick's* *Apologeticus ad praesules Anglicanos* (1636) and William Prynne's* *Newes from Ipswich* (1636) and *Divine Tragedie* (1636). In 1643 the first works from his own pen appeared: *Newes from Heaven of a Treaty of Peace* and *The Life of Faith*. The following year as John Spilsbury's assistant, he was a signatory and possible co-author of the confession of faith issued by seven Particular Baptist churches in London, which suggests that he worked closely with William Kiffin,* Thomas Patient,* Paul Hobson* and other Baptist leaders. The confession was virulently attacked by Daniel Featley in *The Dippers Dipt: or, the Anabaptists Duck'd and Plung'd* (1645), to which Richardson retorted in *Some Brief Considerations on Doctor Featley His Book* (1645). Nevertheless some of Featley's points were taken seriously, and the confession was revised and published in 1646, complete with an epistle to Parliament calling for toleration for the Baptists. With Benjamin Cox,* Richardson distributed copies of the revised confession to MPs in Jan. 1646, but for their pains the two men were taken before the bar of the Commons by the Serjeants-at-Arms, and the Stationers' Company was ordered to suppress the confession.

Richardson's involvement in revising the confession is indicated by his increasing efforts to spread the cause of toleration, beginning with his *Certain Questions* (10 Dec. 1646), subsequently reiterated in his *Fifty Questions Propounded to the Assembly* (21 May 1647) and ultimately his classic, *The Necessity of Toleration* (17 Sept. 1647). Religion, he argued, must be free and flow from 'an inward principle of faith and love.' To establish a church by law and require consent only wounds souls, particularly those of the godly if the religious laws are defective. Moreover public peace is enhanced by toleration. To

Richardson the Westminster Assembly was comprised of 'the men that have often deluded us, and thrust upon us errors for truths'; they are timeservers who once served bishops, and hypocrites who urge others to defend and contribute to the faith while themselves seeking exemptions. 'You have not studied a religion for us out of the word of God; but have borrowed us one out of Scotland,' so that 'we had as good be under the Pope, as under your Presbyterian check.' A copy of this work was in the library of John Milton's* friend, Nathan Paget.

Richardson also became embroiled in other controversies in 1647. His work, *The Saints Desire* (1647?), had been attacked by Homes and Huet, and in response he published a popular doctrinal tract in June entitled *Justification by Christ Alone*. Thomas Kilcop,* a fellow signatory of the first confession, in turn criticized Richardson in a millenarian tract, *Ancient and Durable Gospel* (1648). In 1647 Richardson bought up soldiers' arrears of pay for £1000, but shortly thereafter sustained a major financial loss when royalist privateers captured a ship in which he had a half interest. Loyal to the army, he supported a petition in 1647 in favor of Cromwell and Ireton's* policy of direct negotiations with the King. He subsequently defended Pride's purge and the army – 'the better part, wise and faithful,' of the nation – in Jan. 1649 in *An Answer to a London Ministers Letter* (dedicated to Cromwell and Fairfax*), which also attacked John Geree's *Might Overcoming Right*. His keen dislike of the Presbyterian clergy was again manifested. Another 1649 tract, *Divine Consolation*, carried an epistle by Maurice Thompson,* a leader of the war party in the City.

After the Leveller leaders Lilburne,* Walwyn,* Overton* and Prince* were arrested on 28 Mar. 1649, Richardson visited them in the Tower, hoping on behalf of the Baptists to persuade them to terminate their campaign against the government. According to Lilburne, Richardson, 'one we [had] judged honest and our friend,' was now a person who 'pretending a great deal of affection to the Commonwealth, to Cromwell and to us, pressed very hard for union and peace. . . .' When the mission failed, the Baptist pastors presented a petition to their congregations for subscription on 1 Apr. in which they dissociated themselves from the Levellers and professed their determination to advance the Gospel, not alter the civil government. The following day Richardson probably joined Kiffin, Patient, Spilsbury and others in presenting this petition to Parliament, which in turn assured them of liberty of conscience.

Richardson's concern for social reform was especially evident in his 1653 tract, The Cause of the Poor Pleaded (printed for Livewell Chapman*), in which he lamented that Catholics were more charitable than Protestants, called for an increase in charitable giving and jobs for the unemployed, and praised Cromwell's liberality to the poor. On 21 July 1653 he was appointed to the committee for the hospitals of the Savoy and Ely House. In Sept. 1654 Giles Calvert* published his tract castigating the Fifth Monarchists, An Apology for the Present Government and Governour, in which he declared: 'Whether the ways some take in opposing the present government, doth not declare their opposition is not from God, witness the publishing of a libel, called, A Declaration in the Names of Severall Churches. . . .'' John Spittlehouse* counterattacked in his Answer to One Part of the Lord Protector's Speech. Although Richardson himself had initially opposed the title of Lord Protector, John More's sermon on Nehemiah 9:27 changed his mind, and he distinguished himself as a staunch defender of the Protectorate, admiring its religious toleration and anticipating the abolition of tithes. In Plain Dealing (Jan. 1656), a government-distributed refutation of Vavasor Powell's* charge that Cromwell had betrayed the Good Old Cause, Richardson asserted that Cromwell 'aimeth at the general good of the nation, and just liberty of every man.' Contrary to Powell, he insisted that John Rogers* and Christopher Feake* had not been impris-

oned on a matter of conscience but for the civil peace of the commonwealth. The government duly rewarded him for his service. Fittingly, his final work was a radical theological tract, Of the Torments of Hell (1658), in which he repudiated the orthodox doctrine of perpetual punishment in the afterlife as contrary to 'the nature of the love, goodness and mercy of God.' This elicited various retorts, including a tract entitled Everlasting Fire No Fancy and Thomas Lewis' The Nature of Hell (1720). Richardson was noteworthy for his views on religious reform and his support of Cromwell, and to a lesser degree for his advocacy of social reform and radical theological conceptions.

CSPD, Chas. I, 11:49; CJ, 4:420-21; Lev. Tr.; Richardson, The Necessity of Toleration, in Tracts on Liberty of Conscience and Persecution 1614-1661, ed. E.B. Underhill (1846); Aylmer, SS; Tolmie; Brown; Jordan, 3; DNB; Lumpkin. Papers: O (Rawl. MS A38, f. 487).

R.L. Greaves and B.R. White

RIGBY (or Rigbie), Alexander (1594-1650)

Civil War officer and parliamentary radical, MP SP, LP 1640 (Wigan). Rigby was the eldest surviving son of Alexander Rigby (d. 1621) of Middleton Hall, Goosnargh, Lancs., and Alice, daughter of Leonard Ashawe, of Shaw, Lancs. Rigby was admitted to Gray's Inn on 1 Nov. 1610; he graduated B.A. from St. John's Coll., Camb. in 1614 and M.A. in 1615. He was called to the bar on 19 Nov. 1617, and then became Esquire of the Body to James I. Rigby became an ancient of Gray's Inn on 4 May 1638, the same day as Thomas Hammond.* Rigby served as JP for Lancashire in 1638 and then DL. By 1643 he purchased the Plough Patent at Sagadahock in New England and was owner of Ligonia (or Laconia) there by 1646. John Winthrop* described Rigby in 1643 as 'wealthy and religious.' Rigby's wealth and lands in Lancashire were devastated by the war, as he related early in 1647: 'I have had by the enemy all my mansion houses extremely plundered, defaced and left uninhabitable and even almost all my goods in them and upon my lands taken away . . . and yet during that time I have for the public service laid aside my profession formerly as profitable to me annually as my estate (as many of my countrymen know). . . .' There can be no doubt that Rigby was patriotically motivated. He adds: 'I have never suffered any of my county's money to come into my own hands. . . . I had . . . four weeks' pay . . . this being all that ever I received from the public for two years' service as a commander of horse and foot and sometimes of several regiments at once.' Elected to both Parliaments in 1640, Rigby's great fame as a lawyer brought him onto his first parliamentary committee almost immediately (3 Dec. 1640) to consider the judicial abuses of the Star Chamber and other courts, for which committee he made a legal report. A fortnight later he was on a committee inquiring into Laud, and from then on Rigby was a member of so many committees that he was, whenever in London, possibly the most industrious single MP until Augustine Garland* in the Rump. He delivered a speech in the House on 21 Dec. 1640 (*Master Rigby's Speech in Answer to the Lord Finch*, 29 June 1641), in which, attacking the courts, he called for dire justice against malefactors: 'Shall not some of them be hanged, that have robbed us of all our propriety? . . . [Let us] become not so merciful, that to the generality (the whole Kingdom) we may grow merciless.'

Rigby's military career began with the war itself. With John Moore* and Ralph Asheton, his two closest Lancashire colleagues, Rigby reported to Parliament on 25 June 1642 that they had secured the powder and match at Manchester, mustered and trained troops as DLs in Lancashire, negotiated a partial disengagement with the Royalist Lord Strange, and hindered other royalist maneuvers – all on their own initiative. Rigby was commissioned a colonel, and his success, according to Whitelocke,* was 'the more discoursed of because Rigby was a lawyer.' On 25 Sept. 1643 he captured Thurland Castle with 400 prisoners after a seven-week siege. One of Rigby's best-known exploits was his stubborn but unsuccessful siege of Lathom House, which he raised only on orders. In 1644 Rigby's house was established as part of a postal route for parliamentary communication with Scotland. Rigby was prominent on the Lancashire Committee which sent troops in 1645 to aid Sir William Brereton,* who was apparently a near relative of Rigby in Cheshire. Rigby was named reader at Gray's Inn, but from 1642 until his death never found time to teach law there. In 1648 Rigby again rallied his county in defense of Parliament, where he seems to have created a local force against all odds. Rigby and the future Regicides Challoner,* Scott* and Marten* were on a committee of five or six MPs selected as friends of the Levellers in late 1648 to negotiate with John Lilburne* about an *Agreement of the People*, though only Marten followed through with this entirely. Rigby was made Governor of Bolton (not Boston, as in the *DNB*) and named to the High Court, but declined to attend. On 1 June 1649 he was made Baron of the Exchequer and began his career as a judge. He was given special assignment not only to hold assizes but to act as parliamentary emissary in the West Country, which he did immediately, and on 7 Aug. 1649 wrote a long and remarkable letter to Lenthall,* saying 'we have used our best care and endeavor to improve the interest of Parliament in these parts,' with detailed accounts of his activities, high praise for Sir Hardress Waller,* suggestions that free quarter be abolished, and other helpful ideas to 'infinitely tie and confirm the minds of the people to the Parliament.' Rigby's judiciary travels exposed him to various epidemics, one of which felled him at the assizes of Croydon, Surrey, where he died on 19 Aug. 1650. Rigby left no will. His son Alexander was his lieutenant-colonel, and there was a cousin, Alexander Rigby of Burgh, Lancs., who was a

Royalist. Rigby's wife, Lucy, daughter of Sir Uriah Leigh, survived him. A fine miniature of Rigby by Oliver the Younger was engraved three times in the last century, when it was owned by a descendant, but its present whereabouts are unknown.

CSPD, Chas. 1, 16-20 *passim*; J. Winthrop, *Journal* (1853); *CJ*, 2:44, 52; Whitelocke, *Memorials*; *DNB*; *Clarke Papers*; *A True Relation of the Great Victory Obtained . . . in Lancashire* (1643); Keeler. Papers: L (Harl. MS 2043, ff. 1-7; Add. MS 11,332, ff. 33, 36v, 37r); O (Tanner MSS 56, ff. 89-90; 57/1, ff. 41-42; 59/2); OCC; OAS; OU.

R.K.G. Temple

RIGGE, Ambrose (c. 1635-1705)

Quaker, was born at Brampton, W'land, where he was educated at the free school. A schoolmaster at Brampton and Grayrigg, he was persuaded to become a Quaker at the age of eighteen by George Fox,* which resulted in Rigge's renunciation by his parents. In the spring of 1655 he went to London as an itinerant preacher, and there joined forces with Thomas Robertson of Westmorland for a preaching foray into the southern counties. While witnessing at a Baptist meeting in Rochester they were arrested and imprisoned. In July they suffered the same fate at Basingstoke, Hants., for refusing the oath abjuring papal authority. Rigge also suffered imprisonment at Bristol (with Robertson), on the Isle of Wight, at Southampton (1656), where in 1658 he was whipped as a vagabond and threatened with branding if he returned, and in Southwark (1657).

After the Restoration Rigge was arrested near Petersfield, Hants., and imprisoned in Winchester for refusing the oath. The King's Secretary, Sir Edward Nicholas, was informed of this by Sir Humphrey Bennet on 15 Jan. 1661, at which time Rigge's pamphlets were also sent to the court. Although released later that year, Rigge was apprehended again at the home of Capt. Thomas Luxford at Hurstpierpoint, Sussex, on 20 May 1662, and imprisoned at Horsham, despite promising (but not swearing) faith and allegiance. An appeal to the King on 16 Feb. 1663 was unsuccessful, though other Friends were released. While in prison he engaged in a pamphlet debate with Leonard Letchford, Vicar of Horsham, and married (6 Sept. 1664) Luxford's daughter Mary. Letchford subsequently prosecuted Rigge's wife for refusal to pay tithes, thus confiscating the furniture and cooking utensils in their cell. Although there was a warrant for Rigge's release dated 12 May 1669, he was still in prison on 27 Oct. 1671, when he again petitioned Charles for his freedom, noting that he had now been incarcerated ten years. A warrant for his pardon was issued in Feb. 1672, and he settled at Gatton, Surrey, where he taught in his home. The local vicar, Robert Pepys, prosecuted him in the Exchequer for refusing to pay tithes and charged him in July 1676 with Recusancy. Rigge served as clerk of the Quaker meeting at Reigate, and in 1687 attended a Quaker meeting in London with Fox, George Whitehead,* Charles Marshall* and others. Rigge's first wife, by whom he had five children, died in Jan. 1689, and on 12 May 1690 he wed Ann Bax of Capel, Surrey. The same year he preached at Fox's funeral. Rigge died at Reigate on 31 Jan. 1705, and was buried at Guildford. He was the author of 36 tracts, including the autobiographical *Brief and Serious Warning* (1678), which also attacks the life of a merchant because it often brings reproach on religious witnessing. Rigge's collected works were published in 1710 under the title *Constancy in Truth*.

CSPD, Chas. II, 1:473-74; 3:50; 9:323; 11:450; 12:170; Fox, *CJ*, 1:429, 442; 2 *passim*; Smith, *Cat.*; Besse, 1 *passim*; *DNB*. Papers: LF.

R.L. Greaves

RIGHTON, William (d. 1687)

Colonist and Fifth Monarchist, was husband to Sibilla, father to William, and brother to Stephen Righton, all settlers in Bermuda. Little educated and frequently in trouble with authorities, Righton alternately practiced tailoring, preaching, smuggling and amateur law. Once a servant to Hugh Peter,* he signed a Fifth Monarchist declaration in London in 1654. In Bermuda he was appointed preacher by the Somers Islands Company in Apr. 1655, only to be suspended in May 1656 for creating dissension. Despite previous anti-royalist rhetoric, he took the Oath of Allegiance and Supremacy at the Restoration. In the 1660s he was cited in Bermuda as a smuggler and unlicensed attorney; he also displeased authorities by defending Quakers in 1670. During the 1670s Righton sat in the General Assembly as disputes between the Company and Assembly multiplied. In 1681 he unsuccessfully petitioned the Crown to revoke the Company's charter and in 1683 brought to the Council charges against the acting governor, Henry Durham. In 1684 Righton helped write articles of complaint against the new governor, Thomas Cony. Facing insurrection in 1685, Cony cited 'old William Righton' as a leader of 'the Republican Party.' When in Dec. 1685 Righton was arrested for smuggling, rioting resulted. Righton was tried for treason in 1686 and ordered to England, the probable place of his death. His widow received £300 for damages in 1687 after Cony's dismissal.

Capp, *FMM*; *CSPC*, 7:512; 10:699; 11-12 *passim*; J.H. Lefroy, *Memorials of the . . . Bermudas* (1877-79).

D. Willen

RIVERS, James (1603-1641)

Parliamentary radical, MP SP, LP 1640 (Lewes). Rivers was the eldest surviving son of Sir John Rivers, Bt. (d.c. 1651), of Chafford, Kent, and Dorothy, daughter and co-heiress of Thomas Potter of Westerham. Rivers matriculated at Corpus Christi, Oxf. in 1616 and received his B.A. in 1620. In 1624 he married Charity, daughter and co-heiress of Sir John Shirley of Isfield, Sussex. After his marriage he seems to have lived primarily in Sussex, first at Isfield and by 1636 probably at Combe in Hamsey parish. Rivers served as JP for Sussex. In 1639 he was reported to be a prominent figure among Puritan JPs attempting to settle in civil courts such ecclesiastical questions as the location of communion tables. Rivers was reluctant to pay ship money in 1636 and refused to contribute money for the King's northern journey in 1639. Rivers supported the reformers in the Long Parliament and served on several committees, including those for encouraging preaching and for curbing the ecclesiastical courts and the Court of Star Chamber. He also signed the protestation for the defense of Protestantism in May 1641. Had he lived, Rivers might have become one of the parliamentary leaders, but he died on 8 June 1641 in London, probably of the plague.

Keeler; *Al. Oxon.*; Cokayne, *CB*; Rushworth, 3:914.

T.L. Moir

ROBARTES, John, first Earl of Radnor (1606-1685)

Civil War officer and parliamentary radical, was the son of the first Baron Robartes who had been forced to purchase his peerage by the Duke of Buckingham. Robartes' mother was Frances, daughter and coheir of John Hender. Succeeding his father as baron in 1634, Robartes inherited a substantial fortune from the family tin and other interests in Cornwall. He was one of 25 peers to oppose the King on the question of the precedence of supply over grievances in the Short Parliament. A strong Puritan, he supported Parliament enthusiastically throughout the quarrels with Charles I which preceded the Civil War. He pledged £1000 to its cause in June 1642, and became colonel of a regiment of horse under Essex,* being dispatched to Cornwall where he successfully relieved Plymouth in the spring of 1643. Although his children were taken hostage, his estate sequestered, and his home occupied, Robartes remained firm in his loyalties throughout the war and, in Aug. 1644, became Governor of Plymouth at the request of the town. He fought with conspicuous courage in a number of Civil War battles and was elevated to the rank of Field Marshal. Robartes served as a member of the Committee of Both Kingdoms in 1644 but, although a Presbyterian, he objected to the subordination of the church to Parliament. He also disagreed with the vote of 'no addresses' to the King taken in Jan. 1648. Growing differences with the leadership of Parliament caused him to absent himself from the House of Lords for a number of months in late 1647 and he returned only when fined for his lack of attendance. He sought and obtained leave to retire to Cornwall in Apr. 1648 and thereafter took no role in political affairs during the Interregnum. In 1650, due to negotiations between Charles II and the Scots, Robartes' Presbyterian sympathies made him suspect by the government and he was ordered by the Council of State to remove his residence from the west where he had great influence. He moved to Essex and gave £20,000 surety for his good behavior. He appears to have been in contact with the Royalists throughout the 1650s, although he refused to correspond with any of the exiled supporters of the King. At the Restoration Robartes became a Privy Councillor and Deputy Lieutenant of Ireland. He also served on the Commission for the Treasury and the Committee of Trade (1660), was Speaker of the House of Lords and Lord Privy Seal (1661-73), Lord Lieutenant of Ireland (1669-79) and Lord President of the Council (1679-84). In July 1679 he was created Earl of Radnor. Robartes married firstly (1630) Lucy, daughter of Robert, second Earl of Warwick* by Frances, daughter and heir of Sir

William Hatton, and secondly (1646-47) Letitia Isabella, daughter of Sir John Smith of Bidborough. Contemporaries, including political opponents, agreed on his exceptional abilities, personal integrity and bad temper. There is no biography of Radnor.

Coate; *DNB*; Cokayne, *CP*; Zagorin, *CC*; MacCormack; Hexter. Papers: CCC; O; L (Add. MSS; Harl. MSS; Sloane MSS; Stowe MSS).

J.S. Flemion

ROBERTS, Timothy (d. 1665)

Fifth Monarchist and ejected minister, was born in Wales. Little is known of his family or early life save that his brother, Jonathan, was also an ejected minister deprived of a living in Wales. Roberts matriculated at Jesus Coll., Oxf. on 21 July 1651 and was graduated B.A. from New College on 22 June 1655. A man of great learning, he especially impressed contemporaries with his knowledge of Hebrew and his abilities as a preacher. Roberts was admitted as Vicar of Barton, W'land, a thinly populated parish north of Ullswater and west of Penrith, on 9 Nov. 1655. Unable to accept the Restoration religious settlement, he was ejected in 1663. His successor at Barton was installed on 3 Feb. His involvement as a Fifth Monarchist seems to have occurred mainly after 1660. Following Venner's* rising, Nathaniel Strange* denounced King and government and urged a violent rising of Fifth Monarchists in London, which Roberts assured of support in the north. An informant in Westmorland reported his preaching activities in 1663 and he was imprisoned at Appleby. In London in 1665, he was infected with the plague and died alone along the highway between Shrewsbury and Oswestry, Shrops.

Calamy Revised; Capp, *FMM*; B. Nightingale, *The Ejected of 1662 in Cumberland and Westmorland* (1911).

M.J. Galgano

ROBERTS, Sir William (1605-1662)

City radical and Commonwealth minister. Roberts was the twin son of Barne Roberts (d. 1610) of Willesden, Middlesex, by Mary, daughter of Sir William Glover, a London alderman. Roberts also had mercantile connections on his mother's side. His brother's death in 1619 left him sole heir, and by 1631 he was wealthy. He studied at Queens' and Emmanuel Coll., Camb., under John Preston,* as well as at Gray's Inn, which he entered on 7 Aug. 1622. He was knighted on 18 May 1624. At the outbreak of the Civil War he was appointed DL of Middlesex, and from 1643 was named to every committee or commission concerned with his county. In 1646 he was appointed a contractor for the sale of episcopal lands and in 1649-50 for crown and capitular lands and fee-farm rents. In May 1650 he was designated Militia Commissioner for Middlesex. He served as Trustee for the sale of lands forfeited for treason (1651-53), and was named to the commission for removing obstructions to the sale of crown and church lands (Apr. 1652), the commission for the sale of forfeited estates (June 1653), the Council of State (Nov. 1653), and the commission to inspect the treasuries (Dec.). In the Council he served on various committees, including those for lunatics, ordnance, the mint and the preservation of customs. He was also a commissioner for appeals in excise (1654), a commissioner for the sale of crown lands (1654), a Wine License Agent (1655), an Accounts Commissioner (1655), JP for Middlesex (1655), and Auditor of the Exchequer (1654-60). A Puritan, Roberts was appointed to the Hale Commission for law reform in Jan. 1652. He sat for Middlesex in the Parliaments of 1653 and 1656, and on 9 Dec. 1657 was summoned to sit in the Upper House. With Sir James Harrington, he was un unsuccessful candidate in Apr. 1660 for election to Parliament from Brentford, Middlesex. In 1655 he was set upon by thieves near Tyburn and one of his sons killed. At the Restoration Roberts lost his offices and a £1077 investment in North-amptonshire bishops' lands, but suffered no further penalty. Named to the High Court in 1649, he had prudently declined to serve. He remained in relative favor with the new regime, and on 8 Nov. 1661 his eldest son was created a baronet. Roberts died a wealthy man and was buried on 27 Mar. 1662 at Willesden. He was survived by his wife Eleanor, the daughter and heiress of Robert Atye, esq., of Kilburn, and numerous children.

CSPD, Comm., 2:157; 5:398, 414-15; 6 *passim*; 7:35, 343; 8:51, 94; 9:14; *CCSP*, 4:644; Abbott, 3:120, 417, 509; 4:685, 951; Aylmer, *SS*; *DNB*.

R.L. Greaves and R. Zaller

ROBINS, John (fl. 1650-1652)

Millenarian, left no writings of his own; his views must be reconstructed from essentially hostile sources. Initially a farmer, he sold his land and moved to London with his wife (variously called Joan and Mary) prior to 1650. Apparently poorly educated, he claimed to be the recipient of divine revelation, including knowledge of Hebrew, Greek and Latin. By 1650 he had gathered a group of disciples, the chief of whom was Joshua Garment, author of *The Hebrews Deliverance at Hand* (1651). According to Lodowick Muggleton,* Robins claimed to be God Almighty, the judge of the quick and the dead, and the reincarnation of Adam and Melchizedek. Among his powers was the ability to raise the dead, including Cain and Judas (both of whom were redeemed and happy), Jeremiah and other prophets, and Jacob's son Benjamin. Muggleton averred that he personally saw these people at Robins' house and that 'they owned themselves to be the very same persons that had been dead for so long time.' Clearly Robins' disciples were beguiled into a version of psychical role-playing which initially impressed Muggleton and John Reeve.* The latter was 'overpowered' by Robins' knowledge and language, including his cognizance of the names and nature of angels, and his avowal that Christ was a weak, imperfect savior.

Robins was an illusionist of extraordinary powers. He presented 'the appearance of angels, burning shining lights, half-Moons and stars in chambers and thick darkness, where it was light to the phantasies of people, when they covered their faces in the bed.' The apocalyptic illusions or visions included serpents, dragons, and a messianic figure (who was Robins himself) riding on the wings of the wind with his head in flames. His ascendancy was such that his disciples knelt and prayed to him, and he in turn gave them authority to damn his opponents, who would be destroyed if his apostles clapped their hands and stomped their feet. As part of his plan to mobilize 144,000 men and women to take (with Garment as his Moses) to Mt. Olivet, dividing the Red Sea and feeding them heavenly manna, he made his disciples (in the manner of Acts 4) 'bring in their estates.' When they obeyed his command to abstain from food by degrees as preparation for the assault on the Holy Land, eating only bread, fruit and water, some died. His followers were allowed to switch spouses, as he himself did, though his wife expected to give birth to the messiah.

On 24 May 1651 Robins, his wife, Garment and seven disciples were arrested at a meeting in Long Alley, Moorfields. Taken before Thomas Hubert, a Middlesex JP, Robins disavowed divinity and claimed only to be a vehicle of divine inspiration, though his disciples asserted he was God. When Garment and the female disciples threw themselves at Robins' feet and Garment begged Robins to deliver them, Robins stomped on the floor, clapped his hands and proclaimed, 'Arise and be hanged.' Instead the motley band was incarcerated in New Bridewell, Clerkenwell, where visitors disputed with them.

On 5 Feb. 1652 Muggleton, Reeve and Mrs. Dorcas Boose visited Robins, denouncing him as the head of all false Christs and prophets. After they left,

Robins 'had a burning in his throat, as if he should be burned to ashes,' and an inner voice told him to recant. About two months later he retracted his views in a letter to Cromwell and was released from prison. He returned to the country, repurchased his land, and died in obscurity. In addition to his influence on Muggleton and Reeve, he may have had some impact on Thomas Tany.* Although Muggleton regarded the Quakers as 'the very influence of John Robins' witchcraft spirit,' there is no evidence that he impressed the Friends. Robins had no direct connection with the Ranter movement, though his sexual promiscuity, damnation of opponents, and primitive communism are shared with the Ranters. Probably the closest group to Robins was that which centered around William Franklin* and Mary Gadbury* at Winchester, for it too had a messianic figure and a woman who played the role of Mary.

L. Muggleton, *The Acts of the Witnesses of the Spirit* (1699); J. Reeve, *A Transcendent Spiritual Treatise* (1652); *All the Proceedings at the Sessions of the Peace Holden at Westminster* (1651); G.H., *The Declaration of John Robins the False Prophet* (1651); *DNB*; Morton; Hill, *WTUD*; D.S. Katz, *Philo-Semitism and the Readmission of the Jews to England 1603-1655* (1982).

R.L. Greaves

ROBINSON, Henry (c. 1605-c. 1673)

Educational, medical and legal reformer, was the eldest son of William Robinson of London, merchant, and Katherine, daughter of Gifford Watkins of Watford, Northants. Robinson matriculated at St. John's Coll., Oxf. in Nov. 1621. He did not take a degree but entered into business and was admitted to the freedom of the Mercers' Company (1626) and became a merchant in the Duchy of Tuscany and London. In two works of the early 1640s, *England's Safety* (1641) and *Liberty of Conscience* (1643), he joined with Roger Williams* and John Milton* in a plea for toleration and freedom of conscience. As a successful and wealthy merchant, as business agent for Lord Stanhope and as Comptroller for the sale of crown lands, Robinson commanded great respect in his views on business, especially his opposition to monopoly and his enlightened approach to the promotion of trade and colonization in the 1650s.

Robinson's most radical proposals concerned the law. In *Certaine Considerations in Order to a More Speedy, Cheap, and Equall Distribution of Justice* (1650), Robinson called on Parliament to abolish trial by jury. He believed that justice should not be dependent upon human emotions, which made the jury system unworkable. The law was in need of reform but also in need of removal from popular control. That removal could be established through a decentralized system of county courts staffed by JPs appointed by the Council of State or Parliament and serving for three to five years. Robinson saw such a system eliminating popular control of justice and producing a uniform law throughout the country. Robinson's attack on the juries prompted retorts from lawyers and laymen such as his friend and fellow merchant William Walwyn* in his *Juries Justified* (1650).

In *Certaine Proposals in Order to a New Modelling of the Laws* (1653), Robinson, writing just after the dissolution of the Rump, attacked the lawyers for what he considered their attempt to nullify the work of the Hale Commission (1652). Robinson claimed that the lawyers in the Rump allowed the Commission to proceed only after discoveries were made in the irregularities of the bar. Nevertheless, he believed the Commission itself to have been controlled by the lawyers in Parliament because the Rump was unable to enact any of the proposals sent it by the Commission. Robinson, a close associate of the educational reformers John Dury* and Samuel Hartlib,* urged the founding of a state school system to provide free education to children of both sexes, as well as admission of poor scholars to the universities. Robinson's suggestion for a national system of workhouses to educate as well as employ the poor was later taken up by Hartlib. His proposals for reform of the medical establishment were even more striking. Robinson wished to see 'physicians and chirurgeons . . . appointed in every county throughout the nation . . . at the public charge' to provide their services daily 'without any other fee or consideration, but what the state allows them,' as well as to erect and endow free public hospitals in each county, 'as well to prevent sickness before it comes, as when it hath seized on [the poor].' As Charles Webster points out, 'This ideal not only outstripped the imagination of [Robinson's] contemporaries, but has scarcely approached realization in the modern welfare state.' Dury and Hartlib also entrusted to Robinson their proposal for establishing an 'Office of Address' to serve as a state-run clearinghouse for invention and reform.

Robinson served in several official capacities during the Interregnum as Auditor of Excise and later Secretary to the Excise Commission, Comptroller (1649) for the sale of crown lands and a member of the Committee for Taking the Accounts of the Commonwealth. After the Restoration he claimed to have increased the Post Office Revenues for the crown from £3000 to £30,000 p.a. Robinson's later years are obscure. He died about 1673.

In the breadth of his interests, Robinson had few peers in the period. Like Robert Owen in a later age, he was a successful businessman turned radical reformer who looked on men and institutions alike with a critical and pragmatic eye. The promotion of trade, education and public health were all in his view practical measures designed to augment the wealth and well-being of the commonwealth. It was typical of him that he was equally skeptical of lawyers and lay juries. His ideal, like that of Harrington* and Henry Parker,* was an aristocratic secular republic controlled by the landed and commercial classes and functioning on rational principles.

W.K. Jordan, *Men of Substance* (1942); Prall; Veall; Judson, *TPR*; Worden; *DNB*; Aylmer, *SS*; Webster, *GI*.

A.J. Busch and R. Zaller

ROBINSON, John (1575-1625)

Separatist minister, was born of a substantial yeoman family in Sturton-le-Steeple, and matriculated at Corpus Christi Coll., Camb. on 9 Apr. 1592, receiving a fellowship in 1598 and an M.A. in 1599. After a moderately successful career as Reader in Greek, he resigned his fellowship on 10 Feb. 1604, and married Bridget White. By then Robinson was seeking a position at the parish church of St. Andrews, Norwich. According to a report filed with John Jegon, Bishop of Norwich, Robinson preached in the parish on 5 Aug. 1603; while expressing 'great hope' for the Gospel under the new King, James I, he nevertheless vehemently attacked abuses by the magistrates, the unlearned ministry of 'dumb dogs,' common laywers, and the 'intolerable' corruption of the church courts. The sermon offended Jegon, but after months of negotiations led by several prominent citizens and the Rector of St. Andrews, Robinson was given the curacy. Within a year or two he was suspended, probably during the Norwich deprivations of 1605 and 1606. Robinson began to move gradually in the direction of Separatism, apparently after failing to gain either the Mastership of the Great Hospital or a lease from the city to preach. He reportedly gathered for private meetings a group of laymen from St. Andrews, all of whom were subsequently excommunicated. Active, restless and increasingly troubled, Robinson began traveling between Norwich, Sturton-le-Steeple, Coventry and Cambridge, preaching and seeking advice from other 'forward professors.' At Sturton in May 1605 seventeen people were fined for having been absent from their own parishes in order to listen to Robinson preach. Traveling to Cambridge, Robinson

heard Laurence Chaderton argue on the basis of Matt. 18:17 that power for church discipline resided in the body of the church, and from Paul Baynes* about the importance of separating the godly from the profane (Robinson, *A Manumission* [1615], p. 20). He also attended one of several Puritan conferences at the Coventry home of Sir William Bowes which included Arthur Hildersam,* Richard Bernard and John Smyth,* who by this time had already embraced Separatism and was probably instrumental in leading Robinson into the cluster of Separatists in the Gainsborough and Scrooby area (Robinson, *Justification*, p. 10). While Smyth provided the leadership of the Gainsborough Separatists, Robinson joined the sister church at Scrooby along with William Bradford,* William Brewster* and Richard Clifton. Soon, however, they decided to emigrate because of the persecution they experienced from local ecclesiastical courts. After several months of official harassment, fines and imprisonment, they managed in Aug. 1608 to reach Amsterdam, already the home of the Ancient Separatist church led by Francis Johnson* and Henry Ainsworth.* It was evidently at that time that the Scrooby congregation elected and ordained Robinson as their pastor. They remained in Amsterdam less than a year. The Ancient church had a long history of internal conflict and when in the fall of 1608 John Smyth caused another tumult with his Se-baptism, Robinson and his congregation decided to move on. Early in Feb. 1609 they applied to the burgomasters of Leiden for permission to reside there. By April they were resettled in Leiden, where Robinson wrote all but one of the 29 letters and treatises that make up the corpus of his writings. His major work, *A Justification of Separation* (1610), was essentially an elaboration of the arguments already raised by Smyth and Ainsworth against the anti-Separatist polemic of Richard Bernard. Robinson identified strongly with the tradition of Separatism by referring to the 1598 Latin edition of the Separatist *Confession* as the one 'we published' as 'our testimony,' and writing favorably of Henry Barrow, John Greenwood and Francis Johnson (*Justification*, pp. 47-48, 83-87). In an earlier work entitled 'An Answer to a Censorious Epistle' (c. 1608, known only from the marginal notes of J. Hall, *Common Apologie*), he drew heavily on the writings of Barrow, Johnson and other Separatists. He also used the first person plural, another grammatical mannerism used throughout his writings by which he identified corporately with the tradition.

While Robinson remained a committed Separatist, he nevertheless modified the tradition at two significant points. In 1614, after three years of debate with William Ames* over the issue of religious communion, Robinson subtly shifted his position by making room for private communion with godly members of the Church of England (*Of Religious Communion Private and Public*, p. 14). A decade later he wrote *A Treatise of the Lawfulness of Hearing of the Ministers in the Church of England*, published posthumously in 1635, in which he argued for the lawfulness of occasionally listening to sermons in the Puritan parishes of England. While the reason for these modifications probably stemmed in part from the influence of William Ames, Henry Jacob* and Robert Parker,* who met in Leiden with Robinson in 1610, it is misleading to suggest, as several historians have, that they indicate he had laid aside his Separatism for non-separating Independency. Robinson continued to be convinced that private communion opposed 'no article of our confession' (*Religious Communion*, p.15), and in spite of his modification of 1614 he boldly reaffirmed his commitment to Separatism, arguing that the constitution of even the Puritan parishes remained so evil 'that no engine of wit . . . can so batter it, as to make safe passage through it for good conscience' (*Manumission*, p. 1). While in 1624 he claimed to share one faith and baptism with godly members of the Church of England, this was in fact a common Separatist argument running at least as far back as Barrow. In spite of his tolerant views on listening, Robinson remained persuaded that he could never 'communicate' with the Church of England 'without being condemned of my own heart' (*Lawfulness*, p. 64).

Evidence about Robinson's life in Leiden outside the realm of ecclesiological debate is slim. Alongside his pastoral duties, he became involved in the academic circles of Leiden, matriculating at the University in Sept. 1615. At one time he reportedly disputed with the Arminian Episcopius, putting his opponent, as the story goes, 'to an apparent *non plus*' (Bradford, *History*, 1:48-50). In 1617 the Leiden Separatists began to make preparations to move to New England. The 'Mayflower' sailed in 1620, taking less than half the Leiden congregation. Robinson hoped to join the small community that settled Plymouth Colony, but died while still in Leiden on 1 Mar. 1625. Other major works by Robinson include: *The Peoples Plea for the Exercise of Prophesie* (1618); *A Defence of the Synod at Dort* (1624); *A Just and Necessary Apology* (1625); *Observations Divine and Morall* (1625).

R. Ashton, ed., *The Works of John Robinson*, 3 vols. (1851); W. Burgess, *John Robinson* (1920); T. Barton, ed., *Registrum Vagum of Anthony Harrison*, 2 vols. (1963); A.C. Carter, 'John Robinson and the Dutch Reformed Church,' *Studies in Church History*, 3:232-41; White; R.M. Bartlett, *The Pilgrim Way* (1971); S.J. Brachlow, 'Puritan Theology and Radical Churchmen in Pre-Revolutionary England with Special Reference to Henry Jacob and John Robinson (D.Phil. thesis, Oxford Univ., 1979).

S.J. Brachlow

ROBINSON, Luke (1610-1669)

Parliamentary radical, MP 1645 (Scarborough), 1655 (Yorks.), 1658 (Malton, disputed), 1660 (Scarborough). Robinson was the eldest son of Sir Arthur Robinson, Kt. and sometime High Sheriff of Yorkshire, and his wife Elizabeth, daughter of

William Walthall, Alderman of London. The family descended from John Robinson, a London merchant who settled in the county in late Elizabethan times. Luke Robinson, distinguished as 'of Thornton Risborough,' was educated in a number of local schools having a high incidence of nonconforming masters, matriculated at Christ's Coll., Camb. in May 1627, and was admitted to Gray's Inn in Feb. 1630. He married three times: to Frances, a daughter of Phinias Hodgson, D.D. of York, in May 1633; to Mary, daughter of Edward Pennel of Woodhall, Worcs. in 1636; and to Judith, daughter of Sir John Reade, Kt., of Wrangle, Lincs., after Aug. 1642.

Robinson's first appearance as a radical was as a member of Yorkshire parliamentary committees in 1644, and he was recruited for Scarborough to the Long Parliament in Oct. 1645. There he was extremely active in committees, especially on religious matters, and was named one of the commissioners to deal with the King at Newcastle in May 1646. In Feb. 1649 he was named to the committee to nominate the first Council of State. After the adoption of the list drawn up by the committee, Robinson was added to the Council by the Rump. He served diligently through 1649, and fitfully in the winter of 1650-51, acquiring a reputation for competence in foreign affairs, trade and the navy, and was named to the Commission for the Admiralty and Navy in Mar. 1650. Because his county connections were considered crucial, he was dispatched to York to bolster the committee there and appointed vice-admiral for the county in 1651.

Named to the Barebones Parliament, Robinson refused the summons and apparently reduced his public role until returned for the North Riding to the second Protectorate Parliament. His contributions to the debates in that Parliament reveal the color of his republicanism. He spoke clearly and wittily for tolerance in religion, including a defense of James Nayler,* equality before the law, merciful justice, resistance to special interests, and above all, parliamentary supremacy over judges and even the Protector himself. He stridently opposed the Humble Petition and served as teller for the opposition in divisions on the matter. After the establishment of the Upper House, Robinson refused to consider it as other than an ancillary of the Commons, and together with Thomas Scott* and Arthur Haselrig* sought to restrain the monarchist tendencies of the late Protectorate through parliamentary obstruction. At the same time he supported John Desborough's* motion to create a strong Parliament-controlled militia financed through further liens on former Royalists' estates.

Robinson's unflinching republicanism brought about a challenge to his election for Malton in the Parliament of Richard Cromwell.* John Lambert* spoke in his support but Robinson was unseated by a vote of 173-142. The restoration of the Rump brought him back to Westminster and to the Council of State, and for a brief time in early 1660 Luke Robinson was among the leaders of Parliament. He and Thomas Scott were the chief liaison between the Rump and Monck, and in the discussions for the restoration of the purged members it was Robinson who mediated. The Long Parliament again sitting, Robinson's leadership role was eclipsed, though he retained several committee seats. Returned for Scarborough to the Convention of 1660, he quickly adopted a royalist position, but to little avail, and in June he was expelled from the House and briefly imprisoned, though he made a tearful abjuration at the bar of Commons; he then retired from public life. His friendship toward Quakers was remarked by George Fox.* Robinson died sometime between July and Oct. 1669.

Burton; *CSPD, Comm.*, 1; Cliffe; Davies, *RC*; Gooder; G. Davies, 'The Election of Richard Cromwell's Parliament,' *EHR*, 53:488-501; Worden; Underdown, *PP*. Papers: L (Add. MSS).

J.F. Battick

ROGERS, Daniel (1573-1652)

Puritan minister, was born in Wethersfield, Essex, the eldest son of the Puritan journalist, Richard Rogers.* Daniel and his younger brother Ezekiel, who later emigrated to New England, both attended Cambridge. Rogers cut a brilliant figure as student and fellow of Christ's College; he even downed William Laud in a debate. Soon after receiving a B.D. (1606) and relinquishing his fellowship (1608), he married and began his ministry. His first wife, a quick-tempered woman, died after bearing only one son, also named Daniel. His second wife, Sarah, bore him eight children (the *DNB* is inaccurate; Daniel's daughters did not marry the Rev. W. Jenkyn). The eldest son, Samuel, left a diary from the 1630s that reveals much about the Rogers' family life. Rogers regularly catechized his family and disciplined his children. Samuel himself grew to admire his father's *Practicall Catechism*, one of the best examples of spiritual exercises required for a godly life. In the catechism Rogers urged heads of families to watch out for their children. He imposed such authority on his sons even after they passed beyond age 21, and his demands were a source of ongoing tension in Samuel's diary. As much as Rogers cared for his family, his clerical duties made heavy demands. He lectured at various places in the early 1620s, including the parish church of Adam and John Winthrop* in Groton, Suff. In 1624 he acquired his father's former lectureship at Wethersfield, Essex. There he remained until his death, a busy extra-parochial minister among neighboring laymen and clergymen, and a source of irritation to his old adversary, William Laud. In the later 1620s he met frequently with a 'conference' of Puritan ministers that resembled the Braintree classis in which Richard Rogers had participated during the 1580s. Daniel's conference included such disruptive Puritans as Nathaniel Ward, a half brother of Daniel, minister at Stondon Massey and later of New England; Samuel Wharton of Felsted; and Thomas Weld,* Vicar of Terling and later of New England. The conference also probably included Thomas Hooker,* Jeremiah Burroughs* and John Beadle, all of whom became well known. This conference gave a lectureship at Earl's Colne to Thomas Shepard,* later a famous preacher and autobiographer in New England. Laud suspended Rogers from the Wethersfield lectureship for nonconformity in June 1632, and though Rogers continued to preach in Essex, he may not have officially resumed his lectureship until 1640. Despite his difficulties, Rogers found favor among the leading lay patrons of the area, most notably the Barringtons* and the Earl of Warwick,* whose family members received dedications in books by Rogers. At the crucial election for knights of the shire early in 1640, the Earl of Warwick commanded that Rogers, then silenced by church courts, be seated among the notables. Rogers returned to his lectureship in the 1640s, but, now aged, did not take a major role in the Revolution, though in 1649 he led a protest in Essex against toleration for those who refused to sign the Solemn League and Covenant. Rogers died on 16 Sept. 1652.

DNB; M.M. Knappen, ed., *Two Elizabethan Puritan Diaries* (1933); Haller, *LRPR*. Papers: L (Eg. MSS 2648, ff. 142, 144); S. Rogers' diary, BQ (Percy MSS 7).

K.W. Shipps

ROGERS, Humphrey (fl. 1650-1651)

Mechanic preacher, was involved in a dispute over the right of laymen to preach that took place in Henley-in-Arden, about fifteen miles southeast of Birmingham, Warks., on 20 Aug. 1650. With other mechanic preachers, including Lawrence Williams, a nail-maker, Thomas Hinde, a plough-wright, Henry Oakes, a weaver, and Thomas Palmer, a baker, Rogers, described as (lately) a baker's-boy-public-preacher, debated with Thomas Hall, who argued that preaching by laymen was unlawful and dangerous. Hall saw Rogers and his friends as descendants of the Anabaptists of Münster, turbulent subverters of the very foundations of the state, sowing error and heresy. The mechanics argued that they excelled many ministers in their ability to preach and expound Scripture and were but imitating Jesus. When Hall cited the works of Theodore Beza, William Perkins and John Cotton* against lay preaching, Rogers and his friends cited Acts 8:4, where those who were persecuted went about preaching, Acts 18:24-25, where the story of Apollos is told, 1 Cor. 14:1-31, where instructions are given on prophesying, and 1 Pet. 2:9, where the priesthood of believers is articulated. Hall published his side of the debate in 1651 under the title *The Pulpit Guarded*. There is no further information about Rogers' career.

T. Hall, *The Pulpit Guarded* (1651); Greaves, *PRET*.

T.W. Hayes

ROGERS, John (c. 1572-1636)

Puritan minister, was the second son of John Rogers and a nephew of Richard Rogers,* the Puritan diarist, who helped to raise young John. After degrees at Cambridge University, John became Vicar of Honingham, Norf. in 1592. In 1603 he succeeded Lawrence Fairclough, father of Samuel Fairclough,* as Vicar of Haverhill, Suff. In 1605 he moved to the lectureship of Dedham where he continued until his death. There he gained the reputation as one of 'the most awakening preachers of the age.' His church overflowed on his Tuesday lecture; the preaching drew hundreds from miles around and divinity students from Cambridge. In 1626 Rogers publicly encouraged the townsmen to resist the forced loan of Charles I and in 1629 he was reported as not reading the divine service in a surplice. On two occasions in the early 1630s Bishop Laud called Rogers before him and asked for a

subscription to the Three Articles. Rogers refused the first time but later submitted. Even so, Rogers rarely wore the surplice or used the Book of Common Prayer in services, and he suffered a long suspension in 1635, allegedly because of an infectious plague, but in reality when Bishop Wren found himself unable to escape ecclesiastical disturbances at Ipswich because the citizens had monopolized all available horses to attend Rogers' lecture. The authorities presently allowed Rogers to preach again, but he died on 18 Oct. 1636 before he could resume his duties. Later recollections claimed that Rogers had been the 'prince of all preachers in England.'

DNB; C. Mather, *Magnalia Christi Americana*, ed. K.B. Murdock (1977); K.W. Shipps, 'Lay Patronage of East Anglian Puritan Clerics in Pre-revolutionary England' (Ph.D. diss., Yale Univ., 1971); *Winthrop Papers* (1929-47), 3:58-59. Papers: LG (MS 9331/15, ff. 24-25).

K.W. Shipps

ROGERS, John (1627-c. 1665)

Independent minister and Fifth Monarchist, was born in Messing, Essex, the second son of Nehemiah Rogers (1594-1660), vicar of the parish, and his wife Margaret. As a boy Rogers was tormented by overwhelming fears of sin and eternal damnation. His deep conviction of personal guilt led to 'raging fits' and several suicide attempts before he finally discovered in Puritanism a sense of religious purpose and personal salvation that freed him from emotional turmoil. Rogers' association with Puritans greatly distressed his Anglican father. When Nehemiah was turned out of his living by the Puritans in Oct. 1642, he banished his son, now fifteen, from the family home.

John fled to Cambridge where he was already a student of medicine and a servitor at King's College. Shortly after he arrived parliamentary forces took control of the colleges and dismissed the servitors, which reduced Rogers to eating grass, leather and old quill pens to stay alive. In early 1643 he obtained a teaching position in Huntingdonshire and within a few months gained a favorable reputation as a preacher among the Presbyterian congregations of the district. He was ordained a Presbyterian minister in 1647 and soon thereafter was appointed Rector of Purleigh, one of the best livings in Essex. At age 20 he married Elizabeth, daughter of Sir Robert Payne of Midloe.

Rogers' Puritanism constantly put him at odds with his conservative congregation at Purleigh. Finally, unable to accept the rigidity of Presbyterian doctrine, discipline and custom, he hired a curate to administer his parish, moved to London in late 1648 and renounced his Presbyterian ordination. He began to preach strongly in favor of Independency, arguing that England's oppressive burden of tithes, restrictive social structure and unjust laws were due to the popish influence of Anglicanism and Presbyterianism. In Jan. 1649 he was appointed Independent lecturer at St. Thomas Apostle's Church, London. For the next two years he used the influence of this position to attack the Presbyterians and to support the Independent MPs in their efforts to initiate political, social and religious change. In 1651 the Council of State sent Rogers to Dublin's Christ Church Cathedral to establish a stronghold of Independency in Ireland. He was unable to heal a schism in that congregation, and in Mar. 1652 he returned to St. Thomas Apostle's.

By now the Rump Parliament had proved itself to be a cautious and indecisive body not at all intent on carrying out revolutionary social, religious, legal or economic reforms. Consequently many Independents shifted their loyalties to Oliver Cromwell and the New Model Army. Rogers, likewise disillusioned with Parliament, aligned himself with the Fifth Monarchists. Since the execution of Charles I this collection of millenarians, Antinomians, Puritans and Independents had grown into an influential sect. Intent

on preparing England for the imminent establishment of Christ's kingdom on earth, the Fifth Monarchists added the force of divine directive to demands for the abolition of tithes, the reduction of taxes, revision of the legal system, reform of the clergy and the removal of corrupt government officials. Rogers quickly adopted their approach to his own goals, and by 1653 he had become a recognized leader of the sect.

Rogers was a Fifth Monarchist more from convenience than from conviction. He did not have the intellectual commitment to radical millenarianism that led Christopher Feake,* Vavasor Powell* and John Simpson* to seek merely the destruction of existing political and religious institutions. As a reformer, Rogers believed the saints' responsibilities went beyond destruction to the reconstruction of earthly society. He also realized that Englishmen would not surrender the security of traditional institutions for something as unspecific as godly government. Therefore he proposed that man-made government was acceptable to Christ and could even become godly if its leaders corrected their laws in accordance with divine reason. Such laws would include annual election of government officials, the abolition of exorbitant legal fees, the revision of taxes and the adoption of new standards of accountability for lawyers, public officials and church leaders. In effect, Rogers sanctioned the acceptance of something other than the immediate establishment of the kingdom of Christ on earth, and for this he drew the censure of the more radical Fifth Monarchists.

The dissolution of the Rump Parliament in Apr. 1653 brought the Fifth Monarchists to the height of their activity and influence. Believing Cromwell to be a champion of reform, Rogers led the majority of the sect in supporting the Commonwealth of Saints. Many Fifth Monarchists became members of the Nominated Parliament, and to it they attached all their hopes for a new heavenly order. When Cromwell accepted the resignation of that body in Dec. 1653 and assumed the title of Lord

Protector, these hopes were destroyed. Rogers, however, was not totally convinced of Cromwell's perfidy. Because he realized that the accomplishment of all the reforms he had proposed since 1648 now lay within the power of the Lord Protector, he did not publicly attack Cromwell though he warned him against heeding the exigencies of politics instead of his own conscience. In short he reserved judgment on the Lord Protector to see what use he would make of his virtually unbridled power.

Under the authority of a new Treason Ordinance passed in Jan. 1654, all Fifth Monarchists were subject to close surveillance and almost total censorship by the government. Christopher Feake and John Simpson were imprisoned. In Apr. 1654 Rogers' own house was searched and his papers seized. He was not fully persuaded that Cromwell was an apostate to the cause of Christ and to the principles of civil and religious liberty. In a terse public epistle devoid of Fifth Monarchist exhortations, he likened the Protectorate to the arbitrary government of King Charles, and then demanded that Cromwell demonstrate his commitments to impartial justice, civil liberty, religious freedom and representative government by releasing Feake and Simpson and restoring to all men the right to preach and publish. In July 1654 he was arrested and imprisoned at Lambeth Palace.

With each week of his confinement, Rogers' anger and fanaticism grew. In Feb. 1655 he was granted a personal audience with the Lord Protector. Because he had never been charged with a specific crime, he was anxious to confront the man he held responsible for his imprisonment. Cromwell hoped to persuade Rogers that their goals were still compatible, and to extract a promise from him that he would refrain from public invective against the government, but Rogers was implacable. Imprisonment had transformed the once cautious Puritan reformer and moderate millenarian into a radical Fifth Monarchist saint. He refused to recognize the Protectorate as other than the government of Antichrist, and he pledged to oppose it by preaching, praying, suffering and fighting. Rogers returned to prison. Although his basic animus was personal hatred of Cromwell rather than zeal for the immediate establishment of Christ's kingdom, his cell at Lambeth became the headquarters of Fifth Monarchist activity in London. Consequently the government removed him to Windsor Castle on 30 Mar. 1655, and six months later transferred him to Carisbrooke Castle on the Isle of Wight. He was released in Jan. 1657 and returned to London to resume his public denunciations of the Lord Protector.

Parliament's proposal to make Cromwell king in the spring of 1657 spurred the Fifth Monarchists to new militancy. Thomas Venner* even attempted an armed rebellion. Rogers carefully avoided direct involvement in any conspiracy. After Venner's defeat, all Fifth Monarchists were branded as traitors. To salvage his own position Rogers invited Presbyterians, Baptists, Independents and Seekers to join the Fifth Monarchists in one unified Philadelphian body dedicated to the elimination of evil and corruption in governmental and religious institutions. His proposals drew response only from the Council of State. On 3 Feb. 1658, one day before Cromwell dissolved his second Protectorate Parliament, Rogers was arrested for sedition and imprisoned in the Tower for six weeks.

Cromwell's death freed Rogers to return to his pursuit of reforms. He abandoned his reliance on chiliastic ideology and now attached his demands to Sir Henry Vane's* proposals for a quasi-republican parliamentary commonwealth without king, protector or House of Lords. Convinced that his own reforms could never be realized under a Stuart king, Rogers limited participation in such a government to those who opposed the rule of any single person. In so doing, he reverted to the elitism inherent in Fifth Monarchy thought. For the rule of the saints, he substituted the rule of commonwealth republicans. To assure civil justice and religious liberty, he again called for a government based on Christian principles.

Rogers welcomed the return of the Rump Parliament in May 1659 because he saw it as the only alternative to monarchy, anarchy or military dictatorship. His disaffection with the Rump, however, was soon rekindled by the factious wrangling and indecisiveness of its members. To remove a possible source of trouble from London, the government appointed Rogers in July 1659 to preach the Gospel in Ireland. He was saved from this exile when the Council instead commissioned him as a chaplain in the army sent against Sir George Booth.

The army's success produced no greater unity in Parliament. Tiring of the Rump's impotence, Maj.-Gen. Lambert* forcibly expelled its members on 13 Oct. In one of its last official acts, the Council nominated Rogers to a lectureship at Shrewsbury. He went instead to Dublin, and despite efforts at anonymity, he was imprisoned there for several weeks by army officers. When the Rump regained its temporary ascendancy in December, Rogers was released. Rather than cast his lot with the thoroughly discredited Rump in its third reincarnation, and fearing the rule of military dictators, he fled to Holland in Jan. 1660.

The Restoration forced Rogers to remain among the Dutch for nearly three years. He resumed his study of medicine and received an M.D. degree from the University of Utrecht in 1662. He became convinced of the futility of maintaining any opposition to Charles II in June 1662 when his friend and compatriot Henry Vane was finally executed for treason. Plagued by the insecurity of exile, he sought and was granted permission to return to England in Dec. 1662. He took up the practice of medicine at Bermondsey in Surrey, and in 1664 he was admitted to an *ad eundem* degree of M.D. at Oxford University. In 1665 advertisements appeared in London for an 'experimented preservative against the plague' which point to the work of John Rogers. If it was, this was the last printed word from him. He may have succumbed to the Black Death, or he may have lived on in obscurity until 1670. The register of St. Mary Magdalen parish, his last known residence, lists the burial of one John

Rogers on 22 July 1670. The name was a common one in the district, and the exact date of Rogers' death is unknown.

Rogers' major published works include: *Ohel or Bethshemesh* (1653); *Sagrir* (1653); *Mene, Tekel, Perez* (1654); *Jegar-Sahadutha* (1657); *A Reviving Word from the Quick and the Dead* (1657); *Mr. Prynne's Good Old Cause* (1659); and *A Christian Concertation* (1659).

Capp, *FMM*; R.M. Gibson, 'John Rogers: Religion and Politics in the Life of a Puritan Saint' (Ph.D. diss., Ohio State Univ., 1973); L.F. Solt, 'The Fifth Monarchy Men: Politics and the Millennium,' *CH*, 30:314-24; *DNB*; Woolrych; Zagorin, *HPT*; Rogers.

R.M. Gibson

ROGERS, Richard (c. 1550-1618)

Puritan minister, was probably born in 1550, the son of John Rogers, a humble joiner at Chelmsford, Essex. Rogers' baptism occurred on 29 June 1551 in the Chelmsford parish of Moulsham. In 1566 he entered Christ's Coll., Camb. as a sizar, taking his B.A. (1570-71), and his M.A. from Caius College in 1574. No doubt his education resulted from the beneficence of a wealthy patron who saw the young man's promise; Rogers enjoyed the patronage and protection of such men throughout his career. Having been ordained a deacon and priest in 1571, he returned to Essex and settled in Wethersfield near Braintree where for over forty years he lectured, preached, wrote practical treatises on the Christian life, trained future Puritan leaders, organized private prayer meetings, actively participated in the classis movement and occasionally ran afoul of ecclesiastical authorities until his death on 21 Apr. 1618.

Rogers' radical activities began as early as 1582 when he hosted a Puritan exercise at Wethersfield on 9 Sept., with Edmund Chapman of the Dedham classis as preacher. A year later he joined other

Essex ministers in presenting Archbishop Whitgift with a grievance over the required subscription to Whitgift's three articles: all were summarily suspended for refusing to sign. Two months later Rogers was unconditionally restored through the intervention of a local influential gentleman, Sir Robert Wroth. Rogers was again silenced in 1586 for refusing the surplice, the sign of the cross in baptism and subscription. An admirer of such radical figures as Dudley Fenner, John Field and Edward Dering, Rogers' fear that he would lose his liberty is continually expressed in the personal diary he kept from 1587 to 1590, and some of his activities at the time suggest that he had good reason to worry. He was deeply involved in several Puritan exercises, traveling widely to conferences in London, Cambridge, Halstead and Huntingdon. At one noteworthy gathering (8 Sept. 1587), he met Cartwright, Field, Chaderton and other Puritans in Cambridge to discuss the *Book of Discipline*, ways of avoiding the unlawful discipline and hierarchy of the established church, and means of furthering the classis movement. In the following year, Rogers took his most radical step when in a private home he covenanted with twenty Wethersfield parishioners to forsake their worldly ways and to encourage one another's spiritual estate. While Rogers was at pains to prove his group was not a Brownist conventicle, this act of near separatism provided future non-separating Congregationalists like John Winthrop* with a potent example of a covenanted group within the parish system. In 1589-90 Rogers was betrayed to the High Commissioners by the Vicar of Dedham, only to be rescued by another sympathetic gentleman, Sir Robert Jermyn.

In the 1590s, under increased pressure from the hierarchy, Rogers and the majority of Puritans diverted their religious zeal into the cultivation of personal piety. The author of the first important Puritan guide for daily conduct, *Seven Treatises* (1603), Rogers' book was reissued seven times before 1630 and received wider circulation in the highly popular condensed version, *A Garden of Spiritual Flowers* (1609), and in another abridgment, *The Practice of Christianity* (1618). Rogers may have been temporarily in trouble with the High Commissioners again in 1598, but his last confrontation with the ageing Whitgift occurred in 1604 when he was suspended with six other ministers for refusing the oath *ex officio*. He was released the following spring through the aid of William Lord Knollys. During the remaining years of his Wethersfield ministry, Rogers continued to feel threatened but remained virtually untouched while providing a useful service for the Puritan movement by keeping, as he had always done, a school in his home for young men, such as Paul Baynes,* destined for Cambridge and the more radical Puritan circles of the early Stuart era. Other works by Rogers include *Certain Sermons* (1612), *Commentary upon the Whole Book of Judges* (1615), and *Samuel's Encounter with Saul* (1620). Rogers died at Wethersfield on 21 Apr. 1618, and was buried in his churchyard. His sons Daniel* and Ezekiel both achieved prominence as ministers.

A. Peel, ed., *The Second Parte of a Register*, 2 vols. (1915); M.M. Knappen, ed., *Two Elizabethan Puritan Diaries* (1933); P. Collinson, *The Elizabethan Puritan Movement* (1967); Haller, *RP*; *DNB*.

S.J. Brachlow

ROLFE (or Rolph), Edmund (fl. 1643-1656)

Army officer, was born on the Isle of Wight. Rolfe was first noticed in Oct. 1643 as 'Colonel Cromwell his man,' i.e. presumably manservant. He was subsequently a trooper in Cromwell's regiment and, by Aug. 1644, a cornet. Rolfe joined Col. Hammond's* regiment of foot at its formation in 1645. By 1647 he was a captain and a prominent Agitator, representing the regiment with Capt. Francis Wheeler. Late in that year he was detached to guard the King at Carisbrooke Castle. In June 1648 he was accused of plotting Charles' assassination by one of his attendants, Richard Osborne. He was committed to the Gatehouse on 1 July, though he was so severely wounded he had to be conveyed in a horse-litter. Hammond came to Rolfe's defense and he was acquitted at the Hampshire Assizes in August. The House of Commons discharged him, and on 23 Sept. voted him £150 as compensation (*CJ*, 6:5, 28). Rolfe was apparently disabled from further service by his wounds, but seems to have been Deputy Governor of Bristol for a time (*CSPD, Comm.*, 7:352). He made land purchases at Bradford Manor, Devon and Walton-upon-Thames, Surrey, and in 1654 and 1656 acquired parcels in Theobald Park.

J. Sprigge, *Anglia Rediviva* (1647); *Clarke Papers*; *Lev. Man.*; Brailsford; Firth & Davies; Rushworth, 6:840, 1162; Cobbett, 17:243ff., 259, 268, 274-75, 401-402; 18:293; 22:354, 358; R.W. Stent, 'Thomas Rainsborough and the Army Levellers' (M.Phil thesis, Univ. of London, 1975).

R. Zaller

ROLLE (or Rolles), Henry (c. 1589-1656)

Parliamentary radical and jurist, MP 1614, 1621, 1624 (Callington), 1625, 1626, 1628 (Truro). Rolle was born in Heanton, Devon, the second son of Robert Rolle (d. 1633) and Joan, daughter of Thomas Hele of Fleet. His younger brother John* was the merchant and notable parliamentary radical. Rolle matriculated from Exeter Coll., Oxf. on 20 Mar. 1607, and entered the Inner Temple on 1 Feb. 1609. He was called to the bar in 1618 and practiced successfully in the King's Bench, becoming a bencher (1633), a reader (1637, 1638), Recorder of Dorchester (1636), and serjeant-at-law (10 May 1640). Rolle sat in the last three parliaments of James I and the first three of Charles I, where he strongly urged the impeachment of Buckingham and consistently spoke for redress of grievances before supply. His brother John took over his seat for Truro in the Long Parliament.

Rolle supported the parliamentary cause at the outbreak of war, pledged £100 for the defense in June 1642, and took the Covenant. In Oct. 1645 he became a judge of the King's Bench, and in Nov. 1648 the chief justice of that court. Rolle's name appeared in the first draft of the bill to establish the High Court which tried the King. In its final form, however, both his name and that of the other chief justice, Oliver St. John,* were omitted. Rolle resumed his duties on 8 Feb. 1649, barely a week after Charles' execution, and joined the Council of State on 13 Feb. At the abolition of the monarchy Rolle's court was renamed the Upper Bench; he remained its presiding officer. On 4 Aug. 1654 he was also appointed a Commissioner of the Exchequer.

In Mar. 1655, while at Salisbury on assize business, Rolle was seized by a party of Royalists who had taken over the town. He narrowly escaped hanging, his life being spared by the intercession of Col. John Penruddock. Rolle was permitted to leave Salisbury, losing only his commission of assize. Not long after he applied to Cromwell for his *quietus*, which was granted on 7 June 1655. Rolle had clashed with the Protector on several cases, including that of the merchant George Coney (or Cony), and that of Nathaniel Barnardiston, whom Cromwell was attempting to foist as recorder on the town of Colchester. Rolle survived his retirement only a little over a year, dying on 30 July 1656. He was buried in the church of Shapwick, near Glastonbury, Som., where he owned a home. Rolle married Margaret, daughter of Sir Thomas Foot, Alderman of London, by whom he had one son, Francis, who was knighted in 1665.

Rolle was one of the small group of legal commentators and compilers who included, after the great Coke,* such men as Littleton and Selden.* Rolle compiled many reports and abridgments while serving at the bar; published posthumously, they served as models for later collections of statutes and precedents.

J. Campbell, *The Lives of the Chief Justices of England* (1873-74); *DNB*; E. Foss, *The Judges of England* (1848-64); H. Rolle, *Un Abridgment des Plusieurs Cases et Resolutions*, ed. M. Hale (1668); H. Rolle, *Les Reports de Henry Rolle* (1675). Papers: L (Add. MSS; Harg. MSS); OE.

B.C. Weber

ROLLE (or Rolles), John (1598-1657)

Parliamentary radical, MP 1625, 1626, 1628 (Callington, Corn.), SP, LP 1640 (Truro), sec. (?) 1648. Rolle was christened at Petrockstow on 13 Apr. 1598, the fourth son of Robert Rolle of Heanton, Devon, and his wife Joan, daughter of Thomas Hele of Fleet, Devon. A London merchant involved in trade with the Turks, he joined with Erle* and Seymour in the Parliament of 1625 to limit the King's grant of tonnage and poundage to one year. Rolle refused to pay tonnage and poundage in 1628 and thereupon had goods worth £1517 seized by crown officials. He challenged the legality of this action by suing for return of the goods in Chancery through a writ of replevin, which was blocked first by the Privy Council and then by the Exchequer. On 9 Feb. 1629 he was summoned out of a Commons' committee and served with a subpoena to appear in Star Chamber to answer for his actions, thus complicating the case by the infringement of parliamentary privilege. Although an apology was ultimately tendered to him on the privilege question, the judges ruled against him on the recovery of goods and he suffered imprisonment. The Long Parliament, in which he sat for Truro, resolved in 1644 that he receive compensation of £1517 for lost merchandise, £4944 interest on stock idled when he ceased trading, and £500 for legal expenses. He was very active in the Long Parliament, having 73 committee appointments, and was a proponent of ecclesiastical reform. A Presbyterian, he sponsored Thomas Watson to preach the

monthly fast sermon on 27 Dec. 1648, which proved to be an attack on the Rump (*Gods Anatomy upon Mans Heart*, 1649), in which Rolle did not sit. In 1645 the Puritan John Graunt, who had known Rolle for thirty years, said of him: 'I see you to participate in the best and excellent places of sound doctrine in the way of truth and salvation.' Rolle is sometimes confused with his elder brother Robert, an MP and judge (cf. Worden, *The Rump Parliament*); his brother Samuel* was also an MP. His family ties also included his cousin Sir Thomas Hele, MP, his brother-in-law Alexander Carew, MP, and his father-in-law Sir George Chudleigh of Ashton, Devon. A wealthy man, Rolle owned lands in Ireland and a mansion at Widdecombe, Devon. His will was proved on 13 Jan. 1658.

CD 1625; *CD 1629*; *CJ*, 1:921, 928; 2:154; 3:483; Rushworth, 1:653-54, 658; *DNB*; Keeler; Worden; Russell, *PEP*. Papers: L (Add. MSS; Sloane MSS).

R.L. Greaves

ROLLE (or Rolles), Sir Samuel (c. 1588-1647)

Parliamentary radical, MP 1625 (Grampound), SP 1640 (Callington), 1641 (Devon). Rolle was the eldest son and heir of Robert Rolle (d. 1633) of Heanton Sackville, Devon, and his wife Joan, daughter of Thomas Hele of Fleet, Devon. Rolle's first wife is said to have been Mary, daughter and co-heiress of Sir Edward Stradling of Somerset. Rolle married Margaret, daughter of Sir Thomas Wise, in 1620, and was knighted in 1621. He served as JP for Cornwall and Devon. In 1639 Rolle refused to contribute to the loan for the King's northern journey, and in Oct. 1640 he helped elect his brother-in-law Thomas Wise MP for Devon. Elected MP for Devon in the spring of 1641 after Wise's death, Rolle promptly joined the reformers. He served on committees for discovering, punishing and disarming Recusants, reforming abuses in ecclesiastical courts, and impeaching the bishops. He also signed the protestation for the defense of Protestantism in May 1641, and was appointed to the Guildhall Committee of Safety in Jan. 1642.

Active in the Civil War, Rolle was sent to Devon in July 1642 to help raise and organize the militia for Parliament. In 1643 he served as a commissioner to collect the weekly assessment in Devon, and also served on the Devonshire Committee for Sequestrations. A colonel in the parliamentary army, Rolle took part in the defense of Barnstaple in 1643, raising troops and serving on the Barnstaple Council of War. Rolle fell under suspicion of royalist leanings in 1644, perhaps because when Barnstaple surrendered to the Royalists in Sept. 1643, its defenders asked for, and received, a royal pardon for their rebellion. A parliamentary committee investigated Rolle's conduct, but in Aug. 1644 the House voted to allow him to keep his seat on its recommendation. Despite this suspicion, Parliament appointed Rolle a Civil Commissioner to accompany Fairfax's* army on its western campaign in 1645. In that same year he was voted both a pension and a lump sum by Parliament to compensate him for property losses.

As tension grew betweeen Parliament and the army, Rolle was closely identified with the Presbyterians. By the summer of 1647 the old accusation of having sought pardon from the King was revived. In July 1647 the Commons voted to exclude anyone who had asked for such a pardon. While Rolle was not actually expelled, he, along with others, was effectively intimidated. By this time he seems to have been suffering from ill health, and he died in Dec. 1647.

Keeler; *Al. Oxon.*; R.W. Cotton, *Barnstaple and the Northern Part of Devonshire During the Great Civil War 1642-1646* (1889); Rushworth, 3:913; *CJ*, 2 *passim*.

T.L. Moir

ROSSIER (or Rosier), Edmund (fl. 1636-1652)

Separatist and City radical, was a clothier of Ironmonger Lane, London. In 1636 Rossier took John Lilburne* to meet John Bastwick* in the Gatehouse prison, and Lilburne, after his release by the Long Parliament in Nov. 1640, joined the Separatist church of which Rossier was lay pastor. Rossier was present at the meeting in William Shambrook's* house in May 1644 to discuss the dispute which had erupted in Henry Jessey's* church over baptism. In 1647 he was a witness for the army in its dispute with the Presbyterian-dominated London Militia Committee. The following year, in *Reasons Shewing That the Desires of the Cloathiers*, he attacked the Merchant Staplers on behalf of the Clothiers. According to William Walwyn,* Rossier treated him with respect, yet he was a signatory with William Kiffin* and others of *Walwyn's Wiles* in Apr. 1649. Despite his connections with Lilburne and Walwyn, there is no evidence that Rossier was a Leveller. He was, however, a member of the London Common Council in 1650-52 with such other radicals as Praisegod Barebone* and Samuel Eames.*

Tolmie; J.E. Farnell, 'The Usurpation of Honest London Householders,' *EHR*, 82:24-46; *Lev. Tr.*; Watts.

R.L. Greaves

ROUS (or Rouse, Rowse, Roos), Sir Francis (1579-1659)

Parliamentary radical and mystic, MP 1625 (Truro), 1628 (Tregony), SP, LP 1640 (Truro), 1653 (Devon), 1654 (Truro) 1656 (Corn.). Rous was born at Dittisham, Devon in 1579, the fourth son of Sir Anthony Rous and his first wife Elizabeth, daughter of Thomas Southcote, and he was acquainted early with Sir Francis Drake, a friend of his father. In 1597 he graduated

B.A. from Broadgates Hall (Pembroke Coll.), Oxf., and from the University of Leiden in 1599. In 1601 he proceeded to study law at the Middle Temple until a profound religious experience caused him to return home to Landrake to study theology. In 1616 Rous published his first religious treatise, *Meditations of Instruction*, which combined Calvinist orthodoxy with mystical fervor. Rous' emphasis on a disciplined life, personal piety and godly preaching stamped him as an exemplary Puritan, while through his step-brother, John Pym,* he had excellent connections with the Puritan leadership in Parliament. Rous first sat for Truro in the Parliament of 1625 and joined the growing attack on Arminian influence in the church. In 1626 he published *Testis veritatis*, a response to Richard Montague's *Apello Caesarem*.

Rous led the attack on Arminianism in both sessions of the Parliament of 1628, emerging as one of the leaders of the godly party. In the Short Parliament he took his place again beside Pym, assailing both the Laudian regime and ship money. With the opening of the Long Parliament he launched the attack on Laud's new canons and in Mar. 1641 he delivered the articles of impeachment against John Cosin. A member of numerous committees concerned with religion, Rous was elected one of the lay representatives of the House to the Westminster Assembly in June 1643 and took the Covenant that autumn. Baillie, convinced of his Presbyterianism, worked hard to have his metrical translation of the Psalms adopted by Parliament, the Assembly and the Scottish Committee of Estates. Although never widely used in England, Rous' translation became popular in Scotland and some Psalms are still in hymnals to this day.

Rous was one of the Long Parliament's most active members. He was made Provost of Eton College in Feb. 1644, chairman of the committee for the ordination of ministers in 1644, a member of the committee of appeals on the visitation of the University of Oxford in 1647, and a member of the Derby House committee in 1648. Rous took no part in the King's trial.

While in no sense a doctrinaire republican, however, he advocated collaboration with the Commonwealth in *The Bounds and Bonds of Publique Obedience* (1649) and *The Lawfulness of Obeying the Present Government*. About the same time, and for equally pragmatic reasons, he forsook Presbyterianism, and as a member of the Rump's Committee for the Propagation of the Gospel sought to promote a national church along congregational lines. Rous' combination of long experience, undoubted piety and political flexibility commended him to Cromwell for the speakership of the Barebones Parliament, where he attempted to exert a moderating influence. As a reward for his connivance in the Parliament's dissolution, he became a member of Cromwell's Council of State. In 1654 he served on the Committee for the Approbation of Public Preachers and in 1656 on a committee to discuss kingship with Cromwell. In Dec. 1657 he was made a lord of Parliament. Rous died in Jan. 1659. By his wife Philippa he had one son, Francis (b. 1615).

Rous' emphasis on personal piety and inward experience was combined with his commitment to a national church. Thus he could strive to reconcile Presbyterianism and Independency, abandoning the former when it proved too rigid. Rous was a member of no party as such; he required a well-ordered church and godly preaching as the context of a disciplined preparation for mystical experiences. His mysticism did not undercut his Puritan ethic but drove him into parliamentary activity and enabled him to move from one position to another in search of a religious settlement that would permit and encourage his type of piety.

In addition to the works cited above, Rous' more important books include *The Art of Happiness* (1619), *Diseases of the Time* (1622), *Oil of Scorpions* (1623), *The Only Remedy* (1627), *Mystical Marriage* (1631), *Heavenly Academy* (1638), *Psalms of David in English Meter* (1643), *The Balm of Love* (1648), *Catholic Charity* (1641), *Great Oracle* (1641), and *Treatises and Meditations* (1657).

J.C. Brauer, *Francis Rouse* (1948); *DNB*; G.C. Boase and W.P. Courtney, *Bibliotheca Cornubiensis* (1874), 3; A. Chalmers, *The General Biographical Dictionary* (1812-17); *Ath. Oxon.*; Woolrych; A.A. Wood, *The History of Antiquities*, ed. J. Gutch (1786-90), 2; T. Liu, 'Saints in Power' (Ph.D. diss., Indiana Univ., 1969); Judson, *TPR*.

J.C. Brauer

ROWE, John (1626-1677)

Ejected minister, was born in Crediton, Devon, the son of John Rowe. In 1642 he went to New Inn Hall, Oxf., but the seizure of his college by royal troops forced his removal to Cambridge where he was admitted to Emmanuel (19 Apr. 1644). Two years later he took his B.A. After the war Rowe returned to Oxford, was incorporated B.A. and admitted M.A. He was chosen a fellow of Corpus Christi College in 1649 and began lecturing at Witney, Oxon. On 3 Feb. 1653 the second floor of an inn in which a play was being acted gave way, killing five of the audience. Rowe preached and published three sermons on what he considered the providential failure of the floor. Shortly afterward he became the lecturer at Tiverton, but in June 1654 he was appointed preacher at Westminster Abbey where he also began to serve an Independent congregation. He continued in this ministry until the Restoration when he was deprived. Afterward, he met with his followers in Haberdashers' Hall and then in Bartholomew Close. Their last meeting place was a house on Holborn Street near Gray's Inn Lane where Rowe resided. He was known as a man of 'great gravity in conversation, of strict piety, of diligent researches into the mysteries of religion.' Rowe died on 12 Oct. 1677 and was buried in Bunhill Fields. His published works include *Tragi-comoedia* (1653); *Mans Duty* (1656); *Heavenly-Mindedness and Earthly-Mindedness* (1672); *The Saints Temptations* (1675); and the post-humous *Emmanuel, or the Love of Christ* (1680). Calamy lists several unpublished treatises on the Trinity and the Holy Spirit, and sermons on the first chapter of John's Gospel.

Calamy; *Calamy Revised*; Nuttall, *VS*; Wilson, *HADC*; Wing.

R. Masek

ROWE (or Roe), Owen (c. 1593-1661)

Civil War officer and Regicide, was the son of John Rowe who in 1609 was of Bickley, Ches., but no relation to the Rowes of Macclesfield, Ches. He was related to the Rowes who were Lord Mayors of London in 1568, 1592 and 1607. Rowe's father was possibly the John Rowe who on 28 Nov. 1637 petitioned the King against fraudulent practices in the wool trade. The elder Rowe bound himself for £100 to Edward Pickering on 11 Aug. 1609 to put Rowe to apprentice for the Haberdashers' Company, and he eventually became a liveryman of the Haberdashers, a silk merchant, a member of the Common Council before 1638, and a prominent resident of Coleman Street in the City, where, with Isaac Penington,* he was a leading parishioner of St. Stephen's and a member of its committee to select communicants. By the mid-1630s Rowe had a share in the Massachusetts Bay Company, owned a house, town lot and cattle in Boston, as well as property at New Haven and 200 acres of farmland in Massachusetts, where he intended to settle. He even had sent his eldest son Nathaniel to America in 1635 ahead of him. In 1630, acting as agent with John Alcock for the Bermudas Company, Rowe sold 700 lbs. of tobacco in London, both men becoming by 13 Oct. 1644 members of the Company's governing board. Rowe became Deputy Governor of the Company, an office he lost in 1647 but regained in 1655, holding it until the Restoration. Rowe's colleagues on the board included the Earl of Warwick* and the radicals Cornelius Holland,* Lord Say and Sele,* Francis Allen* and Sir John Danvers* (who was Governor in 1651). Isaac Rowe, a 'kinsman' mentioned in Rowe's brother's will, was on the board by 1653. Rowe was always active in his concerns, and his Bermuda interests were no exception. He tried to restrain the Royalists in those colonies, but his lands and property were confiscated at the Restoration along with those of Holland and Danvers.

Rowe was attracted to military affairs from an early age. He became a lieutenant of the City's Honorable Artillery Company on 26 Oct. 1619. He later became captain and then by 3 May 1642 was serjeant-major in the City's fifth (Green) regiment under Alderman John Warner,* with his brother Francis Rowe as second captain under him. By 31 Dec. 1642 he was a lieutenant-colonel in charge of the City's arms and ammunition magazine at the Tower. The Houses authorized Rowe to spend £5000 to buy arms for Parliament on 6 Sept. 1643. He became the central arms administrator for Parliament under the command of Essex* and had under him the officers of the ordnance. Rowe continued in this role until at least July 1645, during which time he was the acknowledged expert in the country for judging the condition of arms, a crucial matter at a time when entire shipments of hundreds of muskets or firelocks were sometimes found worthless or faulty just prior to a battle. Rowe supplied thousands of arms of every variety to troops all over the country, inspected and loaded arms into the ships for Ireland, and was responsible for organizing his own shipments and deliveries inland. This argued a very considerable degree of efficiency and reliability, and no complaints seem to have been made of Rowe in a most exacting job. The city chose him as a commissioner to Ireland, which the House approved on 18 Aug. 1645. By 1646 he was back in England and was commissioned colonel of the City's Green regiment, and on 23 July 1647 Parliament appointed Rowe one of the Committee for the Militia of London, with his old associates Penington, Warner,

Allen and others. On 7 Aug. 1646 he was granted £2000 by Parliament 'for his long and faithful service' after petitioning for payment. Rowe faced prison for the debts of his brother Francis, for which he had stood surety, and on 4 Mar. 1648 the two petitioned the House for an additional £6457 in arrears to Owen. Francis was by now scoutmaster-general of the New Model Army, but he died in Dec. 1649 at Youghal in Ireland, and in his will named Owen as his executor.

Rowe was named to the High Court, attended nearly all its meetings, and signed the death warrant. Rowe also signed the death warrant on 6 Mar. 1649 of Hamilton and others. Rowe was colonel of the regiment of horse the City raised against the Scots, which he commanded until it was disbanded on 17 Sept. 1651. On 16 Oct. 1651 Rowe was named to the commission for court martial of twenty English prisoners. He had been appointed to a committee to attend the Council of State regarding officers' pay (ironically, since he rarely if ever received his own), and was summoned in this duty again on 30 Dec. 1651. In company with Maj. William Robinson on 19 Oct. 1652, Rowe made a remarkable bid to take over the inland and foreign letter offices, and offered £10,000 cash for control of all postal services, submitting a detailed proposal to the Council of State listing charges of all routes. A committee of the Council of State which included Vane* and Haselrig* favored Rowe's proposal and submitted it to the full Council, but the House had other plans for the postal services, and after six months with no decision, Robinson withdrew the proposal. Rowe was instead appointed on 8 June 1653 to a position at the Customs House. As a Commissioner of Oyer and Terminer he was summoned to the Old Bailey on 17 Aug. 1653. He was a trustee for the sale of dean and chapter lands, and on 2 Mar. 1654 he, Tichborne* and others opposed the Protector's order for settling some lands. Charles Fleetwood* and the Regicides John Jones* and Miles Corbet* tried on 8 July 1654 to persuade Cromwell to honor Parliament's grant of lands in Ireland to Rowe in satisfaction of the long-standing public debt to him of £5065. On 25 Mar. 1656 Rowe was appointed a Commissioner for the Peace in London under Mayor Philip Skippon* and John Barkstead.* Barkstead, however, accused Rowe and others of conspiring against the Protectorate in a letter to Thurloe* on 12 Aug. 1656. In 1659, again commanding his regiment, Rowe opposed Monck. At the Restoration Rowe was tried and imprisoned. He died in the Tower on 25 Dec. 1661, and was buried on 27 Dec. at St. John's Shacklewell, Hackney, traditional burial place for the Rowes. Rowe married three times and had many children; his brother married the daughter of the Regicide Thomas Scott.* Sir Nicholas Crisp, Bt., the Royalist, was Rowe's brother-in-law by his third wife.

DNB; Pearl; *CSPD, Chas. 1*, 18-20 *passim*; 23:661; *Comm.*, 3-7 *passim*; 9:238; *CCAM*; *CJ*, 4:245, 607; 7:317; *HMC, 7th Report*, App.; J.H. Lefroy, *Memorials of the . . . Bermudas* (1877-79). Papers: L (Eg. MS 1048, ff. 158-59); LG (MS 15,860/3); O (Rawl. MSS A. 16, ff. 115-16; B.48, ff. 25r, 29v); LPR.

R.K.G. Temple

RUDYARD (or Rudyerd), Sir Benjamin (1572-1658)

Parliamentary radical, MP 1621, 1624, 1625 (Portsmouth), 1626 (Old Sarum), 1628 (Downton), SP, LP 1640 (Wilton). Rudyard was born on 26 Dec. 1572, the son of James Rudyard of Hartley, Hants., and his wife, Margaret, daughter and heiress of Lawrence Kidwelly of Winchfield. He was educated at Winchester School, St. John's Coll., Oxf., and the Middle Temple. On 24 Oct. 1600 he was called to the bar. Prior to the Civil War Rudyard enjoyed patronage from the Court and especially from the Earl of Pembroke.* From 1618 to 1647 he served as Surveyor of the Court of Wards. Rudyard regarded parliament as a key to order and liberty, and his defense of

parliament became increasingly outspoken, climaxing in his active participation in the debate on the Petition of Right in 1628. Elected to the Long Parliament, he remained in the House until Dec. 1648. By that time he had served as one of the Governors of the Providence Island Company and shown zeal for religious reform. Although not a Presbyterian and a firm believer that the civil magistrate should be a church officer, he took the covenants in 1643 and participated in the Westminster Assembly. Imprisoned at Pride's purge, Rudyard was released the same day, perhaps through Pembroke's influence or in deference to his age. Thereafter he lived in retirement. Rudyard published various poems and literary pieces in his younger years, and was highly regarded as an orator. A number of his parliamentary speeches have also been printed.

DNB; Keeler; *Ath. Oxon.*; *PSP 1640*; Ruigh; *CD 1625*; J.A. Manning, *Memoirs of Sir Benjamin Rudyerd* (1841); Underdown, *PP*. On Rudyard's Pembroke connection see SCL: Elmhirst MSS 1360/1, 1352/2, 1351/1; Sackville MSS ON 131. Papers: O; OU; OQ; OS; C; CS; CCA; L (Add. MSS; Harl. MSS; Lans. MSS; Sloane MSS; Stowe MSS).

E.S. Cope

RUMBOLD, Richard (c. 1622-1685)

Army radical, joined the parliamentary army at the age of nineteen. In Feb. 1649 he was among eight private troopers who petitioned the Council of Officers for the revival of the representative Agitator system of 1647. Five of the petitioners were cashiered but no action was taken against Rumbold. The absence of his name from the Levellers' printed version of the petition suggests that he repented his hasty action. By 1651 he was a lieutenant in Oliver Cromwell's regiment, a relatively rare example of promotion from the ranks and evidence of Cromwell's willingness to forgive a competent soldier his political mistakes. Rumbold was still a lieutenant in the same regiment in June 1659 but may have been promoted shortly afterwards since he later claimed the courtesy rank of captain.

After the Restoration Rumbold married the widow of a maltster and practiced the trade at the Rye House, near Hoddesdon, Herts. In June 1683 he was named as a principal accomplice in the abortive plot to assassinate Charles II and James, Duke of York as they passed the Rye House on the way from Newmarket to London in April of that year. His fellow conspirators, Josiah Keeling and Thomas Walcott,* alleged that Rumbold was responsible for the logistics of the operation, had procured the arms and intended to lead the ambush himself. Ten years before, he was supposed to have planned a similar ambush at the Rye House, also thwarted by providence, and to have contemplated a variation of the Gunpowder plot which would have demolished the Duke of York's playhouse while James and Charles were present. He was also suspected of complicity in Col. Blood's* attempt to steal the crown from the Tower in 1671. At his execution in 1685 Rumbold denied that he had ever directly or indirectly designed the King's death. There is no reason to attach more credibility to his death speech than to the allegations of his fellow conspirators. Rumbold had frequented the company of disaffected radicals for some years before the plot. One-eyed like Hannibal, he was given to bombastic soldierly language and extreme republican sentiments. Bishop Burnet's judgment of the Whig leaders' association with the plot, 'that nothing was ever fixed on: all was but talk,' may apply equally well to Rumbold.

Quick to realize that his circle was under government surveillance, Rumbold escaped to the Netherlands before his indictment for treason in July 1683. He joined the Earl of Argyll's invasion of the Western Highlands in May 1685 with the rank of colonel and command of the horse that Argyll expected to raise on landing. Severely wounded, he was captured and tried at Edinburgh with considerable haste

lest he should die of his injuries. His judges dealt cursorily with his involvement in the Rye House plot, being more concerned to establish whether he was one of Charles I's masked executioners, which he denied. He was condemned and executed in June 1685 for his part in Argyll's rebellion. On the scaffold he claimed to have acted in defense of 'the ancient laws and liberties of those nations.' While maintaining his preference for contractual government by king and a free parliament, he eloquently asserted his belief in the equality of all men and the imminence of the millennium.

ST, 9:496ff., 1008-11; 11:873-88; T. Sprat, *A True Account* (1685 ed.); *Clarke Papers*, 2:193; *CSPD, Chas. II*, 24:195; *DNB*; Earle. Papers: L (Add. MSS).

J.F. McGregor

RUMSEY (or Romsey), John (fl. 1660-1686)

Conspirator, was a veteran of the New Model Army. After serving for seven years with the English forces in Portugal under Lord Schomberg, he returned to England in 1667. Following a trip to Jersey in late February, he was ordered to join the forces fighting the Dutch. When they were disbanded several months later, his return to Portugal was delayed by illness. In 1668 Col. Rumsey was in England awaiting a vacant command, and on 31 Oct. 1669 he was awarded an allowance of £200 p.a., to be paid from Queen Catherine's dowry. By Apr. 1673 he had become the Collector of Customs at Bristol, in consequence of which he was £1600 in arrears in July 1678. In June 1676 he went to Bath to 'wait upon' Maj.-Gen. Thomas Morgan, another ex-Cromwellian officer. Among Rumsey's friends in these years were Sir Robert Southwell and Sir Philip Perceval.

Rumsey became enmeshed in radical conspiracies in the early 1680s. In the fall of 1682 he was involved with Monmouth, William Lord Russell,* Ford Lord Grey,* and Sir Thomas Armstrong in plotting an insurrection, but it had to be postponed due to lack of readiness. In the first half of 1683 he also became intimately involved in the plot to assassinate Charles and James at the Rye House, which he claimed Robert West* initially divulged to him. From the tangled web of testimony that developed after the plot was betrayed in June, it appears that Rumsey himself was the intended assassin, and that he also urged the murder of Monmouth, 'leaving none of the branch alive,' for the Duke 'hated them all in his heart' and stood in the way of the re-establishment of a republic. In the general insurrection he was allegedly to have raised Bristol, and he was also implicated in the plans to divide London into twenty districts to facilitate the rising.

After the Rye House plot was betrayed by Josiah Keeling, Rumsey attended the 17 June meeting with Armstrong, West, Robert Ferguson,* Richard Rumbold,* Nathaniel Wade,* Richard Goodenough* and others at which the decision was made to go into exile rather than launch an insurrection. According to West, Rumsey wanted to assassinate not only Sir Nicholas Butler because of his spy network, but Keeling too. Nevertheless, by the 23rd Rumsey could not be found in his Soho Square lodgings (the same area in which Wade, Richard Nelthorp* and Thomas Walcott* also lived), and a proclamation was issued offering a reward of £100 for his apprehension. Discovered almost immediately, on the 24th he was brought to Secretary Jenkins for examination. Over a period of time he divulged his partly fictional account of the plot, but only after Keeling and West had begun the chain of confessions. According to Ormond on the 26th, Rumsey, 'the most considerable man yet appearing, has some reserve which it seems he would keep for the King's knowledge and his own last refuge.' Charles did examine him personally. Ormond also observed that 'the man has been so highly obliged by the King and the Duke that he has made himself a good fortune . . . and he seemed to me to be more concerned for the infamy of such ingratitude than for his life, of which all men say he was upon service very little careful.' Rumsey's subsequent testimony against Walcott, Russell, Algernon Sidney* and others did indeed bring him opprobrium from other radicals. Rumbold told West on 2 Aug. that he thought Rumsey was the Duke of York's spy and trepan, 'managed by the Duke of Beaufort, ever since he was the lord's privado. . . .' Yet Rumsey, a self-confessed 'vile consulter' in the conspiracy, was under tremendous family pressure. His wife, Anne, was extremely ill the week he was arrested, and his daughter, Elizabeth Smyth, impressed on him the need to confess everything for her sake. The harshness of his imprisonment was gradually mitigated, in part because he contracted small pox in Feb. 1684. However, when James Holloway* was finally captured and made damaging new accusations against Rumsey, including the charge that he had been personally responsible for the assassins, Roger L'Estrange confided to Secretary Jenkins that Rumsey had probably not confessed everything, and on 9 Apr. 1684 he was once again placed under close custody.

After his release Rumsey supported the Monmouth rising, but was returned to prison in July 1685 for conspiring to levy war against the King. He testified against Lord Brandon and Henry Cornish.* In Apr. 1686 he was sent to St. Nicholas Island, near Plymouth, where he had been sentenced to spend the rest of his life.

Col. John Rumsey is not to be confused with the John Rumsey who was town clerk of Bristol, a conservative who favored the repression of Nonconformists and ultimately became a Jacobite.

CSPD, Chas. II, 6:534; 8:152; 9:542, 561; 10:564; 15:178; 16:459, 517, 20:276; 24-27 *passim*; *Jas. II*, 1:269, 272, 406; Luttrell; *HMC 36, Ormonde N.S.*, 7:53-54; *HMC 63, Egmont*, 2:41, 44-46; *HMC 75, Downshire*, 1:56, 59-60; *ST*, 9; Ashley, *JW*; Haley, *FES*. Papers: LPR.

R.L. Greaves

RUSSEL, William (d. 1702)

General Baptist and physician, was the son of John Russel, General Baptist minister at Waddesdon, Bucks. By 1672 he had received an M.D. degree from Cambridge. His one medical publication, *De calculo vesicae* (1691), instances his success in the medical treatment of bladder stone in the 1680s. He is to be distinguished from William Russell, chemist to Charles II, who, while also very involved in the chemical treatment of illnesses, lived elsewhere in London and was dead by 1697.

Russel signed the General Baptist *Brief Confession* (1660). He was living in Chesham, Bucks., when his son Jabez (1662-1672) was born. His only child to reach adulthood was Nehemiah (b. 1663). By 1670 he was resident in St. Bartholomew's Close, near St. Bartholomew the Great's church, West Smithfield, London; by 1691 he was in the Barbican not far away.

His education and skill in disputation brought him into several controversies. He wrote *No Seventh Day Sabbath Commanded* (1663), answered by Edward Stennet.* He attacked Quakers in *Quakerism Is Paganism* (1674). His main activity was in the 1690s. He was a leading member of the Goswell Street General Baptist church, London, until he left in 1697 with several members, alleging that Thomas Kerby, minister since 1687, sympathized with Matthew Caffyn's* opinions on the person of Christ. The new church installed Russel as minister, and after meeting in Dean Street, it made its home at High Hall, West Smithfield. Russel represented it (1698-1701) at the new General Baptist General Association which had been formed over the same issue.

Russel wrote against infant baptism in *An Epistle Concerning Baptism* (1696) and *A Just Vindication* (1701), and against the congregational singing of psalms in *Some Brief Animadversions* (1696). His ability led to involvement with Northamptonshire General Baptists in their dispute over baptism with the Presbyterian minister at Potterspury, for which he wrote *A Vindication of the Baptized Churches* (1697).

Russel became most famous through the Portsmouth disputation. The Portsmouth Presbyterians had lost members to the Gosport Particular Baptist church, and in late 1698 held lectures to oppose the Baptist position. When local Particular and General Baptists both objected, only a public debate would satisfy either side. Russel was invited to lead the Baptist speakers. The disputation was very well attended, lasting from 10 a.m. to 6 p.m. on 22 Feb. 1699. Afterwards each side claimed victory, with a succession of pamphlets until 1701, including Russel's *A True Narrative*, which went to three editions by June 1699, and his *Infant Baptism Is Will-worship* (1700). Such disputations were subsequently discouraged, and only one more took place in England.

DNB; W. Russel, *Life and Death of Jabez Eliezer Russel* (1672); D.C. Sparkes, 'The Portsmouth Disputation of 1699,' *BQ*, 19:59-74; W.T. Whitley, *A Baptist Bibliography* (1916); Underwood.

A. Betteridge

RUSSELL, Francis, fourth Earl of Bedford (1593-1641)

Russell was an important member of the middle group during the years immediately preceding the Civil War. His family's fortunes had been founded by John Russell, the first Earl, who held high office in the government under Henry VIII and Edward VI and who obtained large estates, particularly at Woburn, Tavistock and Thorney, following the dissolution of the monasteries. Francis' father was William Lord Russell of Thornhaugh, a younger son of the second Earl, who made his reputation as a commander of English forces in the Netherlands and in Ireland; Francis succeeded to his father's barony in 1613 and to the earldom upon the death of his cousin Edward, the third Earl, in 1621.

As MP for Lyme Regis (by-elected 1610) Russell had a brief introduction to the House of Commons. He sat in the Lords from 1614. In 1621 he was one of the peers who petitioned James I concerning the prejudice to English noblemen caused by the King's lavish grants of Scottish and Irish titles. During the debate on the Petition of Right in 1628 he supported the position of the Commons and was a member of the committee which investigated the King's right to imprison subjects without showing cause. In 1629 Bedford was briefly imprisoned himself and was brought before the Star Chamber on charges of circulating a pamphlet damaging to the King's cause, but he was released when it was shown that the treatise had been written by Sir Robert Dudley in Italy more than a decade earlier and had merely been copied for the library of Bedford's friend Sir Robert Cotton.*

During the eleven years' personal rule Bedford devoted much of his energy to schemes of improvement in London, at Woburn and in the fens. His development of Covent Garden, immediately to the north of Bedford House in the Strand, was of enormous significance in London's urban planning, for Bedford's architect, the great Inigo Jones, conceived the idea of arranging town houses around an open square or 'piazza' like those he had seen in Italy and in Paris (the Place des Vosges). This established a precedent for the later development of Bloomsbury, which was laid out by Bedford's descendants, and for much of the West End. Jones wished to include a church in his plan; according to legend Bedford insisted that it should be inexpensive, no more than a barn, and Jones responded that he would give the Earl the handsomest barn in the realm. In fact St. Paul's, Covent Garden, is a delightful essay in the Tuscan style of architecture. Its interior is a simple rectangular room, dominated by the pulpit and without a choir screen: it may be that this arrangement reflected the Earl's Puritan taste. Again it proved influential, the same plan being adopted for many of Wren's City churches. Although Charles I may

originally have put pressure on Bedford to develop the Covent Garden site as an imposing architectural unit, and although Bedford paid £2000 for permission to build, the King's financial agents later attempted to fine the Earl for defects in his license. A Star Chamber suit was threatened, and Bedford finally paid a further £2000. All in all the undertaking cost Bedford more than £28,000, but houses were let to members of the aristocracy at high rents, totalling well over £2000 p.a. by the Restoration.

Sometime between 1626 and 1636 the Earl completely rebuilt his country house, Woburn Abbey in Bedfordshire. The original buildings, occupied by Cistercian monks until 1539, had become ruinous, having been ravaged by at least one destructive fire, but when Bedford visited the site while fleeing the plague in London he liked it so much that he determined to make it his principal seat, in preference to his houses at Chenies, Thorney and Tavistock. Charles I and Henrietta Maria visited Bedford at Woburn in July 1636. Little of the fourth Earl's house survives, for Woburn was again rebuilt by the fourth Duke of Bedford in the mid-eighteenth century. It remains in the family and is an important tourist attraction.

In 1630 Bedford signed an agreement in which he undertook to drain more than 300,000 acres of fenland in East Anglia. This area, later known as the Bedford level, included some of the Earl's own land at Thorney. Thirteen co-adventurers associated themselves with Bedford; they were promised 95,000 acres in return for their investment. The combine secured the services of the famous Dutch engineer Cornelius Vermuyden, who supervised the construction of drains and sluices, among them the so-called Old Bedford River, 70 feet wide and 21 miles in length. By 1637 Bedford had spent £100,000 on the project, which was declared to be successful, but contentious fenmen, including Oliver Cromwell, complained to the Privy Council and caused Bedford's group to lose royal favor. They retained 40,000 acres of land, but the King himself undertook supervision of further draining. With the coming of the Civil War the project remained in abeyance, only partially complete.

Bedford's involvement in politics came to a climax between 1639 and 1641, during which time the complexity of his views was revealed. During the Bishops' Wars the Scottish Covenanters sought Bedford's support, believing that his Puritan leanings and his dislike of royal prerogative would make him sympathetic to their cause. Bedford was now a leading member of the group of able moderate reformers – the 'middle group' – which included such men as Pym* and Hampden,* Lords Saye* and Brooke,* and the Earls of Essex* and Holland. In the Short Parliament Pym sat with Bedford's son for the family borough of Tavistock. Following the dissolution of the Short Parliament Bedford was in trouble because Lord Saville had forged his name to a letter encouraging the Scots to invade England.

When the Scottish forces actually crossed the Tweed and defeated English troops at Newburn, Bedford was convinced that only a Parliament could resolve the dilemmas facing the country. He joined with eleven other peers in a petition, dated 28 Aug. 1640, urging Charles to convoke the two Houses and redress grievances, and he went to Hampton Court, along with the Earl of Hertford, to attempt to sway the Council in favor of this policy. The King instead summoned the peers to York in September, and Bedford was named one of the commissioners to negotiate with the Scots. During the meetings at Ripon the Covenanters charged that Bedford had not kept the promises made in the Savile letter, but they were finally convinced that the Earl had no knowledge of it. Following the negotiations at Ripon the commissioners, on their way to London, visited Woburn Abbey. Although the Treaty of Ripon contained the amazing clause which required England to pay the expenses of maintaining the Scottish army until a final settlement could be reached – the clause which necessitated the summoning of the Long Parliament – Charles stated that he did not blame the commissioners, who had done as well as they could.

In Dec. 1640 Bedford conceived a scheme whereby he and his friends in the middle group would manage Parliament for the King. Bedford wished to be appointed Lord Treasurer himself and desired, as further bridge appointments, the position of Chancellor of the Exchequer for Pym and other offices for Hampden and Holles.* In return for this political power Bedford and his associates would undertake to pay the King's debts, increase his revenues and enhance his honor. The plan failed because Charles ultimately proved unwilling to give office to those who had earlier opposed him. Bedford also underestimated Parliament's resistance to voting money, and he misjudged the extent of the clamor for the Earl of Strafford's attainder. In the last weeks of his life Bedford labored to save Strafford's life. He believed Strafford guilty of at least some of the charges against him but still felt that leniency might gain the King's support for a program of conciliation and compromise. Bedford fell ill with smallpox while the attainder was before Parliament, and he died on 9 May 1641. It is unlikely that his policies would have succeeded even had he lived.

The Earl was buried in the family vault at Chenies. He was survived by his wife, Catherine, daughter of Lord Chandos, and by three sons and four daughters (a fourth son had died earlier in 1641). His eldest son,* who had married the daughter of James I's notorious favorite the Earl of Somerset, succeeded to the earldom. All of the daughters married prominent noblemen, the most important alliance politically being that with the Earl of Bristol's son, George Lord Digby.

Bedford's own political position was fascinating. By nature broad-minded and conciliatory, he criticized the extreme positions of the King and the radicals alike. He hated prerogative and arbitrary rule but found attempts to subvert the ancient constitution equally distasteful. In religion, he sympathized with the Puritans and patronized some Puritan preachers, yet he supported the established church and occasionally dined with Archbishop Laud.

Yet Bedford might have been drawn into radical causes had he lived. Clarendon's character sketch is famous: 'The Earl of Bedford [was] a wise man, and of too great and plentiful a fortune to wish a subversion of the government (III.25); . . . [he] proposed and advised moderate courses, but was not incapable, for want of resolution, of being carried into violent ones, if his advice would not have been submitted to (III.194).' The judgment is apt, if possibly over-severe.

J.H. Wiffen, *Historical Memoirs of the House of Russell*, 2 vols. (1833); *DNB*; G.S. Thomson, *Life in a Noble Household* (1937); Thomson, *Family Background* (1949); H.C. Darby, *The Draining of the Fens* (1956); L. Stone, *The Crisis of the Aristocracy* (1965); C. Roberts, 'The Earl of Bedford and the Coming of the English Revolution,' *JMH*, 49:600-16. Papers: Woburn Abbey; L (Add. MSS; Harl. MSS; Stowe MSS).

S.E. Lehmberg

RUSSELL, Francis (fl. 1631-1664)

Army officer and parliamentary radical, MP 1645, sec. 1648, readmitted 1649, 1654, 1656 (Cambs.). Francis Russell of Chippenham was the son and heir of Sir William Russell, Bt. (d. 1654) and his second wife Elizabeth, daughter of Thomas Gerard of Burwell. Sir William had been Treasurer of the Navy and had a long series of associations with overseas trading companies. In 1631 Francis married Catherine, daughter and sole heir of John Wheatly. He may have been admitted to Gray's Inn in 1633 or the Inner Temple in 1635. Russell was a DL in Cambridgeshire when with Oliver Cromwell and Valentine Walton* he secured £20,000 in plate from falling into royalist hands in 1642. At Marston Moor in 1644 he and Cromwell attended Walton's son, who died of wounds suffered in the battle. Russell was a colonel in the parliamentary army but not in the New Model. He served briefly as military Governor of Yarmouth in 1643 and subsequently as Governor of Ely, Lichfield, and the Channel Islands. As recruiter for Cambridgeshire Russell replaced Chichele, his royalist brother-in-law, but in Mar. 1648 Cromwell chided him for his absenteeism from the House. His brother, known as black Sir William, was an ardent supporter of the King. In 1653 Russell was described by the Venetian ambassador as a man of small means but of great influence among the military. His daughter Elizabeth married Henry Cromwell* in 1653 and his son John later married Elizabeth, the daughter of Oliver Cromwell and the widow of Robert Rich. Cromwell elevated him to the Upper House in 1657. Russell died at Chippenham in 1664.

B. & P.; MacCormack; Underdown, *PP*; Abbott; *CSP Venetian*, 29:78; Cokayne, *CB*.

R.H. Gottdiener

RUSSELL, William, fifth Earl and first Duke of Bedford (1613-1700)

Russell was one of the last to seek a negotiated settlement to the Civil War, and the patriarch of the great Whig dynasty active under Charles II and at the time of the Glorious Revolution. The eldest son of Francis,* the fourth Earl, he attended Magdalen Coll., Oxf., and between 1632 and 1634 undertook the Grand Tour under the supervision of a tutor. Although his parents hoped that he would marry a Cecil or a Sidney, he fell in love with Lady Anne Carr, the daughter of James I's Scottish favorite the Earl of Somerset and the infamous Lady Frances Howard, whose scandalous divorce from the Earl of Essex* was soon followed by her implication in the murder of Sir Thomas Overbury. The fourth Earl resisted his son's wishes for more than a year, but in 1636 Charles I and Henrietta Maria visited Bedford at Woburn Abbey and were reported to have secured his consent to the match. Bedford insisted, however, that Somerset provide a dowry of £12,000; this he promised to do, mortgaging his house in Chiswick to raise the initial instalment, and the marriage took place in 1637. The union proved happy and was blessed with eleven children, but Somerset was never able to pay the remainder of the dowry, and an acrimonious lawsuit followed.

In the Long Parliament William Russell was initially elected to the Commons, sitting with John Pym* for the family borough of Tavistock. Upon his father's death he succeeded to the earldom and to a seat in the Lords, which he claimed on 17 May 1641. He sympathized with the Puritans and with the leaders of the Lower House, and during the autumn he proved himself to be one of the more radical members of the Upper House, dissenting from the Lords' order to enforce the established divine service and from their refusal to give immediate attention to a Commons' petition calling for the dismissal of Sir Thomas Lunsford as Lieutenant of the Tower.

As a member of the middle group, reluctant to resort to armed conflict and cognizant of failings on both sides, Bedford found himself in a difficult position after the outbreak of hostilities. Initially he opted for Parliament and was assigned the task of raising the militia in Devonshire. For a time he was successful in a campaign against royalist forces commanded by the Marquis of Hertford, but he failed to win a decisive victory. By the beginning of 1643, perhaps influenced by his brother's death in the siege of Lichfield, he had determined to work for a negotiated settlement. The King's followers were reluctant to receive him at the royalist headquarters in Oxford, but Charles himself welcomed the Earl and Bedford fought for the King at the first battle of Newbury. In December, however, he returned to Parliament. After a few days' confinement he received the Commons' pardon and the restoration of his estates, which had been sequestered. He did not recover furniture and valuable tapestries which had been removed by Parliamentary Commissioners from Bedford House in London.

During the later years of the war and throughout the Interregnum Bedford took no part in national politics. He labored to complete the fen drainage scheme which his father had begun and he concerned himself with the management of his estates, which produced an annual revenue of £8000 just before the war and continued to increase in value as rents from the fenland and from Covent Garden were received. He also interested himself in the education of his children, bringing the Puritan scholar John Thornton from Cambridge to act as their tutor and later placing several of his sons in Westminster School.

Bedford welcomed the return of the Stuarts in 1660. It is said that he had made secret contributions to Charles II during the Interregnum. Certainly he spent lavishly at the Restoration: his ledgers record payments of nearly £1000 for clothing for his family and livery for his retainers on the occasion of Charles' triumphal entry into London and the expenditure of £1500 at the time of the coronation, when Bedford carried St. Edward's sceptre. In 1672 he was made a Knight of the Garter.

But the King's pro-French, pro-Catholic policies soon drove Bedford into opposition. In 1675 he spoke out in the Lords against the proposal that an oath affirming absolute belief in non-resistance be required of all persons elected to the Commons, and in 1681 he petitioned the King not to summon Parliament to Oxford rather than Westminster. Although he supported Shaftesbury's* policy of exclusion he was not as vocal as his son, Lord William,* and he took no part in the Rye House plot of the Whigs. When William was condemned to death for his involvement in this assassination scheme Bedford petitioned the King for mercy, and he allegedly offered a large sum to the Duchess of Portsmouth, one of Charles' mistresses, if she could persuade the King to grant a pardon. These efforts failed; William was executed in 1683. Bedford suffered a further loss the next year when his wife died, distraught with grief.

The Earl never again took an active part in politics. He was not directly involved in the Revolution of 1688 – his nephew, Edward, represented the Russell interest as one of the 'Immortal Seven' – but he did attend the coronation of William and Mary, again bearing the sceptre, and was appointed to their Privy Council. In 1694 he was created first Duke of Bedford and granted the subsidiary title Marquis of Tavistock. He died at the age of 87 on 7 Sept. 1700 and was buried in the family vault at Chenies.

Considering his great wealth and his important political connections, it is surprising that Bedford did not have greater influence in national affairs. His essential moderation – his ability to assess the strengths and weaknesses of political rivals and his commitment to constitutional, parliamentary courses of action – prevented his total adherence to either side in the Civil War and, later, his acceptance of the more radical actions of the Whig party. He was not a dynamic speaker or an effective political organizer, and he must have appeared a man of vacillation rather than loyal to any faction or cause. He is of greatest interest, perhaps, as a forerunner of the Whig landed magnates who dominated England in the eighteenth century: he shared their love of elegance and luxury and their interest in the arts (he patronized Van Dyck and Kneller) as well as their attachment to toleration and constitutional liberties.

J.H. Wiffen, *Historical Memoirs of the House of Russell*, 2 vols. (1833); G.S. Thomson, *Life in a Noble Household* (1937); Thomson, *The Russells in Bloomsbury* (1940); Keeler; *DNB*; Lacey. Papers: Woburn Abbey; L (Add. MSS; Stowe MSS).

S.E. Lehmberg

RUSSELL (or Russel), William, Lord Russell (1639-1683)

Parliamentary radical, MP 1660, 1661 (Tavistock), 1679, 1680, 1681 (Beds.). Russell was born on 29 Sept. 1639, the third son of William Lord Russell,* afterwards fifth Earl (1641) and first Duke (1694) of Bedford, and his wife, Anne, daughter of Robert Carr, Earl of Somerset. His boyhood was passed at Woburn Abbey where, with his elder brother, Francis, he was educated by John Thornton, an ardent anti-Catholic. In 1654 he followed Francis to Cambridge. In 1655 he was admitted to Trinity as a fellow commoner and, at matriculation, was assigned to Magdalene. In 1655 or 1656 Russell left England for a continental tour and the cultural adornments of an aristocratic education. He returned home to Woburn in 1659 and, in 1660, was elected to the Convention Parliament as member for the family borough of Tavistock, Devon. He was returned for Tavistock again in 1661.

On 31 July 1669 Russell effected a major change in estate by marrying, at Titchfield, Hants., Rachel (1636-1723), widow of Francis Lord Vaughan, and daughter and co-heir of Thomas Wriothesley, fourth Earl of Southampton and his first wife, Rachel de Ruvigny. Upon the marriage Russell received a settlement from his father which assured him an annual income of £2000; and to this was added the enjoyment of the considerable wealth of his wife who, two years earlier, had inherited half the estate of her father. Part of that estate was Southampton House in which their four children (Anne [1671-72], Rachel [1674-1725], Catherine [1676-1711] and Wriothesley [1680-1711]) were born.

Russell's emergence as a parliamentary radical coincides with the beginnings of a Country party in 1673. For the next five years he distinguished himself by attacking the French alliance and the King's ministers, first Buckingham in particular, and then Danby. When, in 1678, Danby's French dealings were exposed, the Lord Treasurer sought to mitigate his offense by alleging that Russell, among others, had also treated secretly with the French; and although the accusation was documented, Russell's disingenuous denial was accepted unquestioningly by the House of Commons. Lord Russell (he had succeeded to the courtesy title in Jan. 1678) sat for Bedfordshire in the three Exclusion

Parliaments. He had in 1679, been returned for Hampshire as well, but chose Bedfordshire. At first he showed signs of exerting a moderating influence upon the opposition. In the contest between King and Commons in Mar. 1679 over the election of a Speaker, Russell advanced Serjeant Gregory as an acceptable compromise; and the following month Russell accepted a place on Charles' reformed Privy Council (he was to resign in Jan. 1680). He even considered, during the 1679 Parliament, Halifax's scheme for limitations upon a popish successor, but along with Shaftesbury* he was soon committed to exclusion. On 19 Nov. 1680 he carried the Exclusion Bill to the Lords and again, during the Oxford Parliament, he moved to have the Duke of York disabled.

In June 1683 Russell was implicated in an alleged conspiracy to raise an insurrection and to assassinate Charles II and the Duke of York. He was brought before the Council on 26 June, and tried and convicted of high treason on 13 July. It is unlikely that Russell was active in the 'plot' to kill the royal brothers at the Rye House or elsewhere, but evidence does point to his involvement in general, although perhaps never serious, discussions about the desirability of seizing the King's guards and staging a coup. Russell's defense was that although present, he never participated in any discussion and that he was, at most, guilty of misprision of treason. Pleas for his life were not sufficient to save him from execution on 21 July. He was buried on 2 Aug. at Chenies, Bucks. Lord Russell's official rehabilitation began on 16 Mar. 1689, with the legislative annulment of his attainder; then, on 11 May 1694, Russell's father was created Duke of Bedford, the preamble to the patent celebrating him as the father to 'the ornament of his age.'

Haley, *FES*; *DNB*; Jones, *FW*; D.J. Milne, 'The Results of the Rye House Plot and Their Influence upon the Revolution of 1688,' *TRHS*, 5th ser., 1:91-108; J. Russell, *The Life of William Lord Russell* (1819); G.S. Thomson, *Life in a Noble Household* (1937). Papers: L

(Add. MSS; Harl. MSS); CS.

H.A. Nenner

RYTHER (or Rither), John (c. 1634-1681)

Ejected minister, was the son of John Ryther of York, a tanner who became a Quaker. Having attended a grammar school at Leeds, he was admitted to Sidney Sussex Coll., Camb. on 25 Mar. 1650 as sizar. He became Vicar of Frodingham, including Bromby, on 28 Mar. 1655 and held this living until turned out in 1660, presumably to be replaced by the sequestered incumbent. He moved to Brough but became Vicar of North Ferriby, Yorks., until ejected by the Uniformity Act of 1662. Until forced to move by the Five Mile Act in 1666, he continued to preach when able at his house in Brough and was arrested on 19 Mar. 1666 and imprisoned for several months. Ryther became pastor of the Congregational church in Bradforddale, Yorks, in 1668, and in 1669 was preaching there and at Cross Stone, Sowerby, Coley and Thornton, for which he was imprisoned at least once. In 1669 he moved to London, and a meeting-house was built for him at Wapping, Middlesex. Ordained on 6 Feb. 1670, he preached from then until his death to a congregation including many sailors and their families and became known as the 'seaman's preacher' because he tailored his messages to their needs. Warrants were issued for him several times during this ministry but he was not arrested, possibly because of his popularity with the sailors. His publications, all sermons, include *A Plat for Mariners* (1672), *The Morning Seeker* (1673), *A Funeral Sermon, Occasioned . . . Mr. James Janeway* (1674), *A Looking-glass for the Wise* (1677), *The Best Friend Standing at the Door* (1678), and *The Hue and Cry of Conscience* (1680). He was survived by a son John, a Congregational minister at Nottingham, and a daughter Rachel Dale.

DNB; *Calamy Revised*; Palmer.

M.B. Endy

S

SADLER, John (1615-1674)

Educational, medical and legal reformer, was born on 18 Aug. 1615 at Patcham, Sussex, the son of the incumbent minister, John Sadler, and his wife Elizabeth, daughter of Henry Shelley, also of Patcham. Sadler was admitted pensioner to Emmanuel Coll., Camb. on 13 Nov. 1630. He matriculated the following year, proceeding B.A. in 1634 and M.A. in 1638 with a specialization in Hebrew and Oriental languages, in which he acquired great reputation. In 1639 he was elected fellow. After attending Lincoln's Inn (of which he became a bencher in 1654), Sadler was admitted as Master-in-Ordinary in the Court of Chancery on 1 June 1644, and was also chosen one of the two Masters of Requests. On 9 Sept. 1645 he married Jane, youngest daughter and coheiress of John Trenchard* of Warmwell, Dorset, a recruiter MP. The marriage portion brought Sadler £10,000 and the union produced fourteen children.

Already a member of the Hartlib* circle, Sadler was a trustee for the projected Office of Addresses in 1646 as well as of the Invisible College and, with Nicholas Culpeper,* the chief parliamentary lobbyist for these schemes. In 1649 he defended the Commonwealth in *Rights of the Kingdom* (reprinted 1682), and in the same year became Town Clerk of London. Cromwell offered him the chief justiceship of Munster in December at £1000 p.a., but he declined, becoming instead Master of Magdalene Coll., Camb. (3 Aug. 1650). Sadler was also instrumental in securing the appointment of William Dell* as Master of Caius Coll., Camb. At the suggestion of Sir John Danvers,* Sadler was appointed to the Hale Commission for legal reform in 1652. As MP for Cambridgeshire in the Barebones Parliament, he served both on the Committee for the Advancement of Learning and on the Committee for Lunatics, the treatment of whom was a special interest of his. In that same year (1653) he was appointed to Cromwell's Council of State. Among other activities during the Protectorate, he obtained the right for the Jews to build a synagogue in London, and sat for Great Yarmouth in Richard Cromwell's* Parliament. In Dec. 1659 he was appointed a Commissioner for Probate of Wills. With the Restoration, Sadler was deprived of all his offices as well as the properties he had acquired during the Interregnum, including Vaux Hall on the Thames and the large manor at Bedford Level. In 1662 he retired to Warmwell, Dorset, which he inherited that year. From here he prophesied that London would be destroyed by fire and plague, and in the fire of 1665 he lost his own home in Salisbury Court and other properties. The prophecy is printed in Hutchins' *Dorset* (1:435). Sadler was also the author of *Masquarade du Ciel* (1640), dedicated to Queen Henrietta Maria, and *Olbia, the New Iland Lately Discovered* (1660). He died in Apr. 1674.

DNB; *Al. Cant.*; Webster, *GI*; Worden; Zagorin, *HPT*; Hill, *MER*; Woolrych; M.B. Rex, *University Representation in England, 1604-1690* (1954); D.S. Katz, *Philo-Semitism and the Readmission of the Jews to England 1603-1655* (1982).

R. Zaller

ST. JOHN, Oliver (c. 1598-1673)

Parliamentary radical and Lord Chief Justice, MP SP 1640, LP, 1640-48, 1651-53, 1659, 1659-60 (Totnes). St. John, the son of Oliver St. John of Cayshoe, Beds. and Sarah, daughter of Edward Buckley of Odell, Beds., was admitted to Queens' Coll., Camb. in 1615, where he studied under John Preston,* and Lincoln's Inn in 1619; he was called to the bar in 1626. The first two of his three marriages (to Johanna Altham and Elizabeth Cromwell) brought connections with the influential Barringtons of Essex as well as with the Cromwells. More immediately important was St. John's association with the fourth Earl of Bedford.* It was especially through the Bedford connection that he associated with some of the most prominent critics of the Court, including John Pym,* during Charles I's personal rule. Another point of contact came through his employment as legal advisor to the Providence Island and Saybrook Companies, in the first of which he was a personal adventurer.

In 1629 St. John was sent to the Tower and threatened with the rack for communicating to Bedford a seditious paper from Sir Robert Cotton's* library, and although the charges were dropped, he never, according to Clarendon, forgave the incident. In 1637 his papers were seized on suspicion of his having drawn up Henry Burton's* reply to the Star Chamber accusations against him. In the same year he became a national celebrity as a result of his defense – in association with another Bedford client, Robert Holbourne* – of John Hampden* in the ship money case. While it is dangerous to draw conclusions about the political views of barristers from the evidence of the briefs they undertake, it is likely that the arguments which St. John employed in the case – he made no attempt to challenge the royal right to judge when necessity existed and rested his case on arguments *de modo* as distinct from *de persona* – were more moderate than his own political views on the matter. Certainly there is a marked contrast between his arguments as counsel in 1637 and those which he was to advance on the same matter in both the Short and Long Parliaments, where he led the attack on ship money.

St. John was active in the Short Parliament, but, according to Clarendon, far from despondent at its dissolution, believing that things must get far worse before they got better, and that the Short Parliament 'could never have done what was necessary to be done.' He and Pym were joint authors of the petition of 18 May 1640 asking for a new Parliament and detailing the grievances of the realm. When that Parliament met, he distinguished himself by his attacks on prerogative levies, his central role in the impeachment of both Strafford and the twelve bishops, his opposition to the ecclesiastical hierarchy, and his support for the Militia Bill and Ordinance. To many, including Hyde, his behavior was the more shocking in that he had been appointed Solicitor-General in Jan. 1641, the first of a number of so-called bridge appointments, made probably at Bedford's instigation. The King almost certainly intended it as a conciliatory gesture, perhaps in the hope of saving Strafford's life. If so, it was spectacularly unsuccessful, for the new Solicitor was in the forefront of the proceedings against Strafford, and there is evidence that the possibility of procedure by Bill of Attainder was in his mind a long time before the impeachment began. On its abandonment, St. John acted as the sole manager for the Commons in presenting the Bill of Attainder at the bar of the Upper House in a notorious speech, distorting precedent, and arguing that while the evidence might not be sufficient in law to condemn Strafford, the law was not for beasts of the chase, and 'it was never accounted either cruelty or foul play to knock foxes and wolves on the head . . . because these be beasts of prey.'

In May 1642, following the flight of Lord Keeper Littleton to York, where St. John had refused to go in defiance of an order from the King, the Solicitor made the radical and bitterly contested proposal that a new Great Seal be made. In November he was made one of the Parliamentary Commissioners for the new Great Seal. It is astonishing that it was not until 1643 that Charles I formally dismissed him as Solicitor-General.

St. John was one of Pym's most devoted adherents and became increasingly prominent as a leader of the House as Pym's health deteriorated in the second half of 1643. A particularly eloquent illustration of his middle-group position is the speech made at a Common Hall in the City on 6 Oct. 1643, when he argued forcefully, not against coming to terms with the King, but against doing so before the entry of the Scots into the war would tip the scales decisively in Parliament's favor. Although he seems to have favored primitive episcopacy as the ideal form of ecclesiastical polity in the best of all possible worlds, he was, next to Pym, the most important figure in getting the Solemn League and Covenant through Parliament, recognizing that, in the gloomy circumstances of 1643, the only alternative was defeat. His proposal that the Westminster Assembly should be asked for a formulation which would afford relief to 'those who scruple to take it [the Covenant],' did not bear fruit, and tender consciences had to wait until the Commons' Accommodation Order of Sept. 1644, which, significantly, was proposed by St. John in response to a suggestion from Oliver Cromwell.

St. John endeavored to preserve the continuity of middle-group policies after Pym's death in Dec. 1643. He found support among the war party – and more especially from his friend Sir Henry Vane the younger* – for measures such as the provision of adequate funds for the Scots and the passage and renewal of the Ordinance for the Committee of Both Kingdoms. Yet he continued to cooperate with peace party-men in support of the Earl of Essex* against the continual snipings of the war party. This he managed to do without setting himself against Essex's rival commanders, Waller* and Manchester, although he was less successful on this front than Pym had been. His support for Essex did not survive the debate on the Self-Denying Ordinance early in 1645, though he voted for it only after protesting his devotion to the Earl. It is especially from this time that St. John's distinctive middle-group identity faded as he became more intimately associated with the radicals of the war party in the Independent alliance: at the beginning of 1645 in the Uxbridge Treaty, where Clarendon mentions him as a party to the intimidation of other Parliamentary Commissioners who

'did heartily desire a peace'; and, later in the year, in exploiting Lord Saville's charges against the moderates Whitelocke* and Holles.*

During the period between the end of the first Civil War and the Treaty of Newport, St. John's politics were those of a moderate Independent. In the quarrel between the army and the Presbyterian-dominated Parliament in 1647 he followed the general Independent line of support for the demands of the soldiers, though he later claimed to have known nothing of the plan to abduct the King from Holdenby. He signed the Engagement of 4 Aug. 1647 in support of Fairfax* against the City, and was a member of the committee appointed to enquire into the counter-revolutionary disturbance in London in late July. In the ensuing weeks he aligned himself with Cromwell and the more conservative Independents rather than Marten* and the radicals and favored negotiations with the King, while urging Cromwell to beware of the danger of moving too fast. He opposed Marten's unsuccessful Vote of No Addresses in September while almost certainly concurring in the successful vote of that name of the following January, by which time the situation had been radically altered by the King's flight to the Isle of Wight and his engagement with the Scots. Nevertheless St. John was associated during 1648 with Cromwell in exploring the possibility of negotiations with the Prince of Wales, and even discussed the desirability of fresh overtures to the King himself. He was one of that group of Independents who finally split the party asunder on the issue of peace with the King and the Newport Treaty in the autumn of 1648. His appointment as Lord Chief Justice of Common Pleas in October made it conveniently impossible for him to attend Parliament, and he took part in none of the preludes to revolution at the end of 1648. There is no need to doubt the vigorous repudiation in his post-Restoration apologia of any complicity in Pride's purge. He never made the formal dissent from the vote of 5 Dec. 1648 to continue the Newport Treaty, which was a prime republican shibboleth of the Rump, and he declared himself absolved of all responsibility for the King's death and associated events. His protestations would have carried more conviction if he had resigned his judgeship and refused to sit on any of the five Councils of State of the regicide regime, though his attendance at meetings of the latter body was very sporadic.

The failure of the mission of St. John and Walter Strickland* in Feb. 1651 to negotiate an alliance, and, if possible, a political union, with the United Provinces had as its product the Navigation Act and the first Dutch War, which authorities as diverse as Ludlow* and Clarendon ascribe to St. John's resentment at the behavior of the Dutch commissioners. Another product was the increased animosity resulting from unpleasant encounters with members of the English royal family in the Netherlands, though in view of the assassination of two other Commonwealth envoys abroad, St. John perhaps escaped lightly. After the Restoration he argued, not very convincingly, that it had been no part of his mission to 'treat concerning the exclusion of his Majesty or his title.' Between the embassy and his far more successful mission to Scotland early in 1652 as part of a Parliamentary Commission to prepare the way for Anglo-Scottish union, he had been appointed Chancellor of Cambridge University in Nov. 1651, having 'shown a disposition to protect human learning against the attacks of the fanatics.' St. John was also instrumental in saving Peterborough Cathedral from destruction by purchasing it and giving it to the townspeople for use as a parochial church, a somewhat unwonted act of generosity, if his contemporary reputation for avarice is justified. It may have been his concern for the status and profits of lawyers as well as his judicial eminence which recommended him for membership of the parliamentary committee to draft a bill for law reform in consultation with the Hale Commission.

By now St. John's political stance showed little or no trace of his erstwhile radicalism. In 1651 he had urged on Cromwell the need to conciliate the Presbyterians, and in the conference at the Speaker's house in December had expressed the view that the maintenance of law and liberty was difficult 'without something of monarchical power.' Given Blair Worden's convincing reinterpretation of the circumstance of the end of the Commonwealth, St. John's consciousness of the need to set a period to the life of the Rump can readily be seen as testifying to his conservatism rather than the reverse. But Cromwell's precipitate dissolution of the Rump in 1653, followed as it was by the radical experiment of the Nominated Parliament, was emphatically not what he had hoped for. Nor was the Protectorate, despite its moves back in the direction of stability and the old constitution, and he refused Cromwell's invitation to sit on the Council of State, the Treasury Commission or the Upper House. According to his own account, which is corroborated by Thurloe,* St. John virtually confined himself to his judicial functions, taking off into the country on the ending of each law term. He embarrassed the government by his refusal to recognize all legislation since 1653, and particularly prided himself that he had 'always discharged such as had been committed by the Major-Generals.' He was somewhat less aloof to Richard Cromwell's* Protectorate, but did not resume his parliamentary seat until the fall of Richard and the restoration of the Rump in 1659, an action which is consistent with his post-Restoration asseveration that he had recognized no parliament but that summoned by Charles I in 1640. While it may seem odd to regard the Rump in this light, he claimed to have regarded its restoration, not with the radical expectations of old republicans such as Haselrig* and Ludlow, but as 'a bridge to let in a Free Parliament,' a view which fits consistently with his cooperation with Monck in 1660 and his support for the readmission of the MPs secluded by Pride's purge. There is no evidence to support the contention of both Royalists and republicans that, down to the last moment, he had aimed to set up Richard Cromwell again. It was probably Monck's influence which saved him in

1660, to the great disappointment of Charles II, as it was reported. His post-Restoration apologia is a valuable source of information about his career, for all its special pleading, and presents a notable contrast to the final testaments of the principal Regicides. *Persona non grata* in 1660, he retired to Northamptonshire and went abroad two years later, first to Basle and then to Augsburg. Despite government efforts to procure his return, he died overseas on 31 Dec. 1673.

The Speech of M. St. John's Concerning Ship-money (1641); *An Argument of Law Concerning the Bill of Attainder of High Treason of Thomas, Earl of Strafford* (1641); *Mr. St. John His Speech in Parliament on Monday, January the 17 An Dom 1641* (1641); *The Case of Oliver St. John Esq Concerning His Actions During the Late Troubles* (1660); V. Pearl, 'Oliver St. John and the "Middle-Group" in the Long Parliament, August 1643-May 1644,' *EHR*, 81:490-519; Pearl, 'The "Royal Independents" in the English Civil War,' *TRHS*, 5th ser., 18:75-81; Worden; *DNB*; Underdown, *PP*; Keeler. Papers: L (Add. MSS; Harg. MSS; Harl. MSS; Sloane MSS; Stowe MSS); O; OQ; OAS; OE; C; DT.

R. Ashton

ST. JOHN, Oliver (1603-1642)

Parliamentary radical, MP 1624-28 (Beds.). St. John, son and heir of Oliver St. John, fourth Baron St. John of Bletso and Earl of Bolingbroke (1624), attended Queens' Coll., Camb. as a fellow-commoner, matriculating in 1618 and taking his M.A. degree in 1620. He married Arabella, daughter of John Egerton, Earl of Bridgwater in 1623 and was admitted to Lincoln's Inn in 1627. At the coronation of Charles I, St. John was made a Knight of the Bath.

Little is known of St. John's political career. He was returned to Parliament in 1624 for Bedfordshire, thanks to his father's influence, and represented the county in the Parliaments of 1625, 1626 and 1628. He made little if any mark in his first Parliament, but took a somewhat more active role in subsequent ones, though he cannot be described as belonging to even the second rank of the House of Commons' leadership. St. John served on but three minor committees in the Parliament of 1625, but in both 1626 and 1628 was a member of the powerful Committee of Privileges. In 1626 he also served on three committees that dealt with military affairs, an interest he pursued in 1628 when he served on a committee which investigated complaints against the billeting of troops in Surrey. He also participated in the debate over the Petition of Right. His opposition-ist tendencies brought him the attention of the Crown; following Parliament's dissolution in 1626, he was ordered to surrender his copies of the Commons' declaration against Buckingham. He also came to the Crown's attention when he attempted to visit Sir John Eliot* in prison after the dissolution of Parliament in 1629.

St. John was elevated to the peerage, perhaps as a result of negotiations with Charles I, in Nov. 1639; however, he did not enter the House of Lords until May 1641. There he was a consistent foe of the Crown, protesting against the Duke of Richmond's plea for an adjournment in Jan. 1642, and promising ten horses and his own services to Parliament when war broke out. He proved to be better than his word, raising a regiment. St. John denied the King admission to Hereford, a city he had taken and fortified in Parliament's interest in 1642. In the autumn he joined the Earl of Essex's* army and fought at Edgehill where he was wounded and died, a captive of the King's forces, on 24 Oct. 1642.

St. John's political career may have been marred by his personal habits. Indeed, it is possible that his elevation to the peerage ensued only upon the King's promise of protection from outlawry for his debts which, according to Clarendon, totalled between £50,000 and £60,000 by 1640. His family's gross rental in 1641 was estimated at under £5000; his financial situation was so grim that he attempted in Dec. 1638 to flee to France under a false name in order to escape his creditors. By 1639 he and his father had run up a private debt of over £34,000. In late 1639 thirty-three creditors, who had lent St. John £5900, were petitioning the King over St. John's debts; another creditor, some months later, appealed to Charles for protection against pending legal action. It is possible that Charles, by protecting St. John from his creditors, hoped to win his political loyalty. If that is true, the King was disappointed. St. John was one of two peers who died in Parliament's behalf during the Civil War.

DNB; *CJ*; Clarendon; L. Stone, *The Crisis of the Aristocracy* (1965); *CSPD, Chas. I*, 15:40; 16:177; 17:94-95; 18:366.

    J. Gruenfelder

SALISBURY, second Earl of. *See* Cecil, William

SALLERS (or Sallows), John (fl. 1662), plotter. *See* Tong, Thomas

SALMON, Edward (fl. 1646-1670)

Army officer, was a native of Kingston-upon-Hull, Yorks. He served under Fairfax,* Lambert* and Ireton* before succeeding the deceased Ralph Coatsworth as lieutenant-colonel in Sir Hardress Waller's* New Model regiment of foot at Oxford in May 1646. Salmon was a member of the committee of officers appointed by the Army Council at Putney on 2 Nov. 1647. In the spring of 1648 Salmon was quartered with his regiment at Exeter, where it was refused billeting and its efforts to collect taxes strenuously resisted. Salmon testified that he 'was constrained to quarter one company where hogs usually lay, another in a church porch and yard, a third in a little church appointed by the mayor, the fourth and fifth in an open place under a part of the Common

Hall.' The regiment was obliged to remain in the west for the remainder of the year to keep the peace, but Salmon was active in the deliberations of the Army Council on the fate of the King, attending all but one of the eight meetings held between 14 and 29 Dec. In May 1649 he was transferred to Col. George Fenwick's* regiment at Hull, and became Deputy Governor of the town. Salmon dealt severely with the disturbance caused by the sermons of the local Presbyterian clergy, and banished two of them, Boatman and Styles. At the same time he encouraged the Independent preachers, who declared him 'faithful and religious.'

After a tour with Overton* in Scotland, Salmon was given command of Richard Deane's* regiment on 15 Oct. 1653 following the latter's death at sea, and on 2 Jan. 1655 he married Deane's widow Mary. The new Protectoral Council of State appointed him to the Committee for Irish and Scottish Affairs on 3 May 1653, and he was subsequently made commissioner for managing the post and Governor of Scarborough. On 8 Nov. 1655 he was appointed an Admiralty Commissioner. He was elected to the second Protectoral Parliament in 1656 but did not sit. Salmon invested heavily in sequestered lands, beginning with the purchase of part of the manor of Egham, Surrey and lands in Holderness, Yorks. on 15 Feb. 1651. In Mar. 1653 he bought half of Blandsby Park, Yorks., whose whole value had originally been £5966 7s. 6d., and on 1 Sept. 1654 he acquired the manors of Cardmell, Lancs. and Epworth, Lincs. for £5910 8s. 5d.

Salmon was sent to Flanders in May 1658 to assist in the siege of Dunkirk and garrisoned the fortress after its capture. In November he vigorously suppressed a mutiny in the garrison caused by bad quartering, arrears of pay and general homesickness in some of the troops outside his regiment, and in Jan. 1659 he and his men returned home. Though regarded as a staunch republican, Salmon sided with Lambert and Fleetwood* in the army coup of October. He worked to secure the adherence of Ludlow* and the Irish officers and signed their letter of 20 Oct. urging

Monck to support the action of the Council of Officers. In December he attempted to win over Vice-Admiral Lawson* and the fleet. On 13 Jan. 1660 he was one of the officers ordered to leave London on pain of arrest and in April, as a known confidant of Lambert's, he was arrested on suspicion of complicity in the latter's rising. Salmon frequented Nonsuch House in 1661 together with such old republicans as John Wildman,* James Harrington,* Praisegod Barebone* and Henry Neville.* At his arrest in December a list of 160 disbanded army officers was found on him. He shared imprisonment with Lambert for a time and was still a prisoner on the isle of Guernsey in 1670 when he petitioned unsuccessfully for release. According to Ashley he was subsequently pardoned and drifted into the Earl of Shaftesbury's* camp.

Firth & Davies; *Clarke Papers*; J. Sprigge, *Anglia Rediviva* (1854); Abbott; Thurloe, *SP*; *HMC*, *11th Report*; Ashley, *JW*; R.W. Stent, 'Thomas Rainsborough and the Army Levellers' (M.Phil. thesis, Univ. of London, 1975), *CSPD, Comm., passim.; Chas. II*, 10:53; 11:503; 18:177; Dow.

R. Zaller

SALMON, Joseph (fl. 1647-1655)

Ranter, whose birthplace is unknown, seems to have had connections with Coventry and may have come from that region. He was an army officer when he published his first book, *Anti-Christ in Man* (Dec. 1647), an Antinomian rather than a specifically Ranter book which interprets Scripture allegorically, posing the 'mystery' against the 'history' as Ranters and other religious radicals were inclined to do. The same may be true of *A Rout, A Rout: or Some Part of the Armies Quarters Beaten Up, by the Day of the Lord Stealing upon Them* (Feb. 1649), though this approaches a Ranter position in its ingenious application of Joachite ideas to the contemporary political situation.

God, Salmon argues, was once in the monarchy, then passed to parliament and now 'clothes himself with the army.' Each change brings a higher manifestation of truth and may be said to involve the death and resurrection of God. It was now his will that the army in its turn should lay aside its power and cast itself unarmed upon God who will inaugurate an age of perfect liberty. *A Rout*, while addressed to his fellow soldiers of the inferior ranks, was evidently Salmon's farewell to the army.

Salmon must then have written *Divinity Anatomised*, now lost, in which, he says, his Ranter opinions were mainly vented. Later in 1649 he was arrested in Coventry where George Fox* found him in prison with other Ranters, the first he had met. They said that they were God, and Fox disputed this with them. He adds that Salmon issued a recantation not long after this and was released. This must refer to *Heights in Depths and Depths in Heights*, in which case 'not long' is perhaps misleading, since it did not appear till Aug. 1651. In this work biographical material is mixed with a record of spiritual experience. Salmon was successively Presbyterian, Independent and Baptist, and this 'in the hottest time of persecution.' But he found the world a chaos devoid of security or comfort. There followed a characteristic crisis, after which the heavens opened revealing a new Jerusalem. Salmon became a Ranter but disillusion quickly followed; he 'turned from a king to become a beast . . . to tear and rend the very appearance of God.'

In prison Salmon had had time to reflect, helped by a Maj. Black. Col. Purefoy* had come from London to Coventry with a discharge, conditional upon Salmon's renouncing in print the errors charged against him. These included statements that there was no God, no heaven, no hell and no sin. These he retracted, though adding that if they had been better expressed they might have been better understood. Typical is what he says of God, 'that pure and perfect being in whom we all are, move and live; the secret blood, breath and life that silently courseth through the hidden veins and close arteries of the whole creation.' This, after all, is little different from the pantheism common among Ranters.

Salmon would seem to have reverted to the pacifism so marked in *A Rout*, writing that 'silence hath taken hold of my spirit. . . . My great desire . . . is to see and say nothing.' On promising to issue his recantation he was released from prison in 1650. His silence, however, was not complete, for after his release he passed some years at Rochester where he preached regularly in the cathedral, and, opponents said, 'sowed the seeds of ranting familism.' Perhaps these expressions, the common coin of contemporary polemic, need not be taken too literally. About 1655 Salmon left England for Barbados, after which no more is heard of him.

Hill, *MER* and *WTUD*; Morton; T. Sippell, *Werdendes Quäkertum* (1937); Nuttall, *HSPFE*.

A.L. Morton

SALTHOUSE, Thomas (1630-1691)

Quaker, was born in the parish of Ulverston, then in Lancashire, a younger son of comfortable yeoman stock. He became a Quaker in 1652 while employed as land steward to the household of Judge Thomas Fell* at Swarthmore Hall, and took part in the great Quaker sweep southwards in 1654. Particularly active in the west, he was soon in trouble with authorities who viewed the Quaker drive as little less than a vagrant invasion from the north, all the more dangerous as an invasion of ideas. Salthouse was detained in prison in Exeter for a year, ostensibly for refusing to pay a fine but in reality because, as some of the magistrates said, if given his liberty he would 'seduce the whole country.' Released in mid-1656, he headed for Somerset where he held meetings, reputedly of many hundreds, until seized as 'a wandering, idle, and dangerous person'

and detained again for almost a year. From then on Salthouse led a transient existence, moving between the west, the north and London. In 1670 he married Anne Upcott, a rector's daughter, who provided him with a Cornish base in the form of a comfortable mercer's business in St. Austell. His troubles were not over. In 1682 Salthouse had goods seized to cover a fine for preaching, and in 1683 was charged with *praemunire* with eighteen other Cornish Quakers for refusing to take the Oath of Allegiance. Although released three years later, the prosecutions and his own unwise speculations had taken their toll on his trade. Quaker merchant friends bailed him out, finding the £180 needed to satisfy his creditors, but his finances were still in a delicate state when, during a protracted bout of illness, he died on 29 Jan. 1691.

Salthouse was author or co-author of twelve tracts. He demanded from Somerset justices the 'privilege of a free-born Englishman'; he called in 1660 for compassion towards the supporters of the blighted republic and muttered the old maxim 'this is the honor of all the saints, to bind the kings in chains and nobles with fetters of iron'; he warned the royalist government to 'bring not upon the nation the old Antichristian yoke of bondage, which neither we nor our fathers were able to bear.' Yet his forte was spiritual exhortation rather than political or social diatribe. He developed, perhaps predictably, from the young enthusiast whose adulation of the Quaker leader Margaret Fell* verged on the sycophantic to the older 'Weighty Friend,' the dependable member of the Quarterly and Yearly Meeting establishment. His chief significance was his astonishing energy as a preacher and proselytizer. In 1659 he was averaging from five to six meetings a week, tramping and riding from one country to another; in the 1680s, though older and troubled with recurring fits of the ague, he was able to cover almost a thousand miles in the space of six months. The spread and consolidation of Quakerism in the west of England were in large measure the result of his efforts.

N. Penney, ed., *Record of the Sufferings of Quakers in Cornwall* (1928); Fox, *CJ*; *EQL*; Besse; *DNB*; Braithwaite, *BQu* and *SP*. Papers: LF; CORO (Wills); SRO (Q/SR 95, pt. 2/54-58).

B.G. Reay

SALTMARSH, John (c. 1612-1647)

Army chaplain, was probably born in Yorkshire of an ancient, decayed family in the East Riding. Saltmarsh took his M.A. at Magdalene Coll., Camb. in 1636 and published *Poemata sacra* in the same year. In 1639 he became Rector of Heslerton, Yorks. and in 1640 published *Holy Discoveries and Flames*, conventional meditations dedicated to King Charles. It was not until 1643 that his radical opposition to all forms of a state church and his commitment to the parliamentary cause became clear. Saltmarsh then published an attack on Thomas Fuller's argument that church reformation must be led by the King and gave up his living at Heslerton because of scruples about tithe-taking. When, early in 1645, he took appointment as Rector of Brasted, in Kent, a living worth £200 p.a., he refused the income; he soon came to judge even voluntary gifts improper and stopped accepting them. His *A Peace but No Pacification* (Oct. 1643) argued that the King would keep no promises and that he must therefore be utterly defeated in the field.

In the last three years of his life Saltmarsh sold his books exclusively through the radical bookseller Giles Calvert* and established himself in positions that made him a favorite target of the Presbyterian propagandists. He became known as a vigorous advocate of toleration and sectarianism, of free grace, and of the New Model Army as an independent political force. His principal arguments for toleration appeared in *Dawnings of Light* (1645), *Groanes for Liberty* (1646), *The Smoke in the Temple* (1646), and *Reasons for Unitie, Peace, and Love* (1646). He shrewdly reminded the Presbyterians of their own cries for liberty of conscience by quoting, in *Groanes for Liberty*, the arguments of the Smectymnuans under episcopacy, but his characteristic tone was not aggressive but irenic. One of his favorite strategies was to present fairly the opinions of the several factions concerning controversial issues in the hope that the reader could be brought to respect, and thus tolerate, the opinions of others. This technique is evident in *The Smoke in the Temple*, and it is extensively used in Saltmarsh's masterwork, *Sparkles of Glory* (1647). His ability to present without distortion the positions of those whose views he did not share was a special talent in an age when few men would have understood the purpose of an unbiased survey of opinions.

Although the Presbyterians held his tolerationist views in contempt, they were chiefly scandalized by the Antinomianism they found in Saltmarsh's *Free Grace* (1645). His Antinomianism arose, as it usually did among pious radicals, from his enthusiasm for the life of grace and for the freedom the Gospel promised to those who receive without meriting it the free grace of Christ. For Saltmarsh faith was not a first step in the salvation of a man, nor a culminating step following other necessary steps like repentance, but the only thing needed to receive the 'Spirit of Adoption.' Saltmarsh expressed the freedom of the redeemed man as intemperately as the later Ranters would: 'The Spirit of Christ sets a believer as free from hell, the law, and bondage here on earth, as if he were in heaven; nor wants he anything to make him so, but to make him believe he is so. . . .' It may be noted that since Saltmarsh granted repentance, prayer and other religious duties no role in the salvation experience, he left no important function for a Christian church; indeed, in his later work he showed little interest in the church as an institution except to insist that it must be free from the magistrate's control and must allow its members a dominant role in its activities and its governance.

About June 1646 Saltmarsh became an

army chaplain. Baxter was disturbed to find that Saltmarsh and William Dell* were the most important preachers at the headquarters. He was a popular and 'spiritual' preacher – that is to say, he avoided the schematic and logic-chopping manner so common among university-trained preachers and put forward spiritual insights that his audience found moving. He spoke slightingly of logical and rational systems as barriers to the perception of spiritual truths.

While none of Saltmarsh's army sermons survives, their substance and manner were probably of a piece with the meditations in *Sparkles of Glory*. There Saltmarsh made clear the basis of his radical views of toleration. To an age whose ideal was to reform the church into conformity with the apostolic church, Saltmarsh said that the New Testament churches are not to be seen as models but as 'types,' foreshadowings of the true, invisible (i.e. not institutionally organized) church of believers. The differences among churches all concerned merely outward, 'legal' things, the sort of issues that engaged the Assembly of Divines, where Antichrist pretended to establish the truth by counting the ballots of men. Indeed, for Saltmarsh the Christian is 'taught of God' and, seeing that baptism, the Supper, preaching, and even church fellowship itself are all 'beggarly rudiments,' the true Christian can lead a life in which there is no role at all for visible churches of any kind. Thus Saltmarsh carried the Separatist impulse to its limit and distinguished himself sharply from the Seekers, with whom he is often confused, since the Seekers were waiting for new authorities with apostolic gifts to come and establish a visible church whose way of worship would have divine authority.

Early in June 1647, just after the army defied the Parliament with its *Solemn Engagement*, Saltmarsh published *A Letter from the Army* assuring the people of the army's peaceable intentions and its dedication to the securing of civil justice. Saltmarsh then had sanguine expectations that the army would give effective voice to

the concerns of the common soldiers. By late October, however, Saltmarsh was afraid that the grandees would betray the army's great mission. Writing from Essex, where he lived after he left the army sometime after June, Saltmarsh sent letters to Fairfax,* Cromwell and the Council of War scolding them for not keeping their promises and warning that God required them to heed the common soldiers. While the letters do not have a specific political content, their general thrust suited the Levellers and Capt. Bishop introduced one into the Putney debates. After the events at Corkbush Field, where one Leveller sympathizer was executed and eleven others imprisoned, it seemed even more likely that the interests of the common people would be trodden upon, and on 6 Dec. Saltmarsh arrived at the headquarters at Windsor to follow God's command and tell the army what had been revealed to him in a vision. He told the Council, Fairfax and Cromwell that God was angry with them and required that they release the prisoners and live up to their former promises. Though Saltmarsh spoke with his hat on his head, the army leaders listened respectfully to this sepulchral figure. His visit became the more memorable when, upon his return home on 10 Dec., he told his wife he had finished his course and must now go to his Father, took ill that same day, and died the following day.

Jones, *SMR*; Morton; Solt; D.M. Wolfe, *Milton in the Puritan Revolution* (1941); Woodhouse; Hill, *WTUD*; Greaves, *PRET*; *DNB*.

N.T. Burns

SALTONSTALL, Sir Richard (1586-1658)

Puritan colonist, was born near Halifax, West Riding, Yorks., the son of Sir Peter Saltonstall and the nephew of Sir Richard Saltonstall, Lord Mayor of London in 1597. Saltonstall was knighted at Newmarket on 23 Nov. 1618. He owned manors at Ledsham and Huntwick Grange, Yorks., and was a justice in the West Riding. On 26 Aug. 1629 he and eleven other members of the Massachusetts Bay Company resolved to go to New England within six months to establish a colony. Other members included John Winthrop,* Emmanuel Downing, Isaac Johnson and Increase Nowell. Saltonstall was elected to the Board of Assistants on 29 Oct. 1629. One of the principal patentees for the Massachusetts Bay Colony, Saltonstall left with his five children on the 'Arabella' on 1 Apr. 1630. He founded Watertown, half a mile west of Cambridge, and was twice fined (for absence from court and improperly beating a servant). He left for England on 30 Mar. 1631, leaving his two eldest sons in the colony, but maintained an active interest in colonial events, retained a share in the trading stock and profits, and was one of five men responsible for managing the company's business. On 28 June 1632 he offered to make a map of Salem and Massachusetts Bay for the Council of New England.

In Mar. 1631 Saltonstall secured the rights over land in Connecticut and part of Massachusetts, and then organized a syndicate including Lord Saye and Sele,* Lord Brooke,* Warwick, * John Pym* and John Hampden* as members to establish a colony. Saltonstall was instrumental in organizing the syndicate and securing support for the proposed colony of Saybrook. In May 1635 he personally financed a twenty-man expedition led by Francis Stiles, which was to go to the Connecticut Valley and begin a settlement on the Connecticut shore of Long Island Sound. The expedition was, however, confronted by some Dorchester immigrants, who effectively prevented the establishment of a permanent settlement by the Stiles' party. In 1635-36 Saltonstall protested these acts at Windsor, but was not compensated for his losses, perhaps due to some of his previous activities. In 1633 he was delinquent in paying ship money. In Feb. 1634 he and John Humfrey were summoned before the Privy Council and required to take the Oaths of Supremacy and Allegiance and subscribe to the discip-

line of the Church of England. Although they took the oaths, they did not subscribe. Though Saltonstall had received permission on 23 Nov. 1633 to travel abroad for three years, he did not at first leave, but in 1640 he was living in Arnhem with Philip Nye* and Thomas Goodwin.*

Saltonstall was appointed ambassador to Holland in 1644 and while there had his portrait painted by Rembrandt. His continued interest in colonial affairs is shown by his 1645 petition for the right to establish trading posts north of those already founded. He was granted a twenty-year monopoly with the stipulation that no trading post be built within fifty miles of an English plantation. In 1648 he was one of the commissioners who tried the Duke of Hamilton, the Earl of Hamilton and Lord Capel for high treason. He sided with the Independents in their struggle against the Presbyterians, arguing for greater indulgence toward dissidents. In 1651 he wrote to John Cotton* and John Wilson advocating greater toleration for Quakers, asserting that forced conformity only made hypocrites of the converts. Upon his death in 1658 he willed a legacy to Harvard College. Saltonstall married Grace, daughter of Robert Keyes, and there are indications of two other marriages. His son Richard (d. 1694), who attended Cambridge University, welcomed the Regicides to New England in 1660 and opposed the importation of black slaves to the colonies.

DNB; *CSPC*, 1:112; *CSPD, Chas. I*, 6:296; 10:197; Hexter; Cliffe; Tolmie; *Winthrop Papers* (1929); E. Bacon, *Connecticut River and Valley of the Connecticut* (1906); T. Hutchinson, *History of Colony and Province of Massachusetts Bay* (1914).

D. Mock

SALWAY (or Salwey, Salloway), Humphrey (1575?-1652)

Parliamentary radical, MP LP 1640 (Worcs.). Salway, of Stanford, Worcs., was the eldest son of Arthur Salway, an Exchequer official. He matriculated at Brasenose Coll., Oxf. on 8 Nov. 1590, receiving his B.A. on 16 Feb. 1593. In Nov. 1594 he was admitted as a student to the Inner Temple. He was a prominent JP in the county, and married Anne, daughter of Sir Edward Littleton of Pillaton Hall, Stafford. On 6 July 1630 he was fined £25 for not taking knighthood at the King's coronation.

Elected knight of the shire for Worcester on 21 Oct. 1640 by an overwhelming majority, he sat in the Long Parliament until his death. Salway opposed the royal Commission of Array in Worcestershire, having already joined with Sergeant Hyde on 4 Mar. 1642 to pledge £1000 for the loan, and in June 1642 promised a horse and maintenance for the parliamentary cause. He appears as a Sequestration Commissioner for Worcester in 1643. Parliament appointed him a member of the Westminster Assembly on 12 June 1643, and King's Remembrancer in the Exchequer Court on 3 Aug. 1644 with an income of £400 p.a. He held this post until his death, although authorized to function by deputy in 1651. In Oct. 1644 he was a member of the General Assessment Committee, in June 1646 the Committee on Scandalous Offences, and in May 1649 the Navy Committee. Salway was one of six Parliamentary Commissioners nominated to attend the Scottish army at Hereford on 18 July 1645. As an early Independent he fled to the army in 1647 and probably dissented to the 5 Dec. 1648 vote in Feb. 1649. In Jan. 1649 he was appointed to the High Court, but did not sit. Salway died in Dec. 1652 and was buried in Westminster Abbey on 20 Dec. An order dated 9 Sept. 1661 resulted in his body being removed from the Abbey. The prominent Parliamentarian Richard Salway* was his fourth son.

DNB; Keeler; *Al. Oxon.*; Williams, *Worcester*.

E.A. Andriette

SALWAY (or Salwey, Salloway), Richard (1615-1685)

Parliamentary radical, MP 1645-53 (Appleby), 1653 (Worcs.). Salway was the fourth son of Humphrey Salway* of Richard's Castle, Herefs. Apprenticed to a London tradesman, Salway was identified as a citizen and grocer of the parish of St. Leonard, Eastcheap, in the license for his marriage to Anne, daughter of Richard Waring, in 1641. Waring himself was a prominent radical leader in London, serving as Common Councilman (1638-47), Warden of the Grocers' Company (1646) and Alderman (1649). He was one of the City Committee which drew up the counter-petition against peace in Dec. 1642. Probably influenced by his father-in-law in the early years of the Puritan Revolution, Salway is said to have been the spokesman of the London apprentices in some of their tumultuous petitions to the Long Parliament.

'A man of great parts,' Salway soon proved himself to be an important parliamentary leader and was employed in a variety of capacities during the Civil War and the Commonwealth. In the political sphere he was appointed to the committee for the reduction of Worcester (1644), committees for Irish and Scottish affairs (1647, 1651), the committee for the navy (1648), the High Court of Justice for the trial of the King (1649), and the Council of State (1651-53). He was also on a number of commissions for the counties of Westmorland, Worcester and Hereford. Although not noted as a military man, Salway was a major in the parliamentary army and took part in the siege of Worcester in 1646. He was twice included on the national commission for the examination of scandalous offenses (1646 and 1648).

Salway's London connection appears to have been maintained after his apprenticeship, though it is not known whether he was ever engaged in business in the City. He was appointed to the London Militia Committee (1647, 1649, 1659), and in 1649 he was elected a Common Councilman in

Bridge Ward Within. Salway's interest in trade and his connection with London can also be seen in some other appointments of his complex career: in 1650 he was appointed one of the commissioners for the advancing and regulating of the trade of the Commonwealth; in 1654 he was chosen ambassador to Constantinople; and in 1657 the Lord Mayor of London requested Salway to serve as one of the commissioners in Ireland for the restoration of Londonderry and other Irish lands to the Companies of the City, though he declined the invitation.

Salway was clearly a radical political Independent. Richard Baxter considered him an adherent of Sir Henry Vane's* religious thought. Salway was active in the events of Jan. 1649, helping to draft the republican resolution of 4 Jan., though he did not sit on the High Court and did not take the dissent until May. He was a leading Rumper and a member of the inner circle around Haselrig,* Scott* and Vane. Later he allied himself politically with the Fifth Monarchist John Carew,* as well as his City colleague Francis Allen.* He opposed Cromwell's forcible dissolution of the Rump in 1653, withdrew from the Council in protest on 3 May, and though called to the Barebones Parliament, Salway does not appear to have taken part in its proceedings. Perhaps estranged from Cromwell, Salway was in retirement in the latter part of the Protectorate. It is with the downfall of Richard Cromwell* in Apr. 1659 that he once more appeared on the national scene and took a leading part in the events of the last months of the Revolution. On 7 May he was appointed to the Committee of Safety and later in the month to the Council of State, and he served as the Council's president in September. Salway was also appointed as one of the Commissioners of the Admiralty, the first of the commissioners to manage the revenue of the Commonwealth, a member of the London Militia Committee and a number of other militia committees for various counties. When the army turned out the Rump again in Oct. 1659, the General Council of Officers invited him to serve on a Committee of Safety, but Salway declined the invitation and endorsed the letter: 'I utterly refuse to act as a member of that Committee.' However, he worked with the army officers for a political settlement, and was consequently regarded as a traitor by the Parliament, which, when restored again, ordered him to the Tower on 17 Jan. 1660. Upon his plea of ill health, he was allowed to retire to the country on 21 Jan. At the Restoration, Salway escaped unpunished, though he was constantly under suspicion. He died at the end of 1685.

DNB; *HMC, 10th Report, App., Part IV*, 409-11; Williams, *Worcester*; Davies, *RC*; Firth & Rait; Yule; Woolrych; Worden; Glass. Papers: LG (MS 3461/1); LCRO (Journals of the Common Council, vol. 40); L (Sloane MSS; Stowe MSS).

T. Liu

SANDERS, Thomas (fl. 1648-1696?)

Civil War officer and MP 1653, 1654, 1656 (Devon). Sanders appears as Governor of Exeter Castle from Jan. 1648 until Oct. 1651. He was commissioned as captain of the dragoons in the Devon militia in May 1650, and is consistently called major (1651-58). He was at Plymouth in May 1652, and again as commander of the fort there in Apr. 1654. In the 1653 Parliament he was listed as a moderate. L.F. Brown, followed by others, confused him with Col. Thomas Sanders, the Derbyshire Presbyterian, who was also a major until 1648.

Although alleged by some modern writers to have been a Baptist, Maj. Sanders has not left a record of his views nor does his church allegiance appear. He may be the Thomas Sanders who in 1666 married Silvester Davis, a member of the Broadmead church, Bristol. If so, he was living in St. Ewin's parish, Bristol in 1696, with a personal estate worth £600. This Sanders signed a plea for better prison conditions for Quakers in 1682, and his house was searched for weapons in 1684 on grounds of suspected sympathy with Monmouth. He was not a member of his wife's church.

CSPD, Comm., 2:507; 3:353; 7:86, 134; 12:37; *CJ*, 7 *passim*; Hayden, *RCCB*, p. 303; Woolrych (who suggests a death date of 1659); *Somers Tracts*, 6:248, 339.

A. Betteridge

SANDYS (or Sands), Sir Edwin (1561-1629)

Parliamentary radical and colonizer, MP 1586 (Andover), 1588, 1593 (Plympton), 1604 (Stockbridge), 1614 (Rochester), 1621 (Sandwich), 1624 (Kent), 1625, 1626 (Penryn). Sandys was born on 9 Dec. 1561, the second son of Edwin Sandys, Bishop of Worcester, future Bishop of London and Archbishop of York (d. 1588), and his wife Cicely, daughter of Sir Thomas Wilford of Cranbrook, Kent. He attended Merchant Taylors' School from 1571 and matriculated at Corpus Christi Coll., Oxf. in 1577. He took his B.A. and was elected a fellow of Corpus in 1579. His M.A. followed in 1583, but his supplication for a B.C.L. in 1589 was refused. He entered the Middle Temple in 1590, together with his closest friend, George Cranmer. The Master of the Inn, Richard Hooker, had been his teacher at Oxford, and Sandys later financed the publication of *The Laws of Ecclesiastical Polity*. In 1596 he and Cranmer were members of the Earl of Lincoln's embassy to Hesse, and the two friends remained abroad for a Grand Tour, including a stint at the Academy in Geneva. Sandys visited Italy and France, and ended his travels by writing *A Relation of the State of Religion* (1599), dedicated to Whitgift. This remarkable plea for co-existence between Catholicism and Protestantism was published in 1605, ran through three editions in a few months, and then was ordered burned by the High Commission. The reasons are unclear, but may relate to Sir Edwin's sudden obstreperousness in the 1604 Parliament, his mild Arminianism, or his kind remarks about the Catholics and acerbic ones about

'great persons and princes, of whom it was said . . . that few went to hell, and the reason, because they were few.'

Sandys' career was transformed in the early years of James I's reign. Until 1604 he was a respectable member of the Establishment – connected with the Cecils, knighted by the new King in 1603, and an inconspicuous veteran of three parliaments. In James' first Parliament he emerged as the most powerful and effective opponent of Crown wishes in the Commons. His speech of 19 Apr. 1604 was the first major assault on the King's pet project, the Union between England and Scotland, and the turning point in discussions of the issue. Thereafter his influence in the House was unparalleled for almost twenty years, frequently in opposition to royal positions.

The tone was set from the start. Sandys' effectiveness depended on sober, serious and careful argumentation. He was no fiery rhetorician, but an eminently sensible and persuasive speaker who had a knack for catching the mood of the House and evoking the principles that would sway his colleagues. In the 19 Apr. speech, for instance, he urged delay by stressing the importance of parliamentary deliberation and the need for the approval of the country. These constant themes in Sandys' repertoire appealed powerfully to the gentry MPs.

Why Sandys took the stand he did in 1604 is unclear. He continued to seek Crown favor – hoping for a Secretaryship of State as late as the 1620s – but there was a combination of principle and enjoyment of stature in the Commons that took him into the role of principal opponent of the King in Parliament. Not inappropriately, Wallace Notestein called him the Pym of the Jacobean Commons.

The issues he addressed varied widely. In 1604 he also led the attempt to end monopolies with a free trade bill, and he was prominently involved in the preparation of the Apology of the House. In the remaining sessions of the 1604-10 Parliament he continued to hammer away at the Union until it collapsed; he helped decide the fate of various subsidy proposals, notably the Great Contract of 1610; he made important interventions in the discussions of purveyance; and he busied himself constantly with procedures. He was one of the chief watchdogs of privilege, especially where the confidentiality of debates was concerned, and he played significant parts in the regularization of the official *Journal* and the creation of the Committee of the Whole House.

In the Addled Parliament of 1614, Sandys tried to avoid the collapse of the session so that tangible results could be produced, but his substantive work was along the same lines he had followed for the past decade. He chaired the Committee on Grievances, led the investigation of impositions, and took an important part in the expulsion of Sir Thomas Parry from the House. Although Sandys was not among the four MPs sent to the Tower after the session, some of his documents were burned and he was confined to London for a month.

The decade of the 1610s marked the high point of Sandys' other major interest, colonization. He was a member of the Virginia, East India, and Somers Islands Companies, and a member of the Council of the first two. In 1619 he took over the leadership of the Virginia Company, and in the next three years dispatched over 3,500 settlers to the colony. Although the King forbade his re-election in 1620, his friend the Earl of Southampton* continued his policies, and Sandys remained the Company's guiding spirit. Mismanagement, the Indian massacre of 1622, and rival factions among the adventurers brought about the dissolution of the Company in 1624. Sir Edwin had not handled its financial affairs well, and he had concealed its problems; but Virginia was to flourish as a royal colony, and given the horrendous death rate in Jamestown, it might not have survived if he had not poured settlers across the Atlantic in such numbers, regardless of the cost. In any case, he remained sufficiently respected in London to be considered for the governorship of the East India Company in the mid-1620s.

The Parliament of 1621 was the high point of Sandys' running battle with the Crown. One of the principal managers of the House's business, he took decisive action on many issues, producing a bill against monopolies, surveying the state of trade, gathering petitions of grievance, promoting a bill against Recusants, and much else besides. But the impeachment of Bacon and the growing irritation at Court with parliamentary behavior led to a major quarrel in the last days before summer adjournment, pitting the powerful Master of the Wards, Sir Lionel Cranfield, against Sandys. The latter rashly said he was 'never more afraid' for the future, since 'all things in the country are out of frame,' and after the adjournment he was examined by the Privy Council, primarily for inflammatory remarks and collusion with other MPs, imprisoned for five weeks, and then confined to his country home in Kent. When the session resumed in the autumn, without Sandys, the attempt to find out the reasons for his imprisonment and to justify the Commons' conduct was a major cause of the Remonstrance that led James angrily to dissolve the Parliament.

By 1624 the situation was transformed. Buckingham decided to use Parliament to pressure James to break England's peace with Spain, and the Commons, with this decisive ally at court, were given their heads. Thirty-five bills became public statutes, many of them failed legislation from 1621 and before. The Commons gained the right to discuss foreign affairs, and Sandys was able to steer many of his longstanding proposals to passage, including the Monopolies Act. He also used his new power to impeach Cranfield. Although the alliance of Buckingham with the parliamentary leaders certainly gained the Duke his ends, both sides benefitted, and the session can also be seen as the climax of Sandys' career.

Sir Edwin sat in the Parliaments of 1625 and 1626, but by then he was an old man and participated only sporadically in events. After the promise of 1624, the deterioration of relations between King and Commons must have saddened him, but it was his own activities that had taught his colleagues how to organize opposition and what issues could unite the gentry. He died in Oct. 1629 in Kent, survived by his fourth wife and most of their twelve children.

DNB; T.K. Rabb, 'Sir Edwin Sandys and the Parliament of 1604,' *AHR*, 79:646-70; Moir; Ruigh; *CD 1610*; *CD 1625*; E.S. Sandys, *History of the Family of Sandys* (1930), 1; P.W. Hasler, *The History of Parliament: The Commons 1558-1603* (1982); W. Notestein, *The House of Commons 1604-1610* (1971); Zaller. Papers: L (Add. MSS; Harl. MSS; Lans. MSS; Stowe MSS; Sloane MSS).

T.K. Rabb

SANKEY, Sir Jerome (or Hierome) (c. 1620-c. 1685)

Army officer and parliamentary radical, MP 1654 (Tipperary and Waterford), 1656 (Reigate), 1657 (Marlborough), 1659 (Woodstock). Sankey was born in Shropshire. His father, Richard Sankey, and grandfather, Peter Sankey, were both clergymen of Shropshire who obtained their B.A. and M.A. degrees from Oxford. Sankey received his B.A. degree from Cambridge (1641) and his M.A. from Oxford (1644). He had intended a clerical career, but soon after graduation he joined the parliamentary army and rose to colonel. He was wounded at Nantwich in 1645. Progressively a Presbyterian, Independent and Particular Baptist, Sankey opposed kingship and favored a republican government.

In Mar. 1649 Sankey was created subwarden of All Souls, Oxf. by the Parliamentary Visitors, and University Proctor the next year. In this capacity he received Fairfax* and Cromwell at All Souls in 1649, where they received honorary degrees. Sankey was sent in 1649 to Ireland where he commanded a cavalry regiment with much success, and was shot in the hand. As a reward for his military

and other service in Ireland, he was knighted by Henry Cromwell* on 16 Nov. 1658. Sankey and several other army leaders brought charges of corruption against William Petty,* who had acquired over 15,000 acres of choice land for himself in the process of surveying Ireland. Elected to Richard Cromwell's* Parliament of 1659, Sankey pressed these charges against Petty, but Parliament ended before the issue could be resolved.

In Aug. 1659 Sankey brought his regiment to England to join Gen. Lambert* and was active in various disputes. At the end of Richard Cromwell's Protectorate, he became one of several Baptist members on the Army Council. Sankey was arrested in Dec. 1660, and was one of thirty republicans whom the House of Commons recommended on 24 May 1661 to exempt from pardon and confirmation of estates. He faded thereafter from public view and died in Ireland about 1685.

Underwood; C.G. Hull, ed., *The Economic Writings of Sir William Petty* (1899); W. Petty, *The History of the Survey of Ireland, 1655-56*, ed. T.A. Larcom (1851); R. Bagwell, *Ireland Under the Stuarts*, 2 (1963); Abbott.

R.G. Eaves

SAUNDERS (or Sanders), Thomas (1610-1695)

Army officer, was the eldest surviving son of a well-to-do gentry family established in Derbyshire since the fourteenth century. Educated at Repton, he was admitted to the Inner Temple in 1632. In 1642 he was among the first in his county to raise forces for Parliament under Sir John Gell. He quarreled with Gell, however, who accused him of insubordination, cowardice and Brownism. The dispute reached high command levels, including the Committee of Public Safety, but in Mar. 1646 Saunders was assigned with his troop to the New Model Army. By late 1647 he was the major in Sir Francis Thornhaugh's* regiment of horse, and succeeded Thornhaugh upon his death at Preston. Mrs. Hutchinson* described Saunders as 'a very godly, honest country gentleman' but added that he 'had not many things requisite to a great soldier.' This less than flattering estimate must be set against the fact that John Hutchinson* was in competition with Saunders for Thornhaugh's command. Despite Hutchinson's popularity with the troops, Cromwell's preference for Saunders decided the issue. Saunders' regiment submitted one of the petitions demanding that Charles I be brought to trial, and he attended the Whitehall debates in Dec. 1648.

In May 1649 Saunders was given the guard of Parliament when Cromwell and Fairfax* marched to suppress the Levellers. In October he was ordered to disperse gatherings in Derbyshire and Staffordshire. He was stationed near the Scots border at the battle of Worcester, and assisted Maj.-Gen. Harrison* in pursuing fugitives into Derbyshire and Yorkshire. Later in the year he garrisoned Exeter. In 1652 his regiment was posted to Scotland, remaining there until its phased withdrawal back into England between Oct. 1653 and Feb. 1654.

Saunders was at first a staunch supporter of Cromwell, writing him on 19 Sept. 1650 that 'God hath made you the man of his right hand, strong and successful for himself, his cause and saints.' He supported the Protectorate initially as well, and was elected for Derbyshire to the first Protectoral Parliament in 1654. But in October he joined Matthew Alured* and John Okey* – the former probably a new acquaintance, the latter an associate since the siege of Lichfield in 1643 – in opposing the Instrument of Government as a covert return to monarchy, and demanding the restitution of the republic. The discovery of their petition (probably drafted by John Wildman*) led to the arrest of the three colonels. Saunders was personally dismissed by Cromwell after an interview on 16 Dec. His restoration was authorized by the Committee for Nomination of Officers in June 1659 and approved by the restored Long Parliament on 4 July, but although a roster of officers was named, recruitment appears to have been delayed. Saunders adhered to Parliament during the October coup, and was arrested while trying to raise forces on its behalf in the Midlands. His release was ordered by the House of Commons on 27 Dec., and he was shortly afterward given command of Robert Swallow's* regiment, from which he was removed at the Restoration.

A portrait of Saunders, by Daniel Loggan after Balthasar Flessiers, is extant. He is not to be confused with his namesake, the Thomas Saunders who sat for Devon in the Barebones Parliament and was later Governor of Plymouth, nor with Col. Robert Saunders, also a Derbyshire man and Governor of Youghal and Kinsale, who was briefly associated with the republican agitation in 1654 but made his peace with the regime.

Firth & Davies; *Clarke Papers*; Clarke MSS; J.L. Hobbs, 'The Sanders Family and the Descent of the Manors of Caldwell, Coton-in-the-Elms and Little Ireton,' *Journal of the Derbyshire Archaeological and Natural History Society*, n.s., 21:1-23; B. Taft, '*The Humble Petition of Several Colonels of the Army*: Causes, Character, and Results of Military Opposition to Cromwell's Protectorate,' *HLQ*, 42:15-41; Nickolls; Cobbett; Woolrych; H. Cary, ed., *Memorials of the Great Civil War in England* (1842); *CSPD, Comm.*, 1:337-38; 4:74; 12:375, 378, 389, 394, 396; 13:67, 80, 299; Pole-Gell MSS, *HMC, 9th Report*. Papers: Derbyshire R.O.

R. Zaller

SAY, William (1604-c. 1666)

Regicide, born in 1604, was the second son of William Say of Ickenham, Middlesex, and his wife, Anne, daughter of Sir Edward Fenner, one of the judges of King's Bench. He matriculated at University Coll., Oxf. on 9 Dec. 1619 and graduated B.A. on 29 June 1623. Admitted to the Middle Temple on 15 Aug. 1622, he was called to the bar on 24 June 1631 and became an associate bencher on 5 May 1654. Having supported Parliament, Say obtained possession in 1646 of the sequestered lands of John, Lord Abergavenny in Kent, and enjoyed substantial profits until 1655. He was returned recruiter MP for Camelford, Corn. on 12 Apr. 1647, and on 2 Dec. 1648 was appointed one of the Kent Commissioners of Militia. A leading figure at the trial of Charles I, Say acted as temporary president of the court until Bradshaw's* arrival and afterwards sat regularly on Bradshaw's left as one of his two assistants. He also served on subcommittees which prepared the formal charges, drafted the death sentence and drew up the subsequent account of the trial for presentation to the Commons. At the 1649 trial of Lilburne,* Walwyn,* Prince* and Overton,* Say was one of the counsels for the Commonwealth, and in 1652 was the inappropriate co-author, as a former fenland speculator, of a one-sided parliamentary report on riots in the Isle of Axholme which involved Lilburne and John Wildman.* A member of the Council of State from 12 Feb. 1650 to Apr. 1653, he was appointed to various Rump committees, including the Admiralty, foreign affairs and law reform. As attorney to the Marshal's Court, he drew a modest annual profit which should perhaps have gone to the state. With Ludlow* and three others, Say tried to reconcile the army and Parliament in Nov. 1659 and was reappointed to the Council of State on 31 Dec. 1659. When Speaker Lenthall* was granted ten days 'sick' leave on 13 Jan. 1660, Say was appointed temporary Speaker. Exempted from the Act of Indemnity on 6 June 1660, he escaped to the Continent where he joined Ludlow* briefly at Lausanne in Sept. or Oct. 1662 before moving to Vevey. He remained there until news of the assassination of John Lisle* at Lausanne, and reports of similar action being planned against other Regicides, reached him on 11 Aug. 1664. After seeking refuge in Germany, he finally found a haven at Amsterdam in 1665 where he sought the support of fellow exiles in 1666 for Dutch moves against England. Say probably died in or shortly after 1666 in Holland. He was related by marriage to John Lisle.

DNB; Noble; Ludlow; J. Nalson, *A True Copy of the Journal of the High Court of Justice for the Trial of King Charles I* (1684); R. Temple, unpublished MS material. Papers: L (Add. MSS).

K.J. Lindley

SAYE AND SELE, first Viscount. *See* Fiennes, William

SAYER, John (1590-1658)

Parliamentary radical, MP 1645 (Colchester). Sayer was the eldest son of Sir George Sayer (d. 1630) of Bourchiers-Hall, Essex and of his wife Dorothy, daughter of John Higham of Norfolk. The Sayer family was one of considerable traditional standing in Essex, with lands at Abbots, Aldham and Great Tey, and with an exalted position since Tudor times in Colchester corporation. John Sayer's position in the county, and his return for Colchester may have had more to do with his family's inherited position than with his personal abilities. Though the historian of his county considered him to have been highly active in county committee work under the Commonwealth, Ralph Josselin gave the contrary impression – that Sayer had to be goaded into action, especially in religious matters. Sayer was returned for Colchester as a recruiter member in 1645. He sided with the army in 1647. His parliamentary career was undistinguished; though he was not actually excluded in Pride's purge, he stayed away from Parliament after 1648. Probably a Presbyterian in religion, Sayer died in 1658; the fortunes of his once prosperous family declined rapidly after his death.

B. & P.; P. Morant, *The History and Antiquities of . . . Essex* (1816), 2:194,

199-200; A. Macfarlane, ed., *The Diary of Ralph Josselin* (1976); Underdown, *PP*. Papers: L (Add. MSS; Stowe MSS).

M. Mullett

SCAWEN (or Scowen, Scauen), Robert (1602-1670)

Parliamentary radical, MP LP 1640-53 (Berwick on Tweed), 1659 (Grampound, Corn.), 1662-70 (Cockermouth). Scawen was born on 16 May 1602 in St. Germans, Corn., the second son of Robert Scawen (d. 1628) of Molenick, St. Germans and his wife, Isabella, daughter of Humphrey Nicholls (or Nicoll) of Penvose, St. Tudy, Corn. Scawen acted as solicitor to Francis, Earl of Bedford,* before becoming the Earl of Northumberland's secretary (c. 1640) and probably owed his election as MP for Berwick on Tweed in 1640 to Northumberland's patronage. Although he voted against Strafford's attainder, Scawen soon became a prominent Parliamentarian, probably aided by his kinship with Pym's nephew, Anthony Nicoll. An expert in army matters, he became chairman of the Army Committee and was voted £2000 by Parliament in 1646 in recognition of his exceptional service. Scawen also succeeded Pym* as Receiver-General of Hampshire, Wiltshire and Gloucester. He was one of the Parliamentary Commissioners sent to negotiate with the army in 1647 and, although absenting himself at Pride's purge, he continued to sign army committee warrants until Dec. 1648. His expertise in revenue matters was drawn upon under the Protectorate, and, having been elected MP for Grampound, Corn. to Richard Cromwell's* Parliament, he featured prominently in trade and revenue affairs. After the Restoration he acted as a commissioner for disbanding the army; was MP for Cockermouth (1662-70); and, remaining active in revenue matters, resumed the receiver-generalship (Oct. 1662-67), and served as a commissioner of excise appeals until his death. He married

Catherine, daughter of Cavendish Alsop of London, by whom he had seven sons and two daughters, and in 1658 established the family seat at Horton, Bucks.

Keeler; Bean; Burton, 3, 4; *CSPD, Comm.*, 9:198; 12:382; *Chas. II*, 2:536; 7:168, 431; 10:154. Papers: LPR; L (Add. MSS).

K.J. Lindley

SCOTT, Thomas (c. 1566-1635)

Parliamentary radical, MP 1624, 1628 (Canterbury). Scott was born about 1566, the eldest son of Charles Scott of Godmersham (d. 1596) and his wife Jane, daughter of Sir Thomas Wyatt of Boxley, the rebel leader in 1554. Although little is known about Scott's early life he was probably educated at Canterbury Grammar School before proceeding to Cambridge University for a short stay. Soon after his father's death he married Elizabeth Webbe, heiress of John Webbe, a leading Canterbury merchant; on her death in 1602 he took as his second wife Mary, daughter of John Knatchbull of Mersham, an important county landowner with kin ties to Paul Wentworth, the Elizabethan parliamentary radical. From about 1612 Scott lived mainly in Canterbury, though he maintained the family estate at Godmersham. Admitted a freeman of Canterbury in 1618, he entered the corporation shortly after, remaining a member until the end of 1620 when he was probably forced off the Council by anti-Puritan pressures. He declined to stand for election for the city to the 1621 Parliament but was returned MP for Canterbury in 1624, helped by strong Puritan and anti-oligarchic support, particularly from small freemen and lesser traders in the city. Unsuccessful in the 1625 and 1626 elections, he again served for Canterbury in the 1628 Parliament. Little is known about his activities in Parliament. From 1613, if not before, Scott kept a detailed personal and political diary, large sections of which are extant; he also wrote several unpublished tracts including 'A Discourse of Polletique and Civell Honor' (c. 1618). A committed Puritan like his father, Scott was instrumental in the establishment of a radical lectureship in St. Alphege's parish, Canterbury, and became a close friend of the first preacher there, Herbert Palmer,* the eminent Presbyterian divine. Scott opposed the Court-oriented candidates in the 1614 county elections and later that decade attacked the growing corruption and abuse in town politics, caused by the growth of oligarchy, as well as the sale of honors at Court. The Anglo-Spanish marriage negotiations in 1623-24 and the related resurgence of Kentish Catholicism transformed Scott's earlier preoccupation with the reform of civic politics into an acute concern with national political developments. In 1625 he campaigned vigorously on behalf of the anti-Court candidates in the shire elections for Kent. In 1626 he proposed a detailed scheme of parliamentary reform, including reapportionment, the abolition of pocket boroughs and the exclusion of over 200 non-resident MPs from the House of Commons. In 1627 he argued that Parliament should act against the Duke of Buckingham, if necessary overriding the King's will. In the first half of 1628 he led the Canterbury opposition to the billeting of troops and was briefly detained that summer for his criticism of the regime. In the early 1630s Scott continued to oppose the government, attacking Laudian innovations in the church and resisting militia exactions. His will led to protracted litigation after his death, but the Godmersham estate eventually descended to his granddaughter Dorothea Scott, a Quaker pamphleteer and friend of several Cromwellian radicals.

P. Clark, 'Thomas Scott and the Growth of Urban Opposition to the Early Stuart Regime,' *HJ*, 21:1-26; G.D. Scull, *Dorothea Scott* (1883). Papers: KAO (Knatchbull Papers).

P. Clark

SCOTT, Thomas (1580-1626)

Puritan minister and pamphleteer, was chaplain to James I and the Earl of Pembroke* and Rector at St. Saviour's, Norwich, and St. Clement's, Ipswich. A B.D. was incorporated by Cambridge in 1620. Scott achieved notoriety that year with the publication of *Vox populi*, a satire which purported to be the transcript of a debate in the Spanish Council on how to deceive England and undermine the Protestant religion. It created a diplomatic incident, and the English ambassador to Madrid was forced to convey apologies. Scott's arrest was ordered by an irate James I, but he remained safe in hiding. His next pamphlet, a forged *Speech Made in the Lower House . . . by Sir Edward Cicill* (1621), warns against the political dangers associated with Arminianism, and *The Belgicke Pismire* (1622) emphasizes a theme found in *Vox populi*, that mankind was not created for idleness or to any base or vile employment, but to labor to preserve creation. The ideal justice of Plato's *Republic* and More's *Utopia*, Scott notes, had already been realized in the Netherlands. In *News from Pernassus* (1622) Scott pleads for England to support the Palatinate, and in *A Tongue-Combat* (1623) his Protestant soldier maintains that a brotherly communion would be preferable to episcopal government. *The High-Waies of God and the King* (1623) defends religious moderation and attacks the hypocrisy of ministers, magistrates, lawyers and merchants for enriching themselves at public expense and charges that courtly thieves and monopolists beg patents so they may rob with licence.

In *Digitus Dei* (1623) Scott reaches new heights of indignation; citing Foxe's *Acts and Monuments*, he holds out the Waldenses as a model of Christian piety and links this sect to descendants in Bohemia and the Palatinate. Puritans, he writes, are like Samson, poor honest men who, once united, will pull the house down on idolaters. Such outspokenness necessitated Scott's flight to Utrecht in late 1623. *An Experimentall Discoverie of Spanish*

Practices and *Vox Dei*, both of which urge war against Spain and advise England to develop the New World, appeared before the end of the year. *Vox regis* (1624) defends *Vox populi*, which had gone to five editions, and asserts that just as truth comes sometimes from vulgar people and famine is felt first by the poor, the House of Commons is where the disorders of a state are first felt and soonest discerned. Scott continued the attack on Spain in other pamphlets published in 1624: *The Spaniards Perpetual Designes, Votive Angliae, Certain Reasons and Arguments of Polocie, Aphorismes of State, Englands Joy, Symmachia*, and *Boanerges*. *Vox coeli*, in which Scott creates a celestial conference of English royalty, ran to four editions, and *The Belgick Souldier* not only counsels war against Spain as a check against economic exploitation and moral laxity, but uses the primitive church as an example of how those called heretics (especially the Hussites) have always fought for liberty of conscience.

In the summer of 1624 Scott published *The Second Part of Vox populi*, but because of the previous collapse of the Spanish marriage negotiations and the imminence of war the charges had lost much of their sting. As a result, after bringing out a collected edition of his works Scott appears to have published nothing for over a year. His last pamphlet, *Sir Walter Rawleighs Ghost* (1626), which recalls his *Robert Earle of Essex His Ghost* (1624), pays tribute to Scott's lifelong hero. As he was leaving church in Utrecht on 18 June 1626, Scott was stabbed to death by an English soldier, John Lambert, a former Spanish agent who refused to confess any complicity even though tortured before being hanged. Scott's funeral attracted many dignitaries, and his influence on Puritans of the next two decades is unmistakable.

T. Scott, *Workes* (1624); L.B. Wright, 'Propaganda against James I's "Appeasement" of Spain,' *HLQ*, 6:149-72; Hill, *IOER*; Zaller; C. Steele, *English Interpreters of the Iberian New World from Purchas to Stevens* (1975). Scott's authorship of *Vox coeli* has been challenged in J.H. Bryant, 'John Reynolds of Exeter and His Canon,' *The Library*, 5th ser., 18:299-303, where it is attributed to Reynolds. Papers: L (Add. MSS).

T.W. Hayes

SCOTT (or Scot), Thomas (d. 1648)

Leveller, is not to be confused with his namesake, the Regicide.* Virtually nothing is known of Scott's family background, except that he may have come from Yorkshire, or his life until he rose to prominence in the parliamentary army. As Maj. Scott, he and a captain were voted £100 by Parliament on 13 Jan. 1644 in recognition of their loyal service, and in 1645 he was returned as recruiter MP for Aldborough, Yorks. In Oct. 1646 Scott was granted leave by the House and recommended for service in the army in Ireland but he apparently never left England. There is a possibility that he was the same Maj. Scott who was providing the Royalists with intelligence in June 1647 (0: Clarendon MS 29). In Sept. 1647 he clashed with Ireton* and Cromwell in the House when he accused the army officers of conducting secret negotiations with the King. Scott was arrested by Fairfax* on 15 Nov. 1647 after he had been observed with others inciting the soldiers to mutiny in support of *The Agreement of the People* at the rendezvous at Corkbush Field, near Ware, Herts. Having been sent up to Parliament in the custody of Lieut. Chillenden,* he was ordered to give an account of his actions and was suspended from sitting. He died in prison on 6 Jan. 1648.

DNB; F. Maseres, *Select Tracts Relating to the Civil Wars in England* (1815); *CCSP*, 1:380, 400, 408; *HMC*, *5th Report, Duke of Sutherland MSS*, 173.

K.J. Lindley

SCOTT (or Scot), Thomas (c. 1603-1660)

Regicide and parliamentary radical, MP 1645 (Aylesbury), 1654 (Wycombe), 1656 (Aylesbury), 1659 (Wycombe). Scott was born in Little Marlow, Bucks., the son of Thomas Scott of London and Mary (née Sutton). He was educated at Westminster School and Emmanuel Coll., Camb., where he was admitted pensioner in 1619 and graduated B.A. in 1623 and M.A. in 1626. Scott inherited wealth from his parents and a plentiful estate from his first wife Alice Allanson (m. 1626), who was probably a cousin of Francis Allen.* In 1644 he married Grace, daughter of the future Regicide Sir Thomas Mauleverer.* After her death in 1646 he took a third wife, Alice (surname unknown), who survived him.

Scott was a minor provincial attorney until the outbreak of the Civil War, but his treasurership of the Buckinghamshire County Committee (1644-46) catapulted him to prominence. Returned as a recruiter MP in 1645, he was soon among the emerging republican minority in the House of Commons. In July 1647 he was one of the MPs who fled to the army and, if the inscription on his wife's grave in St. Michael's, London is to be credited, was commissioned a colonel. His relations with the army were unquestionably intimate. He was a prime mover of Pride's purge, and took over from John Gurdon* the measure requiring MPs to register their dissent to the vote of 5 Dec. 1648 for a further address to the King. Appointed to the High Court, Scott was one of the most zealous of Charles' judges, and among the most finally unrepentant. He helped draft both the charge and the final sentence and, confronting his own execution, declared he wished no better epitaph than 'Here lies one who had a hand and a heart in the execution of Charles Stuart, late King of England' (Ludlow, 2:250).

With Cromwell, Haselrig* and Vane,* Scott was one of the chief guiding forces of the Commonwealth. On 7 Feb. 1649 he was appointed to the five-man committee which nominated the new Council of State.

Scott himself served on all five Councils between 1649 and 1653. On 5 Mar. he published *A New Paire of Spectacles of the Old Fashion, for the Scots Commissioners to Helpe Their Eye-Sight*; it was printed anonymously. On 1 July he was made chief of the new republic's intelligence service, which he fashioned into the instrument later so ably wielded by John Thurloe.* It was Scott who broke Love's conspiracy in 1651, though he personally opposed his execution. Withal, he found time to serve as Recorder of Wycombe and, with his colleague Simon Mayne,* dominated Buckinghamshire affairs.

Despite his own radicalism, Scott recognized the need to rally moderate support to the new regime. For this reason, he opposed the disestablishment of the House of Lords, and in the *Declaration of Parliament* which he drafted, he emphasized the common ground between the Civil War Parliament and the Rump. To Cromwell he wrote in 1650, 'England is not as France, a meadow to be mowed as often as the governors please; our interest is to do our work with as little grievance to our new people, scarce yet proselyted, as possible.'

Scott supported Cromwell's initiative for a new representative in the fall of 1651, but he bitterly opposed the dissolution of the Rump and was an implacable foe of the Protectorate. In the first Protectoral Parliament he refused the engagement to the Instrument of Government and urged his fellow MPs to reject it as well. Excluded from Parliament in 1656, he spoke out boldly in favor of a republic and against the Cromwellian Upper House when finally permitted to take his seat: 'Shall I, that sat in a parliament that brought a king to the bar, and to the block, not speak my mind fully here?' Scott was instrumental in deposing Richard Cromwell* in 1659, and took his place in the restored Rump. On 14 May and again on 31 Dec. he was appointed to the Council of State. On 24 May he was made a member of the Intelligence Committee and its chief again on 10 Jan. 1660. Opposing Lambert* and Fleetwood* in the fall of 1659, he entered into correspondence with Monck, and was sent to him as a Parliamentary Commissioner as well as Secretary of State in Feb. 1660. Monck's true attitude to the Good Old Cause was soon revealed. Scott fled to Brussels in April, and surrendered after having been recognized in June. Despite this, and a detailed memorandum he supplied his captors on his intelligence activities, he was excepted from the pardon, tried on 12 Oct. and executed. Scott bore his death with great fortitude, declaring that he died 'in a cause not to be repented of.' His son Thomas was arrested in Ireland in 1663 on a charge of plotting. Another son, William, served as a government spy under the aegis of Aphra Behn; his daughter Alice married William Rowe, the Scoutmaster-General.

DNB; Burton; Nickolls; Underdown, *PP*; Worden; D. Underdown, *Royalist Conspiracy in England* (1971); A.M. Johnson, 'Buckinghamshire 1640-1660' (Swansea M.A. thesis, 1963); C.H. Firth, ed., 'Thomas Scot's Account of his Actions as Intelligencer during the Commonwealth,' *EHR*, 12:116-26; R. Temple, unpublished MS material.

G.S.S. Yule and R. Zaller

SCROPE (or Scroope), Adrian (1601-1660)

Regicide, was the son of Robert Scrope of Wormsley, Oxon., and his wife, Margaret, daughter of Richard Cornwall of London. Scrope entered Hart Coll., Oxf. in 1617, and the Middle Temple in Feb. 1619. In 1624 he married Mary, daughter of Robert Waller of Beaconsfield, by whom he had two sons and two daughters. His mother-in-law was Anne Hampden, aunt of John Hampden.* At the beginning of the Civil War he raised a troop of horse for Parliament, securing a captaincy under the Earl of Essex* in Oct. 1642. By the spring of 1645 he was a major in the regiment of Col. Richard Graves, having been included in the original list of officers appointed for the New Model Army. Two

years later Scrope sided with the army in its dispute with Parliament, after which he was promoted to colonel and given command of Graves' regiment (July 1647). Following the outbreak of the second Civil War, Scrope's regiment was assigned garrison duty in Dorset until June 1648, when Fairfax* recalled him to London to fight against the Earl of Norwich and the Kentish Royalists. After taking part in the siege of Colchester, on 10 July his regiment captured the Earl of Holland and routed his forces. Afterwards Scrope proceeded to Yarmouth in expectation of a royalist landing by the Prince of Wales, but finding the city able to defend itself, moved his regiment back to London where he participated in the Army Council's deliberations during the fall of 1648. He was appointed one of the commissioners for the trial of Charles I, attended all but one of the twenty-three sessions of the High Court, and signed the death warrant.

Scrope's regiment was one of those drawn by lot in Apr. 1649 to go to Ireland. Inspired by Leveller pamphlets, they mutinied at Salisbury on 1 May, demanding a democratically elected Parliament and the restoration of the elected Army Council which had existed in 1647. After Scrope's efforts to negotiate a settlement failed, Cromwell and Fairfax marched against the rebels at Burford and ended the crisis. His active military career virtually terminated by this episode, Scrope became Governor of Bristol Castle in Oct. 1649. When Bristol was ordered demolished in 1655, Cromwell appointed him to the Council for Scotland, with a salary of £600 a year.

At the Restoration Scrope obeyed the royal proclamation and surrendered himself on 4 June 1660. The House of Commons voted to include him in the Act of Indemnity, provided he pay a fine equal to one year's value of his estates. He was released on parole on 20 June, but the Lords adamantly refused to allow Scrope to be pardoned, and in August he was placed in close confinement. At his trial (12 Oct. 1660) he defended himself with considerable dignity and eloquence, maintaining that he had acted by the authority of Parliament, which at that time was deemed the supreme authority in the land, even by some of those who now sat in judgment upon him. However, the court summoned Richard Browne, formerly major-general for the parliamentary army and now Mayor-elect of London, who testified that Scrope had spoken in defense of the King's execution after the return of Charles II. Scrope rightly concluded that it was not his involvement in the execution of Charles I but Browne's betrayal of a private conversation which condemned him. He was executed at Charing Cross on 17 Oct. Contemporary accounts describe Scrope as a man of high principles and strong character, who bore his fate with cheerfulness and courage.

Scrope's eldest son, Edmund, was Keeper of the Privy Seal in Scotland, and Adrian's grandson, John Scrope, took part in Monmouth's rebellion and later became Secretary to the Treasury. A contemporary portrait of Scrope by Robert Walker hangs at Wormsley Hall.

DNB; *Clarke Papers*; Firth & Davies; *ST*; Noble; R. Temple, unpublished MS material. Papers: (Add. MSS).

C.B. Rynder

SEARLE (or Serle), George (d. 1658)

Parliamentary radical, MP LP 1640 (Taunton). Of obscure origins, Searle may originally have been a merchant from Honiton, Devon. He was Mayor of Taunton in 1640, and possibly before then, and was made Mayor again by the Commons in 1649. Probably his duties in the borough precluded a more active parliamentary role. A Presbyterian elder and JP, Searle was a political ally of Col. John Pyne* of Curry Mallet, head of the County Committee in 1645 and effective controller of the institutions of local government in Somerset. During this period, Searle and others bought the Bishop of Winchester's rights in Taunton. By then, he was one of only two

MPs out of the sixteen elected to the Long Parliament for Somerset constituencies who survived death or expulsion. In 1646 he was voted compensation of £2500 for losses in the Civil War. Purged from the Commission of the Peace in 1657, he was among the many radicals replaced by moderates in accordance with the Protector's drift towards settlement and accommodation. After his death on 28 Sept. 1658, the administration of his estate was granted to his widow, Welthian.

Keeler; Underdown, *SCWI* and *PP*; *CJ*, 2:21; *HMC, 4th Report*, 25; Worden.

J.F. Brown

SEDGWICK, Obadiah (c. 1600-1658)

Puritan minister, was born in St. Peter's parish, Marlborough, Wilts., where his father, Joseph, was vicar. Obadiah was the eldest of several brothers (John, Joseph) who entered the ministry and seem to have had Puritan leanings. He matriculated at Queen's Coll., Oxf. about 1619, but soon migrated to Magdalen Hall, eventually proceeding to the B.A. (1620), M.A. (1623) and B.D. (1630). Sedgwick's Puritanism may have been clear from his first employment as chaplain to the Veres. He accompanied Horatio Vere, Baron of Tilbury, to the Low Countries, before returning to pursue the B.D. His first preferment was as lecturer at St. Mildred's, Bread Street, London (1630), but in 1639 he was presented by the Earl of Warwick* to the parish of Coggeshall, Essex, a church that was to have a long history of Puritan activism. While at Coggeshall, Sedgwick gained some notoriety as 'the scandalous and seditious minister' (Wood).

At the outbreak of the Civil War he was for a time chaplain to Sir Denzil Holles'* regiment, while his brother John was chaplain to the regiment raised by the Earl of Stamford. Sedgwick was one of the original members of the Westminster

Assembly (1643) and seems to have voted with the Presbyterians. Possibly to be nearer the Assembly, he resumed his position as lecturer at St. Mildred's, Bread Street, and Wood records the anecdote that in hot weather he would unbutton his doublet so that 'his breath might be the longer.' Wood also records Sedgwick's consistent opposition to episcopacy, noting that in Sept. 1644 he 'told the people several times that God was angry with the army for not cutting off delinquents.'

Sedgwick was very briefly Rector of St. Andrew's, Holborn, but in 1646 obtained the parish of St. Paul's, Covent Garden, and forthwith resigned his living at Coggeshall, where he was succeeded by John Owen.* From the first he pressed for alliance with the Scots (cf. 'Four Speeches,' 1646), and he was one of the licensers appointed to control the press. He was a member of the eleventh Classis of the London Provincial Assembly, but his Presbyterianism did not prevent him from cooperating fully with the Protectorate government. In Mar. 1654 he became one of the Triers in the ecclesiastical settlement of the Protectorate, and later that year a ministerial assistant to the Ejectors. Two years later, however, his health began to fail, and he resigned his living at St. Paul's, Covent Garden to his son-in-law, Thomas Manton. By then a man of considerable wealth, he retired to Marlborough, where he died in Jan. 1658. Sedgwick published a catechism and many sermons.

Ath. Oxon.; *DNB*; *Rel. Bax.*; A.F. Mitchell and J. Struthers, eds., *The Minutes of the Westminster Assembly* (1874); R. Dale, *Annals of Coggeshall* (1863); Hetherington.

R.S. Paul

SEDGWICK, William (c. 1610-1663)

Independent minister, was born in Bedfordshire, the son of William and Elizabeth Sedgwick. Sedgwick matriculated at Oxford in 1625, where he took the B.A. in 1628 and the M.A. in 1631. His first benefice was at Farnham in northwestern Essex, a living he held from 5 Feb. 1634 to 1644. During that time he circulated widely among Puritan ministers, and many of his activities appear in the diary of Samuel Rogers. Sedgwick, like many of his brothers, soon ran afoul of the official church. He preserved his place through the Laudian suppression and, like other Puritans, found a London pulpit early in the 1640s. In Oct. 1641 parishioners of St. Giles-without-Cripplegate hired Sedgwick to lecture on Thursdays. By late 1642 he had become chaplain to the troops gathered by Sir William Constable,* himself a Puritan patron. Sedgwick preached several fast sermons before the Parliament during the first Civil War. Through the assistance of Oliver Cromwell, he was appointed preacher at Ely Cathedral and collected sequestration monies to maintain himself. Sedgwick preached at Ely until Sept. 1649, and during his tenure he moved into more radical currents of thought. One contemporary observer described him as 'a Presbyterian, sometimes an Independent, and at other times an Anabaptist.' He showed millenarian tendencies as well. A 1647 newsletter related that Sedgwick came to London where he prophesied 'that the world will be at an end within fourteen days, Christ then coming to judgment, and that Christ appeared to him in his study the last week at Ely and told him so much.' Several ministers tried to argue with him; some even thought Sedgwick had a temporary mental disorder. When the date arrived, a terrible storm struck in the night which many took as a kind of fulfilment, and earned the prophet the name of 'Doomsday Sedgwick.' Henry Pinnell,* himself no stranger to worldly temptation, saw Sedgwick's prophecy as an attempt to win popular applause and personal glory. Sedgwick continued to be open to radical, prophetic ideas. In such sermons as *Christs Coming* (1648) and *The Leaves of the Tree of Life* (1648), he described England in ecstatic terms as God's elect nation, while decrying the unrelieved oppression of the poor and the avarice of

Parliament. By 1652 he was fascinated by John Reeve.* Sedgwick never joined the Muggletonian sect, but he corresponded with Reeve through 1657. As a Seeker in his own sense, Sedgwick also discussed Quaker ideas with James Nayler.* It is not clear what permanent preaching post, if any, he held during the Commonwealth period, though he was in touch with many key Cromwellian clergymen and lay leaders. Sedgwick died shortly after the Restoration and does not appear as one of those ejected from a place either in 1660 or 1662.

DNB; *Calamy Revised*; Hill, *MER*. Papers: S. Rogers' diary, BQ (Percy MSS 7).

K.W. Shipps

SELDEN, John (1584-1654)

Legal scholar, was born on 16 Dec. 1584 in the hamlet of Salvington near Tarring, a Sussex port-town. The parish register's baptismal note records his father as a 'ministrel.' The Selden clan, widespread in Sussex, was of a sturdy if undistinguished stock. The father's musical talents, it was said, had enabled him to captivate and marry Margaret Baker, only daughter and heiress of Thomas Baker of the knightly Kentish family of Bakers. But Thomas Selden must have been highly regarded in his local parish, being named one of the two church wardens as early as 1581. By the early years of James I, Thomas was identified as a 'yeoman,' indeed one of some substance with rents to an annual value of £23 8s. The material well-being of the family explains the father's ability to send his only surviving son off to the prebendal free school at Chichester where his talents caught the eye of the school master, Hugh Barker, who arranged an exhibition for his prize pupil at Oxford where he matriculated in 1600. After two years, Selden left without a degree, enrolling at Clifford's Inn and thence winning admission to the Inner Temple in 1603. Presumably with his father's continued

support he endured the long years of study preceding the call to the bar in 1613.

It was neither Sussex nor Oxford but London and the associations he made there which formed Selden's interest, outlook and spirit. The Bohemian literary flavor of the Inner Temple's gentlemen attracted young Selden and his chamber-mate, Edward Heyward, to the 'tribe of Ben' and Selden was early identified as among the ardent admirers of Ben Jonson. The bond was as much classical scholarship as poetry, for Selden could not but observe that where Jonson bore the weight of undoubted learning lightly, Selden's poetic muse sank under his own erudition. More enduring and more essential was the interest in classical, legal and historical scholarship that Selden found and nurtured in the company of Sir Robert Bruce Cotton* and the incomparable library he had assembled at Westminster. To that collection Selden was given welcome access and from it he took the materials used in his early scholarly works. Cotton's enthusiasm, width of interest, and generosity – as well as the pattern of the scholar-collector – left a life-long imprint on Selden. The third circle was a sophisticated aristocratic ensemble centering around Elizabeth, Countess of Kent and her two sisters, co-heiresses of the Earl of Shrewsbury and married respectively to Henry Grey, Earl of Kent, Thomas Howard, Earl of Arundel, and William Herbert, Earl of Pembroke.* Selden was to serve for many years as steward to the Earl of Kent and on his death entered into a liaison with the Countess whose personal estate he subsequently inherited. Selden spent the long summer vacations at the Kent estate in Wrest, Beds. and shared the London season with them as well, their town-house, White Friars, being adjacent to the Inner Temple grounds. Arundel patronized him for scholarship, retained him for legal matters, and awarded him a handsome annuity of £50. Pembroke became his political patron, indirectly helping him obtain parliamentary seats in 1626 and 1628. Literature, scholarship and politics were the common threads that ran through all three circles whose boundaries indeed overlapped each other. Strong feelings, strength of character, and intellectual independence and excitement were equally evident in all three and with it a critical – and sometimes openly hostile – reaction to the politics of the Stuart dynasty.

It was scholarship and not poetry that engaged Selden's interest throughout his life. From 1606 until 1629 he authored ten books, edited one, and contributed several pieces to the works of others. The variety of this first scholarly phase reveal an impressive versatility and range of interests. Five dealt with English history: *Analecton Anglo-Britannicon* (1606; printed 1615); *Jani Anglorum facies altera* (1610), *England's Epinomis* (1610); *Eadmer* (1623); and the notes to Fortescue's *De laudibus legum Angliae* (1616), these five revealing his early concern with the period from Anglo-Saxon England to the fifteenth century. If these all in some degree employed legal materials as historical evidence, only the *Duello* (1610), the notes for Fortescue, the *History of Tithes* (1618) and the *Privileges of the Baronage* (1621; printed 1642), were primarily exercises in English legal history while the *Titles of Honor* (1614) drew substantially upon both European and English legal materials. Two of his works – *De Dis Syris* (1617) and *Marmora Arundelliana* (1628) – dealt significantly with aspects of biblical and classical history respectively. And one of them, the notes to Drayton's *Poly-Olbion* (1612), saw the historian exploding most of the myths, fictions and poetic licence which has passed for historical gospel among medieval chroniclers and later writers, a demonstration of the critical, scientific approach to historiography which was to be Selden's special contribution to English intellectual life. Three of these works, *De Dis Syris, Titles of Honor* and *Marmora Arundelliana*, won him immediate international repute while the *History of Tithes* with its undermining of clerical claims to tithes by divine creation, got him into trouble with the ecclesiastical authorities and set Selden in that anticlerical, secular, Erastian posture

which affected his future political career. These were indeed productive years and by his mid-thirties Selden's special brand of English legal humanist history had made a distinctive mark in scholarship; elaborated a critical, scientific theory of history; and demonstrated the early English experience with positive legislation and the primacy of the rule of law in English political institutions and life.

The political implications of Selden's scholarly convictions and interests were essentially crystallized between 1616 and 1618 when he published his edition of Fortescue and the *History of Tithes*. They were undoubtedly aggravated by the divine right theory of monarchy which James I professed and which he and a group of ambitious clerics elaborated. For Selden any conceptualizations, whether by king, judges or clerics, which elevated the royal prerogative above the rule of law undermined his historical vision of popular sovereignty, positive legislation by representative assemblies, and the limits on monarchy guaranteed by the substantive and procedural remedies of the rule of law. Despite these sentiments Selden did not sit in Parliament until 1624. However, it should be noted that his scholarly expertise had earlier involved him with the Parliament of 1621. Selden's *Titles of Honor* had discussed the privileges of the peers as individuals and as a corporate group when they sat in the House of Lords. In 1621 the upper House began an investigation of its privileges and retained Selden and William Hakewill* as consultants for the technical aspects of the research into the records. The revival in 1621 of the impeachment process against Mitchell, Mompesson and Bacon by the House of Commons gave an urgency to Selden's researches which had not been foreseen at the outset. At the same time the House of Commons staked a claim to an original jurisdiction in the action it took against Floyd. The Privy Council apparently believed that Selden had advised or supported the lower House in that move and Selden was arrested and detained for seven weeks before he could convince the authorities that he disapproved of the usurpation of an original jurisdiction by the Commons. It was an ironic preview of a dilemma that was to color the whole of Selden's own political career: at what point did the privileges of parliament rise above the rule of law and the due process which protected the liberties of the subject? and under what conditions were the privileges of parliament above the royal prerogative?

Selden served with increasing activity in the Parliaments of 1624, 1626 and 1628-29. In 1624 Selden was returned for the borough of Lancaster. Befitting a novice, he was not prominent in debate but the House employed him extensively in committee service, particularly in connection with reforms in the law and the courts. He was also involved in the successful maneuver to establish sole jurisdiction of the House over the election and return of its members. There was no occasion for serious constitutional confrontation. With the failure of the Spanish match and the spectacle of a King willing to entertain the threat of war abroad, if not actual hostilities, the relationship of crown and parliament was indeed now more harmonious than it had been since the first session of the Parliament of 1604.

Selden was returned in 1626 for both Great Bedwin, Wilts, and Ilchester, Som. Lady Kent's brother-in-law, William Herbert, third Earl of Pembroke, was Lord Lieutenant of Somerset and also had vast estates in Wiltshire where he was allied with William Seymour, Earl of Hertford, who controlled Great Bedwin. It was for the latter borough that Selden decided to sit. In parliament he was now more active in debate, especially in the attack on the Court of High Commission for imprisoning and excommunicating Sir Robert Howard. Here Selden combined opposition to the arbitrary power of the prerogative courts with hostility to any interference with the independence of parliament. With Coke* and Noy, he searched the medieval legal and parliamentary precedents to justify the parliamentary nomination of treasurers to receive the subsidy and ensure its specific appropriation for the war effort abroad. He

also energetically supported the attempt to impeach the Duke of Buckingham, making the key suggestion to employ 'common fame' and serving as one of the managers of the prosecution in the House of Lords. Selden was particularly emphatic about the dangerous precedent which Buckingham had demonstrated in seizing a merchant ship, 'an example,' he declared, 'to justify all authority without law or legal cause. . . .' To save his favorite, Charles dismissed the Parliament, abandoning thereby the hope of a subsidy and impelling him to undertake the forced loans, a scheme of prerogative taxation which seemed to fulfill Selden's dire prophecy.

Selden's forebodings were soon realized as resistance to the forced loan increased and Charles ordered the arrest of at least 76 'gentlemen recusants of the loan.' More refused than could be committed. Selden's friend, Henry Grey, Earl of Kent, was 'disofficed' as Lord Lieutenant of Bedfordshire when he rejected the royal mandate. The judges paid but refused to acknowledge the legality of the loan. The benchers of the Inner Temple submitted but there is no evidence that Selden, a mere barrister, was invited to participate. To do so would have been inconsistent with constitutional principles he deeply cherished. When some of the prisoners decided to challenge the legality of prerogative arrest by suing for a *habeas corpus* and moving for freedom under bail, Selden served with distinction as counsel for Sir Edmund Hampden in the Five Knights' Case. His attempt to elevate the issue from prerogative arrest to prerogative taxation failed and he built his argument on the issue before the court on medieval precedents and Magna Carta, ch. 29. Although his argument won popular applause, the King's Bench judges seemed sympathetic to Attorney General Heath's 'reason of state' argument. However, they never actually delivered a final judgment, rather remanding the prisoners by an interim resolution while they took the arguments under further consideration. Curiously, the technical distinction between the interim resolution and final judgment seems to have been widely misconstrued by contemporaries, Selden included, who regarded the failure to bail the prisoners as a miscarriage of justice. The challenge now presented to the liberties of the subject dominated Selden's life for the next four years.

The prisoners were released in January as part of the crown's preparation for summoning a parliament in Mar. 1628, in which Selden sat for Ludgershall borough, Wilts., another seat controlled by the Earl of Hertford. In the two sessions of this Parliament Selden played a stellar role along with Coke, Eliot,* Phelips,* Wentworth and Digges in their concerted effort to bring the exercise of the prerogative under the rule of law. In addition to the abuses of prerogative taxation and prerogative arrest, Selden also emphasized the dangers involved in the practice of billeting soldiers on private subjects and especially in the extension of martial law from the military to the civilian population. He was chairman of the committee which searched for precedents to support their position and drafted the reports as well as speaking most effectively both in the Commons and in conferences with the House of Lords. Selden staunchly refused to subordinate the liberties of the subject to the suggestion of some to rely on trust in the King and carried the House with him as he assured them that the procedure by petition of right rather than by bill was equally effective in binding King and judges. He was most forceful in successfully leading the House to reject the compromise modifications diffidently proposed by the House of Lords and equally so in refusing to accept the King's first answer to the Petition of Right. What Selden and his colleagues accomplished in adding the Petition of Right to the statute book in 1628 was as significant symbolically for modern English constitutional history as what the barons achieved in 1215 in wresting Magna Carta from King John – and historically, equally ineffective.

In the second session Selden's distrust of Charles was vindicated when he demonstrated to the House that the King was directly responsible for ordering the printing of the Petition of Right with the rejected first answer. And he informed the House of continuing violations as the King continued to collect tonnage and poundage without specific statutory enactment and despite the injunction of the Petition of Right. On the fateful March 2nd when Charles ordered the Parliament to adjourn, Selden firmly supported Eliot's attempt to move a remonstrance and upbraided the Speaker for refusing to entertain the motion.

The March 2nd incident quickly led to the arrest of Selden and eight of his colleagues, ironically without cause expressed and none forthcoming until Selden's writ for *habeas corpus* produced a return certifying detention for sedition and conspiracy. Thus began a two-year period of trials and legal harassment where despite Attorney General Heath's blunders, Selden was in a kind of legal limbo: neither freed on bail nor convicted. The attempt to gloss over the awkward legal problems by offering Selden and his associates freedom on bail with sureties for good behavior was indignantly rejected as involving an admission of wrong-doing and compromising the privileges of parliament. It was largely the Earl of Arundel's need for Selden's legal services which brought him liberty with the condition of appearing before the judges on the first day of each term. After some years, even this condition was removed.

With the death of Coke, Eliot and Cotton and the acceptance of royal office by Noy and Digges, Selden was now in effect the titular leader of what had been the parliamentary opposition to prerogative government, and not surprisingly the crown made some effort to win his gratitude, if not his open support. It was in this connection, apparently under Laud's prodding, that Selden finally revised and published in 1635 his long-languishing manuscript of *Mare clausum* as a British reply to Grotius' *Mare liberum*. But the effort to win him over to the crown did not succeed. His suspicions of Charles and concern for the rule of law remained equally unchanged.

He had no interest in power for its own sake; had no family responsibilities; and his practice brought him sufficient wealth for his comfortable life-style. When Charles entertained the idea of offering Selden the lord chancellorship, his two young friends, Clarendon and Falkland, who were consulted in the matter and knew full well that Selden 'had never affected' preferment, advised against it to avoid Charles the embarrassment of a rejection. Despite imprisonment and legal persecution Selden never let rancor or the need for revenge becloud his judgment or the pursuit of his own goals. To the confusion of some of the crown's adherents, his deference was never at the expense of his intellectual and political independence.

During the 1630s Selden devoted himself largely to scholarship. He took advantage of the leisure created by his imprisonment to return to his studies, which now took a surprising new turn: the political, legal and social institutions and the legal philosophy of the ancient Hebrews. The works which now issued forth revealed a mastery of Oriental languages and literature, with an especial relevance for legal problems. In 1631 he published *De successionibus ad leges Ebraeorum in bona defunctiorum*; in 1638 *De successione in pontificatum Hebraeorum*; in 1646 *Uxor Ebraica*, whose account of the divorce procedure fascinated John Milton.* In 1640 Selden published *De jure naturali et gentium juxta disciplinam Ebraeorum*, a major work and an ingenious attempt to construct an historical system of natural law which much interested Vico in the next century. Later he edited Eutychius' *Origines* (1642); and in 1644 he published *De anno civili et calendario veteris ecclesiae; seu reipublicae Judaicae*; and the *De synedriis et praefecturis iuridicis veterum Ebraeorum* between 1650 and 1655. Learned Christian Hebraists had multiplied in his day but Selden had no interest in their central dogmatic concerns. If there was a noticeable absence of exposure to a formal Talmudic dialectic and a too easy reliance on rabbinic sources, it was more than compensated for by his extraordinary width of learning and his unusual ability to provide a superior comparative perspective. The cool analytical approach and unconcern for dogma revealed the historian exploring the early history of civilization in broad terms and enhanced Selden's repute both abroad and at home.

The decade of the 1640s was for Selden a busy one intellectually and an unhappy one politically. He sat in the Long Parliament as a burgess for Oxford University, probably owing the seat to Archbishop Laud who also was Chancellor of the University. According to Yonge's diary, there was a rumor that the Privy Council had considered Selden's name for Speaker of the House but the King eventually nominated Lenthall.* If true, it reflected more confidence on the King's part than was justified by Selden's actions. If Selden was opposed to the King's commissions of array, he was less than enthusiastic about the parliamentary Militia Ordinance. He won public obloquy for opposing the attainder of Strafford after it appeared the impeachment effort would not succeed. And he did not participate in the impeachment of Laud. But in the choice between the illegalities of the crown and those of Parliament, Selden reluctantly regarded the latter as the lesser of two evils. Accordingly, he remained in London when the King called his parliamentary supporters to Oxford in 1643, took the Covenant that year, and stayed in the House until the late spring of 1649. For Selden, the King's attempt to undermine Parliament by setting up a rival assembly in Oxford was not in his own best interest. 'When the King's friends are absent,' Selden remarked, 'the King will be lost.'

The prophecy reflected the acute realism of the experienced and casts a poignant light on lost potentialities. As political friction escalated into military combat, Selden well knew that the rule of law would be the chief victim: *Arma leges silenti*. If the King emerged victorious, how would the prerogative be restrained? Selden's convictions and distrust of Charles framed his answer.

Although parliamentary diaries for the

Long Parliament exceed in number as well as in bulk those for 1624 or 1628, they do not permit the historian to follow Selden's activities in comparable detail. There were apparently periods of long absence by Selden and his appointment by the House to serve with the parliamentary delegation in the Westminster Assembly of Divines also took him out of much of the day-to-day activity in the legislature. It is thus difficult to construct much beyond a scrappy account of his activity in the Commons. The best reflection of his convictions at this time – and a further clue to why he stayed in London – is afforded by Selden's table-talk which an amanuensis, Richard Milward, recorded during these years. For good and evident reasons they remained unpublished until the Glorious Revolution of 1688 established a more palatable environment for Selden's trenchant opinions.

Selden dismissed the divine right theory of monarchy with the simple observation that 'a king is a thing men have made for their own sakes, for quietness' sake.' However, 'the King's oath is not security enough for our property, for he swears to govern according to law; now the judges interpret the law; and what judges can be made to do we know.' In the light of contemporary parliamentary actions against the ship-money judges, this was less the cynicism of an individual who knew whereof he spoke by personal experience than the reasoned conclusion of a political element. 'This is the epitome of all the contracts in the world betwixt man and man, betwixt prince and subject; they keep them as long as they like them and no longer.'

Insofar as sense could be made in the fluid world of politics, the ultimate touchstone for Selden was the theoretical foundation of popular sovereignty in shaping the structure of the state, whether in the election of a king, that of a parliament, or in the disciplinary organization of the church. 'All are involved in a parliament . . . all consent civilly in a parliament.' 'All is as the state likes.' But he had no illusions about the perfectability of any human institution, parliament included. 'The parliament men are as great princes as any in the world, when whatever they please is privilege of parliament.' 'No man must know the number of their privileges, and whatsoever they dislike is breach of privilege.' Selden much preferred the sovereignty of law to the sovereignty of parliament. 'The parliament party, if the law be for them, they call for law; if it be against, they will go in a parliamentary way. . . . The parliament party do not play fair, in sitting up till two of the clock in the morning, to vote something they have a mind to. . . . Young men and infirm men go away. Besides a man is not there to persuade other men to be of his mind, but to speak his own heart; and if it be liked – so; if not, there's an end.' It may be questionable whether Selden's myth of parliamentary representation was applicable in 1628; but in the faction-ridden, divisive, tradition-rending politics evident after 1642 it no longer explained the attempt to govern by consensus.

For Selden the political essential was to preserve the rule of law, or the closest acceptable approximation of it. 'Every law is a contract betwixt the king and the people, and therefore to be kept.' 'If two of us make a bargain, why should either of us stand to it?' 'Certainly because there is something about me that tells me *fides est servanda*, and if we after alter our minds, and make a new bargain, there's *fides servanda* there too.' 'To pretend conscience against law, who knows what inconveniency may follow?' 'Keep your contracts.' The legal doctrine of consideration, in which faith in reciprocity was of the essence, was for Selden the foundation of public as well as of private law.

In addition to the reflection of Selden's table-talk his activities in parliament reveal two other motives. He had as little use for divine-right presbytery as he had for divine-right monarchy or episcopacy. Here his Erastian zeal – 'all is as the state likes' – came to the fore as, much to the dismay of the Scots observers, he rallied the secular and Erastian elements in the Commons. Selden, Baillie complained, 'will have no discipline at all in any church, *jure divino*, but settled only upon the free will and pleasure of the parliament.' Additionally, he became the parliamentary spokesman for universities and scholarship. He helped protect and preserve the libraries of the King, Lambeth Palace, Archbishop Ussher, Herbert and others. He could not always completely protect scholars but he did succeed in moderating their difficulties, as in the case of Pococke, Langbaine and Greaves. And to a degree, he blunted the attack on Oxford.

If he was no longer the anti-prerogative radical of 1628, he was still fundamentally committed to the rule of law. It was a posture which frequently put him on a collision course with the majority but Selden was not without some tactical success. There is, after all, some satisfaction in constructive obstruction. Nor did parliament resent his critical posture. It appointed him Keeper of the Records in the Tower (1643), named him one of the twelve Commissioners of the Admiralty (1644), and voted him £5000 for the persecution by the crown in 1629-1631 (1646), a sum which he had some difficulty in collecting. If Selden was thus fundamentally out of sympathy with those who were leading parliament in strange ways and paths, he nevertheless continued to serve in it – perhaps with increasing abstentions – until the late spring of 1649 when he and many others justifiably questioned the legality of a minority element ruling in the name of a majority not present and not represented. Despite his evident abstention thereafter, Selden continued to be treated with respect by the Cromwellian government, which consulted him on several occasions.

In these latter years Selden's scholarly and political involvements generated a vast correspondence, of which some part survives at the Bodleian. In addition, he entertained visiting scholars, both English and foreign, with great hospitality. And he continued his own scholarship, publishing in 1647 his *Dissertatio ad Fletam*, a sprightly and sophisticated survey of the history of Roman law in medieval Europe and England in which, in imitation of Hotman, he constructed a *mos Britannicus* to explain the evolution of English common law. Perhaps his most mature piece of scholarship, it has been strangely overlooked by the historians of English law. He also increasingly encouraged the scholarship of others, especially Ussher, Pococke, Greaves and Twysden, by example, by loan of books and by gifts of money. And he continued to the end to build up that remarkable library which was his own testimony to the example of Cotton. Some 8000 volumes of it are housed to this day at the Bodleian, a monument to the enduring impact of humanist scholarship in English life and learning.

Clarendon, a younger favorite who knew him well in these latter years, has left a 'character' of Selden which he acknowledged was difficult to 'transmit in any expression equal to his merits and virtue. . . . Of stupendous learning in all kinds and in all langauges . . . his humanity, courtesy, and affability was such that he could have been thought to have been bred in the best courts . . . but . . . his good nature, charity, and delight in doing good, and in communicating all he knew exceeded that breeding. . . . He had the best faculty in making hard things easy and present to the understanding of any man that hath ever been known.'

Always delicate in health and failing in his later years, Selden died in his seventieth year, on 30 Nov. 1654, at White Friars, the London residence of the late Elizabeth, dowager Countess of Kent, where he had resided in later years both before and after her death in 1651. His funeral was conducted by Archbishop Ussher, a friend of long standing, and he was buried in the Temple Church, in those precincts where he had been bred in the law and where, pursuing scholarship, he had grown to that fame which Grotius described as 'the glory of the English nation.' After specific gifts to his household staff, to his friends and relatives, the residue of his large estate was shared equally by his executors, Edward Heyward, Matthew Hale,* John Vaughan and Rowland Jewks, who eventually transferred the rich and valuable library to the Bodleian, where largely intact it remains to this day in the basement stacks rather than in the fabled Selden End created to house it. It as well as his scholarly works crystallize the actions and passions of one devoted to the rule of law and the sanctity of contracts in an age which momentarily neglected both. His enduring monument is the vigorous school of English legal history and the Selden Society for which he is the eponymous hero.

Apart from the observations recorded by Aubrey and the 'character' sketched by Clarendon, the first attempt at an extended biographical statement was the *Vita* in Joannis Seldeni, *Opera omnia*, ed. D. Wilkins, 3 vols. in 6 (1726). See also A. Kipnis, ed., *Biographia Britannica* (1778-93), 6:3605-24; A. Chalmers, ed., *The General Biographical Dictionary* (1816 ed.), 17:317-32; J. Aiken, *Life of Selden and Ussher* (1816); G.W. Johnson, *Memoirs of John Selden* (1835); *DNB*; D.S. Berkowitz, 'Young Mr. Selden. Essays in Seventeenth-Century Learning and Politics' (Ph.D. diss., Harvard Univ., 1946); Berkowitz, 'Projects for a Biography and Edition of John Selden's Works, 1654-1766,' *Quarendo*, 4:247-57. Selden's library of printed books and manuscripts, along with some of his working papers, was presented by his executors to the Bodleian Library. However, Sir Matthew Hale, one of the executors, retained some of the legal material and that portion which escaped the great fire was given by him to Lincoln's Inn. Some manuscript materials, traceable to a collateral branch of Hale's family, have come on the market in recent years. The Bodleian, which has Selden's correspondence file, mainly in letters, collects Selden materials. Neither the Inner Temple nor the British Library has much in the way of stray papers.

D.S. Berkowitz

SEWEL, Willem (1653-1720)

Quaker, was born on 19 Apr. 1653 in Amsterdam, the son of Jakob Willemszoon Zeewel and Judith Zinspenning. His grandfather, William Sewell of Kidderminster, Worcs., was a Separatist who sought refuge in Holland and took a Dutch wife in Utrecht. Jakob Zeewel, a citizen and surgeon of Amsterdam, and his wife were Mennonites before they were converted to Quaker principles by William Ames* about 1657. Willem spent ten months in England in 1668-69, during which he visited Stephen Crisp* in prison at Ipswich and also came under the influence of Josiah Coale and George Fox,* whom he heard preach in London. From 1669 to 1674 Sewel served his apprenticeship in Amsterdam, probably to a weaver, and simultaneously developed his considerable linguistic skills. Sewel maintained his contacts with English Friends, partly through extensive correspondence with John Penington of Worminghurst, Sussex, William Penn* and others. He was probably an amanuensis for Fox when the latter visited Amsterdam in 1677 and 1684, and he served as an interpreter for foreign Quakers in Holland. In 1696 Penn urged him to come to Bristol to take charge of a school for Quaker children, but Sewel declined due to a conviction that he had been divinely placed in Amsterdam as a Quaker witness.

Sewel was a prodigious translator and author, whose output included ten of his own books, twenty-seven translations, and one edited work. His translations include a number of Penn's works, Edmund Ludlow's* *Memoirs*, George Whitehead's* *Christian Doctrine*, and works of Bishop Burnet, Robert Boyle, Fox, Stephen Crisp and Juvenal. His principal work, utilizing material he gathered in England, *The History of the Rise, Increase and Progress of the Christian People Called Quakers*, was begun in 1695, with the first edition appearing in Dutch in 1717, and in England in 1722 and America in 1728. In it he argued that the Quaker movement was the consummation of the Protestant Reformation.

Sewel had previously assisted Gerard Croesse, author of the first history of the Quakers.

On 19 Feb. 1681, Sewel wed Jacomina, eldest daughter of the Quakers Willem and Jannitge Boekenoogen of Alkmaar. She bore him a son and three daughters before her death on 4 Feb. 1703. Sewel died on 13 Mar. 1720 after a life of active service as a Quaker scholar and correspondent.

W.I. Hull, *Willem Sewel of Amsterdam* (1933); Hull, *William Penn and the Dutch Quaker Migration to Pennsylvania* (1935); Hull, *RQA*. Papers: LF.

R.L. Greaves

SEXBY, Edward (c. 1616-1658)

Leveller, secret agent and conspirator, may have been the son of Marcus Sexby or Saxbie of London, gent., who was apprenticed to Edward Price of the Grocers' Company in 1632. Sexby himself claimed to be a native of Suffolk who joined Cromwell's regiment in 1643 as a trooper and later served with Fairfax,* while Aubrey suggests that he was Cromwell's kinsman. All these suggestions are conceivably true, and the last would help explain the extraordinary relationship he had with Cromwell; as with much else in Sexby's career, the facts remain uncertain. What is clear is that he emerged from apparent obscurity in 1647 as one of the most active, forceful and articulate Leveller spokesmen. Elected Agitator for his regiment, he presented with two other soldiers a petition from eight regiments to Maj.-Gen. Philip Skippon,* calling upon him to help the army resist its forcible disbandment by the Long Parliament. For this he was called before the bar of the Commons on 30 Apr. Permitted to return to his regiment by the intercession of Independent MPs, Sexby remained the chief link between the Levellers in London and the Agitators in the field. Meanwhile he mapped out a strategy of his own. As early as 4 May he considered control of the King's person a principal objective. He suggested 'keeping a party of able pen-men at Oxford and the army where their presses [may] be employed to satisfy and undeceive the people,' and the holding of 'correspondence with soldiers and well-affected friends' throughout the country to mobilize resistance to the Presbyterian party and maintain the unity of the army. In addition, he urged that a list of army demands be drawn up, including indemnity, the punishment of malefactors, and the 'reformation of civil justice.' It appears highly probable, as Firth suggests, that he was involved in the seizure of Charles I at Holdenby.

Though still a mere private, Sexby took a prominent part in the Reading debates of mid-July. He may well have instigated the election of new Agitators in five regiments of horse (Cromwell's, Ireton's,* Whalley's,* Fleetwood's* and Rich's*) in early October, and helped devise *The Case of the Army Truly Stated*. At the Putney debates he was the opening speaker, and his first remarks contained the genesis of Pride's purge and the regicide: 'We have labored to please a king, and I think, except we go about to cut all our throats, we shall not please him; and we have gone to support an house which will prove rotten studs – I mean the Parliament, which consists of a company of rotten members.' In the same blunt vein, he informed Cromwell and Ireton that their 'credits and reputations had been much blasted' for temporizing. The following day, he stated the heart of the army's case: 'There are many thousands of us soldiers that have ventured our lives; we have had little propriety in the kingdom as to our estates, yet we have had a birthright. But it seems now, except a man hath a fixed estate in this kingdom, he hath no right in this kingdom. . . . If we had not a right to the kingdom, we were mere mercenary soldiers.' Cromwell was particularly nettled at this: 'I confess I was most dissatisfied with that I heard Mr. Sexby speak, of any man here, because it did so much savour of will.' Not to be outdone, Sexby shot back: 'I do not know how we have been answered in our arguments.'

With the collapse of Leveller agitation at Ware, Sexby left the army late in 1647, and again his movements are obscure. But obviously he remained in contact with the Leveller leaders, as well as on terms with Cromwell, for in July 1648 he appeared at Preston with a letter from John Lilburne* to Cromwell, and after the battle was dispatched back with news of the victory, for which he received £100 from Parliament. This mission apparently laid the groundwork for the cooperation between the Cromwellian Independents and the Levellers that fall, and in late September Sexby was again reported in Cromwell's camp as a liaison by a royalist newspaper. In 1649 he rejoined the army as Governor of Portland, Dorset, with the rank of captain. He was also entrusted with a number of sensitive missions by Parliament, among them the arrest of the Scots Commissioners in Feb. 1649. In June 1650 he was ordered to fit part of his regiment for service in Ireland, but was sent instead to Scotland, where he took part in the siege of Tantallon Castle in Feb. 1651.

The circumstances of Sexby's second departure from the army suggest a frameup, though as Aylmer points out direct proof is lacking. In June 1651 Sexby was court-martialled in Edinburgh, the principal charges against him being that he had executed a soldier at Morpeth, N'land without due process, and that he had mustered several men who were absent. The first charge was refuted by Sexby's vigorous defense and a supporting letter from Sir Arthur Haselrig,* in whose command the execution had taken place. A full seven or eight hours' debate on the second count failed, according to William Clarke, to establish more than that Sexby had held back some soldiers' pay to persuade them to ship for Ireland. Such a misdemeanor would scarcely seem enough to embarrass so well-sponsored a career, but Sexby was cashiered.

He was soon again employed however, being sent by the Council of State to La Rochelle and Bordeaux, where republican sentiments were stirring, 'to give an account of the state of that country and the affections of the people.' Sexby's interventions were naturally more direct. Working with a local Leveller counterpart, the *Ormée* of Bordeaux, he produced *L'Accord du Peuple*, a literal translation of the final *Agreement of the People*. A three-man delegation visited Cromwell in Apr. 1653 and received his encouragement, but the Protector's visions of a possible annexation of Bordeaux came to nought in the general collapse of the Fronde.

Sexby returned to England in Aug. 1653 after nearly two years abroad. Discouraged by the French fiasco and disgruntled with the Protectorate, he made contact with an old Leveller comrade with an equal taste for intrigue, John Wildman,* who with Lord Grey of Groby* and others was attempting to foment rebellion among radical officers, including Cols. Alured,* Okey* and Saunders.* With the discovery of this plot Sexby fled in Feb. 1655 from Portland Bill to Amsterdam, where he made contacts with the royalist camp. Hyde described the impression he made: 'For an illiterate person he spake very well and properly and used those words very well the true meaning and signification whereof he could not understand. . . . He was very perfect in the history of Cromwell's dissimulation, and would describe his artifices to the life.' Sexby proposed to enlist Spain in an overthrow of the Protectorate, presenting forged letters from Wildman and others to exaggerate his influence, and was able to gain an audience in Madrid. In June 1656 he was back in England. Despite rumors that Wildman was now a double agent, he concerted an assassination plot with him against Cromwell, employing an ex-soldier, Miles Sindercombe. On 17 Sept. a series of attempts to ambush Cromwell on his way to open Parliament failed, the Protector denouncing Sexby as 'a wretched creature, an apostate from religion and all honesty.' In December Sexby was seeking Don Juan of Austria's help against Cromwell, and on 8 Jan. 1657 a plot to blow up Whitehall, again using Sindercombe, miscarried. In March

Sexby, still abroad, announced his intention of returning to England to compass Cromwell's death or his own, and that spring published (under the name of William Allen) a public incitement to Cromwell's assassination called *Killing No Murder*, which he dedicated to the Protector himself. Perhaps betrayed by Wildman, he was captured on 24 July while returning to Holland on a secret visit to England, and died in the Tower on 13 Jan. 1658, 'having been awhile distracted in his mind and long sick.'

Firth's verdict on Sexby will hardly be challenged: 'There is no more remarkable career in the annals of the New Model Army.' Half-revolutionary, half-desperado, he had the nerve and talent, but neither the rank nor discipline, to have cut a memorable figure. Yet despite the waste, the words at Putney live, and are his monument.

DNB; Firth & Davies; Ashley, *CG*; Aylmer, *SS*; Brailsford; Gardiner, *HCP*; Ludlow; Woodhouse; *Clarke Papers*; Clarendon; R. Scrope and T. Monkhouse, eds., *Clarendon State Papers* (1767-86); G.F. Warner, ed., *The Nicholas Papers* (1886-1920); Thurloe, *SP*.

R. Zaller

SHAFTESBURY, first Earl of. *See* Cooper, Anthony Ashley.

SHAMBROOK, William (d. 1648)

City radical, was a man of substance who lived in the parish of St. Mary Colechurch, London. Sometime between 1636 and 1640 Shambrook joined the congregation of Henry Jessey.* In Oct. 1640 he was in trouble with the High Commission and was bound, with other members of Jessey's church, to appear before it in Michaelmas term. On 21 Aug. 1641 constables apprehended Shambrook and other members of the church as they attended an illegal conventicle; they were bound over to the quarter sessions, but released when the witnesses failed to appear. In May 1644 a group of Separatist and Independent leaders, including Philip Nye,* Thomas Goodwin,* Sidrach Simpson,* Jeremiah Burroughs,* Praisegod Barebone,* William Erbery* and Sabine Staresmore,* met in Shambrook's house to discuss the question of baptism following Kiffin's* defection from Jessey's church. By 1647 Shambrook had become an officer in the London militia, but that spring he was purged by City conservatives hostile to his political and religious views. Following the army's march on London, however, he was appointed lieutenant-colonel of the Tower regiment, commanded by Robert Tichborne,* in Aug. 1647. Shambrook was killed in the siege of Colchester in July 1648.

CSPD, Chas. I, 17:384; *Clarke Papers*, 1:153; Firth & Davies; Rushworth, 7:1179, 1181; Burrage, 1:326; 2:301; *TBHS*, 1:243; Tolmie.

R.L. Greaves

SHAW (or Shawe), John (1601-1672)

Puritan minister, was born at Sick-house in the parish of Ecclesfield, Yorks. He became a pensioner at Christ's Coll., Camb. in 1623 and was influenced by the Puritan sentiments of his tutor, William Chappell, and Thomas Weld,* who emigrated to Boston, Mass. in 1632. Shaw was ordained deacon and priest by the Bishop of Peterborough in 1629 and received his M.A. in 1630. He was lecturer at Brampton, Derby from 1630 to 1633. His Diocesan, Thomas Morton, Bishop of Coventry and Lichfield, gave him a preaching license for the whole diocese without subscribing. He was chaplain to the Earl of Pembroke* before transferring to a lectureship maintained by London Puritans in Chulmleigh Devon, for a term of three years. The lecture was suppressed, probably by Laud's influence. Shaw retired to his property at Sick-house on his father's death in 1636 and was subsequently appointed lecturer at All-Hallows-on-the-Pavement, York. After his first sermon he was summoned for rebuke by Archbishop Neile, who moderated his tone when he heard that Shaw was Pembroke's chaplain. Pembroke presented him with the Vicarage of Rotherham and took him as his chaplain to the siege of Berwick. There Shaw met and befriended Alexander Henderson, one of the Scottish Commissioners, who met the English Commission at Ripon to settle Scottish grievances. Shaw acted as chaplain to the English Commission in 1640. At the outbreak of the Civil War Rotherham was attacked by the King's forces and Shaw fled to Hull, but after preaching there he was excluded by the governor, Sir John Hotham, as an extremist. Shaw preached before Gen. Fairfax* at Selby. Returning to Rotherham he was proclaimed a traitor and fined 1000 marks. On the capture of the town his wife was imprisoned but he fled to Manchester in 1643, where he preached every Friday without pay. Shaw accepted the Rectory of Lymm, Ches., but continued to live in Manchester. He was invited on a preaching mission to Cartmel, Lancs. in 1644, and recorded stories of the ignorance of the district, which was strongly Catholic. He fled to Yorkshire on the approach of Rupert and was chaplain to the standing committee appointed by Parliament for the government of the northern counties. Shaw preached in York Minster at the taking of the Solemn League and Covenant, and was made secretary of the assembly of ministers appointed to cast out 'ignorant and scandalous ministers.' Fairfax gave him the rich living of Scrayingham, Yorks., but he only preached there a short time and returned to Hull as lecturer at Holy Trinity Church with a stipend of £150 and a house from the Corporation (1645-62). There he lectured on Wednesdays and Thursdays and preached to the garrison. Shaw displayed congregational ideas and his parishioners petitioned Parliament about his forming of a particular church. He served as chaplain to Parliamentary Commissions at Newcastle-on-Tyne in 1646, and was appointed Master of the Charterhouse at Hull with an income of £10 p.a. His predecessor refused to surrender his mastership, which Shaw claimed accompanied his lectureship. Parliament forced Styles, the incumbent, to surrender. Shaw had several disputes with the Corporation over the non-payment of his salary and over the mismanagement of the Charterhouse accounts. During the Protectorate he preached frequently at Whitehall; Cromwell admired his eloquence and gave him an augmentation of £100 p.a. At the Restoration he was sworn a royal chaplain. The garrison at Hull complained of the tone of his sermons, and he was prohibited from preaching by royal mandate. He went to London and was introduced to the King by the Earl of Manchester. Charles refused to remove the mandate but allowed him to keep the mastership and promised to provide for him as chaplain. He saw Archbishop Sheldon, who complained that he was no friend to episcopacy. Shaw declared he had never said a word against either. At the passing of the Act of Uniformity he resigned the mastership and lectureship, closed the accounts with the Corporation (which owed him over £1000) and returned to Rotherham. Afterwards he only preached in private houses. Shaw published a number of sermons and a memoir of his first wife.

DNB; *Calamy Revised*; 'The Life of Master John Shaw', in *Yorkshire Diaries and Autobiographies in the 17th and 18th Centuries* (1875); Hill, *S. & P.*

I. Morgan

SHEPARD, Thomas (1605-1649)

Puritan minister and colonist, was born at Towcester, Northants. on 5 Nov. 1605, the son of William Shepard, a grocer. Shepard was admitted as a pensioner to Emmanuel Coll., Camb. on 10 Feb. 1620, and graduated B.A. (1623-24) and M.A. (1627). He was ordained deacon and priest in July 1627, by which time he had already become a Puritan. Shepard left Cambridge to become lecturer at Earls Colne, Essex; the lectureship had been endowed on a rotating basis by the Feoffees for Impropriations and was originally intended for Coggeshall, but Shepard was the first holder. When his term was completed the parishioners provided his maintenance (£40 p.a.). Shepard was summoned to London in Dec. 1630 by Bishop Laud, 'a fierce enemy to all righteousness,' and forbidden to minister in the diocese of London. The next six months were spent with the Harlakendens, during which time Shepard became convinced of the evils of the sign of the cross, kneeling, and the surplice. When Laud ordered him out of the diocese Shepard, through the intervention of Ezekiel Rogers, went to Butter Crambe, Yorks. to serve as chaplain to Sir Richard Darley. When, however, Richard Neile became Archbishop of York, Shepard thought it expedient to accept a call to the church at Heddon, N'land rather than subscribe: 'I came here to read and know more of the ceremonies, church government and estate, and the unlawful standing of bishops than in any other place.'

Continuing threats to his ability to preach soon persuaded Shepard to follow Thomas Hooker* and John Cotton* to America. 'I saw the Lord departing from England . . . and I saw the hearts of most of the godly set and bent that way.' After preaching a farewell sermon at Newcastle, Shepard and his family boarded a collier for Ipswich in June 1634. In October they sailed for New England from Harwich, but were forced back to Great Yarmouth, where Shepard's son died within a fortnight. Departing on the 'Defense' in Aug. 1635, the Shepards arrived in Boston on 3 Oct. Settling at Newtown (Cambridge), Shepard was ordained the pastor of a Congregational church there in Feb. 1636, a charge he held until his death. The following year he was present at the trial of Anne Hutchinson,* whose Antinomianism he deplored. After Hugh Peter* left the colonies, Shepard played a major role in raising his daughter Elizabeth.

Shepard, an admirer of John Harvard, was instrumental in the founding of Harvard College and locating it in Cambridge, and he served on its Board of Overseers. Through his efforts books were obtained from England, 'heathen' learning was defended, and financial support was acquired by his proposal to the Confederation of New England in 1644 to have each family in the associated colonies give the College a quarter-bushel of wheat each year. His efforts for a public confession of faith and a plan of ecclesiastical polity were fulfilled in the synod of 1647. Shepard also advocated evangelical work among the Indians. A noted evangelist himself, he was also a prolific author. In *The Sincere Convert* (1641) and *The Sound Beleever* (1645) he explored the nature of conversion, and his interest in casuistry is reflected in *Certain Select Cases Resolved* (1648). In *New Englands Lamentation* (1645) he attacked the sectaries, and *Theses sabbaticae* (1649) is an exposition of the standard Puritan position on the sabbath. Shepard's concern for the Indians is manifest in *The Clear Sun-shine of the Gospel* (1648) and his version of his friend John Eliot's *The Indiane Primer* (1720). Shepard's case for paedobaptism was enunciated in *Church Membership of Children* (1663). Shepard's autobiography and journal are among the most valuable Puritan documents.

By his first wife (m. July 1632), Margaret Touteville (d. 1636), Shepard had a son Thomas (1635-1677), who became the pastor of the Charlestown church in 1659. Shepard's second wife (m. Oct. 1637) was Joanna (d. 2 Apr. 1646), eldest daughter of Thomas Hooker, by whom he had two surviving sons, Samuel and John. By his third wife (m. 8 Sept. 1647), Margaret Boradel, he had another son, Jeremiah. Shepard died in Boston on 25 Aug. 1649. Neither a militant nor a martyr, Shepard was yet a man whose conscience drove him to a land where Puritan principles could be pursued free of the restrictive oppression of Laudian authoritarianism.

T. Shepard, *Works*, 3 vols. (1853); M. McGiffert, ed., *God's Plot* (1972); S.E. Morison, *Builders of the Bay Colony* (1930); Morrison, *The Founding of Harvard College* (1935); *DNB*; *DAB*; *Al. Cant.*; A. Whyte, *Thomas Shepard* (1909); D.D. Hall, ed., *The Antinomian Controversy* (1968).

R.L. Greaves

SHERFIELD (or Shervill), Henry (d. 1634)

Parliamentary radical, MP 1614, 1621 (Southampton), 1624-29 (Salisbury). Sherfield's family origins and early life are equally obscure, though he is described in the 1623 visitation of Wiltshire as third son of Richard Sherfield, by Matilda, daughter of John Morton of Wiltshire. Sherfield was admitted to Lincoln's Inn, as of Wiltshire, in 1598, and called to the bar eight years later. In 1607 he married Maria, daughter of William Hodson, Alderman of Winchester and widow of George Bedford, clothier of Salisbury, where Sherfield now kept a house in addition to the lands he farmed at Porton and Winterbourne Earls, just north of the city. Maria bore him one daughter, Mathilda, before her death in 1613. By this time Sherfield had become a leading counsel in the Court of Wards, helped by the favor of Sir James Ley, the Attorney of Wards.

Sherfield's parliamentary career began in 1614, when he was returned as a member for Southampton, where he became Recorder in 1618. In 1617 he was appointed steward of the Earl of Salisbury's estates in the West Country, and in the same year he married Rebecca, daughter of Christopher Bailey of Southwick, North Bradley, and widow of Henry Longe, of Whaddon, near Salisbury. Sherfield was again returned for Southampton in 1621, when he spoke on several bills to reform the legal system, but was not otherwise conspicuous. In Dec. 1623 he gained election as Recorder of Salisbury, and represented that city in Parliament the following year, being also

offered a seat by Southampton. Sherfield delivered the Lent reading at Lincoln's Inn in 1624; several copies of his lectures on the Statute of Wills survive in manuscript (e.g L: Harg. MS 402; Stowe MS 424).

Within Salisbury, Sherfield now joined his fellow Puritan vestrymen of St. Edmond's church in promoting ambitious schemes to discipline, employ and relieve the town's poor, sponsoring a bill for that purpose in the Parliament of 1625, where he also drew attention to the 'very dangerous and seditious book' of the Arminian Richard Montague. Sherfield was a prominent critic of Buckingham in 1626, and assisted Christopher Wandesford in drawing up part of the Commons' charge against the Duke; he continued his attacks against the Arminian bishops in Charles' third Parliament and chaired the Commons' Committee on Tonnage and Poundage in 1629.

By this time Sherfield's financial situation had become very serious. Although the knighthood composition of £35 which he paid in 1631 was among the highest in the county, he was arrested that same year for part of the massive burden of debts and suretyships which he had accumulated over the previous decade, not only on his own account but also for his kinsfolk by descent and marriage, especially his elder brother Richard and the improvident Walter Long,* as well as his fellow MPs Sir Thomas Jervoise* and Sir George Wrottesley. Against this background of impending financial catastrophe, Sherfield faced prosecution in the Star Chamber by Attorney-General Noy, a former friend and colleague both in Parliament and on the bench of Lincoln's Inn, for breaking down, in Oct. 1630, a supposedly idolatrous stained-glass window in St. Edmond's church, with the authorization of the vestry but against the command of Bishop Davenant. The personal, local and national tensions which underlay Sherfield's trial and conviction early in 1633 attracted considerable attention to the case, which the defendant himself survived by only one year, dying intestate with debts of some £6000 in Jan. 1634.

DNB; P. Slack, 'Religious Protest and Urban Authority; the Case of Henry Sherfield, Iconoclast, 1633,' *Studies in Church History* (1972); Hill, *S. & P.* Papers: HARO (Sherfield MSS 44M69).

W.R. Prest

SHERLAND, Christopher (d. 1632)

Parliamentary radical, MP 1624, 1625, 1626, 1628 (Northampton). Sherland was born in Easton Maudit, Northants.; an uncle and a grandfather were judges. He was admitted to Gray's Inn on 1 Nov. 1604, was called to the bar in 1617 and became a bencher of the Inn in 1627. In addition he was called to the Grand Company in 1622 and was chosen Reader of the Staple Inn in 1623 and Lent Reader in 1626. As Recorder of Northampton he sat in every parliament between 1624 and 1628. Sherland was a Feoffee for Impropriations for Dunstable, Cirencester and Hertford in 1627, when his activities came under investigation together with those of George Harwood. He was a founding member of the Providence Island Company in 1630 and was closely associated in this and other ventures with Richard Knightley.* Among his other commercial interests was the French Company.

Sherland was one of those who resisted Charles I's demands for supply at the Oxford Parliament, warning with Edward Alford* that they might lead to annual subsidies. He was one of the earliest members to call attention to the dangers of Arminianism and the growth of the ecclesiastical establishment. He reported to the House of Commons the proceedings of the York House conference in 1626, and attacked the Court of High Commission for styling itself a court of record. His vigorous opposition to the Duke of Buckingham was based primarily on his view of the Duke as 'the principal patron and supporter of a semi-Pelagian, semi-popish faction, dangerous to the church and state.' These views however were premature, and as one of the managers of Buckingham's impeachment before the House of Lords on 10 May 1626, he spoke instead to allegations of venality and the sale of honors. In 1628 Sherland played a substantive role in devising the Petition of Right, but he again adverted, with greater success, to the relationship between Arminian influence and violations of the subject's liberty. As Conrad Russell points out, this was 'a new intellectual link: the connection of alteration of religion with alteration of government.' By 1629 Sherland was accusing Arminians of 'treason in the highest degree,' and he called upon the House of Commons to reaffirm the Protestant religion as it had been understood 'till within these 7 or 8 years.'

Sherland's will was dated 5 July 1631 and proved on 16 Feb. 1632. In it he bequeathed £400 for the purchase of impropriations, 200 marks to put the poor of Northampton to work, and £100 to endow poor scholars. According to the funeral sermon preached by Richard Sibbes,* Sherland 'died before he was come to the middle of his years.' Sibbes' portrait is of 'a general scholar' with 'elegant learning' in divinity as well as law, pious but not censorious, and a strict keeper of the sabbath. It is one of the few personal descriptions of this important but elusive figure.

Newton; Russell, *PEP*; R.J. Fletcher, ed., *The Pension Book of Gray's Inn* (1901-10); W.R. Prest, *The Inns of Court 1590-1640* (1972); I.M. Calder, *Activities of the Puritan Faction of the Church of England 1625-1633 (1957); CD 1625, 1628, 1629*; R. Sibbes, *The Saints Cordialls* (1637). Papers: NRO (Knightley MSS).

R. Zaller

SHUTE, Richard (fl. 1640-1658)

City radical, was a haberdasher. His early career is obscure, but he was involved in colonial interloping ventures with Maurice

Thompson,* with whom he presented the citizens' petition to Charles I at York in Sept. 1640 demanding that Parliament be called and grievances redressed. Shute was active in organizing further petitions in 1641. In June 1642 he was appointed a commissioner for the sea adventure to Ireland, to which he subscribed £500. On 13 Nov. Shute led a delegation of 'the most godly and active part of the City' before the House of Commons to protest conciliation with Charles and to offer to raise 1000 light horse and 3000 dragoons for service under Philip Skippon.* The same group also proposed collecting weekly subscriptions, and, a week later, weekly assessments, an idea implemented by Pym* on 26 Nov. On 1 Dec. another petition was presented by Shute, Jeremiah Burroughs,* John Goodwin,* Hugh Peter,* Sir David Watkins* and 95 of their supporters denouncing 'counsels of accommodation' and demanding that the Earl of Essex* be furnished with 6000 dragoons and ordered to march immediately against the King. The petition further proposed that war reparations be paid out of delinquents' estates and that malignant ministers be sequestered. The Common Council refused to subscribe to these proposals and no alderman accompanied the petitioners to Parliament. The petition was referred back to the Council where it was rejected, and a counter-petition was circulated which Shute denounced in terms which alienated the House of Commons (*CJ*, 2:887).

Shute was more successful the following spring. With Watkins and Randall Mainwaring* he drew up the Remonstrance of 30 Mar. 1643, embodying the substance of the previous radical petitions. This passed the Council, while at the same time (12 Apr.) a subcommittee was established at Salters' Hall to raise three regiments of horse and seven of foot, thus giving official status to a group of which Shute had been treasurer since the preceding fall. On 21 Oct. he became a commissioner for the collection of tonnage and poundage, at which time he subscribed £1000 to Parliament. In 1645 he was appointed a Trier to regulate the selection of elders in the Presbyterian classes of London, though by 1651 he had become a member of a gathered church and was a signatory of *A Declaration of Divers Elders and Brethren of Congregationall Societies*. Shute was chosen a commissioner for compounding with delinquents on 8 Feb. 1647. In September he refused to take the traditional East India Company oath of allegiance to the King, and was subsequently part of the Common Council's delegation to Parliament to demand justice against him. He continued active under the Commonwealth, becoming a commissioner for the navy and for customs on 16 Jan. 1649, an assessment commissioner for London on 7 Apr., and a member of the High Court of Justice on 26 Mar. 1650. He was again appointed to this last position on 21 Nov. 1653. Much of Shute's energies in this period were devoted to an unsuccessful attempt to secure the patent of the inland and foreign letter offices with John Hallett of London and Stephen Trevill of Cornwall. On 19 Apr. 1655 he petitioned to be granted an additional £1000 p.a. for his commissionership of tonnage and poundage to bring it to its former value of £1250. Shute was still active in 1658. His son, Hallet, was a merchant with a quarter interest in the frigate 'Welcome.'

Pearl; Tolmie; Manning, *EPER*; Beaven; R.P. Brenner, 'The Civil War Politics of London's Merchant Community,' *P. & P.*, 58:53-107; idem., 'Commercial Change and Political Conflict: The Merchant Community in the English Civil War' (Ph.D. thesis, Princeton Univ., 1970); Firth & Rait, 1:9, 10, 914, 1259, 1261; 2:38, 302, 365, 471, 668, 781, 917, 1015; *CCAM*, 3, 6; *CCC*, 8, 10, 30; *CSPD, Chas. I*, 23:654; *Comm.*, 2:214; 4:445; 5:178, 448; 6:266, 549; 7:425; 8:133; 11:515; *Somers Tracts*, 4:596. Papers: LPR (SP 46/101/274; HCA 24/109/154).

R. Zaller

SIBBES (or Sibbs, Sibs), Richard
(1577-1635)

Puritan minister, was born at Tostock,
Suff., the eldest son of Paul Sibbes,
wheelwright, and his wife Johan. After
studying at the grammar school at Bury St.
Edmunds, Sibbes became a sizar at St.
John's Coll., Camb. in 1595 through the
influence of the Puritan John Knewstub.
Elected a scholar at St. John's, he graduated B.A. in 1599, became a fellow on 3
Apr. 1601, and proceeded M.A. in 1602
and D.D. in 1627. His spiritual commitment stemmed from the sermons of Paul
Baynes.* Sibbes was ordained, appointed
preacher at St. John's (25 Apr. 1609),
awarded the B.D. (1610), and designated
lecturer at Holy Trinity church, Cambridge. His lectureship, which was supported by subscriptions, was very popular,
but was terminated in 1615 under a royal
order prohibiting lectures that might dis-
tract scholars from catechizing. The same
year the High Commission also stripped
him of his fellowship.

Through the influence of Sir Henry
Yelverton, Sibbes became a preacher at
Gray's Inn on 5 Feb. 1617, and in the
ensuing years his auditors included not
only lawyers but aristocrats, merchants
and lesser citizens. His summer sojourns in
the homes of the great carried his message
to the countryside. His appeal became so
great that in 1624 the chapel at Gray's Inn
had to be expanded to accommodate his
audience, and in 1631 the Earl of Warwick*
had a gallery constructed at the chapel's
east end so he could avoid the crush and
still hear Sibbes. Preaching twice each
Sunday, Sibbes was successful – a slight
stammer notwithstanding – largely because
of his fervor, insight and plain style: 'Truth
feareth nothing so much as concealment,
and desireth nothing so much as clearly to
be laid open to the view of all: When it is
most naked, it is most lovely and powerful.' Yet at least one Puritan, Robert
Jenison, lecturer at All Saints, Newcastle,
complained in 1621 that Sibbes was too
timorous.

As early as 1622 Sibbes, John Davenport* and William Gouge tried to persuade
King James to aid the Protestants in the
Palatinate. With Thomas Taylor,* they
issued a circular letter on 2 Mar. 1627
seeking support for 240 preachers and
thousands of laymen in the Upper Palatinate. Laud (who endorsed a copy of the
letter, now deposited in the Public Record
Office) reprimanded Sibbes and Taylor for
this action. In the meantime, in 1626 Sibbes
had succeeded John Hills as Master of St.
Catherine's Hall, Camb., but without
relinquishing his influential lectureship at
Gray's Inn. Also in 1626 he joined with
Gouge, Davenport, Charles Offspring
(Rector of St. Antholin's) and eight laymen
to form the Feoffees for Impropriations. In
their encouragement of godly preaching
they periodically tangled with the government in the courts, as in a 1633 dispute over
advowson rights for All Saints, Worcester.

James Ussher, with whom Sibbes had
corresponded since 1620, offered him the
Provostship of Trinity Coll., Dublin on 10
Jan. 1627, but he declined, as he did again
when Archbishop Abbot renewed the offer
on 19 Mar. Sibbes was on close terms with
Ussher and John Preston,* there existing
between them 'a most entire affection.' In
fact Sibbes, Preston and ten other London
divines urged Ussher to supervise a project
to produce 'a sum of our practical theology.' Sibbes was also a friend of John
Pym* (whom he included in his will), Sir
Nathaniel Rich,* and Sir Horace and Lady
Mary Vere* (to whom he dedicated The
Bruised Reede). Samuel Hartlib* regarded
him as 'one of the most experimental
divines now living,' and his efforts to
relieve Protestants in the Palatinate
received the support of the elder Isaac
Penington.* His sermons influenced such
notables as John Cotton,* Thomas Goodwin* and Hugh Peter,* and he preached
the funeral sermons of Christopher Sherland* and Sir Thomas Crew.

Sibbes remained active in his last years,
not only preaching but serving as a senior
Puritan advisor. When, in late 1632, a
delegation from Colchester sought
approval to have William Bridge* as their
lecturer, Laud grumbled: 'When you want

one, you must go to Dr. Gouge and to Dr. Sibbes, and then you come to me: I scorn to be so used.' Sibbes gave a deposition in 1633 in the disputed election for the Mastership of St. John's Coll., Camb., involving Richard Holdsworth* and Robert Lane. Following the resignation of Thomas Goodwin, he became perpetual Curate of Holy Trinity, Cambridge on 1 Nov. 1633. His last sermon was preached at Gray's Inn on 28 June 1635, and he died there, having never married, on 5 July.

The first of Sibbes' numerous major publications did not appear until 1629: *The Saints Cordialls*, a collection including ten of his own sermons, provided not only a synopsis of his views on the Christian life but an expression of concern for Protestants in Heidelberg, Prague and France. *The Bruised Reede and Smoaking Flax*, published the following year, analyzed the process of conversion and was later a factor in Richard Baxter's conversion. In 1634 came *The Churches Visitation* and *The Soules Conflict*, the latter concentrating on post-conversion spiritual struggles. Sibbes' remaining major works were published posthumously, with a number of them edited by Goodwin and Philip Nye.* Others who aided in their publication were Jeremiah Burroughs,* Arthur Jackson, John Dod, John Sedgwick, Lazarus Seaman, Simeon Ash, James Nalton, Joseph Church and Thomas Manton. With Goodwin, Davenport and Thomas Ball, Sibbes had collected and edited the sermons of Preston. He also edited Thomas Gataker's *Christian Constancy* (1624) and wrote epistles to works by Baynes, Ball, Ezekiel Culverwel, Richard Capel and Henry Scudder.

Although the tone of Sibbes' work was normally devotional rather than controversial, he exercised a significant influence on the direction of English Puritanism through the subjects he stressed and his implanting of radical concepts. The principal themes of his sermons dealt with the strategy and tactics of spiritual war, a subject readily adaptable to conditions in the 1640s. He breathed the spirit of activism: 'When things are clear, and God's will is manifest,

further deliberation is dangerous.' Coupled with this was an emphasis on total commitment: 'Partial obedience is indeed no obedience at all.' He contributed to the development of covenant theology and played a major role in orienting Puritan thought to the working of the Holy Spirit: 'Oh! the Spirit is the life and soul of the word.' The characteristic Puritan tendency toward self-analysis was furthered by Sibbes, who insisted that if 'men would search and plough up their own hearts, they would not need the plowing of God's enemies; we should not need God's judgments, if we would judge ourselves.' He hammered away at the Catholic Church as an apostate institution fitly described as an adulteress and a whore, and he regarded the Pope as Antichrist. To Sibbes the principal enemies of the church were Catholicism, Arminianism and Separatism, and therefore he was a firm believer in preserving the unity of the Church of England as a bulwark against them. Although it was defiled by popish ceremonies and profane persons, there could be no separatism, for 'perfect reforming is for another world.'

Among his radical themes which were magnified in later decades was a belief in toleration, based on the premise that spiritual tyranny is the greatest despotism. Yet Sibbes did not espouse unlimited toleration, particularly for Catholics, for this would lead, he argued, to spiritual anarchy. Like later radicals he was convinced that an illiterate man of any calling could be a better divine than an educated carnal person. He assailed clergy who sought temporal advantage in the spiritual thraldom of others, 'such as raise estates by betraying the church, and are unfaithful in the trust committed unto them,' a theme dear to advocates of anticlericalism. Finally, he warned that people feared kings more than God, and that kings relinquished their realms to Antichrist. Although Sibbes made an exception of James I, when this sermon was published in 1639 under the title, *The Beasts Dominion Over Earthly Kings*, the implications were ominous. Published every year from 1633 to 1641, his works infused the saints with a sense of activism, a hostility to Arminianism and an insatiable hunger for a godly society, all of which boded ill for the Stuart regime.

A.B. Grosart, ed., *The Complete Works of Richard Sibbes*, 6 vols. (1862-64); Haller, *RP*; *DNB*; W.R. Prest, *The Inns of Court under Elizabeth I and the Early Stuarts* (1972); Seaver; Brook; *CSPD. Chas. I*, 2:77; 5:167; 6:192-93, 270, 287; McGee; Nuttall, *HSPFE*. Papers: LPR; L (Add. MSS; Lans. MSS).

R.L. Greaves

SIDNEY (or Sydney), Algernon (1622-1683)

Republican theorist and conspirator. Sidney's career is a paradox, his character an enigma. Of all the major actors of the seventeeth-century revolutions, he was among the most gifted. By birth, talent and ambition he seemed destined for eminence, and for forty years he was a figure to be reckoned with. Yet, among revolutionary regimes no less than royal, he never achieved power, office or responsibility commensurate with his abilities. Proud and isolated, his effect within his own lifetime was almost negligible. Yet his death made him a popular hero, and gave his ideas a currency rivaled only by Milton* and Locke* among the inheritors of the revolutionary tradition.

Sidney was born into the upper ranks of the peerage, the second surviving son of Robert Sidney, second Earl of Leicester, and Dorothy, daughter of Henry Percy, ninth Earl of Northumberland. He was educated at home in Penshurst, Kent, accompanying his father on an embassy to Denmark in 1632 and visiting Paris in 1633. His highstrung character and quick intelligence was noticed early, and he was clearly the family favorite, a fact much resented by his elder brother Philip, Lord Lisle.* Their rivalry continued into adulthood, exacerbating Sidney's always strained finances.

Sidney's career divides naturally into three phases: his service to the revolutionary regimes of the 1640s and 1650s; his prolonged exile at the Restoration; and the final six years of agitation and conspiracy, culminating in his execution for treason. Sidney commanded a troop in the regiment of horse raised by Lord Lisle for service in Ireland in 1642, and was commended for bravery. His adherence to Parliament was largely circumstantial and pragmatic; writing from Ireland in June 1643 he declared that 'nothing but extreme necessity shall make me bear arms in England, and yet it is the only way of living well for those that have not estate.' After returning to England in August he joined the Earl of Manchester's army as captain of a troop of horse, though with the courtesy rank of colonel. The House of Commons voted Sidney £400 for his service in Ireland on 10 May 1644, and he was wounded at Marston Moor, where he 'charged with much gallantry.' Disabled, he was forced to decline the offer of a regiment in the New Model Army, instead accepting the governorship of Chester (10 May 1645). Sidney was returned to the Long Parliament for Cardiff as a recruiter, and on 4 Jan. 1647 was voted a further £2000. He joined his brother again as Lieutenant-General of Horse in Ireland and Governor of Dublin but, failing to obtain a joint command upon the latter's recall, he returned to England in April. This slight was scarcely palliated by an appointment as Governor of Dover, a post Sidney resigned in 1651 under threat of court-martial by 'divers officers of the army.' The circumstances of this affair remain unexplained, but the House of Commons treated it as a breach of parliamentary privilege, leading to a substantial altercation between the Rump and the army. With this Sidney's military career came to a definitive close.

Sidney opposed the execution of the King and declined to serve on the High Court. He took the dissent and resumed his seat in Parliament, where he now assumed a more active role. Though he had resisted Ireton's* demand for an oath of approval for the regicide and the abolition of the House of Lords, he drifted toward the radical faction of Marten* and Morley,* and was instrumental in securing the admission of Henry Neville* to the Rump in October. He served on committees for law reform and union with Scotland, chaired the Committee for Irish Adventurers, and sat on Vane's* committee to provide for a new parliament. Elected to the last Commonwealth Council of State on 25 Nov. 1652, he served assiduously, particularly on the Committee for Foreign Affairs, attending no fewer than 82 sessions. His initial reservations overcome, Sidney was clearly hoping to play a major role in the new republic. Cromwell's expulsion of the Rump once again aborted his plans. Sidney has left perhaps the most convincing and objective account of the scene. He himself was sitting on the Speaker's right hand when Cromwell entered the Commons, and refused to rise until Harrison* and Worsley* clapped hands on him.

Sidney boycotted the Protectorate. In 1654 he visited republican Holland in a pointed gesture of opposition, and in 1656 staged a satire against the regime at Penshurst which enraged Lord Lisle, a staunch Cromwellian. At the fall of Richard Cromwell* Sidney reclaimed his seat in Parliament, and on 14 May 1659 was elected to the new Council of State. Almost at once however he accepted a mission to mediate peace between Denmark and Sweden. Sidney was still abroad at the Restoration and, after a brief hesitation, chose to remain.

In exile, 'the broken limb of a shipwrecked faction' as he described himself, Sidney was still regarded as the new regime's most formidable opponent. He did not deny its legitimacy, as it had been summoned by a Parliament, but he refused 'to submit, to recant, to renounce, and ask pardon' for actions that had been just: 'I had rather be a vagabond all my life than buy my own country at so dear a rate.' In a gesture which could scarcely be misinterpreted, he visited the Regicide Edmund Ludlow* in Vevey and presented him with a brace of pistols. Assassins dogged him, but he found refuge, first in Holland and then in France. To both countries he proposed an invasion of England. Louis XIV offered him 20,000 crowns toward the pupose, but he rejected it as inadequate.

Sidney returned to England in Sept. 1677 under a pledge of good behavior to claim his father's legacy. Though it amounted to only £5100 his elder brother contested it, forcing him into a protracted suit in Chancery. Detained by this, Sidney found himself caught up in the political turmoil of the country: the agitation for a new parliament, the Popish plot and the Exclusion crisis. He stood unsuccessfully for the Commons four times: at Guildford in Dec. 1678 he was defrauded at the poll; at Bramber in Aug. 1679 he stood aside when opposed by his brother Henry; at Amersham his election was voided in Dec. 1680 and Feb. 1681. Sidney had contacts with the venerable conspirator John Wildman* as well as the Quakers William Penn* and Benjamin Furly,* but he was essentially isolated. Refusing to play second fiddle to Shaftesbury,* whom he despised for accepting office, he remained aloof from the Whigs until the latter's flight to the Continent in Dec. 1682. Thereafter Sidney was rapidly drawn toward a vortex of real and pretended intrigue, perhaps through his admirer John Hampden.* On 26 June 1683 he was arrested with the other alleged members of the Council of Six. No second witness against him could be found, but the manuscript of his 'Discourses Concerning Government' was brought forward in evidence, a work which, said Judge Jeffryes, 'contains all the malice, and revenge and treason that mankind can be guilty of; it fixes the sole power in the Parliament and the people.' Sidney was condemned and, despite appeals for a commutation, executed on 7 Dec. According to the Duke of York, not a sympathetic witness, he died 'very resolutely, and like a true rebel and republican.'

Sidney wrote pamphlets and an *Essay on Love* (he never married); his role in drafting the Pennsylvania constitution is disputed. His fame rests on the incomplete *Discourses*, first published in 1698 by John Toland.* The bulk of the manuscript was probably written in 1680-81, prompted (as were works by Locke, Tyrell* and Hunt) by the publication of Filmer's *Patriarcha;* though some notes and drafts may have gone back a number of years, Sidney's own statement that 'so much as is of it was written long since, never reviewed, nor shown to any man' is refuted by internal evidence.

The *Discourses* set out to refute Filmer's theory of absolute monarchy as having no basis in the law of God or nature or the constitution of England. The argument is similar to that in Milton's *First Defense*, and Milton's own praise of Sidney in the *Second Defense* as 'indissolubly attached to the interests of liberty' suggests an exchange of ideas between them. Though Sidney does not reject limited monarchy directly, the whole thrust of his writing is a polemic against the concentration of authority which any form of kingship implies. 'Those governments only deserve praise,' says Sidney flatly, 'who put power into the hands of the best men.' Such a conception is clearly incompatible with a hereditary system, which tends to produce the worst, and constitutes a standing invitation to civil conflict. But elective Caesarism is ultimately no better, for it is the nature of one-man rule to cast off all restraint: as Sidney put it in a phrase with a more than faint autobiographical echo, 'Man is of an aspiring nature, and apt to put too high a value on himself.' Human nature itself guides monarchy toward tyranny.

If monarchy produces tyranny, tyranny fosters servility as its natural counterpart. By contrast, a free republic nurtures valor, self-reliance and virtue, which Sidney defines as 'the dictate of reason, or the remains of divine light, by which men are made benevolent and beneficial to each other.' Such a virtue is both the condition and concomitant of liberty. Thus republics foster the virtue they exemplify, while monarchies spawn the corruption which destroys them. For this reason kingdoms may be conquered in a single battle, republics never – a cardinal point for one who, like Sidney, saw war as the supreme function of the state.

As Sidney idealized ancient Sparta and Rome or the Venice of his own time, so he praised Saxon England, even to the point of denying that the Norman invasion was a conquest. England's true decline dated from the reigns of Henry V and especially Henry VII, 'the Welsh adventurer.' With them, the true nobility of England – which Sidney identified not with the titular peerage but with the public spirit and valor of such families as the Hampdens – had become progressively enfeebled, until the very term had come to imply mere 'empty titles of honor.'

Sidney's ideal was an aristocratic republic consisting of a rotating magistracy, a senate and a popular assembly which directly represented the people and – as power lay ultimately in the whole – constituted the highest authority. The vaguest of these elements was the senate. Sidney conceived of it as chosen rather than prescriptive, though he did not exclude birth as a factor. Elsewhere however he says that he would willingly see a hereditary peerage 'fall.' Essentially he saw his nobility as a meritocracy preserved but not proscribed by family tradition. If by nobility he meant something wider than commonly understood by the term, by the 'whole' people he meant somewhat less – freeholders and merchants rather than the virtueless rabble. Liberty exercised by those who could not distinguish it from license was for Sidney a contradiction in terms.

Sidney's thought is squarely in the classical republican tradition, as Fink and Raab indicate. It shows a fruitful reading of Machiavelli, though it is almost completely impervious to the Florentine's supreme realism; among contemporaries it has clear affinities to Milton, Harrington* and Neville. The one quite unexpected element in Sidney is the frank espousal of the right of revolution. Rebellion and freedom were indissolubly linked; men had not only the right but even the duty to rebel when their liberties were at stake, and any man might justly kill a tyrant. What Locke set out with such great pains to prove, Sidney assumed as a matter of course. Perhaps this hatred of tyranny was as much temperamental as ideological. Sidney was a violent man, of 'overruling temper and height' as Whitelocke* called him. Certainly he accepted no man as his master.

Like Filmer, Sidney benefited from delayed publication. The *Discourses* appeared at a moment when the appeal to virtue and the warning against corruption struck a particularly responsive chord. He was widely read throughout the eighteenth century and profoundly influenced French, German and American revolutionary thought; until well into the nineteenth century he was the quintessential Whig martyr. 'I am persuaded to believe that God has left nations the liberty of setting up such governments as best please themselves,' said Sidney; that statement summed up much of what the next hundred years were to strive for.

J. Robertson, ed., *The Works of Algernon Sidney* (1772); J. Dalrymple, *Memoirs of Great Britain and Ireland* (1771-88); G.W. Meadley, *Memoirs of Algernon Sydney* (1813); R.W. Blencowe, ed., *The Sydney Papers* (1825); A.C. Ewald, *The Life and Times of the Hon. Algernon Sydney* (1873); *DNB*; *HMC, DeLisle and Dudley*; Z.S. Fink, *The Classical Republicans* (1962); M.M. Dunn, *William Penn* (1967); C. Robbins, *The Eighteenth-Century Commonwealthsman* (1961); C. Robbins, 'Algernon Sidney's *Discourses Concerning Government*,' *William and Mary Quarterly*, 3rd ser., 4: 267-96. Papers: C; L (Add. MSS; Sloane MSS; Stowe MSS).

R. Zaller

SIDNEY, Philip, Viscount Lisle, third Earl of Leicester (1619-1698)

Civil War officer and parliamentary radical, MP SP, LP 1640 (Yarmouth, Isle of Wight), 1653 (Kent), 1658 (Upper House). The eldest son of Robert, second Earl of Leicester and Dorothy Percy, and the elder brother of Algernon,* Philip was styled Viscount Lisle from 1626 until he succeeded to the earldom in 1677. Lisle's personal life was clouded by an often bitter relationship with his father whom he believed much preferred his brother Algernon, a view born out by the extremely unsympathetic life which the Earl wrote of his son. Educated at Christ's Church, Oxf. and Gray's Inn, Lisle travelled with his father on diplomatic missions to Denmark and France in the 1630s, spending time in the city of Saumur in 1636-37 for purposes of health and education. Lisle represented Yarmouth, Isle of Wight, in the Short Parliament of 1640 and served in the second Bishops' War under his maternal uncle, the Earl of Northumberland, who praised his actions. He attended Charles I at the Council of Peers at York in Sept. 1640 and in November once again sat for Yarmouth in the Long Parliament.

In Apr. 1642 Lisle was sent in command of 1500 men to help put down the rebellion in Ireland, where his father was Lord Deputy. There he proceeded to harass the rebels, but was also caught up in the political struggles between the Parliamentarians and his superior, the Royalist Marquis or Ormond. In Mar. 1643, at the battle of Ross, he was accused of cowardice when it was claimed, among other things, that he became so frightened he offered up to £20 for a guide from the field. In April an inquiry by a Council of War indicated that, while specific charges were unproven, Lisle's general conduct was questionable. In May, believing that Ormond was obstructing him, he was ready to leave Ireland, and returned to England in August.

Lisle was sent again to Ireland in Feb. 1647, having been appointed Lord Deputy the previous April. Engaged in a bitter struggle with Lord Inchiquin, the Lord President of Munster, Lisle possessed neither the capacity nor the time to deal effectively with the situation, and when his commission expired in Apr. 1647 it was not renewed.

In June 1648 Lisle became a member of

the Derby House Committee. In December, following Pride's purge, he was appointed to the High Court but took no part in its deliberations. Lisle not only continued to sit in the Rump, but was elected to all but one of its Councils of State. In 1650 he took the Engagement to the Commonwealth and in 1652 was appointed ambassador to Sweden. After a long delay, partly caused by the changes of government in 1653, Lisle asked to be excused from the post on the ostensible grounds of ill health.

Lisle represented Kent in the Barebones Parliament, and with the establishment of the Protectorate became a member of its first Council of State in December. He was one of the commissioners for the Dutch treaty in 1654 and served in other capacities. He was also a member of the Council of State created in July 1657 under the Humble Petition and Advice. Lisle sat in the Upper House both under Oliver and during the brief Protectorate of Richard Cromwell,* also sitting on Richard's Council. He sought and received pardon on 30 Oct. 1660, and thereafter seems to have avoided political involvement. In May 1678, after succeeding to the Earldom of Leicester the previous October, he entered the House of Lords. Lisle died on 6 Mar. 1698.

In addition to his political activities, Lisle displayed a lifelong interest in art. In Sept. 1660 he appears to have returned to Charles II a number of paintings and statues which were apparently part of the royal collection. Collins also speaks of him as a patron of Dryden and Wycherly. Lisle's character, formed by childhood resentments, was difficult. His membership in the Barebones Parliament suggests strong religious conviction, but his private life was dissolute, and after the early death of his wife Catherine (née Cecil) he had at least three natural daughters by Grace and Jane Pensac. A cynosure of the Commonwealth and Protectorate – he served on every Council of State but one between 1649 and 1659 – his willingness to serve may have stemmed less from conviction than a desire for recognition.

HMC 77, *De Lisle*, 6:559-624; *DNB*; Cokayne, *CP*; *CSPD, Chas. I*, 16-22 *passim; Comm.*, 1-13 *passim*; Aylmer, *SS;* Woolrych; A. Collins, ed., *Letters and Memorials of State* (1746). Papers: L (Add. MSS; Stowe MSS).

M.L. Schwarz

SIMMONDS, Martha (1624-1665)

Quaker, was born in Jan. 1624 in the parish of Mere, Som., the daughter of George and Elizabeth Calvert and sister of Giles Calvert,* the Quaker printer. She became the wife of Thomas Simmonds, also a well-known Quaker printer. After fourteen years of religious search, Martha became one of the earliest convinced Quakers in London in 1654. By 1655 she was traveling in religious service, appearing in sackcloth and ashes as a 'sign,' and suffering the first of many imprisonments throughout England. All three of her known publications date from 1655-56. She became closely associated with James Nayler,* increasing her influence over him in the troubled period of 1656, and appears to have engineered Nayler's so-called messianic entrance into Bristol in 1656. She was testified against by Friends and imprisoned by the Commonwealth for her part in this episode. In 1657 Simmonds and the largely female following she gathered around her were attacking Quaker leaders, disturbing meetings for worship, and embracing a type of Ranterism. In late 1657 however, she began to undergo a change of heart and was eventually received back into the Quaker movement. She died in 1665, while on her way to Maryland.

Simmonds, *A Lamentation for the Lost Sheep of the House of Israel* (1655); Simmonds, *O England; Thy Time Is Come* (1656); K.L. Carroll, 'Martha Simmonds, a Quaker Enigma,' *JFHS*, 53:31-52. Papers: LF (Caton MSS, III, 364-65, 366-67, 370, 375, 391; Markey MSS, pp. 120-23; Swarthmore MSS, I, 294 [Tr. III, 645], II, 129 [Tr. I, 247], III, 193 [Tr. II, 232], III,

153 [Tr. II, 597], III, 195 [Tr. II, 231], V, 27 [Tr. VII, 125], V, 50 [Tr. VII, 231]).

K.L. Carroll

SIMPSON, John (d. 1662)

Fifth Monarchist, was born in the parish of St. Dunstan in the East, London. In the early 1640s Simpson, already a Baptist and an Antinomian, became lecturer at St. Dunstan in the East and at St. Botolph's, Aldgate. During the Civil War he served as a major in the parliamentary army, and by 1647 became a close friend of Henry Jessey.* It was also in 1647 that he became a 'teacher' at Allhallows the Great. On 14 Jan. and 11 Feb. 1649 Simpson engaged in debates with John Goodwin,* whose Arminian tenets he despised. With Jessey, Christopher Feake,* William Greenhill,* Thomas Brooks,* Hanserd Knollys,* Thomas Harrison* and others, Simpson was a signatory in 1651 of *A Declaration of Divers Elders and Brethren of Congregationall Societies*, calling for Christians to submit to constituted political authority, but favoring the limitation of the franchise to 'visible saints,' including Presbyterians. Sponsored by Harrison, Simpson preached before the House of Commons the same year, but his views were sufficiently provocative to defeat a motion to thank him. In 1652 Simpson was appointed Rector of St. Botolph's, Aldgate, where he maintained an open-membership congregation of Independents and Baptists. Vavasor Powell* visited him there in 1653, the year he was attacked by Arise Evans.* In August Simpson and Jessey were on Blake's* flagship, the 'General,' to celebrate the day of thanksgiving, following which they visited churches in the Yarmouth area. Altogether that summer the two men contacted about thirty congregations in Essex, Suffolk and Norfolk to foster unity.

The dismissal of the Barebones Parliament prompted Simpson to turn against Cromwell, prophesying in Dec. 1653 that he would fall within six months. For this a warrant for Simpson's arrest was issued on 25 Jan. 1654, and on the 28th he and Feake were committed to Windsor Castle. On 7 Feb. Marchamont Nedham* informed Cromwell that Allhallows was 'a dull assembly' without Simpson and Feake, 'for they were the men that carried it on with heat.' The government authorized some of Simpson's parishioners on 26 Apr. to use the income from his living to support his family and hire a replacement. So many people flocked to Windsor to see Simpson and Feake that the Council ordered on 27 May that they be kept close prisoners. From Windsor Simpson urged his congregation in London to 'help Christ to the throne of England.' A warrant for his release was issued on 4 July and he was freed nine days later on condition that he not come within ten miles of London. Imprisonment had moderated his views somewhat, for he was willing to pray for the Protectorate instead of categorically condemning it. Simpson's outlook in 1654 is amply revealed in *The Great Joy of Saints*, a revision of his earlier work, *The Perfection of Justification Maintained* (1648). It includes his vision of the time when the 'wicked, ungodly and unbelieving men shall be raised as slaves and vassals, and be brought forth in chains and fetters before the dreadful tribunal.' In contrast, the saints would govern in the millennium like kings. Simpson's millenarianism was vividly depicted in his visions of the fall of Cromwell ('great O'), who ran towards a crown, sat in a chair of state, sprouted horns, and was cast down and destroyed.

In Dec. 1654 Simpson defied the ban by returning to London to preach at Allhallows. Hoping to persuade him to a moderate course, Cromwell spent the better part of a day listening to Simpson and four companions complain about tithes, Triers and government by a single person. Simpson's continued hostility to the Protectorate led to his removal from St. Botolph's in July 1655, but his influence was such that Arise Evans regarded him along with Feake, Powell and John Rogers* as the demigods of the radical Independents. On 3 Dec. Simpson and Wentworth Day* read the petition *A Word for God* to a meeting of 500 at Allhallows; the petition attacked tithes and heavy taxation and accused the Protector of betraying the Good Old Cause. For Simpson's opposition a warrant was issued for his arrest on 12 Dec., but in February, shortly after his release, he adopted a moderate position, perhaps influenced by Jessey. Simpson preached against Fifth Monarchist tenets, argued that there would be no millennium until Christ reappeared in person, denounced the use of arms against the government, and spoke in favor of the Triers. The impact on his congregation at Allhallows was electric. On 1 June the Fifth Monarchists in the church presented a paper outlining their case against the Protectorate, prompting Simpson and his supporters to seek the advice of other ministers, including Jessey, Knollys and George Cokayne.* After the militants persuaded these men not to intervene, a debate was held with the Simpson faction. Simpson then barred the Fifth Monarchists from the church and appealed for help from others, including Philip Nye,* who investigated the crisis in Jan. 1657. Ultimately the Fifth Monarchists seceded on 1 Sept. 1657.

Simpson was also occupied throughout much of 1657 and the ensuing years by a controversy with the Presbyterian Curate of St. Botolph's, Zachary Crofton, who attempted to stop Simpson's Sunday afternoon lectures. On 10 Feb. 62 of Simpson's supporters successfully petitioned Cromwell to confirm his right to lecture on Sundays and a weekday. Undaunted, Crofton continued to fight, and on 13 Aug. a number of the Common Councilmen and the churchwardens complained of his hostility to Simpson. On 24 Sept. the Council of State, which had supported Simpson, also ordered that his congregation be granted waste ground at the west end of St. Paul's to build a church. On 11 May 1658 the churchwardens and some parishioners of St. Peter, Paul's Wharf, petitioned the Council to allow Simpson to become their minister, but nothing seems to have come of this. On 14 Sept. 1658 members at St. Botolph's petitioned to have Simpson preach for the commemoration of the battle of Newbury, and on 20 Jan. 1659 they petitioned for him to be allowed to preach funeral sermons, in part because of his ability to attract charitable giving on such occasions. Later that year Simpson was again appointed Rector of St. Botolph's, though he was opposed by the restored Rump. His book, *The Herbal of Divinity*, was published the same year.

After Monck arrived in London, Simpson, Powell and others were attacked as fanatics. In Oct. 1660 Simpson preached 'that though the unjust judges now condemned the saints to death, they were justified before God and had acted conscientiously'; regicide had not been wrong. With Knollys and Jessey, Simpson continued to hold services at Allhallows, arguing that the saints must overcome principalities and powers. Finally, on 29 Nov. 1661, a warrant was issued to the keeper of the Gatehouse prison to take Simpson into custody for seditious speech. Simpson took the oaths and was released, but he died in June 1662. His funeral sermon was published anonymously as *The Failing & Perishing of Good Men* (1663). In his millenarianism, political radicalism, hostility to 'heathen' learning, and belief in alchemy, Simpson typified much of the ideological framework of the radical left in the 1650s.

CSPD, Comm., 6-12 *passim*; *Chas. II*, 1:320; 2:87, 97, 133, 162; *Clarke Papers*, 3:13-14; Brook; Capp, *FMM*; Rogers; Brown; Seaver; *TBHS*, 6:225-26; *BQ*, 1:216; *The Old Leaven Purged Out* (1658); J.A. Dodd, 'Troubles in a City Parish Under the Protectorate,' *EHR*, 10:41-54.

R.L. Greaves

SIMPSON, Sidrach (c. 1600-1655)

Independent minister, entered Emmanuel Coll., Camb. as a sizar in 1616. After ordination Simpson became Curate at St.

Margaret's, Fish Street, London, but he fell foul of William Laud's episcopal visitation in 1635 for breaches of the canon law. He made his submission, but about 1638 went to Holland and joined the Independent church in Rotterdam where Samuel Ward* (formerly of Ipswich) was pastor and William Bridge* the teacher. Simpson differed strongly from Bridge, particularly over Simpson's belief that members of the congregation should have the right of prophesying, and 'that the people on the Lord's days should have liberty after the sermons ended, to put doubts and questions to the ministers.' He also disapproved of a ruling elder Bridge had brought in, and the breach was so sharp that Simpson left the church without asking for a letter formally breaking the relationship, and gathered a church himself with four members. Ward apparently sided with Simpson and was deposed in favor of Jeremiah Burroughs.* Simpson's church prospered, largely at the expense of Bridge's congregation. He returned to England in 1641 and resumed his position as lecturer at St. Margaret's, Fish Street. Simpson, Bridge and Burroughs were named as members of the Westminster Assembly when it was called in 1643, and they joined Philip Nye* and Thomas Goodwin* as the nucleus of Independents in the Assembly. These Dissenting Brethren published their *Apologeticall Narration* early in 1644, and their *Reasons* against the Presbyterian system in 1648. They were bitterly attacked by Presbyterians such as Robert Baillie (*Disswassive*) and Thomas Edwards (*Antapologia*; *Gangraena*), who delighted in revealing the Independents' previous disputes in Holland. Naturally the *Apologeticall Narration* put a different interpretation on these events (pp. 16ff). After their return to England Simpson and Bridge gave no hint of any rancor and worked very closely throughout the Assembly. Simpson distinguished himself as an advocate of toleration, and contemplated the possibility of a national assembly whose jurisdiction would be superior to king or parliament.

With the other Apologists, Simpson prospered during the Commonwealth. In 1650 he was appointed Master of Pembroke Hall, Camb., and about the same time became Rector of St. Mary Abchurch in London, a parish that he organized on congregational principles. In 1653 he moved to St. Bartholomew Exchange, preached at the commencement of Cambridge University, and was one of the fourteen ministers appointed to draw up the 'Fundamentals' that were to be the basis of the religious settlement of the Protectorate, and to define the limits of its toleration. In 1654 he became a Trier, but during the last years of his life appears to have been at odds with the Protectorate. He was briefly imprisoned in Windsor Castle for preaching against Cromwell, and died in 1655. His son of the same name became a D.D. of Oxford and a high churchman.

Besides participating in the *Apologeticall Narration* and the *Reasons*, Simpson published a reply to Alexander Forbes' *An Anatomy of Independencie* with *The Anatomist Anatomis'd* (1644), and also wrote Διατριβή, setting out the position of the Reformed churches regarding preaching by unordained persons. This appeared anonymously in 1647.

DNB; T. Edwards, *Antapologia* (1644) and *Gangraena* (1646); R. Baillie, *Disswassive from the Errours of the Time* (1645); *Rel. Bax.*; B. Gustafsson, *The Five Dissenting Brethren* (1955); R. Paul, ed., *An Apologeticall Narration* (1963); Nuttall, *VS*. Papers: L (Add. MSS).

R.S. Paul

SKINNER (or Skynner), Augustine (b. 1593?)

Parliamentary radical, MP LP 1642, 1654 (Kent). Skinner, of Totesham Hall, East Farleigh, Kent, was the second son of Augustine Skinner of Mount Nessing, Essex. Skinner's family was newly arrived lesser gentry. He matriculated at Balliol Coll., Oxf. on 23 Nov. 1610 and in 1611 became a student at the Middle Temple. Skinner supported Sir Edward Dering in the election to the Long Parliament, and later was instrumental in Dering's support when the latter made his peace with Parliament in 1644. A strong Puritan, in 1641 Skinner encouraged Dering to work for a reformed episcopacy, to delete the excesses of the bishop's office, and to promote a sober and learned ministry. He wanted lay patrons retained but greater authority granted to the congregations. Elected in the spring of 1642 to replace the disabled Dering, Skinner promised to forward to the House of Commons the March petition of the Kentish gentry. Skinner served on the County Committee that controlled Kent for Parliament following the Civil War and was seen as one of the *nouveaux-riches* supporters of Sir Anthony Weldon. An early Independent, he fled to the army in 1647. While surviving Pride's purge, Skinner absented himself from the House after 20 Dec., but was readmitted on 28 Feb. 1649 after dissenting from the 5 Dec. vote. Appointed to sit on the High Court, he did not serve. Skinner was actively involved in 1651 in handling matters directed to Kent by the Council of State. He was elected to the first Protectorate Parliament, and sat in the restored Rump in 1659. He bought extensively of church and royalist lands; the manor of Bromley confiscated from the Diocese of Rochester cost £5,665. 11s. 11d. in 1648 and was held until the Restoration. He died in debtor's prison. Skinner was married twice, first to the daughter of a serjeant-at-law, and then to the daughter of a London alderman.

Everitt; B. & P.; *Al. Oxon.*; Underdown, *PP*.

E.A. Andriette

SKINNER (or Skynner), John (fl. 1646-d. 1694)

Particular Baptist and Fifth Monarchist, was Curate of Pauntley, near Dymock,

Glos. (c. 1646); Rector of Munsley, near Ledbury, Herefs. (1647); at Weston-under-Penyard, near Ross-on-Wye, Herefs. (1650), and Rector of Weston-under-Penyard with Hope Mansell (1651-60). He was also lecturer at Ross-on-Wye (1654) and assistant to the Herefordshire Commission (1657). Skinner first appears as a Baptist in 1653, signing a letter from Baptist churches in and around Herefordshire to the Hexham church. He signed as 'teacher' to the church at Weston-under-Penyard, in company with others who held parish livings while being open-membership Particular Baptists, John Tombes* of Leominster and Ralph London of Hereford. The same year Skinner joined with Tombes, London and others in Herefordshire and Gloucestershire to petition Cromwell to appoint ten preachers with liberty to cover the area.

In Dec. 1655 Skinner disputed with Thomas Goodyear in Ross parish church about baptism, and as a result Skinner wrote *Corruption Corrected, or the Ordinance of Baptism Revived* (1655). Capp identified him with the Lieut. or Capt. Skinner who was a leading Fifth Monarchist in London in 1663. He was reported to be assistant to Nathaniel Strange.* Skinner was at such meetings in Bishopsgate and near St. Paul's (Feb. and Mar. 1663), and was the regular speaker on Sundays at Brickendon Bury and elsewhere near Hertford, with attendances of 300. A warrant was issued for his arrest on 30 Dec. 1663, together with Henry Danvers* and Strange. Thereafter Skinner was back near Ross-on-Wye: he was fined for holding a conventicle and then presented at Hereford Assizes in Mar. 1665, as of Hope Mansell, for continuing to meet in such a way. He may have been the Fifth Monarchist preacher from Herefordshire who told their meeting in London to listen to God, turning their thoughts from open rebellion by saying that when God calls 'to seek by prudential policy to avoid danger is the only way to be involved in danger.'

Under the 1672 Indulgence Skinner was licensed as a Congregationalist (in accordance with being an open-membership

Particular Baptist) at his own house at Clearwell, Glos. not far from Hope Mansell. The Weston-under-Penyard church had other leadership, which represented it at the Particular Baptist Assembly in Sept. 1689. The John Skinner who was also at this Assembly (not the General Baptist one, as has been claimed), connected with Hanserd Knollys'* church in London, is unlikely to be the same as the Herefordshire Skinner, who was buried at Ross-on-Wye on 28 May 1694.

Calamy Revised; Capp, *FMM*; G.L. Turner, 'Williamson's Spy Book,' *TCHS*, 5:249, 254-55, 309, 316; J. Stanley, 'Was John Skinner Ejected in 1662?' *TBHS*, 3:117-20; Underhill, *RCCF*, 344.

A. Betteridge

SKIPPON, Philip (c. 1600-1660)

Army radical, was born at West Lexham, Norf., the son of gentry parents, Luke (d. 1631) and Anne Skippon. Skippon served under Sir Horace Vere in the Palatinate and in subsequent campaigns of the Thirty Years' War under Dutch colors. He took part in the sieges of Bois le Duc and Maastricht, was wounded at the siege of Breda in 1625 and again on its recapture in 1637, and returned to England in 1639, where he became Captain-General of the Honorable Artillery Company of London in succession to Marmaduke Rawden. The key role played by the Company during 1640 and 1641 made Skippon the logical choice as commander of the City's trained bands (10 Jan. 1642). On 12 Jan. he was appointed commander of the parliamentary guard with the title of Sergeant-Major-General. Ordered to blockade the Tower, he attempted to surprise it, and won praise in the Commons for his 'great care and faithfulness' as early as 4 Feb. When on 13 May the King ordered Skippon to York, the two houses declared the action illegal and forbade him to go (*CJ*, 2:579). It was with much reluctance that the Common Council acceded in

November to his appointment by Essex* as Sergeant-Major-General of the army.

Throughout the campaigns of 1643 and 1644 – at the siege of Reading, the relief of Gloucester, the two battles of Newbury (particularly the second, where his troops took the palm), and even the disastrous Cornish campaign – Skippon fought with skill and valor. Immensely popular with his troops, he was equally nimble at treading the waters of parliamentary faction, and managed to keep the confidence and respect of all sides. Skippon retained both his rank and regiment in the New Model Army, to which he was appointed on 21 Jan. 1645. He was instrumental in recruiting the remnants of Essex's foot to the New Model, and on 8 Apr. his own command was augmented by two regiments from Manchester's army. Seriously wounded at Naseby, he refused to leave the field, and nearly died en route back to London. Parliament sent two surgeons to attend him, but his convalescence was prolonged, and it was not until 1 May 1646 that he rejoined the army at Garsington, where he was 'received with much joy and many acclamations of the soldiers.' Skippon supervised the siege works at Oxford, and after its surrender on 24 June besieged Raglan Castle, which fell on 19 Aug.

Skippon had been named Governor of Bristol on 3 Dec. 1645 in response to a petition by its inhabitants, and after occupying Newcastle on 30 Jan. 1647 was named Governor there as well. In Dec. 1646 he was deputed to pay off the Scottish army and secure the evacuation of the northern fortresses. A more problematic assignment was the commission offered him in Apr. 1647 as Marshal-General of the proposed Irish expedition. Skippon begged off, pleading infirmity of body and loss of estate, but he cannot have been insensitive to the political implications of dividing the New Model at this point, and the eagerness of the Holles* faction to advance the project. On 30 Apr., the day after taking his seat as MP for Barnstaple, he laid before the Commons a petition of grievances from the Agitators of eight regiments of horse. At Saffron Walden in May and Triploe

Heath in June he tried to mediate between Parliament and the army; that failing, he joined the latter in its march on London in August.

In May 1648 Skippon was appointed commander-in-chief of the London militia at a salary of £600 p.a. On 3 July he was authorized by the Commons to raise an independent command of 1000 horse in the City. Enraged and fearful of a radical coup led by these forces, the Common Council took its case before the Lords, causing a major rift between the houses. Clement Walker spoke of 'Skippon's secret listing of schismatics in the City amongst the congregations of Mr. Goodwin,* Mr. Patient* and others, with power given him to kill and slay,' and accused him of trying to arm the apprentices. There is no doubt that Skippon was representing the interest of the army if not the sectaries, and his control of the local forces was a major factor in the bloodless occupation of London in December and the success of Pride's purge. On 18 Dec. he moved successfully in the House that no citizen who had favored treaty with the King be eligible for the Common Council election three days later, which accordingly returned an overwhelming radical majority and assured the peace of the City during Charles' trial. Despite his own misgivings about the trial (he was named to the High Court but did not attend its sessions) Skippon adhered to the new regime and served on its first, second, third and fifth Councils of State, as well as both Protectoral Councils. He sat for Lyme in the Parliaments of 1654 and 1656 and served, though without enthusiasm, as nominal Major-General for London in 1655. Though disturbed by the Protectorate's drift toward monarchy, he accepted membership in the Upper House in Dec. 1657, and signed the proclamation acclaiming Richard Cromwell's* succession. Nonetheless he retained sufficient credit in the restored Rump to be again appointed Major-General of the London militia on 27 July 1659. It was his last service; he slipped quietly into retirement at the Restoration and, though a note of two oral codicils to his will indicates that he was still alive in June 1660, he presumably died shortly thereafter.

Skippon was the author of three devotional works, *A Salve for Every Sore* (1643: second edition as *A Pearl of Price*, 1649); *True Treasure* (1644); and *The Christian Centurion's Observations* (1645), which contains autobiographical reminiscences of his service in Holland. He was probably a Presbyterian, as his plea for Christopher Love in 1651 and his outburst against James Nayler* in 1656 would suggest. A bluff soldier but by no means an uncomplicated man, Skippon combined personal integrity, religious conviction, political canniness and military loyalty in successfully negotiating twenty years of revolution. His persona of the Christian centurion (which he adopted as the subtitle of his first two books as well as the title of his last) probably comes closest to catching his essential self-conception, with its overtones of duty and witness; it is no accident that two men of honor who bitterly opposed each other, Ludlow* and Clarendon, should both have paid him tribute. Skippon was twice married, first to Maria Comes at Frankenthal on 14 May 1622, and after her death in 1655 to Katherine Philips, a widow. A son by his first wife, Philip, was knighted in 1674.

DNB; Firth & Davies; MacCormack; Aylmer, *SS*; Underdown, *PP*; Burton; Kishlansky; C.E. Lucas Phillips, *Cromwell's Captains* (1938). Papers: LPR; L (Add. MSS; Sloane MSS).

R. Zaller

SLATER, Samuel (fl. 1625-1662)

Ejected Independent minister, began preaching at St. Katherine by the Tower, London, in 1625, and was appointed 'brother' there on 3 Nov. 1628. Slater distinguished himself by remaining in the City during the 1625 plague. On 20 Mar. 1654 he was appointed a Trier. In 1658 Samuel Petto* wrote to him about the doubts of some Congregationalists in Suffolk toward paedobaptism. By 1661 he had been ejected as lecturer of St. Katherine's, but signed *A Renuntiation and Declaration of the Ministers of Congregational Churches* (1661) disavowing Thomas Venner.* By 1662 Slater had become the minister of a Congregational church in Wapping, Middlesex. He married twice: first to Mary, daughter of John Whiting of Hadleigh, Suff., and widow successively of Nicholas Stanton of Ipswich and George Cowper; and secondly the widow Sarah Taylor, whom he married on 1 Oct. 1661 at All Hallows Staining. His son Samuel* was also an ejected minister. Slater was the author of *The Two Covenants* (1644), an exposition of covenant theology. On 6 July 1667 a Samuel Slater was buried at St. Olave's, Hart Street, London, but this may have been the person who had been baptized at this church on 3 Mar. 1629, and who graduated B.A. from Emmanuel Coll., Camb. in 1643.

Calamy Revised; Firth & Rait; F. Peck, ed., *Desiderata Curiosa* (1779); Seaver; *HMC, 8th Report*, App., p. 62.

R.L. Greaves

SLATER, Samuel (d. 1704)

Ejected minister, was the son of Samuel Slater,* lecturer at St. Katherine by the Tower, London. Slater was admitted as a sizar to Emmanuel Coll. Camb. on 28 Jan. 1645, matriculated the same year, and graduated B.A. in 1648 and M.A. in 1658. He was appointed Vicar of Stoke by Nayland, Suff. in 1651, lecturer (by the corporation) at Bury St. Edmunds on 16 July 1654, and assistant to the Suffolk Commission on 10 Dec. 1657. On 11 Mar. 1661 the corporation at Bury determined that Slater and Nicholas Claget, also a lecturer there, should be dismissed because of their refusal to conform. Slater was prohibited from continuing to minister in the parish of St. James, but with Claget was allowed to preach until midsummer in

St. Mary's parish, 'they admitting the Book of Common Prayer to be duly read there during that time.' Claget and Slater were presented at the assizes that year for refusing to read the Book of Common Prayer. On 22 Aug. 1661 Slater was licensed by the Bishop of Norwich to teach grammar and preach. He was preaching in St. Mary's parish, Bury in 1669. Under the Declaration of Indulgence he was licensed as a Presbyterian in Apr. 1672 to teach in his house at Walthamstow, Essex, but his application for a license for the Shirehouse in Bury was rejected. In 1680 he succeeded Stephen Charnock* as co-pastor of the church meeting in Crosby Hall, Bishopsgate, London. In Nov. 1681 Slater, John Owen,* Matthew Meade,* Robert Ferguson,* John Collings* and six others were presented under the Five Mile Act. In Dec. 1687 the Lord Mayor heard Slater preach in Grocers' Hall. Slater contributed £100 to the Common Fund on 15 Sept. 1690, and became one of its managers in 1695. He was married to the widow Hannah Hood, daughter of Harman Sheafe of London. Slater died on 22 May 1704.

Slater was the author of numerous sermons, including those for the funerals of John Marsh and William Rathband. He also wrote *A Treatise of Growth in Grace* (1671), *A Discourse of Closet (or Secret) Prayer* (1691), *An Earnest Call to Family Religion* (1694) and *Poems in Two Parts* (1679). He referred approvingly to Milton's* *Paradise Lost*.

Al. Cant.; *Calamy Revised*; *DNB* (inaccurate); Davids; *CSPD, Chas. II*, 12:308, 337, 356, 410, 433, 606; 22:592, 613; *HMC* 75, *Downshire*, 1:279; Turner.

R.L. Greaves

SMALLWOOD, Thomas (c. 1617-1667)

Ejected Independent minister, was the son of William Smallwood of Sproston, Ches. Smallwood matriculated from St. Mary Hall, Oxf. on 13 Dec. 1633, but apparently did not proceed to a degree. He was appointed Curate of Thurstaston, Ches. in 1638, Curate of Nether Peover, Ches. in 1639, and Curate of Scammonden, Yorks. in 1642. After the outbreak of the Civil War Smallwood served as chaplain to both Thomas Fairfax* and John Lambert,* and in 1653 he became a member of the Congregational church at Woodkirk, Yorks., of which Christopher Marshall* was pastor. On 25 May 1654 Smallwood became Vicar of Batley, Yorks., and in the same year he was appointed an assistant to the West Riding Commission. In July 1659 he was a signatory of the accommodation between Congregational and Presbyterian ministers in Lancashire. With John Owen,* Philip Nye,* William Greenhill* and fifteen other Congregational ministers and laymen he signed a letter to Monck dated 31 Oct. 1659, asking the general to receive a delegation comprising Joseph Caryl,* Matthew Barker,* Edward Whalley* and William Goffe,* in the hope of restoring unity in the army.

Smallwood was ejected from Batley in 1660 and, according to Calamy, from Idle, Yorks. in 1662. In a sermon at Chapel le Brears, Halifax, he used millenarian language to attack the re-establishment of Anglicanism, allegedly asserting that 'the whore of Babylon is rising and setting up . . . meaning the Book of Common Prayer and other seditious words.' For this he was indicted on 29 July 1661 at the York Assizes, and bound over on 25 Mar. 1664. He may have been the Thomas Smallwood for whom a warrant was issued on 6 June 1665, and who was released by 28 June. It was probably later that year that Lord Arlington issued a pass for a Thomas Smallwood to come to London to 'dispose' of his ward, Dorcas, daughter of the late Randolph Dale, to settle accounts with his sisters, and to receive portions due to two of his children.

Smallwood married Martha Brooke (d. 1661) of Birstall, Yorks. in 1642, and secondly Mary, daughter of Thomas Craister, a gentleman of Clayton, Yorks. Smallwood had four children: Joseph, Elizabeth, Samuel and Abigail. He died at Flanshaw Hall, Wakefield on 24 Nov. 1667. His will, dated 2 Nov. 1667, was proved at York on 30 July 1668. He left an unpublished manuscript, 'Nonconformity a Christian's Duty.'

Al. Oxon.; *Calamy Revised*; *Clarke Papers*, 4:81-82; Liu; *Yorkshire County Magazine*, 1:262; *CSPD, Chas. II*, 4:412, 452; 5:178.

R.L. Greaves

SMITH, Aaron (fl. 1677-1699)

Whig lawyer, practiced law in London. Roger North described Smith as a barrister-at-law, and he became solicitor to the Treasury under William III. Smith was associated with various Whig groups during the last quarter of the seventeenth century, including the Green Ribbon Club, and was involved in several Whig plots. He first came to public notice in 1677 by calling for the dissolution of the Cavalier Parliament, and a proclamation was issued for his arrest. He denied the charge, and no record remains of any punishment. Smith was an acquaintance of Titus Oates, and prosecuted some of the alleged conspirators in the Popish plot. In 1681 he became involved in the case of Stephen College,* who was charged with treason in plotting to seize the King in London or Oxford. Smith was questioned about illegally providing College with papers for his defense. He apparently attempted to act as College's attorney before College had pleaded in the case and without receiving assignment from the court to represent the defendant. Smith pleaded not guilty to the charge. The jury found him guilty of delivering the papers, but he escaped into hiding and avoided punishment at this time. Smith had a peripheral role in the Rye House plot, being paid by Algernon Sidney* to travel to Scotland to recruit participants. Smith was arrested but never tried. Instead he was sentenced for his conviction in the College case.

Released from King's Bench Prison in

1688, Smith was appointed solicitor to the Treasury in 1689 by William III, due to the influence of the Earl of Warrington* and Charles Mordaunt. In this post he eagerly prosecuted Jacobite sympathizers, spending large amounts of government money for investigations and informers. The number of convictions in his cases was extremely small, and the amount of money he spent proportionately large. In 1696 he was questioned by the House of Commons about £19,000 in public money that had been issued to him. He failed to make a satisfactory report and was removed from the office in 1696.

T.B. Macaulay, *The History of England* (1898); S.B. Baxter, *The Development of the Treasury* (1957); *Calendar of Treasury Papers, 1689-1699*; *ST*; R. North, *Examen* (1740). Papers: L (Add. MSS).

W.C. Dickinson

SMITH (or Smyth), Erasmus (1611-1691)

Educational philanthropist, was born in 1611, a younger son of Sir Roger Smith (d. 1655) of Husbands Bosworth and Edmondthorpe, Leics., by his second wife Anna, daughter of Thomas Goodman of London. Smith received a sizable allotment for a younger son, but he acquired the bulk of his wealth from his extensive involvement in the Turkish trade. He was a member of the Grocers' Company of London and served as an alderman of the City. He purchased Weald Hall in Essex, married the daughter of Hugh Hare, Lord Colerane, and had six sons and three daughters. Smith seems to have attended to his business during the Civil Wars and remained politically uncommitted. He sold supplies to the King but also provided foodstuffs for the armies in Ireland and Scotland in 1650. As a result of the 'adventure' of £300 he offered to put down the Irish insurgents, Smith received over 650 acres of land in Ireland at the Cromwellian settlement of 1652. In the following years he added extensively to his holdings in Ireland, which reached over

45,000 acres by the 1680s. Out of these lands, Smith settled some 13,000 acres in endowments for the purpose of maintaining grammar and elementary schools. His interest in educational reform became evident in 1655, when he petitioned to create five free schools in Ireland. In 1657 he succeeded in establishing five elementary and five grammar schools. Smith's philanthropy seems to have been motivated by religious zeal, though his particular beliefs are not known. In 1657 he placed the management of the endowment in the hands of a board of eighteen trustees, most of whom were Puritan. By the terms of the new charter Smith received in 1669, the schools came under Anglican supervision. Smith died in 1691 at his manor in South Weald.

DNB; A. Webb, *A Compendium of Irish Biography* (1878); J. Granger, *Biographical History of England* (1824); Beaven.

M.A. Hartman

SMITH, Francis (fl. 1657-1688)

Bookseller and General Baptist, was popularly known as 'Elephant Smith' to distinguish him from several other booksellers of the same name. The sobriquet derived from Smith's place of trade, first at the sign of the Elephant and Castle near Temple Bar and from 1670 at the Elephant and Castle in Cornhill. At the time of Venner's* rising in 1657 Smith was attacked by a mob, which broke into his house and beat him so badly that for some time he was unable to turn in bed. In 1659 he published William Bray's* *Plea for the Peoples Good Cause*, the first work attributable to him. On 15 Mar. 1660 he issued *A Brief Confession* signed by himself with 39 fellow Baptists, affirming their faith and denying rumors that they had secreted arms and planned assassinations. In May he published his own *Symptoms of Decay and Growth to Godlinesse*, a religious treatise prefaced by Henry Jessey,* Henry

Denne* and John Gosnell. With Livewell Chapman* he published Jessey's *The Lords Loud Call to England* on 1 Aug. 1661, which described the plagues and wonders being visited on the ungodly. Several more extensive collections of the same material were published by Chapman and Smith in collaboration with Giles Calvert* and Thomas Brewster* under the title *Mirabilis annus*. For these activities Smith was imprisoned in the Gatehouse, and lost his trade for two years. During the plague he lived with his family at Dorking, and after the great London fire published *A True and Faithful Account*, purportedly the report of a parliamentary committee which blamed the fire on the Papists. In 1666 Peter Lilliecrap, a pursuivant of Sir Roger L'Estrange's, brought two porters to Smith's shop who took away as many books as they could carry. Smith complained that he was 'so often and daily harassed' by L'Estrange that he became delirious and ill. He was also persecuted as a Baptist. Smith was 'teacher' of a congregation of 400 to 500 strong in Goswell Street, and in 1671 was again deprived of his trade for six months for violating the Conventicle Act. Under the Indulgence of the following year he was licensed to meet with a congregation at a former malt-house in Croydon. Smith complained of piracy as well as the Stationers' Company before the House of Lords in 1677, and estimated his losses through fines, suspensions, confiscations and assaults in the preceding twenty years at £1400.

Smith was again active during the period of the Popish plot and the Exclusion crisis. He issued a series of seditious tracts, including *A New Years Gift for the Lord Chief Justice* (Scroggs), *Some Observations upon the Trial of Sir George Wakeman* and *An Act of the Common Council*, but attempts by the Privy Council to prosecute him were repeatedly frustrated by sympathetic juries. Smith published his own account of the proceedings against him over the last-named tract on 16 Sept. 1680. His counsel, William Williams, became Speaker of the second Exclusion Parliament the following month and Smith, who had been arrested in 1673 for illegally publishing parliamentary proceedings, was named printer of the House of Commons on 30 Oct. He promptly capitalized on this by publishing *The Speech of a Noble Peer* (allegedly written, though never delivered, by the Earl of Shaftesbury*), which stated that the King was 'not to be trusted.' The House of Lords ordered it burnt on 4 Jan. 1681. Smith nonetheless reissued it on 19 Sept., for which he was again indicted; a last edition appeared in 1689. In Feb. 1681 he began printing *Smith's Protestant Intelligence*, but this was suppressed on 15 Apr. Smith also printed Stephen College's* scurrilous *Ra-Ree Show*, and according to his own testimony presented another anti-government tract, *Vox populi*, gratis to each member of the Oxford Parliament. Smith for a time fled to Holland and allegedly returned to England in disguise. On 3 Mar. 1684 he was again arrested for nonpayment of fines; these were finally remitted by James II. Plomer identifies him as the Francis Smith, stationer, who was buried in Farnham Surrey on 6 July 1688, but he may have lived on into the succeeding reign, because not only was *The Speech of a Noble Peer* reprinted in 1689 but also *The Case of Francis Smith*, an autobiographical tract. He published a number of works by John Bunyan.*

Plomer, *DBP* and *DPB*; J.G. Muddiman, *The King's Journalist* (1923); Whiting; *CSPD, Chas. II, passim*; F. Smith, *An Impartial Account of the Tryal of Francis Smith* (1680).

R. Zaller and H.T. Blethen

SMITH (or Smyth), Henry (1620-1668)

Regicide, was the only son of Henry Smith of Withcote, Leics. His mother was a daughter of Henry Skipworth of Cotes, Leics. He matriculated at Magdalen Hall, Oxf. on 26 Jan. 1638, and graduated from St. Mary Hall on 9 June 1640. He was admitted to Lincoln's Inn on 11 Apr. 1640. Smith was a major of horse in the

Leicestershire militia. He was Haselrig's* candidate in the by-election when he was elected as recruiter on 20 Nov. 1645 to represent Leicestershire after the elevation of Henry Lord Grey of Ruthin to the peerage. The other county member was Thomas Lord Grey of Groby,* also a future Regicide. Smith's wife was the daughter of Cornelius Holland,* whose Leveller sympathies he shared. In 1648 Smith was on the Committee for Compounding, voted against treating with the King, and signed the King's death warrant (Jan. 1649). A list of radicals published a few days after Pride's purge included his name. Smith followed Holland's lead in the Rump, supporting Henry Marten.* He also sat in the restored Rump in 1659. He was brought to trial at the Restoration and confined in the Tower under the Bill of Attainder against the Regicides. At this trial he pleaded youth and bad influence as responsible for his role in the death of the King. His affiliation with the Greys and their ancient family feuds in Leicestershire as well as their radical Puritan stance and the likely influence of his father-in-law made his defense a plausible one. He was apparently released from the Tower before his death. His daughter Susannah was reputed to have been the mother of the Tory cleric Henry Sacheverell.

Yule; B. & P.; G. Holmes, *The Trial of Doctor Sacheverell* (1973); MacCormack; *ST*, 5; Noble; *DNB*.

W.L. Fisk and R.K.G. Temple

SMITH, Humphrey (d. 1663)

Quaker, was born in Little Cowarne, Herefs., the son of a prosperous farmer. Smith purchased his own farm, married and had at least one child, a son, Humphrey. Apparently well-educated and for a time an Independent preacher of considerable note, Smith became a Quaker about 1654. Particularly active in Gloucester, Worcester and Devon, Smith was imprisoned on several occasions between 1655

and 1661 in Evesham, Exeter, Dorchester and Winchester. Smith established Quaker meetings at Lyme, Hawkchurch and Bridport, Dorset. In 1657 in South Perrot, Dorset, he was whipped as a vagrant on the order of Thomas Bampfield. In Oct. 1661 he was imprisoned for the final time in Winchester jail. He contracted a fever and died there on 4 May 1663. Smith wrote numerous short tracts of prophecies and sufferings, including one in May 1660, a 'Vision' of the London fire of 1666.

H. Smith, *A Collection of the Several Writings* (1683); *FPT*; *EQW*; Besse.

W.G. Bittle

SMYTH, John (c. 1570-1612)

Separatist and Se-Baptist, was the son of John, yeoman of Sturton-le-Steeple, Notts. Smyth matriculated from Christ's Coll., Camb. in 1586, took his B.A. in 1590, his M.A. in 1593 and was fellow from 1594 to 1598. He was ordained at Lincoln in 1594. In 1597 Smyth was in trouble with the university authorities for his criticism of the burial service, the churching of women and the use of the surplice. On 27 Sept. 1600 he was appointed City Lecturer at Lincoln. There he preached the sermons on Psalm 22 later published as *The Bright Morning Starre* (1603). His appointment was terminated on 13 Oct. 1602, probably as the result of a local faction dispute. Smyth was financially compensated for the loss of his lectureship, but in 1603 his preaching license was withdrawn and in 1606 he was prosecuted for reading public prayers in the Gainsborough church. Smyth's next book, *A Paterne of True Prayer* (1605), indicates that he was still anxious to be regarded as a loyal member of the Church of England. It appears that as late as Mar. 1606 he still did not hold clearly Separatist views though he had certainly reached that position by the autumn of 1607 at the latest. By that time the twin congregations at Gainsborough led by Smyth and at Scrooby led by John

Robinson* could have been as much as a year old.

Until he migrated with his congregation to Amsterdam in 1608, Smyth's thinking in ecclesiological matters was largely indebted to the older Separatists, though closer acquaintance with Francis Johnson's* congregation raised new issues. Smyth's *The Differences of the Churches of the Separation* (1608) explained why he believed that Bibles had no place in spiritual worship, why the ministry should not be presbyterian in form but be that of a single pastor with final authority lying with the body of the congregation, and why a church should support its own needy members without help from outside. In the next year or so his thought moved further until he accepted the principle of believer's baptism. His arguments can be traced in *Paralleles, Censures and Observations* (1609) and *The Character of the Beast* (1610). Smyth's unease with infant baptism had probably begun with the issue of the validity of any baptism derived from the, as he believed, false Church of England. He also came to believe that Christ died for all men and so turned from Calvinist orthodoxy.

Believing the Mennonites also to be in error and himself therefore in the midst of a universal apostasy, Smyth's concern for a right church order led him to baptize first himself and then his followers. Both Smyth and his leading supporter, Thomas Helwys,* then concluded that the Mennonites were, after all, a true church. They drew different conclusions, however: Smyth believed that concern for a proper church order meant that he should have sought baptism from them and union with them while Helwys did not. The congregation consequently divided with Smyth and his supporters seeking union with the Mennonites and Helwys' minority forming an independent church. The negotiations were tortuous and when Smyth died in Aug. 1612 they were still incomplete. Union was effected in Jan. 1615.

Contemporaries tended to stress and condemn Smyth's several changes of position but seem not to have noted that each was nevertheless consistent in direction: his aim was to reconstitute the apostolic church in his own day and each of his changes of mind, increasingly more radical and subversive of most contemporary church order, was directed to that end.

H.C. Porter, *Reform and Reaction in Tudor Cambridge* (1958); White; W.T. Whitley, ed., *The Works of John Smyth*, 2 vols. (1915); Tolmie; Watts; W.H. Burgess, *John Smyth the Se-Baptist* (1911); *DNB*.

B.R. White

SNELL (or Snel), George (1582-1656)

Educational reformer, was born at Fremington, Devon, the son of William Snell, gent. Snell was admitted as a pensioner to Caius Coll., Camb. on 31 Jan. 1600; he received the B.A. from St. John's in 1604, the M.A. in 1607 and was named a fellow of St. John's. He was awarded the D.D. in 1620 from St. Andrews. He was Archdeacon of Chester (1619-55) and Prebend of Chester (1622-45), of Wallasey (1619-45), of Great Smeaton (1622-45), and of Waverton (1633-45), all in Cheshire. Snell traveled as tutor to the Earl of Newport, taught at Cambridge, and later kept boarding students in his home. He married Lydia, daughter of Sir Thomas Bridgman of Devon (aunt to Sir Orlando Bridgman, Keeper of the Great Seal) and sired two sons and five daughters. Accused of preaching against the Civil Wars, a charge he denied (*A Looking-glass for England*, 1646), his properties at Gelden, Sutton and Hargreave were sequestered and he was compelled to pay a fine of £330. Snell's interest in education attracted him to Hartlib* and Dury,* to whom he dedicated his plan for a national system of general education (*The Right Teaching of Useful Knowledge*, 1649). He proposed that Parliament found 'rural colleges' in every city and town, to prepare most young men for ordinary life as well as a few gifted ones for the universities. Snell emphasized the speaking and writing of English, practical mathematics and other useful subjects. His scheme aroused no official interest. He died on 5 Feb. 1656 and was buried at St. Mary's, Chester.

Al. Cant.; CCC; Turnbull; Jones, AM.

P.-A. Lee

SNELLING, George (d. 1651)

Parliamentary radical, MP 1645 (Southwark). Snelling was probably a native of Southwark and may have been a brewer; he was described in 1648 as a 'strongwater-man.' From 1643 he was a commissioner for disbursements in Southwark, and entered Parliament as a recruiter MP for the borough in 1645. In 1647 he was appointed to the Southwark Militia Committee, one of the suburban committees which were challenging the conservative monopoly on arms in the City. On 16 Feb. 1648 he was chosen an Irish assessment commissioner, serving for both Southwark and Surrey, and on 29 Aug. became a commissioner for scandalous offenses. In Parliament he was a close ally of his longtime trading partner, Maurice Thompson,* and served on the committees for excise (5 Jan. 1648) and for regulating the price of ale and beer (5 Sept. 1649). He absented himself from Parliament after 20 Dec. 1648, but took his dissent on 22 May 1649 and was named an excise commissioner on 20 Sept. 1650. He died shortly thereafter. Snelling was a Presbyterian elder in his parish of St. Olave's, and was married.

Underdown, PP; Worden; Yule; Shaw, 2:403; Firth & Rait, 2:422; CCAM, 1403; CJ, 6:290, 443; LJ, 9:639.

R. Zaller

SOAME (or Soames), Sir Thomas (c. 1584-1671)

City radical, was the third son of Sir Stephen Soame, grocer, alderman, Lord Mayor and MP for London, by Anne, daughter of William Stone of London. Soame, together with his brother John, was admitted to the Grocers' Company in 1615 and to the livery in 1617. The elder Soame died in 1619, leaving an estate estimated at £6000 in land and £40,000 in goods. By the 1630s, when he began to traverse the cursus honorum of City politics, Soame was a great merchant in his own right, with interests in the Russian and East India companies as well as in trade with the Levant; in 1634 he was part owner of at least one ship. He served on the Court of Requests in 1629 as well as on subsequent commissions for the London area, became an alderman from 1635 and Sheriff of Middlesex in the same year, colonel of the trained bands 1638-42, and President of the Honorable Artillery Company in 1639.

Soame was intimately linked with the eastern Puritan gentry. He knew the Winthrops* and was a brother-in-law of Sir Nathaniel Barnardiston.* He refused to pay the forced loan in 1627 and as sheriff in 1638 declined to proceed against ship money defaulters. After the breakup of the Short Parliament, in which Soame served for London, he and three fellow aldermen were ordered to draw up lists of wealthy residents for a new loan. Resisting, they were imprisoned by the Council on 10 May 1640. Soame compounded his offense by declaring in Star Chamber that he placed his reputation as an honest man above the duty required of him. His defiance made a popular hero of him at once. Put up as an opposition candidate to Sir William Acton in the mayoral election on 29 Sept., Soame headed the poll, but the result was invalidated by the Lord Mayor and the Privy Council.

Elected to the Long Parliament, Soame promptly joined forces with Pym,* retaining his allegiance despite being knighted by the King as part of the aldermanic delegation which attended him on 3 Dec. 1641. He stood again unsuccessfully for mayor in that year. Soame contributed two horses to the defense in June 1642, helped negotiate a substantial loan from the Grocers' Company, and served on the committee with Brooke,* Saye,* Pym and Vassall* to implement collection of the weekly assessment. In 1647 it was ordered that £1440 be repaid him. Soame served on the committee for grievances, for the recess and for maimed soldiers, among others. Though never again in the forefront of agitation, he continued to support the parliamentary cause until his exclusion at Pride's purge. In 1649 he was removed from the aldermanic bench, but with the return of the Rump he regained both his office and his seat in the Commons. Soame died on 1 Jan. 1671 and was buried at Throcking, Herts. He was married to Joan, daughter of William Freeman of Alpenden, Herts., and kin to the poet Robert Herrick, who eulogized him.

Keeler; D'Ewes, *Jour.* (C); Pearl; Beaven.

R. Zaller

SOUTHAMPTON, third Earl of. *See* Wriothesley, Henry

SOWLE, Andrew (1628-1695)

Quaker bookseller, was the son of the yeoman Francis Sowle of the parish of St. Sepulchre's, London. On 6 July 1646 he was apprenticed to the widow and stationer Ruth Raworth. Converted to Quaker principles 'in his young years,' Sowle published early Quaker works, though his imprint does not appear until the 1680s. In 1674 he and Benjamin Clarke* were designated the official printers of the Friends and made responsible to a standing committee which had to approve all publications. Shortly after the expiration of the Licensing Act in May 1679, Sowle and Clarke became associates of Ellis Hookes, who raised funds for printing materials and kept an official record of book titles approved for publication by the Morning Meeting. Beginning in 1681 the printers

were guaranteed a minimum sale of 400 copies of each sanctioned work, and this was later increased to 600 copies. Sowle suffered frequent harassment by the authorities, and on one occasion 'about a thousand reams of printed books' were seized. Sir Richard Brown, the Lord Mayor, even threatened to have Sowle executed. He was imprisoned several times, at least once in Newgate. He died on 26 Dec. 1695, shortly after a visit from his friend William Penn,* some of whose works he had published. By his wife Jane he had two daughters: Elizabeth married William Bradford (d. 1752), who emigrated to America where he printed Quaker books, and Tace (1669-1746), who succeeded her father as a printer and bookseller in 1691. The Quaker printer John Bringhurst was Andrew Sowle's apprentice.

J. Tomkins, *Piety Promoted* (1703), 186-92; Plomer, *DBP*; A. Lloyd, *Quaker Social History* (1950); Fox, *SJ*.

R.L. Greaves

SPARKE (or Sparkes), Michael (d. 1653)

Bookseller, was born at Eynsham, Oxon., the son of the husbandman Richard Sparke. For seven years Sparke was apprenticed to the London stationer Simon Pauley; he first began his own publishing in 1617. His unauthorized publication (with Isaac Jaggard) of Lancelot Andrewes' *Seven Sermons* in 1627 was a matter of concern to the Bishop of London. The following year Henry Burton* admitted to the High Commission on 29 Oct. that Sparke had, without license, issued two of his works. On 20 Apr. 1629 the Commission charged Sparke with the unlicensed printing of Burton's *Babel No Bethel*, to which he responded on 5 May by challenging the Commission's competence to enforce the Star Chamber decree of 1586 on licensing. On 15 Jan. 1630 he again appeared before the Commission, this time to answer for the unlicensed publication of

Christs Confession and Complaint. His
illegal importing of Bibles from the Continent prompted a protest from the King's
printer to the Privy Council in Jan. 1631,
but Sparke challenged the monopoly on
Bibles at common law. The Council
ordered the legal action stopped and had
him arrested in February. He appeared
before the Council again in May 1631 to
answer further charges, but apparently
made a satisfactory defense. Sparke
became embroiled in further difficulty as a
consequence of his licensed publication of
William Prynne's* *Histriomastix* in 1633.
He was condemned in Star Chamber, fined
£500, and required to stand on the pillory
with Prynne on 10 May 1634. To dissociate
itself from the scandal, the Stationers'
Company suspended Sparke from its livery.

Sparke's association with Prynne continued. At Prynne's instigation, Sparke
persuaded Anne Griffin to publish Thomas
Becon's *The Displaying of the Popish
Masse* in 1637, which Laud immediately
ordered seized. Sparke published many of
Prynne's works, probably including a
number of them without a publisher's
name. He is known to have published such
works as Prynne's *Antipathie of the
English Lordly Prelacie* (1641) and
Soveraigne Power of Parliaments (1643),
as well as Hartlib's* translation of Comenius' *A Reformation of Schooles* (1642).
Sparke's *Scintilla, or a Light Broken into
Darke Warehouses* (1641) criticized
monopolies in the book trade, particularly
those relating to Bibles and law books. He
was also the author of *Crumms of Comfort*,
a Puritan devotional manual which had
gone through (according to Sparke) forty
printings and sold over 60,000 copies by
1652, when a second part was issued. In the
1640s Sparke was an active petitioner to
reform the Stationers' Company. He did
relatively little publishing (based on extant
records) after issuing Prynne's *Vindication
of the Imprisoned and Secluded Members*
in 1649, though he compiled and published
The Narrative History of King James in
1651, and his *Second Beacon Fired by
Scintilla* appeared in 1652. He died at

Hampstead on 29 Dec. 1653. His son,
Michael Jr., who had been his partner, died
eight years earlier from a wound received
from his brother.

W.W. Greg, *A Companion to Arber*
(1967), 74-84, 235-88 *passim*; E. Arber,
ed., *A Transcript of the Registers of the
Company of Stationers*, 4 (1877): 35-38;
W.A. Jackson, ed., *Records of the Court
of the Stationers' Company 1602 to 1640*
(1957); C. Blagden, 'The Stationers'
Company in the Civil War Period,' *The
Library*, 13:1-17; Plomer, *DBP*. Papers:
LPR.

R.L. Greaves

SPARROW, John (1615-c. 1665)

Civil War officer and religious mystic, was
born on 12 May 1615 into a lesser gentry
family of Essex. He was the son and heir of
John Sparrow of Stambourne, probably
brother to Drugo (Drew) and Robert
Sparrow, and most likely father of that
John Sparrow of Essex admitted to the
Inner Temple in 1657 and Trinity Coll.,
Camb. in 1659. Sparrow himself matriculated at Trinity in 1631 and was admitted
to the Inner Temple in Nov. 1633, where
he became a barrister. At some point he
served with the English army in Ireland
and during the Civil War served as a
colonel in the Eastern Association. He was
given his rank and regiment by the Essex
Committee of Both Kingdoms, responding
to the ordinance of 12 July 1644. His troops
reinforced Maj.-Gen. Browne's garrison at
Abingdon although Browne complained
that Sparrow's long absences encouraged a
high desertion rate. By Mar. 1645 the
regiment was incorporated intact into the
Eastern Association. In 1647 Sparrow
became preoccupied with the writings of
the German mystic Jacob Boehme and for
the next fifteen years translated Boehme
into English. He also continued his legal
career, for in 1659 he was appointed a judge
for the probate of wills. During the
Protectorate he seems to have known

Samuel Hartlib* and, like Hartlib, desired unity for the various Protestant churches. He was attracted to Boehme's works on these grounds as well, seeing in Boehme's mysticism a way to overcome sectarian dissension in England.

Interest in Boehme had accelerated in England when in 1644 an anonymous *Life* was published and Boehme's manuscripts began circulating. In 1647 Sparrow translated *The Clavis* and *XL. Questions Concerning the Soule*, which Humphrey Blunden published as a single volume. From 1648 until 1662 Sparrow translated ten additional titles, including *Aurora* (1656). He collaborated at times with his relative, John Ellistone of Essex, who was also engaged in translating Boehme, until the latter's death in 1652. The translations contributed greatly to Boehme's vogue in England, though he was criticized by Baxter among others. Sparrow's translations are as noteworthy for their quality as their influence. He worked successfully with both German and Dutch versions and knew Latin and some Greek and Hebrew; his translations are careful and erudite. They established him as the leading Boehmist commentator in England.

Sparrow was not so much impressed with Boehme's implicit anti-intellectual, magical tendencies as he was with the German's emphasis on unity. Boehme taught that 'everything has been in all eternity in God.' The unity of the Godhead contains not only the Trinity but also the primordial origin of all being. From this unity developed what Boehme saw as the law of opposition, reflected in man's very soul as the conflict between good and evil. The soul, itself of divine substance, chooses evil over good whenever it seeks independent existence. Although Boehme's language is complex and allusive, Sparrow cogently argued his merits, seeing in his teachings the means to achieve 'inward peace,' to overcome the disturbing proliferation of sects and heresies, and to resolve the Antinomian controversy. Boehme's writings on the mysteries of nature also provided Sparrow the means to reconcile the Paracelsian tradition with the new experimental philosophy. Finally, Sparrow saw in Boehme's teaching a model for reforming the secular laws. If those who made the law understood 'the spirit of God,' they would make law correspond to the needs and welfare of the citizens. Sparrow was a member of the Hale Commission, as well as serving as a Commissioner of Prize Goods and a trustee for the sale of the King's goods. Sparrow's confidence in Boehme apparently remained unshaken. He issued a second edition of *XL. Questions* in 1665, shortly before his own death.

Al. Cant.; M.L. Baily, *Milton and Jakob Boehme* (1914); J. Boehme, *Aurora* (1656) and *XL. Questions of the Soul* (1647); *CSPD, Chas. I*, 20; Holmes; *DNB*; S. Hutin, *Les Disciples Anglais de Jacob Boehme* (Paris, 1960).

D. Willen

SPEED, Adolphus (fl. 1650-1660)

Pamphleteer, sometimes (mistakenly) referred to as Adam Speed. Nothing is known of Speed's birth or education. In 1650 he printed a set of *General Accommodations* which are not much more than advertisements offering his services in matters of money investment, drawing up of legal documents, even the making of arrangements for those wishing to travel abroad. The pamphlet concludes with proposals for setting up academies for 'young gentlemen' and 'young gentlewomen.' For the former, the study of Hebrew, Greek, Latin and French 'by incomparably more methodical, compendious and facile ways' (not indicated) than were customary in endowed grammar schools, would be supplemented by the study of heraldry, drawing, music, dancing, fencing, horsemanship and the use of arms, as well as 'experimental philosophy' including mathematics, geography, astronomy, perspective, architecture and fortification. For the 'young gentlewomen' provision would be made for the usual accomplishments of French, music, singing, dancing, needlework and embroidery, together with more mundane matters such as writing, cyphering, casting accounts and 'shortwriting,' and an introduction to the 'receipts of physick and chirurgery.' In addition, a solicitor would be available to look after the affairs of any orphans present.

In that same year, Speed produced his *Cornucopia: a Miscellanarium of Luciferous and Fructiferous Experiments, Observations and Discoveries* (1650?), which was merely a list of allegedly 'improved practices' which would make money where money had not been made before, including 'a certainty to raise £2000 per annum *de claro* with less than £200 stock.' Speed's writings and proposals were criticized with some justification by Walter Blith* in his *English Improver Improved* (2nd ed., 1652), in which he complained there were too many like Speed 'who can make good but one quarter of what they affirm.' 'These things are gallant in contemplation,' Blith asserted, 'but more sadly experimented, which you will hardly find by sea or land, nor any other place but in Mr. Speed's chamber.'

In 1659 Speed published *Adam out of Eden*, in which he reminded his readers that Adam was 'placed in Eden not only to enjoy but to labor, without both which no place can be a paradise.' 'England affords land enough for the inhabitants,' Speed asserted, 'and if man did but industriously and skilfully improve and manure it, we need not go to Jamaica for plantations.' He offered a range of 'improved' agricultural practices, citing Hartlib* and Gabriel Plattes* in support, as well as a plan to transport coal along the Trent from the Nottinghamshire pits to Newark. Speed's ideas, while hardly original, typify the range of interests in the Hartlib circle, as well as its faith in rational improvement.

DNB; Webster, *GI* and *SHAL*.

K. Charlton

SPEKE, Hugh (b. 1656)

Political agitator, was the second son of George Speke (d. 1690) of White Lackington, near Ilminster, Som., and Mary, the daughter of Sir Robert Pye.* The elder Speke, a Royalist during the Civil War, was a vocal Country supporter as MP for Somerset in the second Exclusion Parliament, and ostentatiously entertained Monmouth in Nov. 1681. Hugh Speke matriculated at St. John's Coll., Oxf. on 1 July 1672, but left without taking a degree. With his brother Charles, who was later hanged in Monmouth's rising, he was associated with the Green Ribbon Club. In 1683 he published *An Enquiry into and Detection of the Barbarous Murder of the Late Earl of Essex*, suggesting that the Earl* had been assassinated at the behest of the Duke of York. Arrested and detained without bond for eighteen weeks, he was rearrested upon posting bail. On 7 Feb. 1684 he was tried before Judge Jeffreys, who fined him £1000. Refusing to pay this sum, he was imprisoned in the King's Bench until 1687. Speke became counsel for Exeter upon his release. Returning to London in Aug. 1688, he served William of Orange as a double agent. Speke allegedly penned the spurious *Third Declaration of the Prince of Orange*, which called for the disarming of all Papists in London and helped provoke the anti-Catholic and anti-Irish rioting in the capital in December. It was not however until 1709 that Speke claimed credit for the *Declaration* in his *Memoirs of the Most Remarkable Passages and Transactions of the Revolution* (republished in 1715 as *The Secret History of the Happy Revolution in 1688* and dedicated to George I). Speke's reputation was unsavory; he never recovered more than £500 from William, and a further £100 voted him by Queen Anne's Council in May 1703. He was subsequently employed by Harley in Ireland, and was last known residing at High Wycombe in 1719.

DNB; *Al. Oxon.*; *ST*; Luttrell; E. Bohun, *History of the Desertion* (1689);

Sir J. Mackintosh, *History of the Revolution of 1688* (1834); J. Miller, *Popery and Politics in England, 1660-1688* (1973); *idem.*, 'The Militia and the Army in the Reign of James II,' *HJ*, 16:659-79. Papers: L; O.

R. Zaller

SPENCER, John (fl. 1639-1682)

Baptist and Fifth Monarchist, served originally as groom to Lord Saye and Sele* and later as an army officer. Spencer was first identified as a Baptist preacher in 1639 in London, and won notoriety for his public preaching. He published a millenarian justification of the Civil War in 1642, and remained active in London throughout the war years. By July 1647 Spencer was a cornet in Lilburne's* regiment. He attended the meetings of the General Council of the army at Whitehall in Dec. 1648-Jan. 1649. On 10 Apr. 1650 Spencer was commissioned a captain. In 1653 he began his association with Col. William Packer,* receiving a warrant that entitled them, with Capt. William Kiffin* and others, to preach in any pulpit. On 7 Feb. 1654 Spencer joined Samuel Highland* and Henry Jessey,* the Baptist minister, in carrying on meetings in John Simpson's* congregation at All Hallows, the three providing a steadying influence upon the Fifth Monarchists. Although part of an early Fifth Monarchy group in 1652, Spencer remained loyal to the Protectorate. On 5 Dec. 1655 he and Packer, along with other officers, offered advice to Cromwell and were graciously received. The two men subsequently bought a royal estate in Hertfordshire. On 24 Sept. 1657 Spencer was granted £60 p.a. as preacher; this however was adjusted the following March to £50 on his appointment to Theobalds. Spencer was commissioned again as captain under Packer in June 1659 and in November was stationed with the Ayr garrison. There he formed another Baptist congregation with 23 privates and corporals of his company. Spencer and Col. Sawrey were subsequently ousted by Monck. Spencer returned to Theobalds, where he had acquired the manor. The Dutch ambassador reported Spencer in prison in his dispatch of 10/20 Aug. 1665. Spencer was licensed in 1672 for Baptist worship at Cheshunt, Herts., and last appears in 1682. He wrote *The Spiritual Warfare* (1642), but not *The Short Treatise* (1641) formerly attributed to him.

Brown; Capp, *FMM*; *Clarke Papers*; Firth & Davies; W.J. Hardy, ed., *Hertford County Records* (1905); Tolmie.

J.D. Ban

SPILSBURY (or Spilsbery), John (1593-c. 1668)

Particular Baptist, was a cobbler in Aldersgate, London. Possibly as early as 1633 he formed the first Particular Baptist congregation, perhaps by seceding from the Separatist church of John Dupper.* Spilsbury may have been the man who baptized Samuel Eaton* in 1633. In June 1638 six members of Henry Jacob's* church, 'convinced that baptism was not for infants, but professed believers,' were dismissed in order to unite with Spilsbury's congregation. On 23 Apr. 1640 eight women in that congregation, including Magdalen Spilsbury, presumably his wife, appeared before the High Commission, but their case was transferred to the quarter sessions; they were described as 'poor women, schismatics, lately taken at a conventicle.' In 1641 Samuel Chidley* tried without success to reconvert Spilsbury to paedobaptism. By 1642 the latter switched from baptizing believers by sprinkling to immersion, and in 1643 he defended his principles in *A Treatise Concerning the Lawfull Subject of Baptisme* (2nd ed., 1653). Spilsbury's congregation, which met in Cold Harbour, Thames Street, was apparently growing, for in 1644 he was assisted by Samuel Richardson* and George Tipping. In that year he was a signatory and probably the principal author of the Particular Baptist confession, which was also signed by such men as Richardson, William Kiffin,* Thomas Patient* and Paul Hobson.* Prior to this Spilsbury had drafted his own confession of faith in ten articles, which was published with his 1643 *Treatise*. He was also on friendly terms with Benjamin Cox.* In 1646 Spilsbury refuted the Seekers in *God Ordinance, the Saints Priviledge*, arguing that the believer's baptism of the New Testament was not of fire or the Spirit but of water. With Kiffin and fourteen other Baptists, he repudiated the Ranters in *Heart Bleedings for Professors Abominations* (1650).

When the Protectorate was established, Spilsbury did not share the hostility of the Fifth Monarchists. With Kiffin and Joseph Sansom (not Fansom) he appealed early in 1654 to Baptists in Ireland to acknowledge the Protectorate and reject Fifth Monarchist principles. A grateful Henry Cromwell* wrote to John Thurloe* on 8 Mar.: 'I believe they [the Baptists] will receive much satisfaction' from this letter. Cromwell subsequently wanted Spilsbury to come to Ireland to espouse the case for loyalty to the government, but on 19 Feb. 1656 Thurloe informed him that Spilsbury was unable to come because of another commitment. Spilsbury was opposed to Oliver Cromwell's assumption of the crown and signed the petition of 3 Apr. 1657 with Hanserd Knollys,* John Clarke,* Henry Jessey* and others asking him to reject it. During this period his house was the scene of weekly gatherings of Baptist messengers, and in 1658 his church sent a representative to the meeting of the Abingdon Association.

In Dec. 1659 Spilsbury, Kiffin, Knollys, Jessey, John Tombes* and others issued a *Declaration* proclaiming their obedience to the state, their tolerance toward episcopacy, presbyterianism and paedobaptism, their opposition to the Quakers, the Catholics and blasphemy, and their desire for religious toleration for persons who were normally honest and peaceful. This provoked retorts from Henry Adis* (*A Declaration of a Small Society*, 1659),

Richard Hubberthorn* (*An Answer to a Declaration*, 1659), and John Griffiths and other General Baptists (*A Declaration of Some of Those People*, 1660). Spilsbury's church continued to meet after the Restoration, when Jerome Sankey* was a member. The church dissociated itself from Venner's* rising in 1661. Spilsbury probably died about 1668, though it may have been as early as 1662. He is not to be confused with the John Spilsbury who was a Puritan preacher in the 1650s and subsequently was the pastor of a Nonconformist congregation at Bromsgrove, Worcs.; this Spilsbury was the son-in-law of the Baptist minister John Eckels.

Burrage; Tolmie; *CSPD, Chas. 1*, 16:406; Lumpkin; Nickolls, 159-60; Thurloe, *SP*, 2:149; 4:545; *TBHS*, 2:247; 3:252-53; *BQ*, 7:217; 26:25.

R.L. Greaves

SPITTLEHOUSE, John (fl. 1643-1656)

Fifth Monarchist and pamphleteer, probably came from Lincolnshire or Nottinghamshire. He joined the parliamentary army early in the Civil War and fought at Gainsborough (July 1643) and the siege of Newark (Mar. 1644). By his own account Spittlehouse rose to be 'deputy to the Marshal-General' and, after taking part in the battle of Worcester, he left or was discharged from the army in the general reduction which followed it (Oct. 1651). By then he had already written the first of the pamphlets which, between 1650 and 1656, put forward his version of the Fifth Monarchist position. His initial work, *Rome Ruin'd by Whitehall* (Dec. 1650), approved the execution of the King, attacked the aristocracy and expressed considerable dissatisfaction with the Rump for not advancing God's work. In *The Army Vindicated* (Apr. 1653) Spittlehouse applauded the dissolution of the Rump and, since it was improper for the godly themselves to be engaged in politics, urged that the country be governed by a committee chosen by the army officers. The following month, in *A Warning Piece Discharged*, he altered this to a proposal that the government be named by Cromwell, whom God had clearly appointed to lead England as Moses had led the people of Israel.

Spittlehouse presented to the new Parliament early in its session a version of the Fifth Monarchist program in *The First Addresses* (July). Among other things, he called for the abolition of the existing legal system, which embodied 'the corrupt reason of William the Conqueror,' and the election of judges in the new one. Turning to church organization in September, he produced *An Explanation of the Commission of Jesus Christ*, part of a general Fifth Monarchist campaign against tithes.

But the Fifth Monarchists remained a distinct minority in the Nominated Parliament, with which Spittlehouse was soon as dissatisfied as he had been with the Rump. Its dissolution only confirmed his drift into opposition. In Dec. 1653 Spittlehouse was summoned before the Council to explain his seditious attacks on the regime and, though not formally charged, he remained in custody until Apr. 1654. In September, at the opening of the first Protectorate Parliament, Cromwell attacked the Fifth Monarchists as Levellers. Spittlehouse, after a period of silence, had just produced a new attack on the regime, *Certain Queries Propounded to . . . Those Persons Now in Power*. To this he now added *An Answer to One Part of the Lord Protectors Speech* denying the charges of levelling and specifically defending the existing social order. He was promptly re-arrested. The date of his release is not clear, but some time in 1655, perhaps in a period of liberty, he wrote *The Royal Advocate or an Introduction to the . . . Laws of Jehovah*. He was presumably arrested again for not until Feb. 1656 was he released on bond. In the course of that year he produced *A Manifestation of Certain Gross Absurdities* and probably the anonymous *The Picture of a New Courtier*, an attack on Cromwell. The following year saw the appearance of *An Appeal to*

the Consciences of the Chief Magistrates . . . Touching the Sabbath, written with William Saller, and the last pamphlet attributed to Spittlehouse.

The date of his death is unknown but a reference to 'the widow Spittlehouse' in the summer of 1659 suggests, rather inconclusively, that year. Spittlehouse was a major Fifth Monarchist pamphleteer. He exemplified a certain strain of seventeenth century radicalism, ready to overturn church, state and legal institutions utterly in favor of a new theocratic system, but profoundly hostile to religious toleration, social equality or even limited concessions to political democracy.

Abbott; Capp, *FMM*; *CSPD, Comm.*, 7:61-62, 378, 434; 9:155; 13:39; *DNB*; Thurloe, *SP*. Papers: O (Rawl. MS D828).

S.J. Stearns

SPRIGGE (or Sprigg), Joshua (1618-1684)

Independent minister, was born in Banbury, the son of William Sprigge, who was in the service of William Fiennes,* Lord Say and Sele, and was later steward of New Coll., Oxf. Matriculating at New Inn Hall, Oxf., in 1634, Sprigge later went to Scotland, receiving his M.A. in 1639. Returning to England, he served as preacher at St. Mary Aldermary in London and, after taking the Covenant, became Rector of St. Pancras, Soper Lane. During the Civil War he served with Fairfax's* army.

In 1647 Sprigge published *Anglia Rediviva: England's Recovery*, in which he described the campaigns of Fairfax from Apr. 1645 to June 1646. Because of the apologetic handling of Nathaniel Fiennes'* surrender of Bristol in 1643, it was suggested that the book had really been written by Fiennes; but the relationship of the Sprigge family to the Fiennes is explanation enough. More important than the battle accounts, however, was Sprigge's interpretation of their meaning. The victories of Fairfax's army were seen as an empirical sign that God approved the religious diversity in the army as opposed to uniformity. The officers were described as good soldiers and even better Christians. The soldiers were depicted as being more exemplary in their relationships with each other than many who were accounted to be orthodox. All of this gave evidence of God's approval as well as being a practical demonstration that people could deal peacefully with each other despite differing religious positions, and unite for significant action without uniformity of religion. Predictably, he was attacked by the Presbyterians.

Like Fairfax, Sprigge was opposed to the execution of the King. Shortly before Charles' death, he published a tract addressed to members of the High Court, comparing the King's relation to the people with that of Christ to the church, as well as giving a number of prudent reasons for not executing the King. While Sprigge did not condone the injustices committed by Charles, he believed that the task of the High Court was to purify rather than to destroy. The theory of government expressed here is different from the commonwealth theory elucidated ten years later by Sprigge's younger brother, William.* However, William's proposal to abolish a national clergy could certainly have been extrapolated from *Anglia rediviva*. Sprigge's own sermons now had a strongly millennial tone, and he questioned whether the reform of clerical government could accomplish anything beyond mere surface change. The only change that mattered, he asserted, was an inward change toward the new being in the Christ who was soon to appear. Church reform was an indifferent matter compared with that which was soon to come.

In 1649, as a result of his military service, Sprigge was appointed a fellow of All Souls Coll., Oxf., and the following year he was incorporated M.A. and made senior bursar. In that capacity he is reputed to have defaced an ancient carving over the gate that depicted the story of Christ's ascension. He was a friend of the educational reformer John Webster* and wrote a preface to his collected sermons. In Dec. 1656 Sprigge headed a deputation to Parliament which petitioned for the release of the Quaker, James Nayler.* After the Restoration, Sprigge retired to an estate he had purchased at Crayford in Kent. In 1673 he married Frances Cecil, the widow of James Fiennes, Lord Say and Sele. She shared his opinions, and they held conventicles in the house until legal difficulties forced them to move to Highgate, where he died in June 1684, and she two weeks later.

Wing; *DNB*; Nuttall, *HSPFE*; *Ath. Oxon.*

J.C. Spalding

SPRIGGE (or Sprigg), William (fl. 1652-1695)

Political theorist and educational reformer, was born in or near Banbury, Oxon., probably before 1636, the younger son of William Sprigge, a Deddington esquire and JP. The younger William's elder brother was the Puritan minister, Joshua Sprigge,* and his brother-in-law was John Fenwick, the Rector of Somerton, Oxon., who was ejected in 1660. Sprigge matriculated at Lincoln Coll., Oxf. on 2 Oct. 1652, and graduated B.A. ten days later. Upon the recommendation of Oliver Cromwell he was elected a fellow of Lincoln on 11 Dec. 1652, and was made M.A. on 15 June 1655. In 1657 Sprigge was appointed one of four fellows of Cromwell's new college at Durham, in company with Samuel Hartlib's* friend Ezerell Tonge, through whom he likely met Hartlib. After Cromwell's death the college at Durham failed to survive, and Sprigge additionally suffered ejection from his fellowship at Lincoln College in 1660, where he had not lived 'statutably.' On 27 Dec. of that year he unsuccessfully petitioned the House of Commons for his restoration. A member of Gray's Inn since Nov. 1657, he was called to the bar in 1664, and shortly thereafter moved to Dublin, where he married and practiced law. In 1684, following Joshua's death, he returned to England and settled on his brother's estate at Crayford, Kent. Sprigge was a friend of Anthony Wood, who defended him from charges (by Henry Stubbe* and others) that his tracts, *A Modest Plea for an Equal Commonwealth* (1659) and the *Apology for Younger Brothers*, were written by Francis Osborne.*

Apparently influenced by James Harrington,* Sprigge favored a commonwealth in which the gentry exercised dominant authority and political offices were filled by rotation among those qualified. His religious views were those of the left-wing Independents, and he was sometimes vehemently anticlerical. Sprigge argued for religious toleration as long as the laws were obeyed, and moderation and moral honesty upheld. An outspoken advocate of laicization, he favored the abolition of the professional clergy and all clerical garb, which he viewed as a relic of Judaism. Tithes too were to be terminated and lay ministers supported by voluntary contributions.

Sprigge proposed reforming the universities to end the monarchical government by heads in favor of rule by the faculty, thus paralleling the proposed government of the commonwealth. Admission to the universities was to be restricted to sons of the gentry, and education in general was to be provided in accordance with one's socio-economic status. An excessive number of college graduates were, to Sprigge, a threat to the stability of the state, but he supported the decentralization of colleges for reasons of convenience as well as to terminate the alleged power of monarchists and Presbyterians at Oxford and Cambridge. The educational curriculum was to be determined by the Baconian ideal of utilitarianism, and at the university level was particularly to concentrate on studies appropriate to gentlemen, ranging from history, economics and law to agriculture and military science. In keeping with the interest of other educational reformers in the natural sciences, Sprigge gave some emphasis to chemistry, anatomy and medicine. He also proposed

founding a college at Chelsea to refine the English language.

Sprigge's reforming interests also extended to law. Like other Country radicals, he favored decentralizing the courts, so that ultimately each county would have its own registers and judicial system. Like Harrington he advocated that land tenures be reformed to replace primogeniture by gavelkind. Sprigge did not contemplate any general social levelling, but he demanded the abolition of the hereditary nobility, and to benefit the poor he called for the establishment of workhouses throughout the country and the annexation by the state of glebe lands to provide employment. In 1695 Sprigge was still living on his estate at Crayford, Kent.

R.L. Greaves, 'William Sprigg and the Cromwellian Revolution,' *HLQ*, 34:99-113; Greaves, *PRET*; *Ath. Oxon.*; *DNB*; J.C. Davis, *Utopia and the Ideal Society* (1981); *Calamy Revised*. Papers: O.

R.L. Greaves

SPRINT, John (d. 1623)

Puritan minister, was born near Bristol, the son of John Sprint, D.D. (Oxford) and Archdeacon of Wiltshire. Sprint entered Christ Church, Oxf. in 1592, and was imprisoned briefly for delivering a sermon against Anglican ceremonies at the university church. He retracted his statements at convocation. After receiving his B.A. in 1596 and his M.A. in 1599 he was ordained and became Vicar (1610) of Thornbury, Glos. He may have written the *True, Modest, and Just Defence of the Petition for Reformation*, which was presented to James I in 1618 and signed 'The Humble Petitioners.' His name is printed with the 'Anatomy of the Controversed Ceremonies of the Church of England,' a schematic outline of Puritan complaints which precedes the *Petition*. The preface, however, includes a repudiation of Sprint himself. The occasion for this was Sprint's

Cassander Anglicanus, which also appeared in 1618. In it Sprint argued that a minister could not in conscience allow himself to be deprived of his ministry for refusing to conform to the ceremonies of the Anglican Church (specifically, kneeling at communion, baptism with the sign of the cross, preaching in a surplice, and conducting public prayer). This conformism led to Sprint's condemnation by his fellow petitioners.

Sprint's other works include *Propositions Tending to Prove the Necessarie Use of the Christian Sabbaoth* (1607), which insists upon observation of the sabbath by all Christians, in opposition to Anabaptist extremists. The piece is laced with anti-Roman sentiments and citations of Calvin and Beza. His best-known work, *The Christian's Sword and Buckler* (1620; ten eds. by 1650), is an eighteen-page letter, somewhat casuistical in nature, offering rather commonplace theological explanations of human affliction.

Two of Sprint's sons took orders and were eventually ejected at the Restoration. The younger (d. 1692) John Sprint's works, published posthumously, include *Christian Loyalty Revived* (1694), *The Christian Mourner Comforted* (1692), and *The Brides-Woman's Counsellor* (1699).

DNB; *Ath. Oxon.*; Zagorin, *CC*; Seaver (for Sprint, Jr.).

R.E. McFarland

SPURSTOWE, William (d. 1646)

Parliamentary radical, MP, LP 1640 (Shrewsbury), was the eldest son of Thomas Spurstow of Shrewsbury and his wife Catherine. The family was well established in Shrewsbury, where it had engaged in the wool trade since the late fifteenth century. By 1594 Spurstow was a member of the local Drapers' Company and by 1602 one of the company's London brethren, and was probably resident in the capital thereafter. About 1604 he married Damaris Parkhurst, whose brother

Robert, also a cloth merchant, was later Lord Mayor of London. Spurstowe's affairs prospered. He was admitted to the Mercers' Company of London in 1606, and to London citizenship. He took up residence on Coleman Street and became a member of the Puritan congregation of St. Stephen's, of which John Davenport* was vicar. In 1629 he became a member of the Massachusetts Bay Company. Spurstowe joined the East India Company in 1624, and by 1635 was one of its directors. He held numerous City positions, serving as a member of the London Court of Requests in 1624 and 1633, on a commission to deal with policies of assurance on the royal exchange in 1630 and 1631, and as an examiner of the tables of package, scavage, balliage and portage in 1636. In 1627 he refused the forced loan and was detained in Lancashire. Spurstowe secured election to the Long Parliament in 1640 from Shrewsbury, where he had maintained his connections, but was named to most of the liaison committees with London. An early and active proponent of reform in church and state, he pledged £200 for the defense in June 1642. Spurstowe died shortly before 19 Jan. 1646. His will attested his strong Puritan faith. He left much of his wealth to charity, and requested burial in St. Stephen's. His eldest son William* served as a chaplain in the parliamentary army and became a leading London minister, while his second son Henry, also a mercer, became an alderman at the Restoration.

Keeler; B. & P.; *Pearl CJ*, 2 *Passim*; *CSPD, Chas. I*, 9:241.

B.C. Weber

SPURSTOWE, William (c. 1605-1666)

Puritan minister, was apparently born in London, the son of William Spurstowe,* a mercer whose family had moved there from Shropshire. He matriculated at Emmanuel Coll., Camb. in 1623, graduating B.A. in 1626 (incorporated at Oxford, 1628), M.A. in 1630, and D.D. in 1649. He was elected a fellow of Catharine Hall, but resigned in 1637, probably to become Rector of Great Hampden, Bucks. (1638). Spurstowe was connected with the parliamentary reformer John Hampden,* and was later chaplain to Hampden's regiment. With Stephen Marshall,* Edmund Calamy,* Thomas Young and Matthew Newcomen, he was one of the authors of the acronymous 'Smectymnvvs' tracts, the initials of his name providing the last letters (vvs). A member of the Westminster Assembly, in May 1643 he became Vicar of Hackney, Middlesex and in 1645 succeeded Ralph Brownrigg (deprived) as Master of Catharine Hall, Camb.

Spurstowe supported Presbyterian positions consistently in the Assembly, was a leading member of the London Provincial Assembly in 1647, acted as a commissioner to Charles I during the negotiations on the Isle of Wight (1648) and strongly opposed the trial and execution of the King. He also refused to take the Engagement supporting the Commonwealth, which cost him his Mastership of Catharine Hall in 1650.

At the Restoration, with other Presbyterians Spurstowe became a chaplain in ordinary to Charles II, and he took part in the Savoy Conference (Apr.-July 1661) that tried to bring Anglican and Presbyterian ministers together on the Book of Common Prayer. When that failed and the Act of Uniformity became effective (24 Aug. 1662), he resigned his living at Hackney and lived in retirement. He established six almshouses there, survived the plague, but died soon after in 1666. He published sermons.

Ath. Oxon.; T. Fuller, *History of Cambridge University* (1655); *DNB*; Neal; *Rel. Bax.*

R.S. Paul

SQUIBB, Arthur (d. 1680)

Fifth Monarchist and parliamentary radical, MP 1653 (Middlesex). Squibb was the son of Arthur Squibb, Teller of the Exchequer, whose family was from Dorset and Wiltshire. In his early career he was a clerk to Sir Edward Powell. On 29 Jan. 1640 Charles I granted Squibb the place of Teller for life. During the Civil War Squibb's sympathies lay with Parliament, and by 1649 a gathered church (perhaps Baptist) was meeting in his home. On 5 Apr. 1650 he was named to the Committee for Compounding, a capacity in which he served until 1654. In 1653 he was a member of the Committee for Sequestrations, JP for Westminster and MP for Middlesex in the Nominated Parliament. As an MP he was a member of the committee on tithes, the committee to consider a new body of law and the committee to inspect the treasuries. He was also an opponent of the bill to establish a new High Court of Justice. Deeply involved in the Fifth Monarchy Movement, he made his house the center of strategy discussions while Parliament met, and opposed its forced dissolution. On 12 May 1653 the Council of State asked him to examine Lord Falkland, and on 16 Sept. it ordered him to apprehend Catholic priests. He drafted proposals for regulating the mint, yet on 21 Feb. 1654 he sold his tellership to his brother Edmund. His Fifth Monarchist convictions increasingly alienated him from the government, and in Feb. 1655 he was a member of a delegation to Cromwell demanding the release of imprisoned saints. In the winter of 1655-56, he, Clement Ireton,* John Portman* and Thomas Venner* negotiated with the Commonwealthsmen in the unrealized hope of finding a common basis for replacing the Cromwellian regime with a new government. It was probably in connection with these surreptitious meetings that he was arrested and imprisoned on the Isle of Man until Dec. 1659.

After the Restoration a long legal battle over the Tellership ensued, mostly undertaken by his brother. In 1662 Squibb was reported as being 'unfit and unacceptable for the office,' though he was unsuccessfully prosecuting William Pinckney to recover it. Before 1 July 1671 Squibb was one of 35 members of a group of Fifth Monarchists and Seventh Day Baptists meeting near the Tower who were arrested; he refused to take the Oath of Allegiance and was imprisoned in the Tower. A year later, on 28 Oct. 1672, he was licensed under the Declaration of Indulgence to preach at his house in Chertsey, Surrey. He died in 1680.

CSPD, Comm., 5:322; 6 *passim*; 7:272; *Chas. II*, 2:369; 3:121, 582; 11:357; 14:93; Woolrych; Capp, *FMM*; Abbott, 3:615; 4:489. Papers: L (Add. MSS).

R.L. Greaves

STALHAM, John (fl. 1617-1677)

Ejected minister, was reportedly born in Norfolk. Stalham became sizar of Christ's Coll., Camb. in Apr. 1617 and received the B.A. in 1621 and M.A. in 1624. Ordained in Norwich in 1626, he became Vicar of Terling, Essex on 5 May 1632, replacing a deprived minister, and that same year married Ann Powell of London. In 1654 and again in 1656 he was named an assistant to the Essex Commissioners for the removal of scandalous and insufficient ministers. In the summer of 1654 he was appointed by the Council of State to preach in Scotland and money was appropriated for the purpose. By his own acknowledgement he preached frequently in Edinburgh and was long absent from Terling. A Congregationalist and strict Calvinist allied to the Cromwellian establishment, he disputed with Quakers, Baptists and sectarian Arminians, whom he considered dangerously alluring to the godly. Stalham published *The Summe of a Conference* (1644), describing a debate with Baptists (11 Jan. 1644); *Vindiciae redemptionis* (1647), defending particular election and limited atonement; and *Contradictions of the Quakers* (1655), written while in Scotland. Back in Terling in 1657 he answered the Quakers Farnworth* and Hubberthorne* in *The Reviler Rebuked* and *Marginal Antidotes*. Ejected in 1662 (his successor was instituted on 10 Oct. 1662), he remained in Terling as pastor of a Congregational society with no record of molestation by the authorities. He probably died shortly before Aug. 1677 and not in 1680 or 1681 as Calamy thought.

Calamy Revised; *DNB*; Davids; *CSPD, Comm.*, 7:195, 450; *CMHS*, 4th ser., 8:584.

D.D. Wallace, Jr.

STAPLETON, Brian (c. 1589-1658)

Parliamentary radical, MP 1645 (Aldborough). Stapleton was born at Wighill, Yorks., the son and heir of Sir Robert Stapleton, and matriculated from Balliol Coll., Oxf. on 30 Mar. 1604, aged fifteen. After graduating B.A. on 24 Nov. 1606, he studied at the Middle Temple in 1607. From his father-in-law, the Royalist Sir Henry Slingsby, he was receiver of the manor of Wakefield and of the issues and profits of the former colleges, chapels and chantries in Yorkshire in the possession of the Duchy of Lancaster. A substantial squire with an annual income that probably ranged between £500 and £1000, he served as Receiver-General for Charles I. A Puritan, he had a lease of impropriations for the parish church at his county seat of Myton, near Boroughbridge, which stipulated that he provide a minister to preach four sermons a year.

Stapleton's opposition to the Stuart regime began to develop in the 1630s. Initially he had refused to compound for knighthood, and in 1633 he declined to contribute to a muster master's fee. An exasperated Sir Thomas Wentworth referred to him that year as 'a saucy Magna Charta man' and pressed for his dismissal from the Commission of the Peace in the North Riding, though this was delayed until July 1635.

When the Civil War began Stapleton supported the parliamentary cause, and in 1645 was elected as a recruiter for Aldborough. A political Independent, he, William Ashhurst, Robert Goodwin* and John Birch* were dispatched as Parliamentary Commissioners in the spring of 1648 to treat with the Scots with a view to avoiding conflict. In September, Stapleton, Thomas Scott,* John Blakiston* and John Weaver* supported the Leveller cause in the House of Commons, with Stapleton warning his fellow MPs that they must listen to the Levellers. In December he was believed to be in support of the army and was not purged, yet he withdrew from the House and did not take the dissent. Although 'an outright radical' (Underdown), he appears to have retired from national politics. Stapleton was buried at Wighill in 1658. He was a kinsman of Lord Fauconberg.

Al. Oxon.; Cliffe; Underdown, *PP*; Bean; Yule.

R.L. Greaves

STAPLEY (or Stapely), Anthony (1590-1655)

Regicide and parliamentary radical, MP 1624, 1625 (New Shoreham), 1628 (Lewes), SP, LP 1640, 1653, 1654 (Sussex). Stapley was the eldest son of Anthony Stapley (d. 1606) of Framfield, Sussex, by Ann, daughter of John Thatcher of Priesthaws, Sussex. After completing his education at Cambridge and Gray's Inn (admitted 5 Jan. 1609), he married in 1614 a sister of George Goring, the courtier and later Royalist who became Earl of Norwich. She died in 1637. Stapley's allegiances diverged totally from Goring's. In the late 1620s he and his close companion Sir Thomas Pelham,* who married a sister of Sir Henry Vane, Jr.,* helped to set up a Puritan lectureship in Lewes. A JP from 1633, he chaired the Michaelmas quarter sessions in 1639 and urged the bench to challenge Laud's orders to place communion tables altarwise as an ungodly innovation.

Stapley and Pelham were returned as knights of the shire to both the Short and the Long Parliaments and in Feb. 1641 they presented their county's petition for the abolition of episcopacy root and branch.

Stapley was made DL in 1642 and commissioned as a colonel; the eminent Puritan divine Francis Cheynell was for a time chaplain to his regiment. He and Herbert Morley* organized and led a small but effective provincial army and became the dominant influences in county affairs. Stapley was also Governor of Chichester from 1643 to 1645. He readily accepted appointment to the High Court and he signed the King's death warrant. He served on the Rump's first two Councils of State and again on the fourth, though his attendance in the House became very intermittent. Nevertheless he served on its Army Committee from Apr. 1649 until 1653, and twice on the Council's Admiralty and Ordnance Committees, among others.

Stapley evidently approved the expulsion of the Rump, for he accepted Cromwell's summons to the interim Council of State in Apr. 1653 and to the Nominated Parliament in July. Then, after attending regularly, he absented himself from the Council from 13 July until late October, and there is no evidence that he took his seat in the Parliament before 10 Nov., when he was added to the radical committee set up on 19 Aug. 'to consider a new body of the law.' The highly unconventional will which he wrote with his own hand on 12 Oct. 1654 suggests that he had strong views on law reform. A contemporary broadsheet listed him among the religious radicals in the House, but neither his patronage of Cheynell nor his appointment in 1654 as a Cromwellian Ejector suggests an extreme or sectarian position. He died in Jan. 1655, just a year after his second wife, who was born Anne Clarke.

DNB; Keeler; Woolrych; Fletcher. Papers: L (Add. MSS).

A. Woolrych

STARESMORE (or Stasmore), Sabine (fl. 1616-1647)

Separatist and Leveller, was probably the younger son of William Staresmore,

Rector of Frolesworth, Leics. Although influenced by the Puritan minister Richard Mansell, Staresmore repudiated the notion of a formal liturgy and became one of the leaders of Henry Jacob's* London congregation in 1616. In 1618 he was an agent for John Robinson's* Leiden church in its negotiations with the Virginia Company concerning migration to America. In the same year Staresmore was arrested at a conventicle and sought the aid of Sir Edward Coke,* but was released by 1619. In the latter year he published *The Unlawfulnes of Reading in Prayer*, a retort to Mansell's criticism of the Jacob church. Sometime between 1619 and 1621 Staresmore attempted to join the remnants of Henry Barrow's Separatist congregation, now under the leadership of N(icholas?) Lee, but succeeded only in instigating a controversy over the Jacob church's refusal to separate totally from the Church of England. About 1622 Staresmore went to Amsterdam, where his endeavor to join Henry Ainsworth's* church created similar difficulties and led to several years of disturbances. Despite joining John Robinson's Leiden congregation, he persisted in trying to win acceptance in Amsterdam. When Giles Thorpe, the ruling elder and printer for the Amsterdam church died in 1623, Staresmore assumed control of the press until at least 1634. Among the works he published was Alexander Leighton's* *Speculum belli sacri* opposing Separatism, and *An Appeal to the Parliament* (1629) advocating the abolition of episcopacy. He probably knew the Separatist printer Thomas Brewer.* After Ainsworth died, Staresmore published *Certain Notes of M. Henry Aynsworth His Last Sermon* (1630), with an account of Ainsworth's death. Returning to London in 1630, Staresmore joined John Dupper* in seceding from the Jacob-Lathrop* congregation to found a strict Separatist church. By 1633 he was back in Amsterdam, where he was unhappy to find that his congregation had been united with the remnants of Ainsworth's by John Canne.* He was the printer of William Ames'* *A Fresh Suit Against Human Ceremonies in Gods Worship* in 1633, and in 1634 he published and commended William Best's *A Just Complaint Against an Unjust Doer*, attacking John Davenport.* Staresmore returned to England in 1635 and supported Roger Williams* in his pamphlet controversy with John Cotton.* In May 1644 Staresmore participated in the conference of London Independents and Separatists which refused to condemn William Kiffin's* separation from Henry Jessey's* congregation to found a Particular Baptist church. In 1646 he was involved in the controversy stemming from London's Remonstrance against the Separatists. Staresmore was a friend of John Lilburne,* and in 1647 was active with Samuel Highland,* Benjamin Wood, Robert Hall and others in supporting Leveller petitions to the House of Commons.

CJ, 5:179; *Lev. Tr.*, p. 356; Burrage, 1-2 *passim*; Tolmie; Foster; A.C. Carter, *The English Reformed Church in Amsterdam in the Seventeenth Century* (1964); *TBHS*, 1:243.

R.L. Greaves

STARKEY (or Starkie, Sterky, Stirk), George (1628?-1665?)

Medical reformer, was born in Bermuda, the son of George Starkey, an Anglican clergyman of Puritan leanings, and Elizabeth Painter. The elder Starkey died in 1636 but a colleague, Patrick Copland, saw the son off to Harvard College in 1639 with a letter of recommendation to Gov. John Winthrop* of Massachusetts. The boy was intended for the study of divinity but soon showed an interest in medicine and alchemy which he was to follow for the rest of his life. He was graduated B.A. in 1646 and also received the M.A. Later he would call himself M.D. but it is not known where, when, or even if he received that degree. Starkey practiced medicine in Boston and also continued alchemical experiments in which he had the encouragement and assistance of John Winthrop,

Jr. The latter may have been the American 'adept' who was supposed to have confided to him the secret of transmutation of metals and given him a number of alchemical treatises. Starkey also told Samuel Hartlib* that during this period he had been confined for two years on suspicion of being a spy or a Jesuit. In any case he emigrated to England in 1650 where he joined the circle around Hartlib and Dury,* a group with which he was to remain in close contact for some years. Once in England Starkey built up a new practice, claiming medical cures for such ailments as fevers, the stone, epilepsy, dropsy and venereal disease. However his chief interest remained alchemy where he continued to search for the Alchahest, or universal solvent. From these experiments and the knowledge imparted by the American adept, he claimed to be able to make silver from various substances and small amounts of gold from iron – although this did not keep him out of debtor's prison in 1653, 1654 and 1658.

With his medical interests, his combative nature and his taste for personal publicity, Starkey also involved himself as a leading Helmontian in the debate with the Galenists (*Nature's Explication and Helmont's Vindication*, 1657). Although a university graduate, Starkey rejected the traditional curriculum because he believed it put too much emphasis on authority, embodied incorrect opinion and encouraged speculation divorced from reality. He attacked the medical establishment as a conspiracy to 'monopolize the lives of men' and maintain exorbitant fees. He favored a broadly practical and scientific medical education which would eschew theology and emphasize the experimental study of nature. A firm Helmontian and a friend of Robert Boyle (to whom he dedicated *Pyrotechny Asserted*, 1658), he published numerous tracts on his medical and alchemical interests. His medical radicalism was not, however, associated with extreme radicalism in other spheres. Although his religious sympathies seem to have been Presbyterian, his politics (at least when put into print at the Restoration)

were discreetly royalist. He may have been the G.S. who published *The Dignity of Kingship Asserted* early in 1660, and he was certainly the author of *Royall and Other Innocent Bloud Crying Aloud to Heaven for Due Vengeance*, which appeared later the same year. Starkey also appears to have been the author of a series of alchemical treatises compiled as *The Marrow of Alchemy* (1654-55) under the pen name Eirenaeus Philalethes, although authorship has been attributed to John Winthrop, Jr. and others. Starkey is said to have died in 1665, having remained in London with other Helmontians to treat victims of the plague. He was married to Susanna, daughter of Israel Stoughton (d. 1662).

DNB; *Dictionary of Scientific Biography*; Greaves, *PRET*; Jones, *AM*; G.H. Turnbull, 'George Stirk, Philosopher by Fire (1628?-1665),' *Publications of the Colonial Society of Massachusetts, Transactions, 1947-1951*, 38:219-51; R.S. Wilkinson, 'Further Thoughts on the Identity of Eirenaeus Philalethes,' *Ambix*, 14:204-208; Webster, *GI*.

P.-A. Lee

STEELE, William (1610-1680)

Independent, law reformer and Lord Chancellor of Ireland, was born in Cheshire, the son of Richard Steele. He was admitted to Caius Coll., Camb. on 25 Sept. 1627, and was a scholar from 1629 to 1631. Steele entered Gray's Inn on 13 June 1631 and became a member of the bar on 23 June 1637. On 17 Aug. 1644 Parliament appointed him as one of the commissioners for the execution of martial law, and less than three years later Steele conducted the prosecution of Capt. John Burley for attempting to rescue Charles I from the Isle of Wight. On 10 Jan. 1649 Steele was appointed solicitor on behalf of the Commonwealth in the trial of King Charles, but was too ill to attend the trial. Apparently his indisposition was real and not feigned as was that of so many absentees from the High Court. He regained his health by 9 Feb. 1649, in time to take a leading role in the prosecution of the Duke of Hamilton, the Earl of Holland and several other Royalists. Steele subsequently published his argument on Hamilton's case in a pamphlet entitled *Duke Hamilton, Earl of Cambridge, His Case*. He became Recorder of London on 25 Aug. 1649.

In July 1653 Steele's position as Recorder enabled him to take part in the trial of John Lilburne,* and in May 1654 he was one of the commissioners in the murder trial of Don Pantaleon Sa. He became serjeant-at-law on 25 Jan. 1654, was also MP for London that year, and was finally appointed Chief Baron of the Exchequer. In 1655, judging the case of Manasseh Ben Israel, Steele was one of only two judges who certified that there was no law forbidding the Jews to return to England. Steele served as well on the Hale Commission, and in 1659 a reformed code of Irish equity, *Rules and Orders to Be Observed in the Proceedings of Causes in the High Court of Chancery*, appeared under his authority, though his degree of participation in it is unclear.

Steele was appointed Lord Chancellor of Ireland on 26 Aug. 1656, and traveled to Dublin the following month. His long devotion to Cromwell earned him a summons to Cromwell's Upper House in Dec. 1657, although Steele's duties in Ireland could not free him to accept. With the death of Oliver Cromwell, Steele took part in the proclamation of Richard Cromwell* in Ireland. Steele's relations were considerably less cordial with Richard's brother Henry,* Lord Deputy in Ireland. He strongly favored toleration of the sects and with equal vehemence opposed Henry Cromwell's alliance with the Old Protestants. By 1658 he had emerged as the leader of the Irish Independents and his quarrel with Cromwell had reduced the government, in the words of a recent scholar, 'to virtual paralysis.'

After the fall of Richard Cromwell and the recall of Henry, the restored Long Parliament appointed Steele as one of five commissioners to govern Ireland (7 June 1659). In October Steele was named to the Committee of Safety. Steele returned to England at the appointment (much to the detriment of Irish affairs, several said), but then refused to sit on the Committee, counseling Fleetwood* and other officers to leave constitutional questions to Parliament.

At the Restoration Steele sought shelter in Holland. He later returned to England and died in Dublin in 1680. His will was proved on 19 Oct. 1680 and described him as living in Hatton Garden, Middlesex. Steele had married Elizabeth, daughter of Richard Godfrey of Wye, Kent on 15 Mar. 1638. He later remarried, this time to Mary Mellish, widow of Michael Harvey. His wives gave him three sons, Richard, William and Benjamin. Steele was 'generally esteemed to be a man of great prudence and integrity,' according to Ludlow;* more impressive is the testimony of an enemy, Bishop Griffith Williams, who declared that 'although he hated my person, he said, though I deserved it not, I should have justice, and so he did me justice presently. . . .'

Al. Cant.; *DNB*; Firth, *LYP*; Gardiner, *HCP*; Masson; F.E. Ball, *The Judges in Ireland* (1926); Barnard. Papers: L (Add. MSS 21,247, ff. 172, 174).

W.W. MacDonald

STENNETT (or Stennet), Edward (d. 1705)

Seventh Day Baptist, was a chaplain in the parliamentary army. In the 1650s he affiliated with John Pendarves'* Particular Baptist church at Abingdon, Berks. Stennett was present at the Fifth Monarchist rally that followed Pendarves' death in Sept. 1656, and may have been a Fifth Monarchist himself. He was in any case a millenarian until at least 1667. His wife Mary (née Quelch) was probably related to the Fifth Monarchist Richard Quelch (d.c. 1666), an Oxford watchmaker who attended the Abingdon rally.

Stennett adopted sabbatarian views by 1658. His son Joseph* was born at Abingdon in 1663, so presumably it was after that date when he moved to Wallingford Castle, Berks. There he practiced medicine and ministered to a Seventh Day Baptist conventicle, protected by the legal tradition which rendered the castle immune from search except on a warrant from a Lord Chief Justice. His exposition of sabbatarian tenets appeared in 1664 under the title *The Seventh Day Is the Sabbath*, which included a preface by John Belcher* and repudiated William Russel's* *No Seventh Day Sabbath Commanded* (1663). In *The Royall Law Contended for* (2nd ed., 1667) Stennett explored the proper understanding of the Hebraic judicial laws. In 1671 and 1674 he corresponded with Seventh Day Baptists in Rhode Island. He was licensed under the Declaration of Indulgence in Aug. 1672, and in 1677 he published *The Insnared Taken*, a refutation of John Cowell's *The Snare Broken*, reaffirming the Saturday sabbath. With his son Joseph, whose liberal education he had carefully nurtured, he reorganized the former Seventh Day Baptist congregation of Francis Bampfield* in London in 1686. His elder son, Jehuddah, the author of a Hebrew grammar, had joined this congregation during Bampfield's ministry. Stennett was still at Wallingford in 1690, and died in 1705. He may have been a descendant of the Mr. Stinnet, a minister, who was attacked by Theophilus Brabourne in 1631, in *A Defence of That Most Ancient and Sacred Ordinance of God's, the Sabbath Day*.

E.A. Payne, *The Baptists of Berkshire* (1951); Capp, *FMM*; *TBHS*, 2:54-55; 3:9; 7:231; *BQ*, 14:161; 25:11; *DNB*, s.v. 'Stennett, Joseph'; Whiting; *CSPD, Chas. II*, 13:462. Papers: ORP.

R.L. Greaves

STENNETT, Joseph (1663-1713)

Seventh Day Baptist, was born at Abingdon, Berks., the second son of Edward Stennett* and Mary (née Quelch). Stennett was educated at the Wallingford Grammar School, and at age 22 he went to London, where he became a tutor. On 28 Sept. 1686 he and his father reorganized the Seventh Day Baptist congregation formerly associated with Francis Bampfield* at Pinners' Hall, where he was ordained on 4 Mar. 1691 by Hanserd Knollys* and others. Stennett opposed the efforts of James II to win the support of the Dissenters, urging them to repudiate the Declarations of Indulgence in hostile verse printed and distributed at Nonconformist meetings. He lectured at the Devonshire Square church, and sometime prior to 1695 became Sunday-morning lecturer to the Baptist congregation at Paul's Alley, Barbican. The latter, however, requested in 1698 that he refrain from preaching Calvinist doctrines. Following the Turnham Green plot in 1696 Stennett signed the association to defend William. In Dec. 1701, after an introduction by the Earl of Peterborough, he presented the King with an address by Baptist ministers in London critical of Louis XIV's support of the Old Pretender. On various occasions Whig peers sought Stennett's advice. In Mar. 1706 the General Baptist Association requested that he write a history of the Baptists, and though he gathered material, ill health prevented him from completing the assignment.

Stennett was the author of a wide variety of works, the most popular of which were his hymns. His *Hymns in Commemoration of the Sufferings of Our Blessed Saviour . . . for the Celebration of His Holy Supper*, published in 1697, reached a second edition in 1705 and a third in 1709. He also wrote baptismal hymns. Although initially opposed to congregational singing, he entered the debate in its favor, and his work ultimately influenced Isaac Watts. Stennett's *Advice to the Young* (1695) urged early conversion. As a controversialist he wrote *An Answer to Mr. David Russen's Book, Entitul'd Fundamentals without a Foundation* (1704), defending Baptist principles. He preached funeral sermons for the minister John Belcher* (*The Groans of a Saint*, 1695) and John Piggott (*The Rest of the People of God*, 1713). Among his other published sermons were those preached to commemorate the victory at Blenheim (1706) and the union of England and Scotland (1707). He also published a biblical paraphrase entitled *A Version of Solomon's Song of Songs* (1700) and various translations from French.

In 1688 Stennett married Susanna, the younger daughter of George Guill, a Huguenot refugee; her sister married the Nonconformist minister Dr. Daniel Williams, who became Stennett's friend. By Susanna he had four children. His eldest son, Joseph (1692-1758), who was born in London, served as a Baptist minister in Exeter and, commencing in 1737, at Little Wild Street, Lincoln's Inn Fields, London. Stennett died on 11 July 1713 at Knaphill, near Hughenden, Bucks., and was buried in the local graveyard.

The Works of the Late Reverend and Learned Mr. Joseph Stennett, 4 vols. (1732); *DNB*; Burrage, 1:354; Whiting; L.F. Benson, *The English Hymn* (1915), *TBHS*, 7:184, 231; W.T. Whitley, 'Seventh Day Baptists in England,' *BQ*, 12:253-58.

R.L. Greaves

STERRY, Peter (1613-1672)

Independent minister, was baptized at St. Olave's, Southwark, on 19 Sept. 1613, the son of Anthony Sterry, a cooper. Sterry was educated at Emmanuel Coll., Camb. (B.A. 1634, M.A. 1637), where he became a fellow in 1637. He was a close friend of his contemporary Benjamin Whichcote and was associated with the Platonist movement which had its beginnings at Emmanuel. Sterry left Cambridge without being ordained, apparently because of disaffection with the established church. By the winter of 1639-40 he was chaplain to Lord Brooke.* In May 1643 Sterry was named to the Westminster Assembly,

where he was soon identified with the Dissenting Brethren. About this time he became an intimate friend of Sir Henry Vane, Jr.* Richard Baxter, who was no admirer of Vane or his party, later wrote that in Sterry's preaching, 'vanity and sterility were never more happily conjoined.'

When the Presbyterian ascendancy began to wane after 1645, Sterry was one of the Independents invited to preach before Parliament. His fast day sermon before the Commons on 26 Nov. 1645, published as *The Spirit Convincing of Sinne* (1646), made a sharp distinction between reason and spirit, laying heavy stress on the importance of the latter. At a thanksgiving sermon before the Commons on 5 Nov. 1651, published as *England's Deliverance from the Northern Presbytery Compared with Its Deliverance from the Roman Papacy* (1652), he argued that the Presbyterians, like the Catholics, overvalued particular forms of polity and doctrine and thus fettered the work of the Holy Spirit. Other sermons, also published, were preached before the Commons on 27 Oct. 1647, before the Lords on 29 Mar. 1648, and before the Commons on 1 Nov. 1649.

Sterry was appointed chaplain or preacher to the Council of State on 16 Feb. 1649, and thereafter preached regularly at Whitehall. After Cromwell became Lord Protector, Sterry served at Whitehall. After Cromwell became Lord Protector, Sterry served as one of his chaplains, a responsibility he continued to fulfill until the Protector's death. During these years Sterry was one of a small group which served to advise the government on religious matters. Cromwell not infrequently called upon him for assistance. At the end of Nov. 1653 Cromwell asked Sterry, whose own writings had a pronounced millenarian strain, to try to reconcile the Fifth Monarchy Men to the government. In Dec. 1655 Sterry was a member of a conference intended by Cromwell to prepare the way for the readmission of Jews to England. He also served as a Trier for the approbation of public preachers beginning in 1654, and a member of the committee to raise money for the distressed Protestants in Piedmont beginning in 1656. Sometime after Cromwell's death, Sterry became chaplain to Philip Sidney, Viscount Lisle,* eldest son of the Earl of Leicester.

With the Restoration, Sterry's influence diminished sharply, to the delight of longstanding antagonists such as Robert Baillie. Sterry exercised his ministry in conventicles in Hackney and elsewhere in London. Under the Indulgence of 1672 he secured a license to preach at several locations, surprisingly as a Presbyterian. Sterry died on 19 Nov. 1672 and was buried at Little St. Helen's, Bishopsgate. In addition to the sermons published during his lifetime three works were published posthumously: *Discourse of the Freedom of the Will* (1675), with a preface stating a notably charitable and tolerant theory concerning religious differences, *The Rise, Race and Royalty of the Kingdom of God in the Soul of Man* (1683), and *The Appearance of God in the Gospel and Other Sermons* (1710). Sterry was a philosopher, theologian and prose stylist, with a practical capacity to deal with ecclesiastical problems. He may be considered one of the chief architects of Cromwell's religious policies.

Rel. Bax.; F.J. Powicke, *The Cambridge Platonists* (1926); V. de Sola Pinto, *Peter Sterry* (1934); R.S. Paul, *The Lord Protector* (1955); Wilson, *PP*; Nuttall, *HSPFE*; *DNB*. Papers: C.

W.B. Patterson

STIRREDGE (or Sterridge, Sturge), Elizabeth (1634-1706)

Quaker, was the daughter of William Tayler of Thornbury, Glos. She was reared in a rigorous religious environment, her father 'being one of those called Puritans.' After a childhood and adolescence characterized by spiritual unrest and dissatisfaction, she was convinced during the period of John Audland* and John Camm's* journey through the west in 1654

and William Dewsbury's* visit to Gloucestershire in 1655. On 6 May 1663 she married fellow Quaker James Stirredge the younger of Somerset (North division). In 1665, ten years after her convincement, she began to speak in public meetings and entered into an active preaching ministry.

Stirredge's testimony was particularly directed against the persecution of the Quakers. Vociferous in reminding persecuting officials of the leveling nature of God's judgment, she gained notoriety as a Quaker prophetess. In a testimony delivered to Charles II in 1670 she urged him to fear God, 'for of his righteous Judgments all shall be made Partakers; from the King that sitteth upon the Throne to the Beggar upon the Dunghill.' During her imprisonment at Ilchester jail, Som. in 1683 she charged the JPs at the Brewton sessions with the destruction of godly people, their livelihoods and families, and warned that persecutors would not evade an eternal justice meted out on the basis of their deeds.

Deeply concerned with the unity of the Quaker movement, Stirredge condemned the Wilkinson*-Story* schismatics (c. 1672) for their abandonment of public meetings in favor of 'Christian prudence' under persecution. When she confronted Story in Bristol she testified against his departure 'from the Cross' and his denial of the validity of women's preaching. *Strength in Weakness Manifest* (1711), the autobiography which she completed in 1692, illustrates her concern for the future integrity of the movement in the hands of 'careless' and 'indifferent' professors of truth. She feared the falling away of the new generation of Quakers by nurture, and wrote her autobiography for the use and guidance of her six children. She concluded that work, 'Lord keep my Family, and thy People; let not one of them be lost. . . .'

In 1688 the Stirredges moved from Chew Magna, Som. to Hemel Hempstead. During the later years of her life she was active in neighboring meetings in Hertfordshire, and continued to visit Bristol and attend yearly meetings in London. She died on 7

Sept. 1706 and was buried at the Friends' burial ground at Wood-End.

Minute Book of the Men's Meeting of the Society of Friends in Bristol 1667-1685 (1971); F. Budge, *Annals of the Early Friends* (1877, 1879); Besse; J. Godber, *Friends in Bedfordshire and West Hertfordshire* (1975).

P.B. Volkman

STONE, Samuel (1602-1663)

Independent minister and colonizer, was born in Hertford, the son of John Stone. He was educated at Hale's Grammar School and Emmanuel Coll., Camb., proceeding B.A. in 1623 and M.A. in 1627, and was ordained deacon and priest at Peterborough in 1626. Suspended as Curate of Stisted, Essex in 1630, Stone served as a lecturer in Towcester (1630-33), and emigrated to New England in 1633 with John Cotton* and Thomas Hooker.* Stone helped Hooker found Hartford (named after his own birthplace) in 1636, served as chaplain to Maj. John Mason in 1637, and was Hartford's minister from 1647 to 1663. Stone's work at Hartford was marred in 1656 by a controversy with that church's ruling elder, William Goodwin, regarding baptism, church membership and the rights of church members. Goodwin ultimately withdrew secessionist members of the church to Hadley in 1659. Stone died at Hartford on 20 July 1663. He was twice married, the second time (1641) to Elizabeth Allyn, by whom he had a son and four daughters.

Stone was a firm advocate of Congregationalism, as indicated in his only published work, *A Congregational Church is a Catholic Visible Church*, which appeared with a preface by Samuel Mather* in 1652. In it, Stone presents an argument for Congregationalism on the basis of Aristotelian logic. At the same time, as his controversy with Goodwin reveals, Stone was not a proponent of ecclesiastical democracy.

DNB; *Al. Cant*; C. Mather, *Magnalia Christi* (1902); J. Winthrop, *The History of New England* (1825).

R.J. VanderMolen

STONEHAM (or Stonham), Benjamin (c. 1612-1676)

Independent minister and Fifth Monarchist, was probably born in Lincolnshire, though place and date of birth are unknown. He was entered at St. Catharine's Coll., Camb. in 1633, and graduated B.A. (1636) and M.A. (1640). Stoneham served as house preacher to Sir Anthony Irby* of Boston, Lincs. before the Civil War, as Rector of Oakley, Suff. from 1644 to 1650, and as lecturer or curate at St. Peter's Church, Ipswich, in 1651. He founded an Independent church there with the support of a Puritan lawyer, William Hanby, and his wife, Mary. A Fifth Monarchy agent in Suffolk in 1656-57, Stoneham was an MP in the Barebones Parliament. Disillusioned by Cromwell's failure to establish the rule of the saints, he helped organize opposition to him in East Anglia. He was silenced in 1662 and went to London where he preached in his lodgings, for which he was committed to Newgate jail at the time of the plague in 1665. The Fifth Monarchists saw the plague as divine retribution on the country for restoring the monarchy and allowing the return of the bishops. Stoneham did not take out a preaching licence in 1672 at the Declaration of Indulgence and died in Mar. 1676, aged 64 years.

His Fifth Monarchy activities brought him early into contact with Christopher Feake.* With Feake in 1659 he published *A Serious Proposal*. Stoneham seems to have muted his Fifth Monarchy views after 1662. He became more interested in the millenarian views of Thomas Brightman, who identified the Pope with Antichrist, through his studies of Revelation and Daniel. He retained his millenarian beliefs until his death, though he was not certain whether the millennium was near or far off. In 1664 he published *The Voice of a Cry at Midnight*, an appeal to Independents to preach in a 'usual known place' and not retreat into private houses, which quotes from Thomas Brightman. In 1676 in *Saul and David Compared Together* and *The Parable of the Ten Virgins*, Stoneham reaffirms his faith in the millennial reign of the saints.

Capp, *FMM*; *Calamy Revised*; Nuttall, *VS*; Thurloe, *SP*, 4:687, 727.

I. Morgan

STORY (or Storey), John (d. 1681)

Quaker, was an agricultural laborer at Goosegreene, Preston Patrick, W'land. After his conversion at Firbank in 1652, he and John Wilkinson* carried the Quaker message to southwestern England commencing in 1654, with most of their work concentrated in Wiltshire, Bristol and Gloucestershire. They achieved some success, partly in Baptist circles, but as early as 1654 their emphasis on the Inner Light in individuals was attracting the Ranters, as at Kidsley Park, Smalley. Story defended Quaker principles in *Babilons Defence Broken Down* (1660) and *A Short Discovery of Certain Truths* (1664), and seems to have been well regarded in Quaker circles. An early Quaker account observes that 'while he kept humble and low [he] was very serviceable, especially in the defence of truth against opposers thereof, in several disputes to the advantage of truth, being well read in holy scripture' (*FPT*, 256).

In the 1670s friction developed between Story and George Fox* over the institutionalization of Quakerism, particularly the extent of women's meetings and the harnessing of the Inner Light in individuals to the sense of the Quaker meeting. Relations worsened in the aftermath of Story's return from the south in 1672, and in 1674 Fox charged that Story and Wilkinson had 'run out and drew many

after them by subscriptions and otherwise.' When the Story-Wilkinson group established their own business meeting in May 1675, it was denounced by the Yearly Meeting of Ministers at London. Efforts to mediate the dispute were made, including the session in Apr. 1676 at the home of John Blaykling near Sedbergh, Yorks. At Swarthmore Fox pressed Story and Wilkinson to terminate the schism, as did the Yearly Meeting of Ministers in May 1676, but instead Story traveled south to increase his base of support. To this point the schism had largely been confined to Westmorland and involved only the business meetings, but matters were exacerbated in June 1677 when the Yearly Meeting, urged on by Fox, withdrew meetings for worship from the houses of those involved with the schismatic business meetings. That summer Bristol Friends sided with Story and Wilkinson, and others followed in Wiltshire, Reading, Hertford, York and the East Riding. Passions were further enflamed by William Rogers' denunciation of Fox in *The Christian-Quaker Distinguished* (Nov. 1680). To opponents of Story and Wilkinson, their followers were looked on as libertines, and indeed from the very beginning Story's appeal had been to those more prone to spiritual excitement and individual expression than was typical among most Quakers. At the time of Story's death on 22 Nov. 1681 the schism remained unhealed. A vindication of his position by Wilkinson and other supporters appeared in 1683 under the title, *The Memory of That Servant of God, John Story, Revived*, but to this Thomas Camm retorted by defending the orthodox position in *The Line of Truth*.

FPT; *EQL*; Fox, *CJ*; *EQW*; Braithwaite, *SP*; Hill, *WTUD*. Papers: LF (Swarthmore MSS).

R.L. Greaves

STRANGE, Nathaniel (d. 1665)

Particular Baptist and Fifth Monarchist,

served as a lieutenant in Robert Lilburne's* regiment. In the later 1650s he was the pastor of a Particular Baptist church at Barnstaple, Devon, and from 1656 to 1658 he played an active role in the Baptist Western Association with Thomas Collier,* John Pendarves* and Thomas Glasse.* He signed four circular letters of exhortation to Association members and was probably a co-author of the Association's *A Confession of the Faith of Several Churches of Christ in the County of Somerset, and Some Churches in the Counties neer Adjacent* (1656). He was at the Dorchester meeting in May 1658 when William Allen,* John Carew* and John Vernon* argued for the union of the Baptists and Fifth Monarchists.

Strange himself did not manifest Fifth Monarchist views until after 1660 when he moved to London. There he quickly became involved in the radical underground, for a warrant was issued by Secretary Nicholas for his arrest on 25 Oct. 1661 for seditious words and actions. At that time he was living in Southwark. On 2 June 1662 Nicholas was informed that Strange, 'a dangerous man,' was holding a conventicle in Trinity Lane, and that at a meeting in Southwark he and his followers identified the King with the beast in the Apocalypse. The following day another warrant was issued for his arrest on the grounds that he was a threat to the public peace. The same year he associated with a conventicle in Duke's Place, London, and during the summer he was at Aylesbury, Bucks.; a warrant for his arrest there was issued on 11 July. Again the authorities missed him, enabling him to participate in the plotting for the Yorkshire rising in 1663. Warrants for his arrest and that of John Skinner* were issued on 30 Dec., and these were followed on 21 Mar. 1664 by a warrant to arrest Glasse and Strange. The government learned on 2 June that a thousand copies of *Mene Tekel*, thought to be by Strange, had been printed in Holland and sent to Scotland and Ireland. Other warrants followed in July 1664 and Mar. 1665. Strange was now using the alias Capt. L'Estrange, and this 'rash heady

person' even tried to persuade the saints to attack Whitehall. In early May he met with an unidentified MP at the Black Swan Court to determine the intentions of Parliament. To the end he eluded the state, but on 22 Oct. 1665 Lord Arlington learned that Strange was either sick or dead of the plague. Although known as a 'scholar and linguist,' he was one of the most active leaders in the underground.

CSPD, Chas. II, 2-4 *passim*; 5:24; Capp, *FMM*; G.F. Nuttall, 'The Baptist Western Association 1653-1658,' *JEH*, 11:213-18; Thurloe, *SP*, 7:140; *A Memorial on the Death of . . . Nathaniel Strange* (1666); *TBHS*, 6:65-69; *ARPB*. Papers: ORP.

R.L. Greaves

STRANGER (or Stringer), Hannah (fl. 1656-1680)

Quaker, was, with her first husband, the London combmaker John Stranger, a disciple of James Nayler.* Using extreme language she referred to Nayler as 'the everlasting Son of Righteousness' and 'thou fairest of ten thousand, thou only begotten son of God.' In similar fashion her husband wrote that 'thy name shall be no more James Nayler, but Jesus.' As early as Sept. 1656 George Fox* denounced the Strangers and Martha Simmonds* to Nayler as liars and slanderers who did not possess the truth, but Nayler refused to repudiate them. On 24 Oct. 1656 Hannah Stranger and Martha Simmonds held the reins of Nayler's horse and John Stranger preceded them on the controversial procession into Bristol. With Nayler and the others Hannah Stranger was imprisoned in Bristol and transferred to London in November. When Nayler was placed in the pillory on 27 Dec., nine days after his cruel scourging, Hannah Stranger, Martha Simmonds and Dorcas Erbery, daughter of William Erbery,* were with him – in imitation, John Deacon wrote, of the women at the cross. In 1666, by which time Stranger's first husband was deceased and she had married Henry Salter of London, she repented her role in the Nayler episode and was received back into the Quaker fellowship at Bristol. With Martha Fisher she appealed to Charles II in 1671 to release Margaret Fox* from prison. Subsequently she went to America, where she acquired property in New Jersey. In 1679-80 she was living as a widow in Tokany, Del.

Fox, *CJ*; *EQL*; *EQW*; M.B. Brailsford, *A Quaker from Cromwell's Army: James Nayler* (1927); J. Deacon, *The Grand Imposter Examined* (1656); Brailsford, *BQu*. Papers: LF (Swarthmore MSS).

R.L. Greaves

STREATER (or Streeter, Streator), John (fl. 1642-1687)

Army radical, pamphleteer and bookseller, joined the parliamentary army in 1642 and fought at Edgehill and Newbury. In 1650 he went to Ireland as quarter-master general of foot, where he was also employed designing siegeworks and fortifications. Streater was on leave in England in Apr. 1653 when the Long Parliament was dissolved, and he immediately challenged Cromwell in a pamphlet, *Ten Queries*, for which he was court-martialed and cashiered. Undaunted, he followed this with *The Grand Politic Informer*, an indictment of one-man rule. On 11 Sept. the Council of State committed him to the Gatehouse, and on 21 Nov. the Barebones Parliament denied his petition for *habeas corpus*. He sued for it successfully in the Upper Bench however, and in Feb. 1654 was ordered released by Justices Rolle* and Aske. Streater continued to attack the Protectorate in *Observations . . . upon Aristotles First Book of Political Government* (April) and the *Politick Commentary upon the Life of Caius July Caesar* (May), both of which suggested the desirability of assassinating Cromwell, and despite the patronage of Cromwell's brother-in-law

John Desborough* and an engagement taken on 18 Oct. against further criticism of the regime, he was imprisoned again in November by order of Parliament. Arguing that the order had lapsed with the expiration of the Parliament, he was again upheld in court, and released early in 1655 on a bond of £500. Streater then resumed his old civilian profession of printer and bookseller, which he had practiced at Budge Row (Watling Street?) in 1646 if not earlier, and was soon involved in controversy over the publishing of a Bible. Abbott suggests that he may have been the author of the anti-Protectoral tract, *The Picture of a New Courtier* (1656), also attributed to John Spittlehouse,* and he was probably responsible for the republication (with additions) of Edward Sexby's* *Killing No Murder* in 1659.

Streater published his apologia, *Secret Reasons of State Discovered . . . in John Streeters Case*, with the fall of the Protectorate in May 1659. About this time he became official government printer, later in collaboration with John Macock; on 11 Apr. 1660 they received a warrant for £528 13s. 3d. for printing acts and orders. Streater resumed his military career as well. On 30 July 1659 he was given command of the Artillery Train by the Council of State. He remained loyal to Parliament during Lambert's* coup (*The Continuation of the Session of Parliament Justified*, signed J.S.), and was part of the abortive plot of 12 Dec. to seize the Tower on its behalf. On 12 Jan. 1660 he was given command of John Hewson's* regiment, and later stationed by Monck at Coventry. In April he led 500 foot in the suppression of Lambert's rising. Streater lost his command in July, but remained with the regiment until its disbanding in the fall. He was briefly arrested in Nov. 1661 but in 1662 was exempted from the provisions of the Printing and Printers Act, a mark of apparent favor. However he was soon printing anti-government tracts again, for in Mar. 1663 he engaged to print nothing critical of the regime after being arrested. Streater obtained a patent for printing law books as one of the assigns of Richard and

Edward Atkyns, but in 1664 was again imprisoned with others by the Stationers' Company for infringing their privileges. In 1666 he testified against Samuel Speed for selling law books printed during the Commonwealth, and in 1669 defended his patent in *The Kings Grant of Privilege for Sole Printing Common Law Books Defended*. In July 1670 he was arrested once more as the author of a 'seditious libel,' *The Character of a True and False Shepherd*. Streater is last noticed in 1687; the Joseph Streator listed as the printer of *Sylvias Revenge* (1688) was perhaps his successor.

Plomer, *DBP* and *DPB*; *DNB*; Firth & Davies; Abbott; Thurloe, *SP*; Aylmer, *SS*; J.G. Muddiman, *The King's Journalist* (1923); Woolrych; *CJ*, 7:353, 714, 810, 878; *CSPD, Comm., Chas. II, passim*. Papers: L (Harl. MS 5928).

R. Zaller

STRICKLAND, Walter (fl. 1640-1660)

Parliamentary radical, MP LP 1646 (Minehead), 1653 (Yorks.), 1653 (East Riding), 1656 (Newcastle), 1659. Walter Strickland, brother of Sir William Strickland,* was a younger son of Walter Strickland (d. 1636) of Boynton, Yorks., by his wife Frances, daughter of Peter Wentworth of Lillingstone Lovell, Oxon. Strickland attended Queens' Coll., Camb., and Gray's Inn. Little else is known of his life until 1642, when he was appointed Parliament's agent to the States General of Holland. That diplomatic assignment and others kept Strickland abroad for most of the Civil Wars and throughout the King's trial and execution. In Feb. 1650 Parliament again enlisted Strickland's skill in foreign affairs. Along with Oliver St. John* he was chosen ambassador extraordinary to the United Provinces for the purpose of negotiating a political as well as an economic union (a mission that failed, despite his efforts). After returning to England Strickland was entrusted with further diplomatic tasks. Between 1653 and 1656 he defended England's interests in negotiations with Portugal, Holland, France and Sweden, and helped engineer the treaties signed with the latter three nations. In addition to his successful career as a diplomat, Strickland also made his mark in domestic politics during the Commonwealth and Protectorate. He was elected to the Council of State in Feb. 1651 and again in Nov. 1652, and his record of attendance as well as his appointment to numerous parliamentary committees suggest that he was an active member of the Rump. Strickland achieved his most prominent position in the government during the Protectorate, becoming one of Cromwell's most loyal supporters. After the dissolution of the Rump, Strickland was chosen to sit on the army's Council of Thirteen. From then until the restoration of the Long Parliament in 1659 he was elected to every Parliament and Council of State, including those under Richard Cromwell.* He attended the Rump during the summer of 1659 and was appointed to the Committee of Safety that ruled England between Oct. and Dec. 1659. Strickland's absence from England during the critical years of civil war and the lack of recorded speeches, writings or other sources of his opinions makes assessment of his political and religious radicalism difficult. Although he registered opposition to Quakerism during the parliamentary debates over the fate of James Nayler,* he also strongly cautioned against religious persecution. Yet it is not clear whether he was expressing his own views or defending Cromwell's policy of toleration. Strickland's acceptance of every political authority between 1649 and 1659 and his absorption with administrative and diplomatic responsibilities suggest that he was primarily a man who rode along with the revolutionary current of the 1640s and 1650s. Indeed, he was attacked by contemporary pamphleteers as a 'courtier' who served the government only in order to advance his own selfish ends. In Jan. 1660 Parliament ordered Strickland to attend the House and give an account of his actions, but at the Restoration he escaped punishment.

DNB; Abbott; R. Sherwood, *The Court of Oliver Cromwell* (1977); Woolrych; B. Carroll, "The Diplomatic Career of Walter Strickland" (M.A. thesis, Vanderbilt Univ., 1959); Worden. Papers: L (Add. MSS; Stowe MSS).

M.A. Hartman

STRICKLAND, Sir William (c. 1596-1673)

Parliamentary radical, MP LP 1640 (Hedon), 1654, 1656 (Yorks.). Strickland was born in Boynton, Yorks., the elder brother of the diplomat and politician Walter Strickland.* He attended Queens' Coll., Camb. and Gray's Inn and was a JP in the East and North Ridings of Yorkshire. Elected to the Long Parliament, he vigorously supported the parliamentary cause. Strickland was a staunch Presbyterian who continued to sit during the Speaker's absence in 1647. He was not secluded at Pride's purge but refrained from taking his seat. Ludlow* says he carried the news of the battle of Dunbar to London. Strickland represented Yorkshire in the Protectorate Parliaments of 1654 and 1656 where he spoke out strongly against James Nayler.* He received a writ of summons to Cromwell's Upper House. He took his seat in the restored Rump Parliament but took little part in the proceedings and did not attend after the secluded members were restored. Retiring from public duty at the Restoration, he was left unmolested until his death in 1673.

DNB; Keeler; Masson; Whitelocke, *Memorials*.

H.R. Engstrom

STRODE, William (1599?-1645)

Parliamentary radical, MP 1624, 1625, 1626, 1628, SP, LP 1640 (Beeralston). Strode was the second son of Sir William Strode of Newnham, Devon, and his wife Mary, daughter of Thomas Southcote of Bovey Tracey, Devon. Strode entered the Middle Temple in 1614, but was never admitted to the bar. He matriculated at Exeter Coll., Oxf. in 1617, and received his B.A. in 1619. Strode never married. After denouncing martial law in the debate over the Petition of Right, Strode emerged in the parliamentary session of 1629 as a vehement opponent of Crown policy. He demanded that goods seized for non-payment of tonnage and poundage be returned before any consideration for authorizing the levy, and denounced the leniency shown the Catholic priests arrested in Clerkenwell. In the disorderly scene that accompanied the conclusion of Parliament in 1629, Strode played a prominent part, demanding that the Speaker read Eliot's* resolutions and calling on the members to signify their assent by standing up. Summoned before the Privy Council the next day, Strode refused to come, but was soon arrested and imprisoned. Rejecting the jurisdiction of the Star Chamber and declaring that he was responsible only to the Commons for his actions there, he remained in prison until Jan. 1640.

The King released Strode from imprisonment as a conciliatory gesture prior to the Short Parliament. There he argued, with John Hampden,* to have grievances precede supply. In the Long Parliament Strode was an active opponent of the King, working closely with Pym.* Strode's prominence rested largely on his role as a stubborn martyr to parliamentary liberties and on his fiery oratory. As a parliamentary leader he did not rank with Pym and Hampden. Strode served as one of the managers of Strafford's impeachment and bitterly attacked Lord Keeper Finch. He opposed the bishops, and vehemently supported the protestation in defense of Protestantism in May 1641. Strode was a member of the committee to investigate the army plot. He also introduced a bill for annual parliaments, demanded that ministerial appointments should be submitted to Parliament, and was an early advocate of the Grand Remonstrance. In Nov. 1641 he moved that Parliament should undertake to put the kingdom in a posture of defense and should take command of the militia. One of the five members impeached by the King in Jan. 1642, on the King's approach Strode refused to leave St. Stephen's until he was dragged from the chamber by his friend and relative Sir Walter Erle.*

More vehement than ever against the King following the attempt on the five members, Strode opposed any compromise once the Civil War began. He was present at Edgehill and gave the Commons an account of the battle. In 1643 his property in Devon suffered so severely from royalist depredations that he was compensated by Parliament. In Parliament Strode spoke of the King with open contempt and insulted the House of Lords. He was bitterly critical of Essex* and the peace party. In 1643 he was a member of the committee to supervise a military force to be raised and controlled by the City. Strode was an active enemy of Laud. When the Commons sent him to the Lords in 1644 to urge Laud's execution, Strode threatened them with mob violence to hasten their compliance. In Jan. 1645 he was made a member of the Assembly of Divines. Strode died on 9 Sept. 1645 in London.

Strode should not be confused with William Strode (1602-1645), the poet and dramatist, or with William Strode (1589?-1666) of Barrington, Som., who fought for Parliament in the Civil War and was MP for Ilchester from 1646 until Pride's purge.

DNB; Keeler; *Al. Oxon.*; D'Ewes, *Jour.* (C); T. Moore, *The History of Devonshire from the Earliest Period to the Present* (1829); *CD 1625*. Papers: L (Add. MSS); CS.

T.L. Moir

STRONG, William (d. 1654)

Independent minister, was born in Durham and educated at St. Catharine's Hall, Camb., of which he was elected a fellow in 1631. In 1640 Strong became Rector of More Critchell, Dorset, but was driven out by the Royalists in 1643. Coming to London, he soon became one of the prominent Puritan ministers in the City and at Westminster. In 1644 he was chosen as lecturer in the Puritan-inclined parish of St. Dunstan in the West. In 1645 he was appointed to succeed Edward Peale as a member of the Westminster Assembly of Divines. Two years later, upon the resignation of Andrew Perne from the Rectory of St. Dunstan's, Strong became its minister. It appears that Strong left St. Dunstan's in mid-1650, and was chosen later in the year as pastor of an Independent congregation meeting at Westminster Abbey.

During these years in London Strong's religious position showed clear tendencies towards radicalism. His election in 1644 as lecturer was a good indication, for the leading parishioners of St. Dunstan's were Alexander Normington, William Perkins, Francis Allen* and Col. Richard Browne, all of whom were radical and civic leaders during the early years of the Civil War. Strong's radicalism in these years was also revealed in the sermons he frequently preached before Parliament. In 1647, for instance, in sermons before the Lords and the Commons, he called for a 'perfect' reformation in religion and society. He used eschatological interpretations of current events and advocated toleration for the saints. Strong elaborated on these themes in a sermon he preached on 29 Aug. 1649, probably before Commons. His Congregationalism can be seen in his sermon preached on 9 Dec. 1650, when he was chosen pastor of the Independent congregation at the Abbey Church.

Like many of his Independent brethren, Strong turned towards a more conservative position after 1651, probably in fear of the rising influence of Baptist churches and the Fifth Monarchy Men. In 1653, the year of the Barebones Parliament, Strong attacked the radicals and their 'unruly and inordinate thoughts' in his sermons at St. Paul's and the Abbey Church. Later in the year, in a sermon preached before the Lord

Mayor and Aldermen of the City, Strong denounced Separatism.

In 1652 Strong joined his Independent brethren in presenting to the Parliament *The Humble Proposals* for the establishment of a broad Independent state church, and in early 1654, when the Trier system was founded, he was included on the Commission. Strong died in June 1654 and was buried in Westminster Abbey, but his remains were dug up and thrown into a pit after the Restoration. His wife Damaris survived him and prepared his manuscript sermons and tracts for publication. According to Henry Wilkinson, who appears to have been related to his widow, Strong had 'a good skill' in the original languages of Scripture and his treatment of the covenant doctrine 'arrived to an excellency and height . . . beyond the most that ever I read or knew.'

DNB; Nuttall, *VS*; W. Strong, *The Way to the Highest Honour* (1647); *The Trust and the Account of a Steward* (1647); *Babylons Utter Ruine, the Saints Triumph* (1649); *A Voice from Heaven, Calling the People of God to a Perfect Separation from Mystical Babylon* (1654); *XXXI Select Sermons* (1656); *The Humble Proposals of Mr. Owen, Mr. Tho. Goodwin, Mr. Nye, Mr. Simpson, and Other Ministers* (1652); Firth & Rait. Papers: LG (MSS 2968/3; 3016/1).

T. Liu

STUBBE, Henry (1632-1676)

Political theorist and pamphleteer, was born on 28 Feb. 1632 in Partney, near Spilsby, Lincs., whence his family moved to Ireland. In 1641 his mother settled with him in London and sent him to Westminster School, where his exceptional intelligence won the notice of Richard Busby, the headmaster, and the patronage of the younger Sir Henry Vane.* With his aid Stubbe went to Christ Church, Oxf. in 1651, where he earned a reputation at once for impudence and proficiency in Greek.

He graduated B.A. in 1653, served in the parliamentary army in Scotland from 1653 to 1655, returned to his studentship at Christ Church, and graduated M.A. in 1656. In 1657 he became second Keeper of the Bodleian Library through the influence of John Owen,* the Vice-Chancellor, for whom Stubbe had written against Owen's enemy, the Presbyterian John Wallis. Stubbe remained at both Christ Church and the Library until ejected in early 1660.

From 1656 Stubbe became a leading spokesman in the university for the Independents and for Vane's principle of religious toleration. Stubbe also blended Vane's republican ideals with the philosophies of Thomas Hobbes* and James Harrington.* In 1656 Stubbe undertook to translate *Leviathan* into Latin but did not succeed. From Hobbes he accepted the necessity of an arbitrary sovereign, but Harrington's *Oceana* supplied him with a republican model for the way this sovereign should behave. From Hobbes, Harrington and John Selden* he derived his natural religion and his Erastian views. Stubbe made his own contribution to constitutional theory when he argued in *An Essay in Defence of the Good Old Cause* (1659) that provision must be made against the restoration of monarchy and so called for a senate to be elected only by those certified as true patriots. This senate would be responsible for preserving the polity, which in all else would be a Harringtonian republic.

After the Restoration Stubbe conformed outwardly to the established church, accepting the failure of the republican cause and the necessity for some form of monarchy. He became a physician, having studied medicine in the university, and Charles II sent him to Jamaica in that capacity in 1663. Returning two years later, he established a practice in Warwick and Bath. He had become a retainer of Viscount Conway by 1667 and of the Earl of Kent by 1673 at the latest.

Stubbe never gave up his love of polemics or his radicalism, despite the repression after 1660. In *The Miraculous Conformist* (1666) he compared the cures for scrofula (the king's evil) recently performed by Valentine Greatrakes to the miracles of Christ and the Apostles and was accused of crypto-republicanism for slighting the royal touch. In 1670-71 Stubbe published a number of tracts attacking the Royal Society for undermining church, state and the universities. On the surface he appears in this assault as a conservative defender of established institutions against the destructive onslaught of the new science. But as Joseph Glanvill, his chief adversary, was quick to point out, Stubbe's purpose was again subversive: his own view was of a church made subservient to the state and of a state and civil religion that were essentially Hobbesist. This is made clear in Stubbe's masterpiece, written during the period of his attacks on the Royal Society, *An Account of the Rise and Progress of Mahometanism* (not published until 1911, but widely circulated among freethinking Whigs in the late 1670s).

In 1673 Stubbe joined the Country opposition; the last things he wrote attack the popery of the Court. On 12 July 1676, he fell from his horse between Bath and Bristol, and drowned.

Ath. Oxon.; Zagorin, *HPT*; P.M. Holt, *A Seventeenth-Century Defender of Islam* (1972); J.R. Jacob, *Robert Boyle and the English Revolution* (1977). Papers: L (Add. MSS 32,553; 35,838); LPR.

J.R. Jacob

STUBBER, Peter (fl. 1647-1661)

Civil War officer, served in Ireland, from where he was sent in 1647 as emissary from the army in Munster to the English Parliament. Adhering to Parliament in Apr. 1648, he attended meetings of the Council of Officers between Nov. 1648 and Mar. 1649 as an adjutant-general. He was given command of a regiment of foot in Ireland and was Governor of Kinsale in 1649-50. By Apr. 1652 he commanded the parliamentary forces in County Clare. As

Governor of Galway from 1652 to 1656, Stubber transported to Connaught those Irish considered dangerous by the army. In 1648 he was greatly feared among the Irish for his transportation of opponents of the army and women judged as vagrants to the West Indies, and he persecuted Catholics harshly. His regiment was disbanded in Aug. 1655; in 1657 Stubber petitioned Parliament for £2000 for his Irish service previous to 1649. Retired since 1656 on his considerable estates around Galway (he also owned land in Co. Tipperary), he sided with the army in Dec. 1659. On 11 Mar. 1661 Parliament ordered Irish lands acquired by Stubber returned to their original owner. In 1661 the Irish Parliament proposed to except him from the Act of Indemnity because he had commanded the halberdiers who had guarded Charles I at his trial, but on 4 Dec. Stubber was granted a license to remain in London, notwithstanding his status as a disbanded officer, in order that he might 'settle a trade into Ireland.'

CSPI, 1647-60, 1660-62; Firth & Davies; Dunlop; T. Carte, *The Life of James, Duke of Ormond* (1851); *ST*, 5:1126, 1147; J.T. Gilbert, *A Contemporary History of Affairs in Ireland* (1880).

L.S. Popofsky

STUBBS, Francis (d. 1662), plotter. *See* Tong, Thomas.

STUBBS, John (c. 1618-1674)

Quaker, was born in Ulverston, Lancs. He attended school until the age of sixteen or eighteen and was skilled in Latin, Greek and 'Oriental' languages. While in Cromwell's army Stubbs was garrisoned at Carlisle during Fox's* imprisonment there in 1653 and became a Quaker. His wife Elizabeth, by whom Stubbs had four children, was also converted. Dismissed from the army for refusal to take an oath,

Stubbs began an extensive itinerant ministry. With William Caton* in Kent in 1654 he convinced Luke Howard and Samuel Fisher.* The two shared an imprisonment in Maidstone. After a journey to Scotland, Stubbs and Caton traveled to Amsterdam in 1655, possibly the first Quakers to do so. Stubbs visited Turkey with Samuel Fisher between 1657 and 1658. With Henry Fell* he visited various Mediterranean locations between 1660 and 1662, including Rome and Egypt. In 1671 Stubbs left England for the American colonies, spending two and a half years in the West Indies, in New England, where he shared a brief period of imprisonment with Solomon Eccles in Boston in 1672, and in the Middle Colonies. Returning to England in Jan. 1674, he died a few months later. Stubbs shared many of Fox's journeys and imprisonments. He wrote five Quaker tracts including, with Fox and Benjamin Furly,* *A Battledoor*, an attempt to show the historical accuracy of 'plain language' to which his own linguistic knowledge undoubtedly contributed much.

Hull, *RQA*; Braithwaite, *BQu*; Fox, *CJ*; J. Gough, *A History of the People Called Quakers*, 4 vols. (1789-90); *FPT*; *EQW*; Besse.

W.G. Bittle

STUBBS, Thomas (d. 1673)

Quaker, like so many of his co-religionists was a New Model man who left the army to spread the Quaker message. We know nothing of his early life, except that he was from Dalston, Cumb. and was one of the first to be converted in 1653 during the initial wave of Quakerism in that county. Although active in other areas, his main significance lies in his tenacity as a preacher and proselytizer in the midlands in the mid-1650s, where indeed he suffered several terms of imprisonment (sometimes of dubious legality), and where he came to the attention of the rigid Maj.-Gen. William Boteler,* who detained Stubbs and other Quakers after 'great meetings' in the Edge Hill area. He was in Scotland in 1657 and wrote a pamphlet in 1659, a year of renewed radical activity, but disappears from view after 1660, apparently returning to Cumberland where he died in 1673. He was the author of two tracts.

FPT; Braithwaite, *BQu*; H.J. Cadbury, ed., *Letters to William Dewsbury* (1948); Besse. Papers: LF.

B.G. Reay

STUCLEY (or Stukeley, Stuckley), Lewis (c. 1622-1687)

Ejected Independent minister, was the son of John Stucley, a gentleman of Afton, West Worlington, Devon. Stucley matriculated from Wadham Coll., Oxf. on 19 May 1637, was a scholar from 1637 to 1647, and graduated B.A. on 18 Mar. 1641. He was appointed Rector of Newton Ferrers by the Devon County Committee on 11 July 1646, lecturer at Great Torrington the same year, and Vicar of Tiverton, Tidcombe and Clare portions, in 1651. In the previous year he organized a Congregational church in Exeter. Stucley was appointed an assistant to the Devon Commission in 1654 and the next year he joined the Devon Association. On 2 Dec. 1656 he concluded an agreement with the corporation of Exeter to divide the cathedral into two portions for use by the Independents and Presbyterians. Stucley's first book, *Manifest Truth* (1658), dealt with the controversy which erupted over the excommunication of two women in his congregation who defected to the Presbyterians.

In 1660 Stucley was ejected as preacher of Exeter Cathedral, though he did not give his farewell sermon until 14 Aug. 1662 in St. Laurence's, Exeter. Apparently he had also been Curate of St. Sidwell's. Stucley remained in Exeter after his ejection, and in 1665 was one of three Independent ministers holding conventicles in the city. With his former colleague Thomas Mall* he was a signatory of the 1666 petition on the Devon ministers protesting the Oxford Oath. His second book, *A Gospel-glasse Representing the Miscarriages*, appeared in 1667, followed by a second edition in 1670. In 1669 he was reported preaching at Netherexe, Cruwys Morchard and Crediton, Devon. Under the Declaration of Indulgence he was licensed on 2 Apr. 1672 to preach as a Congregationalist at a house in Exeter, the licenses for Crediton and Bideford followed in August and September respectively. After the Declaration was cancelled, he continued to preach at Bideford, but when he went to Exeter to preach he was fined £20 on 8 Nov. 1674. In the period 1672-75 he was a regular correspondent of Lord Wharton.*

By his first wife, Ruth, whom he married after resigning as scholar of Wadham College in Feb. 1647, Stucley had a daughter, Ruth (b. 22 July 1655; d. Aug. 1664), and a son, John (b. 15 Nov. 1656). He married his second wife, Susanna Dennis (d. 1692) on 6 Jan. 1673 at Abbotsham, Devon, and by her had three sons, Dennis (b. 10 Feb. 1674), Thomas and Lewis, and a daughter, Sarah. Apparently Stucley was related to Gen. Monck (cf. L: Add. MS 4460, f. 60).

CSPD, Chas. II, 12:272-73, 555; 13:473; *Calamy Revised*; Turner; Nuttall, *VS*.

R.L. Greaves

STURGEON (or Sturgion), John (fl. 1653-1662)

General Baptist, appears as a member of Edmund Chillenden's* congregation in 1653 and a signatory of a publication questioning the rite of laying on of hands (J. More, *Lost Ordinance*, 1654, p.1; Griffith, *Gods Oracle*, p. 37). While serving in Cromwell's bodyguard he secretly published *A Short Discovery of his Highness's Intentions Concerning Anabaptists in the Army* (1655), in which he accused the Protector of intending to purge the army of Baptists; at least a thousand copies were apparently distributed by Fifth Monarchists. Sturgeon was apprehended in Aug. 1655 and despite denying his involvement in the affair, was discharged from the Life Guard and imprisoned. By May 1656 he had been released and appeared in Reading preaching nightly to large crowds and, according to a report filed with Thurloe* by William Goffe,* had treated an army officer with disrespect. In the same year Sturgeon, along with other Baptists and Levellers, wrote to Charles urging him to return to England. They promised their loyalty on the condition that Charles re-establish the Long Parliament, champion the 'liberties of the people,' never establish an episcopal or presbyterian hierarchy, allow religious toleration, abolish tithes, and grant a general amnesty to all citizens except loyal Cromwellians. Thurloe suspected Sturgeon was involved in the Sindercombe plot to assassinate Cromwell. Sturgeon then slipped to Holland and joined Edward Sexby* who had just published *Killing No Murder*, a pamphet advocating the assassination of the Protector. In May Sturgeon was back in London where he and the Fifth Monarchist Edward Wroughton were apprehended trying to smuggle about 1500 copies of *Killing* into the country. Sturgeon proved uncooperative; according to the arresting officers, he not only lied about his name and refused to talk, but also carried a pistol 'which had four barrels, and was charged ready for execution.' He was examined and imprisoned in the Tower where he remained on suspicion of high treason. Released at the Restoration, Sturgeon became a Messenger of the Exchequer. Following the royal proclamation against religious conventicles on 10 Jan. 1661, Sturgeon wrote *A Plea for Tolleration of Opinions and Persuasions in Matters of Religion* (1661) in which he sought to dissociate Baptists from Venner's* rebellion, reaffirm their loyalty to the Crown and plead for freedom of conscience. Nevertheless, he retained his position in the Exchequer until 1 Oct. 1662, when he resigned because of ill health.

J. Griffith, *Gods Oracle* (1665); Crosby; Capp, *FMM*; Thurloe, *SP*; *Clarke Papers*, 3:145; *CCSP*; *CSPD, Comm.*, 12:582; *Chas. II*, 1:144; 2:513.

S.J. Brachlow

SWALLOW, Robert (fl. 1643-1665)

Army officer, was a native of Norfolk. He commanded the eleventh troop of horse in Cromwell's regiment, called the 'Maiden Troop' because it was raised in 1643 at Norwich with the help of some of the young women of the town. Swallow had difficulty in maintaining it. He was obliged to borrow £184 17s. at one point from a relative, Richard Swallow, and in Jan. 1645 had to send men home 'for want of horses.' When the Ironsides was incorporated into the New Model Army, Swallow joined Col. Whalley's* regiment, and in the autumn of 1645 succeeded Christopher Bethell as major. In 1648 Swallow took part in the preparations to seize Charles I at Newport and bring him to trial. He served continuously throughout the Commonwealth and Protectorate, on 6 July 1659 succeeding Whalley as commander. Swallow joined John Lambert* in suppressing Booth's rising in August, and adhered to him in the disbanding of the Rump in October. Cashiered at Lambert's fall, he remained suspect after the Restoration. On 20 Nov. 1662 he was committed to the Tower, and was again arrested in Norwich in Aug. 1665.

Firth & Davies; Kishlansky; *CSPD, Chas. II*, 2:564, 569; 4:543.

R. Zaller

SWYNFEN (or Swinfen), John (1613-1694)

Parliamentary radical, MP 1645, 1659 (Tamworth), 1660 (Stafford), 1661, 1679, 1681 (Tamworth), 1690 (Beeralston). Swynfen was born at Swinfen, Staffs., the eldest son of Richard Swynfen (d. 1659). The family had originally lived in Leicestershire. Swynfen was elected to Parliament at a by-election on 30 Oct. 1645. He was appointed in 1645 as one of the Staffordshire Commissioners for Compounding, served on the committee responsible for the ejection of ignorant and scandalous ministers, and was an agent of Sir William Brereton.* Swynfen was a leader of the moderate political Independents in 1647-48 who sought a negotiated peace with the King upon secure terms, but with other Presbyterians he was adamant in refusing to consider the return of episcopacy. Secluded at Pride's purge, he was detained for more than a month. He took no part in national politics during the Protectorate, but returned to represent the borough of Tamworth in the Parliament of Richard Cromwell* in 1659. He was denied his seat when the Long Parliament was resumed that May, but Monck restored him to his seat on 21 Feb. 1660, presumably for Stafford. On 30 Mar. 1660 he was elected to the Convention Parliament for Stafford, where he was instrumental in getting Sir Harbottle Grimston elected Speaker. Swynfen sat again for Tamworth in the Cavalier Parliament, where he established himself as an opponent of the Court and a supporter of toleration.

In 1659 Swynfen was asked by Richard Baxter to help develop regulations for parliamentary elections which would have limited office to church members. He was described in 1663 as a 'rigid Presbyterian,' but his activity in the House indicated a more moderate position. By 1668 Swynfen seemed to be in general agreement with the doctrines of the Anglican Church, and although he continued to demur on grounds of ceremony, he urged that the law comprehend those who dissented from the church over ceremony only. Swynfen's strongest stands in the 1660s were aimed at Popery and the bishops who would not enforce the laws against Recusancy. His opposition to the Court was not strong enough for some; in preparing a list of 125 friends and 21 moderate supporters, Lord Wharton* omitted Swynfen. As early as

1664 Swynfen diverged from his fellow Presbyterians in supporting the repeal of the Triennial Act of 1641, arguing that the King should not be coerced into calling a parliament. In 1672, however, Swynfen strongly urged that the Declaration of Indulgence be embodied in statute, fearing the potential abuse of the dispensing power. He joined in opposition to the Court over the long prorogation of Parliament prior to the 1677 session, arguing that whether this constituted a dissolution should be debated before the House turned to any regular business. Swynfen also urged that year that the Lords' concurrence with the Address of the House over the King's foreign policies was more important than any quarrel with the upper House over money matters, and strongly opposed the raising of an army. He stood firm for the rights of the Commons on money questions and, along with John Maynard,* was appointed to manage the conference with the Lords over a tax bill the latter had amended.

Swynfen was elected to the first Exclusion Parliament and to the Oxford Parliament, again for Tamworth. His failure to secure election in 1679 was probably the result of a late candidacy; he did not enter the race until August and was defeated by a single vote. Swynfen served on the committee which drew up the first Exclusion Bill and took an active part in the debates surrounding it. Swynfen was among those who journeyed to Chester, ostensibly for a horse race, in Sept. 1682, but under the pressures of the discoveries of the Rye House plot a year later, the trip was seen as part of the test of support to be given to the Duke of Monmouth who had appeared in Cheshire at the same time. There is, however, no evidence that Swynfen was part of any plot to meet with the Duke, support his resistance to the Crown, or join in any insurrection in the country.

Swynfen was in the service of William Paget, sixth Baron of Boreatton, until the latter's death in 1678. They were also friends and political allies, Swynfen staying at Lord Paget's house near Westminster when Parliament was in session. He remained friends and a political ally with Lord Paget's son, William, the seventh Baron. Swynfen was also closely allied in the House with Hugh Boscawen, John Hampden,* William Prynne* and other notable Presbyterian and Independent members. His last service in the House came in the first Parliament of William and Mary, when he represented Beeralston, Devon. Swynfen died on 12 Apr. 1694, survived by his wife, three sons and one daughter; he was buried at Weeford, Staffs.

DNB; CSPD, Chas. II, 23:362; S. Pepys, Diary (1936), 1:306, 470; Lacey; MacCormack; B. & P.; D.T. Witcombe, Charles II and the Cavalier House of Commons (1966); Underdown, PP. Papers: SS (Salt MS 454 [Swynfen MSS]).

F.D. Barrows

SYDENHAM, William (1615-1661)

Parliamentary radical and army officer, MP 1645 (Weymouth), 1653, 1654, 1656 (Dorset). Sydenham was the eldest son of William Sydenham of Wynford Eagle, Dorset, by Mary, daughter of Sir John Jeffrey of Catherston. He and his three younger brothers fought hard for Parliament in the Civil War; he was a colonel by Apr. 1644, and by June Governor of Weymouth. From the ranks of the lesser Dorset gentry he rose to such prominence that by 1649 he and his friend John Bingham,* with their common father-in-law John Trenchard,* were largely running the county. That year Sydenham was made Governor of the Isle of Wight, at first jointly with Charles Fleetwood,* but by Jan. 1650 on his own. Although elected to Parliament in 1645, his military duties often kept him away from the House, and he was in Dorset when the King was brought to trial. On 6 Feb. 1649 he acted as a teller against the abolition of the House of Lords, but he waited until August before qualifying to retain his seat by registering his dissent from the Commons' vote of 5 Dec.

1648 for pursuing a settlement with the King.

It was undoubtedly his record as a soldier-administrator which commended Sydenham to Cromwell after the dissolution of the Rump. He was appointed to the interim Council of State in Apr. 1653 and summoned to the Nominated Parliament. There he made his mark, serving on many committees of both the House and the Council, to which he was twice re-elected. A moderate, undogmatic Puritan himself, he consistently opposed the religious extremists. He was a teller in the first and last divisions in the assembly's five-month session: in the first, in favor of calling it a parliament, against the millenarian zealots for whom the name stank of 'carnal' government, and in the last in favor of proposals for a broad established church, against the Separatists to whom any publicly maintained parochial ministry was anathema. For the moderates the narrow defeat of these proposals was the last straw, and Sydenham played an active part in their carefully staged resignation of the Parliament's authority to Cromwell on 12 Dec. 1653.

Sydenham was one of the original members of the Protectoral Council of State, and one of the busiest. Milton* praised him in his *Defensio secunda*. Sydenham was soon made a Commissioner for the Treasury, which together with his governorship and his Councillor's salary made him a rich man. Yet he kept his independence of view. In the Parliament of 1656 he spoke many times against the arbitrary and cruel treatment of James Nayler,* though he deplored Quaker activities generally. 'That which sticks with me most,' he said, 'is the nearness of this opinion to that which is a most glorious truth, that the spirit is personally in us.' Later in this Parliament he was a teller against giving a reading to the proposal to make Cromwell king, and he opposed it vehemently thereafter. That did not deter Cromwell from elevating him to the Upper House in 1657.

Sydenham remained a Councillor under Richard Cromwell,* but served him less well. Allying with Fleetwood, Desborough* and the other military grandees, he participated prominently in their disastrous overtures to the republican opposition in Mar.-Apr. 1659. When Richard in consequence was overthrown and the Rump restored, Sydenham was placed on the new Council of State and given a regiment of foot. He sided with the army when it again interrupted the Rump in October, and served on its ill-fated Committee of Safety. For this he was expelled from the Rump on 17 Jan. 1660. After the Restoration the Act of Indemnity permanently incapacitated him from office, but by then he had less than a year to live.

DNB; Burton; Ludlow; Bayley; B. & P.; Woolrych; Firth & Davies. Papers: L (Add. MSS; Stowe MSS).

A. Woolrych

SYMONDS (or Symons), Richard (1609-1660?)

Independent minister, was the son of Thomas Symonds of Abergavenny, Mon. He matriculated at Exeter Coll., Oxf., on 18 Feb. 1627 and graduated B.A. on 5 Feb. 1629. By 1635 he was a schoolmaster at Shrewsbury. Like Walter Cradock* and Henry Walter,* he periodically journeyed to Bristol to preach in the mid and late 1630s. Before 1638 he became a schoolmaster at Brampton Bryan, Herefs., where he expounded upon the Puritan sermons of the local rector, Stanley Gower, in the home of Sir Robert Harley, and engaged in private fasts at which Gower preached and prayed *ex tempore*. In Feb. 1638 he was described as a 'suspended priest' who had been driven out of North Wales. Symonds and three other Monmouthshire ministers sent a certificate to Cromwell, Haselrig,* Pym* and D'Ewes on 23 Mar. 1642 complaining about Catholic strength in the county. When the Civil War commenced Symonds went to London where he preached in various City churches as well as in Sandwich, Kent. In Aug. 1645 the

House of Commons determined that £300 p.a. be set aside from the lands of the bishops, deans and chapters of Llandaff and St. David's to enable Symonds, Cradock and Walter to preach itinerantly in South Wales. On 6 Aug. of the following year, the Lords consulted the Westminster Assembly about their qualifications, but Cradock and Walter left without the Assembly's approval in accord with a Commons' request of 28 Oct. The Lords' approval came on 17 Nov. Symonds had preached before Commons on 30 Sept. 1646, a day of public humiliation, and he returned to do this again on 26 Apr. 1648. He also preached before Sir Thomas Fairfax* at Bath. Under the provisions of the Act for the Propagation of the Gospel in Wales (1650) he was appointed an Approver. In the early 1650s he preached mostly in Glamorgan, and about 1655 he was at St. Fagan's, near Cardiff. On 15 Sept. 1657 the Trustees for the Maintenance of Ministers were told by the Council of State to settle an augmentation of £50 on Symonds to lecture at Llandaff Cathedral. He was an advocate of religious toleration and was accused of Antinomianism by Thomas Edwards.

Symonds appears to be commonly confused with Richard Symmonds (d. 1669 or 1670), a Puritan who was appointed lecturer at Andover, Hants. on 14 Feb. 1642. The vicar's objections were so intense that on 24 Aug. the House of Commons had to order that Symmonds be allowed to preach there without hinderance. By 1654 he had become Curate of Southwick, Hants., and in that year he was made an assistant to the Hampshire Commission. Symmonds was ejected in 1662, but continued to live in Southwick until his death.

CJ, 2:735; 4:678; 5:545; *CSPD, Chas. I*, 12:249; *DNB*; *LJ*, 8:463, 569. For the Symmonds of Hampshire see *Calamy Revised*, p. 443.

R.L. Greaves

T

TALBOT, Thomas (fl. 1643-1659)

Army officer, was from Yorkshire, and served under Thomas Fairfax* in the first Civil War. In 1643 Capt. Talbot, along with other officers, petitioned for increased supplies for the army; in 1645 he signed a petition pledging loyalty to Fairfax. In 1655 the Protector promoted Talbot to colonel, succeeding Matthew Alured,* in a regiment of foot which was quartered in the south of Scotland until 1658. Talbot brought his wife with him to the headquarters at Dalkeith. He was a regulator for the Scottish assessment in 1653 and a JP for Dumbartonshire in 1656. When commissioners remodeled the army in the summer of 1659, Monck's request that his own regiment and Talbot's be left unchanged because of the confidence he reposed in their officers was denied by Parliament. However, when Monck declared for restoring Parliament, Talbot sided with Lambert.* On 25 Oct. 1659 Lambert and Fleetwood* sent Talbot as a mediator to Monck to propose negotiations. Talbot won Monck's respect in this mission, the latter promising to preserve Talbot's regiment for him if he would remain neutral in the sturggle between the army and Parliament. Talbot, then in England, continued to adhere to Lambert, and signed a protest of army officers sent to Monck on 15 Nov., although his regiment in Scotland firmly supported Monck.

Firth & Davies; *Clarke Papers*; Ludlow; *Fairfax Corr.*; F. Maseres, ed., *Select Tracts Relating to the Civil Wars in England* (1815); Davies, *RC*.

L.S. Popofsky

TANKERVILLE, Earl of. *See* Grey, Ford.

TANY (or Tani, Tannye), Thomas (*alias* Theaurau John) (fl. 1649-1655), millenarian and pantheist, was a goldsmith on the Strand in London. Tany's family lived in the parish of St. Mary Aldermary, which had a history of religious radicalism. His parents, he asserted, were poor. Tany was living at the Three Golden Keys without Temple Bar when, on 23 Nov. 1649, he claimed to have received a divine command to change his name to Theaurau John, as a Jew of the tribe of Reuben. Tany thereupon taught himself Hebrew. His first publication was a broadsheet which appeared on 25 Apr. 1650, *I Proclaime from the Lord of Hosts the Returne of the Jewes*. In it he announced the repatriation of the Jews to Palestine, the rebuilding of the temple, and his own role as the Lord's high priest. According to Lodowick Muggleton* he was serious enough about this to circumcise himself. The broadsheet was sold by Giles Calvert,* with whom Tany had a continuing relationship. On 20 Dec. 1650 Tany proclaimed he was the Earl of Essex, descended from Henry VII, and the heir to the throne of Charles I.

Early in 1651 Tany published *The Nations Right in Magna Charta Discussed with the Thing Called Parliament*, and there announced: 'Know that I am a madman.' Tany began to develop pantheistic ideas, probably after reading Jacob Boehme. In *Theauraujohn His Theous-Ori Apokolipikal* (1651), which was sold by Calvert, Tany asserted that God was in everything and man's salvation was assured. The same year he was indicted with Capt. John Norwood for blasphemy and briefly imprisoned in Newgate. In Mar. 1652 Tany published *Theauraujohn High Priest to the Jewes, His Disputive Challenge*, in which he condemned all religion as a deceit and a lie, and asserted that the only truth was love. Adopting the myth of the Norman yoke, he averred that in the aftermath of the Civil War the English could throw off their subjection and claim their rightful inheritances. He also called on Cromwell 'to stand with us for the liberty of the Gospel and the laws of the land.' The same year Tany published *Theauraujohn Tani His Second Part of His Theous-Ori*, a second edition of which was published in 1653.

On 4 Feb. 1652 Muggleton, John Reeve* and Thomas Turner unsuccessfully endeavored to persuade Tany to relinquish his illusions, and a month later sentenced him to eternal damnation. Undaunted, Tany went in April to Eltham, Kent, to make tents for an expedition to the Holy Land. Later that spring he issued two more broadsheets, *Hear O Earth* and *Thau Ram Tanjah His Speech*; he now claimed the crowns of France, Rome, Naples and Jerusalem. At the end of the year, in a bonfire at St. George's Fields, Lambeth, he burned his tent, sword, pistols and Bible 'because the people say it is the Word of God, and it is not;' 'the Bible is letters, not life.' An irate crowd was ready to stone him. On 30 Dec., when his attempt to deliver a petition to Parliament was frustrated, he drew his rusty sword and attacked the doorkeeper and others, allegedly moved by a vision to slay the MPs. Mistakenly regarded as a Quaker, he was imprisoned in the Gatehouse after an appearance before the bar of the Commons, though he was bailed with John Biddle* on 10 Feb. and discharged on 28 May 1655. His last work, *Theauraujohn His Aurora*, appeared the same year and was sold by Calvert. His mission then led him to the Jews in the Netherlands, but either on his way or after his arrival he drowned.

Tany was variously regarded as 'a blasphemous Jew,' a Quaker and a Ranter. He shared many of the ideas of radical sectaries, including the denial of the Bible as the word of God, hell and heaven as places, eternal punishment, and the devil. His pantheism was in the tradition of Boehme and John Pordage* (with whom he stayed), his eccentricity akin to that of John Robins* and Muggleton, and his interest in the Jews shared with many, including his friend Robert Norwood, whose *Proposals for the Propagation of the Gospel, Offered to Parliament* (1652) advocated the readmission of the Jews to England.

Tany was clearly unbalanced, yet there was often method in his madness. Like others who claimed special vision or personal divinity, he took the millennial ideas of his time to their logical conclusion, and acted out their implicit contradictions. In declaring himself the messiah and claiming the royal succession, he attacked the secular oligarchs who controlled the Rump from both a Fifth Monarchist and divine right perspective, thus constituting himself as a metaphor for the entire spectrum of dissent to the new regime. His subsequent pantheism was a logical extension of this. If God were present in all men, by what right did any presume to govern their fellows? Those who did were necessarily usurpers, and therefore to be dealt with as the former usurper, Charles I, had been. From this point of view Tany's quixotic assault against the members of Parliament in 1654 can be seen as inspired guerilla theatre, a symbolic act of assassination in which a single avenger slew many tyrants as the regicide had been a collective repudiation of one. Perhaps more than any other manifestation of the period, it embodied the contradictions of a world turned upside down in which authority, cast down from its pedestal, was present in all men but prescriptive in none. Others burned bibles and claimed divinity (like William Franklin*) or royal descent (like Cornelius Evans, who claimed in 1648 to be the Prince of Wales), but in its combination of madness and insight no career cast a more oddly penetrating light on the crisis of the Interregnum than Tany's.

DNB; Hill, *WTUD* and *P. & R.*; *Ath. Oxon.*, 3:599; *A Perfect Account*, 209 (3-10 Jan. 1655), p. 1666; C. Fowler, *Daemonium meridianum* (1654); Burton, 1:cxxv-cxxvii; Whitelocke, *Memorials*;

D.S. Katz, *Philo-Semitism and the Readmission of the Jews to England 1603-1655* (1982); Abbott, 1:191.

R.L. Greaves and R. Zaller

TATE, Zouch (1606-1650)

Parliamentary radical, MP SP, LP 1640 (Northampton), sec. 1648. Tate was born in Mar. 1606, the eldest son of Sir William Tate (d. 1617) of Delapré, Northants., and his wife Elizabeth (or Eleanor), daughter of Edward Lord Zouch of Harringworth, Northants. Tate's father was JP, DL and MP. Tate married Catherine (d. 1700), daughter of Sir Giles Allington of Horseheath, Cambs. and grand-daughter of Thomas Cecil, Earl of Exeter. He was educated at Trinity Coll., Oxf. and the Middle Temple, and traveled in France in the early 1620s. During the 1640s Tate was JP in Northamptonshire. He was active in the Long Parliament, particularly on committees concerning the management of the parliamentary army. Tate was chairman of a committee on army reform and a committee to select officers for the New Model Army. He supported the establishment of the Committee of Both Kingdoms in 1644, and chaired a committee named in that year to purge unreliable officers in Essex's* army. Tate recommended the appointment of Manchester as lieutenant-general and Lord Robartes* as field marshal in Mar. 1644. His committee on army reform heard testimony between 25 Nov. 1644 and 6 Jan. 1645 from almost every ranking officer. Tate found the army so corrupt that it needed a complete overhaul, Tate's perspicacity has been slighted in accounts of evidence' of the indwelling Christ. Chris-Cromwell. Previous opinion notwithstanding, Tate's proposal for the Self-Denying Ordinance was not influenced by Cromwell. Tate had indicated a strong opposition to Independency in the army and elsewhere; he was unlikely to have cooperated in a plan to oust Manchester while retaining Cromwell. Indeed, Cromwell offered to drop his charges against Manchester on 9 Dec. 1644 because of Manchester's effective testimony before Tate's committee. Tate's reasons for proposing the Self-Denying Ordinance were thus different from Cromwell's – Tate believed a truce was necessary to prevent a further split in the parliamentary ranks.

Tate was assessed by Baillie as one of the firmest Presbyterians in the Commons. In Oct. 1644, when Henry Vane, Jr.* and Oliver St. John* proposed toleration for Independents, Tate violently opposed the measure. He supported wide powers of excommunication for ministers and also regularly advised Scottish Presbyterians on plans to have Presbyterianism adopted in England. Tate's religious views and his opposition to the army Remonstrance led to his seclusion in Dec. 1648, but he remained a JP until his death in Dec. 1650. Tate's inheritance included two manors in Northamptonshire and one in Warwickshire in addition to his being co-heir to three manors in Hampshire. His estate at Delapré was valued at £1500 p.a. in 1660. Tate was buried at Hardingstone, Northants.

L. Kaplan, *Politics and Religion during the English Revolution* (1976); A.N.B. Cotton, 'Cromwell and the Self-Denying Ordinance,' *History*, 42:211-31; MacCormack; Keeler; Kishlansky. Papers: L (Harl. MSS; Cotton MSS; Lans. MSS).

D.W. Hollis, III

TAYLOR, Christopher (c. 1620-1686) and Thomas (c. 1617-1682)

Quakers, were born at Carlton near Skipton, Yorks., and educated at Oxford. The brothers became priests and returned to the northwest. By 1650, having rejected tithes and parochial livings, Thomas was minister to a Separatist congregation at Preston Patrick chapel, W'land, where the Seeker community paid him a stipend of £50. He had rejected the legitimacy of infant baptism in a public debate at Kendal, but resumed the practice in 1651, apparently due to the influence of Baxter's

Association movement. This led to some coolness between him and his Preston congregation. Thomas accepted a call from a similar community 45 miles away in Swaledale and became lecturer at Richmond, Yorks. in the spring of 1652. Meanwhile George Fox,* having crossed Pendle Hill, won many followers among Thomas' former congregation, including Francis Howgill* and John Audland,* two of the lay preachers. In September Thomas was invited to Judge Fell's* Swarthmore Hall in Lancashire where Fox challenged him to testify whether his calling was indeed from Christ. Initially Fox's challenge silenced him, but Fox accompanied him to Newton and a day later Thomas testified that 'truly . . . I find through the great grace of my God a principle springing up in my soul that doth really give evidence' of the indwelling Christ. Christtopher was convinced shortly after, the two being among the very small number of university trained ministers to become Quakers. Both became itinerant preachers of the movement and, during their frequent imprisonments, prolific publishers of tracts. Both were imprisoned at Appleby in 1654, where Thomas had interrupted a church service, and Thomas was subsequently imprisoned at York, Leicester and Coventry, Margaret Fell* supporting his wife and six children during his frequent incarcerations. He accompanied Fox to Leominster in 1657, where the two debated John Tombes,* the resident Baptist minister. In 1658 Thomas preached at St. Mary's, Oxford, where he was arrested but generously released by Dr. John Owen,* the Vice-Chancellor, on learning that Taylor was a graduate.

The Restoration brought a divergence in the brothers' careers. In 1661 Thomas was imprisoned at Stafford where he remained until 1672, when he was released along with most Friends on a general pardon obtained after the Declaration of Indulgence was issued. While in prison he taught school, preached from a window in the jail, and published; his wife had taken a house in Stafford, and on his release they lived there until his death in 1682. Like most Puritans,

the early Friends opposed games and sports as implying a 'levity' unbecoming in a 'professor of truth.' To this traditional objection, Thomas added an objection to blood sports which he viewed as contrary 'to the tender nature of Christ and all Christians, truly so-called.' At the Restoration, if not before, Christopher became a schoolmaster, keeping a Friends' Latin school at Hertford in the 1660s and becoming the first master of the Friends' coeducational school at Waltham Abbey where he was arrested in 1670 for teaching without a license. In 1676 he translated into Latin as *Institutiones pietatis* a primer and catechism written by Fox and Ellis Hookes, to which he added a Latin grammar, and in the following year with the help of John Matern, a Silesian Quaker, he published the *Compendium trium linguarum*, a text of instruction in Greek, Latin and Hebrew, which used only biblical passages rather than classical texts. In 1679 the school was moved to Edmonton where the sons of Isaac Penington* were among Christopher's students. In 1682 he turned the school over to George Keith* and followed Penn* to Pennsylvania, where he became Registrar-General of the colony and a member of the Council of State until his death in 1686.

Braithwaite, *BQu*; Fox, *CJ*; Cadbury; *FPT*; *DNB*. Papers: LF.

P.S. Seaver

TAYLOR, Daniel (c. 1614-1655)

Independent and London radical, was a central figure in the Arminian congregation of John Goodwin.* Taylor had ties to many London Independent politicians and was an active supporter of the army during the Commonwealth. A Londoner and freeman of the Haberdashers' Company, Taylor also invested heavily in land. At the time of his death in 1655, he owned tenements in London and estates in Leicester, Middlesex, Essex and Cheshire.

Taylor was a resident of Goodwin's parish of St. Stephen's, Coleman Street, and a member of Goodwin's gathered church from at least 1644. In 1645 he published a letter defending Goodwin from the aspersions of John Vicars.* When Parliament ejected Goodwin from his parish living, Taylor apparently withdrew from the parish church with him. In 1647 he signed the congregation's defense of Goodwin, *An Apologeticall Account of Some Brethren*. In 1652 he signed the congregation's declaration of Arminianism, *The Agreement and Distance of Brethren*. His will, written in 1655, reveals close personal and business ties to almost every leading member of Goodwin's gathered church, notably John Price* and Alderman Mark Hildesley.

Taylor's political career seems to have begun only in the months following the second Civil War. He may have joined other Goodwin followers in an intermittent alliance with the Levellers between 1645 and 1648, but no direct evidence for his participation survives. He counted Col. Robert Tichborne* and Capt. Thomas Juxon, his brother-in-law, among his close friends. Possibly for that reason as well as from ideological conviction he became active on behalf of the army Independents in the fall of 1648. At the request of Cromwell, who hoped to placate the Levellers, Taylor, Price and Tichborne organized a meeting of representatives of the army, the Levellers, and the London Independents to discuss Leveller proposals for constitutional reform. Taylor participated in the subsequent meetings, held at Windsor, where the *Second Agreement of the People* was drafted. In 1649 Taylor was made a member of the High Court of Justice that tried the five royalist peers. That same year he and Hildesley were named Customs Commissioners by the Commonwealth government, and Taylor was also elected to the London Common Council. He became a trustee for the sale of dean and chapter lands in 1650. On 22 Sept. 1651 he was elected alderman and discharged for a £400 fine the same day.

In Nov. 1651 Taylor published his only pamphlet of political significance, *Certain Queries or Considerations*. The views he expressed reflect the goals of the Goodwin circle then sitting on the Common Council. He timed the tract to coincide with the debate over dissolution of the Rump. In its place Taylor advocated a parliament composed of representatives of the godly churches of England. He also suggested various social, economic and legal reforms to revitalize the economy of London, improve justice and, in general, foster godliness. He wanted an end to the wool monopoly, extension of Customs officers' hours, regulation of lawyers' and doctors' fees, simplification of copyhold laws, and swifter punishment of criminals. One of his highest priorities was the abolition of tithes. Maintenance of the ministry and propagation of the Gospel, he felt, should be matters of national policy attended to promptly by Parliament. Taylor died in 1655. He was survived by his second wife, Margaret Locke, sons William, Edmond and Samuel, and daughters Katherine, Rebecca and Margaret.

E.S. More, 'The New Arminians: John Goodwin and His Coleman Street Congregation' (Ph.D. diss., Univ. of Rochester, 1980); Beaven; Tolmie; *Lev. Tr.*

E.S. More

TAYLOR, George (d. 1696)

Quaker, was an ironmonger of Kendal, W'land. Shortly after the Kendal Fund was established in June 1654 to assist Quaker preachers, Margaret Fell* designated Taylor and Thomas Willan of Underbarrow its co-treasurers. Money collected was dispensed to itinerant Quakers in England, but beginning in 1655 modest amounts (initially about £45 a year) were channeled to support Friends witnessing in Scotland, Ireland, Venice, the Netherlands and Germany. Financial details were provided in a series of letters from Taylor and Willan to Margaret Fell (1654-59). Taylor was troubled by the practice of some Friends marrying privately and called for weddings to be performed in the presence of local meetings. In 1658 Taylor was in prison at

Ilchester and had not paid his fine, but on 27 Nov. a committee of the Council of State recommended that he be pardoned. When the restored Rump asked Quakers in May 1659 for lists of persecuting JPs, moderates and Friends qualified to serve as JPs, Taylor was instrumental in compiling the information for the northwestern counties. He may be the George Taylor whose commital was noticed by the Council of State on 27 July 1659, and was probably the George Taylor imprisoned with James Parke* and others in 1667 for attending a Quaker meeting at Harwich, for which he was fined £1. In 1684 Taylor and Thomas Wilson suffered distress of goods worth 19s. for attending a Friends' meeting at Kendal. He is not to be confused with the George Taylor who was a Quaker at Chesterton, Cambs., or the Quaker of the same name who was sentenced to banishment at the Old Bailey on 16 Jan. 1665 and died of the plague at Newgate before the sentence of banishment was executed.

CSPD, Comm., 12:199, 360; 13:44; Braithwaite, *BQu*; *EQL*; Besse. Papers: LF; LPR.

R.L. Greaves

TAYLOR, Thomas (1576-1633)

Puritan minister, was born in 1576 at Richmond, Yorks., where his father was the town recorder and a friend to Puritans. Taylor excelled at Christ's Coll., Camb. where he graduated (B.A. 1595, M.A. 1598), was fellow (from 1599-1604) and Wentworth Hebrew Lecturer (1601-4), and proceeded D.D. (1628); he was incorporated D.D. at Oxford in 1630. At Cambridge Taylor became one of the many disciples of William Perkins. He began preaching at age 21 and became a famous preacher and a prolific writer. Taylor along with others (Perkins, Bownde, Preston,* Sibbes,* William Gouge, Richard Baxter) can be seen as representative of the mainstream of pre-Civil War Puritan thought.

When only about 25 Taylor delivered a sermon at Paul's Cross before Queen Elizabeth. In 1608 he delivered a sermon at Great St. Mary's in which he attacked Bancroft's repressive policies. For this Archbishop Harsnet silenced him and threatened him with degradation. By 1612 Taylor was living in Watford, perhaps as vicar, and later moved to Reading where his brother, Theophilus Taylor, served as pastor from 1618 to 1640. Here Taylor maintained 'a little nursery of young preachers, who under his faithful ministry flourished in knowledge and piety.' On 22 Jan. 1625 he was elected curate and lecturer at St. Mary Aldermanbury, London, where he preached vigorously. While at St. Mary's Taylor signed a circular letter soliciting voluntary support for the 'godly preachers' and other Protestants in the Palatinate, which earned him a reprimand from Laud and the High Commission. He preached at St. Mary's until about 1630 when ill health forced him to retire to Isleworth, where he died in Jan. or Feb. 1633, leaving a widow. He was buried at St. Mary Aldermanbury, with his disciple William Jemmat preaching the funeral sermon.

Wherever Taylor ministered people described him as 'a precious seeds-man,' 'a guide to others,' 'a walking Bible,' and 'a kind of poet in the pulpit.' Collected, though not complete *Works* were issued in several editions. A characteristic discourse is *The Pilgrims Profession*, a funeral sermon which likened the carriage of the saint through this life to the journey of a traveler going home through a strange country.

Haller, *RP*; Hill, *S. & P.*; Seaver; M. Walzer, *The Revolution of the Saints* (1965); *DNB*.

R.G. Kyle

TEMPLE, James (b. 1606)

Regicide, was the son of Sir Alexander Temple (d. 1629) of the Longhouse, Chadwell, Essex, and of Etchingham, Sussex, by his first wife Mary, daughter of John

Somers and widow of Thomas Peniston of Leigh, Sussex. Temple entered Lincoln's Inn with his brother John (1603-1627) in Nov. 1622 and may have accompanied him on the expedition to Rhe, where the latter was killed in hand to hand combat with the French Commander General. Temple succeeded to the family estate on his father's death and was later of Clapham. With Edward Whalley,* a friend and relation by marriage, he speculated in land in the early 1630s, and Whalley leased Temple's home at Chadwell. Temple joined the parliamentary army as a captain of horse under the Earl of Bedford* in 1642. The following year he was appointed captain of the fort at West Tilbury, of which his father had formerly been governor, and was named both to the Committee of the Ordinance of Association and the Committee for Sequestrations in Sussex. As Governor of Bramber Castle he repulsed a strong royalist assault on 12 Dec. 1643; Francis Cheynell reported that his courage in this action was 'the wonder of all the country,' and a plaque commemorates it to this day. In Feb. 1645 Temple was appointed a commissioner to raise supplies for the Scottish army in Sussex, and in 1646 a JP for the Rape of Bramber. Returned to Parliament in Sept. 1645 as a recruiter MP for Bramber, he was sent to Munster in 1647 as a joint commissioner with his friend and close colleague Thomas Challoner.* By 1648 he was living at Chadwell again, but his main residence appears to have been a sequestered estate at Michelgrove, Sussex. Temple also served as a Militia Commissioner for Sussex and continued to garrison the fort at Tilbury, of which he was named governor in May 1649. Named to the High Court, he attended nine sessions, and signed the King's death warrant.

Temple was an active member of the Rump, serving on the committees for Ireland and the navy. He presented a series of proposals 'for prevention of the export of gold or other coin, and the business of melting down coin' to Parliament in Apr. 1649, but seems to have encountered financial difficulties himself, and was apparently imprisoned briefly for debt in 1653. On 14 July of that year he was ordered to Ireland by the Council of State. He took his place in the restored Rump in 1659 and was given lodgings in Whitehall. Excepted from the Act of Oblivion in 1660, he attempted to flee to Ireland but was seized in Coventry and committed to the Tower. At his trial on 16 Oct. he argued that he had been duped into joining the High Court and had signed the warrant under duress. There is no evidence that this was so, but Temple was able to produce affidavits attesting his loyalty to the royalist cause and escaped execution. Confined in the Tower, he was last mentioned as a prisoner on Jersey in 1668.

Temple first married Mary (née Busbridge) of Haremore Hall, Etchingham, Sussex, by whom he had five sons and a daughter, Mary, who married Admiral Cornelius van Tromp. Temple himself later married into this family, taking as his second wife Johanna, daughter of Admiral Martin van Tromp. His eldest son John entered Lincoln's Inn on 4 May 1646, and his second son Alexander was a captain of dragoons raised in Sussex in 1651. Aside from Whalley, Temple's relations on the High Court included Peter Temple,* a distant cousin, and Simon Mayne.* He was the nephew of Lord Say and Sele* and first cousin of both Nathaniel Fiennes* and Sir Peter Temple, Bt., who was nominated to the High Court but refused to sit.

DNB; Ludlow; *ST*; Underdown, *PP*; Fletcher; *HMC, 7th Report*; *CCC*; *CSPD, Chas. I*, vol. 22, *passim.*; *Comm.*, vols. 1, 2, *passim.*; *CSPI*.

R. Zaller and R.K.G. Temple

TEMPLE, Sir John (1600-1677)

Master of the Rolls in Ireland, was born in Ireland in 1600, the eldest son of Sir William Temple (d. 1627), Provost of Trinity Coll., Dublin, and Martha, daughter of Robert Harrison of Derbyshire. Educated at Trinity (B.A. 1617; fellow 1618; M.A. 1620) and Lincoln's Inn (admitted 22 June 1620), Temple entered the personal service of Charles I and was knighted on 16 July 1633. Appointed Master of the Rolls in Ireland and a Privy Councillor in 1641, he took a leading part in provisioning Dublin following the outbreak of rebellion and was elected MP for Meath on 23 July 1642. He was imprisoned in Dublin Castle for opposing the 1643 cessation until exchanged for a parliamentary prisoner. Returning to England, his patrons the Sidneys* helped secure his election as recruiter MP for Chichester in 1645 and in 1646 he published his *Irish Rebellion*, a propagandist work written to stir up support for Lord Lisle's mission. A Commissioner for Munster in 1647 and a Commissioner of the Great Seal of Ireland in 1648, Temple was secluded at Pride's purge and took no further part in public affairs until appointed a commissioner of forfeited estates in Ireland on 21 Nov. 1653. He was returned MP for Sligo, Roscommon and Leitrim on 28 July 1654; resumed the Mastership of the Rolls in June 1655; served on commissions concerned with forfeited lands (1655-56); and was rewarded with two substantial leases in Counties Carlow and Dublin in 1658. Appointed to the Council of State in 1660 and elected MP for Tregony, Corn., on 20 Apr. 1660 he was confirmed as Master of the Rolls; returned MP for county Carlow on 4 May 1661; and acted as Vice-Treasurer of Ireland (1673-74). He died on 14 Nov. 1677. Temple married Mary (d. 1638), daughter of John Hammond of Chertsey, Surrey, royal physician, by whom he had four sons and three daughters.

Underdown, *PP*; F.E. Ball, *The Judges in Ireland, 1221-1921* (1927); *DNB*; A. Webb, *A Compendium of Irish Biography* (1878).

K.J. Lindley

TEMPLE, Peter (1600-1663)

Parliamentary radical and Regicide, MP

LP 1645 (Leicester). Temple was the third son of Edmund Temple (d. 1616) of Sibbesdon, Leics., and Elizabeth, daughter of Robert Burgoine of Wroxhall, Warks. He was apprenticed to a linen-draper in London, but succeeded to the family estates following the deaths of his brothers, Paul and Jonathan. In Dec. 1642 he was appointed a member of the committee for the defense of the midland counties (though the Association was stillborn) and the following month of the committee to oversee the Leicestershire militia. He was commissioned in 1642 as a captain of the horse. The House of Commons appointed him High Sheriff of Leicestershire on 30 Dec. 1643, and in that capacity he repressed the local Baptists. In Feb. 1645 he was named to the committee responsible for raising supplies for the Scottish army in Leicestershire. He was not present at the siege of Leicester by the Royalists that spring, but did become military Governor of Cole Orton, Leics. On 17 Nov. 1645 he was elected to represent the borough of Leicester in the Commons. One of the most active judges of Charles (20 sessions), he was present when the death sentence was passed and he signed the warrant. On 13 June 1649 he was named to the Committee for Compounding. A Rumper, he petitioned Parliament on 21 July 1649 with respect to the losses he sustained in the war and was awarded £1500 from sequestrations in his county. The Council of State ordered him on 12 Dec. 1650 to return to Leicestershire to preserve the peace as a Militia Commissioner. He was not chosen for the 1653 Parliament. In 1659 and 1660 Temple was in London, where the Council provided him with lodgings. Excluded from the Act of General Pardon and Oblivion (June 1660), he surrendered to the Speaker of the House on 12 June and was imprisoned in the Tower. He pleaded not guilty at the Old Bailey on 10 Oct., but subsequently admitted his role in condemning Charles. Sentenced to hang, he successfully pleaded the benefit of Charles' proclamation, but remained in the Tower until he died of dropsy on 20 Dec. 1663.

CJ, 3:354, 576, 638; 6:267; 8:61, 63, 139; CSPD, Comm., 2:468; 13:30, 96, 325; Chas. II, 2:247; 3:383, 450; DNB; Abbott, 1:728. Papers: L (Stowe MSS 190; Add. MSS).

R.L. Greaves

TEW (or Tue), Nicholas (fl. 1629-1647)

Leveller bookseller, was the son of the London gentleman William Tew. On 6 Sept. 1629 he was apprenticed to Henry Bird, a London stationer. Tew took up his freedom on 1 Oct. 1638. Before Mar. 1643 he provoked the ire of Edward ('Codpeece-Ned') Dobson, a London bookseller of Catholic and royalist sympathies, who physically beat him before fleeing to Oxford. According to Dobson, Tew was at that time a girdler at the Exchange, and was teaching daily in a chamber at Whitechapel. Tew was a member of the General Baptist church of Thomas Lamb.* By 1644 Tew and Richard Overton* had set up a secret press in Coleman Street. When Tew was arrested in Jan. 1645 for printing a libelous work against Essex* and Manchester, he admitted he had a printing press in his home which was used by various Independents. He was imprisoned in the Fleet. In 1647 Tew was a supporter of the March Petition which recognized the Commons as the supreme authority in the state and urged the abolition of tithes without compensation. When the Levellers brought a certificate to the Commons' committee attesting the genuineness of the petition, only to be rebuffed, Tew read the certificate to a group assembled in the Court of Requests. On 19 Mar. the Commons ordered that he be committed to the custody of the Serjeant-at-Arms during the House's pleasure. Subsequent petitions protested his imprisonment in Newgate, and his suffering was further recalled in *Walwyns Just Defence* and in *The Hunting of the Foxes* (1649) by Robert Ward and others. The Levellers regarded him as one of their martyrs.

CJ, 5:118; Lev. Man., pp. 133, 170, 369; Plomer, DBP; Brailsford; Tolmie; E. Dobson, XIV Articles of Treason and Other Misdemeanors (1643); H.R. Plomer, 'Secret Printing During the Civil War,' The Library, N.S., 5:375-81.

R.L. Greaves

THIMBLETON (or Thymbleton), Walter (fl. 1653-1686)

Fifth Monarchist, was unknown until he emerged as a member of Morgan Llwyd's* North Wales congregation at Wrexham in 1653. In that year he was one of the signers of the Denbighshire letter to Oliver Cromwell, approving Cromwell's dissolving of the Rump and his calling for a Parliament of Saints. Two years later, Thimbleton appeared as a signatory of A Word For God (1655), the remonstrance drafted by Vavasor Powell* accusing the government of deserting the Good Old Cause of religion and parliament. Thimbleton's last known activity during the Interregnum was as captain of a company of foot sent by the Council of State to Scotland in Sept. 1659.

After the Restoration Thimbleton appears to have been active in Fifth Monarchist meetings in the London area, in consequence of which a warrant to seize him and his papers was issued in Nov. 1662. Three years later (Jan. 1666) Capt. Thimbleton was again reported active, this time in Essex, as one of the 'restless fanatic party' ready to support any insurrection that might arise in London. No more of Thimbleton is heard until the 1680s, although in 1677 he may have been living in London as a merchant. In 1682 he was reported in the frequent company of Henry Danvers* and Titus Oates, and suspected of plotting insurrection. In 1685, following the accession of James II, both Thimbleton and his wife were sought by the government, presumably for their suspected involvement in the early planning of Monmouth's rebellion. Thimbleton was convicted in 1686 for different and lesser offenses. In February he was found guilty of holding a conventicle in his house in Stepney, his second such offense, for which he was fined £40, and in June he was convicted of publishing a libel concerning the death of the Earl of Essex,* for which he was fined £100 and sentenced to the pillory. His request for an abatement of the fine, owing to poverty, was refused on procedural grounds.

Capp, *FMM*; A.H. Dodd, 'A Remonstrance from Wales, 1655,' *Bulletin of the Board of Celtic Studies*, 17:279-92; *CSPD, Chas. II*, 23:405; *Jas. II*, 1:136; 2:174, 183, 191.

H.A. Nenner

THOMASON, George (c. 1602-1666)

Bookseller, was the son of George Thomason of Sudlow, Bucklow, Ches., a husbandman. In Sept. 1617 he was apprenticed for nine years to Henry Fetherston (or Fetherstone), a bookseller in St. Paul's churchyard, whose niece Katherine Hulton he later married. On 5 June 1626 he took up his freedom as a member of the Company of Stationers, and his first book entry was recorded in the Registers on 1 Nov. 1627. Between 3 Nov. 1640 and 23 Apr. 1661 he attempted to collect every work of quarto size or less concerning contemporary events published in London, even in the face of the 20s. fine levied upon anyone caught purchasing a 'scandalous' pamphlet after 1649. The resulting 'Thomason Tracts' include some 14,942 pamphlets, 97 manuscripts, and 7216 newspapers. His efforts were well enough known so that John Milton* sent him many pamphlets, and in the fall of 1647 Charles I asked to borrow one.

At the outbreak of the Civil War Thomason was a member of the Presbyterian group which supported Parliament. In 1642-43 he was appointed an official Parliamentary Collector of the sums levied upon citizens to support the war effort, and he was elected a Common Councillor of the City for 1647-48. Thomason was a supporter of Lord Mayor Sir John Gayer and, sharing his growing fear of the Independents after the surrender of the King, threw his support to Charles. In 1648, in the aftermath of Pride's purge, he was removed from office along with others who advocated a personal treaty with the King, and in Apr. 1651 he was arrested and charged with being a member of the Love conspiracy which aimed at uniting Scottish and English Presbyterians to restore Charles I. He was imprisoned at Whitehall until 27 May when he was released on £1000 bail; on 14 June the Council of State dropped the charges.

Thomason appears to have withdrawn from political life after this episode, his attention turning more to the affairs of the Stationers' Company. He had been active since 1645 in the Commonalty's efforts against the secret ballot election of Master and Wardens which weakened the power of the Commonalty. In July 1651 he was elected an Assistant, and in July 1657 he became a Junior Warden. He died in Holborn in Apr. 1666, was buried on the 10th, and his will proved on the 27th. He left four sons, George, Edward, Henry and Thomas.

Fortescue; L. Spencer, 'The Politics of George Thomason,' *The Library*, 5th ser., 14:11-27; Spencer, 'The Professional and Literary Connexions of George Thomason,' *The Library*, 5th ser., 13:102-18.

H.T. Blethen

THOMPSON (or Thomson), George (c. 1603-c. 1691)

Parliamentary radical and sectary, MP 1645 (Southwark). Thompson was the second son of Robert Thompson of Wotton, Herts. and Elizabeth, daughter of John Harsnett, also of Wotton. He emigrated to Virginia in 1623, three years after his elder brother Maurice,* and by 1629 had become a member of the House of Burgesses for Elizabeth City as well as a JP and lieutenant. Subsequently he returned to England, and settled in Southwark as a merchant. With his brothers Maurice and William, Thompson subscribed to the Irish adventure in June 1642. Enlisting in the parliamentary army, he served under the Earl of Bedford* as a captain of horse in 1643. By 1644 he was campaigning in the west with his own regiment of horse under Waller,* but lost a leg in action and retired from active service. In 1645 he was returned to Parliament as a recruiter MP, where he worked closely with his brother Maurice and others, including his fellow Southwark member George Snelling,* on commercial policy. Thompson served as a commissioner for compounding, for the sale of bishops' lands and for the Irish assessment, and was a militia commissioner for Southwark. He assumed a prominent role under the Commonwealth, serving on the commissions for the Admiralty, the Great Seal and the customs, as well as committees for trades and plantations, Scottish and Irish affairs, ordnance and the security of the Tower. At the same time he vigorously promoted the commercial interests of the London radicals. In Feb. 1651 he was elected to the Council of State.

Thompson opposed the dissolution of the Long Parliament and was abruptly stripped of his offices on 18 May 1653, though he was sufficiently acceptable to be appointed a commissioner for the ejection of scandalous ministers in Aug. 1654. He was apparently associated with Fifth Monarchist and other sectarian groups, and it was reported that in 1659 he gathered 'with some thousands in St. George's-in-the-Fields, Southwark, and with Bibles in their hands, and good swords also, they declared for King Jesus, which signified what they pleased, except King Charles' (CSPD, Chas. II, 5:457-58). With the return of the Long Parliament, he was appointed to the Council of State and the Committee for Intelligence, and on 18 Aug. 1659 was authorized to raise a regiment of volunteers in London. Thompson took refuge with his brother Maurice at Lee in Kent at the Restoration. He

remained under suspicion, and a warrant for his arrest was issued on 31 Oct. 1661. Thereafter he lived in obscurity, though Pepys reported that he had been nominated to the Commission for Accounts in 1668. Thompson's will, dated 15 Dec. 1690 and proved on 17 Jan. 1691, declared his residence to be in St. James Clerkenwell. He was survived by his wife Abigail, to whom he left £100 p.a. and the manor and parsonage of Brickinsley, Essex, and was buried in St. Olave's church, Southwark beside his first wife Elizabeth, daughter of James Brickland of Thorncliff, Ches.

DNB; Waters; Underdown, PP; Worden; Firth & Rait; CCC, 137, 801; CSPD, Comm., 1-6 passim; Virginia Magazine of History and Biography, 1:188-90; R. Brenner, 'The Civil War Politics of London's Merchant Community,' P. & P., 58:53-107.

R. Zaller

THOMPSON, Maurice (d. 1676)

City radical and colonizer, was the eldest son of Robert Thompson of Wotton, Herts. and Elizabeth, daughter of John Harsnett, also of Wotton. Thompson emigrated to Virginia in 1620 and soon established a lucrative trade in slaves and tobacco between the Guinea coast of Africa and St. Kitts, where he received a grant of 1000 acres in 1627. By 1632 he was one of the official factors for the entire Virginia tobacco crop. In 1629 he entered the Canadian fur trade in defiance of both English and French monopolies, and with William Courteen interloped on the East India Company trade in the 1630s. At the same time he was the chief agent of the Providence Island Company, and in 1642 he helped the Earl of Warwick* finance a privateering expedition to the same area, acquiring a large property on Barbados for a sugar plantation. By the Revolution, Thompson had established himself as the most resourceful and aggressive colonial merchant of his day.

With Richard Shute,* Thompson presented the citizens' petition to Charles I at York in Sept. 1640, demanding that a parliament be called and grievances redressed. A member of the Honorable Artillery Company, he was appointed to the Militia Committee in Jan. 1642, and was a key financier of the parliamentary war effort. Thompson remained a foe of establishments, whether clerical or lay; when in 1643 the parish of St. Dunstan's decided to replace the closed vestry with churchwardens of their own choosing, they elected Thompson, his brother-in-law William Tucker and his business associates William Allen and Richard Bateson. Thompson himself was a parochial Independent in religion, but his daughter joined William Greenhill's* gathered church and in 1649 he contributed a commendatory epistle to the Particular Baptist Samuel Richardson's* pamphlet, *Divine Consolation*.

The Commonwealth was Thompson's opportunity. He dominated the committee of merchants set up on 16 Jan. 1649 to purge the navy and the customs, and the Trinity House Commission where he worked closely with Samuel Moyer.* He became a treasurer of customs, a prize ship commissioner, an assessment commissioner for Ireland and, in 1650, a member of the Board of Trade. Thompson was principally responsible for drafting the Navigation Act of 1651 and, with the help of his brother George,* seeing it through Parliament. The Act reflected his scheme for an integrated national trade that would replace the old chartered monopolies, but that was only the beginning of his vision. Having developed a successful triangular trade in the West Indies, Thompson dreamed of reproducing it on a far larger scale. He had joined the East India Company in the 1640s and become the recognized leader of its expansionist faction. He now proposed that the Company promote colonial settlement, particularly in Assada on the northwest coast of Madagascar, which he saw as a second sugar-producing Barbados. With West African slave marts supplying labor, he believed the Company could ultimately engross the entire carrying trade between India, the Malay peninsula, China and Japan. To this end he urged the government to revive its claim to the spice islands in the first Dutch War.

The dissolution of the Long Parliament only briefly interrupted these plans. Thompson joined other City radicals in demanding restitution of the Parliament on 1 May 1653, but by November he had accepted membership on Cromwell's High Court of Justice. Though he failed to implement his reorganization of the East India Company at a climactic meeting on 10 May 1654, he presided over a highly successful recapitalization of the Company three years later, and in Dec. 1657 became the first governor under its new charter. Thompson was now more than ever a financial mainstay of the government, and one of his last acts as governor was to negotiate a £15,000 loan with the Council of State in June 1659.

Thompson retained the bulk of his wealth if not his influence after the Restoration, though his brother William served as Governor of the East India Company under Charles II. He was suspected of intriguing with the Dutch, and an intelligence report described him as 'always violently against kingly government.' He was still active in 1675 when he was named as an executor of Thomas Sprigge's will; his own was proved on 9 May 1676. Thompson married Dorothy, daughter of John Vaux of Pembrokeshire, by whom he had a son John (b. 1647), later Baron Haversham, and at least four daughters. He left his entire estate to John, including property in England, Ireland, Barbados, Antigua, St. Kitts, Virginia and 'the Carebee Islands and elsewhere,' excepting only certain estates in London. In addition he bequeathed 20s. each 'to one hundred poor silenced ministers.' Thompson's extraordinary career lacked only adequate scope; had he belonged to the eighteenth century his name would have been a famous one. As it is he is one of the most significant and exemplary figures of the revolutionary period, and the lack of a biography is one of the most conspicuous lacunae of modern Stuart scholarship.

Pearl; Tolmie; Waters; *Virginia Magazine of History and Biography*, 1:188-90; J.E. Farnell, 'The Navigation Act of 1651,' *Economic History Review*, 2nd ser., 16:443-46; R.P. Brenner, 'The Civil War Politics of London's Merchant Community,' *P. & P.*, 58:53-107; idem., 'Commercial Change and Political Conflict: The Merchant Community in Civil War London' (Ph.D. diss., Princeton Univ., 1970); J.P. Cooper, 'Social and Economic Policies under the Commonwealth,' in Aylmer, *Int*; M. Ashley, *Financial and Commercial Policy under the Protectorate* (1962); S.A. Khan, *The East India Trade in the XVIIth Century* (1923); *Cal. Court Minutes of the East India Company, 1644-59, passim*; *CSP, West Indies 1570-1650*, 8-10 *passim*; *CSPD, Comm., passim*; Firth & Rait.

R. Zaller

THOMPSON, Robert (d. 1694)

Army radical, was the fifth and last son of Robert Thompson of Wotton, Herts. and Elizabeth, daughter of John Harsnett, also of Wotton. Among his brothers were two future directors of the East India Company, Maurice* and William, and the Civil War officer and MP George.* Thompson emigrated to America after his brothers and bought a 'stone house' at Guildford, Conn. from the Rev. Henry Whitefield and property at Nipmugg. In 1649 he was appointed a naval commissioner with the rank of major in the new Commonwealth regime, and was reputedly close enough to Cromwell to have been a prospective son-in-law. By the end of the Protectoral period he had become a colonel, though he was commonly addressed as 'Major Thompson' in later life. Thompson was reported plotting against the government in 1666 when an informant, Hugh Squier, supplied the following sketch of him: 'he began with nothing, rose high enough to

purchase £2200 in bishops' lands, and lost it on the Restoration, so that he brags that he hates not the persons but the office of bishops; he is bold, full of malice, and embittered against the government; he was six or seven years a navy commissioner for the Protector, so that he knows all the ways of the navy, and is thus able to commit this treason.' No action was apparently taken against Thompson at this time. He owned lands in Suffolk, Lincolnshire and Kent as well as Middlesex, where he resided. Thompson was survived by his wife, a son Joseph, daughters Elizabeth, Marian and Susan, and a grandson, William, the son of his deceased son William.

Waters; *CSPD, Comm.*, 1-13 *passim*; *Virginia Magazine of History and Biography*, 1:188-90.

R. Zaller

THOMPSON, William (d. 1649)

Army radical and Leveller, was a corporal of Capt. Pitchford's troop in Col. Whalley's* regiment. In Sept. 1647 he was cashiered by a Council of War for his violent conduct during a tavern brawl, and the Council ordered him broken at the head of his regiment. Thompson, however, refused Maj. Swallow's* order to dismount, charged the Council with injustice, and contended that the use of martial law violated the army's *Engagement* of June 1647. Soldiers in the ranks supported this view, and Thompson remained with or near the regiment for six weeks, circulating tracts and attempting to incite disaffection among Fleetwood's* troops as well as Whalley's (*The Justice of the Army against Evill-Doers Vindicated*, June 1649, pp. 7-9). Arrested and imprisoned in Windsor Castle, Thompson published a tract addressed to Fairfax* in which he denounced the use of martial law in time of peace, particularly in the case of a civilian such as he now was (*Englands Freedome, Souldiers Rights . . . or, The Just Declaration . . . of William Thompson*, Dec.

1647). Permitted to go to London on parole, Thompson prepared another attack on the Council of War and was again secured when sighted in Whitehall by Cromwell and Ireton.* Sentenced to death by the army Council, Thompson was reprieved and committed to prison (*A Vindication of . . . Cromwell and Ireton, against . . . a Posted Libell Signed by One Tompson*, Mar. 1648; *A True and Impartial Relation . . . Concerning the Proceedings . . . against W. Tompson*, Mar. 1648). He escaped and became an outlaw. In 1649, assuming the title of captain, Thompson and a gang of armed men engaged in violent robbery in Essex, and on at least one occasion Thompson killed a man. He was again captured, but this time was delivered to the civil magistrate for trial. He was bailed by John Lilburne* and again escaped (*The Justice of the Army*, p. 9; *Clarke Papers*, 2:199). In May, having gathered a few score men together in Banbury, Thompson published a manifesto, *Englands Standard Advanced*, which denounced the government and urged all who had honor, courage and love of country to set the people free. The call to arms was eloquent, the final *Agreement of the People* was appended, and it is unlikely that Thompson drafted the appeal without considerable help – probably from Lilburne. Thompson's forces were easily routed by Col. Reynolds' troops, and while some of the rebels joined the related resistance at Burford, Thompson escaped to Northamptonshire, where he put up a valiant fight until he was killed (*The Moderate*, 8-16 and 15-22 May). Thompson's brother James, a cornet, was one of three rebels executed in connection with the Burford mutiny. In addition to physical courage and strong temper, Thompson possessed some skill in expression. His protest against military discipline after he had been cashiered was valid and well stated, and Lilburne may have assisted his preparation of the argument. Lilburne evidently admired and valued Thompson and gave him important moral and practical support throughout his short and turbulent career.

Fortescue; Wing; Brailsford; Firth & Davies.

B. Taft

THORNAUGH (or Thornhagh), Francis (c. 1616-1648)

Civil War officer, was the eldest son of Sir Francis Thornaugh of Nottinghamshire. He attended the free school at Lincoln with John Hutchinson* and other gentlemen's sons, where he received some training in arms from an old soldier. At the outbreak of the Civil War his father, Sir Francis, was commissioned a colonel and empowered to raise a regiment of horse in Nottinghamshire. He appointed his son as his lieutenant-colonel. At about this same time, Thornaugh was appointed to the County Committee. Lucy Hutchinson describes him as upright and faithful to God, his people and his country's true interests, a man of valor and noble daring. Thornaugh was captured after the siege of Gainsborough in 1643, disarmed, wounded and left for dead. He managed to reach the house of one of his tenants and then escaped to Lincoln. He was elected to the Long Parliament as a recruiter from East Retford in 1645 but did not play a prominent role there. During the second Civil War Thornaugh commanded the Nottinghamshire horse under Cromwell. He was killed at the Battle of Preston leading a charge against the Scots. Ludlow* praised his great courage on this occasion as well as his devotion to the parliamentary cause.

Hutchinson; MacCormack; Ludlow. Papers: L (Add. MSS).

H.R. Engstrom

THORPE, Francis (1595-1665)

Parliamentary radical, MP 1645 (Richmond), 1654 (Beverley), 1656 (West Riding). Thorpe was probably born at Birdsall, Yorks. He matriculated at St. John's Coll., Camb. in 1610 and took his B.A. in 1613-14. He was admitted to Gray's Inn in 1611 and called to the bar in 1621. He quickly established a successful legal practice in London and in the north, becoming Recorder of Beverley (1623-49) and later of Hull (1639-48). In Mar. 1641 he was a witness at Strafford's trial, and at the outbreak of war accepted a commission in the parliamentary army, rising to the rank of colonel. He was a recruiter MP to the Long Parliament from Oct. 1645. Though appointed a commissioner to try the King in Jan. 1649 he never attended the trial. Despite his obvious doubts about the new commonwealth he performed a useful service for it by accepting an appointment as judge on the northern circuit and, on 20 Mar. 1649, delivered a charge to the jury at York which vigorously defended the regime and the execution of the King, declaring that 'the people (under God) is the original of all just power.' The statement was quickly published and widely circulated, and Thorpe received the thanks of the House of Commons. Thorpe himself was responsible, together with another judge, John Puleston, for the execution of a Royalist named Marris who had seized Pontefract Castle for the King in the second Civil War. In Apr. 1650 he was named one of the commissioners for establishing a High Court of Justice. As a successful lawyer he was unenthusiastic about legal reform. He may have begun flirting with royalist opposition groups as early as the spring of 1650 but, if so, he was not discovered, for he did not reach an open breach with the regime until well after the fall of the Rump. He sat in the first Protectorate Parliament and, in the spring of 1655, was the presiding judge who tried those involved in the western rising. Shortly after, however, when Cromwell called him in about trying the cases in the Yorkshire rising Thorpe raised so many procedural objections that he was allowed to retire. By then his differences with the Protectorate were quite obvious and when he was returned to the second Protectorate

Parliament (Sept. 1656) he was excluded, though he was allowed to sit during its second session (Jan.-Feb. 1658). The Rump, in power again, restored him to the bench for a brief interim. At the Restoration he pleaded for a special pardon on the ground that he had opposed the King's execution and refused to try the Yorkshire rebels. Though Prynne* called for his execution the indemnity was granted and he died peacefully at home in 1665.

Al. Cant; Nuttall, *Yorks.*; *CSPD, Comm.*, 1-2, 4, 6-9 *passim*; 11:186; 12:375; *DNB*; Aylmer, *SS*; Thurloe, *SP*. Papers: LPR.

S.J. Stearns

THURLOE, John (1616-1668)

Secretary of State, was born on 12 June 1616, the son of Thomas Thurloe, sometime Rector of Abbots Roding, Essex. Thurloe's career began in legal services to Oliver St. John,* through whom he became a secretary to the Parliamentary Commissioners at the Uxbridge negotiations in 1644. Though he seems to have been enrolled at one of the so-called Chancery Inns, Furnivall's, he gained admission to Lincoln's Inn only in 1646, being called to the bar in 1653. Minor offices accrued but Thurloe took no direct part in politics and his later claim to be 'altogether a stranger' to the events of 1649 rings true. In 1651 St. John, with whom he would always maintain good relations, took him on his embassy to the United Provinces and in Mar. 1652 he was appointed rather unexpectedly successor to Gualter Frost as Secretary to the Rump's Council of State. The influence of Oliver Cromwell, for whom he had been doing private legal work, may be detected here. Thurloe was then successively secretary of the Council to the Barebones Parliament and to the Protectorates of Oliver Cromwell and Richard Cromwell,* and in 1657 became a member of the Council. Dismissed by the restored Rump in May 1659, he came back briefly under Monck on the eve of the

Restoration. It is a remarkable though by no means unique instance of continuity in administrative personnel during the Interregnum. En route, Thurloe collected other jobs, notably Postmaster General and, not unconnected, head of the intelligence service. He is best known and praised for the latter work, but in fact was rather the heir of the pioneer work of Thomas Scott* and George Bishop* than an initiator.

Thurloe has been variously assessed: a master-spy, close confidant if not *eminence grise* to Oliver Cromwell, a mediocre amanuensis, a peculatory timeserver, never a revolutionary. He seems to have been an industrious civil servant, tireless drafter and filer of correspondence, not all of it his own, respectful to his political masters, in no way original or, indeed, ambitious of being an independent force in politics. By the standards of the day he was not corrupt, though naturally he rewarded himself well for his pains. His network of agents, British and foreign, most of them venal, weakened royalist prospects but perhaps did little more, though the documentation is a quarry of miscellaneous information which tends to exaggerate his influence. Thurloe was a welcome channel between foreign diplomats and the Protector but it is doubtful if he himself formulated foreign policy. Oliver, he said, chose men for his places and what the Protector found in Thurloe was a prudent, indefatigable, loyal, comforting bureaucrat, a willing screen between himself and the importunate. Close though the relationship was, Thurloe was not privy to Cromwell's inmost thoughts – both repudiation of the major-generals and rejection of kingship took the Secretary by surprise. He was never a statesman nor in the parliamentary sense a politician, though he served in the Protectoral Parliaments of 1654, 1656 and 1659, in the first two for Ely, the latter for Cambridge University. He reflected rather than formulated the outlook of the 1650s regimes – generally conservative, limited, seeking first of all security, continuity and mere stability, ready only then for positive advance in settlement. Thurloe's frequent bouts of ill-health and depression are a symptom of the difficulties of even that limited program.

Thurloe had many connections – in the City, in the army and almost every area of civilian life. Among his correspondents were Henry Cromwell* and the reformer Samuel Hartlib,* through whom he made contact with men such as John Pell* and John Dury,* advocate of reunion in European Protestantism. Through Dury Thurloe made moves that led to the readmission of the Jews to England. But Thurloe seems generally to have been less interested in the reformers' own ideological aspirations than in the information they could give him of comings and goings and opinions, particularly royalist, on the Continent. His work and comments on both domestic and foreign policies do not suggest that he was a deeply religious man, but rather that he had a cool, lay attitude that may have complemented Oliver's own. He condemned equally the Levellers and the restlessness of army men as different as Okey* and Lambert.* More of his stamp were the Kinglings: Broghill significantly supported his return as Secretary in 1660. He might have served Charles II as he had the various governments of the 1650s, but having survived a treason charge he preferred to retire to private practice to his old Inn, Lincoln's. He died there in his chambers on 21 Feb. 1668. His papers, apparently comprehensive but possibly reduced in number, were found years afterwards above a false ceiling in his chambers – a reflection at once of his natural caution and his bureaucratic respect for paper.

Thurloe was twice married, first to a lady of the family of Peyton who bore him two sons who died in infancy, and second to Anne, third daughter of Sir John Lytcott of East Moulsey, Surrey, by whom he had four sons and two daughters.

Aylmer, *SS*; Burton; *DNB*; Thurloe, *SP*; Turnbull. Papers: O (Rawl. MSS A1-73); L (Add. MSS 415-19; Lans. MSS; Sloane MSS; Stowe MSS); EN.

I. Roots

THURSTON, Thomas (c. 1622-1693)

Quaker, was born near Bristol, Glos., and was one of the very first to proclaim Quakerism in Gloucester in 1654. In July 1656 he was a member of the second Quaker group to reach New England, where he was incarcerated in Boston before being banished to England. Accompanied by Josiah Coale,* Thurston labored in Virginia and Maryland in 1657-58 and was imprisoned in both places and then banished. Thurston and Coale, accompanied by Thomas Chapman of Maryland, made a very difficult journey through the wilderness to enter New England by the 'back door,' since it was now against the law for ship-masters to bring Quakers into Massachusetts. A second visit to Virginia and Maryland in 1659 brought great suffering upon Thurston: whippings, other physical abuse and imprisonment. Still another visit to Maryland in 1661 preceded his settlement in Maryland in 1663. Having fallen under the spell of John Perrot,* Thurston was a very disturbing influence on Maryland and Virginia Quakerism between 1663 and 1673. George Fox*, while in Maryland in 1673, met with Thurston and, for a time, brought him back into the Quaker fold. Thurston was in South Carolina between 1681 and 1683, having followed his fellow Maryland Quaker William Fuller there. Thurston then returned to Maryland in 1683, becoming a 'renegade' Quaker testified against by Maryland Friends. In 1688, still calling himself a Quaker even though testified against, he was elected to the Maryland Assembly and was allowed to occupy his seat without taking the required oath. He was still an object of controversy in his seventieth year, serving as the chief military officer in Baltimore County until forced out of the office less than a year before his death there early in 1693.

Archives of Maryland, 3:331, 347-50, 352-53, 362, 364; 4:268-69, 287, 322, 331, 333, 339, 394-400; K.L. Carroll, 'Thomas Thurston, Renegade Maryland Quaker,' *Maryland Historical Magazine*, 62:170-92;

EQL; F. Howgill, *The Deceiver of the Nations Discovered and His Cruelty Made Manifest* (1660). Papers: LF (A. R. Barclay MSS, XIII).

K.L. Carroll

TICHBORNE, Robert (d. 1682)

Regicide, army officer and parliamentary radical, MP 1653 (London). Tichborne was the eldest son of Robert Tichborne of London by Joan, daughter of Thomas Bankes. He was probably born in the early 1620s, for though old enough to be a captain in the London militia in 1643 he pleaded his lack of years in 1649 when he was tried at the Restoration. When Fairfax* faced the threat of a Presbyterian counter-revolution in London in 1647, he made Tichborne colonel of a specially raised militia regiment, and on occupying the capital in August appointed him Lieutenant of the Tower. Originally a draper, Tichborne took part in both the Putney and Whitehall debates of the Council of Officers (1647-48), expressing the views of a radical Independent but not of a Leveller. Nevertheless he joined in negotiations with Levellers after the second Civil War, sharing their dread of a reactionary political settlement, and sat with them on the Committee of Sixteen which drafted the second *Agreement of the People*. On 15 Jan. 1649 he presented a petition from London's Common Council to the Rump, calling for rigorous justice upon the King and all other authors of the late wars. He himself attended the High Court assiduously and signed the King's death warrant. Tichborne became a Sheriff of London in 1650, and was one of eight commissioners appointed by Parliament on 23 Oct. 1651 to go to Scotland and make arrangements preparatory to its union with England.

Like his fellow-alderman John Ireton,* Tichborne worshipped in George Cokayne's* congregation, but the two lengthy devotional works which he published early in 1649, *A Cluster of Canaans Grapes* and *The Rest of Faith*, show little of Cokayne's millenarian preoccupations. Their main theme is the profession of a saint, and they breathe a rather emotional piety, quite free of fanaticism. Tichborne dedicated the first to Fairfax and the second to Cromwell, who summoned him to the Nominated Parliament of 1653. He became one of its most active members, sitting on numerous committees of both the House and the Council of State, to which he was elected in July and again in November. He sided with the religious moderates, opposing both the immediate discontinuance of tithes and the abolition of lay patronage, on which issue he was a teller on the opposite side from John Ireton. He is said to have been one of the members who engineered the assembly's resignation.

Tichborne worked closely with the Protectorate, as a judge for probate of wills, a commissioner for approbation of public preachers (Trier), an Ejector, and a commissioner to try treasons against the Protector's person. His employment (since 1649) as a Customs Commissioner, however, was terminated in 1656, though whether because of alleged non-payment of large arrears to the Exchequer or suspicion of misappropriation in a business concerning smuggled gold bars is uncertain. Nevertheless he became Lord Mayor of London in Oct. 1656 and was knighted by Cromwell, who also named him to his new Upper House. He apparently kept in favor with the Rump when it was restored in 1659, serving as a Militia Commissioner and as colonel of a regiment of volunteers that was raised during Booth's rising. When the army again interrupted the Parliament in October it appointed Tichborne to its short-lived Committee of Safety, which led to his disgrace when the Rump returned. He surrendered at the Restoration. His plea of ignorance in the King's death was belied by the facts; he had been one of the most aggressive and persistent of the Regicides both in and out of the High Court. But his life was to be spared, although he was formally sentenced to death. He lost all the considerable lands and goods he had acquired, however, and remained a prisoner until his death in 1682.

DNB; *Second Narrative of the Late Parliament* (1659); *London's Triumph* (1656); Beaven; Tolmie; Woolrych; Wedgwood, *CKC*; Firth & Davies. Papers: L (Add. MSS).

A. Woolrych

TILLAM, Thomas (fl. 1637-1668)

Particular Baptist, Fifth Monarchist and Seventh Day publicist. Tillam left the Catholic church about 1637 and eventually became a member of Morgan Llwyd's* gathered church at Wrexham. There he was excommunicated on a charge of seeking to divide the church, perhaps over believer's baptism, since he next appears as a member with Hanserd Knollys* in Swan Alley, Coleman Street, London. Tillam had for a while been an apothecary, but in 1651 he published *The Two Witnesses*, a millenarian exposition of Rev. 11. He was sent out the same year as an evangelist from Knollys' church, 'a messenger of one of the seven churches in London,' to Hexham, N'land, where he held a lectureship established by the London Mercers' Company worth £80 p.a. and received a further £40 from the Committee for Augmentations. He arrived in Hexham on 27 Dec. 1651 and founded the Particular Baptist church there on 21 July 1652 by baptizing eleven men and five women and adding his wife Jane by transfer from a Cheshire church. The manuscript records show that he did not practice laying on of hands from the beginning. The following month others were baptized including Edmund Hickeringill* (or Hickhorngill), who was sent in December as an evangelist to Scotland. On a visit to London Tillam received the laying on of hands from Peter Chamberlen* and in Apr. 1653 a member from Chamberlen's church joined Hexham. These are the first indications of links with the Seventh Day men. During this year Tillam engaged in missions in Cheshire, Yorkshire and Northumberland. At Stokesley the minister William Kaye and nineteen of his people were baptized. Tillam was deceived by a pretended Jew who professed conversion and was baptized; Tillam provided his account in *Banners of Love* (1654). More serious tensions arose with the Newcastle, N'land congregation led by Paul Hobson* and Thomas Gower* who had been pioneers among the London Particular Baptists. It seems that the issues included that of the laying on of hands, the presentation of children for blessing (in place of infant baptism), and the singing of psalms 'with the world' (this was probably regarded as praying with the unconverted). In addition, during July 1653 Tillam's congregation apparently developed links with open-membership churches, including those of Henry Jessey* and John Tombes.* In Feb. 1655 Tillam signed a petition of support for the Protector, *The Representation and Petition of Christ's Servants*, which would have further displeased Hobson. By June 1655 attempts to patch up the differences with the Newcastle congregation had failed and Knollys' Coleman Street church seems to have disowned Tillam, who then departed from Northumberland for Colchester, Essex. There he enjoyed the use of the parish church and engaged in public debate in July 1655.

By the following year Tillam had gathered a considerable congregation who supported his Seventh Day Baptist views. In *The Seventh-Day Baptist Sought Out* (1657), a response to a pamphlet by William Aspinwall,* he claimed a congregation of 200 adherents and published three hymns for congregational singing. After a period in prison Tillam was released, and in London in 1658 he shared in a public disputation with Chamberlen and Matthew Coppinger against Jeremiah Ives* on the sabbath question. His own position was attacked by Edmund Warren in *The Jews Sabbath Antiquated* (1658). At the Restoration Tillam was again imprisoned briefly

(by June 1660), and during this period wrote *The Temple of Lively Stones*, with an epistle by Christopher Pooley.* Thereafter Tillam can occasionally be glimpsed as a proponent of the Fifth Monarchy who in 1661 urged his associates to emigrate to the Palatinate to avoid the fearful judgment he believed would soon fall upon apostate England. In 1664 he was at Rotterdam, and in 1666 he was in Ireland, allegedly associating with Thomas Blood.* The last known references to him (in 1667 and 1668) indicate that such English Seventh Day Baptists as Edward Stennett* had disowned him and that he and his friends had adopted circumcision and other Jewish rites together with a community of goods and, according to some rumors, of wives. As late as 1668 recruits from East Anglia and the north left to join his community. According to Payne, he died about 1676.

E.A. Payne, 'Thomas Tillam,' *BQ*, 17:61-66; Underhill, *RCCF*; Capp, *FMM*; Howell, *NPR*; *CSPD, Chas. II*, 2, 6-8 *passim*; T. Weld, *Mr. Tillam's Account* (1657); *TBHS*, 3:177-89.

B.R. White

TILLINGHAST, John (1604-1655)

Fifth Monarchist and Independent minister, was the son of John Tillinghast (d. 1624), Rector of Streat, Sussex (B.A. 1582; M.A. 1585, Clare Coll., Camb.), and elder brother of Robert Tillinghast (B.A. 1631, Christ's Coll., Camb.). Tillinghast, who was christened on 25 Sept. 1604, attended the grammar school at Newport, Essex, before becoming a pensioner at Caius Coll., Camb. on 24 Mar. 1621. He graduated B.A. in 1625, and became Rector of Tarring Neville, Sussex, in July 1636, moving in Sept. 1637 to become Rector of Streat as his father's successor. In 1643 he went to preach in London and was converted to the Independents no later than 1650, when he joined the Independent church at Syleham, Suff. He accepted an invitation in Feb. 1651 to become an assistant minister to William Bridge* at Great Yarmouth. In Jan. 1652 he became pastor of an Independent congregation and Rector of Trunch, Norf., but left for London in 1655. He presumably knew George Cokayne,* whose congregation included Tillinghast's uncle, the Regicide Robert Tichborne,* but by this date Cokayne had relinquished his Fifth Monarchy views. Nathaniel Brewster, an Independent and Rector of Alby *cum* Thwaite, Norf., introduced Tillinghast to Cromwell in the spring of 1655, only to have Tillinghast 'bear his testimony to his face . . . in such a way of plainness, and pity towards him, who was guilty of such open abominations.' At Windsor Castle Tillinghast visited Christopher Feake,* who edited the former's *Eight Last Sermons* (1655). Tillinghast died in June 1655. He was succeeded at Trunch by Richard Lawrence, son-in-law of William Bridge.

Tillinghast was the most learned of the Fifth Monarchists and the only one capable of publishing a systematic analysis of the prophetic texts that were basic to the movement. His *Knowledge of the Times* (1654) argued that Christ's personal appearance, the dissolution of the fourth monarchy, and the beginning of the millennium would occur in 1701, but he was also convinced that God would perform natural wonders in 1654 or 1656, when the beast's (the Papacy's) reign would end and the Jews would begin to stir preparatory to their final conversion and restoration in 1701. His millennium had an evening phase, consisting of a kingdom founded and ruled by the saints preparatory to the establishment of the morning phase when Christ would appear. Tillinghast preached a highly activist Christianity combining missionary outreach (especially to Ireland, India, Turkey, Northumberland and Cumberland) and military aggression (against the Turks, the Papacy and the Continental Catholic states). As early as 1653 he warned against Absalom-like treachery at home and looked with disfavor on the establishment of the Protectorate. Affairs of state were to be managed only by holy men, and he came to doubt Crom-

well's inclusion in that category.

Tillinghast's *Eight Last Sermons* were intended in part to shore up the convictions of those who were beginning to doubt the imminence of the fifth monarchy. One sure sign was 'the defection and apostacy of eminent leading men in the churches,' including the Triers and the clergy who accepted positions in the universities. Feake's imprisonment and the defection of Parliament, the New Model and Cromwell from the cause of the godly were among the other signs. The saints' responsibility, as Tillinghast conceived it, was to bring down lofty men, overthrow the Antichrist and establish godly rule. His thought turned increasingly apocalyptic between 1653 and 1655, as witnessed by the additions he made to *Generation Work* (1653, 1654, 1655).

Capp, *FMM*; Nuttall, *VS*; Abbott, 3:756-57; DNB; Capp, in *Puritans, the Millennium and the Future of Israel*, ed. P. Toon (1970), pp. 68-70.

R.L. Greaves

TINDAL, Matthew (1657-1733)

Deist, was baptized on 12 May 1657 at Bere-Ferris (or Bere-Ferrers), Devon, the son of John Tindal, a minister, and Anna Hulse. Tindal matriculated at Lincoln Coll., Oxf. in 1673, but moved to Exeter College before receiving his B.A. in 1676. He won a fellowship in law at All Souls in 1678 and proceeded B.C.L. in 1679 and D.C.L. in 1685, when he became an advocate at Doctors' Commons. He remained a fellow of All Souls until his death on 16 Aug. 1733. Probably after the accession of James II, Tindal became a Roman Catholic and apparently sought the wardenship of his college. He later claimed that this conversion was due to his youthful susceptibility to the clergy, but he was nearly thirty years old when he reverted to the Church of England (as he claimed) before James fled the country in 1688. Whatever reasons lay behind his Roman

Catholicism, Tindal became a staunch Whig of impeccable anti-Catholic and low-church credentials.

After involvement in several cases of international law, Tindal published *An Essay Concerning the Law of Nations* (1694) and *An Essay Concerning Obedience to the Supreme Powers* (1694), which argued that political power is derived from the people and ought to be controlled by them to guarantee liberty of conscience. He is reputed to have written *A Letter to the Reverend Clergy of Both Universities* (1694) and *Reflections on the XXVIII Propositions Touching the Doctrine of the Trinity* (1695), both of which attacked defenders of Trinitarian doctrine and were printed in the Unitarian *Third Collection of Tracts*. In 1697 Tindal published *An Essay Concerning the Power of the Magistrate,* which set forth a Lockean theory of religious toleration. He wrote in favor of a free press in 1704 and 1709, and created considerable controversy in 1706 with *The Rights of the Christian Church*, an attack on the high church party, which brought many replies and two defenses from Tindal. He continued his assault on high-church policies with *New High Church Turned Old Presbyterian* (1709) and, not dissuaded by the Commons' burning of *The Rights of the Christian Church* with Sacheverell's sermon in 1710, he published within that year *The Jacobitism, Perjury, and Popery of High-Church Priests, A High-Church Catechism* and *The Merciful Judgments of the High-Church Triumphant*. For some years thereafter his writings tended to concentrate on political affairs. His attack upon Robert Walpole's resignation and call for Whig unity in *Defection Consider'd* (1717) seems to have gone through six editions within the year, but upon Walpole's return to government Tindal published his praise and support in 1721 and 1722.

At the ripe age of 73 Tindal published his most famous work, *Christianity as Old as the Creation* (1730), a thorough summary of Deistic doctrines and arguments. Asserting that the goodness of God and the immutability of human nature require that the means to human happiness and the fulfilment of divine obligations be universally known, he argued that reason operating on the nature of things, or natural religion, must provide a complete knowledge of human duty. This natural religion, he concluded, differs from historical revelations such as that of Christianity only in the means by which it is communicated. Tindal proceeded, however, to level at Christianity the common Deistic charges of superstition, priestly imposition of absurd beliefs, and the difficulty of agreeing on the text and interpretation of Scripture, with the clear implication that natural religion is superior to the Christian revelation and that it should serve as a corrective to Christianity. While not an original work, Tindal's 'Deist's Bible' elicited dozens of replies, some of which, like those of William Law and Joseph Butler, signaled a significant change in the course of English religious thought.

J. Hunt, *Religious Thought in England* (1871); G.V. Lechler, *Geschichte des Englischen Deismus* (1841); L. Stephen, *History of English Thought in the Eighteenth Century* (1962); *DNB*.

J. Biddle

TOLAND, John (1670-1722)

Radical Whig and religious thinker. Toland was born in Ireland, probably of poor and Catholic parents, but became a Protestant Dissenter sometime in his youth. He attended university first in Glasgow and then at Edinburgh where he received his M.A. in 1690. Among his tutors was the Newtonian, David Gregory. The earliest available comments about him by contemporaries associate him with freethinking as well as with cabals and secret societies. Indeed records indicate that he belonged to what was probably a Masonic Lodge headed by Sir Robert Clayton* in London during the 1690s. He also participated in or headed a 'Socratic Society' whose ritual is described in his *Pantheisticon* (1720). In

1692 Daniel Williams' Presbyterian congregation sent Toland to Holland where he attended classes at Utrecht and Leiden. His personal and intellectual contacts in the Netherlands played a vital role throughout his life. He knew Pierre Bayle and Benjamin Furly* and after 1709-10 he associated with another semi-clandestine group of French refugees located at the Hague. When Toland returned to England after his first sojourn in the Netherlands he did so not as the Presbyterian minister his sponsors had hoped he would be but, as Furly described him in a letter to Locke,* as 'a free-spirited ingenious man [who has] now cast off the yoke of spiritual authority, that great bugbear.'

But Toland had little visible means of support. Locke shied away from him although Toland may have belonged to his 'college,' a group of Whig confreres including John Freke, possibly Matthew Tindal,* and Edward Clarke, among others. The Whig party after 1688-89 was heavily factionalized and Toland associated with one of its most radical factions. To maintain a livelihood he wrote pamphlets and edited, among other works, Harrington's* *Oceana* (1700). Though he subscribed to its major tenets, Toland's republicanism defies easy characterization. He appears to have been willing to accept monarchy, if severely limited and Protestant. His practical politics, however, should not obscure the highly radical nature of both his personality and his religious thought. Of all the Deists of his time Toland was most feared and hated by the church, perhaps because his contemporaries sensed an anger in him against ecclesiastical authority and most legitimate social authority which marked him in their eyes as dangerous.

Toland had no flair for political organization or mass movements. His greatest interest lay in constructing an alternative to Christianity; he was, to use the word he invented, a Pantheist. In 1696 he published *Christianity Not Mysterious*, although it had been written two years earlier. Locke saw a portion of it in manuscript form and probably wrote *The Reasonableness of Christianity* (1695) to counteract it. *Christianity Not Mysterious* attacked all tenets of prevailing orthodoxy for which verification rested ultimately on faith; in short it attacked Christianity at its root and branch. The book brought him censure and notoriety but little financial gain.

During the reign of Anne, Toland was occasionally employed by Robert Harley to write anonymous pamphlets expressing Country sentiment. Toland needed the work and on some issues Country Toryism and radical Whiggery could be made compatible. Despite this compromise (which occasionally disturbed him), Toland did not hesitate to attack both Latitudinarian and Highchurchmen. He even attempted to use Newton's ideas to support his own pantheistic materialism, and Samuel Clarke attacked him ferociously in the Boyle Lectures (1704-5). That confrontation sharply delineated the social message embodied in Newtonianism as well as enlisted Newton's science in the struggle against Deism and atheism.

Letters to Serena (1704) is Toland's most philosophically acute work, indicating his familiarity with the thought of Spinoza, Newton and Leibniz, but largely indebted to his reading of Giordano Bruno. Toland stands as a major link between the pagan naturalism of the late Renaissance and the pantheistic and materialistic aspect of Enlightenment thought. It may be the case that Toland's greatest impact was made on the Continent, particularly in the radical and libertine circles of French refugees in the Netherlands. Toland made his mark as far away as Vienna where clandestine manuscripts of his were brought by the Baron Hohendorf, Prince Eugene of Savoy's intimate friend and librarian. Toland may have admired Maj. Wildman* and other radicals of the 1650s but his mature thought owed more to his highly individual reading of Bruno, Spinoza, Locke and even Newton than it does to Puritanism *per se*.

Toland died relatively young and during his last years of illness he received financial support from Robert Molesworth* and Anthony Collins.* In previous years he had received assistance from Anthony Ashley Cooper, third Earl of Shaftesbury. By 1720, if not before, Toland seems to have been preoccupied with his brotherhood and with refining its liturgy and ritual. He was probably a Freemason of sorts, but his philosophy and politics were far more radical than that espoused by the Grand Lodge founded in 1717.

G. Carabelli, *Tolandiana* (1975); M.C. Jacob, *The Newtonians and the English Revolution, 1689-1720* (1976); F.H. Heineman, *John Toland and the Age of Enlightenment* (1944); A. Lantoine, *John Toland* (1927); J.P. Kenyon, *Revolution Principles* (1977); R.E. Sullivan, *John Toland and the Deist Controversy* (1982); C. Robbins, *The Eighteenth-Century Commonwealthsman* (1961). Papers: L (Add. MSS 4295; 4465); LLP (MS 933); VNL (MS 10,325); KU (Trenchard-Simpson Correspondence).

M.C. Jacob

TOMBES, John (1603-1676)

Baptist minister, was born in Bewdley, Worcs. He matriculated at Magdalen Hall, Oxf. in 1618, and took his B.A. in 1621, M.A. in 1624 and B.D. in 1631. He became Vicar of Leominster, Herefs. in Nov. 1630. Tombes' doubts about the validity of infant baptism dated back to 1627. In 1641 he admitted that he had begun to omit the use of the surplice and cross in baptism, and that he had turned the table at Leominster rather than leave it in an altar-like position. A sermon, later printed as *Fermentum Pharisaeorum, or, The Leaven of Pharisaicall Wil-Worship* (1641), in which he advocated the purging of human inventions from worship, is said to have exposed him to the rage of the church party. Thus early in the Civil War he was obliged to leave Leominster for Bristol when royalist forces arrived in Herefordshire, and as Vicar of All Saints in Bristol he was further obliged to leave for London in 1643 when the city fell into royalist hands. In London he also found himself at odds with the Presbyterian party, for in 1642 he debated the subject of infant baptism with a Baptist in Bristol and subsequently adopted antipaedobaptist views himself. He communicated these views to the Westminster Assembly but was disappointed by the lack of response. Yet there was sufficient reaction later against his antipaedobaptist arguments to cause the loss of his positions as Master of the Temple (gained only after an interview with Stephen Marshall* in Jan. 1645 in which he had promised not to preach his views) and Rector of St. Gabriel, Fenchurch Street. In 1646 he was made Rector of Ross, Worcs. and perpetual Curate at Bewdley where he regularly attended Richard Baxter's Thursday lectures given at nearby Kidderminster. Although he found in Bewdley the freedom to organize a Baptist church and to foster others in western England, it was not until 1649, after Presbyterian dominance had ended, that he returned to Leominster where he continued to serve as vicar until his ejection in 1662.

Tombes was an active disputant both in the pulpit and in print. His most notable public debate was against Baxter on the subject of infant baptism. It took place before a large audience at Bewdley chapel on 1 Jan. 1650, and lasted from 9:00 a.m. to 5:00 p.m. with Tombes apparently emerging victorious. Such public debates on this and other subjects were interwoven with his polemical tracts, which often provoked replies. His *An Examen of the Sermon of Mr. Stephen Marshall About Infant-Baptism* (1645), *Anti-paedobaptism* (1652) and *Felo de Se* (1659) received replies from Marshall, Baxter and others. His anti-Quaker tract, *True Old-Light* (1660) brought responses from George Fox* and other Quakers, and his *A Serious Consideration of the Oath of the Kings Supremacy* (1660) supporting the lawfulness of oaths was attacked by both the Quaker Richard Hubberthorne* and the Baptist Henry Adis.*

In 1646 Tombes had an interview with Oliver Cromwell and gave him copies of his works, and in 1654 he was among the 38 central Triers appointed for the approbation of preachers. At the Restoration his tracts on the lawfulness of oaths for the king's supremacy and his *Saints No Smiters* (1664) denouncing violence against civil powers enhanced his friendship with Lord Clarendon, who introduced him to Charles II. Nevertheless, his refusal to conform as a minister cost him his living at Leominster, though he did conform as a lay communicant. Having taken as his second wife Elizabeth, the wealthy widow of Wolstan Abbot of Salisbury about 1658, he moved to Salisbury where his house was licensed as a Presbyterian place of worship in 1672. He died on 22 May 1676 and was buried in the churchyard at St. Edmund's.

Rel. Bax.; *DNB*; *Calamy Revised*; Tolmie; Palmer; Crosby; A.S. Langley, 'Seventeenth Century Baptist Disputations,' *TBHS*, 6:216-43; P.J. Anderson, 'Letters of Henry Jessey and John Tombes to the Churches of New England, 1645,' *BQ*, 28:30-40. Papers: LW; MWA.

T.L. Underwood

TOMLINSON (or Thomlinson), Matthew (1617-1681)

Army officer, was a native of Yorkshire, the second son of John Tomlinson and Eleanor, daughter of Matthew Dodsworth. In 1642 he was among the gentlemen of the Inns of Court who enlisted under Philip Stapleton in the Earl of Essex's* lifeguard. On 25 Mar. 1645 he defeated a party from Wallingford garrison, and shortly thereafter he entered Sir Robert Pye's* regiment of horse with the rank of major. Tomlinson presented the army's remonstrance to the House of Commons on 25 June 1647. The following month he replaced Pye and took part in the council at Reading, and in August he led his regiment into London. On 28 Oct. he was one of the officers deputed to negotiate with the Levellers at Putney. As the second crisis between Parliament and the army loomed,

Tomlinson was appointed by the General Council of Officers on 28 Nov. 1648 to draw up a declaration justifying the occupation of London. On 23 Dec. he was ordered to convey the King from Windsor to London and thereafter had command of his person up till the day of his execution. Tomlinson was also appointed a member of the High Court but avoided attendance at its sessions, pleading his duties. He is thrice recorded as having sat on 27 Jan. 1649, and another entry for a 'W. Tomlinson' is presumably a mistaken reference to him, but he denied ever attending the Court at the trial of the Regicides. Of Charles' captors he was by far the most civil. At the King's request he accompanied him onto the scaffold and was given a gold toothpick and case as a keepsake. Unable to reach the crowd and surrounded by his executioners, Charles addressed his last words to Tomlinson.

In Apr. 1649 Tomlinson's troops were stationed in Hampshire, where they were ordered to desist exacting payments from the population. In August, Tomlinson put down risings in Kent. He accompanied Cromwell to Scotland in 1650, and took part in the battle of Worcester. In Jan. 1652 he was appointed a member of the Hale Commission. With the expulsion of the Long Parliament, Tomlinson assumed a prominent role. He was appointed to the Council of State in May 1653, became a Commissioner of Excise and of Accounts, and served on committees to receive intelligence, sequester estates, deal with embassies, victual the fleet and investigate prison abuses, among other matters. On 5 July he was named to the Barebones Parliament. Tomlinson became an Irish Councillor in Aug. 1654 and served under Fleetwood* and Henry Cromwell.* The latter knighted him on 24 Nov. 1657, but referred to him sarcastically in a letter to Thurloe* as 'one no ways famous for his formal affection to me.' Tomlinson was named to the Other House in Dec. 1657 but, having been continued in his duties, was unable to sit. He opposed the growing conservatism of Henry Cromwell's regime, and was appointed one of the five commissioners of the successor government on 7 July 1659. Adhering to Ludlow* and the army that fall, he was arrested in the seizure of Dublin Castle. On 19 Jan. 1660 he was impeached by Parliament, but permitted to remain at liberty on condition that he not disturb the existing government.

Excepted from the order to arrest the King's judges in May, Tomlinson was nonetheless imprisoned with John Jones* and Miles Corbet* in July. He narrowly escaped trial, and was required to give evidence against Hacker* and Axtell.* Thereafter he lived in retirement until his death on 3 Nov. 1681, and was buried in the church of East Malling, near Maidstone. Tomlinson married Pembroke, daughter of Sir William Brooke and heiress of the Cobham estates (d. 1683), by whom he had two daughters, Jane (d. 1703), wife of Philip Owen, and Elizabeth, who died a spinster. Tomlinson's sister Jane married Sir Thomas Twysden, a judge of the King's Bench.

DNB; *Clarke Papers*; Ludlow; Thurloe, *SP*; Abbott; Barnard; Wedgwood, *CKC*; Firth & Davies; Firth & Rait; *ST*; *CSPD*, *Comm.*; *CSPI*, *passim*; *HMC*, 7:123; M. Cotterell, 'Interregnum Law Reform: the Hale Commission of 1652,' *EHR*, 83:689-704; Woolrych; A.W. McIntosh, 'The Numbers of the English Regicides,' *History* 67: 195-216.

R. Zaller

TOMLINSON, William (fl. 1653-1696)

Quaker, was one of the more radical members of the early movement, but one about whom we know tantalizingly little. A former Separatist preacher, possibly the William Tomlinson admitted as a sizar to Trinity Coll., Camb. in 1632, and, as all the evidence suggests, a North Riding man, he was probably converted in 1653 during the sect's early activity in Yorkshire. He may have been the man who was dismissed from the army in 1650 on ideological grounds, and who was trying unsuccessfully for readmission during the heady days of 1659. He was almost certainly the man whom George Fox* contemplated placing in charge of a Quaker school of language and herbalism. Ten of Tomlinson's tracts appeared in print. They include *Word of Reproof* (1653) and *Seven Particulars* (1657). The latter tract sounds a note of Winstanley-like radicalism that is rare among Quakers: 'Woe to the oppressors of the earth, who grind the faces of the poor, who rack and stretch out their rents till the poor with all the sweat of their brows and hard labor can scarce get bread to eat.' Great families, Tomlinson suggested, were founded on 'tyranny, cruelty [and] oppression.' His later writing was too radical for the increasingly conservative Quaker hierarchy. During the 1670s and 1680s six potential tracts were either 'corrected,' 'considerably altered,' or 'laid by' by the Monthly Meeting.

Al. Cant.; Braithwaite, *BQu*; Davies, *RC*; Cadbury. Papers: LF.

B.G. Reay

TONG (or Tonge), Thomas (d. 1662)

Plotter and republican, served in the English military as an ensign and captain prior to becoming a distiller and tobacco merchant at Tower Ditch, London. In 1662 he became involved in a plot (which now bears his name, though he denied conception or leadership) to restore a republican government. Charles II, the Dukes of York and Albemarle, and Sir Richard Brown were to be assassinated (either in Whitehall Palace or en route to Greenwich), the Tower assaulted, and Windsor Castle seized by friendly forces within. A declaration was to be issued opposing bishops and the Book of Common Prayer and supporting liberty of conscience. Government agents uncovered the plot in which a host of radicals, including Edmund Ludlow,* Anthony Palmer,* Nathaniel Strange,* Col. Robert Danvers* and Philip

Nye* were allegedly involved, though the government lacked evidence to prosecute them. Tong and five cohorts – Sgt. George Phillips (a London yeoman), Nathaniel Gibbs (a London feltmaker), Francis Stubbs (a London cheese merchant), John Sallers (or Sallows, a London compass maker) and James Hind (a ship's gunner from London) – were found guilty of high treason at the Old Bailey on 11 Dec. 1662. Tong had confessed, but at the trial pleaded not guilty and repudiated the confession on the grounds that it was extorted through threat of the rack. The six were sentenced to be hung, castrated, drawn, beheaded and quartered; the sentence was carried out on Tong, Gibbs, Phillips and Stubbs on 22 Dec., and their heads placed on poles in or near the Tower. Sallers and Hind were reprieved.

Tong had favored a republican government with a parliament and electorate composed solely of committed republicans. Parliament would be restricted to sitting no more than one year and would have no power in ecclesiastical matters. To support monarchy, a House of Lords or any form of one-man rule would be high treason. Tong conceived of the basis of power as a grand alliance of Fifth Monarchists, Levellers, Independents, Baptists, Quakers and Presbyterians.

CSPD, Chas. II, 2:541, 588, 591, 602; W. Hill, *A Brief Narrative of That Stupendous Tragedie* (1662); W.C. Abbott, 'English Conspiracy and Dissent,' *AHR*, 14:513-14; Capp, *FMM*. Papers: LPR; cf. L (Add. MS 23,904).

R.L. Greaves

TOOKEY, Job (1616-1670)

Ejected Independent minister, was born on 11 Dec. 1616, the son of Job Tookey, Vicar of St. Ives, Hunts. Tookey matriculated as a sizar from Emmanuel Coll., Camb. in 1631 and graduated B.A. in 1635 and M.A. in 1638. After serving as chaplain to Lady Westmorland and tutor to her sons, Lord Townshend and Sir Horatio Townshend, he was appointed lecturer at St. Ives on 19 Feb. 1642, and vicar on 28 Apr. 1643. He was also Rector of St. Martin, Vintry, London, and, commencing Dec. 1648, preacher at St. Albans Abbey, a living controlled by the mayor and corporation. He organized a Congregational church during his tenure in St. Albans. On 22 Mar. 1652 Tookey, recognized as a man of 'gifts and abilities,' was appointed teacher of the Congregational church at Yarmouth, Norf. of which William Bridge* was the minister. Tookey was also town preacher at Yarmouth until ejected in 1661. Tookey and Bridge had no objections to receiving state funds as remuneration for their work as town preachers, but they rejected the corporation's proposal to levy a rate for their maintenance as contrary to the Gospel. Imprisoned very briefly, Tookey was subsequently excommunicated for recusancy. Faced with a writ *de excommunicato capiendo*, Tookey moved to Bunhill Fields, London in 1665. He died on 20 Nov. 1670. By his wife Anne he had two sons, Job (b. 10 Mar. 1650) and Jonathan, and three daughters, Rebecca, Hannah and Sarah. His will, dated 10 June 1669 at St. Giles, Cripplegate, was proved on 6 May 1671. Tookey was the compiler of an unpublished concordance to the Bible.

Al. Cant.; *Calamy Revised*; Nuttall, *VS*; PCC, Wills; Shaw; J. Brown, *History of Congregationalism . . . in Norfolk and Suffolk* (1877); Watts.

R.L. Greaves

TOPPE (or Topp, Tappe), James (d. 1661)

Baptist and millenarian, was a schoolmaster and leader of the Baptist church at Tiverton, Devon, which had been founded by 1626. Toppe married Israel, widow of the pewterer William Cockram (or Cockeram, d. 1623), sometime between 30 Sept. 1628, when she was fined 4s. as an Anabaptist under the name Israel Cockram, and 9 Feb. 1629, when she paid a fine of 4s. for her husband, Toppe. The latter paid a fine of 8s. for both of them on 14 Mar. 1629. Early the following year he wrote to the English and Dutch Mennonite church at Amsterdam. In the reply, dated 13 Sept. 1630, the Mennonites were critical of the rejection of pacifism by the English, and they expressed their view that it was not an excommunicable offense to hear sermons by the parish clergy. Toppe and his wife responded (a Dutch translation of their letter was made on 5 June 1631), asserting that the parish clergy were 'false prophets' and those who listened to them deserved excommunication. They also blamed the Dutch for the failure of the two groups to unite. Sometime after this Toppe was taken before the High Commission and subjected to a 'long and tedious imprisonment' in Newgate, London, during which he frequently petitioned for release, but apparently refused to take the required oath. He petitioned again on 7 Aug. 1639, offering to post bail, and was subsequently released. On 30 Jan. 1640, however, the High Commission ordered him to appear before the end of the term in March or be attached. Historians have suggested that the John Fort of Tiverton fined £500 by the High Commission on 17 Oct. 1639 for Anabaptism was really Toppe, but this is erroneous since Fort was a clothier.

Sometime prior to 1647 Toppe wrote, at the request of a friend, a 'few lines to prove Christ's monarchical reign over all the kingdoms of this world.' With John Archer's* *The Personall Reigne of Jesus Christ upon Earth* (1642), his work was attacked by Leonard Busher* in Delft. No millenarian, Busher refuted the idea that Christ would reign in person, for he was the sovereign of a heavenly kingdom. Toppe retorted in 'Christs Monarchicall and Personall Reigne uppon Earth' (1648?), asserting that 'Christ shall reign over all the kingdoms of this world . . . during the time of 1000 years and more, to begin after his second and next coming.' Relying on Daniel and Revelation, he contended that the Jews would soon return to Palestine and rebuild the Temple, only to be driven out. Returning again, they would be threatened by the Turks, but Christ would reappear to save them and usher in the millennium.

Toppe died in 1661 and his will was proved on 3 July. An inventory of his goods totalled £23 4s. 10d. His heirs were his daughter, Mary Hawkey, and his step-daughter and sole executrix, Abigail Saunders.

W.H. Burgess, 'James Toppe and the Tiverton Anabaptists,' *TBHS*, 3:193-211; *TBHS*, 3:3-5; Burrage; B. Evans, *The Early English Baptists*, 2 vols. (1862-64). Papers: L (Sloane MS 63, ff. 36-57); Mennonite Archives, Amsterdam (MS B.1377).

R.L. Greaves

TOWSE, John (d. 1645)

City radical, was enrolled in the Honorable Artillery Company from 1615, and a member of the Grocers' Company from at least 1627. He held neither municipal nor company office until joining the Common Council in 1639, though he was rated one of the wealthiest men in his ward. He rose rapidly thereafter. In June 1640 he was elected sheriff as the candidate of the Common Hall, and from Nov. 1640 until his death in 1645 was alderman for Cripplegate. In 1642 he was elected to the Militia Committee and made colonel of the Orange Regiment of the trained bands. He gave evidence against Sir Richard Gurney, the deposed Lord Mayor, and was apparently a candidate to succeed him. Towse was one of the most prominent parliamentary financiers, both giving and raising large sums. He was one of the four collectors of taxes and loans appointed by Parliament, and a treasurer for the Irish loan, the weekly assessments, and the collection of money and plate. In 1643 he was appointed Excise Commissioner, and with his fellow commissioners had raised £14,000 by the end of 1644. He was one of the sponsors of the Remonstrance of 30

Mar. 1643, which declared the sovereign power to lie in the people and their representatives in Parliament. Towse died at Hampstead on 28 May 1645, leaving a much-depleted estate of £4250.

Pearl; Firth & Rait; *CJ*, 3:330, 362, 442, 465, 618, 868. Papers: LSH (Rivers 74).

R. Zaller

TRAPNEL, Anna (fl. 1642-1660)

Fifth Monarchist, was the daughter of a pious London shipwright, William Trapnel, of Poplar, Stepney and possibly the sister of Ursula Adman,* another Fifth Monarchist. Trapnel later maintained that she did not understand her first visions at age nine because, as an Anglican, she still labored under the false doctrine of works. In her late teens she began attending various Puritan congregations, including John Simpson's* church in 1642. In 1645, after her parents' death, she became a house companion to a Mrs. Harlow in the Minneries, Aldgate. It was probably in the summer of 1646 that she had what she described as her first true visions while under a high fever and following a bout with Satan. Soon afterwards she was reported as one of the witnesses to the miraculous 53-day trance of Sarah Wight in 1647. By now she was having visions, including political prophecies, on a regular basis. In 1647 Trapnel left Mrs. Harlow and moved in with a relative, Mrs. Wythe, on Fenchurch Street. Meanwhile her struggle with 'legalism' came to an end. Embracing the covenant of grace, she joined Simpson's Baptist congregation in 1650, and after a brief involvement with the Familists in 1652, became a champion of Fifth Monarchy ideas.

By 1654 Trapnel was a public personality. On 7 Jan. 1654, while accompanying Vavasor Powell* to an examination at Whitehall, she fell into a twelve-day trance; she lay in bed with 'her eyes shut, her hands fixed,' and delivered a series of visions in verse of the coming Kingdom of Christ coupled with a denunciation of Cromwell for his 'great pomp and revenue, while the poor are ready to starve.' Two accounts of what transpired at Whitehall appeared in 1654, *The Cry of a Stone* and *Strange and Wonderful News*. Visitations during the trance by some notables, including Col. William Sydenham* and Thomas Allen,* brought the Trapnel phenomenon to the attention of the newspapers and of Cromwell himself. Since her attacks on the Protector were somewhat muted at this point, no action was taken against Trapnel until Simpson's congregation sent her on a propaganda mission to Cornwall. Her activities in the west aroused both the local clergy and the central government; she was arrested on 23 Mar., imprisoned in Plymouth, transferred to Portsmouth, and then to Bridewell before being released on 26 July. These experiences were set forth that summer in two tracts, *Legacy for Saints* and *Anna Trapnel's Report and Plea*. Despite her earlier commitment to believer's baptism, only now was she formally baptized. Late the next year she made a second sojourn to Cornwall, ostensibly to visit the imprisoned John Carew.* Summoned before the local JPs, she was unable to appear because of another trance. Trapnel escaped arrest this time, but her mission was reported as being unsuccessful and she may have contemplated migrating to America. Another source of disappointment was that during her absence (Dec. 1656 to May 1657) a split occurred within Simpson's church.

These reverses were the backdrop to what proved to be a trance of monumental proportions and perhaps support an earlier view that she was 'of a troubled mind.' For some ten months, from Oct. 1657 to Aug. 1658, lying in bed and sustained only by a daily 'little small beer' and an occasional piece of toast, she poured forth a torrent of prophecies in a series of fifty-odd sessions that are recorded in two works, *Voice for the King of Saints* (1658) and a thousand-page folio with a missing title-page now in the Bodleian Library. In addition to her continued criticism of the Protectorate, these works also attacked the Quakers,

Ranters and the recent Vennerite plotters. Trapnel was herself attacked in print in 1660, but there is no further confirmed record of her activities.

C. Burrage, 'Anna Trapnel's Prophecies,' *EHR*, 26:526-35; Capp, *FMM*; Woolrych; *CSPD, Comm.*, 6-7 *passim*; *Mercurius Politicus*, 312 (29 May-5 June 1656); *Several Proceedings*, 225 (12-19 Jan. 1654); Hill, *WTUD*. Papers: O.

A. Cohen

TRAPP, John (1601-1669)

Puritan minister, was born at Croome d'Abitot, Worcs. on 5 June 1601, the son of Nicholas Trapp of Kempsey, Worcs. He was probably educated by his uncle Simon Trapp, Vicar of Stratford-upon-Avon, as well as by John Ballam, pastor of Evesham, and then as a king's scholar at the free school at Worcester. He matriculated at Christ Church, Oxf. on 15 Oct. 1619, proceeding B.A. on 28 Feb. 1622 and M.A. on 17 June 1624. Trapp returned to the Worcester school as usher to the headmaster in 1622 and on 2 Apr. 1624 succeeded him; on 29 June he married Anne or Mary Gibbard, by whom he had eleven children. He continued his duties with the Worcester school until 1638 and also conducted occasional services at the chapel at Luddington, where he was presented to the living by Edward Lord Conway in 1636. In 1637 he published his first work, *God's Love Tokens*, dedicated to Anne, Countess of Middlesex, and in 1639 was presented to the vicarage of Weston-on-Avon, Glos., two miles from Stratford, by the Earl of Middlesex, where he remained until 1662. Trapp adhered to the parliamentary cause and took the Covenant in 1643; he was roughly handled when royalist troops occupied the area. Subsequently he served for two years as chaplain to the parliamentary garrison at Stratford. In 1646 he was given the rectory of Welford, where he was opposed by the ejected royalist minister, Dr. Bowen, who regained his post in 1660. Trapp was also an assistant to the Triers and Ejectors of Warwickshire. He was not ejected in 1662. Trapp's major work was his series of biblical commentaries, the first set of which, the *Exposition of St. John the Evangelist*, appeared in 1646; they were collected as *Annotations upon the Old and New Testaments*, beginning in 1662. A new edition was published in the nineteenth century, with a brief life prefixed to the third volume. Trapp was also noted as a preacher. He died on 17 Oct. 1669 and was buried in the church at Weston-on-Avon, leaving an estate of £116. Among his children were Joseph (1638-1698), whose son was professor of poetry at Oxford, and John (1635-1684), who succeeded Trapp as vicar.

DNB; A.B. Grosart, ed., *A Commentary on the Old and New Testaments* (1867-68); *Al. Oxon.*; *Fasti Oxon.*

R. Zaller

TRASKE (or Trask), John (1585-1636)

Sectary, was born in Somerset where he taught school and was ordained about 1611. He was a preacher at Axminster, Devon, before leaving for London about 1615. Royal intervention allegedly procured his preferment in a London church, perhaps because he offered James I a miraculous cure for the gout. His congregation was, however, virtually independent of the established church, and soon began to adhere literally to Old Testament prescriptions. Traske considered himself a second Elias whose mission was to unmask the Antichrist. He insisted on the necessity of fulfilling the entire Jewish law and demanded strict observance of the sabbath, including a ban on lighting fires and cooking. A true minister, in his judgment, was incapable of teaching error. Traske laid his hands on four disciples, including Hamlet Jackson and Returne Hebdon, to proselytize for him. In 1617 his Hebraic views led to imprisonment by the High Commission. When he refused to recant, he was summoned before Star Chamber in June 1618, where he was degraded from the ministry and sentenced to be whipped, placed in the pillory, branded with a 'J' (for Jew), fined £1000 and imprisoned for life. Not content with this, Lancelot Andrewes preached a sermon against him.

Traske finally recanted in 1620 before the High Commission and in *A Treatise of Libertie from Judaisme*, though his second wife Dorothy (née Coome; m. Feb. 1617) refused to submit and remained in prison. By 1623 Traske had become a preacher at Tillingham, Essex, but in 1627 he was again embroiled in controversy. After the execution of Joshua Purcas, a sectary accused of rape, a request was made for Traske to preach the funeral sermon, but in the charged atmosphere Bishop Montaigne refused permission and subjected Traske to an examination on 9 Aug. Suspended and imprisoned, Traske petitioned Laud on 13 June 1629, admitting he had erred and claiming he had already confessed his earlier Hebraic errors in print and in the pulpit. He was, he claimed, not a person prone to rail at bishops. In the 1630s Traske, again free, adopted Antinomian views and joined the Jacob*-Lathrop* congregation in London. He died in 1636.

Dorothy Traske was still in the Gatehouse prison in 1645 for refusing to recant her sabbatarian views. Convinced that borrowing and begging were curses, she refused all gifts in prison. An ascetic, she was a vegetarian and drank only water, and even refused to cohabit with her husband while they were imprisoned together. Paul Best* ultimately converted her to his views about 1645, and she died shortly thereafter.

CSPD, Chas. I, 2:278, 281, 289; 3:576; 7:121; 14:466-67; 21:549; E. Pagitt, *Heresiography* (1661 ed.); W.T. Whitley, 'Trask in the Star Chamber,' *TBHS*, 5:8-12; B.R. White, 'John Traske (1585-1636) and London Puritanism,' *TCHS*, 20:223-33; Whiting, 314-16; D.S. Katz, *Philo-Semitism and the Readmission of the Jews to England* *1603-1655* (1982). Papers: LPR; O (Rawl. MS. C. 303, f. 38).

R.L. Greaves

TRAVERS, Rebecca (1609-1688)

Quaker. Travers, the daughter of apparently zealous Puritans, was the wife of a Watling St. tobacconist, William Travers, and an active Baptist at the time of the first Quaker incursion into London in 1654. Like many other women she was attracted to a creed which offered her sex that measure of equality denied by most sects and by society in general. Unlike most of her co-religionists (and indeed her husband who also became a Quaker) she attained a prominent position in the movement. James Nayler* was responsible for her conversion in London in the mid-1650s. After the Restoration she issued an uncharacteristically non-pacifist warning against the implementation of the Conventicle Act: 'I say unto you, remember what the Prophet said, *If God speak war, who can speak peace?*' Yet she became a dependable member of the sect's organizational establishment, siding with George Fox* against John Perrot* and other schismatics, playing an active role in women's meetings and the Six Weeks Meeting (a disciplinary committee of 'grace and ancient' Friends), and occasionally acting with the sect's self-imposed board of censors, the Morning Meeting, which frequently met at her home. She wrote seven pamphlets as well as some verse and prefaces to two of Nayler's tracts. She died intestate and apparently in debt in London on 15 June 1688.

J. Whiting, *Persecution Expos'd* (1715); Besse; R. Travers, *This Is for All* (1664); Fox, *CJ* and *SJ*; Braithwaite, *BQu*. Papers: LF; LG (MSS 9051/15; 9053/16).

B.G. Reay

TREBY, Sir George (1643-1700)

Parliamentary radical, MP 1677, 1679[1], 1679[2], 1681, 1689, 1690 (Plympton). Born in Plympton, Devon, the son of Peter Treby and his wife Joan, Sir George Treby enjoyed a political and legal career which placed him squarely in opposition to the late Stuart Kings. He began his legal education at the Middle Temple in 1663 and his political career in 1677, when he was returned to Parliament for Plympton. He held this seat, with the exception of the 1685 Parliament, until his elevation to the bench in 1692.

Treby's radicalism was evident early, Shaftesbury* considering him 'thrice worthy.' A vigorous supporter of exclusion, he served in the three Exclusion Parliaments, where he was named to more than thirty committees, including the one charged with formulating the Bill of Exclusion. Treby defended exclusion by reminding the House of the massacres of Protestants in France, the persecutions under Mary Tudor and the threat of foreign invasions. As he put it, to oppose exclusion was 'in plain English, to have our throat cut.'

Probably in an attempt to mollify his opposition, Treby was appointed Recorder of London in Dec. 1680 and knighted in Jan. 1681. In 1683 he defended the city's charter in the *quo warranto* proceedings. He based his learned and lengthy presentation on the doctrine of prescription: the commonalty, citizens and Mayor of London were 'a body politic time out of mind,' whose customs and privileges were confirmed by acts of Parliament and charters. Moreover, he insisted on the high power of Parliament: the King alone could not dissolve a corporation. Such an action must be accomplished by Parliament.

That Treby subscribed to the doctrine of coordination, which placed legal sovereignty in King, Lords and Commons, and not in the King alone, appears likely from his service as counsel for the defense in the trial of the seven bishops (1688). Here the royal dispensing and suspending powers were successfully attacked on the ground that the legislative power was in the King, Lords and Commons jointly and that, therefore, the King possessed no power of dispensing with or suspending statutes. On the contrary, Treby asserted that laws must be suspended or dispensed with by the authority which made them, namely Parliament.

Active in promoting the cause of the Prince of Orange, Treby once again accepted the recordership of London (Dec. 1688) which he had relinquished following the *quo warranto* proceedings. He figured prominently in the making of the revolution settlement, serving in the Convention Parliament and being named to sixty committees. His most important assignments included serving as the first chairman of the committee which prepared the Declaration of Rights and serving on the committee dealing with the Oaths of Supremacy and Allegiance and the Coronation Oath. In the debates over the settlement, Treby argued against the use of the word 'deserted,' insisting that James II's actions constituted abdication.

Treby's service to William and Mary was duly rewarded. In 1689 he was named Solicitor General and then Attorney General, in which latter capacity he carried the Declaration of Rights to the Lords on 9 May 1689. Named Chief Justice of Common Pleas in 1692, he frequently replaced Somers as Speaker of the House of Lords during the latter's illnesses (1695-1700). Treby died in Dec. 1700 and was buried in Temple Church. Married four times, he was survived by a son from each of his last two marriages.

ST, 8, 10; B.D. Henning, ed., 'Draft Biographies for the History of Parliament Trust, 1660-1690;' M. Landon, *The Triumph of the Lawyers* (1970); L.G. Schwoerer, *The Declaration of Rights, 1689* (1981); *DNB*. Papers: L (Add. MSS; Harg. MSS).

J. Greenberg

TRENCHARD, Sir John (1640-1695)

Parliamentary radical, MP 1679-80, 1681 (Taunton), 1689 (Dorchester), 1690 (Poole); Secretary of State (1692-94). Trenchard was born at Lytchett Matravers, near Poole, on 30 Mar. 1640 and graduated from New Coll., Oxf. on 15 Aug. 1665. In Nov. 1682 Trenchard married Philippa Speke, daughter of George Speke. Their union produced seven children, including four sons. Although Trenchard played no major role in the actual revolution of 1688, he managed to secure the goodwill of William III and was subsequently knighted, made Chief Justice of Chester, and in 1692 appointed Secretary of State. Sir John died on 27 Apr. 1695 after a year of failing health.

Trenchard entered Parliament in 1679 and promptly associated himself with the Exclusionist faction. He became intimately linked with such revolutionaries as Aaron Smith* and Hugh Speke,* and, as a member of the Green Ribbon Club, actively sought anti-Catholic legislation. In Nov. 1680 Trenchard brought before Parliament the first Exclusion Bill, which maintained that the Crown was subject to statute law and that Parliament could legally ignore the hereditary claims of James.

With the dissolution of the Oxford Parliament in 1681 he joined the Rye House plotters. When the time came to act, however, Trenchard's pusillanimity became a source of great amusement among the conspirators. In July 1683 he was arrested for his involvement in the plot, but charges against him were dropped when Lord William Russell* refused to give evidence against him. Fearing the possibility of rearrest, Trenchard spent two years on the Continent in exile and returned to England only when assured of a pardon through the office of William Penn.*

DNB; L. von Ranke, History of England, 4-6 (1875); T.B. Macaulay, History of England 4 (1858); Lacey; Jones, FW; Trench; Earle; J.B. Burke, A Genealogical History of the Dormant . . . and Extinct Peerages (1831), 4; H. Horwitz, Parliament, Policy and Politics in the Reign of William III (1977). Papers: L (Add. MSS).

W.M. Bledsoe

TREVOR, Sir John (d. 1673)

Parliamentary radical, MP 1621 (Denb.), 1624, 1625 (Flint), 1628 (Great Bedwin), LP 1640 (Grampound), 1654 (Arundel), 1656 (Steyning), 1659. He was the son of John Trevor of Trevalyn, Denb. and Margaret, daughter of Hugh Trevanion of Cornwall. Trevor was admitted to Queens' Coll., Camb. on 13 May 1612, and entered the Inner Temple in 1613. In 1619 he was knighted and in that same year married Anne, eldest daughter of Edmund Hampden of Buckinghamshire, one of the five knights imprisoned for opposing the forced loan prior to the Petition of Right, and a relative of John Hampden.*

Sir John had close contacts with the Court until 1639 when he evinced some reluctance to accompany the King to the north. He probably obtained his seat in the Long Parliament through his Cornish relatives and was closely associated with John Hampden. An ardent Presbyterian, Trevor was a patron of Stephen Marshall* who dedicated his The Sinne of Hardnesse of Heart (1648) to him. Though not himself secluded, his son John was, and Trevor protested Pride's purge, absenting himself from Parliament until 28 June 1649. Thereafter, however, he was an active Rumper and a strong supporter of Herbert Morley.* He sat in Cromwell's first and second Parliaments, was a member of the Council of State in 1651 and 1652 and advocated the crown for Cromwell. He sat in Richard Cromwell's* Parliament, and then supported the Restoration.

Trevor was a part owner of the Newcastle coal farm and lost his position as surveyor of Windsor Great Park. He was an example of a Parliamentarian whose business interests tempered his political loyalties.

His son, Sir John Trevor the younger (1626-1672), was elected for Flintshire to the Long Parliament in 1646. He later sat in the Convention and Cavalier parliaments and bought a Secretaryship of State. He showed Nonconformist leanings during the Restoration. He also served Charles II during the conduct of diplomatic relations with France but seems to have been uninformed on the King's intentions in diplomacy. His wife was Ruth Hampden, fourth daughter of John Hampden.

Chamberlain; Keeler; B. & P.; *DNB*; MacCormack; Underdown, *PP*; Worden. Papers: L (Add. MSS).

W.L. Fisk

TRYON, Thomas (1634-1703)

Sectary, was born on 6 Sept. 1634 at Bibury, Glos., the son of the tiler and plasterer William Tryon and his wife Rebeccah. Tryon's religious visions commenced about the age of six. While apprenticed to a London hatter Tryon adopted his master's Baptist convictions, about 1654. After reading astrological and medical works he gave up his Baptist associations for a life of mystical asceticism about 1657. His diet was vegetarian and he drank only water. Fasting and silence were deemed important, and he manifested a preference for country living, a distaste for smoking and drugs, and an abhorrence of war. He hoped, without success, to establish a society of ascetics known as 'The Society of Clean and Innocent Lives,' for which he drew up rules mandating strict observance of the sabbath, pacifism, the wearing of veils in public by females over seven, nine-hour workdays, and the rejection of plays, romances and love songs. His followers were not to eat meat or fish or even cook in vessels used for the preparation of meat. It was also forbidden to use animal skins for

gloves, shoes and saddles. Women were required to forbear doing all heavy or dirty work, including labor in the fields. Tryon married in 1661, but his wife Susanna did not share his religious convictions. Subsequent to his marriage he visited Barbados as part of his mercantile concerns. His interests in astrology, alchemy and asceticism are reflected in his numerous writings, beginning with *The Way to Health, Long Life, and Happiness* in 1682, and including subsequent works on education, Pythagorean philosophy, dreams and visions, diet and health. Before his death at Hackney on 21 Aug. 1703, he had composed personal memoirs covering all but the last two decades of his life.

Some Memoirs of the Life of Mr. Tho. Tryon (1705); *DNB*; Whiting, pp. 310-14.

R.L. Greaves

TUTCHIN, John (1661?-1707)

Pamphleteer, claimed to have been born in London and was probably the grandson of Robert Tutchin, a Presbyterian minister of the Isle of Wight, who was ejected with his three sons in 1662. He was educated at a free school in Lymington and at the Stepney academy. At the age of 25 on 30 Sept. 1686 he was licensed in London to marry Elizabeth, daughter of John Hickes,* a Presbyterian minister.

In 1685 Tutchin began both his literary career with a volume of poems and his Whig activism by participating in Monmouth's rebellion. He joined with Titus Oates and John Dunton in publishing several versions of a work generally known as 'The Bloody Assizes,' which contained a false account of his trial and sentencing by Judge Jeffreys. His eulogies of William III in *An Heroick Poem* (1689) and Archbishop John Tillotson in *A Congratulatory Poem* (1691) may have earned him a government clerkship in the vitualing office, which he held until 1695 when he was unable to support a charge of corruption against his superiors. In 1696 Tutchin published *A Pindarick Ode in Praise of Folly and Knavery*; thereafter he may have served for a time in the army in Ireland. Back in London by the summer of 1700, he published *The Foreigners*, a poem attacking the King and his Dutch connections. He was soon arrested and several responses were published, including *The True-born Englishman* by Daniel Defoe,* who later became Tutchin's ally in assaulting high-church policies. In Nov. 1701 Tutchin published *The British Muse*, a satire of recent elegies of James II, and two months later he wrote *The Mouse Grown a Rat* in defense of William Fuller, who later accused Tutchin of instigating a plot to discredit the King and members of the government. From 1 Apr. 1702 Tutchin published *The Observator*, which after the first eight weekly issues appeared twice a week until his death in 1707. Consistently advocating Whig policies, he bitterly and satirically attacked the Tories, high-churchmen, the government and the immorality of the day. Between 1702 and 1707 over sixty pamphlets were directed against him and Defoe. He was threatened with prosecution no less than three times in 1703, and in Jan. 1704 he fled to the country in the face of a warrant and a reward for his arrest on the charge of seditious libel against an MP. Tutchin subsequently surrendered and was tried and convicted; however, an appeal on legal technicalities led to his release. He probably wrote *A Letter of Advice to a Friend in London* (1704) and *The Hog Toss'd in a Blanket* (1705), both defending the freedom of the press against government suppression. In Feb. 1707 he was attacked by six men in a public house and severely beaten, but his death in September of that year, while in prison for debt, was apparently unrelated to those injuries. Tutchin contributed significantly both to early English journalism and the freedom of the press to criticize the government without prosecution for libel.

G. Cambell, *Impostor at the Bar* (1961); L.S. Horsley, 'The Trial of John Tutchin, Author of the *Observator*,' *Yearbook of English Studies*, ed. T.J.B. Spencer, 3:124-40; Horsley, 'Rogues or Honest Gentlemen: the Public Characters of Queen Anne Journalists,' *Texas Studies in Literature and Language*, 18:198-228; J.G. Muddiman, *The Bloody Assizes* (1929); Keeton; J.P. Kenyon, *Revolution Principles* (1977).

J.C. Biddle

TWYN, John (d. 1664)

Bookseller, was of Smithfield. He took up his freedom on 4 Sept. 1640, and operated a small press at Cloth Fair. In 1663 Twyn was approached, probably through Elizabeth Calvert,* to print 'A Treatise of the Execution of Justice.' This tract, timed to coincide with a general rising in London and the north on 12 Oct., called upon the saints to sell their garments and buy swords with which to execute justice upon judges and magistrates as well as the House of Stuart. It was seized in press on 9 Oct. by Sir Roger L'Estrange; no complete copy remains. The plot was easily suppressed, some thirty to forty armed men being captured at Farnley Wood near Leeds. Twyn was tried for high treason at the Old Bailey on 20 Feb. 1664, the chief witnesses against him being his apprentice Joseph Walker, a printer, Thomas Mabb, and L'Estrange. At the trial Twyn also confessed to having printed *Mene Tekel* at the alleged instance of Giles Calvert,* a tract asserting popular sovereignty and the right of rebellion. Twyn was offered his life in return for information about his fellow conspirators, but he refused and was accordingly executed at Tyburn on 24 Feb.

Plomer, *DBP*; J.G. Muddiman, *The King's Journalist* (1923); Ashley, *JW*; *An Exact Narrative of the Tryal and Condemnation of John Twyn* (1664); *ST*.

R. Zaller

TYRRELL, James (1642-1718)

Whig pamphleteer and historian, was born on 5 May 1642 in Great Queen Street, St. Giles-in-the-Fields, Middlesex, the eldest son of Sir Timothy Tyrrell of Shotover, near Oxford, and Elizabeth, only daughter and heiress of James Ussher, Archbishop of Armagh. Tyrrell was educated in the free school at Cumberwell, Surrey. He was admitted to Gray's Inn on 7 Jan. 1656, and on 15 Jan. 1657 he matriculated from Queen's Coll., Oxf., from which he proceeded M.A. on 28 Sept. 1663. Tyrrell was called to the bar from the Inner Temple in 1666 but did not practice, settling instead on his estate at Oakley, near Brill, Bucks., where he served as a JP and DL until removed from office in 1687 by James II for refusing to subscribe to the Declaration of Indulgence. Later he moved to Shotwell within access to the libraries at Oxford. He died on 7 June 1718, and was buried in Oakley Church. Tyrrell married Mary, daughter of Sir Michael Hutchinson of Fladbury, Worcs. on 18 Jan. 1670; their son, James (d. 1742) rose to the rank of lieutenant-general in the army and was MP for Boroughbridge from 1722 until his death.

Tyrrell's first important publication, *Patriarcha non monarcha, or the Patriarch Unmonarched* (1681), was a refutation of the absolutist theories of Sir Robert Filmer. Like Locke,* Sidney* and Richard Hunt, who also entered the lists against Filmer, Tyrrell rejected the latter's attempt to derive monarchy from the succession of Adam, as well as his analogy between paternal and political authority. To equate these forms of authority was to confuse the proper distinction between the 'economical' and 'civil' functions of society, a point Tyrrell elaborated on in his later *Bibliotheca politica*. Even in families, obedience to fathers was 'not merely natural, from generation, but acquired by their performance of that nobler part of their duty.' Moreover, while the dependence of children made their subjection to parental authority inevitable, it by no means followed that men must be similarly subject to their governments. Political authority was rooted in consent: 'a man without his own act or consent can never lawfully fall into the power or possession of another.'

Tyrrell's critique of Filmer won high praise from William Atwood* in 1690: 'The difference between a patriarchal and a monarchical authority is so well stated and proved by my learned friend, Mr. Tyrrell, that few besides the unknown author of the two late *Treatises of Government* [i.e., Locke] could have gained reputation after him. . . .' Between 1691 and 1694 Tyrrell published a series of thirteen dialogues between Meanwell, a Tory, and Freeman, a Whig, later collected under the title *Bibliotheca politica* (1718, second ed. 1727, repr. 1973). Fair and judicious in tone, it is a veritable compendium of Whig opinion on the major legal and constitutional questions of the day. Tyrrell's defense of the Glorious Revolution is cautious. An advocate of limited monarchy, he preferred to compare 1689 to 1660 rather than 1641. This was a far cry from the theoretical boldness of his friend and mentor Locke; but it is easy to forget how insecure the revolution still appeared in the early 1690s, and such moderate justifications also served the turn. In 1692 Tyrrell published *A Brief Disquisition of the Laws of Nature*, a translation and abridgement of Richard Cumberland's *De legibus naturae disquisitio philosophica*. His purpose here – a common project with Locke, Sidney and Matthew Tindal* as well – was to refute the Hobbesian denial of a common interest in society. Each man, Tyrrell asserted, seeks his own happiness, which by knowledge of his own nature he may understand and achieve. Since all men share a common nature, it is possible to deduce 'what things or actions will conduce not only to our own happiness and preservation but to all others of the same kind.' Private happiness and public welfare were therefore compatible, 'the chief and necessary medium to the common good' being 'the constitution of a distinct property in things, in the labors of persons.'

Tyrrell set himself as his *magnum opus* a

General History of England, Both Ecclesiastical and Civil, which he intended both as a vindication of the authority of the House of Commons and a refutation of Robert Brady's royalist *History*. Three volumes appeared between 1696 and 1704, but the project, which he meant to bring down to his own time, got no further than Richard II. Among his other works were a dedication to Charles II affixed to Ussher's *Power Communicated by God to the Prince* (1661), a vindication of Ussher in Parr's *Life of Archbishop Ussher* (1686), and a translation of *Toxaris, or a Dialogue of Friendship* by Lucian of Samosata (1711). Not an original thinker, Tyrrell was nonetheless a representative one, and one of the important Whig scholars and polemicists of his generation.

DNB; J.W. Gough, 'James Tyrrell, Whig Historian and Friend of John Locke,' *HJ*, 19:581-610; J. Daly, *Sir Robert Filmer and English Political Thought* (1979); J.H. Franklin, *John Locke and the Theory of Sovereignty* (1978); J.A.W. Gunn, *Politics and the Public Interest in the Seventeenth Century* (1969); C. Robbins, *The Eighteenth Century Commonwealthsman* (1959); G.J. Schochet, *Patriarchalism in Political Thought* (1975); E.S. de Beer, ed., *The Correspondence of John Locke* (1976-); M. Cranston, *John Locke* (1957). Papers: O.

R. Zaller

V

VACHELL (or Vachel), Tanfield (1601-1658)

Parliamentary County Commissioner, was born in 1601, the only son of John Vachell (d. 1640) of Burghfield, Berks. and his wife Mary, daughter of Clement Vincent of Peckleton, Leics. He matriculated at Exeter Coll., Oxf. on 17 Dec. 1619, graduated B.A. on 27 June 1622, and was admitted to Lincoln's Inn on 21 Mar. 1633. His uncle, Sir Thomas Vachell of Coley, having been predeceased by his two sons, made Tanfield his heir, but protracted lawsuits followed Sir Thomas' death in 1638. His widowed aunt, Lettice, married John Hampden* in 1641. Vachell served as High Sheriff of Berkshire (1641-45), but when ordered in Nov. 1642 to raise the county for the King, he refused and declared for Parliament. On 1 Apr. 1643 he was appointed one of the sequestrators of royalist estates in Berkshire, and from 27 June 1644 served on the County Committee, but his collection of pictures, books and curios proved his major preoccupation in these years. He was returned MP for Reading after a disputed recruiter election in 1645 but did not take an active part in the Commons' proceedings and, although not secluded, ceased to sit at Pride's purge. His first wife was Anne Cos (d. 1651), the widowed daughter of a city merchant, and his second, Rebecca (d. 1671), daughter of Sir William Leman, Bt.* He died without issue and was buried in St. Mary's, Reading, on 1 June 1658, his property descending to a cousin, Thomas.

B. & P.; A. Aspinall et al., Parliament through Seven Centuries (1962); I. and A.C. Vachell, A Short Account or History of the Family of Vachell (1900); G.P. Crawford, 'Vachell of Coley, Reading,' Berkshire Archaeological Society Journal, 3:2, 32, 64, 87.

K.J. Lindley

VALENTINE, Benjamin (d. 1652)

Parliamentary radical, MP 1628, LP 1640 (St. Germans). Valentine's background is obscure. His only known estate was in Cheshire, and he may have come from that county. He married Elizabeth, daughter of Matthew Springham, and had at least one son, Matthias. Valentine was a member of Sir John Eliot's* circle by 1628 when, through Eliot's influence, he was chosen as MP for St. Germans. He supported Eliot's condemnation of the Duke of Buckingham in June 1628 and, on 2 Mar. 1629, he and Denzil Holles* held Speaker Finch in his chair in order to prevent him from adjourning the House before Eliot could present a prepared statement of grievances. Valentine and the other major participants in the 2 Mar. episode were examined by the Council and committed to the Tower. Nearly a year of legal maneuvering followed before judgment was pronounced against Valentine on 12 Feb. 1630. Since he refused to make submission or acknowledgment of his offense, he remained in confinement until released in Jan. 1640. Again elected to sit for St. Germans in the Long Parliament, Valentine was appointed to the Committee of Privileges, regularly served as messenger between the House and the Lord Keeper during the first years of the Parliament, took the Protestation on 5 May 1641, pledged two horses for the defense in June 1642, took the Covenant on 25 Sept. 1643, and continued to sit after Pride's purge, but never appears to have become very active as a committee-man or speaker. Between Oct. 1644 and Jan. 1647 the House ordered several payments to be made to Valentine in reparation for his former sufferings and the loss of income from his Cheshire estate during the war.

DNB; Keeler; CJ, 1-7 passim; H. Hulme, The Life of Sir John Eliot (1957); Underdown, PP. Papers: L (Add.

MSS).

W.B. Bidwell

VALENTINE (or Valentyne), Thomas (1588-1664)

Puritan minister, was baptized at Eccles, Lancs. on 15 July 1588, the second son of Thomas Valentine, a gentleman of Bent-cliffe, Lancs. Valentine matriculated as a sizar from Christ's Coll., Camb. (Easter 1603) and graduated B.A. (1607) and M.A. (1610). He was ordained a deacon in London in Sept. 1610, appointed lecturer at the Almshouse, Watford, Herts. in 1613, and admitted to Gray's Inn on 6 Aug. 1615. Valentine was appointed Rector of Aldingham, Lancs. on 23 Aug. 1623, and instituted as Rector of Chalfont St. Giles, Bucks. on 26 July 1625. For refusing to read the Book of Sports, Valentine was suspended in Oct. 1635 by Sir John Lambe and subsequently excommunicated, but an appeal to John Williams, Bishop of Lincoln, brought absolution on 7 Oct. He had also been cited on 21 Aug. 1635 for allowing his chancel to be in a state of disrepair. Valentine continued to be the center of controversy, still refused to read the Book of Sports, and was again suspended. He petitioned Laud on 20 Dec. 1636, 3 Nov. 1637 and 11 July 1638, was supported by a petition from 28 parishioners on 18 Jan. 1637, and was finally absolved from suspension and sequestration by the Court of Arches on 13 July 1638 until the feast of St. John the Baptist.

Valentine became lecturer at Wendover, Bucks. on 17 May 1642. He preached monthly fast sermons to the Commons on 28 Dec. 1642 (*A Sermon*, 1643) and 29 Sept. 1647 (*Christs Counsell to Poore and Naked Souls*, 1647), and to the Lords on 30 Apr. 1645 and 26 May 1647 (*A Charge Against the Jews, and the Christian World*, 1647). A member of the Westminster Assembly, he was appointed Rector of St. Mary's, Whitechapel, Middlesex in 1645, and a Trier in Mar. 1654. Valentine was

ejected from his living at Chalfont St. Giles in 1662. His will, dated 28 June 1662 at Chalfont St. Giles, was proved in June 1664. He owned property in Rickmansworth, Herts. and Ireland. His legatees included a daughter, Sarah Goodall, and a son-in-law, John Hammond. Samuel Cradock* witnessed his will.

CSPD, Chas. I, 8-12 *passim*; *Calamy Revised*; PCC, Wills; Firth & Rait; *Al. Cant.*; Shaw; Wilson, *PP*. Papers: LPR.

R.L. Greaves

VANE, Sir Henry, Sr. (1589-1655)

Parliamentary radical, MP 1614 (Lostwithiel), 1621, 1624, 1626 (Carlisle), 1628 (Retford), SP, LP 1640 (Wilton), 1654 (Kent). Born on 18 Feb. 1589, the eldest son of Henry Vane of Kent, Vane attended Oxford University and Gray's Inn and was knighted in 1611. Beginning life with modest holdings, Vane acquired numerous offices of state and great wealth. According to his account, he inherited land worth only £460 p.a., but his marriage to Frances Darcy and his cultivation of well connected persons at Court like Sir Thomas Overbury led to his rapid advancement. By 1629 he acquired land in Kent for £4000 and estates in Durham for about £18,000. In addition, he continued to purchase land during the Interregnum, and in 1649 he estimated his income at £3000 p.a. One of the wealthiest members of the Long Parliament, the elder Vane was probably the richest Roundhead. Much of Vane's substantial wealth derived from his various Court positions. Starting off with the purchase of a carver's place for £5000, he then bought a one-third share of the subpoena office in Chancery. In 1625 he became co-Cofferer of the King's Household and five years later he advanced to Comptroller and was made a member of the Privy Council. In 1632 he obtained appointment as one of the Commissioners of the Admiralty and in 1636 he became one of the Commissioners for the Colonies.

Moreover, Vane frequently received special assignments of some importance, including a mission to Gustavus Adolphus of Sweden to restore the Palatinate. Although negotiations broke down, Charles I expressed satisfaction with Vane's performance. Sir Henry continued to hold the King's confidence throughout the 1630s. At the end of the decade described by the opposition as 'eleven years of tyranny,' Vane continued to be rewarded with high office. In Sept. 1639 he was made Treasurer of the Household and a few months later, in Feb. 1640, he reached his highest post, that of Secretary of State.

In all parliaments in which he sat Vane supported royal policies, earning him the reputation as 'a good King's man.' Although he managed to quarrel with the royal favorite, Buckingham, in 1624, this disagreement was resolved by Apr. 1625, and within two months Charles rewarded him with a household office. Vane's support of the King extended well into 1640 when he advanced Charles a loan (or gift) of £2000 in May and offered his bond for an equal amount to be loaned in November. More to the point, Vane acted as Charles' spokesman in the Short Parliament, informing the assembled body that the King would surrender his claim to ship money in return for twelve subsidies.

If Vane shared any of his son's Puritan sympathies he kept his beliefs well hidden. In 1634 and 1637 he attended Star Chamber proceedings against the prominent opponent of bishops, William Prynne,* and supported both the decision of the court as well as the harsh penalty administered. In 1640, when the royal court divided into two factions, one led by Strafford and the other by the Catholic Queen, Vane sided with the latter. In fact, he owed his appointment as Secretary of State to this faction. Vane's personal distaste for Wentworth may have stemmed from his resistance to efforts to reform the royal bureaucracy carried out as part of the policy of 'Thorough.' It is more likely that the main point of contention between the two men occurred when Strafford got Charles I to create him Baron Raby as his second title, an honor Vane thought should be his own, considering that he already possessed the estates belonging to the barony.

Vane's hatred of Strafford led him to testify for the prosecution during the Earl's trial; he was the only Privy Councillor to do so. Vane claimed that at a Privy Council meeting after the dissolution of the Short Parliament (5 May 1640), Strafford had advised the King to employ the Irish army 'here to reduce this kingdom,' meaning England. During the procedure devising a Bill of Attainder, John Pym* produced a second-hand copy that Sir Henry Vane, Jr.,* had made from his father's original notes of the 5 May meeting, the two original versions possessed by the Vanes allegedly having been destroyed. The elder Vane showed great annoyance at his son's betrayal of confidence, but most Royalists disbelieved these protestations.

Apparently Vane believed that Strafford's execution would improve relations between the King and Parliament and possibly serve to further his own status at Court. He judged wrongly. Charles, although determined to rid himself of Strafford's betrayer, delayed relieving him of his official positions, most likely because of the difficulty of finding reliable successors. Vane even carried out royal missions, accompanying Charles to Scotland in Aug. 1641. Three months later, however, he was dismissed from his many offices at court.

With little delay, Vane joined forces with the opposition and was appointed Lord Lieutenant of Durham as well as to various parliamentary committees, including the important Committee of Both Kingdoms in Feb. 1644. Despite the fact that he did not play a prominent role in the Long Parliament, he was held in high regard in that body. At the Uxbridge negotiations Parliament requested that he be made a baron. Sometimes identified with his more radical son, Vane repeatedly took a more moderate stance, and we find father and son in disagreement over certain issues. Vane Sr. remained hostile to the Scots throughout the period of their intervention, and the pamphlet, 'Westminster Projects' (1648), places him with the royal Independents mainly because of his anti-Scottish position. His moderation in politics was exemplified in July 1647 when he decided not to flee to the army along with other parliamentary Independents. He also favored resuming negotiations with Charles after the conclusion of the second Civil War, and as a result he was secluded by the army at Pride's purge. On 10 Feb. 1649 he took the dissent and rejoined the Rump, yet he remained one of the body's least active members. An attempt to appoint him to the Council of State in Feb. 1650 failed as he was opposed by the radicals Marten* and Ludlow.* He sat for Kent in the first Parliament of the Protectorate. Vane died in May 1655. Vane's adherence to the parliamentary cause was clearly self-interested, and in later years he was overshadowed by his eminent son. Nonetheless, his testimony against Strafford was crucial to the radical strategy in the spring of 1641, and his status as one of the highest-ranking royalist defectors conferred on him a lasting prestige.

Aylmer, *KS* and *SS*; V. Rowe, *Sir Henry Vane the Younger* (1970); Underdown, *PP*; *PSP 1640*; Keeler; *DNB*; C.V. Wedgwood, *Thomas Wentworth, First Earl of Strafford* (1961); Worden; Zagorin, *CC*. Papers: L (Add. MSS; Harl. MSS).

L. Kaplan

VANE, Sir Henry, Jr., Kt. (1613-1662)

Vane was the eldest son of the wealthy courtier-statesman, Sir Henry Vane* of Hadlow, Kent, and his wife Frances Darcy, daughter and heiress of Thomas Darcy Tolleshunt D'Arcy, Essex. Educated at Westminster School under Lambert Osbaldeston, who later defied Archbishop Laud, Vane underwent a conversion experience at the age of fourteen or fifteen which was to shape the remainder of his life. After a brief period at Magdalen Hall, Oxf., followed by a year's term as Governor of Massachusetts Bay where he supported Anne Hutchinson* in the Antinomian controversy, Vane became one of the most important figures of the English Revolution. Although knighted and then appointed joint Treasurer of the Navy by Charles I in 1639, in the 1640s he helped bring down the Earl of Strafford, worked hard for the passage of the Root and Branch Bill, led the war party in the House of Commons, modified the Solemn League and Covenant with the Scots to reflect the Independent or congregational form of church government, secured with Cromwell the passage of the Self-denying Ordinance which led to the creation of the New Model Army, and, except for one short respite, controlled the direction of naval affairs until Dec. 1650. Vane sided with the army in their quarrels with Parliament, but he strongly opposed Pride's purge and refused to participate in the execution of Charles I. In the 1650s he sat on all Commonwealth councils of state, campaigned tirelessly for religious liberty, fiercely objected to Cromwell's dissolution of the Rump Parliament, declined to serve in the Barebones Parliament, and then retired from political life to write his major works on church and state. Returning to politics in 1659, he helped engineer the overthrow of Richard Cromwell,* and served in the recalled Rump Parliament until its second dissolution by the army.

Despite the attention Vane has received from biographers and historians, certain aspects of his writings and career have remained puzzling. In his major religious work, *A Retired Mans Meditations* (1655), Vane anticipated the second coming of Christ and the rule of the saints. Yet in his major political work, *A Healing Question* (1656), he advocated a republic governed by representatives of the 'people.' Although he repeatedly condemned magistrates for pursuing 'self interests,' he himself fell victim to the same charge during his later years as Treasurer of the Navy. In addition, although Vane had supported Parliament against Charles I, Oliver Cromwell and Richard Cromwell, he upheld Lambert's* dissolution of the Rump in Oct. 1659, and participated in the military council that replaced it. In view of such seeming inconsistencies, contemporaries and later historians have varied widely in their assessments of the man. Richard Baxter called him a 'fanatic democrat,' while David Hume labeled him a 'perfect enthusiast.' Because Vane was at once a skilled administrator and diplomat, an ardent millenarian, a shrewd parliamentarian and a serious political theorist, he emerges as a compelling but enigmatic figure whose religious and political ideas resist simple classification. And yet, if one examines his writings, it becomes evident that his religious and political radicalism stemmed from his millennial view of history. From the 1630s until his death, Vane's belief in an ongoing struggle between Christ and Antichrist and his view of the saint's role during the final days inspired a commitment to religious liberty, molded his theories of government and influenced his political career.

In a general sense, Vane shared his millennial ideas with other radicals of the Puritan Revolution. Like many of his contemporaries, Vane interpreted the religious and political turmoil in England as a manifestation of the greater conflict between the forces of Christ and Antichrist. He supported Parliament against the King in part because he associated royal 'tyranny' and political corruption with Antichrist. He opposed the Cromwellian Protectorate on similar grounds. In Vane's mind, Cromwell – like Charles I – had deserted the cause of Christ and used government to serve his own interests. Even after the Restoration Vane, unlike most of the revolutionary generation, retained a strong belief that England's history signaled the triumph of Christ and his saints over Antichrist, and the advent of the millennium.

Although Vane did not fully expound his ideas on politics and the millennium until the mid-1650s, signs of his later views on these subjects were evident as early as the 1630s. In the autumn of 1635 Vane left England 'for conscience-sake' and migrated to Massachusetts Bay. There he quickly formed a close friendship with the Puritan preacher and millenarian, John Cotton.* It is unclear how much Cotton reinforced Vane's millenarianism or encouraged Vane's inclination to seek inner revelation, but when the Antinomian Anne Hutchinson was arraigned before the Massachusetts General Court in 1637, Vane immediately took the side of his fellow seeker of inner truth. Fearful of the spread of Antinomianism, the Court issued an order which prohibited all new arrivals to the colony except those approved by the magistrates. In his *Brief Answer*, Vane attacked this ruling on grounds that would become familiar to parliamentary revolutionaries of the next decade. The order, Vane declared, violated the laws of Christ and infringed upon the rights and liberties of men as English subjects. It was tyrannical and arbitrary because it left admission or exclusion to the personal discretion of the magistrates, rather than to the law of God. 'That law which gives that without limitation to man, which is proper to God,' he asserted, 'cannot be just.'

Although the broad outlines of Vane's millennial thought resembled that of other Puritan revolutionaries, many of his more specific eschatological ideas did not. Sometime before the 1640s Vane read or otherwise absorbed certain doctrines associated with Jacob Boehme. Like Boehme Vane identified three distinct periods of human history, each associated with a person of the Trinity. In each age God showered forth a special dispensation of grace, increasing man's knowledge of him. Vane believed that his own world stood on the brink of the Age of the Spirit, when through a glorious outpouring of the Holy Ghost, the church and indeed all creation would 'be restored to its primitive purity' and Christ would rule with his saints for a thousand years. Further, from this framework of progressive spiritual revelation in history, Vane propounded the notion of similar dispensations within the consciences of men in every age. It was this doctrine that formed the basis for his view of government and his demand for religious freedom.

All men, Vane argued, received one of three measures of inward light: natural, legal or evangelical. Those of the first dispensation, or with a natural conscience, encompassed heathens. They lacked knowledge of Christ but could still establish good government by following the 'right principles' or reason written in their hearts. The second group, men of a legal conscience who were saved for a time but would eventually fall away, Vane frequently called 'children of the first covenant.' They demanded adherence to form and structure in religion rather than the essence of Christ's death and resurrection. But they too could rule justly if they followed the 'pattern of Christ's natural life and perfection.' Lastly, in every age the Lord's truth was carried forth by a few men of the third or evangelical conscience. These 'children of the second covenant' represented God's chosen saints whose salvation he had determined from all eternity. They alone would inherit Christ's kingdom and rule the world with him.

Vane believed that the more 'illuminated' the magistrate's conscience, the better qualified he was to rule. Further, he fully expected that the elect would bring government near its primitive pattern in the latter days. In recognition of their superior talents and wisdom, Vane called for the rule of the saints or 'honest party.' But if he looked forward to godly rule in the last days, he nevertheless also believed that until the proper time arrived. God had given all men a set of fundamental principles through which to govern justly. Even magistracy exercised by heathens, he insisted, could please the Almighty. This was possible because either through reason, God's law or God's spirit, each individual had received the fundamental principles of government. How closely any civil authority conformed to God's perfect rule depended upon how nearly magistrates adhered to the right principles the Almighty had given them.

In setting out these right principles, Vane put forth arguments familiar to and accepted by many parliamentary – and royal – apologists of his time. He rooted government upon popular consent, insisting that 'by nature' and 'the judgment of common reason and sense' each man knew what was good, just and in conformity to God's law. Like most of his contemporaries, Vane's concept of popular consent was far from democratic. At most the 'people' consisted of the middling and upper classes, not the common rabble. Vane also considered civil obedience a Christian duty and an essential condition for the *res publica*. At the same time, he recognized the potential for tyranny in any form of government and upheld the subject's right to refuse civil commands contrary to God's law.

Perhaps uniquely among the political theorists of his time, Vane was fundamentally indifferent to the form government took. Unlike Harrington,* Hobbes* or Filmer, Vane did not believe that a particular constitution, in and of itself, would be more likely to insure popular liberties and advance the public good. Nevertheless, he clearly was convinced that God had sanctioned Parliament's cause, and for virtually all of his political life he supported parliamentary government. In justifying the Revolution after the Restoration, Vane would write that there was 'more of the wisdom and will of God in the public suffrage of the whole nation, than any private person or lesser collective body.'

At the same time that Vane preached the prime importance of 'right principles' in government, he also stressed that the saints would soon restore society to its pristine condition. Not surprisingly, therefore, he worked within the restraints of the existing political order to place government in the hands of godly men. In order to understand Vane's political changes during the 1650s, his disregard for forms and his millennial expectations must be kept in mind. The military successes of the 1640s, the abolition of episcopacy, and the establishment of a large measure of religious toleration all led Vane to support the Long Parliament and then the Commonwealth. Even though Vane opposed Cromwell's dissolution of the Rump, he nevertheless intended his *Healing Question* to lead the Lord General back to the Good Old Cause, reunite the various groups which had supported the Revolution, and restore right principles in government. Vane retained his faith in the remnant of the Long Parliament through most of the 1650s. Still, his foremost loyalty was never to that institution, but rather to the revolutionary aims the Long Parliament had espoused. When, as in Oct. 1659, Vane lost confidence in the Rump, he could turn without contradiction to the saints in the army to carry on the Good Old Cause of the Revolution.

Vane's millennial ideas not only influenced his theory of government, but also led him to demand liberty of conscience. Although he divided all mankind into three spiritual states, or dispensations, he nevertheless asserted that an individual might and often did progress from one stage of conscience to another. Like the Apostle Paul, the elect might remain hidden for a time and even work against Christ before they awakened into a higher conscience. In order for the Holy Spirit to work unhindered, Vane insisted, man's conscience must not be restrained by civil authority. Religious liberty, he declared, was 'a supreme law, sealed and confirmed in the blood of Christ unto all men.' Maintaining that the civil magistrate must not intrude into the 'office and proper concerns of Christ's inward government and rule in the conscience,' Vane argued that any violation of religious freedom infringed the sovereignty of Christ.

During the brief period in 1659 when Vane served as a member of the restored Rump, he took up the task of settling the republic upon a permanent foundation acceptable to Parliament and rooted upon right principles. Faced with demands by republicans for a popular assembly on the one hand, and calls for rule of the saints by millenarians on the other, Vane put forth a plan that embraced both ideas. In a tract entitled *A Needful Corrective or Ballance to Popular Government*, he applauded certain aspects of Harrington's bicameral model of government but attacked Harrington's proposal for broad popular suffrage. It was evident, Vane argued, that if left completely free, the 'depraved, corrupted and self-interested will' of the people inevitably led them to betray, not uphold 'their true public interest.' In light of corruptible human nature, popular government required the 'balancing and ruling motion of God's Spirit.' This 'needful corrective' could be provided by limiting the vote for at least 'a season' to visible saints or those known to be well affected to the republic.

Neither the restored Rump nor the military council that replaced it in October succeeded in establishing the just, righteous government Vane or his fellow revolutionaries sought. Nevertheless, he refused to believe that the millennium would not soon be realized. Even after 1660, as he faced imprisonment and then execution, he continued to write optimistically about the glorious victory Christ would bring to his battered, suffering saints. Vane's persistent faith in the coming millennium, in addition to his political prominence, made him look dangerous to Charles II and his advisors. As a result, Vane became the only revolutionary who had not participated in the execution of Charles I to suffer the death penalty (14 June 1662). Still, in awaiting his own death, Vane found a kind of triumph. He looked upon it as a sacrifice for the Good Old Cause of Christ, and in his last writings he confidently expected the destruction of Antichrist and the advent of the millennium.

G. Sikes, *The Life and Death of Sir Henry Vane Kt.* (1662); J. Forster, *Sir Henry Vane* (1838); J.K. Hosmer, *The Life of Young Sir Henry Vane* (1888); M.A. Judson, *The Political Thought of Sir Henry Vane the Younger* (1969); V. Rowe, *Sir Henry Vane the Younger* (1970); J.H. Adamson and H.F. Folland, *Sir Harry Vane* (1973); *DNB*; Underdown, *PP*; Worden. Papers: L (Add. MSS; Stowe MSS).

L.F. Solt and M.A. Hartman

VASSALL, Samuel (1586-1667)

Parliamentary radical, MP SP, LP 1640 (London), sec. 1648. Vassall was baptized on 5 June 1586, the son of John Vassall of Stepney, Essex, and his wife Anna Russell. Vassall's father was a sailor of French Huguenot extraction, an Alderman of London, and a commander against the Spanish Armada. Vassall was married and had at least one son. He became a member of the Drapers' Company of London in 1619, assistant (1636), and master (1645), and directed eighteen apprenticeships during his lifetime. His merchant ventures included the Levant-East India trade and the newer American market. He was an original subscriber to the Massachusetts Bay Company. Vassall was a member of the Court of Requests and Alderman of London. He evidenced early opposition to the Crown and was arrested sixteen times, e.g. for refusals to pay a forced loan (1627), to pay tonnage and poundage (1628 and 1636), and to pay ship money (1635). In Sept. 1639 his house was searched by order of the Council and incriminating papers found. In June 1640, after the dissolution of the Short Parliament, he was ordered 'committed to some prisons in remote parts for seducing the King's people,' but October saw him re-elected to Parliament for London. In Jan. 1647 the Commons voted Vassall £10,445 damages for his prior imprisonment, but he received none of the monies. An active member of the Long Parliament, Vassall served on the Committee for Plantations and Trade, the Committee of Both Kingdoms, and a committee to investigate piracy and other obstructions to the Mediterranean trade. After he took the Covenant in Sept. 1643, Vassall represented a minority of London merchants who were political Presbyterians and supporters of the peace party, but he was not a member of a Presbyterian congregation. After his removal from Parliament in 1648, Vassall fell on hard times; he claimed a debt of over £20,000 in 1654. After the Restoration he traveled to America and apparently died in Massachusetts in 1667.

Pearl; R. Brenner, 'The Civil War Politics of London's Merchant Community,' *P. & P.*, 58:53-107; D'Ewes, *Jour.* (C); Keeler; *DNB*; *CSPD*, *Chas. I*, 14:25. Papers: L (Add. MSS).

D.W. Hollis, III

VAUGHAN, Rice (fl. 1630-d. c. 1672)

Law reformer, was the son of Henry Vaughan of Machynlleth, Mont. Vaughan was admitted to Gray's Inn in Aug. 1638. His well-known *Discourse of Coin and Coinage* (1675), in J.R. McCulloch, ed., *A Select Collection of Scarce and Valuable Tracts on Money* (1856), was actually written about 1630, but published after his death by his relative Henry Vaughan. Vaughan's views on law reform are contained in two pamphlets, *A Plea for the Common Laws of England* (1651) and *Certain Proposals Humbly Presented to the Parliament* (1652). His *Plea* was an answer to the radical law reformer Hugh Peter,* who had attacked the lawyers and the common law in the tract, *A Good Work for a Good Magistrate* (1651). Vaughan had been, until the publication of Peter's work, a supporter of Peter and the law reformers. Vaughan thereupon did an about face in his *Plea*, maintaining that the common law was the best possible law because it had not been imposed on the people and that nearly all defects in the law had been eliminated by common consent. Those which remained, he asserted, could be removed by Parliament. In *Certain Proposals* Vaughan sought to convince Parliament to establish a committee or commission to assume the judicial function of the state. Parliament would thus have responsibility for and exercise of the judicial authority of the state. Furthermore, he suggested, all justice should be dispensed in public sessions according to the dictates of the Bible. Vaughan died before or in 1672, the year his guide for attorneys in Wales, *Practica Walliae*, was published posthumously.

Veall; Prall; *DNB*; Solt.

A.J. Busch

VENN (or Ven), John (1586-1650)

Regicide and parliamentary radical, MP 1641 (London). Venn pursued a political career which was remarkable for its uncompromising and unalloyed extremism. The second son of Simon Venn of Lydeard St. Lawrence, Som., whose family was of old yeoman stock, Venn was apprenticed to the Merchant Taylors' Company in 1602 and admitted to the freedom of the company in 1610. In the next thirty years he established himself as a well-to-do London merchant, trading in silk and wool, who gradually began to acquire a notable position in public life. The degree to which he immersed himself in City politics, however, and the nature of the interests he pursued, were far from typical and illuminate the direction which his parliamentary career later took.

By the time the Civil War broke out, Venn was a Warden of the Merchant Taylors' Company and had been since at least 1638 a prominent member of the Common Council of London, serving on all its major committees. He was, further, Deputy President of the Honorable Artillery Company, with which he had been associated throughout the 1630s and in which he held the rank of captain-sergeant-major. At this time too he still held shares in the Massachusetts Bay Company, of which he had been a founding member, and belonged to the congregation at All Hallows, Bread Street, long preëminent among London churches for the Puritanism of its clergy, where he had been churchwarden in 1631. Still more remarkably, it would appear, he had established a rapport with the politically alert apprentices and small shopkeepers of London so that, even before his first appearance in the Long Parliament, he had acquired a considerable reputation, thereafter carefully cultivated, as the inciter and controller of the powerful London mob (R. Chestlin, *Persecutio undecima* [1648], pp. 63-64; cf. J. Venn, *A True Relation of a Most Wise and Worthy Speech* [1641]). It was Venn who led the mob in support of Strafford's condemnation and later, while an MP, on behalf of the Grand Remonstrance. But Venn also used his influence to quell untimely demonstrations, as for example the anti-episcopal riots in Dec. 1641.

Venn's career in the Long Parliament began in June 1641, when he replaced Matthew Cradock* as one of the four members for the City of London. He played a key role in 1641-42 in bringing the Common Council and City militia of London under radical control. Even before he entered Parliament, Venn had become known as a sponsor of petitions from the London citizenry; these he now helped to fashion into a formidable instrument for the radicalism of parliamentary policy, especially with regard to ecclesiastical reform, until by 1643 he and his allies had outdistanced the coalition led by Pym,* whose interests they had served. He was one of six members who, with those charged with treason, were excepted from the King's pardon on 17 June 1642. Venn was commissioned a colonel of foot and fought at Worcester on 23 Sept. On 28 Oct. he was sent to take command of Windsor Castle, repelling a thrust by Prince Rupert on 7 Nov. and remaining as governor until 1645. On 26 Apr. 1646 he received the thanks of the Commons for his military services.

Venn was a member of many parliamentary committees in the 1640s, among them the Committee for the Sale of Bishops' Lands, and aroused antagonism for his work on the Committee for Scandalous Offenses and the Committee of Examinations (R. Chestlin, *op. cit.*, pp. 34-35; C. Walker, *The History of Independency*, pt.1 [1648], p. 53). As Governor of Windsor Castle he was alleged to have made considerable gains from plunder and pillage (C. Walker, *op. cit.*, p. 83). Venn purchased bishops' lands and early in 1648 was granted £4000 by Parliament to defray his expenses at Windsor. He was appointed to the High Court, was diligent in his attendance and signed the death warrant. In 1649 he became a Governor of Westminster School, and at the time of his death, on 28 June 1650, he was chairman of the Committee for the Army.

Venn was deeply influenced by the Presbyterian preacher Christopher Love, who became chaplain to his regiment shortly after being expelled from Oxford in 1642, and attended his sermons at the Church of SS. Anne and Agnes, Aldersgate, where Love became minister in 1645. In 1648, however, he became disenchanted with Love and, it was asserted, with his religion too, though during the Rump debates on religion he is thought to have favored a Presbyterian settlement. Venn was twice married, to Mary Neville (d. 1625) and to Margaret, daughter of John Langley of Colchester and widow of John Scarborrow. By Mary he had a son Thomas, afterwards Mayor of Bridgwater, and by Margaret a son John and daughter Anne. Several other children died in infancy.

Pearl; Keeler; G. Bate, *The Lives, Actions, and Execution of the Prime Actors* (1661); *DNB*; Firth & Rait; Worden; Manning, *EPER*; Yule. Papers: L (Add. MSS).

C. Polizzotto

VENNER, Thomas (c. 1608-1661)

Fifth Monarchist plotter, came from Littleham, Devon, but was working as a cooper in London by 1633, and probably became a freeman of the Coopers' Company in that year. In Jan. 1637 Venner, described as a wine-cooper, aged 28, gave evidence before the High Court of Admiralty in the company of the Separatists Praisegod Barebone* and Stephen More, testifying that in Oct. 1635 he had supplied 473 gallons of wine to a ship bound for Virginia. In 1637, he emigrated from Allhallows, Barking, to Salem, Mass., where he was admitted to the church and

made a freeman early in 1638. Venner sold the land allotted to him and worked as a cooper, but he failed to fit into the community and made efforts to persuade some of the settlers to remove to Providence or the Bahamas. About 1644 he moved to Boston where, perhaps significantly, he did not join the church. In 1648 he led the coopers of Boston and Charlestown in forming a company to govern their trade; he was also a member of the Artillery Company. Venner returned to England in the autumn of 1651, and it is clear that his relations with the Boston authorities had not been harmonious.

Venner next emerges in 1655, working in London as a master cooper at the Tower. He was arrested in June and dismissed from his post; he was alleged to have talked of murdering the Protector, and was suspected of planning to blow up the Tower. His imprisonment was short, and the following winter Venner and other militant Fifth Monarchists held a series of meetings with disaffected Commonwealthsmen, among them Col. John Okey* and Capt. Thomas Lawson, to find a basis for common action against the government. Nothing materialized. Thomas Harrison* and Nathaniel Rich,* who were approached, declined to take part, and most of those who did participate were arrested in the summer of 1656, before the meeting of Parliament. Venner escaped the search.

By 1656 Venner was head of a congregation meeting in Swan Alley, off Coleman Street. Some of the members had formerly belonged to John Rogers'* congregation, and Rogers had frequent though unfriendly contacts with Venner. A group also met at Venner's house, in Catherine Lane, near the Tower. The rising which he planned during the winter of 1656-57 was based on his own followers, though there were negotiations with the militant Fifth Monarchist/Baptist church led by John Portman.* Harrison and John Carew* were aware that some violent action was being prepared, and attempted to dissuade the plotters; Rogers also condemned it. There was dissension even among the conspirators over tactics and timing, and one of the group appears to have suspected that Venner was an *agent provocateur*, perhaps from the recklessness of the proposal. The plotters obtained horses, arms and armor, and printed a manifesto (*A Standard Set Up*) which was to be spread throughout the country. Their ultimate aim was to topple the regime and establish a theocracy. The immediate plan was to meet in groups at Shoreditch and elsewhere, and rendezvous at Mile End Green; they would proclaim their cause at Chelmsford on 10 Apr., and then proceed to Suffolk and Norfolk, where they expected to find most support. In the event the plan failed miserably. Thurloe* was informed when they began to meet on the evening of 9 Apr., and a group of about twenty were arrested by soldiers at Mile End. Venner was carried before Cromwell, where he defiantly harangued the Protector on the Fifth Monarchy. The plotters were not put on trial, but Venner and two others were kept in the Tower until at least Feb. 1659.

Venner's lasting notoriety sprang from his second rising, shortly after the Restoration, when he was able to take the government by surprise. On the evening of Sunday 6 Jan. 1661 an armed band left the meeting-house in Swan Alley, with the cry, 'King Jesus and the heads upon the gates.' They marched to St. Paul's, defeated a detachment of the trained bands, proceeded through Bishopsgate and finally left the City and went into hiding in Ken Wood, near Highgate. The next day soldiers under Monck searched the area and seized about thirty sympathizers, but the main body of rebels reappeared and burst into the City once more before dawn on Wednesday 9 Jan. There was fierce fighting, especially in Wood and Bishopsgate Streets, and the City was in a state of panic for several hours. The rebels drove back the trained bands and even a detachment of the Life Guards, but eventually they were all killed, captured or dispersed. Probably not more than fifty had taken part; twenty of those captured alive, including the badly-wounded Venner, were tried for treason on 17 Jan. He pleaded not guilty but his conviction was a mere formality, and on 19 Jan. he was hanged, drawn and quartered outside the meeting-place in Swan Alley.

The rebels' manifesto in 1661, *A Doore of Hope*, appealed to all former Parliamentarians to join against the restored monarchy and the bishops, and made much of the danger of revived Popery. In practice his rising played into the hands of those who wished to portray all Nonconformists as fanatics and rebels. Though Venner became the best-known of all Fifth Monarchists, his conspiracies showed that his approach was highly untypical. Most Fifth Monarchists used language of extreme violence, but Venner's group was almost alone in its willingness to use physical force.

Venner married, probably before 1637, and three children are known: Thomas, born at Salem in 1641, Hannah, born in 1644 at Boston, and Samuel, born there in 1649. Alice, Venner's widow, died in 1692 in the parish of St. Dionis Backchurch, and was interred at Tindalls burial ground. His daughter married William Medley,* who took part in the rising of 1657. In 1661, when he was living in Seething Lane, he was described as secretary and accountant of the Fifth Monarchy organization. Medley later moved to the Netherlands, visiting London again as a Dutch agent in 1672-74. He survived until at least 1682, when he met Shaftesbury* in Amsterdam. Venner's son Samuel was by 1674 serving under Sir Walter Vane, with other English volunteers, in the army of William of Orange. He was with Medley in 1682, probably returned to England at the Glorious Revolution, and in 1691 was made Colonel of the 24th Regiment of Foot. He served in Ireland, Flanders and the Brest expedition of 1694, but was dismissed after a court-martial in Mar. 1695.

DNB; Capp, *FMM*; C.E. Banks, 'Thomas Venner,' *New England Historical and Genealogical Register*, 47:37-44; Banks, *Topographical Dictionary of 2885 English Emigrants* (1963 ed.); C. Burrage, 'The Fifth Monarchy Insurrections,' *EHR*, 25:722-47; Thurloe, *SP*; Rogers;

D.O. Shilton and R. Holworthy, eds., *High Court of Admiralty Examinations 1637-1638* (1932).

B.S. Capp

VENNING, Ralph (1621?-1674)

Independent minister, was born in Devon, possibly at Kingsteignton, and was the first convert of George Hughes,* the Puritan Vicar of Tavistock. Venning entered Emmanuel Coll., Camb. in 1643, graduating B.A. (1646) and M.A. (1659). He became one of the lecturers at St. Olave's Church, Southwark, where he made a great reputation as a preacher, particularly of charity sermons, and often preached before the Lord Mayor of London. Venning also served as chaplain at the Tower of London (1647-48) and was lecturer at St. Mary Magdalen, Milk Street (1658), as well as an assistant to the Surrey Commission in 1657. He signed the Declaration against Thomas Venner.* Venning was ejected in 1662, but was appointed a colleague of Robert Bragge (1627-1704) as preacher to an Independent congregation which met at Pewterers' Hall, Lime Street. He remained there until his death in 1674.

Venning was also reported as preaching at the Wild Man Inn, Cannon Street, in 1664, and was licensed to preach in St. Clement's Church, Eastcheap, in 1672, two years before his death. He was much in demand as a preacher, and his published sermons were also popular, some going into five and six editions. After his death a broadsheet was issued with the title *The Dead Yet Speaketh or Mr. Venning's Living Sayings*, followed by two other broadsheets, *Alarm to the Unconverted Sinners* and *Venning's Remains* (1675). His interest in preaching and the Bible encouraged him to edit with others the first New Testament Greek lexicon giving the meanings in English. Venning is noticed in John Edwards' *The Preacher* (1705-7), which remarked that 'he turns sentences up and down and delights in little cadences

and chiming of words.' Venning's works remained popular into the ninteenth century and cheap reprints of some were issued in 1891. Cotton Mather included *Choice Evangelical Paradoxes Taken out of the Works of Mr. Ralph Venning* in the second edition of his published lecture *Signature*.

Calamy Revised; *DNB*; Shaw, 2:568; Tolmie.

I. Morgan

VERE, Lady Mary (1580-1670)

Puritan patron, was the daughter of Sir William Tracy, Kt., of Toddington, Glos. She first married William Hoby, and in Oct. 1607 Sir Horace Vere, later the senior commander of English forces in Holland. During the 1620s and 1630s Lady Vere supported important Puritan ministers in England and Holland. In the early 1620s she helped to obtain the ministerial services of John Davenport* at St. Stephen's, Coleman Street, London. Lady Vere was an intimate of many famous Puritan ministers: John Preston,*William Ames,* William Stoughton, John Goodwin,* John Dod, Joseph Simonds and William Spurstowe.* When Davenport's conscience would no longer allow him to observe Anglican ceremonies, the parish of St. Stephen's obtained Goodwin, who was ministering at East Rainham, Norf., the advowson of Lady Vere's son-in-law Sir Roger Townshend. One of her favorite ministers was Obadiah Sedgwick,* who had served as chaplain to Baron Vere. In 1637 she chose as chaplain Samuel Rogers, the son and grandson of two famous Puritans, Daniel* and Richard* Rogers. Early in 1638 she met and gave support to Josiah Glover, who is credited with obtaining the funds for and equipment of New England's first printing press. By 1650 Lady Vere held eight advowsons in the county of Essex alone, making her the third most important lay person in the county after the Earl of Warwick* and Sir Henry

Audley. In the biographical sketch on Lady Vere that appeared thirteen years after her death, her support of Puritan ministers through public and private courses received the chief attention.

Lady Vere's religious influence was also manifested in the matches for her five daughters, all by Baron Vere. The eldest, Elizabeth, married John Holles, the second Earl of Clare and supporter of the parliamentary cause. The second, Mary, was married first to Sir Roger Townshend, Bt. and prominent Puritan parliamentarian in Norfolk, and second to Mildmay Fane, an Emmanuel College graduate and later the second Earl of Westmorland. The third daughter, Catherine, married Oliver St. John of Lydeard Tregoze. Anne, the fourth daughter, wed Sir Thomas (later Lord) Fairfax,* the parliamentary general. Dorothy, the youngest, married John Wolstenholme, eldest son in the Puritan family of Sir John Wolstenholme, Bt. of Nostal, Yorks. Lady Vere lived at Clapton in the parish of Hackney, Middlesex, where she died at the age of ninety.

S. Clarke, *Lives of Eminent and Sundry Persons* (1683); I.M. Calder, ed. *The Letters of John Davenport* (1937); K.W. Shipps, 'Lay Patronage of East Anglian Puritan Clerics in Pre-revolutionary England,' (Ph.D. diss., Yale Univ., 1971); Diary of Samuel Rogers (BQ: Percy MSS 7). Papers: L (Add. MSS 4275, 4276).

K.W. Shipps

VERNEY, Sir Ralph (1613-1696)

Parliamentary radical, MP SP, LP 1640 (Aylesbury), 1680, 1685, 1689 (Buckingham). Verney was born on 9 Nov. 1613 at Sir Thomas Denton's estate, Hillesden, Bucks. His father was Sir Edmund Verney and his mother Margaret, the daughter of Sir Thomas Denton. Verney was the eldest of twelve children. In May 1629 he was wed to thirteen-year-old Mary Blacknall, daughter and heiress of John Blacknall of

Abingdon. In 1631 Mary moved to the Verney estate at Claydon while Ralph was studying at Magdalen Coll., Oxf. After his schooling he returned to manage the estate for his father. Verney served as MP for Aylesbury in both the Short and the Long Parliaments, and in 1641 he was knighted. Influenced by the Puritan atmosphere of Magdalen, Verney sided with Parliament in its struggle with the King. His father joined the Royalists and died as the King's standard-bearer in the battle of Edgehill. Verney himself was a man of non-violent character, never taking part in the battles of the Civil War, though he contributed two horses to the parliamentary army. Verney supported the execution of Strafford in 1641 and armed resistance to the King because 'reason will not prevail' (*HMC, Seventh Report*, p. 441). Loyal to the Church of England, he was the only MP who refused to subscribe to the Covenant, and voluntarily exiled himself to France.

In his absence he was expelled from Parliament in 1645 and Claydon was sequestered in 1646. Only after Mary's return to England and her heroic plea before Parliament was the estate returned in Jan. 1648. Her body weakened by her efforts to save the estate and by tuberculosis, she died in 1650. Verney returned to England in 1653, only to be imprisoned two years later by Cromwell. Confined in the Tower, Verney was released after four months. In 1656 the decimation tax was applied to Sir Ralph, and he was forbidden to enter town for six months. Verney was defeated in his bid for a Parliament seat in 1660, but he was made DL in 1661 and was created baronet that year. He sat as a Whig in the 1680 Parliament, and was elected for the same seat in 1685, fighting the questionable tactics of Judge Jeffreys to win seats for the King's candidates. In 1687 Verney was dismissed from the Commission of the Peace by James II. He sat in the Convention Parliament of 1689, and voted against making William and Mary joint monarchs, preferring Mary alone. Verney died in 1696, having fathered three sons and three daughters by his wife Mary. Two of the sons died before their father, and Sir Ralph was succeeded by his second son, who became Sir John Verney, then Baron Verney and finally Viscount Fermanagh.

Verney was one of the copious correspondents and chroniclers of the seventeenth century. He carefully arranged and preserved his own volumes of letters, and he recorded many of the events of the times in his painstaking notes.

F.P. and M.M. Verney, *Verney Memors*, 4 vols. (1892-99); J. Bruce, *Letters and Papers of the Verney Family to 1639* (1853); R. Verney, *Notes of Proceedings on the Long Parliament* (1845); Gardiner, *GCW*; P. Verney, *The Standard Bearer* (1963); Underdown, *PP*; Keeton.

W.C. Dickinson

VERNON, John (d. 1667)

Particular Baptist, Fifth Monarchist and army radical, was the author of *The Young Horseman* (1644), a drill manual for the parliamentary cavalry. In the mid-1640s Vernon and William Allen* helped establish the Particular Baptist church at Dalwood, Devon, and in Dec. 1648 Vernon attacked Pride's purge in *The Swords Abuse Asserted, or a Word to the Army*. The Council of State ordered his attendance in Aug. 1649 when one of its committees considered Col. Fleetwood's* petition regarding pay. The following year Vernon was a signatory of *Heart-Bleedings for Professors Abominations*. Assigned to Ireland, Maj. Vernon was active in Baptist affairs, helping Allen and other Particular Baptists to break up John Rogers,* mixed congregation in Dublin. Vernon and Allen, who belonged to the Baptist congregation in Waterford, were also members of a committee to further Protestant preaching in Ireland. Vernon, who had been serving as a secretary to the Lord Deputy, was appointed a commissioner for Ireland with Col. Vincent Potter* and Henry Herbert on 29 Apr.

1652. On 12 May Vernon, Allen, Jerome Sankey,* Daniel Axtell,* Richard Lawrence* and others signed a treaty with the Irish. After writing to Baptist churches in London in June 1653, Vernon returned to England. Cromwell had complained to him that Thomas Harrison* and John Lambert* coerced him to dissolve the Rump, but Vernon was delighted by the summoning of the Barebones Parliament. In Sept. 1653 he petitioned the government for permission to transport some Irish children to England, presumably to foster Protestantism and perhaps to assist the indigent.

Vernon's disaffection with the Cromwellian regime commenced with the dissolution of the Barebones. In a letter to Cromwell dated 10 Mar. 1654, Vernon warned the Protector to 'be careful that you entrench not upon the government entrusted only unto Christ.' In 1655-56 Vernon preached in such places as Kilkenny, Clonmel and Waterford, criticizing the government and proclaiming that 'it was a great judgment for the people of God to be under young or wicked governors.' He and Allen tried to counter the impact of a letter from London Baptists which urged support for the Protectorate. After a brief trip to England Vernon returned to Ireland in Aug. 1656, though he lacked Cromwell's permission; his family, however, remained in England. In December he and Allen dramatically resigned their commissions. The meetings which they held in 1657 concerned the government because of their republican sentiments. At the Dorchester meeting of Baptists and Fifth Monarchists in May 1658, Vernon and Allen urged unification, but Thomas Collier* and William Kiffin* successfully opposed them. From Dorchester Vernon and Allen went to Exeter, where they planned another large meeting when Cromwell died. After the Protector's death the government received a report that 'they are persons of as much venom and revenge as any whatever and will not spare to adventure on anything that may give them the least hope of success.' In the same year Vernon wrote an epistle to Allen's *The Captive Taken from the Strong* in which he asked the saints to 'wait still in weeping, in supplication until the times of refreshment' arrive.

Under the restored Rump Vernon was appointed quartermaster-general by the Committee of Safety on 8 July 1659. He was a supporter of the Wallingford House party. With Allen, Henry Danvers,* Henry Jessey,* Robert Overton* and others, Vernon was a signatory of *An Essay Toward Settlement* (Sept. 1659), which called for a republican constitution, liberty of conscience, the abolition of tithes, and the removal from office of all supporters of the defunct Protectorate. A warrant for Vernon's arrest was issued on 13 Apr. 1660, but he was released from Newgate in June 1661 on security of £1000 provided he go into permanent exile. Instead he remained in England, practicing medicine at Epsom, Ewell and Newington, and preaching in Thomas Glasse's* London congregation. Warrants for Vernon's arrest were issued on 3 Jan. 1663, 21 Mar. 1664 and 2 Mar. 1665. His final work, *The Compleat Scholler*, was published in 1666. He died on 29 May 1667; Allen contributed to his elegy. Vernon and Allen had married daughters of James Huish of Sudbury, Devon. Vernon was one of the leading republican critics of the Protectorate, though his hostility stopped short of revolutionary action against the government.

CSPD, Comm., 1:262; 3:266; 4:229; 6:140-41; 13:13, 573; *Chas. II*, 2:12; 3:2, 524; 4:233; Abbott; Brown; Capp, *FMM*; *TBHS*, 3:254-55; 4:130-31; 7:236; *BQ*, 3:237-39; 4:268; 19:299-307. Papers: LPR; L (Add. MSS).

R.L. Greaves

VICARS, John (c.1580-1652)

Puritan pamphleteer, was born in London about 1580 of poor parents whose ancestors were from Cumberland. He was educated at Christ's Hospital, London, and Queen's Coll., Oxf., before commenc-ing his career as Usher of Christ's Hospital. In 1637 he gave John Lilburne* a copy of Bastwick's* *Letany* to have printed. A Presbyterian, Vicars called in *Englands Remembrancer* (1641) for a purge of the universities, insisted on the observation of the sabbath, condemned the High Commission and the 'impious prelates,' warned that the Catholics and bishops were trying to force a war with Scotland, and urged Charles to fight in the Palatinate as an ally of Denmark and Holland. In *A Looking-Glasse for Malignants* (1643), a piece of parliamentary propaganda, he blamed the Irish rebellion on the King's evil counsellors, attacked episcopacy, Arminianism and Antinomianism, and defended the Scottish alliance. His *Jehovah-Jireh* (1641 and later eds.) and supplementary works provided a highly partisan account of the Long Parliament and Civil War, which he viewed as part of an historic struggle between the forces of Christ and Satan going back to Eden.

Before 1645 Vicars' ire had been directed primarily toward 'the rotten-hearted Royalists and atheistical crew of impious Oxonian malignants,' but that year he lashed out against the Independents in *The Picture of Independency*, as again in *The Schismatick Sifted* (1646). Hugh Peter's* attack on the Presbyterians early in 1646 disrupted the friendship between the two men. Vicars' most celebrated attack was directed against John Goodwin* in *Coleman-Street Conclave* (1648); Goodwin derisively referred to him as 'Rabshakeh Vicars.' In *England's Worthies* (1647) Vicars provided a secular hagiography of the radical leaders. Among his associations were the elder Isaac Penington,* Sir John Wollaston,* John Warner* and Sir Matthew Brand, Sheriff of Surrey. The minutes of the London Provincial Assembly indicate that Vicars was a ruling elder in the First Classis of the London Province. Vicars died on 12 Apr. 1652, aged 72, and was buried in Christ Church, Newgate Street. His many works do not include *A Discovery of the Rebels* (1643) and *The Great Antichrist* (1643), which have been erroneously attributed to him. He is not to be confused with the John Vicars who was a preacher at St. Benet Paul's Wharf (1602), or the Curate and Lecturer at St. Michael Cornhill and, from 1600 to his death in 1633, Rector of St. Augustine Paul's Gate, London. (The latter was apparently associated with the Feoffees for Impropriations; see Seaver, pp. 178, 359-60).

DNB; *Ath. Oxon.*, R.P. Stearns, *The Strenuous Puritan* (1954); Haller, *RP*.

R.L. Greaves

W

WADE, Nathaniel (d. 1718)

Wade, a conspirator, was the third son of John Wade of Arlingham, Glos., a major in the New Model Army and Governor of the Isle of Man during the Protectorate. Wade's wife, whose maiden name was Lane, died on 19 May 1678 at Arlingham, and was buried with her eldest son at St. Stephen's, Bristol, on 22 May according to the records of the Broadmead Church. The *DNB* is erroneous in stating that Nathaniel Wade was born about 1666, for on 4 Oct. 1677 Sir Joseph Williamson reported that the Privy Council would discuss information on seditious words spoken by Wade. 'Considering the ill principles of the man,' he observed, 'methinks he should at least be bound to good behavior and a strict eye had to his carriage.' Sir Richard Head had Wade bound over to answer the charges at the assizes. Wade could not have suffered much, for he entered New Inn on 11 June 1678.

By 1680 Wade was back in Bristol, where he actively engaged in Nonconformist activities. At a meeting of the Broadmead Church on 1 Aug. 1680 he and his brother William, a grocer, were arrested and imprisoned in Newgate. A certificate issued on the 11th bound him to appear at the Wells Assizes, charging that he had been guilty of seditious practices for three years, particularly as the ringleader of a group of at least sixty Dissenters who, without authorization, armed themselves and engaged in training exercises. Moreover he had 'lately resisted a justice in disturbing a conventicle, for which he has been convicted and fined at the quarter sessions, and . . . on Sunday, the 1st instant [1 Aug.], he resisted another justice in disturbing a conventicle. . . .' Again his punishment was not severe, for on 16 June 1681 Wade entered the Middle Temple. He used his legal skills at Bristol on 28 Aug. 1681 to defend William Harford, co-pastor with Andrew Gifford* of the Pithay

Particular Baptist Church. According to Macaulay, during his early career Wade worked on a plan involving emigration to New Jersey.

Wade was enmeshed in Whig politics in Bristol and was a member, like Ichabod Chauncey,* of the Castle Green Independent Church. His brother-in-law, Joseph Whetham, kept the records of a political club in the city, to which Wade and Chauncey belonged, that supported Sir Robert Atkins, an Anglican MP sympathetic to Nonconformist causes. In the spring of 1683 Wade was entangled in the insurrection allegedly planned by the 'Council of Six,' i.e. Monmouth, Essex,* William Lord Russell,* Algernon Sidney,* John Hampden* and Lord Howard of Escrick.* As Wade understood it, this insurrection was to redress grievances and have Monmouth declared Prince of Wales, but not assassinate the King or Duke of York. The government's discovery of the Rye House plot disrupted their plans, and Wade, who was the link between the more moderate 'Council' and the Rye House conspirators, was in an impossible position. He was then living in Soho Square, London, and meeting with Capt. Thomas Walcott,* a Rye House plotter, Col. John Rumsey,* the lawyer Robert West* and Richard Goodenough,* who were supposedly concerned about a popish rising in London. At a meeting at Walcott's on 17 June, Wade, Richard Nelthorpe* and Edward Norton* argued in favor of an immediate insurrection in London and the west, but Russell dissuaded them. Although the government arrested Russell, by the 20th Wade, Rumsey, Goodenough and other conspirators had fled, and on the 23rd a royal proclamation was issued for the apprehension of Wade, Rumsey, Goodenough, Nelthorpe, Walcott, Col. Richard Rumbold* and others. On the 27th West testified that Wade and Rumsey were involved in a conspiracy at Bristol, and the Mayor of Bristol, Thomas Eston, ordered a search for Wade's papers, but found nothing more recent than 1679. By then Wade's brother William had also gone into hiding. Abraham Holmes* testified on the 29th that Wade was an honest, peaceable man, but the state was not persuaded, and on 1 July Wade was reported en route to Exeter. During the course of the month testimony before the King and Privy Council further implicated Wade. According to the lawyer Zachary Bourne, Wade, Rumsey and James Holloway* conspired to get the prominent citizens out of Bristol and seize their wealth, while Rumsey confirmed that Wade and Holloway were the leading conspirators in Bristol. On the 8th Walcott admitted that Wade, Rumsey, Robert Ferguson* and others had resolved to flee to the Netherlands when the conspiracy was discovered. Although the state had three witnesses against Wade on 12 July, he had fled to Rotterdam, and thence to Amsterdam.

Wade's flight did not deter the government's investigation, and Sir Leoline Jenkins was determined to discover how he escaped, correctly believing it was via Scarsborough. The investigation turned to Wade's brother-in-law, Sir William Clutterbuck, Mayor of Bristol in 1683 and a member of the Bristol Merchant Venturers' Society. Although his examination on 21 July turned up no evidence of complicity in Wade's conspiracy, the Earl of Worcester complained to Jenkins on the 24th that Clutterbuck 'has a general character of a very seditious fellow' and probably knew more than he revealed. On 29 Aug. more damaging testimony was provided to the Privy Council by the merchant Thomas Shepheard, who asserted that Wade and West had discussed the assassination of the King with him. West himself testified on 2 Feb. 1684 that at Rumsey's request he and Wade had drafted a statement of principles to present to the 'Council of Six.' Although Rumsey promised to convey it to the 'Council' he gave it to Ferguson instead. The state still sought William Wade, issuing warrants for his arrest on 7 and 24 Apr. 1684.

By Jan. 1684 Nathaniel Wade had gone to Switzerland to consult Edmund Ludlow.* He also served as an emissary between Monmouth and Archibald Campbell, Earl of Argyll. Of the latter's plan to raise Scotland, Wade subsequently remarked that it was 'kept very private, and the greatest difficulty was to hide it from our own party.' With Argyll and Ford Lord Grey of Werk,* he persuaded Monmouth to commit himself to the 1685 rebellion. In late May he sailed with Monmouth from the Netherlands, and though he had no military experience, commanded the Red Regiment. Landing at Lyme Regis on 11 June he supervised the landing of the arms and stores, and subsequently saw action in all the engagements involving the foot. At the council of war called at Taunton by Monmouth on the 14th, he initially opposed the idea of the Duke declaring himself king, but then reversed himself. After the defeat at Sedgemoor he fled with over a hundred of his men to Bridgwater, where some fifty of them got their horses, rode to Ilfracombe and seized a coasting ship, only to be forced back to harbor by two frigates. Wade fled to Brendon, Devon, but was shot several weeks later trying to escape. Taken to London, he was committed to Newgate prison on 5 Oct. and two weeks later turned King's evidence. In late November he, Goodenough and James Burton requested pardon at the bar of King's Bench, but were remanded to Newgate. Wade testified against Lord Delamere* in Jan. 1686. On 25 May 1686 (Luttrell gives 4 June) he was pardoned.

In Jan. 1687 James II sent Wade to Bristol with the Council's order for remodelling the corporation, hoping he could win the support of the Dissenters. By royal nomination he was appointed town clerk, but served only until Oct. 1687. Out of loyalty to his former comrades, he petitioned MPs in 1701 to reverse the attainder of Monmouth's men. Queen Anne's charter to Bristol of 24 July 1710 confirmed him in his office of steward of the sheriff's court, and in 1714 he commanded the Bristol militia against the Kingswood colliers. He died early in 1718 and was buried on 14 Mar. in the Redcross Street cemetery.

CSPD, Chas. II, 19:391; 21:597-98; 24-26 *passim*; 27:18; *Jas. II*, 1:311, 312, 349, 394; 2:143; *HMC 49, Sackville*, 1:22-23; *HMC 75, Devonshire*, 1:64; *HMC 78, Hastings*, 4:307; *DNB*; Hayden, *RCCB*; Trench; Earle. Papers: L (Harl. MS 6845), reprinted in *Hardwicke State Papers* (1778), 2.

R.L. Greaves

WAITE (or Wayte), Thomas (fl. 1634-1668)

Regicide, was the eldest son of Henry Waite of Wymondham, Leics. He entered Gray's Inn on 5 Mar. 1634. In 1642 he joined the parliamentary forces, serving initially as captain and later as colonel of a regiment of horse under Thomas Lord Grey.* Waite's regiment distinguished itself in several engagements during the first Civil War, including the defeat of royalist forces at Sproxton Heath in Dec. 1643. He was Governor of Rutland in 1643, Governor of Burley House in 1644, and MP for Rutland from July 1646 until the dismissal of the Long Parliament. The summer of 1648 found Waite in the field again, suppressing a royalist uprising at Peterborough in June, and participating in the pursuit and capture of the Duke of Hamilton after the battle of Preston in August. Waite was named to the High Court in Jan. 1649, but attended only three meetings and was among the last of the 59 commissioners who signed the death warrant. He apparently tried to avoid involvement altogether by returning home to Leicestershire, and, according to testimony given at his own trial in 1660, even attempted to suppress republican petitions there and in Rutland. Waite claimed that Cromwell and Ireton* tricked him into attending the final session of the court and then forced him to sign the document.

During the Interregnum Waite took little part in the affairs of state, occupying himself instead with recouping his wartime losses. In lieu of monies owed him for military expenditures, on 31 July 1650 Parliament authorized the sale to Waite of confiscated lands in Rutland formerly belonging to the Duke of Buckingham. Three years later Waite became embroiled in a controversy with his tenants, whose commons and pastures he had enclosed and whose rents he had doubled, violating an earlier agreement not to do so. The villagers of Hambledon presented a petition to the Council of State claiming that unless Waite's oppressions ceased, more than one hundred families would likely be evicted. It is not known if the petition was successful.

As a Regicide, Waite was excluded from the general pardon at the Restoration, and he surrendered himself in accordance with the King's proclamation. He was tried on 10 Oct. 1660, found guilty and condemned to death; however the sentence was not carried out. He spent his remaining years in prison, during which time his impoverished wife Jane petitioned unsuccessfully for his release. Waite was still a prisoner in Jersey in Feb. 1668, but the date of his death is unknown.

DNB; *ST*; James; Underdown, *PP*.

C.B. Rynder

WALCOTT (or Walcot), Thomas (1625-1683)

Plotter, served as a captain of dragoons under Sir H. Ingoldsby, and later was a captain-lieutenant in Ludlow's* troop, serving with Ludlow in Ireland in the early 1650s. Burnet refers to him as a 'gentleman of £1000 per annum in Ireland,' while Luttrell called him an Irish gentleman of £1000, but neither can be substantiated. Walcott was a Baptist and was licensed to preach at Bungay, Suff. in 1672.

Walcott was heavily involved in the Rye House plot and, according to his own testimony, was drawn into the conspiracy by Shaftesbury,* who led him to believe they were engaged in protecting the liberties of the people. He first learned of the conspiracy in the early fall of 1682 when he met Robert Ferguson* and others connected with the plot at the home of Robert West,* a lawyer of the Middle Temple. Ferguson appeared to Walcott to be the leader behind the scheme. In Nov. 1682 Walcott went with Shaftesbury and Ferguson to Holland. He witnessed a codicil of Shaftesbury's estate in Holland after the latter died in Jan. 1683. When Ferguson returned to England, Walcott accompanied him and met with fellow conspirators. According to the testimony of others, Walcott was supposed to attack the King's guards as the royal party approached the Rye House moat. Walcott's own testimony denies that he ever agreed to such a scheme on the grounds that to attack the King's guards would have left the King defenseless and so have constituted a crime against his person. He did testify, however, that the plans included a general insurrection to be raised throughout England and Scotland in Oct. 1682, but was delayed because the country was not then ready. Later, in the spring of 1683, the attack on the King and Duke of York was to be the signal for the general insurrection.

Walcott was apprehended in Essex in early July, and gave his testimony before the King and Council on 8 July 1683. He wrote to Secretary Jenkins on 5 July requesting an audience with the King; the audience was apparently arranged because Jenkins' reply contained elaborate directions on how to proceed to the King's chambers. Walcott was tried at the Old Bailey on 12 July, and was executed on the 20th, refusing to admit that he had been a party to the conspiracy. His son obtained his father's body by petition on the 26th, although the head was set up on Aldersgate.

CSPD, Chas. II, 24-26 *passim*; Luttrell, 1:267-70; Underwood; Morley; Ashley, *JW*; Keeton.

F.D. Barrows

WALLER, Edmond (1652-c. 1699)

Quaker, was born on 6 Jan. 1652 at Hall Barn, Beaconsfield, Bucks. to Edmond (1606-1687), poet and MP, and his second wife Mary (née Bracey). He had one step-brother and three brothers, but death and disinheritance left him as heir to his father's estate. He matriculated at Christ Church, Oxf. on 17 Dec. 1666 but left without taking a degree. On 20 Apr. 1668 he was admitted to the Middle Temple and was called to the bar on 14 May 1675. In 1684 Coleshill manor, Herts. (now part of Bucks.) was conveyed to Waller by Henry Child for £200. On 10 July 1686 Waller married Abigail, daughter of Frederick Tilney of Rotherwick, Hants., but the marriage had ended by 1698. In 1687 Waller's father died, leaving him the Hall Barn estate. In 1688 he was admitted as a 'foreign burgess' to Chipping Wycombe, where from 1689 to 1695 he served as recorder. From 1689 to 1698 he was a JP in Buckinghamshire and was also elected MP for Agmondesham (now Amersham) in the Parliaments of 1689, 1690-95 and 1695-98. Apparently he did not stand for the next Parliament. Waller's voting record in 1696 indicated strong Tory principles. However, his father's parliamentary activities on behalf of the Quakers along with the close proximity of Hall Barn and Coleshill manor to the Quaker communities at Chalfont St. Giles and Hunger Hill led Waller to develop close ties with such leading Friends as William Penn,* George Whitehead,* Thomas Ellwood* and Henry Gouldney. Thus on 7 Feb. 1696, at the behest of Whitehead, he introduced in the House of Commons a petition from the Quakers to be allowed to affirm rather than take oaths. The House ordered him to prepare and bring in the bill, which subsequently became law. On 12 Feb. 1696 Waller was elected a bencher of the Middle Temple, and was to have read at Lent 1698, but at his request his reading was deferred for twelve months, and in fact never took place. By 1698 Waller ceased to attend Parliament and retired to Hall Barn, suffering from severe gout and consequent melancholia. At the same time he was attending Quaker meetings and became convinced. In Apr. 1698 William Penn held a meeting at Hall Barn, and Waller was leaving his house only to attend meetings. In that year Thomas Lower and his wife Mary (née Fell) actively promoted a possible marriage between Waller and their daughter Margery, but to no avail. The following year Waller wrote several letters sharply renouncing any proposals he had made to Margery and went to Bath to cure his gout. Some Quakers were angry with the letters, but it was rumored that on his return he intended to rectify matters. Before he could return, however, Waller died at Bath, probably late in Dec. 1699. He was buried at the Quaker cemetery there, having left £50 in his will for that purpose to the elders of the Quaker meeting nearest to where he should die.

G. Locker Lampson, ed., *A Quaker Post-Bag* (1910); *Al. Oxon*; *CJ*, 11:434, 452, 456, 461; *Middle Temple Bench Book* (1807); PCC, Wills (108). Papers: LF (Gibson MSS; Toft MSS); L (Add. MSS).

C.W. Horle

WALLER, Sir Hardress (c. 1604-c. 1666)

Civil War officer, Regicide and parliamentary radical, MP 1654 (Kerry), 1656 (Limerick), 1659 (Clare). Waller is said to have been the son of George Waller of Groombridge, Kent, and Mary, daughter of Richard Hardress. Knighted in 1629, he married Elizabeth, daughter of Sir John Dowdall of Kilfinny about 1630, thereby acquiring an estate in Ireland at Castletown, Limerick.

Waller was an MP in the 1640 Irish Parliament. Ruined by the Irish rising of 1641, he took a commission in the Munster forces. Waller approached both King and Parliament in England unsuccessfully for support against the rebellion. In 1644 he was Governor of Cork and commander in Munster. Back in England in Apr. 1645, he received command of a New Model Army

regiment and fought at Naseby. In 1645 and 1646 he pursued royalist forces in Cornwall and Devon. One of several Munster landholders who had proposed an attempt in their province in Dec. 1646, Waller accompanied Lord Lisle,* Lord Lieutenant of Ireland, to Cork in Feb. 1647. This farcical expedition exacerbated Presbyterian – Independent quarrels in England and those between Waller's former commander Lord Inchiquin, Parliamentary Lord President of Munster, and Lord Broghill, Waller's patron, both of whom looked to the two parliamentary factions for support. Inchiquin frustrated Waller's efforts to extend his commission beyond Lisle's term of authority, and he returned to England.

Waller participated in the Reading and Putney debates in 1647 in the Army Council and its committees. He stood firmly behind Gen. Fairfax* in these disputes, supporting military authority. The second Civil War saw him again in the west where his efforts to quarter troops in Exeter provoked an incident. He faced only some insurgency in Cornwall and an attempted betrayal of Pendennis Castle. Waller joined the army's march on London in early Dec. 1648 and was one of Pride's* chief associates in the purge of the Commons. Hostile to further negotiations with the King and opposed to the Levellers, as were the other grandees, he intervened in the Whitehall debates over liberty of conscience and the *Agreement of the People*, drawing attacks from the Levellers. Waller attended all sessions of the High Court except one, signed the death warrant, and helped arrange the King's execution.

After another command in Devon and Cornwall, Waller followed Cromwell to Ireland. Between 1650 and 1652, rising to major-general of foot, he commanded at the taking of Carlow, participated in both sieges of Limerick, wasted the barony of Burren, and helped reduce Kerry. He served on a committee regarding the survey of forfeited lands and participated in the transportation to Connaught. The Rump voted him lands in 1653, but they were not settled on him until 1657.

The only general present when Charles Fleetwood* proclaimed Cromwell Protector in Dublin, Waller was returned for all three Protectoral Parliaments. Secure during Fleetwood's deputyship and Henry Cromwell's* lord lieutenancy, in 1659 he was caught between the republican Edmund Ludlow,* his commander, and officers inclined towards Restoration. Embittered by Ludlow's appointment of John Jones* to command, Waller supported a coup by Monck's group in Dec. 1659. When he saw that Monck's Parliament meant a Restoration, he seized Dublin Castle in Feb. 1660, but failing to rally the army, he surrendered. Imprisoned briefly, then released, Waller fled to France. Upon Charles II's proclamation he surrendered, bolted, but finally rendered himself into custody. Tried under the Act of Indemnity in Oct. 1660, he reluctantly pleaded guilty and was sentenced to the penalties of treason, fairly secure that they would not be fully imposed. He was imprisoned in the Tower and then at Orgueil Castle, Jersey, dying there probably in the autumn of 1666.

Cobbett; *DNB*; *HMC, Egmont MSS*; Ludlow; Kishlansky; Woodhouse. Papers: L (Add. MSS).

T.M. Coakley

WALLER, Sir William (1598-1668)

Parliamentary general. The son of Sir Thomas Waller and Margaret Lennard, Waller was born at Knole, Kent and baptized in Dec. 1598. He was educated at Oxford, traveled in Italy and served briefly in Bohemia (1620). Knighted in 1622, he married Jane, daughter and heiress of Sir Richard Reynell of Devon, where Waller settled, playing a minor role in county affairs. On Jane's death (1633) he married Anne, daughter of Sir Thomas Finch, first Earl of Winchelsea. Waller was strongly influenced by her Puritanism. He stood for Andover in Nov. 1640 but the result was disputed and he did not take his seat until Apr. 1642. He was at once put on the Committee for Adventurers raising money for Ireland. In June 1642 Waller contributed men and horses and was soon a colonel of horse under Essex.* From July he was a member of the Committee of Safety. Waller took up arms 'defensively' to force the King to resume working with Parliament to preserve the natural order in state, society and church. He was a moderate Puritan, opposed to Laud but finding a limited episcopacy or a decent presbytery equally acceptable. Waller described the war as 'this tragedy,' and from the first supported peace negotiations, but he fought vigorously (if cautiously) in the field and condemned neutrality as destructive to both localities and the kingdom. He lost a number of engagements, but for his success in 1643 in denying Hampshire and Sussex to the Royalists he was named 'William the Conqueror.' His actions in the west and the Severn Valley earned him the respect of war-party men like Henry Marten* who saw him as a possible counter to the dictatorial Essex. Waller stressed military skill rather than godliness; even so his troops were described by Royalists as a rabble of 'rebellious Brownists.' Failure to relieve Essex in the west weakened Waller's popularity. By 1645 he was weary of the drudgery of war 'notwithstanding those temptations of honor and profit' that went with it. Casting his vote for the Self-Denying Ordinance, he stayed on only as caretaker general of the discontented army of the west – Cromwell was one of his subordinates – and was glad to be relieved in Apr. 1645.

Waller was now in financial difficulties, with his estate in royalist hands and pay in arrears. He contemplated service abroad but politics (as MP, member of the Committee of Both Kingdoms and member of the Hampshire County Committee) proved more attractive. As the war ended Waller became prominent among the Presbyterians who wanted a conservative accommodation with the King. He charged Ireton* with inciting the army to disobey the order to disband. Aware of professional grievances, he objected to an independent political role for the troops. Waller was one of the eleven MPs impeached in June 1647 who commanded the City forces in 'London's counter-revolution.' When the army entered in August, he fled to the United Provinces. Though suspected of complicity in the second Civil War he boldly returned in Aug. 1648 to the Commons and backed the Newport Treaty. At Pride's purge he was imprisoned and was among the last of the secluded members to be released (Mar. 1652). His *Vindication*, written in captivity, condemned his treatment as a breach of parliamentary privilege and fundamental law. He denied having tried to 'kindle a new flame of war.' Meditating on church and state he condemned 'a promiscuous toleration' as a principal cause of atheism and stressed decent outward observance as promoting spiritual unity. Monarchy in association with parliament he thought the best guarantee against the 'exorbitances' of recent years. The Rump – 'a confusion called a commonwealth' – was 'a mere assumption and tyranny.' Waller kept these thoughts to himself during the Protectorate, and though arrested on suspicion of plotting in 1657 and 1659, it was not until after Booth's rising that he renewed his interest in politics. When the Rump was restored for the second time (Dec. 1659) he was among the secluded members demanding readmission and on Monck's arrival in Feb. 1660 he took his seat, becoming a member of the Council of State. In March he voted for the dissolution and was elected for Westminster to the Convention. Curiously he did not take his seat. Charles II offered no encouragement and Waller himself turned away from public life. Probably he had committed himself too much to restoration on the old Newport terms and was disappointed. His last eight years were devoted to his *Divine Meditations* (published in 1680). Although essentially a moderate, Waller's chief significance lay in the vigorous generalship which, prior to the emergence of Cromwell, was crucial to the parliamentary cause in the Civil War.

J.F. Adair, *Roundhead General* (1969); Kishlansky; V. Pearl, 'London's Counter-Revolution,' in Aylmer, *Int.*; Sir W. Waller, *Divine Meditations* (1680); *Vindication* (1793). Papers: LPR; L (Add. MSS; Sloane MSS).

I.A. Roots

WALLER, Sir William (d. 1699)

Parliamentary radical, MP 1679[2], 1681 (Westminster). Waller, the son of the Civil War general, Sir William Waller,* by his second wife Anne Finch, was born in Westminster, Middlesex. He was a gentleman commoner at Wadham Coll., Oxf. He was alleged to be frequenting a Presbyterian conventicle in Westminster in 1676. Nothing came of the Lord Chancellor's recommendation in Aug. 1678 that Charles II appoint Waller minister to Hamburg. After news of the Popish plot broke that October, Waller, as a Middlesex JP, zealously pursued and arrested Catholics, publicly destroyed their books and vestments, and once even invaded the Spanish embassy in pursuit of a priest. In Feb. 1679, the month he was defeated as a parliamentary candidate at Westminster, an informal Catholic tribunal allegedly sentenced him to death. His psychopathic pursuit of Catholics brought him sufficient popularity to win his seat in the September elections, but he was in such financial straits that a public subscription subsequently had to be raised to provide relief from his debts. Waller played an active role in the investigation of the Meal Tub plot in Oct. 1679, which was intended to implicate the Whig leaders in a treasonous plot. A temporary imprisonment in the Gatehouse in Feb. 1680 for the illegal seizure of goods, followed by the improper release in April of a prisoner committed for treason, gave the King the opportunity to remove him from the Commission of the Peace.

Waller fled to Utrecht, where an informer alleged that he had contracted for 4000 pair of horse pistols and 2000 firelocks to be delivered to English conspirators in Rotterdam. Early in 1681 Waller was back in Westminster, where he served as foreman of a grand jury and won election in February as an MP for Westminster. He was a member of the Green Ribbon Club. In the trial in April of Edward Fitzharris, Waller was a principal witness for the prosecution. Despite possessing a writ of privilege, Waller was briefly imprisoned for debt in May 1681, but that fall he was stirring up support for the Country's cause in the Taunton area and mapping out strategy with William Lord Howard of Escrick,* the Earl of Shaftesbury* and William Bedloe. By Jan. 1683 he was in Amsterdam, and in April was reportedly seeking protection from the French ambassador to the Hague. After visiting Copenhagen in the summer, Waller went to Bremen where he established a woolen factory and gathered around him a circle of exiled radicals. In Jan. 1685 it was reported that he had been made Governor of Lünenburg.

Waller was with William of Orange when he invaded England and served with him at Exeter. On 13 Feb. 1689 Waller arrested Lord Chief Justice Wright for high misdemeanors, and the following month he was given a warrant to apprehend Catholics hiding in London and Westminster. William III, however, refused to reward Waller with a government post, and in July 1689 even rejected him as a potential Governor of the Leeward Islands. Waller died in July 1699. He published the anti-Catholic polemic, *The Tragical History of Jetzer* (1679).

CSPD, Chas. II, 20-27 *passim*; *Wm. III*, 1:1-2, 19; *DNB*; Luttrell, 1 *passim*; 4:538; Lacey. Papers: LPR.

R.L. Greaves

WALLOP, Sir Henry (1568-1642)

Parliamentary radical, MP 1597 (Lymington), 1601 (Hants.), 1614 (Stockbridge, election voided 11 May), 1621 (Hants.), 1624 (Whitchurch), 1625 (Andover), 1626, 1628, SP, LP 1640 (Hants.). Wallop was born on 18 Oct. 1568, the son and heir of Sir Henry Wallop, Treasurer at War and Lord Justice of Ireland (d. 1599), by his wife, Catherine, daughter of Richard Gifford of Hampshire. He was tutored by Nicholas Fuller,* matriculated at Oxford in 1584, received his B.A. from Hart Hall in 1588, and was a student at Lincoln's Inn in 1590. He served as deputy to his father in Ireland in 1598 and was knighted at Dublin in Aug. 1599.

In addition to the family estate at Farleigh Wallop and other manors in Hampshire, Wallop owned property in Ireland, Wiltshire, Devonshire and Somerset. His marriage (prior to 1601) to Elizabeth, daughter and heiress of Robert Corbet of Morton Corbet, brought him numerous manors in Shropshire. In 1628 he was referred to as one of the three wealthiest members of the House of Commons. This wealth assured Wallop a prominent position in his county. He was Sheriff of Hampshire in 1603-4 and again in 1629-30, as well as for Shropshire in 1606. He was named to various local commissions, including that for martial law in 1626-27, and often functioned as JP in Hampshire and Shropshire.

Wallop received numerous grants and honors during James' reign, was appointed to the Council of the Marches of Wales in 1617, and was recommended for a peerage in 1619. During Charles' reign Wallop demonstrated opposition to court policies. He protested against contributing to the loan in 1626 and refused to contribute to the Crown in 1639-40. In the Parliament of 1628 he complained against billeting, and as sheriff in 1630 he did not summon his full quota for knighthood composition.

In nearly all of his parliaments Sir Henry was appointed to a few important committees but otherwise does not appear to have been very active or vocal. His advanced age probably prevented greater participation in the Long Parliament, but he clearly supported Parliament's cause. He offered bond of £1000 as security for the loan in Nov. 1640, and presented a petition to the

House complaining of Strafford's unjust proceedings in Ireland. His attendance in the House may have ceased before May 1641 for he did not take the Protestation in that month and there is no evidence of a later appearance, although he and his son offered maintenance for eight horses in June 1642. Despite his absence, Wallop's influence was undoubtedly felt in the House through the work of his more radical son, Robert,* and numerous other like-minded members with family connections to Sir Henry, including his sons-in-law, William Heveningham* and Sir Henry Worsley, as well as Sir William Lytton* and Sir Thomas Barrington,* whose own network of MP friends and relatives was large. Wallop died on 15 Nov. 1642.

Keeler; R. Warner, *Collections for the History of Hampshire* (1795), 3:125-31; *CSPD, Jas. I*, 8-11 *passim*; *Chas. I*, 1-4 *passim*; *Al. Oxon.*; B. & P. Papers: LPR; L (Add. MSS).

W.B. Bidwell

WALLOP, Sir Robert (1601-1667)

Parliamentary radical, MP 1621, 1624 (Andover), 1625, 1626 (Hants.), 1628, SP, LP 1640 (Andover), 1654, 1656, 1659 (Hants.), 1660 (Whitchurch), excluded. Sir Robert was the eldest son of Sir Henry Wallop (d. 1642)* of Farleigh Wallop, Hants. and Elizabeth, daughter of Robert Corbet (d. 1642) of Morton Corbet, Shrops. He entered politics shortly after his matriculation from Hart Hall, Oxf. in 1615, for as the heir of one of the wealthiest commoners of the day, he was returned to Parliament in 1621 and began to serve Hampshire as JP, colonel in the county militia, and commissioner to enforce martial law in 1627. The meeting of the Long Parliament in 1640 placed Wallop in the forefront of the opposition to the Crown. On 4 May 1641 he signed the protestation of the House of Commons and early in 1642 was appointed to the Committee for Irish Affairs. With the outbreak of the Civil War

Wallop served on the County Committee for Hampshire. A member of the Committee of Both Kingdoms, he argued for a vigorous prosecution of the war and was not dismayed by the failure of the Parliamentary Commission, of which he was a member, to treat for peace with the King at Uxbridge in 1645. Wallop's animosity towards Charles I did not extend to abetting the King's death for, though appointed to the High Court, he sat on only three occasions and did not sign the death warrant.

Under the Commonwealth Wallop was elected annually to the Council of State with the exception of 1652, but he was notably absent from parliamentary sessions. Along with three other Rumpers he was notorious for his appearance only on those days when the government chose to discuss issues touching his interests, especially financial ones, as he was heavily indebted by this time. In 1649 he was partially compensated for the £50,000 he claimed to have expended in the parliamentary cause, with a grant of £10,000 from the confiscated estates of the Marquis of Winchester. Wallop was an ardent and outspoken republican, and during Oliver Cromwell's Protectorate he retired from politics although he was officially returned in the first and second Protectorate Parliaments for Hampshire. He was returned to Richard Cromwell's* Parliament and was a member of the Council of State in the restored Rump, but like his fellow republicans was unable to stem the drift to a restored monarchy. In the spring of 1660 Wallop hurriedly made preparations for the restoration of Charles II. He helped further the escape of Edmund Ludlow,* the notorious republican and Regicide, to the Continent; he sought a seat in the Convention Parliament, only to be excluded upon his election for Whitchurch; and he negotiated with the interim government for a pardon, only to be exempted from the Act of Oblivion. Brought before the bar of the House of Commons in 1660, Wallop was attainted of high treason and sentenced to life imprisonment and the annual degradation of being 'drawn from the Tower of London . . . to and under the gallows at Tyburn' in commemoration of Charles I's death sentence. Nonetheless he was fortunate in that his marriage to Anne, the sister of Thomas Wriothesley, fourth Earl of Southampton and a staunch Royalist, saved the Wallop estates from confiscation. The Earl received the estates by a royal grant that permitted him to make them available to his sister and her son and heir, Henry. Wallop died a prisoner in the Tower on 19 Nov. 1667 despite numerous appeals for his release on the grounds of poor health.

B. & P.; Ludlow; Goodwin; Keeler; DNB. Papers: L (Sloane MSS; Stowe MSS).

R.E. Shimp

WALSINGHAM, Sir Thomas (1594-1669)

Parliamentary radical, MP 1614 (Poole), 1621, 1624, 1625, 1626, 1628, SP, LP 1640 (Rochester). Walsingham was born at Scadbury in Chislehurst, Kent. He was the son and heir of Sir Thomas Walsingham the courtier (d. 1630) and Ethelred, the daughter of Sir Ralph Shelton of Norfolk. He was probably a student at King's Coll., Camb. in 1606, and was knighted in 1613. Walsingham married Elizabeth, the daughter of Sir Peter Manwood of Hackington in 1616. In 1634 he married Elizabeth, the daughter of Richard Bourne of London and widow of Nathaniel Master, a London merchant. Walsingham served as a commissioner for the loan in 1626-27 and for knighthood compositions. He was Vice Admiral for Kent from 1626 at least until 1639, a DL as early as 1630 and a JP for many years. Walsingham was on poor terms with the Court in the 1630s, as is shown by his being summoned before the Council in 1637 for allegedly grubbing out part of a royal wood. He repeatedly refused to subscribe £500 to a royal loan in the spring of 1640. He entered the county elections for Kent in 1640 but withdrew in favor of Sir Henry Vane, Sr.* He joined the opposition in the 1640 Parliaments and served as a parliamentary DL during the war. He was a member of the committee for the city of Rochester and subsequently for the county of Kent, where he played a prominent role. Walsingham was captured during the Kentish rebellion of 1643 and was later awarded reparations. His son was one of the rebels. He remained in Parliament until 1653. Walsingham had financial difficulties. He was arrested for debt, and his estates in Kent were sold in 1650 and about 1655.

Everitt; Keeler; Al. Cant.; CSPD, Jas. I, 11:444; Chas. I, 1-15 passim; Underdown, PP; E.A. Webb, G.W. Miller and J. Beckwith, The History of Chislehurst (1899). Papers: L (Add. MSS; Stowe MSS).

R.H. Gottdiener

WALTER, Henry (1611-1678)

Independent minister, was the second son of John Walter, esq., of Piercefield Park, Chepstow, Mon. Walter matriculated at Jesus Coll., Oxf. on 12 Apr. 1633, and graduated B.C.L. on 22 Oct. 1633. He came from an Anglican family and was made Curate of Mounton by his elder brother, who inherited the patronage from their father. Under the influence of William Wroth,* Walter adopted Puritan views; their relationship was close, and Walter was named executor of Wroth's will. In 1636 Walter succeeded the Puritan Marmaduke Matthews as Vicar of Mynydd Islwyn, Newport, Mon. At the outbreak of the Civil War he fled to London with Walter Cradock,* settling at All Hallows the Great with other Welsh refugees. On 15 Aug. 1645 the House of Commons ordered that £300 p.a. be provided from the diocesan lands of Llandaff and St. David's to support the preaching of Walter Cradock and Richard Symonds.* Following the Commons' wishes, Walter and Cradock proceeded to Wales in 1646 without waiting for the approval of the Westminster Assembly. On 17 Nov. 1646 the Lords approved the trio as itinerant ministers for South Wales. The Act for the Propagation of the Gospel in Wales made Walter one of the 25 Approvers responsible for providing Puritan ministers, and his own work was undertaken primarily in Glamorgan and Monmouth. When the Act was not renewed in 1653, he became Vicar of St. Woollos, Newport, staying until his ejection in 1660. In 1666 he was living at Parc y Pil, Llantarnam, and ministering to conventicles in the area. Under the Declaration of Indulgence in 1672, he was licensed as an Independent to preach at his house. He was the spiritual leader of some two hundred Nonconformists in this period, and in 1675 visited the Nonconformist congregation at Broadmead, Bristol.

CJ, 2:735; 4:678; 5:545; *CSPD, Chas. II*, 13:198, 203, 247; *DWB*; T. Watts, 'Henry Walter, a Seventeenth Century Minister at Newport,' *TCHS*, 20:174-76.

R.L. Greaves

WALTON (or Wauton), Valentine (c. 1594-1661?)

Regicide and parliamentary radical, MP LP 1640 (Hunts.) Walton came of an old county family. The son of Nicholas Walton, he inherited the family manor of Great Staughton, Hunts. in 1606 and married Margaret, sister of Oliver Cromwell, in 1617. The radicalism Walton later manifested in his political and military career was already evident in the 1630s when he resisted the Crown's attempts to enforce the collection of nonparliamentary revenues. He prevaricated when required to compound for knighthood in Sept. 1630, opposed ship money later in the decade, and suffered imprisonment for failing to pay his full assessment. By the time the Long Parliament was summoned in 1640, his actions had brought him sufficient local popularity to ensure his election as member for his county against the nominee of one of its two most powerful landowners, Sir Henry Cromwell. Whatever

prominence Walton would later owe to his connection with the Cromwells, his election to the Long Parliament was clearly on his own merits; the first of his family to be elected to Parliament, he was also the last to serve in it.

In Aug. 1642 Walton helped frustrate the King's attempts to gain custody of the plate belonging to the colleges at Cambridge. He raised a troop of horse to serve under the Earl of Essex* and was taken prisoner at Edgehill. Having gained his freedom in July 1643, he was made colonel of a regiment of foot in the army of the Eastern Association that autumn, becoming also Governor of King's Lynn. His appointment as governor, according to Clement Walker, was part of a plan by Cromwell and his associates to secure King's Lynn and the surrounding countryside as a stronghold, should they ever be forced into wholesale retreat. (*The History of Independency*, pt. 1 [1648], p. 147). This rumor was doubtless fueled by the fact that the town was until late in 1644 the main depository for the arms and ammunition of the Eastern Association. Walton lost his eldest son, Valentine, at Marston Moor. Cromwell himself wrote the letter that informed him, and in which he penned his celebrated description of the battle, 'God made them as stubble to our swords. . . .'

As a member of the Long Parliament, Walton was active on committees for religion and on the recruitment committee, and in liaison work between Parliament and the leaders of the Eastern Association. In Nov. 1648 his regiment was among those which petitioned Parliament for the punishment of Charles I. A member of the High Court, Walton was conscientious in his attendance at its sessions and signed the King's death warrant. In Feb. 1649 he was appointed to the Council of State, serving on all five Councils down to the dissolution of the Rump. He was appointed to the Committee for the Army in Jan. 1652 and reappointed in December of that year. From the dismissal of the Rump to the fall of Richard Cromwell,* Walton's career was in abeyance, though he unsuccessfully sought election to Richard's Parliament.

His complete absence from the Parliaments and Councils of the Protectorate, together with the accusation of hostility to the government which was leveled against him at the time of his parliamentary candidature, suggests strong republican sentiments.

Richard Cromwell's deposition in Apr. 1659 brought Walton a brief return to public life. He was restored to his seat in the Long Parliament, elected to the Council of State and appointed a Commissioner for the Admiralty. He was one of the seven commissioners to whom Parliament gave control of the armed forces on 12 Oct., and he afterwards participated in the siege of Portsmouth, which declared for Parliament in Dec. 1659. In Feb. 1660, however, Monck deprived him of the regiment of horse whose command he had recently been given, and this brought his career to an end. At the Restoration he escaped to the Continent, where he is believed to have died in 1661. Walton's second wife died in 1662. He is alleged to have written a history of the Civil Wars which was still extant in 1733.

DNB; Keeler; Holmes; Firth & Rait; Yule; B. & P.; Underdown, *PP*; *VCH, Hunts.*; Noble; Ludlow; Abbott. Papers: L (Add. MSS; Sloane MSS).

C. Polizzotto

WALWYN, William (1600-1680)

Leveller, was the second son of a Worcestershire gentleman and grandson of a Bishop of Hereford. He was apprenticed to the London silk trade and later became a member of the Merchant Adventurers' Company. Of moderate means, he lived with his large family surrounded by friends and books, and was stirred into public controversy unwillingly. His political activity was temperate compared with the flamboyance of Lilburne* and Overton;* his influence was through quiet conversations, discreet lobbying and pamphlets which were more measured and intellectually coherent than those of his colleagues. Walwyn was a firm opponent of royal absolutism and spent most of his writing life indicting religious intolerance and other restrictions on personal freedom imposed in turn by King, Parliament and Presbyterians. He was acquainted with the doctrines of a wide range of religious dissidents, and it was on their behalf that he first pleaded for toleration (*The Humble Petition . . . of Brownists*, 1641; *Some Considerations*, 1642; *The Power of Love*, 1643). No sectarian himself, he remained loosely attached to his Presbyterian parish church of St. James, Garlic Hill (near Moorfields). Before the outbreak of war he had achieved the reform of his parish, as well as organizing successfully the return of 'well-affected' councillors and a parliamentarian alderman and had tried to encourage Parliament to spell out 'certain infallible maxims of free government' (*A Whisper in the Eare*, 1646). In 1643, working through Salters' Hall – the meeting place of the political radicals – Walwyn joined Henry Marten* in attempting a general rising of volunteer troops free from the conservative Militia Committee in London. He met Lilburne in 1645 when both were in trouble before Parliament for trying to charge Speaker Lenthall* with corruption. More philosophical than the pragmatic Lilburne, Walwyn admired and defended him on abstract principles of reason, equity and justice (*England's Lamentable Slaverie*, 1645; *A Pearle on a Dounghill*, 1646).

Walwyn's general justifications for liberty of conscience and the dangers of claiming doctrinal infallibility were sharpened when applied to particular controversies such as his attack on Prynne's* apostasy (*A Helpe to the Right Understanding*, 1645), the damaging salvos against *Gangraena* (*A Whisper in the Eare; A Worde More*, 1646; *An Antidote*, 1646; *A Prediction of Mr. Edwards His Conversion*, 1646; *A Parable*, 1646), the defense of Thomas Hawes, accused of Arianism (*The Afflicted Christian*, 1646) and the spirited *A Demurre to a Bill* (1646) against a proposed bill for preventing heresy by branding and death. With the fear of Presbyterian imposition of religious uniformity Walwyn came back to general philosophical arguments for toleration in his most cogent piece, *A Still and Soft Voice* (Apr. 1647).

As a Leveller activist, Walwyn drafted the 'Large' Petition to Parliament in Mar. 1647 which echoed his own earlier writings in proposing the supremacy of the Commons in secular as well as religious matters, the need for toleration, the abolition of tithes, law reform, freedom of speech and freedom from arbitrary arrest, and a cessation of public begging. When the Petition was condemned to be burned Walwyn singled out those responsible – the Lord Mayor, corrupt MPs (*The Poore Wise-mans Admonition*, 1647) and, more specifically, lawyers, monopolists and relatives of the Lords in the House of Commons (*Gold Tried in the Fire*, 1647). Although true 'commonwealthsmen' remained in principle the repository of the people's power in Parliament, their defeat in the Commons must account for Walwyn's new involvement with the army (Brooke, *The Charity of Churchmen*, 1649; Walwyn, *The Fountain of Slaunder*, 1649), now seen as the smiter of corrupt MPs and the savior of just causes (*The Poore Wise-mans Admonition*). The *Agreement of the People*'s similarity to the 'Large' Petition makes it probable that Walwyn was a party both to its formulation and to the political activities of 1648 linking the army with the London Levellers. However, between mid-1647 and Aug. 1648 Walwyn's writings ceased. Interrupted by the second Civil War, the Leveller program was revised in *The Bloody Project* (1648), where Walwyn reiterated the fundamental principle of the sovereignty of the people through regularly elected parliaments – duly restricted in power over individuals' rights.

Unlike the other leaders who courted the notoriety of jail, Walwyn managed to stay free until he was arrested with three other Levellers in Mar. 1649 for his suspected part in *The Second Part of England's New Chains*. In typical Leveller fashion, Walwyn, though probably innocent, refused to incriminate himself and would say nothing. Though given much gentler treatment than Lilburne or Overton, he was devastated at his incarceration (*The Fountain*). From the Tower the Levellers issued *A Manifestation* (1649), an apologia – probably written by Walwyn – which denied extreme interpretations of Leveller doctrine such as economic levelling, atheism and naturalistic interpretation of Scripture, while stressing equality of opportunity and individual freedoms. This was followed in May by the third *Agreement*, which made specific franchise proposals while reaffirming the supremacy of Parliament – characteristically restricted in order to safeguard individual rights – as the only true representative of the people.

While the four were still in the Tower John Price,* an Independent pamphleteer, published *Walwyn's Wiles* (Apr. 1649) in which he cleverly analyzed Walwyn's rhetorical tactics and plausibly alleged his atheism, anti-scripturism, blasphemy and moral corruption. Henry Brooke, Walwyn's son-in-law, took up his defense (*The Charity of Churchmen*), and he was followed by Walwyn's own *Fountain of Slaunder* and *Walwyn's Just Defence* (May 1649). Brooke throws light on Walwyn's unorthodoxy but ingenuously presents him as a simple, sincere Christian reformer wanting simple doctrine and equity and social justice on biblical grounds. No sign of the Machiavellian Walwyn here. Walwyn's own justificatory writings sketch his dealings with past persecutors; clearly, he considered his religious views more in need of defense than his political stance.

After the Leveller defeat Walwyn emerged from prison, and remained silent until 1651 when he entered the controversy over the jury system. In *Juries Justified* he defended them as a bastion of English liberty, based as they were on conscience 'which some think, have been as frequently found under felt hats and worsted stockings, as with people of a finer stuff.' Sometime in the 1650s Walwyn changed occupations and turned physician. Apparently not a graduate, it is likely that he practiced more as an apothecary – perhaps aided by Dr. Henry Brooke, his constant supporter. In 1667 he published *A Touchstone for Physick*, recommending mild, commonsense treatment of the sick and advertising his own medicines by listing cases of happily cured patients saved from diseases ranging from indigestion to the plague. After his death this pamphlet was republished in 1681 with a different list of successful cures.

Most writers – with the notable exception of Schenk – present Walwyn as a rationalist who lived 'by reason alone' (Pease, p. 247). Yet his autobiographical sketch (*A Whisper in the Eare*) made it clear that the humanist authors he read were unable to resolve his problems of conscience. 'I found much disconsolation therein, great uncertainty and at last extreme affliction of mind' (p. 3), stated Walwyn, until he read the Scriptures and, literally, saw the light. With the victory of the Gospel over the Law he became transformed into a man of faith and fervor to do God's will in his public and private life. A Protestant's faith, not a humanist's reason, was the source of his inner peace. 'God only persuades the heart' (*A Whisper*) and 'things divine . . . could never have been perceived by . . . nature and reason' (*A Prediction*). Indeed, Walwyn's belief in God was not arrived at by rational argument but 'is an unexpressible power, that in a forcible manner constrained my understanding and . . . hath pierced my judgment and affection' (*A Still and Soft Voice*). His self-confessed Antinomianism – belief in free, universal justification – he owed to the working of grace within him, empowering him to preach this liberating doctrine to overcome the universal corruption of mankind. Unlike most Antinomians, he did not feel freed from the Word and he castigated claimants of direct inspiration who treated Scripture as a dead letter (*The Vanitie*, 1649). Claims for immunity from the Law made sectaries intolerant, distracting them from true religion, the pursuit of Christian love and compassion for the poor. Walwyn

was pragmatically suspicious of political action based on direct inspiration – 'consideration,' not heady illumination, would show how church and state should be settled (*A Word in Season*, 1646). But although Walwyn was alien to those directly inspired by the Spirit he cannot be classed as a rationalist, for, like other Puritans, he saw the word of God as forming 'a new creature' (*The Vanitie*). Like many Antinomians, Walwyn believed in an internal heaven and hell, for though reason denied there should be everlasting fires 'for a little small sinning in this world,' yet the Scriptures insist, and 'we both submitted our reasons to God's Word' (*The Charity of Churchmen*).

Walwyn's political thinking stemmed directly from his religious transformation which must have occurred prior to 1641. Realizing that free justification meant that all were potentially saved, Walwyn applied this to a doctrine of love and 'practical Christianity' which stressed the need to glorify God through good works for our fellows (*The Vanitie*). His inner transformation through reading Scripture led directly to the decision to do Christ's will 'and that in a more public way' (*A Whisper in the Eare*). Involvement in ward politics and petitioning Parliament followed. From this early spur to political action Walwyn continued to oppose oppression – the natural outcome of a Puritan's inner conviction of the need to do God's will. The commandment 'to feed the hungry, clothe the naked . . . delivering the captive and setting the oppressed free' (*The Vanitie*) followed directly from reading Scripture; while realizing Christ's love in the world led to 'real' religion (*A Manifestation*). Hence, true Christians defend 'the just liberties of their country' and hate tyranny and oppression (*The Power of Love*).

The translation of religious doctrine into political action came at first as a defense of Separatists' and sects' freedom of conscience against incursions by established ministers and politicians acting in the interests of religious unity. Walwyn's case rested on the moral necessity of each man coming to an understanding of Scripture for himself. In just this way had Walwyn come to his own *unum necessarium*. His spirited defense of Lilburne (*England's Lamentable Slaverie*), which based people's rights not on Magna Carta but on reason, equity and justice confined its examples of oppression to continued compulsion in worship and restrictions on religious freedom. Oppressions such as censorship, monopolies, arbitrary committee proceedings and self-incrimination as required by the Lords were soon included in the further defense of Lilburne (*A Pearle*), but restrictions on free conscience again bore the main thrust of the attack. The 'Large' Petition with its secular list of grievances also complained against the suppression of religious groups and their publications and against tithes.

As the Leveller campaign against corruption in Parliament intensified and spread to the army (*The Poore Wise-mans Admonition*), Walwyn's religious and political radicalism became fused. The vengeance of corrupt parliamentarians was now directed against men of widely differing opinions, while opponents of tyranny were branded as heretics and schismatics.

By the time of the first *Agreement* concern for positive reform rather than complaints against oppression had crystallized into a secular program of constitutional reform, though even here pride of place was given to religious freedom. Walwyn stressed toleration again in *The Bloody Project*, adding to it a 'practical Christian' concern for providing for the poor. Finally, the clinching link between political and religious freedom appeared in Dec. 1648 in *No Papist No Presbyterian* (attributed to Walwyn), where 'free-born people and English natives' would lose their birth-right with the loss of liberty of conscience. *A Manifestation* justifies 'community happiness' and levelling on Christian terms.

The inspiration behind Walwyn's thought stemmed from the enlightenment that came to him through reading Scripture, and was the source of both his temperate concern for freedom to act according to one's conscience and the program of social and political reform most in keeping with the precepts of 'practical Christianity.' The issues he tackled broadened gradually to include a wider set of personal freedoms and political and social changes for which the justifications were God-given reason, equity and common justice. As in so many thinkers of the period, secular reform had its origin in religious inspiration.

Morton; W. Schenk, 'A Seventeenth-Century Radical,' *EHR*, 14: 74-83; Tolmie; Brailsford; T.C. Pease, *The Leveller Movement* (1916); Haller, *Tr.*; *Lev. Man.*; *Lev. Tr.*; D.M. Wolfe, *Milton and the Puritan Revolution* (1941); *Gangraena*; J. Vicars, *The Schizmatick Sifted* (1646); *DNB*; Frank; Hill, *MER* and *WTUD*.

L. Mulligan

WARD, Patience (1629-1696)

City and parliamentary radical, MP 1679, 1680, 1681 (Pontefract), 1689 (London). Ward was born on 7 Dec. 1629, the eighth son of Thomas Ward of Tanshelf, Yorks. and his wife Elizabeth. He apparently owed his name to his father's frustrated desire for a daughter. The latter died when Ward was aged five, and he was raised by his mother for the ministry. He entered Cambridge for that purpose in 1643, but though his brother Leonard founded the first Congregational church in Pontefract, Ward had another calling. In 1646 he was apprenticed to Lancelot Tolson of St. Helen's, Bishopsgate, a Merchant Taylor and Merchant Adventurer trading in France. Ward was received into the Merchant Taylors' Company in 1655, and was its Master in 1671-72. He married (8 June 1654) Elizabeth, daughter and coheiress of William Hobson, haberdasher, and set up shop in St. Lawrence Pountney Lane. Ward ultimately amassed considerable wealth but his early years may have been difficult; he was repeatedly admonished by the Merchant Taylors for failing to take up his livery and in 1663 paid a £50 fine on that account. By 1670 however he was sufficiently prominent and prosperous to gain election as Alderman of Farringdon Within and as Sheriff of London. About the same time he became a DL for Middlesex, and in 1671 a member of the Honorable Artillery Company. On 29 Oct. 1675 Ward was knighted, and he capped his civic career as Lord Mayor of London in 1680-81.

As early as 1664, Ward had been briefly imprisoned for a 'seditious' petition about customs, and after 1670 he emerged as the leader of a merchant group, many of Huguenot origin, whose demands for redress against Colbert's tariffs were a catalyst for religious and political opposition to France as well. With the publication of the 'Scheme of Trade' on 29 Nov. 1674 (*Somers Tracts*, 8:32), a highly colored attack on the state of Anglo-French trade, the group emerged as a potent lobby, and its cause was taken up by Shaftesbury.* Ward testified as its spokesman before the Lords' Committee of Trade on 13 July 1676, urging an embargo of all French imports if a new commercial agreement were not reached. A provision for such an embargo was incorporated into the Poll Bill of Mar. 1678.

By this time, Ward was an implacable opponent of the Court. Elected to Parliament in 1679, he sat on sixteen committees, including those for elections and privileges and for the removal of Papists from London, and supported exclusion. Ward's election as Lord Mayor was a major embarrassment to the government. He dovetailed an aldermanic petition for exclusion with the presentation of the second Exclusion Bill in Nov. 1680, and joined the parliamentary committee which sought the removal of his Recorder, George Jeffreys, for opposing it. Ward was taken ill shortly before the Oxford Parliament, and probably did not attend it. But he remained a thorn in the government's side, refusing a direct request from Charles II not to call a Council meeting to petition for a new parliament, and personally delivering such petitions to Hampton Court on 19 May and 7 July 1681. Among his other acts

as mayor was to erect an inscription blaming the Great Fire on the Papists, and he received a warm address from the Council at the expiration of his term. On 18 Jan. 1682 he was appointed a member of the Council committee to protect the City charter against the writ of *quo warranto*. The Court meanwhile struck him from the assessment lists (1680) and removed his deputy lieutenancy (1681).

In May 1683 Ward was tried before the now Judge Jeffreys for perjury in the trial of Sir Thomas Pilkington.* Found guilty and sentenced to the pillory, he took refuge in the home of Bateman, a surgeon implicated in the Rye House plot, and later fled to Holland, where he corresponded with Thomas Papillon* and contributed £500 to Monmouth's invasion. Despite this, James II made overtures to him in 1687. Ward did not return however until the conquest. He was at once restored to his aldermanic seat, which he occupied until his death, and elected to the Convention Parliament for London. In 1689 he became (again until his death) Commissioner of Customs, and in 1689-90 and 1694-96 was colonel of the Blue regiment. In Parliament Ward sat on thirty committees, including three to raise City loans for the new government. He was also active on the committee to reverse the *quo warranto* judgment. Defeated for the same constituency in 1690, he did not stand again for Parliament. He continued active in City affairs, subscribing loans and furnishing intelligence through his Huguenot contacts. Ward died on 10 July 1696, and was buried in St. Mary Abchurch. His wife predeceased him on 24 Dec. 1685. Lacking direct issue, he left his manor of Hooton Pagnel to his grand-nephew Patience Ward. A nephew, Sir John Ward, was Lord Mayor of London in 1718-19. Ward supported toleration for the Dissenters but was not, as has been asserted, a Quaker. The breadth of his interests is indicated by his election as a Fellow of the Royal Society in 1681. A Tory pamphlet unsympathetically described him as having 'a long and meager' face with the expression of 'one squeezing over a close stool.'

C.E. Whiting, 'Sir Patience Ward of Tanshelf,' *Yorkshire Archaeological Journal*, 34:245-72; M. Priestley, 'London Merchants and Opposition Politics in Charles II's Reign,' *BIHR*, 29:205-19; *DNB*; Beaven; *ST*; *Grey's Debates*; Luttrell; *CSPD, Chas. II, passim*; A.F.W. Papillon, *Memoirs of Thomas Papillon* (1887); History of Parliament, draft biography.

R. Zaller

WARD, Samuel (1577-1640)

Puritan minister, was born in Suffolk, the son of John Ward, minister of Haverhill, and educated at Cambridge (B.A. 1597, M.A. 1600, B.D. 1607), attending first St. John's Coll., then Sidney Sussex, where he was elected one of the first group of fellows in 1599. After serving as lecturer in Haverhill, Ward was elected lecturer or town preacher at Ipswich, Suff. on 1 Nov. 1603, where he officiated for over thirty years. In 1621, when the Spanish match was being negotiated, Ward was imprisoned for having drawn a caricature in which the King of Spain was pictured as an enemy of England and in league with the devil. In 1624 Ward and his fellow Ipswich minister John Yates,* alarmed over the spread of Arminianism, gathered questionable points from the work of Richard Montagu to present to Parliament, thus helping to make innovation in religion a public issue. By 1634 Ward's preaching at Ipswich was credited with encouraging substantial numbers of religious dissidents to emigrate to New England. At the insistence of Archbishop Laud, Ward was censured in the High Commission on 2 Nov. 1635 on a variety of counts, chiefly for disparaging the new ecclesiastical dispensation. After suffering imprisonment Ward withdrew to the Netherlands where he and William Bridge* served as pastors to the English congregation at Rotterdam, then under Independent influence. He returned to Ipswich about 1638.

On 8 Mar. 1640 he was buried at the church of St. Mary-le-Tower, where he had so often preached.

P. Heylyn, *Cyprianus Anglicus* (1671); Gardiner, *HE*; H.R. Trevor-Roper, *Archbishop Laud* (2nd ed., 1962); Seaver; *DNB*.

W.B. Patterson

WARNER, John (d. 1648)

London radical, was the second son of John Warner of Bucknell, Oxon. He and his younger brother Samuel owned a druggist firm in the City, and in 1627 John Warner acquired membership in the livery of the Grocers' Company. The following year Samuel was charged by the East India Company with undertaking private trade with the East Indies, which led to his trial in the Exchequer Court and incarceration. Presumably John shared his hostility to monopolies. John was elected sheriff in Sept. 1639 and alderman in 1640 (as was Samuel three years later). On the advice of Christopher Rogers, Principal of New Inn Hall, Oxf., and the tutor Henry Cornish,* in 1639 Warner made Christopher Love his chaplain, but the effort of the parish of St. Anne and St. Agnes, Aldersgate, to make Love a lecturer failed when Bishop Juxon refused to license him due to his refusal to accept episcopal ordination. Love subsequently married Warner's ward, Mary Stone. In May 1640 Warner defied the Crown's request to submit a list of the richest men in his ward, and in December he signed the Root and Branch Petition. Both John and Samuel were elected to the Militia Committee in Jan. 1642, and that spring John was made colonel of a regiment in the trained bands. The same year he provided evidence against Sir Richard Gurney. Apparently an adept administrator, John served as Parliamentary Treasurer for Irish Subscriptions, for receiving subscriptions of plate and money, for collecting weekly assessments, and (commencing 31. Mar. 1645) for war.

John and probably Samuel were political Independents. With the army's support John became Lord Mayor in Sept. 1647, in which capacity he suppressed royalist and Presbyterian upheavals, though he was unable to secure Independent control of the City government. John Warner died in Nov. 1648, leaving a legacy of £100 to ten poor godly ministers and their families.

CSPD, Chas. I, 14:534; 17:306; 19:37; 20:377; 22-23 passim; CJ, 2:465, 618, 868; LJ, 2:246; Pearl; Seaver. Papers: LPR; L (Sloane MSS 3945).

R.L. Greaves and D. Mock

WARR, John (fl. 1642-1686)

Leveller and law reformer, made his mark with three major pamphlets, Administrations Civil and Spiritual (1648), The Corruption and Deficiency of the Lawes of England (1649), and The Privileges of the People (1649). In Corruption and Deficiency, Warr took up the theme of the Norman Yoke, which he shared with John Hare* and other critics. Warr asserted that the Norman Conquest had given all power to the king under the title of prerogative, and none to the people. Prerogative was therefore not, as prerevolutionary jurists had thought, the legitimate authority of government, but a usurpation of freedom, while liberty existed not in balance to prerogative but opposition to it, representing concessions 'exorted from princes by fury of war and incessantness of address.' Between prerogative and freedom there could only be war to the death, until 'either prerogative and privilege he swallowed up in freedom or liberty itself be led captive by prerogative.' Warr denounced the concept of fundamental law as an attempt to disguise oppression by antiquity, and declared that 'the very law is a badge of an oppression, its proper interest being to enslave the people.' In The Privilege of the People, Warr warned that the privilege of Parliament was no more valid an authority than the prerogative of kings had been.

Freedom, like truth, was indivisible; 'Tis not possible for a people to be too free,' wrote Warr grandly. True law could only spring from freedom, for 'at the foundation of governments justice was in men before it came to be in laws.' For Warr, this was more than a mere approach to contract theory. As Christopher Hill has pointed out, Warr saw history as a perpetual struggle between Equity (i.e., innate justice) and Form, whether represented by custom, government or established religion. The distinction between clerical and lay was thus an abuse of Form just as much as the distinction between government and people. Indeed no institution, as the embodiment of Form, could claim permanent legitimacy. Warr saw legal reform as the prelude to spiritual reform, and the attainment of an ultimate condition of enlightenment in which Equity would definitely prevail, and 'the principled man' would have 'his freedom within himself,' knowing 'no bounds but his own, even Equity.'

Warr believed this process must be gradual, and based on the reform rather than the mere overthrow of existing institutions. He urged codification of the laws, decentralization of courts, simplification of procedure and greater authority for juries. The right of the individual was transcendent. Justice must be made available to all, and all be permitted to plead their own cause. Law had been the instrument of oppression; properly understood, it was the recourse of the poor against the mighty. Only in this spirit could justice prevail. Like other reformers of the period, Warr was especially scathing in his criticism of Chancery, whose purpose was 'merely to elude the letter of the law, which though defective yet had some certainty; and, under a pretense of conscience, to devolve all causes upon mere will, swayed by corrupt interest.' Law itself could not be reformed by more law, but in the last analysis depended upon the innate sense of justice which, however obscured by interest or ignorance, was the birthright of all.

Warr's life is almost wholly obscure. It is known that he was a purchaser of expropriated crown lands in southwestern England and Wales.

Harl. Misc.; Hill, *WTUD* and *P. & R.*; Veall; James.

A.J. Busch and R. Zaller

WARREN, Edward (d. 1663)

Army officer and conspirator, was the son of a Dean of Ossory. In 1649 he was a lieutenant in Col. Whalley's* regiment of horse, in which his brother Abel, later Mayor of Kilkenny, was a captain. Warren distinguished himself at the battle of Glascarring in Nov. 1649, and by 1650 was a captain. He served throughout the Commonwealth and Protectorate, and in 1659 was a major in Fleetwood's* former regiment of horse. Both Warrens opposed Ludlow* in Ireland and are frequently mentioned in his *Memoirs* (2:147, 185-86, 195, 202, 210, 471). Warren was one of the chief actors in the surprising of Dublin Castle on 13 Dec. 1659 for Parliament. He opposed Ludlow's return to command, and was sent to England where he laid articles of impeachment against him in Jan. 1660. He failed however to obtain a looked-for regimental command. After the Restoration he was involved in anti-government conspiracies in Ireland, which led to his arrest and execution on 15 July 1663. Warren defended the republican cause on the scaffold, 'which now lieth in the dust and some days would have terrified the greatest monarchs,' while supporters rioted on his behalf. Lt.-Col. John Warren was also a brother. A committed republican, he was arrested in the retaking of Dublin Castle in Feb. 1660.

Firth & Davies; T. Warren, *A History and Genealogy of the Warren Family* (1902); *CSPI*, 3:692, 695, 706, 709, 710, 4:45; 5:111, 112, 121, 148-49, 154, 163, 170, 176-77.

R. Zaller

WARREN, Elizabeth (fl. 1645-1649)

Pamphleteer, was a gentlewoman of Woodbridge, Suff. and a Latin scholar. In *The Old and Good Way Vindicated* (1645, 1646) she castigated mechanic preachers and those who repudiated the universities and the necessity of traditional learning for the ministry. Her own learning was used in defense of the Puritan clergy, including Henry Burton,* and had the blessing of her minister, Robert Cade, Curate of Woodbridge (1623-66) and a signatory of the petition of Presbyterian ministers in Suffolk in 1646. Cade wrote a commendatory epistle to her *Spiritual Thrift* (1647), a series of meditations on Christian living in which she condemned all intemperance and explained the Civil War as divine punishment for the people's quest for material possessions. She expressed sexual deference (probably *pro forma*) in her 1649 tract, *A Warning Peece from Heaven*, which attacked the Cromwellian usurpers who broke the Covenant by flouting the rights of the King and the people. Warren was essentially a moderate Puritan and was of a different cast than such committed radicals as Mary Gadbury,* Anne Hutchinson* and Anna Trapnel.*

E.M. Williams, 'Women Preachers in the Civil War,' *JMH*, 1:564-65; K. Thomas, 'Women and the Civil War Sects,' *P. & P.*, 13:49.

R.L. Greaves

WARRINGTON, first Earl of. *See* Booth, Henry.

WARWICK, second Earl of. *See* Rich, Robert.

WASTELL, John (c. 1593-1659)

Civil War officer, was born at Scorton, Yorks., the eldest son of Leonard Wastell, a gentleman of modest means. He was admitted to Sidney Sussex Coll., Camb. in

Feb. 1611 and then to Gray's Inn in 1613. Wastell pursued a legal career in his native Yorkshire, and was elected Recorder of Ripon in 1626, an office he held until his death, and of Richmond in 1631. Later he served as a JP in the North Riding. During the 1630s he became known in Yorkshire for his Puritan views and opposition to Strafford. In 1640 he was made Master in Chancery for North Allerton, and, at the end of the year, was returned by that borough to the Long Parliament, where his sympathies lay with the moderate reformers. During the Civil War he accepted a commission and was made colonel. In May 1645, in the campaign which led to Naseby, Fairfax* sent him to serve in the north under Lord Leven. During the second Civil War he had a regiment of foot and fought with Cromwell against the Scots at Preston (Aug. 1648). He adhered to the Rump 'belatedly' and perhaps reluctantly after Mar. 1649, and in May his regiment was disbanded. Little is known of his views about national politics in the 1650s but he continued to be a figure of local significance until his death in 1659.

Abbott; *Al. Cant.*; *CSPD, Chas. I*, 5:26; *CJ*, 2:100, 151, 196; Keeler.

S.J. Stearns

WATKINS, Sir David (fl. 1620-1661)

City radical and merchant, may have been the David Watkins knighted on 5 Nov. 1620. One of the heaviest of the Irish investors, he subscribed £2025 to the Irish adventure in Apr. 1642 and £375 for the sea adventure in June, adding a further £600 in 1646 under the provisions of the doubling ordinance. With this he was able to claim 10,000 acres in Queens and Eastmeath counties. With Richard Shute* and others, he delivered on 1 Dec. 1642 a petition to the House of Commons demanding active prosecution of the war, the immediate levying of 6000 dragoons, payment of war reparations from delinquents' estates and the sequestering of malignant ministers.

(*The True and Original Copy of the First Petition Which Was Delivered by Sir David Watkins*, 1643). The petition was referred back to the Common Council where it was rejected, but its substance was incorporated in the Remonstrance of 30 Mar. 1643, which Watkins helped draft and lobby through the Council. A ruling elder of St. Andrew Undershaft and a leading member of the Grand Committee of the London Provincial Assembly, Watkins was closely allied with Hugh Peter* and John Goodwin,* and in 1645 was named a Trier for regulating the selection of elders in the Presbyterian classes of London. In 1644 he was accused of defaulting on a promised subscription by Sir John Clotworthy, who called him 'a beggarly unworthy fellow,' but John Ashe* and William Strode* testified that he had advanced £8492 for Scotland and an additional £2000 for other purposes, and on Denis Bond's* motion the House ordered Clotworthy to apologize publicly to Watkins and declared itself 'well satisfied of his good affection.' In Dec. 1646 however the House cited him for remarking loudly in the exchange that the army should deal with citizens who petitioned to Parliament against the gathered churches, indicating his own conversion to Independency. Watkins also had ties to the Hartlib* circle, as is indicated by his patronage of the young Oxford scholar Thomas Danson, a pupil of Hartlib's friend Christian Rave. In 1648 he became a trustee for the raising of £50,000 for the relief of Ireland, and with the Commonwealth was appointed to the Committee for the Posts. On 4 Jan. 1653 Watkins presented a paper before the Irish and Scottish Affairs Committee, 'The State of the Foreign Letter Office,' in which he claimed rights to the office based on a grant by the Earl of Warwick* in 1642. He pursued this claim with great pertinacity in the Council, the courts and, after the Restoration, with Charles II, but was unable to vindicate it.

Pearl; Tolmie; MacCormack; Webster, *GI*; K.S. Bottigheimer, *English Money and Irish Land* (1971); W.A. Shaw, *The*

Knights of England (1906); T. Liu, 'The Founding of the London Provincial Assembly, 1645-47,' *Guildhall Studies in London History*, 3:109-34; *CCAM*, *passim*; *CCC, passim*; *CSPD, Chas. I*, 19:227; 21:84; 22:98; 23:661, 666; *Comm.*, 2:175; 3:467; 4:15, 444; 5-7, *passim*; *Chas. II*, 2:228.

R. Zaller

WAUGH, Dorothy (b. 1636)

Quaker, came from Hutton, W'land, and with her sister Jane (d. 1674) was a servant in the home of John and Mabel Camm* at Camsgill farm, Preston Patrick, W'land. With their master, they became Friends at Firbank in 1652. As an itinerant preacher Dorothy witnessed in Cumberland, Lancashire and Norfolk (1654), Cambridgeshire (where she and Anne Blaykling* met with James Parnell*), Hampshire and Cornwall (1655), and Berkshire (1656). With Mary Fisher,* John Whitehead* and William Dewsbury* she was one of the first Quakers to preach in Buckinghamshire. As a consequence of her preaching she was imprisoned at Norwich (1654), Truro (1655) and Reading (1656). With Mary Prince,* Sarah Gibbons,* Mary Wetherhead, William Brend, John Copeland, Christopher Holder and Thomas Thurston* she arrived at Boston on 7 Aug. 1656, two days after Mary Fisher and Anne Austin had been expelled. They were immediately examined by the authorities and imprisoned until the captain who brought them was ready to take them on the return voyage. While in prison the group engaged in friendly correspondence with the sectary Samuel Gorton of Warwick, Rhode Island. In 1657 Dorothy Waugh was part of a contingent of twelve Friends that returned to America, and she and four others began their ministry at New Amsterdam. The following spring she and Sarah Gibbons left Newport on foot for Salem and Boston, where they were whipped. That August Dorothy and five others left for Barbados. While in New England she had urged Friends not to have children because they hindered the Quaker cause. She subsequently married William Lotherington of Whitby, Yorks.

Jane Waugh (d. 1674) was, with Elizabeth Fletcher,* Elizabeth Leavens* and Thomas Holme,* a Quaker worker in Cheshire and southern Lancashire in 1654, though she was illiterate. During the course of her ministry she was imprisoned at Manchester, Cambridge and (with Anne Audland) at Banbury, Oxon. In 1664 she married Thomas Whitehead (d. 1691) of South Cadbury (and later Bruton), Som. She was also imprisoned in that county for her Quaker activities.

Fox, *CJ*, 2 *passim*; Jones, *QAC*; Braithwaite, *BQu*; *EQW*; *FPT*. Papers: LF.

R.L. Greaves

WAVEL (or Wavell), Richard (1633-1705)

Ejected Independent minister, was born on 3 Apr. 1633, the younger son of Major Wavel of Limerston, Isle of Wight, a Royalist. Wavel matriculated from Wadham Coll., Oxf. on 9 Dec. 1653 and graduated B.A. on 15 Feb. 1658. Shortly thereafter he became an assistant to William Reyner, Vicar of Egham, Surrey, but was ejected in 1662. For a time he taught in his own grammar school until stopped by official harassment. He maintained a conventicle in his house at Egham (for which he was not licensed in 1672) until he succeeded Anthony Palmer* as minister of the Congregational church at Pinners' Hall, London in 1679. John Bunyan* preached to his congregation in 1682. Frequently arrested as a Nonconformist in 1683-84, Wavel promised his congregation that 'he would venture his person if they would venture their purses, which they did, and it was no small expense they were put to.' He was aided in his legal difficulties by his relative, Sir Henry Tulse, Lord Mayor of London. Sir John Shorter, a member of Wavel's congregation, became

Lord Mayor in 1687. Wavel was a member of the Happy Union, formed by more than eighty Congregational and Presbyterian ministers in 1691, and a founder of the Congregational Fund Board on 17 Dec. 1695, which assisted ministers and ministerial candidates. His assistant at Pinners' Hall was Richard Taylor. Wavel died on 19 Dec. 1705. He had married Anna Bold, apparently Reyner's stepdaughter, on 2 Feb. 1659 at Egham.

Calamy; *Calamy Revised*; R.T. Jones, *Congregationalism in England* (1962); J. Brown, *John Bunyan* (rev. ed.; 1928).

R.L. Greaves

WAYTE (or Waite), Thomas (d. 1695)

Quaker bookseller, converted to the Friends about 1651. Tracts by George Fox* (*Truth's Defense*), James Nayler* (*A Lamentacion*), Richard Farnsworth* (*England's Warning-peece*) and William Tomlinson* (*A Word of Reproof*) were printed for him in 1653 and were sold at his home in York. He also acted as a local agent for Quaker authors. When, in 1664, the government intercepted a list of 44 Quakers who were dispensing books in the the only professional bookseller on the list was Wayte. He was active in the York Meeting, and in Mar. 1672 was instrumental in providing financial assistance to William Dewsbury.* Early in 1677 he provided hospitality to the itinerant George Fox. His wife Mary, sister of the York tanner Richard Smith, 'labored much in the ministry and in laying friends' sufferings before such as were in authority.' In 1686 she was a co-signer, with other female Friends, of *A Testimony from the Yearly Meeting at York* addressed to the monthly meetings in Yorkshire, and she co-signed another document from the York Quakers in 1688. Mary Wayte died in 1689, and her husband in 1695. Together they were among the most influential Friends of Yorkshire.

Fox, *SJ*; Plomer, *DBP*; Braithwaite, *SP*; *FPT*.

R.L. Greaves

WEAVER, John (fl. 1631-1684)

Parliamentary radical, MP 1645, 1654, 1656, 1659 (Stamford). Weaver is thought to be the son of a northern family which had been financially embarrassed in several lawsuits. His enemies claimed he was the son of an innkeeper. In 1631 Weaver was admitted a freeman of Stamford, obtaining a place in the town government before the Civil War. The possibility that he had some legal training is suggested by his holding, *in commendam*, the office of Judge Advocate in the army.

Weaver was one of the treasurers for the Eastern Association appointed by Manchester and headed the organization for the reassessment of the Fifth and Twentieth part. He also acted as the Association's financial agent in several other transactions, including the sale of goods seized or captured from Lincolnshire delinquents. In 1645 he testified against Manchester during the investigation of Cromwell's charges. In Parliament Weaver was considered one of the extreme Independents, and Clement Walker thought him to be typical of that group. Weaver staunchly opposed the reinstatement of the Presbyterian MPs excluded in 1647. He joined forces with the City radicals Isaac Penington* and John Venn* to oppose a treaty with the King, supported the Leveller petition of Sept. 1648 and called for the King's trial. Nevertheless, he refused to sit as one of Charles' judges. But Weaver continued to sit in the Commons and on 1 Feb. 1649 took the dissent. He played a key role in formulating the Rump's legislation against moral and religious license. In 1649 he was appointed a commissioner for the civil government in Ireland. There he vigorously promoted the propagation of the Gospel, but ran afoul of some army officers, particularly Sir Hardress Waller,* with whom he had a bitter and protracted quarrel. Weaver returned to England in May 1652 where he was active in blocking Lambert's* appointment as Cromwell's deputy in Ireland, but on 17 Aug. he himself was denied reappointment following an army petition for his removal. Parliament rewarded his services by voting him Scottish lands to the value of £250, but later commuted this for a payment of £2500.

After 1653 Weaver was associated in Parliament with Sir Henry Vane* and the Commonwealthsmen. He was excluded from the House in Sept. 1656, but was readmitted with the other excluded members and began the attack on the Upper House. In Richard Cromwell's* Parliament Weaver joined with fellow republicans such as Ludlow,* Neville* and Scott* in opposing the new Protector. Later in the year he was one of the men active in securing the Tower for Parliament. He was subsequently elected to the Council of State and appointed commissioner for the government of Ireland and the management of the navy. Since Weaver refused to take the oath abjuring monarchy, he never actually attended the Council meetings.

Weaver was re-elected to the House in 1660, but his election was annulled. In 1672 John Richardson, the Nonconformist, preached in his house. He was buried on 25 Mar. 1685 at North Luppenham.

DNB; Holmes; C. Walker, *The History of Independency* (1660); Yule; Worden; Burton; MacCormack; Underdown, *PP*.

R.H. Gottdiener

WEBBE (or Webb, Web), Thomas (fl. 1646-1660)

Ranter, was from an old Wiltshire clothing family originally from Bromham; Nathaniel Webb, an ejected minister, was a relative. The family were devoted supporters of the Baptist cause in Devizes. In the 1640s Webbe was Rector of Langley Burrell, a living he allegedly obtained by promising

not to accept tithes from his parishioners. He was involved in radical activity in Wiltshire as early as 1646 and was probably connected with sympathetic elements in the parliamentary army. Webbe answered the first part of Thomas Edwards' *Gangraena* in a tract of May 1646 entitled *Mr. Edwards's Pen No Slander* and was one of the sectaries Edwards attacked in the *Second Part of Gangraena* (1646). Webbe spoke for John Lilburne* and against Parliament during Lilburne's trial in 1649. He also praised Abiezer Coppe,* the Ranter, and carried on a friendly correspondence with Joseph Salmon,* soldier and Ranter pamphleteer. Webbe professed and practiced Ranter principles toward sin and sex and in 1650 was put on trial for adultery, but to the disappointment of local authorities was acquitted. In Sept. 1650 he was ejected from his position by the Committee for Plundered Ministers, apparently for his Leveller sympathies. In 1652 he was denounced as the leader of a Ranter community in Wiltshire by Edward Stokes in *The Wiltshire Rant*. Webbe is last heard of in 1660 prophesying the downfall of Charles II in *A Lasting Almanack for the Raigne of the Fifth Monarchy* and calling himself Mad Tom.

Hill, *WTUD*; M.E. Reeves, 'Protestant Nonconformity,' *VCH, Wilts.*, 3; E. Pagitt, *Heresiography* (1654).

C.W. Wood, Jr.

WEBSTER, John (1610-1682)

Educational and medical reformer, was born on 3 Feb. 1610 in Thornton, Craven, Yorks. He stated that he had studied at Cambridge but there is no record of his having been a student there. More important is his testimony that he had learned chemistry (c. 1632) under the direction of the Hungarian alchemist, John Hunyades (1576-1650), who had come to London in 1623. Like other chemists of his time, Webster's chemical interests were closely associated with medicine and religion. He was ordained a minister sometime after July 1632 and by 1634 was Curate of Kildwick in Craven.

As a medical chemist and surgeon, Webster was attracted first to the work of Paracelsus and then to that of Jean Baptiste van Helmont (1579-1644). The complete works of the latter were first published in 1648 and rapidly attracted interest in England and elsewhere. These texts detailed a chemical cosmology and on a practical level urged the use of chemically prepared remedies which were highly valued by military surgeons. During the Civil War Webster, then a Puritan, served both as a surgeon and chaplain with the New Model Army. By 1648 he had become a Nonconformist. After the Restoration he supported himself as a 'practitioner in physick and chirurgery' and died in Clitheroe, Lancs. on 18 June 1682.

Webster's concern with the educational training of future ministers inspired him to write *The Saints Guide* (1653). Here he attacked the schools which taught worldly wisdom through books and disputations. Any true understanding of Gospel truths, he argued, required God's Spirit through the grace of the Holy Spirit. He returned to this subject again in his *Academiorum examen* (1654), noting here that the traditional emphasis on the 'heathen authors' Aristotle and Galen was improper for Christians. It was far more fitting for them to contemplate the wonders of nature (and thus, the Creator) through observations and personal experience. Yet natural phenomena were not best understood through mathematical abstraction (then of increasing interest among mechanical philosophers), since Webster felt that this approach perpetuated the deductive logic of the schools. A far more useful key to created nature seemed to exist in the laboratory methods of the chemists. The *Academiorum examen* is deeply indebted to Robert Fludd's Rosicrucian apology, the *Tractatus apologeticus* (1617), and Webster pointed to Fludd and to Francis Bacon as the most reliable guides in the formulation of a new philosophy of nature.

Webster was answered by Seth Ward and John Wilkins in the *Vindiciae academiorum* (1654) and by Thomas Hall in the *Histrio-Mastix. A Whip for Webster* (1654). In the former, Webster was taken to task for not having properly understood Bacon or Descartes, and he was accused of having plagiarized the critiques of Aristotle prepared earlier by van Helmont and Pierre Gassendi. He was particularly censured for his defense of Robert Fludd. Hall's tract is really an appendix to his much longer *Vindiciae literarum* and in both works he upholds the existing educational system. He placed great stress on the importance of deductive logic, a tool that had been rejected by the followers of Paracelsus and van Helmont. It seemed to Hall that Webster sought to sweep away the most glorious achievements of the ancients and to substitute in their place alchemy, astrology and natural magic which to him were forms of diabolical magic. The exchange between these authors involved mechanical philosophy, chemical philosophy and the scholastic tradition in education. It clearly reveals the sharp division then existing between the proponents of these different views.

Webster believed that the aim of true natural magic was to uncover the 'secret effects' of nature and he was convinced that this should be the goal of the Royal Society. Although the work of the fellows was more in line with the convictions expressed earlier by Ward and Wilkins, there is little indication that Webster was ever disappointed by the course taken by the members. He referred with approval to the work of the Society in his last two works, the *Metallographia* (1671) and *The Displaying of Supposed Witchcraft* (completed 1673, published 1677). The first is an important compendium of information on then current views on the growth and properties of metals and their ores. Here again Webster made evident his deep veneration of Paracelsus and van Helmont. This work was favorably reviewed in the *Philosophical Transaction of the Royal Society of London* (12 Dec. 1670). Later in the century Daniel Georg Morhof praised the *Metallographia* in his *Polyhis-*

tor (1st ed. 1688-92) for its completeness.

In *The Displaying of Supposed Witch-craft* Webster replied to Joseph Glanvill and Meric Casaubon. The former, a member of the Royal Society and a staunch Anglican, was aware that the mechanical philosophy had been subjected to the charge of atheism. Glanvill encouraged the Royal Society to investigate the spirit world since he was convinced that the existence of a demonic agency in the natural world confirmed the existence of spirits. Such beings invalidated the charge of mechanical atheism and seemed to confirm the truths of established religion. Webster was convinced that the new defense of witchcraft by Glanvill and Casaubon was associated with the old charges of diabolical magic that had been levelled at the chemical philosophers. Accordingly he argued that unexplained phenomena would eventually be explained by natural means. Webster believed that continued scientific advance through the efforts of virtuosi such as those of the Royal Society would result in the eventual confirmation of the macrocosm-microcosm universe of the Paracelso-Helmontian philosophers. Webster's *Discovery of Supposed Witchcraft* together with the works of his opponents may thus be seen in their full context as one more encounter in the continuing debate between the mechanical and the chemical philosophies.

It would be wrong to picture John Webster as a scientist of major stature, but his work remains of significance, for it reflects important themes in a period of transition. His three major publications set forth the religious, educational, medical and scientific goals of the English chemical philosophers of the mid-seventeenth century who sought thorough reform in many areas. If Webster neither held important positions nor received the recognition for his views that he desired, there is little doubt that his work did provoke controversy. It was seen as a threat both by those who represented the old establishment in education, religion and science as well as by those who sought a new science through the development of the mechanical philosphy.

A.G. Debus, *Science and Education in the Seventeenth Century* (1970); Debus, 'The Webster-Ward Debate of 1654,' *L'Univers à la Renaissance*, Travaux de l'Institut pour l'étude de la Renaissance et de l'Humanisme (Brussels), 4:33-51; Hill, *WTUD*; Webster, *GI*; Greaves, *PRET*; T.H. Jobe, 'The Role of the Devil in Restoration Science: The Glanvill-Webster Witchcraft Debate.'

A.G. Debus

WELD (or Welde, Wells), Thomas (1595-1661)

Independent minister and colonizer, was born in Sudbury, Suff., the fourth son of Edmund Weld, a linen draper, and his wife Mary. He matriculated pensioner at Trinity Coll., Camb. in 1611, commencing B.A. in 1614 and M.A. in 1618. Having taken orders in the Anglican church, he was successively Vicar of Haverhill, Suff. and Terling, Essex. While at Terling he signed a petition to Laud (10 Nov. 1629) on behalf of Thomas Hooker.* In Nov. 1631 Weld was deprived for nonconformity. He emigrated to New England, arriving in Boston on 5 June 1632. By July he had been installed as the first pastor in Roxbury, Mass. Weld soon became a leading minister in the Bay Colony. With John Eliot and Richard Mather,* he brought to the press the first book to be printed in America, the *Bay Psalm Book* (1640). He participated in the synod which condemned John Wheelwright and Anne Hutchinson* of Antinomianism, and Mrs. Hutchinson was kept a prisoner in his house before being exiled. In Aug. 1641 Weld returned to England with Hugh Peter* to seek financial aid for the colony. Although their efforts were successful, Peter went into Parliament's service and Weld became involved in English affairs. On 1 Oct. 1645 both agents were dismissed by the colony. In 1644 Weld published *An Answer to W. R. . . .*

Defending New England's Church Ways,
but the following year he was in trouble
with the Independents for having edited
Winthrop's* account of Antinomian troubles as *A Short Story of the Rise, Reign
and Ruine of the Antinomians*. By accepting Presbyterian advice to emphasize the
intolerance of Congregational churches, he
put Independency in a bad light. He was
himself suspect as a Presbyterian sympathizer until his *A Brief Narration of the
Practices of the Churches in New England*
(1645) appeared. For a time he was Rector
of Wanlip, Leics. and may have been at
Terling as well. On 1 Feb. 1650 he was
installed at St. Mary's, Gateshead,
Durham, from which church he may have
resigned by 1657, in spite of Calamy's
statement that he was turned out by John
Laidler, who was not presented until Mar.
1661. Laidler had been the incumbent for
some time, having a presentation from
Bishop Morton of Durham. Weld was in
London to sign *A Renunciation and
Declaration of the Ministers of Congregational Churches* (1661). Other published
works include *A False Jew* (1653), *A
Further Discovery of That Generation of
Men Called Quakers* (1654), and *The
Perfect Pharise* (1654).

Calamy; *Calamy Revised*; *DNB*; Nuttall, *VS*; B. Hanbury, ed., *Historical
Memorials*, 3 vols. (1839-44).

R. Masek

WENTWORTH, Sir Peter (1592-1675)

Parliamentary radical, MP LP 1641 (Tamworth). Wentworth was born in 1592 in
Lillingstone Lovell, Bucks. (then Oxon.).
He was the son and heir of Nicholas
Wentworth, himself the son of the
Elizabethan Puritan MP Peter Wentworth,
and his wife Susannah, daughter and
coheiress of Roger Wigston of Wolston,
Warks. Educated at Magdalen Hall, Oxf.
(B.A., 16 Dec. 1611) and Lincoln's Inn,
Wentworth was knighted at the coronation
of Charles I in 1625. He subsequently

became a JP in Oxfordshire and served as
sheriff there in 1634-35. As a result of his
difficulties in collecting ship money, he
was questioned by the Council in 1638. In
1639 he was noted as having failed to
respond to the King's summons to join the
army against the Scots.

After his election to the Long Parliament
on 18 Dec. 1641, Wentworth devoted
himself to the parliamentary cause. His
demonstrations of zeal were numerous. He
made the substantial subscription of £100
and three horses for defense in June 1642,
promptly took the Parliamentary Covenant in the following June, took the Solemn
League and Covenant in Sept. 1643, and
regularly voted with the war party. In
Parliament he sat on many committees,
including those for sequestration, plundered ministers, and the commission for
sale of delinquent estates. On a number of
occasions he proposed preachers for the
fast sermons. In religion Wentworth was
an Erastian. He was the probable author of
A Packe of Puritans (1641), where he
quoted a number of early reformers and
attacked pluralism, non-preaching ministers, and ministers who assumed temporal
authority.

Wentworth was also active in Parliament's behalf in Warwickshire, where he
likewise served on a number of important
committees and commissions. Among
these were the Committee for Executing
the Militia Ordinance, the committees for
assessment and sequestration, and the
Committee for Raising and Maintaining
the New Model Army. Denzil Holles*
severely criticized him when he acquired
part of the estate of a Royalist. Wentworth
nevertheless escaped more formal charges
of peculation which were levied against
some MPs at the time.

Wentworth continued to sit in the Long
Parliament until at least 14 Dec. 1648.
Although widely described as an extremist
and named to the High Court, he withdrew
from Parliament during the King's trial and
declined to serve. Wentworth wrote to the
Speaker, explaining that he was kept at
home by sprains, falls and other physical
disabilities. After the King's execution he

returned to politics. Elected to the second, fourth and fifth Councils of State, Wentworth took an interest in foreign affairs and became friendly with John Milton.* Wentworth's differences with Cromwell became evident in Apr. 1653, when Cromwell on the occasion of the dissolution of the Rump named Wentworth and Henry Marten* as members whose immorality disgraced the House. Wentworth attempted to answer but was prevented from doing so by the entrance of the army. He remained outside the governing circles of the Protectorate and in 1655 publicly opposed one of the regime's taxes on the grounds that taxes could only be imposed by consent in Parliament. Wentworth was called before the Council for causing two assessors of the tax in Coventry to be arrested. He first defended himself but submitted when Cromwell ordered him to do so. In May 1659, after Cromwell's death and Richard's* fall, Wentworth returned to the Rump and sat with the Parliament until it ended in Mar. 1660. Thereafter he retired. He died unmarried on 1 Dec. 1675, and was buried at Lillingstone Lovell.

DNB; Keeler; Underdown, PP; Abbott; Worden; J.C. Wedgwood, A Parliamentary History of Staffordshire, 2 vols. (1919-20). Papers: L (Add. MSS).

E.S. Cope

WENTWORTH, Thomas (c. 1568-1627)

Parliamentary radical, MP 1604, 1614, 1621, 1624, 1625, 1626 (Oxford City). Wentworth was the third son of Peter Wentworth of Lillingstone Lovell, Bucks. (then Oxon.) and his second wife, Elizabeth, sister of Sir Francis Walsingham. He matriculated at University Coll., Oxf. in 1584 and entered Lincoln's Inn in 1585, being called to the bar in 1594. In 1604 he was elected borough member for Oxford, a seat he retained for the rest of his life, and in 1607 became recorder of the city.

Wentworth carried on his father's parliamentary tradition of opposition to the Crown. He sat on the subcommittee for the Apology in 1604, and expounded frequently on Parliament's responsibility for the laws and liberties of the subject thereafter. He vigorously opposed impositions and attacked the use of Bate's case as a precedent, urging the King to curb expenditures rather than impose new taxation and raising medieval precedents for an outside monitoring agent. The royal domain, he declared, was 'a piece of holy land assigned to the Prince so that he should not tax his people.' Religion was an equally persistent concern. Wentworth backed Puritan-sponsored bills and grievances, deplored the impoverishment of deprived ministers, and denounced the canons of 1604, especially the bishops' power to declare heresy. In the midst of debate on the Great Contract in 1610, he grumbled about the overturning of a widow's will that had attempted to provide for deprived ministers. James ordered Wentworth's imprisonment at the end of the session, but he was spared by conciliar protection, probably Salisbury's. The King had his way however in June 1614, after Wentworth had exulted in Parliament that the Kings of France and Spain had 'died like calves upon the butcher's knife.' The French ambassador lodged a protest, and Wentworth was sent to the Tower.

The Thirty Years' War, whose shadow dominated the parliaments of the 1620s, brought out all Wentworth's instincts as a Puritan and a survivor of '88. He supported war against Spain in the Parliament of 1621, defending the Commons' petition against the Spanish match in an emotional speech in which he recalled the Gunpowder plot and asked whether '36 barrels of gunpowder under these walls do not require this.' To the King's demand that the Commons cease to discuss matters of state, Wentworth retorted that he had 'never yet read of anything that was not fit for the consideration of a Parliament.' In 1624 he was again in the forefront of war supporters, pleading for any sacrifice on behalf of religion. In the event, however, Country caution got the better of Protestant zeal, and Wentworth moved only two subsidies and four fifteenths for the war, less than a quarter of the sum realistically required.

By 1625 Wentworth had become disillusioned by the prosecution of the war and alarmed by the growth of Arminian influence at Court, and in 1626 he joined the attack on Buckingham. Unlike many of his Country colleagues, however, he seemed increasingly convinced that the root of military failure was the inadequacy of the Crown's financial base. In his last Parliament, he joined a select group in urging a settlement of the King's estate, and even proposed to legalize impositions by Act of Parliament.

Wentworth had a long relationship with Lincoln's Inn; he served as its Lent reader in 1612 and was nominated treasurer in 1621. His association with his university was stormier. Oxford had grown increasingly High Church as the municipality had become more Puritan, and Wentworth attacked its franchise. Matters came to a head in 1621 when the university supported the corporation in its attempt to exclude freemen from the ballot, and when Wentworth took the popular side, he was discommoned. Simultaneously the corporation withdrew from its previous practice of electing its recorder to Parliament. Wentworth was defeated in an initial poll, but managed to regain his seat, presumably with the support of his allies.

Wentworth died in Sept. 1627 (*Oxford Council Acts, 1626-1665*, p. 7). He was married to Dorothy, daughter and coheiress of Thomas Keble of Newbottle, Northants., by whom he had seven sons and two daughters. His eldest son, Thomas, succeeded him in Parliament in 1628. Wentworth was the nominal author of *The Office and Duty of Executors* (1641), but the attribution is disputed.

PP 1610; *CD 1610*; *CD 1621*; Notestein, *WIHC*; Zaller; Ruigh; Moir; Russell, *PEP*; Hirst; *DNB*; H.E. Salter, ed., *Oxford Council Acts, 1583-1621* (1928).

L.M. Hill and R. Zaller

WEST, Edmund (1608-1683)

Parliamentary County Commissioner, was born at Marsworth in 1608, the eldest son of Edmund West (d. 1618) of Marsworth, Bucks. and his second wife, Theodosia, daughter of Sir Edward Tirrell of Thornton, Bucks. West matriculated at Brasenose Coll., Oxf. on 6 Dec. 1622 and was admitted to the Inner Temple in Nov. 1623. He was appointed a member of the Midland Association for Buckinghamshire in Dec. 1642 and, in recruiter elections held in Nov. 1645, was returned as one of the knights of the shire for the county though the election was subsequently referred to the Committee of Privileges and not upheld until 26 July 1647. In the interval, West had been elected MP for Wendover (c. Nov. 1646) but opted to serve for the shire. He was one of the two Buckinghamshire MPs sent by the House into the county in Dec. 1647 to remedy grievances arising from the quartering of soldiers and was also appointed a Commissioner for Assessments in Buckinghamshire on 22 Dec. At Pride's purge, West absented himself but later accepted the *fait accompli* and was an inactive member of the Rump. Under the major-generals, he was one of the Buckinghamshire Commissioners associated with Fleetwood* in the government of the county. He married Anne, daughter of Henry Beake of Castle Acre, Norf., by whom he had two sons and two daughters, but Edmund, his heir, dying on 27 Feb. 1682, Marsworth passed to the second son Roger.

Underdown, *PP*; *VCH*, *Bucks.*; *Harl. Soc.*, 58:119, 125; *CJ*, 4:326, 335; 5:258. Papers: L (Sloane MSS).

K.J. Lindley

WEST, Robert (fl. 1680-1685)

Conspirator, was a barrister of the Middle Temple, a self-acknowledged student of Machiavelli and a radical Whig. One contemporary called him an avowed atheist, but he was probably a Nonconformist. He may have been the Robert West, son of James West of Banbury, Oxon., who matriculated at Magdalen Coll., Oxf. on 1 Dec. 1665 at age fifteen, where he remained as a demy until 1668, and became a barrister at Gray's Inn in 1674. In any case the future conspirator married Sarah, daughter of Thomas Cox. Stephen College,* a joiner indicted (and ultimately executed) for treasonous speech while the Oxford Parliament was in session, requested that West be one of his attorneys. West himself was questioned by the authorities in Mar. 1681 for spreading a rumor that Holborn would be burned and the streets would run with blood. With other Whigs he armed himself in the fall of 1682; a swordcutler in Fleet Street revealed in November that he had made a sword for West, 'a good honest Whig.' In early 1683 he became extensively involved in the radical underground with such men as Richard Rumbold* (for whom he had rendered legal services), Richard Goodenough,* Col. John Rumsey* and Sir Thomas Armstrong. In March he and Richard Nelthorpe* studied the defenses of the Tower with a view to capturing it. About the same time he informed John Wildman* in the Exchange that he had a plantation in America 'where the churchmen never had had a footing,' and that if forced into exile he would go there. Given to brash talk, he reportedly told Edmund Waller that Monmouth and the Protestant lords were cowards, and he bragged on other occasions of assassinating James and calling 'the Lord Keeper to an account.' He was enmeshed in the spring of 1683 with the schemes that involved both the assassination of Charles and James – a plot largely planned by West himself – and the general insurrection. His own role in the latter included the acquisition of arms and the recruitment of naval captains. He also concealed the Duke of Monmouth – 'the only great man that faithfully would serve the nation' – in his chambers in the Middle Temple.

West has been accused by Maurice Ashley of fabricating the Rye House plot with John Rumsey in order to profit by revealing it, but this does not square with his earlier commitment to radical causes, his involvement in the general insurrection conspiracy or the later testimony of Rumbold. Five days after Josias Keeling divulged the outline of the plot to Lord Dartmouth on 12 June, West attended a meeting of conspirators in Capt. Thomas Walcott's* lodgings. Robert Ferguson,* Rumsey, Rumbold, Goodenough and Nathaniel Wade* were among those present, and there was a debate over launching an insurrection or going into exile. They opted for the latter, and three days later (20 June) the government learned that West and the others had absconded. In fact, however, West was either unable to escape or became panic-stricken, for on the 21st he wrote to the Earl of Rochester begging for his intercession and claiming that 'an unhappy curiosity first betrayed me' into knowledge of the plotting. The following day he told Rochester he would reveal what he knew, and on the 23rd he surrendered to Judge Jeffreys, who took him to Hampton Court to be interrogated by the King and Council. The tale West spun in the ensuing weeks was a contrivance of fact and fiction, which made his interrogators increasingly suspicious. On the 26th the Duke of Ormond observed to the Earl of Arran that West was 'a man of a quick wit and fluent tongue, and though esteemed fearful does not appear to be so much daunted as the other [Rumsey], possibly as not having so much sense of honor, nor so many obligations to the King.'

On 1 July West was committed to Newgate on charges of high treason. He informed Secretary Jenkins on the 4th that he would do anything to save his life, even offering the next day to testify against William Lord Howard* and the other 'great men' he blamed for ruining him. He petitioned Charles to banish him to the colonies rather than execute him, but instead he was pardoned so he could testify. This he did on 12 July against Walcott and on 21 Nov. against Algernon Sidney.* Illness led him to petition the

King on 9 Jan. 1684 to be confined in his own house rather than the Marshalsea, where he had been transferred, and he was moved to the home of Thomas Atterbury. On 5 Dec. 1685 he received a pardon for all treasonous offenses committed prior to that date.

Ashley paints a damning portrait of West as a two-faced, self-serving and unprincipled man who was an 'unscrupulous liar' and 'the *alter ego* of Titus Oates.' A more reasonable assessment was made by Rumbold in a letter to West on 2 Aug. 1683. Although dismayed by the effect of West's testimony, Rumbold praised him for not divulging some conspirators and for belatedly revealing others, giving them time to escape. 'It is not unknown to any of us with what zeal and sincerity you led us on, whilst there were any hopes of succeeding. . . .'

CSPD, Chas. II, 21:423; 22:218; 23:538; 24-27 *passim*; *Jas. II*, 1:104; *ST*, 9; Luttrell, 1:266, 267, 289; *HMC* 36, *Ormonde N.S.*, 7:54, 65; Haley, *FES*; Ashley, *JW* and *James II* (1977); T. Sprat, *A True Account . . . of the Horrid Conspiracy* (1685). Papers: LPR.

R.L. Greaves

WESTLEY (or Wesly, Wesley), John (d. 1670)

Navy chaplain and ejected Independent minister, was the son of Bartholomew Westley, Rector of Charmouth, Dorset, who was himself ejected as Curate of Allington, Bridport, Dorset in 1662; Bartholomew was married (1619) to Anne, daughter of Sir Henry Colley of Carbury, co. Kildare, and granddaughter of Adam Loftus. Westley matriculated from New Inn Hall, Oxf. on 23 Apr. 1651 and graduated B.A. (23 Jan. 1655) and M.A. (4 July 1657). According to his diary, to which Calamy had access, Westley was 'sent to preach the Gospel' by a congregation at Melcombe, Dorset, and subsequently preached at Radipole and Turnworth in

that county. He was also chaplain of the 'Triumph,' for which the Admiralty approved remuneration of £100 p.a. on 3 Dec. 1657. On 30 June 1658 he was appointed Vicar of Winterborne Whitchurch, Dorset, for which the Council of State voted him an augmentation of £40 on 1 July. According to depositions made against him on 5 Feb. 1661, he had used the pulpit to condemn Charles I and his posterity, to castigate the prelates, and to extol Cromwell, deeming him superior to David and Solomon. At Turnworth he had allegedly asserted that hell was paved with children's skulls, and he had had the church bells rung to celebrate the defeat of Booth's rising. It was probably about this time (Feb. 1661) that Westley was first imprisoned; though released he was again arrested on 2 May 1661 under orders from the Duke of Richmond. Westley petitioned the King and Privy Council on 26 June, but was not released until the end of July, after he had taken the Oaths of Allegiance and Supremacy. In this period no charges had been filed, nor had he received a hearing.

Westley was imprisoned at Blandford Forum early in 1662, though he was released and bound over to appear at the assizes. There he was accused of failing to read the Book of Common Prayer, bound over to the next assizes, and finally acquitted in the winter of 1663. In the meantime he had preached his farewell sermon at Winterborne Whitchurch on 17 Aug. 1662, and the living was declared vacant on 26 Oct. He tried to relocate at Melcombe Regis in Feb. 1663, but was prohibited by the corporation and fined 5s. a week as long as he remained there. He then drifted between Bridgwater, Ilminster and Taunton, Som. Although a member of the gentry provided him with a haven at Preston, Som., he considered going to Surinam or Maryland. Instead he preached to conventicles, refused the Oxford Oath, and then accepted the pastorate of a congregation at Poole, Dorset. Westley was imprisoned three months for preaching at Shaftesbury, Dorset with Francis Bampfield* in July 1663, for six months at Poole, and for shorter periods on two other occasions. In 1669 he was reportedly preaching at Turners Puddle, Dorset. After his death the following year, the Vicar of Preston refused to permit the burial of Westley's body in his church. By his wife, a daughter of John White (1574-1648) and a niece of the church historian Thomas Fuller, Westley had four children: Timothy (bap. 17 Apr. 1659), Elizabeth (bap. 29 Jan. 1661), Samuel (bap. 17 Dec. 1662) and Matthew (d. 1737). Samuel's son John was the founder of the Methodist movement.

Calamy; *Calamy Revised*; *CSPD, Comm.*, 11:474; 12:81; *Chas. II*, 1:504; *Al. Oxon.*; Whiting.

R.L. Greaves

WESTON, Benjamin (1614-c. 1673)

Treasury Commissioner, was born on 4 Aug. 1614 at Roxwell, Essex, the fourth son of Richard, first Earl of Portland (d. 1635) and his second wife, Frances, daughter of Nicholas Waldegrave of Borley, Essex. With his elder brother Nicholas, he was made a burgess of Yarmouth, Isle of Wight, in Aug. 1634, and was MP for Dover from about Feb. 1641. Both he and Nicholas voted against Strafford's attainder but they later took opposing sides. On 5 Aug. 1641 Weston married Elizabeth (d. 1662), the widow of Buckingham's brother, the Earl of Anglesey, and daughter of Thomas Sheldon of Howby, Leics., and became possessed in her right of Ashley Park, Walton-on-Thames, Surrey. He was listed as a Presbyterian elder in the Kingston-on-Thames Classis in 1648 and, although subsequently named as one of the King's judges, never attended the trial. Yet he was appointed a Treasury Commissioner in 1649 and was a member of the Rump, albeit an inactive one. Holles* suggests that Weston's allegiance had been bought by the revival of substantial arrears of a pension formerly enjoyed by his wife. He may have been MP for Midhurst, Sussex, in 1658, and resumed his seat in the Rump in 1659. After the Restoration he acted as an agent of Ludovic, Lord d'Aubigny, in securing him an income from the trade in woollen goods. He died without issue in St. Andrew's Holborn, in or before 1673.

Keeler; Underdown, *PP*; Cockayne, *CP*, 1:132-33; *CSPD, Chas. II*, 1:605; 4:28; 16:539.

K.J. Lindley

WHALLEY, Edward (d. 1675?)

Regicide and Civil War officer, was the second son of Richard Whalley of Kirkton and Screveton, Notts., and Francis, daughter of Sir Henry Cromwell, and thus Oliver's cousin. Whalley became a woollen draper in Chadwell, Essex. He probably served in Essex's* army, and by 1643 was a major in Cromwell's regiment. At the battle of Gainsborough Whalley fought 'with all gallantry becoming a gentleman and a Christian,' and he saw action at Marston Moor, Naseby, Bristol and Banbury. Whalley was promoted to lieutenant-colonel, and was active in voicing Agitator views of his regiment. In 1647 he was placed in charge of Charles I at Hampton Court. After he showed his charge a letter Cromwell sent him warning of threats on the King's life, Charles decided on flight. Persuading Whalley to pull back his sentries, Charles slipped out of Hampton Court early on the morning of 11 Nov. He left behind letters stating that Whalley had treated him well. During the second Civil War Whalley fought at Maidstone and the siege of Colchester. He was prominent in the deliberations that led to Pride's purge and the King's trial. Whalley was appointed a Commissioner of the High Court, attended all but one of its sessions, and signed the death warrant. In 1650 Whalley went to Scotland with Cromwell, and fought with distinction at the battle of Dunbar, where he had three horses shot from under him. Whalley also fought at Worcester. On 13 Aug. 1652, now commissary-general, Whalley put before Parliament a major reform program on

Cromwell's behalf. He represented Nottinghamshire in Cromwell's first two Parliaments, and was created major-general for Nottinghamshire, Lincolnshire, Warwickshire, Derbyshire and Leicestershire on 31 Oct. 1655. He was active in suppressing alehouses, dissident Royalists and indolent ministers, but he allowed racing at Lincoln on the grounds that the government had no intention of denying gentlemen their sport. Responding to county pressure Whalley introduced legislation in Parliament in 1656 against enclosures, but at its first reading it was thrown out as 'the most mischievous bill that was ever offered to this house.' Whalley also lacked support in the county: none of the larger Nottinghamshire gentry, for instance, served as his commissioners. He opposed attempts to make Cromwell king in 1657, but accepted a seat in his Upper House. He supported Richard Cromwell* in 1659, even though his regiment refused to fight for the Protector's son. At the Restoration Whalley was proclaimed a Regicide. He fled to New England with his son-in-law, Maj.-Gen. William Goffe.* Arriving at Boston on 27 July 1660, they were politely received by the Governor of Massachusetts and took up residence, first in Cambridge and later at New Haven. In 1674 he was reported alive and 'patiently suffering all things,' but so infirm that it is unlikely that he lived much longer than 1675.

According to Clarendon, Whalley was 'a man of rough and brutal temper.' Warwick called him 'a ridiculous fanatic, as well as a cracked-brained fellow, though he was a gentleman of good family.' He rose to prominence due to his military abilities and courage as well as his connection with Cromwell, whom he served loyally in peace and war.

Abbott; Rushworth, 7:871-72; Burton, 1:175-76; I. Roots, *The Great Rebellion* (1966); Clarendon; P. Warwick, *Memoires of the Reigne of King Charles I* (1701); Underdown, *PP*; Ashley, *CG*; E. Styles, *A History of Three Judges of King Charles I* (1839); *DNB*.

C.H. Carlton

WHARTON, Philip Lord (1613-1696)

Political radical, succeeded his grandfather as fourth Lord Wharton in 1625 and attended Exeter College, matriculating at Oxford in 1626. He married three times, first to Elizabeth Wandesford in 1632 and secondly to Jane Goodwin, the daughter of the wealthy Arthur Goodwin* of Winchendon, Bucks., in 1637. This latter marriage, which linked him to a reform-minded family with a reputation for opposition to the Crown, may have played a substantial role in forming Wharton's developing political views. His third marriage, in 1661, was to Anne Carr Popham. Wharton, a man of ample means and property, held lands in Yorkshire, Cumberland, Westmorland and Buckinghamshire and developed a sophisticated interest in architecture and gardening. He spent large sums on his principal residence, Woburn, and built up a fine art collection which included works by Van Dyck and Lely.

Wharton was a Puritan whose religious beliefs remained, throughout his life, the mainspring of his actions. By May 1640 he appears as a staunch member of the opposition and helped to prepare the Yorkshire petition against the billeting of troops in the summer of 1640; although not an original signer of the petition of the twelve peers of Aug. 1640, he readily supported the petition's demands. In the autumn he was appointed a commissioner to the Scots to negotiate the Treaty of Ripon and soon won their approval and respect. He consistently supported the opposition leadership in the Long Parliament and has been described as an associate of Pym* and his middle group. Wharton was a leader of the opposition in the House of Lords and served on many of its committees. He was an unrelenting foe of the Earl of Strafford. Wharton was appointed to the Lord Lieutenancies of Lancashire and Buckinghamshire by Parliament in 1642 and, although he hoped for some kind of conciliation between the King and Parliament, became a commander in the army of the Earl of Essex* and participated in the battle of Edgehill.

An original member of the Committee of Both Kingdoms, Wharton was also a member of the Westminster Assembly where he originally supported Scottish hopes for religious conformity between England and Scotland. Although political reasons occasionally prevented him from being more outspoken on the issue of religious toleration, he was a strong supporter of liberty of conscience, a principle he observed in the appointment of clergy to the various livings he controlled. His religious views soon outdistanced those held by the Scots until he even sought the dissolution of the Westminster Assembly.

Wharton's support for the war against the King remained strong; he backed the formation of the New Model Army and supported the appointment of Fairfax* over Essex as general. He avoided any public commitment in the controversy between Parliament and the army in 1647; in 1648-49, however, he opposed both Pride's purge and the King's execution. He remained on good terms with Oliver Cromwell although Cromwell's letters, urging Wharton's return to politics following Charles I's death, went unheeded, and in 1652 they discussed a possible marriage alliance between their two families.

After the Restoration, Wharton resumed an active political role. He assumed leadership and patronage of Presbyterian and Congregationalist MPs in the Cavalier Parliament, and sought to broaden their base by appealing to moderates. Wharton led opposition to the Clarendon Code, the Conventicle Act of 1670 and the Non-resistance Oath of 1675. He denounced the prorogation of Parliament and, refusing submission, was imprisoned in the Tower between Feb. 1677 and Feb. 1678. He returned to give strong support to the Habeas Corpus Act in the latter year, supported electoral reform in 1679, and was an active exclusionist. Following James II's accession, Wharton left England for Flanders and Germany. He espoused the cause of William of Orange and was made a Privy Councillor in 1689.

Wharton was for five decades a major figure in reform and revolutionary politics. His leadership of the Nonconformist cause after 1660 has obscured his strong interest in political reform. He wished to see royal ministers, members of the Privy Council and some judges subject to parliamentary confirmation, as well as newly appointed members of the House of Lords. He also proposed that freeholders be empowered to nominate sheriffs, JPs and militia officers, and hoped to see the Protestant cause furthered by a union of England, Scotland and the United Provinces. His close association with radicals like Shaftesbury* and Dissenters like John Owen* helped bridge the gap between political and religious protest under Charles II.

G.F. Trevallyn Jones, *Saw-Pit Wharton* (1967); *LJ*; *DNB*; *PSP 1640*; Underdown, *PP*; Lacey. Papers: O (Carte MSS); L (Add. MSS; Sloane MSS).

J. Gruenfelder

WHEELER, William (c. 1619-c. 1672)

Ejected Independent minister, received a B.A. from Lincoln Coll., Camb. on 2 July 1639 and an M.A. on 5 May 1642. He signed the nomination of Bedfordshire representatives to the Little Parliament on 13 May 1653. In 1661 he was ejected from his post of Rector of Cranfield, Beds., and his successor was instituted there on 15 Oct. 1661. He was jailed later on a charge of preaching without a license in his own house in Cranfield. A quarter sessions jury cleared him of the charge, but he was still in jail about 1670 when he petitioned the King for release. His wife Frances and daughter Sarah died before Wheeler, who was buried at Cranfield, probably on 13 Feb. 1672, though another William Wheeler was buried there on 28 Apr. 1674.

Calamy; *Calamy Revised*; *CSPD, Chas. II*, 10:632; R.L. Greaves, 'The Organizational Response of Nonconformity to Repression and Indulgence: The Case of Bedfordshire,' *CH*, 44:472-84.

D.L. Clark

WHETHAM, Nathaniel (1604-1668)

Civil War officer. Whetham, of Drimpton, Dorset, came to London in 1620. He married Joanne Terrill in 1632, and in 1633 was baker to the Inner Temple and Steward of the Company of Whitebakers. In the 1630s Whetham, known for his Presbyterian views, was active in Warwick* and Gorges' colonizing venture for Maine, 'The Company of the Plough,' but remained in England. He joined the parliamentary army in 1642 as captain of a London company of dragoons, and from 1643 to 1646 was Governor of Northampton, concerned with the supply and defense of the Eastern Association. He fought in the first and second sieges of Banbury (1644 and 1646). In Jan. 1649 Whetham acquired royalist lands in Chard, Som., and in April was a trustee for the sale of dean and chapter lands. He was military governor of the naval base of Portsmouth from 1649 to 1655, and in May 1650 was appointed JP for Hampshire and colonel of the Hampshire militia. In 1655 he helped suppress unrest arising from Penruddock's rebellion. Whetham was MP for Portsmouth in the Parliament of 1654, in which he opposed proposals to make the Protectorship hereditary. In 1655 Cromwell removed him from Portsmouth and appointed him to the Council of State for Scotland, where Whetham became a firm supporter of Monck. He served as JP for Edinburgh and, as member for Fife in 1656 in the second Parliament of the Protectorate, spoke in favor of union with Scotland. He was elected to Richard Cromwell's* Parliament in 1659 on a double return. He was reappointed Governor of Portsmouth in May 1659 by the army Committee of Safety, but in November signed a remonstrance against the latter; in December he adhered to the Parliament against the army. Whetham supported Monck by admitting Haselrig,* Walton* and Morley* to Portsmouth on 3 Dec. 1659, and helped to secure the garrison for Parliament against Fleetwood's* troops. He joined Monck in his march to London in Jan. 1660, and in February the House voted him £200 p.a. in lands for his service and commissioned him colonel of a regiment of foot. In Feb. 1660 he was again a Commissioner for Scotland. Whetham retired to Chard in June 1660, where he engaged in a legal battle over his lands with John Lord Poulett until his death.

C.D. and W.C.D. Whetham, *A History of the Life of Colonel Nathaniel Whetham* (1907); Ludlow; Firth & Davies; *Clarke Papers*; *HMC, Leyborne-Popham MSS*; J. Nicoll, *A Diary of Public Transactions and Other Occurrences Chiefly in Scotland* (1836); *CJ*, 7:807-8, 850; Whitelocke, *Memorials*; Davies, *RC*; Dow.

L.S. Popofsky

WHITACRE (or Whitaker), Lawrence (c. 1579-1654)

Parliamentary radical, MP 1624, 1625, 1626, 1628 (Peterborough), LP 1640 (Okehampton). Whitacre was probably born in Somerset, but his family origins are obscure. He married first Margaret, daughter of Sir John Egerton of Cheshire and Northamptonshire, and second Dorothy, daughter of Charles Haskins of Holborn, Middlesex. Whitacre was educated at St. John's Coll., Camb. where he received the B.A. (1597) and M.A. (1600). He was incorporated at Oxford in 1603 and admitted to the Middle Temple in 1614. By then Whitacre had moved to Drury Lane, London as secretary to Edward Phelips, Master of the Rolls. In 1615 Whitacre, known as a man of learning and an occasional poet, went into the service of the Earl of Somerset. Between 1619 and 1623 Whitacre received fee farm rents from crown lands in a dozen counties. He served as JP in Middlesex and Westminster, and

Clerk of the Privy Council during the 1620s and 1630s. Along with Inigo Jones, Whitacre was a commissioner for buildings in London in the 1630s. He was sentenced to one week in the Tower for searching Sir John Eliot's* chambers in 1629, but resumed an active role afterwards. His conversion to the opposition in the Long Parliament was due in part to his patron Lord Mohun. He voted against the Earl of Strafford, took the Covenant in Sept. 1643, and served on several committees. Whitacre was a leading diarist, first in the 1626 Parliament, and later produced a continuous diary of the Long Parliament's proceedings from 8 Oct. 1642 to 9 July 1647. Whitacre was not extremely wealthy; his income was probably less than £500 p.a. He had a country estate at Chiswick, former residence of the Earl of Somerset, as well as property in London and Lambeth, manors in Somerset, and a rectory in Lincoln. Whitacre died on 15 Apr. 1654 without direct heirs and was buried at St. Giles'-in-the-Fields.

Whitacre's inclination to assist the Crown prior to the Long Parliament was in large part because of his offices as JP and Clerk of the Council. He served on commissions to collect a forced loan in Middlesex (1626) and to collect compositions for knighthood (1630). Whitacre equivocated on the issue of whether the Commons' grievances had precedence over the King's supply in 1628. Later Whitacre supported taxation for domestic expenses, and assistance to foreign allies and against foreign enemies, but he also cited royal prodigality. Whitacre agreed with the general principles of the Petition of Right. On religious matters, he was more categorical. He defended Parliament's right to discuss religion, warned against condoning religious error, and favored parliamentary discipline of bishops. By the time of the Civil War Whitacre was probably an Independent in religion. He served on committees to reform ecclesiastical courts and regulate popish Recusants. Whitacre has been regarded as essentially neutral on political disputes in the Long Parliament, yet he was a member of the committee which determined that the King must be tried (Dec. 1648), though he did not serve on the court.

Keeler; *CD 1628*; Yule. Papers: Earl of Moray MSS, Donybristle; L (Add. MSS 31,116 – Whitacre's Diary).

D.W. Hollis, III

WHITAKER, William (c. 1594-1646)

Parliamentary radical and law reformer, MP 1624 (Motcombe), 1625, 1626, SP, LP 1640 (Shaftesbury). Whitaker was the son and heir of Henry Whitaker of Westbury, Wilts., gent., and Judith, daughter of William Hawkins of Plymouth. He matriculated to the Middle Temple on 23 April 1602, where he was bound with John Pym* and Francis Rous.* Called to the bar on 27 Nov. 1611, he became reader and bencher in 1627 and treasurer in 1635. Assigned half the upper chamber of Francis Tate, Whitaker became a leading figure in the Middle Temple and in the west country. He married Honora, daughter of Edward Hooper of Boveridge, Dorset, and lived in Shaftesbury from 1626. A JP and member of the Sewers Commissions, he served as MP for over twenty years, becoming recorder of the borough in 1640. In London he associated with the Temple group of parliamentarians, especially Pym, Rous, Erle,* Harley and Rudyard.* A devout Puritan, his life was frugal, and considerable time was spent in the spiritual development of his alleged nine children. But he remained loyal to the Anglican church, a position which caused him to fall from parliamentary favor in the mid 1640s.

Whitaker participated little in parliamentary debates, and no writings have been found to date. He was, however, committed to the reform of the courts, the law and legal education. He was one of the major figures in the administration of the Middle Temple for nearly thirty years. Preferring the admission of devout young men, he tried to increase the dialogue between lawyers and students, and was on many committees for the management of the Inn. He participated in the committee to reform the Inns in 1641, and helped pull down the communion rails of the Temple Church in May 1643. In the Long Parliament he became a member of the middle group, remaining close to the center, and was a trustee of Pym's will. Whitaker supported the Civil War at the beginning, but with the growth of armies and increased bloodshed retreated prior to his death in Oct. 1646. Whitaker's son Henry succeeded him as Recorder of Shaftesbury and sat for the borough both in 1659 and in the Cavalier Parliament.

C.T. Martin, ed., *Middle Temple Record: Minutes of Parliament* (1901), 1-3; Keeler; J. Hutchins, *History and Antiquities of the County of Dorset* (1867-70), 3-4; Bayley; *CSPD, Chas. 1, passim*; B. & P. Papers: L (Add. MSS; Cotton MSS).

L.A. Knafla

WHITE, Francis (d. 1657)

Army radical, was a captain in Sir Thomas Fairfax's* regiment of foot. He appears to have been a yeoman or a yeoman's son. White first gained prominence during the army agitation in the spring of 1647. On 15 May he presented the soldiers' grievances to the six Parliamentary Commissioners at Saffron Walden. He continued thereafter to agitate in his regiment despite pressure from his superiors, and was singled out for his activity: 'There is one Captain White who is the most active man in this business and issues out orders as if he were the lieutenant-colonel.' In June White was promoted major in the reorganization of the regiment. He represented it on the Council of the Army, from which he was expelled on 9 Sept. for insisting that there was 'now no visible authority in the kingdom but the power and force of the sword.' White pressed this singularly unwelcome viewpoint on the army gran-

dees again at the Putney debates, and a week later wrote Fairfax that in trying to reach agreement with the King 'they were repairing an old house, and that when they were laying the top stone it would fall about their ears.' Despite this he was readmitted to the Council on 21 Dec. in a general attempt to placate the radicals.

In Nov. 1648 White was one of the six Independent representatives at the Nag's Head tavern meetings with the Levellers. He supported the army's right to depose Charles and return power to the people, 'its original fountain next under God.' By the same token however he denied the legitimacy of the High Court and opposed the King's execution: 'I do not understand any essential good can accrue to the people, by the taking of his life.' The Levellers took White to heart, praising him in *The Second Part of Englands New-Chaines Discovered* (1649) and complaining about his failure to secure promotion. This made White a logical go-between in the final Leveller mutiny of May 1649. On 12 May Fairfax sent him with other officers to persuade the rebels in Scrope's* and Ireton's* regiments to lay down their arms. White himself drafted their reply, in which they repeated their demand for a General Council but promised to abide by its decisions. He then led them to Burford where, hearing that Cromwell and Fairfax had attacked the town with 2000 dragoons, he rushed out into the night to find Fairfax. Taken prisoner in the street, he was released but forced to return to his quarters. The Levellers accused White of betraying them in *The Levellers (Falsly So Called) Vindicated*, to which he replied in *A True Relation of the Proceedings in the Business of Burford* (17 Sept.), asserting that he had authority only to deliver their message and await a reply. White subsequently distinguished himself at Dunbar, and was chosen by Cromwell to carry news of the victory to Parliament along with the captured enemy colors, for which he was awarded £300 and promoted at last to lieutenant-colonel. In Dec. 1650 he was a commissioner to treat for the surrender of Edinburgh Castle, and in Jan. 1651 jointly commanded the abortive attempt to capture Burntisland with John Mason.* On 12 Dec. 1653 White and Col. Goffe* forcibly dispersed the remnant of the Barebones Parliament. In Oct. 1657 he was sent to Flanders as governor of Mardyke Fort. While returning to England in December he was drowned in a shipwreck. Parliament subsequently voted his three daughters £200 apiece.

Firth & Davies; Brailsford; *Clarke Papers*; Gardiner, *GCW*; Abbott; Thurloe, *SP*; *The Copies of Severall Letters Contrary to the Opinion of the Present Powers* (1649); Woolrych.

R. Zaller

WHITE, Jeremiah (1629-1707)

Independent minister, the son of a clergyman, was admitted to Trinity Coll., Camb. in 1646 (B.A. 1649, M.A. 1653). White's religious depression as a student was eventually resolved by his adoption of a 'universalist' position. Though details are unclear he attracted attention early, preaching before the Council of State and becoming one of Cromwell's chaplains. He was said to have been neatly outsmarted by the Protector when he attempted to marry Frances Cromwell. He is also believed to have opposed Cromwell's pro-French policy. This independence of mind was apparent at the Restoration when he refused to swear to the new government, although well affected towards it, because he said he could not be sure it would not degenerate. It is uncertain how he maintained himself for the rest of his life: he held no living, either Anglican or Dissenting, though he is known to have preached at an Independent meeting house in Rotherhithe built soon after the 1688 Revolution. He was noted for his good humor, charity and avoidance of controversy. During the Interregnum he relieved distressed clergymen and later compiled a list of sufferers from the persecution of the restored Church of England. He is said to have refused tempting offers to publish this in James II's reign. After the Revolution he acted as chaplain to the Calves-Head Club, a satirical republican group which met on the anniversary of Charles I's execution.

Theologically White rejected all limits on the efficacy of God's love and grace. It was God's will that all should be saved and God willed nothing that he did not work. None was excluded forever from salvation even though God's justice was severe: it was the retention of punishment for sin which enabled White to rebut the charge that universal salvation encouraged licentiousness. As a further defense he held that men were wearied by too much pleasure and claimed that his view of God had converted even the Earl of Rochester to a good life. Although the operation of divine grace did not exclude the need for human industry, White rejected what he regarded as the Arminian position of absolute free will. He attempted, with disputed success, to reconcile his universalism with predestination, election and reprobation. His theological position was naturally linked with aversion to religious polemics and a strong support for toleration. He was not indifferent to religious forms but held that Christians should stress their own, not others' fallibility. He even went so far as to state that there had not been such contention in the world till Christ came into it. White contended that uniformity of spirit, not uniformity of worship, was proper to a Christian community.

White's sermons were said to be delivered *ex tempore* and he relied much less on authorities than was usual, but he had close intellectual links with the Cambridge Platonists, particularly Peter Sterry.* His introduction to one of Sterry's works was later expanded as his *Perswasive to Moderation*, a powerful plea for toleration and reconciliation among Christians. His other notable published work, *The Restoration of All Things*, sets out most fully his universalist position and answers objections. A number of his manuscript works are lost, a posthumous proposal to publish them not having been carried out.

DNB; *Monthly Miscellany* (1707): 83-85, 116-20; J. White, *A Perswasive to Moderation and Forbearance in Love among the Divided Forms of Christians* (1708, 1725?); White, *The Restoration of All Things: or, a Vindication of the Goodness and Grace of God* (1712, 1779, 1798).

M.J. Hawkins

WHITE, John (1590-1645)

Parliamentary radical and law reformer, SP 1640 (Rye?), LP 1640 (Southwark). White was born on 29 June 1590, the second son of Henry White of Henllan in Rhoscrowther, Pemb., and Jane, daughter of Thomas Fletcher of Bangor. White was descended from a wealthy Tenby merchant family that dated from at least the fifteenth century. He matriculated to Jesus Coll., Oxf. on 20 Nov. 1607 and to the Middle Temple on 6 Nov. 1610, being called to the bar on 19 June 1618. His family had contributed several Templars in the past, and White continued this tradition by having his son and those of several families from Pembrokeshire and elsewhere specially admitted. He had a chamber in Brick Court from 1624 and a house in Holborn, but did not distinguish himself in the government of the Inn. White was however a very successful lawyer. Counsellor to several Puritan families including the Winthrops, he was a stockholder and counsellor for the Massachusetts Bay and Providence Island Companies, drafted the former's charter, and organized a group of feoffees to purchase lay impropriations. A devout Puritan from his youth, he patronized Independent and Presbyterian ministers, and supported the disestablishment of the Church.

From the beginning of the Long Parliament White was an outspoken opponent of the King's religious and legal policies. His influence was due perhaps to his association with other prominent parliamentary Templars such as Edward Bagshaw, Sir Simonds D'Ewes, William Drake and Richard Seaborne. He was chairman of the committees for inquiring into the immorality of the clergy and for the advancement of new ministers, and spoke vigorously against the established Church. He believed that no canons or ecclesiastical policy could be made without Parliament, that prelates could and should be excluded from Parliament, and that all corrupt or immoral priests should be discharged from their livings. He also opposed arbitrary arrests and the prerogative courts. Equating law with common law and common law with liberty, he declared that liberty was life itself. Thus White stood not only for the abolition of the prerogative, but also the conciliar courts, and opposed the right of any arrest or imprisonment without complete due process.

White was chiefly noted for his speeches and writings on the Church, however, which comprised four works written and published in the years 1640-44. The most famous of these was *The First Century of Scandalous, Malignant Priests* (1643), which earned him the nick-name 'Century White.' This book outlined the evidence collected by his parliamentary committee on 100 ministers in the southeastern counties. Calling his work an investigation into 'the gall and wormwood of the episcopal government,' his biographical sketches portray a feast of crimes: murder, rape, assault, adultery, prostitution, buggery, etc. The book was in instant sensation. It had some five editions in the first year, and led to the dismissal of approximately 1600 ministers. White's supporters were so embarrassed that they refused to allow him to publish a second volume. He kept in the limelight that year by pulling down the basins, candlesticks, rails and crosses from the Temple Church. He died on 29 Jan. 1645. The House of Commons attended his funeral at the Temple Church, under whose high altar he was buried. The inscription placed over his bust was an apt assessment of his impact: 'Here lyeth John, a burning, shining light, His name, life, actions, were all White.'

C.T. Martin, ed., *Middle Temple Record: Minutes of Parliament* (1901), 2; Keeler; *DNB*; D'Ewes, *Jour.* (C); *Massachusetts Bay Society, Transactions* (1906-7). Papers: O (Bodleian MSS; Rawl. MSS).

L.A. Knafla

WHITE, William (1606-1662)

Parliamentary radical and Civil War officer, MP 1645 (Pontefract), 1659?, 1660 (Clitheroe), was born on 16 Feb. 1606, the son of William White of Duffield, Derby by his second wife Sarah, daughter of Matthew Cradock of Stafford. White was the last scion of a prominent Hampshire family; his grandfather had been MP for Clitheroe in 1588, and his father became a tenant of the Duchy of Lancaster. He began his career as a clerk in the Court of Wards, and about 1629 married Margaret, daughter and coheiress of Thomas Talbot of Bashall, Yorks., thereby acquiring an estate at Bashall which, worth £332 p.a. in 1620, had been improved to £500 by 1649. In that year he married again, to Frances or Francisca, daughter of Sir Edward Barkham, first Baronet of Tottenham and a Surrey squire.

White stood for Parliament unsuccessfully at Clitheroe in Sept. 1640. He may have been a lieutenant in the Earl of Stamford's regiment of foot in 1642-43, but thereafter attached himself to the Fairfax interest, becoming a colonel by 1644 and Treasurer-at-War for the northern army. In 1645 he was returned for Pontefract, again through Fairfax influence. He served as well as JP for the West Riding of Yorkshire from at least 1640 and as a commissioner for assessment, sequestration and militia in the county; was a clerk of the assize on the Oxford circuit from 1643 to 1646 and subsequently on the northern circuit, and a commissioner for obstructions from 1648 to 1651. In 1646 he entered the Inner Temple.

White was an intermediary in negotiations between Parliament and the army in 1647, warning that only Royalists could profit by their dissension. In June he was dispatched with Sir Thomas Widdrington* to add instructions to the twelve Parliamentary Commissioners negotiating with the army, and on 2 July he was one of the eight commissioners representing Parliament in the talks at Wickham. In Parliament itself, however, he took a hard line in dealings with the King. At Charles' flight to the Scots in 1646 he was described as one of those who 'made bold with foul expressions' in the House of Commons, and on 10 Oct. 1648 he supported the radical motion to try all delinquents 'from the highest to the lowest without exception,' going the sponsors one better by suggesting it be done by martial law.

White was absent from the Commons during the King's trial and execution. On 1 Mar. 1649 he wrote Speaker Lenthall* excusing himself as 'sick of a fever at York,' but at last took his dissent on 14 May. He was inactive during most of the Protectorate, but probably sat for Clitheroe in Richard Cromwell's* Parliament and returned with the Rump, serving as well as a commissioner for arrears of revenue and for customs and excise. White was returned to the Convention Parliament, where Christopher Clapham charged that he had offered to cut off Charles I's head. An investigation cleared him, but he was shortly after unseated on a dispute over his election, and at the same time removed from the commission for the peace. White's will, dated 6 Sept. 1660, was proved on 3 Sept. 1662.

Clarke Papers; Fairfax Corr.; R. Bell, ed., *Memorials of the Civil War* (1849); Firth & Rait, 2:119, 662, 1277, 1350, 1353, 1424; Underdown, *PP*; MacCormack; Pink MSS; History of Parliament draft biography.

R. Zaller

WHITE, William (fl. 1654-1665)

Fifth Monarchist and Particular Baptist,

was described as a cutler in the town of Abingdon, Berks. in 1654 and later (1656) of the Longworth congregation which separated itself from the Abingdon church. Along with many other Abingdon Baptists he espoused Fifth Monarchist views in the early 1650s, probably due to the influence of the famous Baptist preacher and Fifth Monarchist, John Pendarves,* who preached in the area for a number of years. White attended the massive rally of Fifth Monarchists in Abingdon in 1656 at Pendarves' funeral. The meeting drew adherents from all over England who debated for three days how they could bring about their goals. Before being dispersed by Cromwell's soldiers they endorsed the use of violence if necessary to bring about the rule of the saints. After the Restoration White reappeared briefly in official records when he, along with several others, was fined 13s. 4d. for failure to attend the established church in Abingdon. The following year he was jailed on a similar charge. Under the provisions of the Declaration of Indulgence of 1672 the Abingdon congregation took out a licence as a Baptist congregation but whether White remained a member at this date is unknown. No biographical details of White's life are known.

A.E. Preston, *The Church and Parish of St. Nicholas, Abingdon* (1929); Capp, *FMM*; Brown.

J.S. Flemion

WHITEHEAD, George (1637-1724)

Quaker, was born at Sun Bigg in the parish of Orton, W'land, of poor farming parents. Educated at Blencoe free school in Cumberland, he was raised a Presbyterian but rejected his family's worship at the age of fourteen. He was convinced several years later by the preaching of George Fox.* The prosaic calm of his conversion, which he attributed to his relative youth, set the pattern for the rest of his life. Having developed his spiritual gifts in contests with the local clergy, he moved south as an itinerant preacher at the age of seventeen. Apart from a visit home in 1657 when he was reconciled with his parents, he was occupied until 1661 with Richard Hubberthorne* evangelizing the eastern counties. Despite his youth he asserted himself as leader in disputes with the local clergy, claiming that the Lord gave him the power to discern false syllogisms. He also began a publishing career which was to produce before his death over one hundred tracts, mostly controversial. During several lengthy periods of imprisonment he acquired considerable legal knowledge in defending himself against charges of vagrancy and disturbing religious services. He was principally responsible for establishing by example the propriety of Quakers knowing and asserting their rights in law. Much of his autobiography is given over to turgid descriptions, with copious documentary evidence, of his legal battles. His proud account of besting the Recorder of Norwich occupies over one hundred pages. In 1661 he emerged from rigorous confinement in Newgate where prison fever had carried off Hubberthorn and Edward Burrough.* He subsequently operated from London, although not until 1670 did he decide that his mission was to marry and settle there. By 1680 he was trading as a grocer in Houndsditch. Although frequently convicted under the Conventicle Act, he was rarely imprisoned for long but regularly had his goods distrained for non-payment of fines. Fortunately he was never indicted on a third offense, for which the penalty was banishment.

The death from plague or the rigors of confinement of all the established Quaker leaders except Fox partly explains Whitehead's rise to prominence by 1670, but he also provided the movement with the industrious, pragmatic skills needed to develop the formal institutions of Quakerism. He was a mainstay of the central business meetings, based in London, which had emerged by 1680. A faithful disciple of Fox, his compromising temperament was a useful foil to his leader's autocratic irascibility, particularly in dealing with internal dissent. Such skills, and his residence in London, gave him leadership of the Quaker lobby at court and Parliament. After the first of a number of interviews with Charles II in 1672, he persuaded his reluctant brethren by dubious reasoning that accepting a pardon under the Declaration of Indulgence was no admission of guilt. After the death of Fox in 1691 Whitehead emerged as the acknowledged leader of the Quakers. His principal mission was to gain legal recognition of Quaker objections to oaths which deprived them of most of the benefits of the Toleration Act of 1689. Whitehead's lobbying produced the Affirmation Act of 1696, a poor compromise which offended the scruples of many Friends. The issue continued to disturb the movement until a Hanoverian Parliament legislated for an acceptable form of affirmation a few years before Whitehead's death.

Longevity may ultimately have assured Whitehead his prominent place in Quaker history but he had substantial qualities of more evident worth during the period of consolidation after 1660 than in the first phase of enthusiastic expansion. An expert grasp of legal technicalities and the ability to treat deferentially but firmly with a succession of English monarchs were rare gifts among the First Publishers of Truth.

The Christian Progress of George Whitehead (1725); G. Whitehead, *Jacob Found in a Desert Land* (1656); Braithwaite, *SP*; *EQL*; *FPT*; *EQW*; *DNB*. Papers: LF; OQ.

J.F. McGregor

WHITEHEAD, John (1630-1696)

Quaker, was born of Puritan parents at Owstwick, Yorks. in 1630. He joined the Cromwellian forces at the age of eighteen, and in 1652 was converted to the Quaker cause by William Dewsbury* at Scarborough Castle. He first preached at Malton, Yorks. in Dec. 1652, and the following spring in Butterwick. After leaving the army in the summer of 1653, he preached in the Yorkshire moors and established meetings at Whitby and Cleveland. The following year his itinerant witnessing took him from Coventry to Huntingdon. In November he had to be rescued by troops from a hostile crowd when he tried to preach in Lincoln Cathedral, and the next month he was imprisoned at Leicester. Whitehead, Dewsbury, Mary Fisher* and Dorothy Waugh* were the first Friends to preach in Buckinghamshire, where Whitehead met with the Baptists in Jan. and Feb. 1656, on one occasion debating with the apothecary and lay preacher, William Hartley.* Whitehead's preaching at Wellingborough, Northants., involved him in a public debate with Thomas Andrews, the vicar. Whitehead was arrested for vagrancy on 14 Mar. 1656 and committed to the Northampton jail, though he was freed in Jan. 1657 by an order from Cromwell. After further preaching in Berkshire and London, Whitehead was imprisoned at Boston, Lincs. in 1658, the year in which he engaged in a pamphlet war with Thomas Moore's sectarian congregation at Gainsborough.

After the Restoration Whitehead was imprisoned in Jan. 1661 at Aylesbury, Bucks., for refusing to take the Oath. Following his arrest at Binbrook, Lincs. on 13 Nov. 1661, he spent three months in Lincoln Castle, to which he was recommitted on 9 July 1662 until his release in May 1663. His response to Viscount Saye and Sele's* condemnation of Quaker views appeared in 1662 under the title, *A Manifestation of Truth*. Whitehead suffered further imprisonment in 1663 at Hull, Yorks., and Spalding, Lincs., and he was instrumental in 1664 in procuring the release of George Fox,* with whom he had traveled the previous year in Derbyshire, from Scarborough Castle. In 1675 Whitehead formulated a petition to the King seeking relief for imprisoned Yorkshire Quakers. Two years later he was with Fox in York on behalf of the Friends' cause. On 22 May 1682 Whitehead was committed to Lincoln Castle, charged with being a Jesuit for refusing to take the Oath of Allegiance. After his release in July 1684 he presided over a disciplinary meeting at Fulbeck, Lincs., but JPs discovered the conventicle and fined the Quakers £72 13s. 2d. His last incarceration was at the Poultry Compter in London on 11 Feb. 1685 for preaching at Devonshire House. In the 1690s Whitehead settled at Fiskerton, near Lincoln. He was one of the group of thirteen Friends designated by Fox to see that his journal was published, and to this end the group sought assistance in the epistle of the 1691 Yearly Meeting. Whitehead died at Fiskerton on 29 Sept. 1696, and was buried in Lincoln on 1 Oct. Of the 22 tracts he wrote, the most important is his spiritual autobiography, *The Enmitie between the Two Seeds* (1655). His collected works were published in 1704 under the title, *Written Gospel-Labours*. He is not to be confused with the Belfast merchant of the same name who was detained at Penzance, Corn. in Mar. 1681 for refusing to take the Oath of Supremacy.

Fox, *CJ*; Besse; *EQL*; *FPT*; *EQW*; *DNB*; Braithwaite, *BQu*. Papers: LF.

R.L. Greaves

WHITEHURST, Richard (1637-1697)

Congregational minister and Fifth Monarchist, became Rector of Askham, Notts. on 28 July 1658, then Vicar of Laughton en le Morthen, Yorks. in 1660, from whence he was ejected. Whitehurst kept a conventicle and was protected by Anthony Hatfield, esq., of Westhall, Hatfield. He was licensed there as a Congregational minister on 1 May 1672. Whitehurst also served the Congregational church at Lydgate, Kirkburton, as minister. His Fifth Monarchy views among other differences involved him in protracted disputes with his congregation in 1678-79. Heywood described the efforts made to reconcile those differences. Whitehurst moved to Bridlington in 1695 and died there on 5 Sept. 1697.

O. Heywood, *Autobiography* (1881-85); Capp, *FMM*; J. Hunter, *Rise of Old Dissent* (1842); J. Lister, *Autobiography* (1842); Palmer, 3; *Calamy Revised*.

J.D. Ban

WHITELOCKE, Sir Bulstrode, Kt. (1605-1675)

Parliamentary radical and law reformer, MP 1626 (Stafford), LP 1640 (Great Marlow), 1654, 1656 (Bucks.). Whitelocke was the son of Sir James Whitelocke, Kt.* of Fawley, Bucks., a lawyer and justice of the King's Bench, and Elizabeth Bulstrode (1575-1631), the daughter of Edward Bulstrode of Hedgerley Bulstrode, Bucks. Whitelocke married three times: the first in 1630 to Rebecca Bennet (d. May 1634), the daughter of Thomas Bennet, Alderman of London, with one son as issue: the second in 1634 to Frances Willoughby (d. 16 May 1649), the daughter of Lord Willoughby of Parham, with nine children as issue; the third in 1650 to Mary Wilson (d. July 1684), the widow of Rowland Wilson,* with seven children as issue. Whitelocke attended Merchant Taylors' School (1615) and matriculated at St. John's Coll., Oxf. in 1620, where he was befriended by the president, William Laud, and William Juxon, later Bishop of London. He left Oxford without a degree and entered the Middle Temple in 1622, where he met Edward Hyde, later Earl of Clarendon, and was much influenced by John Selden.*

Whitelocke was elected to Parliament in 1626 for Stafford and kept a diary of the proceedings. He was called to the bar of the Middle Temple in the same year and served as Master of the Revels for 1628, an office which advanced him socially. Whitelocke was never the dour Puritan that he has sometimes been portrayed; he enjoyed music and dancing, directing the music for the production of the famous royal masque in Feb. 1634. Despite these Court connections, however, he opposed the extension of the forests and the expansion of ecclesiastical jurisdiction in the 1630s, and was consulted by John Hampden* and his lawyers in the ship money case. He was defeated for election to the Short Parliament from Abingdon, Bucks., but was returned for the Long Parliament for Great Marlow, Bucks. after a disputed contest. Whitelocke served as chairman of the committee to impeach the Earl of Strafford. He was disturbed by the drift to Civil War, however, even opposing the Grand Remonstrance. But in 1642, as matters reached a crisis, Whitelocke came down firmly on the side of Parliament. He favored the Militia Ordinance, was a member of the Committee of Safety and supported the Nineteen Propositions. He accepted the office of DL for Berkshire and Oxfordshire though not a commission. In the fall of 1642 his home at Henley-on-Thames was severely damaged by Prince Rupert's men. But Whitelocke remained an advocate of compromise and in 1643 became one of the commissioners to treat with Charles I at Oxford, later being accused of duplicity in those negotiations by Edmund Waller. Whitelocke again served as a commissioner to meet the King at Oxford after Marston Moor (1644). In the House he became clearly identified with the moderate party. He bitterly opposed the radical-sponsored ordinance to try political delinquents by martial law, demurred at the Self-Denying Ordinance, and was again accused of treasonable correspondence at Uxbridge. Yet on religious matters, Whitelocke was just as clearly joined with the radicals. He played an important part in denying the *jure divino* claims of the Westminster Assembly, consistently opposed the powers of the presbytery, supported (and later practiced) lay preaching, and stood fast for toleration and freedom of conscience.

In 1648 Whitelocke was chosen by Parliament to serve as one of the Commissioners of the Great Seal, an appointment renewed by the Commonwealth in Feb. 1649. He refused service on the High Court, but continued to sit in Parliament between Pride's purge and the King's execution, and took the dissent in February.

Whitelocke's major responsibility during the Interregnum was that of the Chancery where he served as a commissioner until his resignation in June 1655. He served in that capacity again briefly in 1659, and from June 1655 to 1659-60 he was a Commissioner of the Treasury. Whitelocke distinguished himself as the Protector's ambassador to Queen Christina of Sweden (1653-54), a role which has often overshadowed his accomplishments in the Chancery. Because he was deprived of the Great Seal by Cromwell in 1655 after refusing to implement the Chancery Reform Ordinance (1654), Whitelocke has usually been depicted as opposed to law reform. However, his attempts to reform Chancery through his *Orders of the Commissioners of the Great Seal* (1649), his authorship of the Hale Commission's 1652 bill on country registries and Chancery reform, and his service on the parliamentary committee for regulating the law demonstrate a willingness to work for reform. His dismissal by Cromwell was more likely prompted by a fundamental disagreement with Cromwell over the role of the 1654 Protectorate Parliament and the enforcement of the Chancery Ordinance and others in 1655 as laws not adopted by Parliament. Whitelocke was compensated by Cromwell with the Commission of the Treasury and remained a close confidant of the Protector and his son, Richard Cromwell.* He served as a lord in Cromwell's Upper House after 1657.

Whitelocke survived the Restoration in 1660 but was ostracized from public life. He was often in London during the 1660s but never achieved his former prominence. Financial reverses and a profligate family kept him occupied with creditors. Thereafter, he busied himself with writing, studying, and managing family affairs and estates from his headquarters at Chilton Lodge, Wilts. He lived to age 70 and died on 27 or 28 July 1675 at Chilton Lodge; he was buried at Fawley Court, near Henley-on-Thames.

Whitelocke, *Memorials*; Kishlansky; J. Lord Campbell, *The Lives of All the Lord Chancellors* (1845-47); R. Spalding, *The*

Improbable Puritan (1975); *DNB*; Worden; A.J. Busch, 'Bulstrode Whitelocke and Early Interregnum Chancery Reform,' *Albion*, 11:317-30; Keeler; Whitelocke, *Lib. Fam.* Papers: Longleat; L (Add. MSS 37, 334-37, 347; 4992; 53,726 [Personal Journal]; Lans. MSS; Royal MSS; Sloane MSS; Stowe MSS); B; OE.

A.J. Busch

WHITELOCKE, Sir James (1570-1632)

Law reformer and parliamentary radical, MP 1610, 1614, 1621 (Woodstock). Born the youngest son of Joan Brockhurst of Hertfordshire and her second husband Richard Whitelocke, Sir James studied at Merchant Taylors' School, at St. John's Coll., Oxf., where he was elected a fellow, and at New Inn and Middle Temple. He joined the Society of Antiquaries and was admitted to the bar in 1600. He married Elizabeth Bulstrode of Buckinghamshire who bore him five daughters and two sons.

Chosen Recorder for Woodstock in 1606, Whitelocke represented the borough in Parliament in 1610. Already a man of reputation, he quickly assumed a prominent role. His famous assertion in the debate of 2 July on impositions that the King's 'power out of Parliament is subordinate to his power in Parliament' was a daring formulation of Parliament's sovereign role. Whitelocke's attack on purveyance and his role in the negotiations concerning the Great Contract brought him the unfavorable attention of the Crown. In 1613 Whitelocke again angered the authorities by advising a client on devices to frustrate the proceedings of a royal commission seeking to reform the administration of the navy. While the commission lacked sufficient evidence to penalize Whitelocke as the author of a list of 'exceptions' to its proceedings, the government found other means to chastise him. When Whitelocke attempted to transfer a different matter from Chancery to the Marshall's Court, he was charged with impeaching the royal prerogative, committed to Fleet prison on 18 May, and not released until his written submission was accepted on 13 June.

In the Parliament of 1614 Whitelocke continued his attacks on the abuses of impositions, opposed the granting of new revenues without redress of grievances, and so angered the government that he was examined by the Privy Council and ordered to burn all his speeches after the dissolution of Parliament. Subsequently Whitelocke was deprived of his employment by the Court of King's Bench and King James personally removed his name from a list of candidates to be considered for Recorder of London in 1618. Desiring advancement, Whitelocke modified his activities, acquired land, secured local office and strengthened his association with Chancellor Bacon and others. Subsequently he was invested with the coif, knighted, selected recorder for four boroughs and appointed Chief Justice of Chester. His independence and opposition to the abuse of royal prerogative prompted a dispute with Lord Northampton which resulted in his transfer from Chester to the Court of King's Bench in Oct. 1624.

Continued in office by Charles I, Whitelocke remained independent and joined Sir Ralph Carew in refusing to acknowledge the legality of forced loans. He also advised the abandonment of the practice of securing judges' opinions on an issue before it was considered in Parliament. In 1627 he helped to force Lord Treasurer Marlborough to promise to pay the judges their overdue salaries. When Marlborough's promise proved false, only Whitelocke and two others had the temerity to issue writs which secured the delinquent payments.

After the turbulent Parliament of 1629, the judges disappointed the government by sidestepping the major legal and constitutional issues posed by the imprisonment of nine members who prevented the Speaker from adjourning Parliament. While Whitelocke supported the government's right to try them in Star Chamber Court, he did not want to deny bail as a means to eastern shores of North America, ranging from Maryland and Virginia to Long Island and Rhode Island. Widders won the respect of his associates for his religious fervor, and his wife Jane seems to have been devoted to him. Fox thought highly of Widders and called him 'one of God's valiants' as well as 'a thundering man against hypocrisy, deceit, and the rottenness of priests.'

The Life & Death, Travels and Sufferings of Robert Widders (1688); Fox, CJ; EQW; EQL; Besse; DQB; FPT; Cadbury. Papers: LF.

B.C. Weber

WIDDRINGTON, Sir Thomas (c. 1600-1664)

Parliamentary radical, MP SP, LP 1640 (Berwick), 1654 (York), 1656 (N'land), 1660 (York), 1661 (Berwick). Widdrington was the eldest son of Lewis Widdrington of Cheeseburn Grange, N'land, and Katherine, daughter of William Lawson of Little Usworth, Durham. In 1634 he married Frances, daughter of Ferdinando, Baron Fairfax, MP for Yorkshire in the Long Parliament, and by her had six children, a son who predeceased him and five daughters. His wife died in childbed on 4 May 1649. Widdrington was graduated from Christ's Coll., Camb. in June 1620, was admitted to Gray's Inn, and was later called to the bar. He became Recorder at Berwick in 1631 and served as JP there in 1640. On the recommendation of Justice Hutton, Widdrington was named Recorder at York in 1637. His welcoming speech to the King at York on 30 Mar. 1639 so pleased Charles that Widdrington was knighted. A well respected lawyer, he was named respectively an ancient (1639), bencher (1639), Lent reader (1640) and serjeant (1641) of Gray's Inn.

Returned for Berwick early in 1640, Widdrington sought election from York to the Long Parliament; however Strafford's endorsement worked against his candidacy

coerce submission. In a private audience, Whitelocke secured the King's approval to allow bail if the members posted a bond. While the defendants rejected this arrangement and Whitelocke concurred with the final verdict, he issued a separate opinion which condemned the defendants on the basis of their legal obligations as private citizens without accepting the prerogative claims of the Crown. When the Long Parliament examined this incident in 1640, his son Bulstrode* so effectively defended his position that Whitelocke's lands were exempted from the fund created to provide compensation to the defendants.

J. Whitelocke, Collection of Curious Discourses, ed. T. Hearne (1771); Whitelocke, Liber Fam.; Moir; CD 1610. Papers: O (Ashmolean MSS; Ashburnham MSS); L (Add. MSS; Harl. MSS; Stowe MSS).

S. Hanft

WIDDERS (or Widder, Withers), Robert (c. 1618-1686?)

Quaker, was born in Over Kellet, Lancs., of substantial parentage. A yeoman, he was convinced by George Fox* near Sedbergh in 1652 and soon thereafter began the missionary work he continued zealously for the rest of his life. In 1654 Widders accompanied Fox to Cumberland and Northumberland, but he was imprisoned at Lancester later that year and was not released until William West, a Lancashire JP friendly to the Quakers, issued a writ on his behalf in 1656. Widders then journeyed to Scotland with Fox in 1657-58. Several times the two were banished by the Scottish Council. During Sir George Booth's rising Widders informed the rebels that 'the Lord with his rod of iron would break them to pieces.' Widders and Fox preached in London in 1660 and in Devon in 1663. In Aug. 1671 Widders left London with Fox and other Friends for a missionary journey to Barbados, Jamaica and the and forced him to retain his previous seat. This was his initial rebuff by the citizens of York. Although never a prominent debater Widdrington frequently served on committees and conferences where his legal expertise could be employed. He was involved in the dispute over tendering the Oaths of Allegiance and Supremacy to the Queen's Capuchins and introduced a measure for the more rapid conviction of popish Recusants in 1641. Earlier that year he had drawn up impeachment charges against Matthew Wren, Bishop of Ely. Widdrington noted that Wren, while Bishop of Norwich, had only preached once in the diocese, had encouraged his subordinates not to preach, and had suspended conscientious ministers, placing superstitious priests in their livings. Widdrington's emphasis on the preaching function of the ministry and his hostility to the Book of Sports also suggest his Puritanism.

A Commissioner of the Great Seal and a member of the middle group, Widdrington served on the parliamentary committee charged with restraining the army in 1648. After Pride's purge, though not secluded, he and his fellow commissioner, Bulstrode Whitelocke,* remained away from the House, negotiating behind the scenes for the release of the seized members. Widdrington's personal efforts secured the freedom of Thomas Lane* and Henry Pelham. Throughout December, working with Whitelocke and Speaker Lenthall,* he sought to effect a compromise with Cromwell to restore the secluded MPs, provide the officers with moderate backing and frustrate the Levellers. The attempt failed by 25 Dec. and Widdrington retired from London. Once the High Court commenced its preliminary deliberation he resumed his seat in the Commons on 8 Jan. and continued to issue writs under the Great Seal on the sole authority of the lower House. He took the dissent on 1 Feb. 1649; however, he claimed ill health and 'scruples of conscience' and resigned the Seal on 8 Feb. to pursue private practice. Widdrington accepted the execution of the King and would continue to serve both the Commonwealth and Protectorate.

Widdrington was appointed a serjeant for the Commonwealth and became a member of the Council of State in 1651. A monarchist at heart, he urged that the Duke of Gloucester be named King with limited powers at a meeting to discuss the settlement of the nation after Worcester. Along with Whitelocke he was a vigorous opponent of legal reform during the Commonealth and spoke out against the dissolution in 1653; yet Sir Thomas stood for election to both Cromwellian Parliaments and was designated Speaker in 1656. He strongly supported Cromwell, presided at his second inauguration as Protector, served on many lucrative commissions in the Interregnum and was returned for both the Convention and Restoration Parliaments. Prior to the election of 1661 he offered to dedicate his *Analecta Eboracensia* to the Mayor and Corporation of York. Their refusal wounded him grievously and he withheld his history of the town from publication. Widdrington died in London on 13 May 1664 and was buried there.

D'Ewes, *Jour.* (C); *DNB*; Keeler; Underdown, *PP*; Whitelocke, *Memorials*; Sir T. Widdrington, *Analecta Eboracensia*, ed. C. Caine (1897). Papers: L (Harg. MSS 38-39; Lans. MSS 1083, 1092; Add. MSS 18,979); O.

M.J. Galgano

WIGAN, John (d. 1665)

Baptist and Fifth Monarchist, was a curate at Heapey near Manchester in 1642 until removed by royalist forces in 1644. After 1644 he was at Birch Chapel. At first a Presbyterian, Wigan established Baptist/ Fifth Monarchist churches in Manchester and Cheshire, planting the first ones in 1648 within a month after Robert Lilburne* suppressed a rising in Lancashire. In 1651 he became a captain of a troop of horse, probably in Col. Grosvenor's regiment in Lancashire, and early in 1653 became a major in Cromwell's regiment. Opposed to the signing of the Instrument of Government, he debated it with Cromwell, and because of his opposition to the Protectorate he resigned his army commission in Jan. 1654 and returned to his duties as a minister in the Manchester area. Although in 1654 Wigan's name was among those of ministers to be ejected, in 1656 he received an augmentation of his income as a minister. In 1659 he was among petitioners against rule by a single person and demanded that all former supporters of the Protectorate be removed from office. At the fall of Richard Cromwell,* he expected restoration to his former military position and was bitterly disappointed when offered instead a commission as lieutenant-colonel in Robert Overton's* regiment. Although he accepted the commission he complained that he knew few of the men in his new regiment and doubted their fitness to serve. He also condemned the Commissioners for the Nomination of Officers for their discrimination against Fifth Monarchist. In 1663 he was involved in the Fifth Monarchist plot, for which he was imprisoned in Lancashire in 1663-64. George Fox,* with whom Wigan had debated in London in 1658, was in the same prison and they renewed their argument about the Light within. As a result of this dispute Wigan published the pamphlet *Anti-Christ's Strongest Hold Overturned, or the Foundation of the People Called Quakers, Bared and Razed* (1665). Tendered the Oath of Allegiance at the assizes, Wigan requested and received time to consider taking it. Released on bail, he was permitted to go to London where in 1665 both he and his wife died of the plague. Fox, who once described Wigan as a very wicked man, declared his death to be punishment for the afore-mentioned anti-Quaker pamphlet. Wigan must have been married twice because a wife Ann was buried in Manchester in 1661. He had two daughters, Elizabeth who married Dan Dunbaven, a draper of Warrington, in Feb. 1657, and Lydia who married William Morris of Manchester in June 1658.

Calamy Revised; Capp, *FMM*; Brown; Firth & Davies; W.T. Whitley, *A History of British Baptists* (1932); Firth & Rait, 2:972; *CSPD, Comm.*, 9:156; 10:31; 11:239; 12:265; 13:36, 45, 46.

J.D. Neville

WIGHTMAN, Edward (d. 1612)

Sectary, was the last person to be burned for heresy in England. In his parish, Burton-on-Trent, Staffs. as well as in neighboring parishes, he was active in prophesyings. In these meetings he vociferously expressed Anabaptist views. According to his chief prosecutor, Richard Neile, Bishop of Coventry and Lichfield, Wightman also advocated anti-Trinitarianism, and at times claimed to be the Paraclete – while on other occasions hinting that he was the messiah. More moderate friends tried unsuccessfully to dissuade Wightman from his radical views, but he persevered, and in early 1611 presented a petition calling for radical reforms to James I at Royston. The King sent him to Westminster where he was committed to the Gatehouse and examined by Bishop Neile. Neile was an experienced inquisitor, having been one of the examiners for the last heretic burned at Smithfield. Together with his chaplain, William Laud, from early April until mid-October Neile interrogated Wightman who, under examination, became even more obstinate in his heresy.

In late 1611 James ordered that Wightman be tried in the Consistory Court at Lichfield under the presidency of Bishop Neile. At the conclusion of a trial which lasted several days, Neile pronounced sentence on 14 Dec. 1611, condemning Wightman to be burned as a heretic. The primary charge was that he had denied the Trinity, and before sentencing Neile preached a sermon refuting blasphemies against the Trinity (*CSPD, Chas. I*, 15:83-85). The commission for Wightman's execution was issued on 9 Mar. 1612, and the Sheriff of Lichfield immediately brought Wightman to the stake.

As soon as he felt the flames, Wightman cried out that he would recant. After having been rescued by the crowd, a formal recantation was shown to him, which he accepted before being unchained from the stake. Imprisoned once again, Wightman appeared a few weeks later before the Lichfield Consistory Court to formalize his recantation. Dramatically, he refused and his writ of execution immediately was renewed. This time his courage did not fail, and he was executed totally unrepentant either on 18 Mar. or 11 Apr. 1612.

ST, 2; *CSPD, Jas. 1*, 9; *Chas. 1*, 15; *DNB*; Burrage; R. Wallace, *Antitrinitarian Biographies*, 2-3 (1850); Hill, *MER*.

G.A. Drake

WILD (or Wyld, Wylde), Edmund (c. 1614-1696)

Parliamentary radical, MP 1645 (Droitwich). Wild was born on 10 Oct. 1614 (1616 according to John Aubrey), the eldest son of Sir Edmund Wild of Kempsey, Worcs., and his wife Dorothy, daughter and heiress of Sir Francis Clarke of Houghton Conquest, Beds. A royal ward in 1632, Edmund matriculated at Christ Church, Oxf. the following year. Recruited to the Long Parliament for Droitwich, he survived Pride's purge and was named to the High Court. Wild is listed as present at only two sessions of the Commission (17 and 25 Jan.), both in closed session, and in later years he went to great lengths to persuade William Dugdale and Elias Ashmole to delete his name from accounts of the trial on the grounds that he had never sat in Westminster Hall, only in the Painted Chamber, thus he never participated in the trial per se. According to his reminiscences to Aubrey, Wild influenced the selection of Sir William Petty* to undertake the survey of Irish lands, and of Jonas Moore, the mathematician, as sur-

veyor for the Duke of Bedford's* Great Level of the Fens, but he manifested no hint of loyalty to any particular radical leader or group during a brief parliamentary career which ended with the ouster of the Rump. Content to live down his association with the Puritan rebellion, Wild re-emerged in the 1670s as a resident of Bloomsbury Square, London, an estate owner in Shropshire, Bedfordshire and Essex, a horticultural experimenter, a raconteur, and patron of the then penurious Aubrey, who dedicated his *Remaines of Gentilisme and Judaisme* (1686) to Wild.

Aubrey; A. Powell, *John Aubrey and His Friends* (1948); E. Ashmole, *Autobiographical and Historical Notes*, ed. C.H. Josten (1966).

J.F. Battick

WILDE (or Wylde), John (1590-1669)

Parliamentary radical and jurist, MP 1621, 1624, 1625, 1626, 1628, SP 1640 (Droitwich), LP 1640 (Worcs.), 1659 (Droitwich). Wilde was the son and heir of George Wilde of Kempsey, Worcs., serjeant-at-law, JP and MP for Droitwich, and Frances, daughter of Sir Edmund Huddleston of Sawston, Cambs. He matriculated at Balliol Coll., Oxf. on 18 Jan. 1605, graduating B.A. on 20 Oct. 1607 and M.A. on 4 July 1610. Admitted to the Inner Temple in Nov. 1602, Wilde was called to the bar in 1612, elected a bencher in 1628, created serjeant-at-law in 1636, and on 4 Aug. 1636 appointed Understeward of Kidderminster. From 1627 he was a legal counsel to the city of Worcester, and in Mar. 1640 became its recorder.

Wilde was an outspoken figure from his first Parliament, when he scandalized the Commons by declaring the King to be 'deluded' in his negotiation with Spain and called for its denunciation as an enemy. He strongly supported the Spanish war and was a severe critic of Buckingham's conduct of it, in 1626 seconding Selden's* argument that the Duke might be impeached on the basis of common fame. Wilde was returned for the county in the Long Parliament in a contest with the Royalist Sir Thomas Littleton, where his legal expertise rapidly pushed him to the fore. He was appointed chairman of the impeachment committee against the thirteen bishops engaged in the Canons of 1640. In Dec. 1641 he chaired the committee to investigate the alleged army plot, and on 6 Jan. 1642 was named to head the committee set up to consider measures for the safety of the Kingdom and City in the wake of the attempt to arrest the Five Members. Later in the month he conducted the impeachment proceedings against the Attorney General, Sir Edward Herbert. In June Wilde offered two horses and £1000 for the defense. He was named DL for Worcestershire, and in the following year a Sequestration Commissioner. Wilde was a lay member of the Westminster Assembly and served, with some vigor, in the impeachment of Laud.

In Feb. 1643 Parliament included the nomination of Wilde as Chief Baron of the Exchequer in its proposals to the King. On 19 June 1646 he was appointed an assize judge and on 12 Oct. Chief Baron, a post he retained until his dismissal by Cromwell in Oct. 1653 in favor of William Steele.* Wilde was a lay member of the Westminster Assembly and served, with some vigor, John Burley to death for attempting to rescue Charles from the Isle of Wight while helping to secure the acquittal of Maj. Edmund Rolph,* accused of attempting to poison the King. He used his powers on the assize to promote petitions against further treaty with the King in Somerset in Mar. and Sept. 1648, and on 10 Oct. joined Cornelius Holland* and Thomas Hoyle* in demanding justice upon all delinquents 'without exception' in the House of Commons.

Wilde absented himself from the King's trial with the other judges at Westminster. He welcomed the new regime with enthusiasm however. In Feb. 1649 he joined the Council of State, and on 17 Mar. delivered a 'gallant speech' on behalf of the government at Exeter, though only seven of forty JPs attended it. When the Mayor of Exeter threw the proclamation of the Commonwealth into the gutter, Wilde fined him £200. Wilde prospered during these years, allegedly trafficking in forged debentures for fee-farm rents. After his dismissal from the bench, he confined himself to county politics, but was returned in 1659 to Richard Cromwell's* Parliament, sat in the restored Rump, and was reinstated as Chief Baron on 17 Jan. 1660. At the Restoration he was absolved by the Act of Indemnity and lived in retirement until his death in 1669. Wilde was buried on his son-in-law's estate at Wherwell, Hants. He married Anne, daughter of Sir Thomas Harries, by whom he had one daughter, also named Anne. William Pierrepont* was his brother-in-law.

DNB; Keeler; Clarendon; Gardiner, *HCP*; *Fasti Oxon.*; Zaller; Worden; Underdown, *PP*; Williams, *Worcester*.

W.W. MacDonald and R. Zaller

WILDMAN, Sir John (1623-1693)

Leveller, conspirator and pamphleteer, was born in Berkshire. Nothing tangible is yet known about his early life. He was said to have studied at Cambridge and the Inns of Court, but the records are silent. He had become a soldier by 1647, an officer in 1649 and a major by 1653. Wildman first emerged as an Agitator in the autumn of 1647, when he contributed to *The Case of the Army*, opposing negotiations with Charles I. He then helped draft *The Agreement of the People*, a paper which contained the first constitutional program of the Levellers: a single legislature, manhood suffrage, biennial elections, freedom of religion and conscience, equality under the law, and an unregulated economy without special privileges. With four colleagues, William Allen,* Robert Lockyer,* Maximilian Petty* and Edward Sexby,* he urged this program in the Putney debates. The movement for a democratic commonwealth failed and when Cromwell began his purge of Leveller influence, Wildman produced a vitriolic attack that became one of his best known works, *Putney Projects*. Arrested for sedition in Jan. 1648, he was released in August. When the other Leveller leaders attempted to compromise that autumn with a new revised *Agreement*, Wildman refused, for which he was considered by many a traitor to the cause. He took no part in the formation of the new republic, though legend later placed him on the scaffold with Charles I, and devoted the next five years chiefly to economic speculation. Purchasing perhaps some fifty small parcels of land in various counties at distress prices from Royalists, clergymen and Recusants, he created the foundations of a prominent landed estate.

Wildman continued his political agitation as well however. In 1650-51 he led the London Common Council as legal advisor in an unsuccessful move to democratize the City government. Elected to Parliament in 1654 for Scarborough, his exclusion led him to publish several pamphlets denouncing Cromwell and his government, and an attempt with Sexby to assassinate the Lord Protector which earned him another spell in prison (Feb. 1655-July 1656). Wildman was released on bail of £10,000 with full recovery of his lands in return for agreeing to spy for the government against the Royalists in France. In Europe he tried to woo (and fleece) Charles and the French and Spanish governments into supporting an uprising against Cromwell's government. In the meantime he was working for a popular revolution and, discovered on his return in an attempt to blow up Whitehall Palace with gunpowder, he was arrested again in Jan. 1657. Wildman read Harrington's* recently published *Oceana* in jail, and on his release he wrote several pamphlets under its influence. He held meetings at his pub, the Nonsuch House in Bow Street, which grew into the Commonwealth Club, an association of more than eighty members including such veteran republicans as Marten* and Haselrig.* Wildman opposed Lambert's* coup in the fall of 1659 and

seized Windsor Castle in the name of Parliament. But though as late as 15 Apr. 1660 it was reported that Wildman was still holding out for a republic, he gained favor with the new government of Charles II.

Wildman was wealthy by 1660, and he purchased an office in the Royal Post. His proposal to use the post office for police and undercover surveillance was accepted, and gradually he came to control significant parts of the operation. Arrested for using the system to advance the republican movement, he was charged with treason in Nov. 1661 and sent in exile to the Scilly Isles until Oct. 1667. Wildman then joined forces with the Duke of Buckingham with whom he had intrigued under the Protectorate. He became the Duke's legal advisor and trustee, and after the latter's fall from favor, he joined the old republicans Shaftesbury* and Algernon Sidney* in 1678. After a period of renewed agitation which included his election for Great Bodwin in the third Exclusion Parliament (1681), Wildman attempted once more to bring the democratic revolution to fruition by assassination. On 28 June 1683 he was arrested and imprisoned in connection with the Rye House plot. Released the following 12 Feb. for lack of evidence, he made contact with the Duke of Monmouth and was implicated in the uprising which followed. He fled to Holland in June 1686. He patronized William, Prince of Orange, styling himself the leader of the English common folk and of soldiers who would give him their unswerving loyalty. Wildman was not impressive at the Hague, but at the Revolution he was elected to Parliament for Great Bedwin (1689) and Wootton Bassett (1690), chosen alderman of London (1690), given the freedom of the City, and appointed Postmaster-General (1689). He was soon involved in the Jacobite Montgomery plot, which he regarded as a vehicle for a republican revolution. Discovered, he was dismissed from the Post Office in Feb. 1691. Nonetheless, he was knighted the following year and became DL for Middlesex. He died on 4 June 1693.

Wildman's lifelong purpose was to disestablish church and state. Reflecting the interests of the artisans and yeomen, he revealed a hatred of monarchy, the Church and status groupings. He believed that the English people were slaves under the Norman Yoke, and that only a total revolution could restore freedom. He seems to have had a blind faith in Magna Carta and the liberties of the past, as well as his ability to influence others. Wildman believed that there was a natural law above the divine that all men would come to accept in the end. No philosopher, he was derivative in his thought, and relied largely on the work of Henry Marten, John Lilburne,* James Harrington and Algernon Sidney.

Law, money and pamphleteering were also strong interests in Wildman's life. He was one of the most profilic pamphleteers of his time. A few of his pamphlets, like *Putney Projects, Truth Triumphs* and *The Declaration of the Free*, were effectively and pungently written. But most were collections of arguments and precedents, poorly arranged and thought out. One must remember however that most of his writings were dictated to servants, and that he had little time for composition. There is also no established canon of what he did write as he used pseudonyms frequently. Wildman always claimed to be a legal expert, and indeed he did serve as one in several instances. However, his knowledge of law, despite the praise of some contemporaries, was not good. His cases and arguments reveal no logic, legal reasoning or legal scholarship. He lost almost every suit he counselled, and his legal knowledge was out of date. The assertion that he was educated at the Inns may be apocryphal, as well as the compendium of the laws of England on which he was allegedly working in his later years. What should be emphasized is that his ideas on law reform were both radical and in places original. He wanted the language of the law in English, common law procedure completely revamped and codified, property and estate law simplified, the influence of judges restricted, capital punishment largely abolished, corporal punishment curtailed and prisons reformed. He obviously gained many of these ideas from grim experience.

Wildman's ultimate principles present a serious question. He made large profits not only from distressed Anglicans, papists and vulnerable aristocrats, but also from London artisans, Midland yeomen and Lincolnshire fenmen. He offered to assist some Gloucestershire men in gaining reparations from the Civil War but only for one-third recovered, which they declined. There is also the question of his fidelity to the Good Old Cause. While his biographer believes he was loyal to people and issues to the end, and always loved by those who fought with him, the evidence is not convincing. Recent works on Wildman's colleagues reveal they placed little confidence in his friendship, particularly after 1655. The habit of double agentry he acquired at this time appears to have become second nature, and there seems little doubt that he betrayed Sexby, who died in prison. His role in the late 1640s has also been revised downwards. What cannot be doubted is the support he received from his wife and son, who preferred to be in prison with him rather than outside without him. Whatever the judgment on Wildman, however, he was a man of considerable industry and courage, one of the genuine survivors of the seventeenth century.

Ashley, *JW*; *DNB*; *Grey's Debates*; *Clarke Papers*; Hill, *WTUD*; Beaven; Brailsford; L.G. Schwoerer, *The Declaration of Rights, 1689* (1981). Papers: O (Bodleian MSS; Clarendon MSS).

L.A. Knafla

WILKINSON, John (d.c. 1683)

Quaker, was a farmer at Millholme, New Hutton, W'land. After trying the Independent way in religion, he was converted to Quakerism in 1652 by George Fox* at Firbank. Beginning in 1654 he actively carried the Quaker message with John Story* to Wiltshire, Gloucestershire, Bristol and Somersetshire. In 1655 he was arrested at Marshfield and imprisoned at Gloucester, where the grand jury 'brought in a petition . . . that Ranters, Levellers and atheists, under the name of Quakers, made a disturbance, and petitioned some speedy course might be taken' (*EQL*, 173). He may be the John Wilkinson who, with John Audland,* was arrested at a meeting in Bristol in 1662 and was imprisoned for refusing the Oath of Allegiance, as well as the person who was apprehended at a Quaker meeting at Anlaby in Aug. 1666. There was, however, another John Wilkinson (d. 1675) active in Quakerism in this period; he had, as a Puritan minister at Brigham, Cumb., converted in 1653.

It was the John Wilkinson of Westmorland who supported Story's break with Fox in the 1670s, though he appears to have been a gentle person. An early Quaker source says that he 'at first seemed tenderly to accord with faithful Friends in encouraging faithful Women's Meetings . . . and also in Friends care and inspection' (*FPT*, p. 267); but he accepted Story's opposition both to the extent of Women's Meetings and to the control of meetings over the lives of Friends. Like Story, he stressed the role of the Spirit within. After Story's death in 1681 he vindicated their cause, in collaboration with others, in *The Memory of That Servant of God, John Story, Revived* (1683). It was apparently not long after this that he died and was buried at Kendal.

FPT; *EQL*; Fox, *CJ*; *EQW*; Braithwaite, *SP*; cf. Besse. Papers: LF (Swarthmore MSS; Barclay MSS).

R.L. Greaves

WILLIAMS, John, *alias* **Skimington or Lady Skimington (fl. 1631-1637)**

Enclosure resister, was a miner or laborer of English Bicknor in the Forest of Dean. Williams was a leader in the anti-enclosure riots of Mar. and Apr. 1631 in the Forest of Dean, and was reported leading the revolt in Braydon Forest in north Wiltshire in June which was said to have involved more than a thousand men. The Privy Council, describing him as 'the most principal offender and ringleader in those rebellions and riots,' took an active interest in his apprehension. At one point a posse of 120 men led by the Undersheriff of Gloucestershire attempted to surprise him in bed but, forewarned, he fled. Attempts to bribe the people of the countryside to betray him failed. Williams may have been involved in a riot at Cannop Chase in Dean in Jan. 1632, threatening royal agents there. He was finally caught in March by William Cowse, one of the King's commissioners for the sale of log wood. Cowse was subsequently forgiven a debt of £379. 7s. 8d. owed to the Exchequer in recompense. For the time being however he was a highly unpopular figure. On 8 Apr. he and a fellow commissioner, William Rolles, were attacked in church though they had entered armed. Williams' wife was summoned before the Council in connection with this incident but dismissed for lack of evidence. Williams himself was conveyed under tight guard first to Gloucestershire Castle and then to Newgate, with the Council threatening condign punishment for anyone permitting him to escape. He does not appear to have been tried. After languishing for more than five years in Newgate, he was released on petition to the King and Council in Aug. 1637 under a bond of £2000 for good behavior put up by Robert Wood of Clerkenwell, Middlesex, William King of St. Sepulchre, London, and Thomas Slape of Fetter Lane, London, the former a gentleman and the latter two fishmongers. Their relation to Williams is unclear.

Ironically, the government itself may have done the most to create the legend of this Robin Hood-like rebel. As Buchanan Sharp has shown, at least three distinctly identifiable John Williamses were involved in the riots of 1631-32, while the name 'Skimington' was a common folk *alias* used by a number of other agrarian rebels and deriving from the local custom of raising a 'skimington' or tumult against termagant wives.

B. Sharp, *In Contempt of All Authority* (1980); D.G.C. Allan, 'The Rising in the West, 1628-1631,' *Economic History Review*, 2nd ser., 5:76-85. Papers: LPR; O (Bankes MSS).

R. Zaller

WILLIAMS, John (fl. 1646-1681)

Fifth Monarchist, was a minor Welsh squire. He fetched Vavasor Powell* from Dartford to Wales in 1646 and became an elder of his church and one of his most devoted followers. Williams served as a captain of militia. He was a member of the County Committee for Radnorshire and served as sheriff and sequestrator in the county and as a Commissioner for the Propagation of the Gospel in Wales. In 1652 Williams and three others were accused of having not accounted for property and rents sequestered in 1649. Nevertheless, he was nominated for the Barebones Parliament and served on its Council of State where he supported the principle of voluntary tithes. Reports reached the government in 1653 that Williams had preached a sermon at Cannigull, Radn. in which he denounced Cromwell as a tyrant. Williams was a signatory of Powell's *Word for God*. In 1658 he was rumored to be planning an uprising. After the Restoration he was not known as a Fifth Monarchist and may have been a Congregationist. He was arrested as a Conventicler in 1664 and in 1681 on a writ *de excommunicato capiendo*. Williams was released from prison in 1681 because of ill health and died shortly thereafter. He was denied burial in the churchyard of Llangollen.

Capp, *FMM*; Dodd; T.C. Richards, *Wales Under the Penal Code* (1925); Thurloe, *SP*, 2:46.

R.H. Gottdiener

WILLIAMS, Roger (c. 1603-1683)

Separatist and colonist, was born in London, the son of James Williams (d. 1621), merchant tailor, and his wife Alice Pemberton (1564-1634), daughter of Robert and Katherine Stokes Pemberton of St. Albans. Sir Edward Coke,* the jurist, sponsored Williams at Charterhouse School and at Pembroke Hall, Camb., where he received his B.A. in 1627. In 1629 Williams became chaplain to Sir William Masham* at Otes, High Laver, Essex. Here Williams became acquainted with parliamentary opponents to Charles I, and met with John Winthrop,* Thomas Hooker* and John Cotton.* He married Mary Bernard on 15 Dec. 1629, and embarked from Bristol on the ship 'Lyon' on 1 Dec. 1630, arriving at Massachusetts Bay in Feb. 1631. Gov. Winthrop at that time noted that he was 'a godly minister.' Williams refused the office of teacher in the Boston church, holding the congregation to be an unseparated people unrepentant for having had communion with the Church of England. For this and for asserting that the civil magistrates should not punish a breach of the first four Commandments, the Bay leaders prevented Williams from accepting a position at Salem. Williams went to Plymouth colony, where he assisted the church and prepared to be a missionary to the local Indians, learning their language and forming lasting friendships with their leaders. In 1633, after returning to Salem to assist the dying pastor, Williams sent a treatise (since lost) to colony leaders protesting the European monarchs' practice of granting tracts of land inhabited by Indians as though they, the kings, had rights of ownership. This document implicitly contested the legal basis of colonial settlement.

The action which Williams believed caused his irreconcilable conflict with the government was his objection to the resident's loyalty oath, to be required after Apr. 1634 of all inhabitants who did not have status as freemen. The penalty for refusal was banishment. Williams contended that since an oath was an act of religious worship, to force persons who by Puritan definition were unregenerate to take an oath was to support taking the name of the Lord in vain. So many inhabitants refused the oath that the Bay leadership backed down and the proceeding was dropped.

In July 1634 Williams was in court for protesting the use of civil power to compel uniform church discipline. The Bay clergy were also angry because the Salem church had called Williams to become pastor without seeking their approval. Two factors weakened Williams' defense: his temporary illness, and pressure on the town of Salem, which was seeking confirmation of a land claim. On 9 Oct. 1635 the General Court banished Williams, giving him until spring to leave.

Later the Bay leaders decided to arrest Williams and ship him back to England. When they came for him, he had already departed on his midwinter trip to Wampanoag territory and his friend Massasoit. A letter from Edward Winslow in April indicated that in the interest of continuing good relations with the Massachusetts Bay colony, the Plymouth leaders wished him to move out of their claimed territory to the west side of Narragansett Bay. Here the town of Providence was established in late spring 1636 by Williams and other later refugees from Salem. Salem's land claims were confirmed by the Massachusetts magistrates one month after Williams' departure.

The colonies ejecting Williams received an undeserved benefit from his new location. Williams used remarkable diplomatic skill in preventing an alliance between the Pequots and the Narragansetts which could have proved fatal to the colonies in the Pequot War.

Even though the refugee inhabitants of the new settlement could be trying, Williams maintained the principle of freedom of religious conscience. His image of the community was of a ship holding passengers and crew of varying religious beliefs. People were free to worship or not to worship as they pleased, but they were not free to refuse their required civil duties

upon the ship or to question the civil authority of the ship's officers. Williams was prepared to use the civil sword when necessary.

When Massachusetts Bay authorities became aggressive in asserting their claims to land around Providence, Williams traveled to England in 1643 to negotiate a charter from the English government. On the way he stopped long enough in New Amsterdam to negotiate a peace between that colony and neighboring Indians.

In England, Williams had access to leading members of the parliamentary government through his connection with Sir William Masham. In the face of a rival negotiator from Massachusetts Bay who had come within two signatures of obtaining a Narragansett Patent for his colony, he was able to obtain a charter by which the Narragansett Bay settlements were granted power to rule with their own civil government.

The publication in 1643 of Williams' *Key into the Language of America* helped move the Parliamentary Commissioners in Williams' favor as regards the charter, for it demonstrated that in one English settlement progress was being made in evangelizing Indians. Fortunately Williams had received the charter before the publication in 1644 of *The Bloudy Tenent of Persecution for Cause of Conscience*. Attacking the concept of a national church and upholding religious liberty as a right for Christian, Jew or pagan, he held that the duty of magistrates was to protect the right of a citizen to freedom of worship and not to determine whether his religion was true or false. The book was roundly denounced by the Westminster Assembly and ordered burnt by Parliament on 9 Aug.

Returning from England Williams was able again to avert war between the now United Colonies and the Narragansett Indians. However, this negotiation proved no more final than did obtaining a charter put a stop to the other colonies' attempt to encroach upon Rhode Island. Added to this was a continuing struggle to form a coherent government out of the disparate individuals of the colony.

After another trip to England between 1652 and 1654 (during which he renewed the toleration controversy in *The Bloudy Tenent Yet More Bloody*, 1652) Williams returned to serve as President of Rhode Island. Quakers moved in during this period and though Williams disagreed with their views, he maintained their right to freedom of conscience; he also affirmed the right of Jews to settle in the colony. With the accession of Charles II a new charter was obtained in 1663 and Williams served as assistant to the governor. In 1677 he refused re-election, but continued to serve in the town government of Providence. During Philip's uprising in 1675-76, Williams had warned his Indian friends of the suicidal nature of their armed protest against white land fever, but he also served as a captain of the militia which defended Providence and barely kept it from destruction. His funeral in 1683 was observed with militia firing guns over his grave, an ironic end for a peacemaker.

What set Roger Williams apart from Puritan contemporaries was his rejection of the notion that the nation was in a covenant relationship with God. Not believing in the city set upon a hill, Williams lived out the logic of other Puritan concepts, including the most extreme statement of toleration made by an Englishman in the seventeenth century.

R. Williams, *The Complete Writings* (1963); J. Garrett, *Roger Williams* (1970); E.S. Morgan, *Roger Williams* (1967); O.E. Winslow, *Master Roger Williams* (1957); W. Coyle, *Roger Williams: A Reference Guide* (1977); E.W. Coyle, 'From Sinner to Saint: A Study of the Critical Reputation of Roger Williams' (Ph.D. diss., Univ. of Massachusetts, 1974); W.C. Gilpin, *The Millenarian Piety of Roger Williams* (1979). Papers: L (Add. MSS).

J.C. Spalding

WILSON, Rowland (1613-1650)

Parliamentary radical and Civil War officer, MP 1646 (Calne). Wilson was born in London in Aug. 1613, the only son of Rowland Wilson (d. 1654) of Gresegarth, W'land and London, and his wife, Mary, daughter of John Tiffin of London. A wealthy and influential merchant, Wilson became lieutenant-colonel of the Orange Regiment of the London trained bands soon after the outbreak of the Civil War. In Oct. 1643 his regiment was attached to the army of the Earl of Essex,* and aided in the occupation of Newport Pagnell. By 1646 he had risen to the rank of colonel. He was subsequently elected MP for Calne (June 1646), Alderman of London (28 Nov. 1648), and Sheriff of London (13 July 1649). An Independent, Wilson retained his seat in the Commons after Pride's purge (6 Dec. 1648), and was named to the High Court which tried Charles I, but did not participate in the court's deliberations and refused to sign the death warrant. Despite lingering doubts about the High Court's actions, Wilson accepted election to the first Council of State (7 Feb. 1649). On 12 Feb. 1650 he was again chosen to sit on the Council, but died a week later (19 Feb.). At the time, his death was rumored to be a suicide. Wilson's widow, Mary (m. 1634), daughter of Bigley Carleton of London, became the third wife of Bulstrode Whitelocke* in 1650.

DNB; *CJ*, 4-6 *passim*; Noble; Underdown, *PP*; Yule; Beaven.

C.B. Rynder

WINSTANLEY, GERRARD (c. 1609-1676?)

Digger, the most remarkable of the radical thinkers of the English Revolution, was born in Wigan, Lancs., the son of a mercer of Puritan sympathies. Apprenticed to a cloth merchant in London in 1630, he became a freeman of the City in 1637. In 1640 he married Susan King. He worked in some branch of the cloth trade in London until 1643 when his business failed and he went to live at Cobham in Surrey, earning his living as a farm laborer. The activities and writing (about twenty pamphlets, letters and broadsides), for which he became widely known to his contemporaries and is now famous, were all crowded into the years 1648-51. Nothing certain is known of his life after 1660 although it is possible that a Gerrard Winstanley, Quaker and corn chandler who died in 1676, may be the same person.

Winstanley's first pamphlets were in the tradition of radical religious mysticism. He seems to have begun as a serious Puritan within the Church of England and moved rapidly through the Separatist rejection of a national church (he was certainly a Baptist for a time) to the extreme sectarian position of those 'seekers' who rejected all ecclesiastical institutions.

The 1640s in England saw an outburst of popular preaching and publishing which was unprecedented in the history of the world. This outburst was an efflorescence of a Christian tradition going far back into the Middle Ages, and the distinguishing character of the movement in the 1640s was not the development of radical and mystical religious beliefs, but their popularization to a wide audience of poor and previously inarticulate persons.

Winstanley's religious beliefs were similar to those of all the people whom seventeenth-century conservatives lumped together as Quakers, Familists, Antinomians, Anabaptists, Ranters and the like. He refers to no book except the Bible and mentions the names of no teachers or masters, nor is he mentioned by any other radical religious writer of the period. He did hear the 'prophesyings' of inspired laymen and discussed religion in private meetings with like-minded seekers. It is easy to imagine how he absorbed the popular religious beliefs of many poor Englishmen who had suddenly become religiously intense and articulate.

Had Winstanley written only his five primarily religious pamphlets, he would be known today as one of the most interesting of the many propagandists of radical mysticism. The first four, published between May and Nov. 1648, are passionate and rhapsodic statements of his religious beliefs and contain no hint of his later communist doctrines. Winstanley stressed the importance of relying entirely on the voice of the Spirit or Christ within each person and of rejecting all traditional Christian theology and all doctrine learned second-hand from books and teachers. He substituted the word Reason for God in order to cut all his ties to traditional religion. But Winstanley was not Voltaire. For him Reason was synonymous with Spirit and Love and these were the opposites of Flesh and Imagination. History he saw as the struggle between Spirit and Flesh and the same struggle, he wrote, goes on within each individual. Winstanley was a universalist, insisting that the Spirit would eventually triumph within each individual soul as well as in the cosmos, and he despised Calvinist doctrines of eternal damnation.

Winstanley was convinced that the overthrow of the monarchy was the beginning of the final victory of the Spirit and he used the apocalyptic language of Revelation and millenarianism to indicate that the last age, the Kingdom of God on earth, was at hand. The regeneration of the world, he thought, would renew the world of nature as well as the world of man. Winstanley came near to being a Pantheist, seeing the Spirit in the whole creation, and he expected the victory of the Spirit would increase the fertility of the soil, destroy weeds and pests as well as the tooth-and-claw violence of the animal world. The lion would lie down with the lamb, and the earth would be the Peaceable Kingdom.

Reliance on the Spirit within each person led Winstanley, as it had led others, to deny the authority of the Bible and the human learning required to interpret it. He regarded the Bible as a collection of allegorical tales and moral precepts which probably recorded real revelations of the Spirit to various persons in the past but which could be authenticated only by the Spirit within each reader. He had no use for supposedly scriptural doctrines such as life after death. He was convinced that the fear of hell led to mental disorders and was a cynical tool used by the rich to cheat the poor of their happiness in this world. The resurrection is not, he said, an historical event of the first century A.D., but an allegory of the Spirit rising every day in the hearts of those who listen intently and humbly. Winstanley stressed the need for meditation – listening to the Voice within – and he himself had revelations while in a trance. He despised teaching by hired ministers trained in special schools or at the universities. The Spirit, he thought, spoke most often to the poor and the uneducated and not to their rich oppressors – clergy, lawyers, landowners, rulers. From here to radical theories of politics and economics was but a short step.

Like the Baptists Winstanley believed in universal religious toleration and opposed the use of force in matters of conscience, but unlike them he had no interest in founding exclusive congregations of saints, and he is unique in that, when he came to write about government, he did not want to restrict the suffrage to persons who shared his religious views. Like the Quakers he was a pacifist.

The decade of the 1640s was one of great hardship – economic depression, the ravages of war, inflation, poor harvests, and the collapse of the old political order. Winstanley was one of the victims. Bankrupt, a townsman forced to retreat to the country and herd other men's cows, he began to ruminate about the shape of that reign of love which would replace the reign of Charles I and which would be the true Second Coming, the reign of Christ.

His vision of the new secular order of justice and how it would come to be, makes him unique and justly famous. The vision came to Winstanley in a trance somewhere near the end of 1648. The new secular order he saw was communistic. Winstanley proclaimed his revelation, which he said he had neither read in any book nor heard from any man, in *The New Law of Righteousness* (1649). The vision showed him that men could be free only when private property in land was abolished, when all men had access to the land and worked it in common, and when no man worked for wages. Winstanley's later writings are all restatements of that original revelation. The voice also directed Winstanley, and the men and women of the neighborhood whom he convinced to follow him, to start digging and planting the commons and wastes at St. George's Hill, near Cobham in Surrey. The work began on 1 Apr. 1649. A small tract published in the same month, *The True Levellers Standard*, announced the purpose of the digging in Surrey to the whole world and has anachronistically been called the first Communist Manifesto.

The local landowners, alarmed at the attack on property, appealed to the Council of State in London, and the Commander-in-Chief, Lord Fairfax,* was ordered to investigate. Fairfax and his officers found nothing alarming in a dozen poor families digging up some unused common land. The landowners, however, persisted, pursuing the Diggers in court and leading a mob to trample their crops. In the autumn the Diggers moved nearby to Cobham Manor and began a new communal planting. The landowners again harassed them with acts of hooliganism and court actions. In the early summer of 1650 the Diggers were finally driven out. Meanwhile their activities, and those of several similar groups which seem to have been inspired by Winstanley, created a great stir. Their doings were widely reported in the press and the central government in London was concerned. Other radical groups hastened to disown any connection with Diggers. Defeated in his actions, Winstanley decided to try to convince Cromwell of the truth which had been revealed to him, and his last and most elaborate work, *The Law of Freedom in a Platform* (1652), is dedicated to Cromwell. After this, Winstanley disappears from history for more than 250 years. He was almost completely unknown both to radical thinkers and to historians until the twentieth century, when he was rediscovered by Eduard Bernstein, the German Social Democrat. He has become a hero and a major part of the 'useable past' for socialist and communist theorists of the present.

For modern students Winstanley's proposal for creating a just society in

England, *The Law of Freedom in a Platform* is his most important work. More secular in tone and more systematic in exposition than any of his other works, *The Law of Freedom* describes a communal economic society. All the people work to produce the necessities of life which are then put in storehouses from which individuals can draw as they have need – very near to the socialist principle of 'from each according to his abilities, to each according to his needs.' All buying and selling is abolished as are those traditional ruling orders which Winstanley had come to detest. Winstanley's pamphlets are violently anticlerical and he is particularly forceful in attacking academic learning and theology, as well as the obscurantism of the law, as mere tools in the hands of the rich to oppress the poor. In his new society only the practical arts and sciences are taught and there is no learned class set apart from the people. Winstanley's ideal commonwealth is agrarian, democratic and communist. He defends it with some of the myths about the Norman Yoke, Magna Carta, and providence overthrowing Charles I, which other non-communist radicals used.

Winstanley was not a proto-Marxist or a creator of humanistic utopias. He was a religious mystic who hated those he conceived as oppressors – clergy, lawyers, landowners, royal tyrants – because they denied the Spirit which taught that all men were the children of God and all to be loved as brothers. Many of his contemporaries were also religious mystics who had Winstanley's horror of the powers that be, but they were mostly content to withdraw into private religious societies. Winstanley was unique in wanting to change the outside world. Other men who were less religiously motivated also wanted to change the world outside and they were variously democrats, republicans, believers in limited government and civil liberties, and respecters of the property which a man accumulated by his own efforts – they were the prophets of liberal capitalism. In an age in which bourgeois individualism was the major doctrine and the wave of the future,

Winstanley rejected competition and individualism totally and preached the religious duty and virtue of communal effort and cooperation. This was a remarkable achievement and he does, in the end, appear to have been a unique personality with affinities to the Christians described in Acts 5:32-37, a text which he knew, and to the socialists of the twentieth century, whom he neither knew nor envisioned. A powerful writer of poetic prose, Winstanley belongs squarely in the English tradition of radical prophets which includes Langland, Milton* and Blake.

G. Sabine, ed., *The Works of Gerrard Winstanley* (1941); O. Lutaud, *Winstanley* (1976); R.L. Greaves, 'Gerrard Winstanley and Educational Reform in Puritan England,' *British Journal of Educational Studies*, 17:166-76; G. Juretic, 'The Mind of Gerrard Winstanley' (Ph.D. diss., Northern Illinois Univ., 1973); Juretic, 'Digger No Millenarian,' *JHI*, 36:263-80; L. Mulligan, J.K. Graham, J. Richards, 'Winstanley: A Case for the Man as He Said He Was,' *JEH*, 28:57-75; Hill, *WTUD* and *C. & C.*; R.T. Vann, 'The Later Life of Gerrard Winstanley,' *JHI*, 26:133-36; J. Alsop, 'Gerrard Winstanley's Later Life,' *P. & P.*, 82:73-81; R.T. Vann, 'From Radicalism to Quakerism: Gerrard Winstanley and Friends,' *JFHS*, 49:41-46; C. Hill, ed., *The Law of Freedom and Other Writings* (1973); T.W. Hayes, *Winstanley the Digger* (1979); P. Hardacre, 'Gerrard Winstanley in 1650,' *HLQ*, 22:345-49; W.S. Hudson, 'Gerrard Winstanley and the Early Quakers,' *CH*, 12:191-94; D.W. Petegorsky, *Left-Wing Democracy in the English Civil War* (1940); L.H. Berens, *The Diggers* (1906); C. Hill, 'The Religion of Gerrard Winstanley,' *P. & P.*, Suppl. 5:1-57; J.C. Davis, 'Gerrard Winstanley and the Restoration of True Magistracy,' *P. & P.*, 70:76-95; idem., *Utopia and the Ideal Society* (1981); K.S. Amoroso, 'Gerrard Winstanley' (Ph.D. diss., Univ. of Toronto, 1976).

R.B. Schlatter

WINTER, Samuel (1603-1666)

Independent minister, was born at Temple Balsall, Warks., the son of Christopher Winter, yeoman. Deciding at age twelve that he would be a minister, he prepared himself by attending the free school in Coventry and, being admitted sizar at Emmanuel Coll., Camb. in Jan. 1623, he continued his studies, commencing B.A. in 1632. He went to Boston to work under John Cotton,* who arranged his protégé's marriage to Mrs. Ann Beeston. After a serious illness he took a living at Woodborough, near Nottingham. From here he went to York as a lecturer, and at the outbreak of the Civil War he settled in Cottingham, near Hull, where he organized a Congregational church. His first wife having died and with five sons to raise, he married Mrs. Elizabeth Weaver. In 1650 he resigned his pastorate and went to Ireland as the household chaplain to the four Parliamentary Commissioners. He preached in and around Dublin, gaining a reputation for his effective ministry and piety. About 3 Sept. 1651 he was made Provost of Trinity Coll., Dublin and was confirmed in the office the following June by Cromwell. He aided the college financially and took an M.A. in 1654. When recalled to England in 1659 and set aside as provost, he suffered considerable personal loss. It is not known when he returned to England and there is no record of his ejection. He died on 24 Dec. 1666 and was buried in North Luffenham, Rutl. Biographical sketches of his life depend heavily on the *Life* (1671) written by J. Weaver, his brother-in-law. His own work was *The Summe of Diverse Sermons*, published in Dublin (1656).

Nuttall, *VS*; *DNB*; *Calamy Revised*; Calamy.

R. Masek

WINTHROP, John (1588-1649)

Colonist and first Governor of Massachusetts Bay, was the son of Adam, lawyer and gentleman (d. 1623), and Anne Browne (d. 1629), daughter of a local clothier. Winthrop was raised at Groton, Suff., a manor purchased by his grandfather Adam, a clothier, from the Crown in 1544. The first forty years of his life were those of a conscientious squire. He matriculated at Trinity Coll., Camb. in 1603 but withdrew in 1605 for an arranged marriage to Mary Forth, an heiress. Winthrop's Puritanism dates from several years spent at her estate at Great Stambridge, Essex, where Ezechial Culverwell preached. Winthrop was admitted to Gray's Inn in 1613. In 1615 Mary died, leaving four surviving children. Late in 1615 Winthrop married Thomasine Clopton, who died within the year. In 1618 he married a third time to Margaret, daughter of Sir John Tyndal of Great Maplestead, Essex, a match which proved notably congenial until her death in 1647. Winthrop finally married a Boston widow in 1648.

By 1620 Winthrop was practicing law in London, as well as managing Groton, where he also served as JP. In 1626 he sought to increase his income by becoming an attorney in the Court of Wards, probably through the influence of his brother-in-law, Emmanuel Downing, also an attorney there. Winthrop's affairs reached a crisis in 1629. He was obliged to endow half his estate to three sons who were of age; he lost or resigned his attorneyship; and the growth of Arminianism, capped by the disastrous dissolution of Parliament, convinced him that England was subject to a terrible divine judgment. The Massachusetts Bay Company, already chartered, seemed to offer prospects both of godly service and of a safe shelter. At the end of July Isaac Johnson proposed transporting the charter along with the emigrants; a month later Winthrop and eleven others signed an agreement at Cambridge to sail for New England; and on 20 Oct. Winthrop was elected governor. In Apr. 1630 he sailed on the 'Arbella,' reaching Endicott's settlement at Salem in June and settling at Boston where more than 2000 colonists arrived during the first year.

Massachusetts, the product of 'a special overruling providence,' was to be 'as a city upon a hill,' an example to all. The attempt to discipline the rapidly growing Bay Colony to this transcendent mission occupied the remainder of Winthrop's life. The task of the magistrate to protect the reformed orthodoxy of the Congregational (but professedly nonseparatist) churches involved Winthrop in a series of struggles, first with his friend, Roger Williams,* who was banished in 1636; then in 1637 with Anne Hutchinson,* whose supporters at one point included a majority of the church of Boston and Gov. Henry Vane;* then in the early 1640s with the 'familist' followers of Samuel Gorton; and finally in the 1650s with the Quakers.

Godly rule presented even more formidable problems. Believing that man has 'a liberty to that only which is good, just and honest,' and that corruption could only be avoided by due 'subjection to authority,' Winthrop nevertheless acquiesced in a series of limitations on magisterial power. In 1631 the franchise was extended beyond the stockholders of the company but limited to church members; in 1634 the 'fundamental right' of the freemen to legislate was acknowledged, as was the right of the deputies, as well as the magistrates, to a veto in 1635. In 1641 the General Court authorized a written constitution – the Body of Liberties – and in 1648 a 'Book of General Laws' limiting the magistrates' discretion, both measures Winthrop opposed but never sought to reverse once passed. Governor again in 1646, he spent his last years defending a more liberal state than he desired against interference from England: the radical idealism of 1630 had given way to embattled conservatism.

T.H. Breen, *The Character of the Good Ruler* (1970); R.S. Dunn, *Puritans and Yankees* (1962); E.S. Morgan, *The Puritan Dilemma* (1958); R.E. Wall, Jr., *Massachusetts Bay, 1640-1650* (1972); *DNB*; *DAB*. Papers: MHS.

P.S. Seaver

WINTHROP, Stephen (1619-1658)

Civil War officer, was born at Groton, Suff., the fourth son of John Winthrop,* first Governor of the Massachusetts Bay Colony, and Margaret Tyndall. Winthrop went to New England with his father in 1630, and became Recorder of Boston. He returned to England in Mar. 1646 and served as captain of a regiment of New Model horse at Worcester. He attended meetings of the army Councils in Dec. 1648 and Feb. 1649. Although his troops were involved in the Leveller rising of May 1649, Winthrop was neither implicated nor blamed for his men's conduct. Winthrop served in Wales in 1651-52 as a commissioner under the Act for the Better Propagation and Preaching of the Gospel, although reportedly without much zeal, and later as a Trier. In Jan. 1654 he became colonel of a regiment which served in Scotland until Oct. 1656; Winthrop, however, was allowed to return to England in May 1654 because of ill health. He represented Banff and Aberdeen in the second Parliament of the Protectorate. Winthrop married Judith, sister of Col. Thomas Rainsborough,* and purchased a home in Marylebone Park in Aug. 1652. His ill health prevented him from fulfilling his repeatedly expressed desire to return to New England, where he owned property at Narragansett and near Boston.

Firth & Davies; *CMHS*, 5th ser., 8 (1882); *Clarke Papers*; *Winthrop Papers*, 5 (1947), *passim*; Burton, 2:268, 293; *CSPD, Comm.*, 10:24, 214.

L.S. Popofsky

WISE, James (fl. 1662-1672)

Fifth Monarchist, was a clothworker whose preaching aroused the ire of the authorities in Southampton around Michaelmas 1662, leading to his incarceration in the common jail. From there he continued his preaching through a grated iron gate, attracting considerable numbers of hearers, a circumstance which necessitated his removal to Calshot Castle. In 1669 Wise was reported to be the teacher and head of a congregation of Fifth Monarchists in Southampton, one of seven such congregations reported in the Episcopal Returns for that year. The Episcopal Return for Southampton listed nine dissenting congregations there with the notation that 'the same persons frequent several conventicles.' Wise applied for and obtained a license to preach as a Baptist under the terms of the Indulgence of 1672 in Salisbury and at West Cowes on the Isle of Wight. His millenarianism had evidently become by this time the less activist kind professed by the Baptists and other sects.

Mercurius Publicus, 49 (4-11 Dec. 1662); *CSPD, Chas. II*, 12:314, 354, 447-48; 14:259; Turner; Capp, *FMM*.

W.B. Patterson

WISE, Laurence (c. 1624-1692)

Independent and Baptist minister, was the son of Laurence Wise of London. On 5 Apr. 1639, at the age of fifteen, he matriculated at Magdalen Coll., Oxf., graduating B.A. from Magdalen Hall on 10 Nov. 1642. He was appointed Rector of St. James Garlickhithe, London, in 1649, and on 29 Mar. 1654 the Admiralty Committee named him to succeed William Adderley, a navy chaplain as preacher at Chatham, a position Wise held until his ejection in 1660. He was also made an assistant to the Kent Commission on 16 Mar. 1658, and was preaching at Aldgate in 1659. After the Restoration charges of immorality were made against him and he was suspended from communion, but he repented and on 6 Feb. 1661 petitioned the navy commanders for an opportunity to respond to accusations slandering him. Later that year he was preaching at Allhallows the Great, but on 6 June 1662 a warrant was issued to apprehend him for seditious speeches. These may have been Fifth Monarchist, for in 1663, when he was living in

Moorfields, he was holding conventicles and associating with the Fifth Monarchists Anthony Palmer* and Carnsew Helme.* He subsequently adopted Baptist principles. In 1672 he was reportedly one of those to whom Charles II granted an audience when he issued the Declaration of Indulgence. Wise was imprisoned in Newgate for six months beginning in Nov. 1682 for preaching at Goodman's Yard in the Minories, and in 1685, when he was living in Stepney, he was convicted of being at an illegal conventicle. He died in 1692.

CSPD, Comm., 6:360; 7:467; 13:511; *Chas. II*, 1:504; 2:400; *Calamy Revised*; G.L. Turner, 'Williamson's Spy Book,' *TCHS*, 5:253. Papers: LPR.

R.L. Greaves

WITHER (or Withers), George (1588-1667)

Poet and pamphleteer, was born on 11 June 1588 at Bentworth, near Alton, Hants., the eldest son of George Wither and Mary (née Hunt). Wither was tutored by his cousin Ralph Starkey and by John Greaves, Rector of Colemore. He went up to Magdalen Coll., Oxf. about 1603, but took no degree. After settling in London about 1610 he studied law, and in 1615 was admitted to Lincoln's Inn. Already recognized as a lyric poet, his satiric bent was revealed in *Abuses Stript and Whipt* (1613), which with characteristic bravado he dedicated to himself. The book went through at least five editions in a year, but cost Wither several months in Marshalsea prison. He was again imprisoned in 1621-22 for *Withers Motto*. The satirist in Wither was never silenced, but his later work was increasingly pietistic and moralizing in tone. The bulk of his mature writing was devoted to translations and commentaries on the Scriptures, notably *A Preparation to the Psalter* (1619), *Hymnes and Songs of the Church* (1623), *The Psalmes of David* (1632), *A Collection of Emblemes* (1635) and *Halelujah* (1641). Less esteemed than his early lyric verse, it nonetheless occupies a significant place in the Puritan literature of the early seventeenth century.

In 1623 Wither challenged the monopoly of the Stationers' Company by publishing his hymnal without its license. He defended his action and attacked the Stationers in *The Scholers Purgatory* (c. 1624). Still under the Stationers' ban, he printed his *Britains Remembrancer* (1628), a graphic account of the plague of 1625 interspersed with denunciations of impiety and prophecies of further disaster. *The Psalmes of David* were printed abroad and dedicated to Wither's patron Elizabeth of Bohemia, with whom he sojourned in the early 1630s.

The dispute with the Stationers was finally settled in 1634. Shortly after Wither retired to Farnham, where he issued *The Nature of Man* (1636), a tract dedicated to Selden.* In 1639 he joined the expeditionary force against the Scots, but in 1642 he adhered to the parliamentary cause, and sold his estate to raise a troop of horse. Wither was appointed captain and commander of Farnham Castle on 14 Oct. 1642, and was captured in its fall. Apparently he faced charges, but the waggish Cavalier commander Sir John Denham interceded for him, saying that while Wither lived there would be at least one poet in England worse than himself. Wither later repaid the compliment by sequestering Denham's estate. He was freed in the recapture of the castle by Waller* on 1 Dec. and subsequently promoted to major, but probably saw no further service. On 9 Feb. 1643 he was awarded £2000 by Parliament in compensation for his estate.

Throughout 1643 Wither produced a spate of verse and propaganda on behalf of Parliament, including an anti-Royalist version of *Mercurius Rusticus*. In 1644 however he was removed both from his nominal command and from the commission of the peace in Surrey for accusing Sir Richard Onslow of betraying Farnham Castle and sending money secretly to the King. He pursued his attack in *Justicarius justificatus*, for which he was fined £500 and imprisoned (1646), though both penal-ties were soon remitted. With the advent of the Commonwealth, Wither constituted himself the panegyrist of the new regime, while indefatigably pursuing further monetary claims and seeking official employment. After years of solicitation he was appointed a commissioner for the sale of the King's estate and, in 1655, a clerk of the recognizances in Chancery. Wither hailed Cromwell in such poems as 'The Statesman' (1653) and 'The Protector' (1655), though he expressed some disillusionment with him in the elegy 'Salt upon Salt' (1659).

Wither's public forebodings about the return of the monarchy made him suspect at the Restoration. In Aug. 1660 he was imprisoned after the discovery of a paper highly critical of the Convention Parliament, first in Newgate and, after an arraignment before the House of Commons on 24 Mar. 1662, in the Tower. Wither was released, untried, on 27 July 1663; the offending tract, *Vox vulgi*, was not published until 1880. He lived to blame another great plague, that of 1665, on the corruption of the time (*Memorandum to London Occasioned by the Pestilence*), and opposed the Dutch War in *Tuba pacifica* (1664) and *Sighs for the Pitcher* (1666). Wither died on 2 May 1667 and was buried in the church of the Savoy Hospital in the Strand. He married Elizabeth, daughter of John Emerson or Emerton of South Lambeth, a poet in her own right and 'a great wit' according to Aubrey. She survived him, as did only two of their six children, Robert (d. 1677) and Elizabeth (d. 1708), the wife of Adrian Barry of London and Thame, Oxon.

Wither's career was an unstable mixture of piety and irascibility, sycophancy and candor, self-seeking and impulsive sacrifice. At his best, as in his lines on the battle of Rathmines, he expressed the genuine fervor of the Puritan cause; at his bluntest, he could chide members of the Long Parliament by reminding them, 'are you not some of those,/who made the burghers drunk when you were chose?' Many faults may be forgiven a man who has the nerve to tell his employers that.

DNB; Aubrey; Ath. Oxon.;
J.M. French, 'George Wither' (Ph.D.
diss., Harvard Univ., 1928); idem.,
'George Wither in Prison,' Publications of
the Modern Language Association,
45:959-66; idem., 'Thorn-Drury's Notes
on Wither,' HLQ, 23:379-88; N.E. Carl-
son, 'Wither and the Stationers,' Virginia
Univ. Studies in Bibliography, 19:210-15;
C.V. Wedgwood, Poetry and Politics
under the Stuarts (1960); W.M. Clyde,
The Struggle for the Freedom of the Press
from Caxton to Cromwell (1934);
B.K. Lewalski, Protestant Poetics and the
Seventeenth-Century Religious Lyric
(1979); D. Bush, English Literature in the
Earlier Seventeenth Century (1962);
J.C. Creigh, 'George Wither and the
Stationers: Facts and Fiction,' Papers of
the Bibliographical Society of America,
74:49-57.

R. Zaller

WOGAN, Thomas (fl. 1646-1666)

Regicide and parliamentary radical, MP
1646 (Cardigan), 1660 (Pemb.). Wogan was
the son of John Wogan of Wiston who sat
for Pembrokeshire in the Long Parliament
until his death in Dec. 1645. Thomas
Wogan's service for Parliament began as a
lieutenant in his home county in 1644. On
24 Aug. 1646 he was recruited for the
borough of Cardigan solely upon his war
record, and quickly became identified with
the circle of army and Cromwellian radicals, though more as a spear-carrier than as
a leader. Service in the field removed him
from active participation in Parliament,
and while absent he was ordered by the
Derby House Committee to settle the
peace in southern Wales, and especially to
investigate the loyalty of the garrison of
Pembroke Castle under Capt. John Poyer
and to persuade the forces in the shire to
disband peacefully. In the course of this
duty Wogan was caught up in the maneuvering which culminated in the battle of St.

Fagan's in Glamorganshire on 13 May
1648. He personally carried news of the
victory to Parliament, for which service he
was voted thanks and the sum of £300 in
arrears of salary. At the same time Oliver
Cromwell wrote the Derby House Committee that he desired now Col. Wogan be
appointed Governor of Aberystwyth Castle. In the growing tensions of that year
Wogan remained loyal to Cromwell, survived the purge and was named to the High
Court. He attended sessions of the commission on 18, 20, 22, 23, 26 and 27 Jan. and
his name appears on the death warrant, but
he is said to have refused to sign it
(Wedgwood, CKC, p. 139, citing J. Nalson, Journal of the High Court [1684], and
Yule, p. 126; but cf. B. & P., p. 245, and
Keeler, p. 399). Soon thereafter, however,
he may have been appointed Governor of
Duncannon, but instead served in the
struggle against the Scots. In June 1651 he
was named to a thirty-member High Court
of Justice to keep the peace in southern
Wales where the parliamentary regime was
becoming increasingly unpopular. Wogan
seems to have spent virtually the entire
period of the Protectorate at that task,
returning to London in 1659 to sit in the
restored Rump.

In the elections for the Convention in
1660, Wogan was sent by the shrinking
minority of Pembrokeshire republicans but
was not allowed to sit and his name was
excepted from the Act of Pardon. He
surrendered on 27 June 1660 but execution
for attainder was suspended pending
further consideration, probably because he
was able to cast doubt upon his willing
complicity in the King's death. Nevertheless, his lands were forfeit and he was held
in York Tower until he managed to escape
in July 1664 and flee to the Continent,
whence he was reported to be in Utrecht in
1666. Local legend has Wogan dying of a
broken heart, under an assumed name, in
the vicinity of Walwyn Castle.

Dodd; MacCormack; Noble; Williams,
Wales; Yule; D. Underdown, 'Recruiter
Elections,' EHR, 83:259.

J.F. Battick

WOLLASTON, Sir John (d. 1658)

City radical, was descended from Staffordshire gentry who had established themselves in London; his father, brother and brother-in-law were all aldermen. Wollaston probably began as a goldsmith; by 1630 he was Melter in the royal mint and a wealthy man, and in 1635 shared in the gold and silver refiners' patent. From at least 1630 he sat on the Common Council, and other honors soon accrued: Deputy Governor of the Irish Society in 1633-34 and 1636-37, and Governor from 1654 to 1657; sheriff (with Isaac Penington*) in 1638-39 and Prime Warden of the Goldsmiths' Company the following year, and an alderman, chiefly from Farringdon Without, from Feb. 1639 until his death. Like many other radicals, he was also a member of the Honorable Artillery Company. In 1639 Wollaston refused to lend to the King, and in May 1640 to provide a list of wealthy residents in his ward. He was rumored to have signed the Root and Branch petition in Dec. 1640, and he and his fellow patentees were probably spared punishment in 1641 due to his known support of the parliamentary cause. On 3 Dec. 1641 Wollaston was knighted with several fellow aldermen at Hampton Court, but in Jan. 1642 he became a member of the Militia Committee, vigorously supported the Militia Ordinance in March, and as colonel of the Yellow Regiment of the trained bands closed London Bridge against royalist petitioners from Kent in April. In June he ignored a summons from Charles to join him in the north. Wollaston became a major financier of the parliamentary war effort, and served as a treasurer for the advance of money and plate, for the weekly assessments, the Irish subscription, and as Treasurer for War. He was also a trustee for the sale of bishops' lands and himself expended nearly £8000 in purchase, for which he was satirized in a booth play in 1649. Wollaston became Lord Mayor in 1643-44, after unsuccessfully contesting Penington in 1642. He was notably more moderate than his erstwhile colleague in the shrievalty, and was reported to be dickering with the Presbyerians in 1646. It may have been this which spared him in the Presbyterian purge of May 1647, but he quickly rejoined the Independents as the tide turned back in their favor, and in July 1648 was reported gathering signatures for a petition against further treaty with the King. Wollaston supported both Commonwealth and Protectorate, and remained a prominent figure until his death on 26 Apr. 1658. He served as President of Bethlehem and Bridewell (1642-49) and of Christ's Hospital (1649-58). His steadfast Puritanism was indicated by the bequest of a £100 annuity to Emmanuel Coll., Camb., as well as a gift of £10 to the minister Joseph Caryl.*

Pearl; Beaven; H. Stewart, *History of the Worshipful Company of Gold and Silver Wiredrawers* (1891); Tolmie. Papers: LSH (Wootton 248).

R. Zaller

WOLSELEY (or Wolsley), Sir Charles, Bt. (c. 1631-1714)

Parliamentary radical and Protectorate official, MP 1653 (Oxon.), 1654, 1656, 1660 (Staffs.). Wolseley was the son of Sir Robert Wolseley of Wolseley, Staffs., and Mary, daughter of Sir George Wroughton of Walcot, Wilts. Because Sir Robert was a Royalist, his estate was sequestered, forcing Sir Charles to pay £2500 for its discharge in Oct. 1647. The following May Sir Charles married Anne, youngest daughter of William Fiennes, Viscount Saye and Sele.* In the Nominated Parliament he normally associated with the moderates except on the issue of law reform, where he espoused radical views. On 19 Aug. 1653 he was one of the tellers for the majority on the motion to adopt a completely new body of law. The radical attack on tithes, however, was viewed by Wolseley as a threat to property, and he played a crucial role in the moderates' surrender of power to Cromwell in December.

From 14 July 1653 until the collapse of the Protectorate Wolseley was very active in the Council of State. Among the host of committees on which he served were those dealing with ordnance, foreign affairs, taxes, the Mint, foreign plantations, Whitehall preachers, trade, tithes, Piedmont Protestants, Scottish and Irish affairs, Durham College and the disannulment of Charles II's title. He was also a commissioner to negotiate with the Dutch (1653, 1654, 1656) the Spanish (1653), the Danes (1654) and the Portuguese (1657), a Militia Commissioner for Staffordshire (1655), and a member of the committees delegated to deal with the Fifth Monarchists Feake,* Simpson* and Rogers* (1654). The signatories of the warrant to the Lord Mayor of London proclaiming Cromwell Lord Protector (17 Dec. 1654) included Wolseley. In 1655 he chaired the committee for the Commissions of Oyer and Terminer, and in November he was appointed to the committee to consider readmission of the Jews to England. As MP for Staffordshire in 1656, he opposed the death penalty for Nayler,* questioning Parliament's right to impose such punishment. He urged Cromwell to accept the crown in Apr. 1657, but questioned the imposition of a new Oath of Fidelity under the Instrument of Government in June. Cromwell summoned him to sit in the Upper House in December, and Whitelocke* asserts that Wolseley was a confidant of both Oliver and Richard Cromwell.* He was also a signatory of the proclamation recognizing the latter as Lord Protector, and was consulted on the dissolution of the 1659 Parliament.

Through the intervention of Lord Mordaunt and Sir Robert Howard, Wolseley was pardoned by Charles II at the Restoration and retired to his country home. Monmouth's rebellion led to Wolseley's brief imprisonment at Chester, but James II ordered his release on 2 July 1685. A Nonconformist, Wolseley supported James' repeal of the penal laws, and on 4 Feb. 1688 was appointed DL of Staffordshire, a position he continued to hold as late as the reign of Anne. James recommended that he run for Parliament from New Woodstock on 15 Sept. 1688. Wolseley died on 9 Oct. 1714 and was buried at Colwich, Staffs. He was the author of a number of works, including tracts on the liberty of conscience and a popular attack on atheism, *The Unreasonableness of Atheism Made Manifest* (1669), which underwent three editions in six years.

CSPD, Comm., 6-12 *passim*; *Jas. II*, 1:242; 3:141, 275; Abbott, 3-4 *passim*; *CJ*, 5:328; 7:284-85, 304, 344; Woolrych; *DNB*. Papers: L (Add. MSS; Lans. MSS); LPR.

R.L. Greaves

WOOD, Seth (fl. 1626-1670)

Independent minister, was the son of John Wood, Vicar of Lenton, Notts. He matriculated at Magdalene Coll., Camb. in 1626 and proceeded B.A. (1629) and M.A. (1632). Wood held various livings – Vicar of Lavington, Lincs. in 1639, Rector of Melford, Suff. in 1645 – before becoming Vicar of Christ Church, Newgate St., London in 1654. In the following year he entered upon his assistantship to John Rowe* at Westminster Abbey, and at least as early as 1657 he became one of the preachers at St. Margaret's, Westminster. In 1659 Wood joined with other Independent ministers in London in an appeal to Gen. Monck. He lost all his London appointments in 1660. In 1661 he again joined with his fellow Independent ministers in *A Renunciation and Declaration* (1661), dissociating themselves from Venner.* Between 1660 and 1662 Wood was assistant minister to Matthew Barker* at St. Leonard's, Eastcheap, from which both were ejected in 1662. In the years from 1662 to 1670, Wood appears to have been affiliated with London conventicles in Watling Street, Westminster and Meeting House Lane, Blackfriars. In 1670 he was convicted of preaching at the latter conventicle under the terms of the Corporation Act. He was said to be living then near the

Red Lion, Gray's Inn Lane. There is no record of his having applied for a license to preach in 1672. By 1674 he was dead. He was buried at St. Leonard's, Bucks. Although much of Wood's life remains obscure, his persistent Independency and his reputation as a preacher are clear.

Wilson, *HADC*; *CSPD, Comm.*, 6:136; 10:247; 11:239; *Chas. II*, 10:221; *Calamy Revised*. Papers: LW (G. Lyon Turner MSS).

R. Harvey

WOODALL, Frederick (1614-1681)

Ejected minister, was born at Brome, the son of Thomas Woodall. He attended Corpus Christi Coll., Camb., received his B.A. in 1637 and his M.A. in 1640, and was made Rector of Brome on 8 Oct. 1641. In 1652 Woodall was appointed pastor of a Congregational church in Woodbridge, Suff., but it was reported to Cromwell on 15 June 1654 that he had no state maintenance. The following year he wrote in support of the Independent view that scriptural authority, not ordination, should be the basis of ministerial calling. The pamphlet is apparently no longer extant, but it is summarized in an attack on it by Christopher Atkinson and George Whitehead* entitled *Davids Enemies Discovered . . . A Brief Reply unto Frederick Woodall's Three Principles and Resolves* (1655). To the Quakers, the Spirit alone was adequate authority for preaching; education in scriptural exegesis was unnecessary. On 10 July 1656 Woodall's parishioners petitioned the Council for a grant for him. In 1658 Woodall again entered the ordination controversy; this time, together with John Martin, minister at Edgefield, Norf., and Samuel Petto,* friend of Increase Mather and Rector of South Elham St. Cross in Sandcroft, Suff., he wrote *The Preacher Sent, or a Vindication of the Liberty of Publick Preaching*, which develops a theory of mediate calling through natural law and Scripture and rejects the necessity of an ecclesiastical institution. Ordination is required to administer the sacraments, Woodall asserted, but not to preach. Since preaching is an act of natural worship, the people acting together have the ability to judge a man's fitness for the ministry. This lengthy book was immediately attacked by John Collings* in *Vindiciae ministrii evangelici revindicatae, or the Preacher (Pretendedly) Sent, Sent Back Again, to Bring a Better Account Who Sent Him, and Learn His Errand* (1658), and again by Matthew Poole in *Quo warranto, or a Moderate Enquiry into the Warrantablenesse of the Preaching of Gifted and Unordained Persons* (1658, 1659). Ejected from his ministry soon after the Restoration, Woodall and his large family suffered considerably until he was made Headmaster of Woodbridge School in 1669. He became curate there on 1 May 1672 and served in that capacity until his death on 1 Dec. 1681.

Calamy Revised; Nuttall, *VS*; R.L. Greaves, 'The Ordination Controversy and the Spirit of Reform in Puritan England,' *JEH*, 21:225-41.

T.W. Hayes

WOODWARD, Ezekias (or Hezekiah) (1591?-1675)

Educational reformer, was one of nine children and the youngest of five sons. His father died when he was about a year old and his early years were also made difficult by a speech defect (*A Childes Patrimony*, 1640). Nevertheless he attended a grammar school in Worcestershire for six and a half years, then proceeded to Balliol Coll., Oxf. where he matriculated in June 1610 and from which he graduated B.A. in Feb. 1612. Despite an able and conscientious tutor, Woodward was unhappy at the university. He complained that although he obtained some rude knowledge of the arts he did not gain a unifying knowledge of the disciplines. In addition he criticized the system of disputations as too trivial and too much concerned with artificial matters. Woodward found it difficult to settle upon a career, as his speech impediment seemed to bar him from advancement in either the church or the law. Desperate, he considered manual labor, and he twice went overseas, probably to the court of the Elector Palatine at Heidelberg (*A Light to Grammar*, 1641). By 1618 or 1619 he was back in England and opened a school at Aldermanbury, London. In 1644, continuing his teaching career, he became Master of St. Saviour's Grammar School, Southwark. A follower of the educational ideas of Comenius and a friend of Hartlib,* Woodward believed the student should have a sound knowledge of English before commencing Latin, stressed the importance of natural science, and put great emphasis on sensible and humane methods of instruction, even to the avoidance of 'vilifying words [which] hurt much and sad[den] the spirit.' In *A Light to Grammar* he espoused universal education and stressed the value of personal judgment and experience. Rejecting the grammar school model of his youth, he argued that a child could 'do his work playing, and play working.'

In religion Woodward was at first an active supporter of Presbyterianism, although by the mid-1640s he was leaning toward Independency. His anonymously published *Inquiries into the Causes of Our Miseries*, which appeared without license in 1644, caused him to be examined before two judges and only released on bond. In 1649 Cromwell presented him to the living of Bray near Maidenhead where he wrote on education and religion, and preached against malignants and the abuses of the Church of England until the Restoration. He also impoverished himself by refusing to accept tithes and attempting to live on the free offerings of his congregation. After 1660 Woodward went to Uxbridge but continued to preach. On 13 May 1672 he was licensed to preach in a Presbyterian meeting-place. He died at Uxbridge on 29 Mar. 1675. He was married (his wife Frances died in 1631), and the father of at least four children.

DNB; *Al. Oxon.*; *Ath. Oxon.*; C.B. Freeman, 'A Puritan Educator: Hezekiah Woodward and his "Child's Patrimony," ' *British Journal of Education*, 9:132-41.

P.-A. Lee

WORSLEY, Benjamin (c. 1617-1677)

Agricultural and trade reformer, was born and educated in London, the son of a nonarmigerous family of Kineton (near Edgehill), Warks. He probably took service with Strafford in Ireland and was surgeon in the army at the outbreak of the Irish rebellion. In 1643 he entered Trinity Coll., Dublin. By 1645 he was back in England, at which time he was apparently a prisoner for debt. He was soon taken up however by a powerful Anglo-Irish interest that included the Boyle family, Sir John Temple* and, later, Viscount Lisle.* In late 1645 or 1646 he began an enthusiastic correspondence with young Robert Boyle on chemical subjects. Worsley and Boyle were the original projectors of the 'Invisible College' which was to serve as a clearing-house for scientific information through a network of correspondence. In 1646 Worsley proposed to manufacture saltpetre from turf, ferns and firs in *De nitro theses quaedam*, suggesting that it might be used not only in gunpowder but for manuring, preserving fish, combating crop diseases and improving wool. The project attracted support both in Parliament and among the London aldermen; its failure did not diminish Worsley's credit. In *Proffits Humbly Presented to This Kingdome* (1646 or 1647), a tract reflecting the utopianism of the Hartlib* group, he linked agricultural and technological innovation to increased trade and productivity, which would in turn free the nation's energies for law reform, the advancement of learning and the propagation of the Gospel (Webster, pp. 539-46).

Worsley was appointed Surgeon-General to the army in Ireland on 17 July

1647 (*CJ*, 5:247) but failed to take up his post, visiting Holland instead. Back in England in 1649, he cultivated Henry Vane the Younger,* Walter Strickland,* Sir John Trenchard,* and other commercial contacts. He broached to John Dury* a new scheme to replace the royalist governor of Virginia with a parliamentary commission to foster 'free preaching of the Gospel, civility and industry.' The instructions to the new Council of Trade bear the stamp of his influence, and in August he was appointed its secretary at a salary of £200 p.a. He played a key role in drafting the Navigation Act of 1651 and defended it in two pamphlets, *Free Ports: the Nature and Necessity of Them Stated* and *The Advocate*, both of 1652. They are reprinted in Hinton. The Council lapsed, and in 1652 Worsley was appointed secretary to the Parliamentary Commissioners in Ireland, perhaps through Vane's influence. The opportunity to accompany Lord Lisle on his embassy to Sweden brought him back to England in 1653, but the mission was postponed, and Worsley returned to Ireland as Surveyor-General of lands. The project for a survey of Irish lands combined agronomic improvement and settler greed; it was also an immensely complex undertaking, and soon degenerated into a quarrel between Worsley and William Petty,* who held his former secretaryship with the Irish commissioners. By Dec. 1654 Worsley had been effectively supplanted, though he retained his title and continued to oppose Petty. His connection with Vane made him suspect, however, and his career languished. By 1658 he had been forced to resign, remaining only a JP for Queen's County. The Rump's return rekindled his prospects (he is said to have succeeded Thurloe* at the Post Office, though this is uncertain), and his contacts with the Boyles and Sidneys stood him in good stead at the Restoration. Another avenue was the Earl of Clarendon, who consulted him on colonial matters; Worsley, who now styled himself 'Doctor,' presented Lady Clarendon with an autobiography. He also corresponded with the younger John Winthrop. In 1668 he became a member of the Select Committee on Trade, in 1670 Assistant Secretary of the Trade Council, and in 1672 Secretary and Treasurer to the Trade and Plantations Council. This remarkable second career was ended by the Test Act, which forced him to resign in Sept. 1673. He was dead by Sept. 1677, and in May 1678 his library of 5000 volumes was put up for auction.

Worsley has suffered unfairly from comparison with the brilliant (but often spiteful) Petty, who denounced his work on the Irish survey as 'absurd and insignificant.' In fact his eclipse seems to have owed more to suspicions of his religious and political radicalism. He was probably a Socinian; he corresponded with William Rand about the doctrine and owned a number of rare Socinian tracts. There is a hint too of Fifth Monarchist sentiment (of the more passive kind) in his description of himself as mere dirt in God's eyes; 'what is dirt he should think himself so good, and so great, as to take upon him to judge what designs were fit to be promoted in the world. . .?' But ultimately his temperament was more robust. A Baconian in science, he declared in 1648 that he would believe 'only that which is immediately deduced from, or built up on, real, or certain experiments'; and in 1657 he decried the continuing influence of Aristotle in the universities. Mystic and impressario, inventor and projector, a republican who flourished under the Restoration, Worsley's career touched virtually every aspect of radical thought and action in the middle decades of the century; but his ultimate skill was survival.

Aylmer, *SS*; Barnard; Webster, *GI*; J.B. Whitmore, 'Dr. Worsley Being Dead,' *N. & Q.*, 185:123-28; L.F. Brown, *The First Earl of Shaftesbury* (1933); R.W.K. Hinton, *The Eastland Trade and the Common Weal in the Seventeenth Century* (1959); T. Birch, ed., *The Works of the Hon. Robert Boyle*, vol. 6 (1772); W. Petty, *Reflections on Some Persons and Things in Ireland* (1660). Papers: L (BL 11906 e. 5 and C. 120.c.2(5)); O

(Clarendon MSS 75, ff. 300-301); SUL (Hartlib MSS).

R. Zaller

WORSLEY, Charles (1622-1656)

Army radical, was born on 24 June 1622, the eldest son of Ralph Worsley of Platt, Manchester, by Isabel, daughter of Edward Massey of Manchester and widow of Alexander Ford of Wigan. Ralph Worsley was a prosperous merchant who sought to establish himself as a landed gentleman. His son Charles became a captain in a regiment of Lancashire troops in 1644 and two years later zealously began to inform against those who concealed portions of their estates from sequestrators. The regiment of foot of which he was made lieutenant-colonel in June 1650 was placed under Cromwell's direct command in October after fighting with him the previous month at Edinburgh, and was sent to the Isle of Man in Oct. 1651 with Col. Robert Duckenfield* and Col. John Birch.* Worsley was a signatory of *A Declaration of the Armie*, which was presented to Parliament on 13 Aug. 1652 and called for dissolution of the Rump, the cessation of tithes, replacement of immoral office-holders, and law reform. A staunch Cromwellian, he led the thirty to forty musketeers who dissolved the Rump on 20 Apr. 1653, personally expelling Algernon Sidney* and taking the mace into his custody. That November he took part in the treaty negotiations chaired by Cromwell with the Dutch envoys. When Capt. Thomas Dutton and others plotted to assassinate the Protector, Worsley seized them on 14 Feb. 1654. Worsley sat as MP for Manchester in the 1654 Parliament.

As major-general in charge of Lancashire, Cheshire and Staffordshire beginning in Oct. 1655, Worsley demonstrated a thoroughness and severity largely unmatched by his colleagues. The key to his behavior was his religious zeal; of his officers' work he wrote, 'I plainly discern the finger of God going along with it.' He restored and encouraged the Committee for Ejecting Scandalous Ministers and Schoolmasters; he strove to enforce the laws against drunkenness, swearing and sabbath-breaking; and he prohibited horse races and public meetings (partly for security reasons). Alehouses, 'the very bane of the counties,' were suppressed in large numbers – over 200 in the hundred of Blackburn alone – causing a flood of petitions. Royalists were disarmed, the petty constables were purged and the decimation tax was rigorously levied. Even minor delinquents were dealt with severely. Those who violated the new marriage law were imprisoned. Worsley was concerned with the shortage of suitable JPs, and his administration was characterized by the prominence of low-born but 'godly' men. He was not tolerant of Quakers and sought advice from Thurloe* on their suppression. He was also involved in the conference granted by Cromwell to John Rogers* in Feb. 1656.

Physically exhausted by his responsibilities, Worsley died at St. James' on 12 June 1656 and was given an impressive state funeral before being buried the following day in Henry VII's chapel at Westminster Abbey. His first wife (m. 18 Sept. 1644), Mary, daughter of John Booth of Manchester, had died on 1 Apr. 1649, and his second wife (m. 6 Oct. 1652), Dorothy, daughter of Roger Kenyon of Park Head, Whalley, married Col. Waldine Lagoe* in 1659, who also inherited his regiment. Worsley's responsibilities as a major-general were delegated to Tobias Bridges.*

Firth & Davies; Thurloe, *SP*, 4-5 *passim*; Abbott, 2-4 *passim*; *CSPD, Comm.*, 2:308; 4:352; 7:165-66; 8:275, 378; 10:28; *DNB*; Morrill. Papers: LPR; L; O; MR; CCRO.

R.L. Greaves

WRIOTHESLEY, Henry, third Earl of Southampton (1573-1624)

Parliamentary radical and colonizer, was

born at Cowdray House in Sussex on 6 Oct. 1573. Upon the death of his father, the second Earl of Southampton, in Oct. 1581, he succeeded to the earldom and became a ward of Lord Burghley. For four years he lived in Burghley's London mansion and befriended members of the Cecil family and other wards, including the second Earl of Essex and the Earl of Rutland. He entered St. John's Coll., Camb. in 1585 and received an M.A. in 1589, whereupon he entered Gray's Inn. Through the influence of Burghley and Essex, Southampton frequently appeared at the court of Queen Elizabeth, consorted with the social elite, and became a beneficent patron of several literary figures, including Thomas Nashe, Gervase Markham and William Shakespeare. He also became romantically involved with Elizabeth Vernon, the Queen's lady-in-waiting and Essex's cousin, whom he eventually married. In 1596 and 1597 he joined Essex's expeditions to Cadiz and the Azores respectively, and in 1599 he served under Essex as General of the Horse in Ireland. The following year he fought briefly under Lord Mountjoy, Essex's successor in Ireland, and unsuccessfully sought the governorship of Connaught. Disappointed by the Queen's rejection, he returned to England in Sept. 1600 and joined Essex in London. Several months later he actively participated in Essex's abortive rebellion, only to be apprehended, convicted of high treason, attainted and sentenced to death. In the eleventh hour, however, the Queen spared his life. After James I's accession Southampton received a royal pardon and several favors. He was installed a Knight of the Garter, restored to his title, and regularly attended the King. But, never fully trusted because of his role in the Essex conspiracy, Southampton received no high office from James and exercised little political power, except in Parliament. In the House of Lords he gradually became the acknowledged leader of a faction opposed to the King's policies and to royal favorites such as Northampton, Suffolk and Somerset. He also used his influence to secure the election of MPs supportive of his views. In the Parliament of 1614 he developed close ties with the opposition in the House of Commons and in 1621 worked with country leaders such as Sir Edwin Sandys,* his close associate in the Virginia Company, to bring about the impeachment of Sir Francis Bacon and attack the patents of monopoly. He also led the abortive attack on the Marquis of Buckingham. On 16 June, shortly after the adjournment of Parliament, Southampton was arrested together with Sandys and John Selden,* and closely questioned about his connections in the House of Commons as well as clandestine dealings with the ambassador of the Elector Palatine Frederick V, who had been strongly lobbying for a Spanish war. The Earl's role in the revival of parliamentary impeachment, the major constitutional innovation of the decade, was attested in his interrogatories, where he was asked whether he did not 'wish that the House of Commons had power of judicature.' At first Southampton stood on his parliamentary privilege, but when threatened with the loss of his pensions, worth £3000 p.a., he submitted and subsequently retired to his estates for the remainder of the Parliament.

In the interval between parliaments, Southampton interested himself in the affairs of the Virginia Company, of which he was treasurer and chief patron. In Oct. 1623 a crisis occurred when James supported the efforts of a faction headed by the Earl of Warwick* to wrest away control of the company and moved to revoke its charter. The episode had considerable repercussion in the Parliament of 1624. Southampton exerted his electoral influence to the full; some 10% of the MPs returned were shareholders in the company. But support also came from an unexpected quarter as Buckingham and Prince Charles, now resolved on war, assiduously courted the Earl. Clear evidence of their collaboration in 1624 is apparent, though doubtless it would have proved temporary, as in the case of Pembroke,* Sandys, Phelips* and other opposition leaders.

In Aug. 1624 Southampton led a contingent of English soldiers against the Spanish in the Low Countries. In autumn contagion struck his regiment, then stationed at Rossendaal. His son and heir, Lord Wriothesley, succumbed on 5 Nov., and five days later, while transporting his son's body back to England for burial, the Earl himself died at Bergen-op-Zoom. Father and son were buried in the Titchfield parish churchyard on 28 Dec. Southampton's premature death removed a potent figure. As colonizer, connoisseur and military commander, he was a man of Elizabethan scope. A superb parliamentarian, his influence in the Commons was unrivalled except by Pembroke, and he would surely have been prominent in the political crisis of Charles' early reign.

C.C. Stopes, *The Life of Henry, Third Earl of Southampton, Shakespeare's Patron* (1922); A.L. Rowse, *Shakespeare's Southampton* (1965); G.P.V. Akrigg, *Shakespeare and the Earl of Southampton* (1968); Ruigh; 'New Light on the Last Days and Death of Henry Wriothesley, Earl of Southampton,' *HLQ*, 37:59-69; Zaller; *DNB*; *Cabala sive scrinia sacra* (1691 ed.); Chamberlain.

V.F. Snow

WRITER (or Wrighter), Clement (fl. 1627-1658)

Seeker, was a Worcester clothier who was persuaded to relinquish his Presbyterian views for Independency about 1638 after reading the works of John Robinson.* He continued his spiritual pilgrimage by adopting General Baptist views. In 1641 he toured Gloucestershire with Thomas Lamb,* whose church he joined. He then apparently fell under the influence of Richard Overton's* *Mans Mortalitie* (1644), and by 1645 he was in London asserting the mortality of the soul and professing Seeker (and soon Leveller) principles. He was also attending public meetings of other sectaries to encourage petitions to Parliament and distributing literature asserting his views. Among his friends was William Walwyn.* About 1653 Writer had a conference with Richard Baxter, who injudiciously labelled him an infidel, a Papist and a Seeker. From Baxter he subsequently received a copy of *The Unreasonableness of Infidelity* (1655), in which Baxter repudiated his assertions that no one had to believe in Christ's miracles unless he saw them. Writer promptly annotated the book to show Baxter his errors and returned it to him in Dec. 1655. Writer then turned his attention to composing *Fides divina: The Ground of True Faith Asserted* (1657), in which he argued that the Bible was fallible due to errors of transcription and translation. He also raised the question of canonicity by pointing to disagreements on which books were inspired. Baxter responded by inviting him to Worcester, but failed to shake Writer's unorthodoxy and attacked him in *A Second Sheet for the Ministry*, to which Writer retorted with *An Apologetical Narration* (1658). Writer was living in London in Sept. 1658.

Writer, who claimed not to have been formally educated, professed to write for 'the middle sort, and plain-hearted people, who are sincere lovers of truth.' He was extremely chary of the use of human learning in understanding Scripture, pointing out that Catholics perverted the Bible despite their learning. Saving faith was only possible by divine evidence (e.g. miracles): 'No unconverted . . . man, is bound by God upon pain of damnation to believe and obey the Gospel, without divine evidence, to attest unto him the truth thereof.' It was thus only natural that he commended Samuel How's* *The Sufficiencie of the Spirits Teaching*, though he also spoke well of John Goodwin.* Writer was scathing in his condemnation of Presbyterian polity: 'I perceive their government is imperial and king-like: their parishes their kingdoms, . . . and their silly parishioners their subjects and vassals.' A corollary of this was his political conviction that just power derives from the consent of the governed.

Rel. Bax., 1:116; *Gangraena* (3rd ed., 1646), pt. 2, pp. 27-28; *DNB*; Hill, *WTUD*; Tolmie.

R.L. Greaves

WROTH, Sir Thomas (1584-1672)

Colonizer and parliamentary radical, MP 1628, 1645, 1656, 1659, 1660 (Bridgwater). Wroth was born in London, the eldest son of Thomas Wroth (d. 1610), a lawyer of the Inner Temple, and Joan, daughter and heiress of Thomas Bulmer of London. Wroth's grandfather was the prominent politician Sir Thomas Wroth (d. 1573). He was baptized at St. Stephen's on 5 May 1584, and matriculated as a commoner from Gloucester Hall (later renamed Worcester College), Oxf. on 1 July 1600. Wroth left Oxford without a degree, and entered the Inner Temple as a student with his brother Peter in 1606. With the death of his father, Wroth inherited a great deal of wealth, with which he purchased the Somerset estates from his bankrupt cousin Sir Robert Wroth, where he subsequently resided at Petherton. On 14 Oct. 1613 he was knighted. Wroth joined the Virginia Company in 1609 through his brother-in-law Sir Nathaniel Rich,* and became a leading member of the Warwick* faction which opposed Sir Edwin Sandys* from 1621 to 1624. He became a Council member for New England on 3 Nov. 1620, and after serving in this post for many years was made commissioner for the government of the Bermudas on 25 June 1653.

Wroth entered Parliament in 1628 as MP for Bridgwater. In Sept. 1635 the government seized a letter in which Wroth lamented the state of religion and hinted at violent resistance. His post as Sheriff of Somersetshire in 1639-40 debarred him from the Short Parliament, but he delivered the Somerset petition against episcopacy to the Commons on 25 Feb. 1642. Wroth served under the Earl of Stamford in the Civil War (Jan. 1643), raising forces in western Somerset, and sat on the County Commission as an influential ally of John Pyne.* In Dec. 1645 he was returned to Parliament for Bridgwater, whose recorder he was, succeeding his brother Peter (d. 1644). On 3 Jan. 1648 Wroth made the motion that the King should be impeached and the country settled without him in a violent speech in which he demanded 'any government rather than that of kings.' He was subsequently appointed one of the judges to try Charles, but attended only one session. Wroth was appointed a Militia Commissioner in Somerset and raised forces against the Levellers in the spring of 1649. A Presbyterian elder, he distinguished himself in the second Protectorate Parliament by demanding the death penalty against Nayler* in a speech whose ferocity again recalled the nickname of 'Wrath' which opponents had given him. Wroth sat again in Richard Cromwell's* Parliament, the restored Rump and the convention Parliament.

With the Restoration Wroth lived in retirement on his Somerset estates. He died at the age of 88 on 11 July 1672. He left no children, and his estates passed to his grand-nephew Sir John Wroth. Wroth had a literary turn, writing *The Destruction of Troy, or the Acts of Aeneas, Translated out of the Second Booke of the Aeneads of Virgil*, and *Abortive of an Idle Hour, or a Centurie of Epigrams* in 1620. His only other work was an account of his wife Margaret, daughter of Richard Rich of Leighs, Essex, who died of a fever on 14 Oct. 1635. This work was included in the Duke of Manchester's *Court and Society from Elizabeth to Anne* and also published separately in 1635.

DNB; Gardiner, *GCW*; Underdown, *PP* and *SCWI*; Worden; Barnes.

W.W. MacDonald

WROTH, William (1576-1642)

Puritan minister, was born near Abergavenny, Mon. He attended three Oxford colleges: he entered New Inn Hall on 27

Nov. 1590, received a B.A. from Christ Church on 18 Feb. 1596, and an M.A. from Jesus Coll. on 26 June 1605. In 1613 Wroth was presented to the rectory at Llanfihangel Roggiatt, and in 1617 (or possibly in 1611) to the rectory at Llanvaches (both in Monmouthshire). Wroth's early Puritanism emerged from the tradition of strong support for the Reformation in sixteenth century South Wales. In his time Wales still suffered widespread abuse in church discipline and an extreme scarcity of competent preaching ministers. Puritan zeal in the 1620s and 1630s and the influence on South Wales of the Bristol churches generated a new surge of reforming spirit in the region where Wroth served. As one of the earliest ministers instrumental in establishing and maintaining contact with English Puritanism, Wroth was associated with St. Philip's parish in Bristol as early as 1613, and from it imported reform ideas.

In the 1620s and early 1630s Wroth opposed Archibishop Laud's efforts to discipline the clergy and to enforce the ritual and the Book of Sports in Wales. His opposition induced the Bishop of St. David's to call him before the Court of High Commission on 20 Oct. 1635. A three-year trial – with many charges, rebuttals and adjournments – followed, and Wroth was expelled (or he resigned) from his living.

That event marked the turning point in his career. Together with Walter Cradock,* who had been suspended from St. Mary's, Cardiff, Wroth formed the first Independent congregation in Wales, at Llanchaves, in Nov. 1639 with the help of Henry Jessey,* pastor of the parent Independent congregation in London. Wroth's congregation continued to maintain close contact with the Puritan church at Bristol, at which Wroth frequently preached. According to William Erbery,* the new Llanvaches church, of which Wroth was now chief pastor, was formed 'according to the New England pattern,' a loosely structured gathered congregation.

Wroth's later doctrine was radically simplified. He saw himself simply as a 'preacher of God's Word,' and when denounced for 'uncanonical practices' by the Bishop of Llandaff in 1635, replied, 'there are thousands of immortal souls around me thronging to perdition, and should I not use all means likely to succeed to save them?' His emphasis on simple Gospel truth and the saving of souls, which flew implicitly in the face of rites and ritual, authority and hierarchy, made him a major forerunner of revolutionary religious thought, although he continued to believe that separation was not irrevocable.

Wroth died early in 1642. His congregation moved that year to the parliamentary city of Bristol, and then in 1643 to London, where it continued to flourish. Wroth was granted his final wish to die before the 'trump of war' had sounded, but he had, by that time, paved the way for the future growth of the Independent churches in South Wales. When he died, the man whom his successor Walter Cradock* called the 'blessed apostle of South Wales' willed his three acres of land to an endowment for the poor of the parish. He was buried at his request in the chancel of the Llanvaches church, rather than the meeting-house he founded and for which he is remembered.

DWB; J.W. James, *A Church History of Wales* (1945); Richards, *PMW*; H.L. Short, 'Wales and the Ejection,' in *The Beginnings of Non-Conformity* (1964); H. Thomas, *A History of Wales* (1972); Hayden, *RCCB*.

N.F. Collins

Y

YATES, John (c. 1590-1660)

Independent minister, was admitted sizar at Emmanuel Coll., Camb. in 1604, and commenced B.A. in 1608, M.A. in 1611 and B.D. in 1618. John Robinson's* *The Peoples Plea for the Exercise of Prophecy* (1618), written against Yates, identifies him as a preacher in St. Andrews, Norwich (1616-22). In 1622 Yates was presented to the Rectories of St. Mary with St. John, Stiffkey, Norf., by Sir Nathaniel Bacon.* He held St. Mary's until 1658. Both he and Samuel Ward,* who attacked Richard Montagu for his Arminianism, are identified as preachers in Ipswich in 1624 by Peter Heylyn. Yates' reply to Montagu's *Appello Caesarem* appeared in 1626 as *Ibis ad Caesarem*, yet his hostility to popish and Arminian views had clearly been established in *Gods Arraignment of Hypocrites* (1615). Besides these works he published *A Short and Briefe Summe of Saving Knowledge* (1621), which was expanded in 1622 as *A Modell of Divinitie* and further enlarged in 1623. Yates assisted William Greenhill* and William Adderly in editing Jeremiah Burroughs'* writings and brought out William Bridge's* works. He was a signator of *A Renunciation and Declaration of the Ministers of Congregational Churches . . . in the City of London* (1661), a denunciation of Venner's Fifth Monarchy plot.

B. Hanbury, *Historical Memorials Relating to the Independents* (1839); *DNB*; Nuttall, *HSPFE*; P. Heylyn, *Cyprianus Anglicus* (1668).

R. Masek

YAXLEY, John (c. 1615-1687)

Ejected minister, was born at Cambridge, the son of John Yaxley. He was educated at Perse School and on 22 Feb. 1632 entered Christ's Coll., Camb., graduating B.A. in 1636 and M.A. in 1639. At Peterborough Yaxley was ordained deacon (12 June 1636) and priest (4 June 1637), and in 1639 became Rector of Stibbington, Hunts. After the outbreak of the Civil War he was appointed Rector of Thornhaugh, Northants. (5 Dec. 1642), but was ousted by royalist forces, prompting an appeal to the Committee for Plundered Ministers on 16 May 1646. He became Rector of Conington, Cambs. in 1644, resigning in 1647. When William Hunt was ejected as Rector of Kibworth Beauchamp, Leics., Yaxley took his place on 14 Apr. 1647, but Hunt was restored on 8 July. The rectory was again given to Yaxley on 22 Sept. 1654, but Hunt sued in the assize, claiming Yaxley had had him forcibly ejected by soldiers. An assize verdict in Hunt's favor was stayed by the Council of State on 13 June, but on 12 Feb. 1655 the Council approved a compromise giving Yaxley the rectory in return for paying Hunt £120 the first year and thereafter £80 p.a. for life. Yaxley was an assistant to the Leicestershire Commission in 1654. At the Restoration he preached that 'hell was broke loose,' which resulted in accusations of treason against him in the House of Lords on 12 July 1660. He was ejected from Kibworth Beauchamp sometime prior to 23 Aug. 1660, and thereafter preached near West Smithfield. Under the Declaration of Indulgence Yaxley was licensed in 1672 as a Congregational minister, at which time he was living in Holborn, London. By his wife Priscilla he had a son John, who became an Anglican minister, and two daughters, Ann and Rebecca. His will, dated 7 Sept. 1687, was proved on 13 Dec. 1687.

Al. Cant.; Calamy; *Calamy Revised*; *LJ*, 11:89; *CSPD, Comm.*, 7:207-208, 382-83, 403; 8:36-37; *Chas. II*, 13:377. Papers: LPR.

R.L. Greaves

SUPPLEMENTARY BIBLIOGRAPHY

Ainsworth, Henry M.E. Moody. ' "A Man of a Thousand": The Reputation and Character of Henry Ainsworth, 1569/70-1622,' *HLQ*, 45:200-14

Alford, Edward P.W. Hasler, *The History of Parliament: The Commons*, 3 vols. (1981) (hereafter: Hasler); R. Zaller, 'Edward Alford and the Making of Country Radicalism,' *JBS*, 22 (1983): 59-79. N.B.: Alford served for Beverley in the Parliament of 1593.

Allen, Francis A.W. McIntosh, 'The Numbers of the English Regicides,' *History*, 67 (1982): 195-216 (hereafter: McIntosh)

Andrewes, Thomas McIntosh

Alaby, John Woolrych

Bampfield, Francis R.L. Greaves, *Saints and Rebels* (1985) (hereafter: Greaves, *SR*)

Barebone, Praisegod Woolrych

Barrington, Sir Francis Hasler; A. Searle, ed., *Barrington Family Letters 1628-1632* (Camden Society, 4th Series, vol. 28, 1983) (hereafter: Searle)

Barrington, Sir Thomas Searle

Bellers, John J.C. Davis, *Utopia and the Ideal Society* (1981) (hereafter: Davis)

Bennet, Robert Woolrych

Blake, Robert Woolrych

Blount, Thomas Woolrych

Bourchier, Sir John Searle

Browne, John Woolrych

Bunyan, John R.L. Greaves, 'John Bunyan and the Fifth Monarchists,' *Albion*, 13 (1981): 83-95

Calamy, Edmund Greaves, *SR*

Caley, Jacob Woolrych

Carew, John Woolrych

Chamberlen, Peter Davis

Clarke, John R.L. Greaves, 'A Colonial Fifth Monarchist? John Clarke of Rhode Island,' *Rhode Island History*, 40 (1981): 41-47

Clarkson, Lawrence D.G. Greene, 'Muggletonians and Quakers: A Study in the Interaction of Seventeenth-Century Dissent,' *Albion*, 15 (1983): 102-122 (hereafter: Greene)

Coke, Sir Edward Hasler

Cooper, Anthony Ashley Woolrych

Courtney, Hugh Woolrych

Croft, Sir Herbert Hasler

Cromwell, Henry Woolrych

Culmer, Richard	R.L. Greaves, 'A Puritan Firebrand: Richard Culmer of Canterbury,' *Historical Magazine of the Protestant Episcopal Church*, 50 (1981): 359-68; Greaves, *SR*
Danvers, Henry	R.L. Greaves, 'The Tangled Careers of Two Stuart Radicals: Henry and Robert Danvers,' *BQ*, 29 (1981): 32-43; Greaves, *SR*; G.F. Nuttall, 'Henry Danvers, His Wife and the "Heavenly Line",' *BQ*, 29 (1982): 217; Woolrych
Danvers, Robert	R.L. Greaves, 'The Tangled Careers of Two Stuart Radicals: Henry and Robert Danvers,' *BQ*, 29 (1981): 32-43
Duckenfield, Robert	Woolrych
Dury, John	D.S. Katz, *Philo-Semitism and the Readmission of the Jews to England, 1603-1655* (1981) (hereafter: Katz)
Evans, Arise	Katz
Finch, Sir Henry	Hasler
Fleetwood, George	Woolrych
Fuller, Nicholas	Hasler
Gerard, Sir Gilbert	Searle
Goodwin, John	E.S. More, 'John Goodwin and the Origins of the New Arminianism,' *JBS*, 22 (199): 50-70
Griffith, George	Greaves, *SR*
Hakewill, William	Hasler
Hammond, Thomas	McIntosh
Hampden, Richard	L.G. Schwoerer, *The Declaration of Rights, 1689* (1981)
Harvey, Edmond	McIntosh
Hastings, Sir Francis	Hasler
Helwys, Thomas	B.R. White, *The English Baptists of the Seventeenth Century* (1983)
Heveningham, William	McIntosh
Hobson, Paul	Greaves, *SR*
Holland, Cornelius	McIntosh
Jessey, Henry	B.R. White, 'Henry Jessey, a Pastor in Politics,' *BQ*, 25: 98-110; B.R. Dailey, 'Youth and the New Jerusalem: The English Catechistical Tradition and Henry Jessey's *Catechisme for Babes* (1652),' *Harvard Library Bulletin*, 33: 25-54
Knollys, Sir Francis	Hasler
Lawson, George	C. Condren, '*Sacra* Before *Civilis*: Understanding the Ecclesiastical Politics of George Lawson,' *Journal of Religious History*, 11 (1981): 524-35
Lisle, John	McIntosh
Locke, John	N. Wood, *The Politics of Locke's Philisophy: A Social Study of "An Essay Concerning Human Understanding"* (1983)
***Love, Nicholas**	McIntosh
Luke, Sir Oliver	Hasler
Masham, Sir William	Searle
Martin, Richard	Hasler
Milton, John	A.N. Wilson, *The Life of John Milton* (1983)
Muggleton, Lodowick	Greene
Owen, Sir Roger	Hasler
Perrot, Sir James	Hasler
Reeve, John	Greene

Robinson, John   T. George, *John Robinson and the English Separatist Tradition* (1982)

Sandys, Sir Edwin   Hasler

Simpson, John   Greaves, *SR*

Sterry, Peter   N.I. Matar, 'Peter Sterry and the Ranters,' *Notes and Queries*, 29: 504-6

N.I. Matar, 'Peter Sterry. The Millenium and Oliver Cromwell', *Journal of the United Reformed Church History Society*, 2:334-42.

*Wallop, Sir Henry Hasler

CORRIGENDA

vol. 1, p. 1, col. 2, l. 4	Tillingham
vol. 1, p. 4, col. 1, l. 27	Warmsworth
vol. 1, p. 9, col. 2, l. 10	Yeovil
vol. 1, p. 16, col. 1, ll. 29-33	read: In 1644 Amyraut . . its publication
vol. 1, p. 16, col. 1, ll. 43-44	read: a resolute Puritan
vol. 1, p. 21, col. 1, l. 30	Levellers
vol. 1, p. 30, col. 1, l. 46	Hewson's
vol. 1, p. 38, col. 1, l. 6	There is also a 1642 edition.
vol. 1, p. 40, col. 2, l. 7	Ketton is the colloquial for Kedington
vol. 1, p. 42, col. 1, l. 11	Leighs
vol. 1, p. 42, col. 2, l. 16	Francis'
vol. 1, p. 49, col. 1, l. 39	Wood
vol. 1, p. 51, col. 1, ll. 9-10	Wetherfield
vol. 1, p. 52, col. 1, l. 22	Little Easton
vol. 1, p. 53, col. 1, l. 36	Oundle
vol. 1, p. 56, col. 2, l. 4	Wokingham
vol. 1, p. 60, col. 1, l. 9	Hutton
vol. 1, p. 61, col. 1, l. 11	Elmswell
vol. 1, p. 64, col. 1, l. 39-40	Witham Friary
vol. 1, p. 68, col. 1, l. 4	St. Augustine's
vol. 1, p. 70, col. 2, l. 2-3	Southcote, Reading, Berks.
vol. 1, p. 77, col. 2, l. 44	Delete: Blower then founded . . . members.
vol. 1, p. 78, col. 1, l. 1	
vol. 1, p. 78, col. 1, l. 11-12	Read: Northampton, whose covenant was signed by about 164 members; William Shepherd . . .
vol. 1, p. 80, col. 2, l. 3-4	Hardness
vol. 1, p. 80, col. 2, l. 46-47	read: Sidney* sent by Richard Cromwell's* government to mediate
vol. 1, p. 83, col. 2, l. 35	Beningbrough
vol. 1, p. 85, col. 1, l. 12	Henry Burton*
vol. 1, p. 85, col. 1, l. 35	brothers
vol. 1, p. 92, col. 1, l. 11	Mitton
vol. 1, p. 92, col. 2, l. 45	Sedbergh
vol. 1, p. 93, col. 2, ll. 29-30	read: Vavasor Powell* visited Praisegod Barebone* and Breman . . .
vol. 1, p. 97, col. 2, l. 3	1646
vol. 1, p. 98, col. 1, l. 17	Bawtry
vol. 1, p. 99, col. 1, l. 14	delete: based
vol. 1, p. 102, col. 2, l. 2	read: vicar of Tenbury, Worcs.
vol. 1, p. 102, col. 2, l. 40	*Mistery*
vol. 1, p. 102, col. 2, l. 48	delete: presumably
vol. 1, p. 102, col. 2, ll. 50-51	delete: though the earlier edition has not survived.

vol. 1, p. 105, col. 2, l. 25	Bayly's
vol. 1, p. 120, col. 1, l. 7-8	Friends House
vol. 1, p. 120, col. 2, l. 17	Sedbergh
vol. 1, p. 127, col. 1, l. 9	Samuel
vol. 1, p. 127, col. 2, l. 46	forewords
vol. 1, p. 136, col. 2, l. 42	for Richard Brewer, read Thomas Brewster*
vol. 1, p. 141, col. 1, l. 6	Christ Church
vol. 1, p. 148, col. 1, l. 44	Golding
vol. 1, p. 151, col. 1, l. 26	Edmondson

vol. 1, p. 151, col. 1, l. 38-40;
           col. 2, l. 17;
  p. 152, col. 1, l. 36;
           col. 2, l. 23
	Bletchingley

vol. 1, p. 153, col. 2, l. 33	Kendal
vol. 1, p. 156, col. 1, l. 8	read: near Hungerford, Berks.
vol. 1, p. 159, col. 1, l. 26	Henley
vol. 1, p. 163, col. 1, l. 33	Nether
vol. 1, p. 165, col. 1, l. 51	Bridlington
vol. 1, p. 165, col. 2, l. 3	Tadcaster
vol. 1, p. 168, col. 2, l. 43	More
vol. 1, p. 173, col. 1, l. 28	Carrickfergus
vol. 1, p. 174, col. 1, l. 53	Barnes
vol. 1, p. 177, col. 1, l. 18	1665
vol. 1, p. 179, col. 1, l. 17	read: in Boston, Lincs.
vol. 1, p. 179, col. 2, ll. 43-44	Theddingworth
vol. 1, p. 181, col. 2, l. 22	read: to the
vol. 1, p. 184, col. 2, l. 26	Peverell
vol. 1, p. 187, col. 1, l. 15	add: Cradock's patron was the Earl of Essex.*
vol. 1, p. 187, col. 2, l. 43	Llanvair Waterdine
vol. 1, p. 192, col. 2, l. 15	Hilborough, Norf.
vol. 1, p. 193, col. 2, l. 29	read: Richard Cromwell's government ordered him
vol. 1, p. 195, col. 2, l. 7	Wicken
vol. 1, p. 195, col. 2, l. 26	read: Royston, across the county line in Herts.
vol. 1, p. 201, col. 1, l. 9	politicking
vol. 1, p. 201, col. 1, l. 35	at
vol. 1, p. 206, col. 1, l. 18	Goodnestone
vol. 1, p. 207, col. 2, l. 1	for Kent, read Surrey
vol. 1, p. 208, col. 2, l. 24	Alphege
vol. 1, p. 211, col. 1, l. 9	Moddershall
vol. 1, p. 214, col. 1, l. 22	Northallerton
vol. 1, p. 218, col. 2, l. 35	(fl. 1647-1661)
vol. 1, p. 223, col. 1, l. 40	Pirton
vol. 1, p. 225, col. 2, l. 26	for Mon., read Glos.
vol. 1, p. 235, col. 1, l. 30	Leyton
vol. 1, p. 235, col. 1, l. 46	Dukinfield
vol. 1, p. 235, col. 2, l. 39	ejecting
vol. 1, p. 238, col. 2, l. 34	Quendon
vol. 1, p. 239, col. 2, l. 28	Coggeshall
vol. 1, p. 240, col. 1, ll. 9, 17	Much Hadham
vol. 1, p. 244, col. 1, ll. 1-2	Dukinfield

vol. 1, p. 244, col. 1, l. 35	Largan
vol. 1, p. 250, col. 1, ll. 38-39	Llandecwyn
vol. 1, p. 250, col. 2, ll. 2, 17	(now Dolgellau)
vol. 1, p. 250, col. 2, l. 28	Barwick-in-Elmet
vol. 1, p. 251, col. 1, ll. 8, 11	Waddesdon
vol. 1, p. 254, col. 2, l. 19	who
vol. 1, p. 272, col. 2, l. 14	Heidelberg
vol. 1, p. 276, col. 1, ll. 10-11	read: all of whom (except George)
vol. 1, p. 284, col. 2, l.42	Sowerby
vol. 1, p. 292, col. 2, l. 38	Kirkby
vol. 1, p. 294, col. 2, ll. 43-46	delete: telling Thomas Hooker, 'you were as good yield to the English bishops as to the Dutch classes.'
vol. 1, p. 301, col. 1, l. 8	bewitchment
vol. 2, p. 3, col. 2, l. 23	for at, read with
vol. 2, p. 3, col. 2, l. 18	St. Benet
vol. 2, p. 6, col. 1, l. 28	Bishop's
vol. 2, p. 6, col. 1, l. 31	Draycot
vol. 2, p. 9, col. 2, ll. 20, 27	Edgmond
vol. 2, p. 17 col. 2, l. 47	(or Bletchingley)
vol. 2, p. 29, col. 2, ll. 17-18	Delamere
vol. 2, p. 36, col. 1, l. 27	(or Hevingham)
vol. 2, p. 36, col. 2, l. 12; p. 37, col. 1, l. 15	Bridgford
vol. 2, p. 43, col. 1, l. 38	Dronfield
vol. 2, p. 44, col. 2, l. 48	Carisbrooke
vol. 2, p. 48, col. 1, l. 26	Mainwaring
vol. 2, p. 60, col. 2, l. 45	Orlestone
vol. 2, p. 68, col. 1, l. 37	Melbourne
vol. 2, p. 69, col. 2, l. 36	Noseley
vol. 2, p. 69, col. 2, l. 41	Lilford
vol. 2, p. 70, col. 1, l. 45	Lansdowne
vol. 2, p. 70, col. 1, l. 50	Cheriton
vol. 2, p. 82, col. 2, l. 24	Wilts.
vol. 2, p. 87, col. 1, l. 46	Martock, Som.
vol. 2, p. 95, col. 1, l. 46	Surrey
vol. 2, p. 109, col. 2, ll. 10, 14, 46	Markshall
vol. 2, p. 113, col. 1, l. 29	Noseley
vol. 2, p. 129, col. 1, l. 25	Isleham
vol. 2, p. 143, col. 1, l. 24	Droylsden
vol. 2, p. 171, col. 2, l. 7	Sandford
vol. 2, p. 175, col. 1, l. 17	Isleham
vol. 2, p. 185, col. 1, l. 8	to the bar of Lincoln's Inn
vol. 2, p. 185, col. 2, l. 38	the Commonwealth
vol. 2, p. 190, col. 1, l. 29	Offerton
vol. 2, p. 198, col. 1, ll. 37-38	Ilchester
vol. 2, p. 198, col. 2, l. 12	Albemarle
vol. 2, p. 199, col. 1, ll. 45, 46 p. 199, col. 2, l. 11	Eton
vol. 2, p. 201, col. 1, l. 12	Youghal
vol. 2, p. 201, col. 1, l. 39	Stratton

vol. 2, p. 207, col. 2, l. 20	Bóteller
vol. 2, p. 212, col. 2, l. 39	Blythburgh
vol. 2, p. 212, col. 2, l. 44	Cookley
vol. 2, p. 214, col. 2, l. 16	Carlow
vol. 2, p. 217, col. 1, l. 12	Essex
vol. 2, p. 222, col. 1, l. 19	Colaton Raleigh
vol. 2, p. 226, col. 2, l. 41	Totnes
vol. 2, p. 232, col. 1, l. 9	Hedgerley
vol. 2, p. 235, col. 1, l. 29	Romford
vol. 2, p. 253, col. 1, l. 12	St. Germans
vol. 2, p. 265, col. 1, l. 19	Dorset
vol. 2, p. 265, col. 2, l. 9	Chaddleworth
vol. 2, p. 271, col. 1, l. 3	Wednesbury
vol. 2, p. 271, col. 1, l. 3	Sedgeley
vol. 2, p. 276, col. 2, l. 4	(now Cullompton)
vol. 2, p. 282, col. 1, l. 18	
p. 283, col. 2, l. 18	Stadhampton

INDEX

This index is restricted to radicals who are the subjects of entries in the Dictionary. Except for his own entry, Oliver Cromwell is not indexed. Other radicals are indexed only on their first appearance in any given entry.

Firmin, Thomas, *1:282-84*; 1:172; 2:74,
236, 269
Fisher, James, *1:284*; 1:195
Fisher, Mary, *1:285*; 2:108; 3:64, 295, 315
Fisher, Samuel, *1:285-86*; 1:130; 2:91, 166;
3:217
Fitch, Thomas, *1:286-87*
Fitten, James, *1:287*
Flavel, John, *1:287*
Fleetwood, Charles, *1:287-89*; 1:5, 11, 30,
45, 58, 59, 67, 69, 133, 149, 154, 155, 167,
194, 201, 210, 219, 226, 290, 298; 2:31, 62,
68, 83, 85(2), 148, 169, 204, 232, 274, 283;
3:1, 68, 117, 133, 149, 161, 204, 220, 223,
235, 246, 272, 280, 293, 302, 308
Fleetwood, George, *1:289-90*; 1:189, 295
Fletcher, Andrew, *1:290-92*; 2:253
Fletcher, Elizabeth, *1:292*; 2:107; 3:295
Foley, Paul, *1:292-94*
Forbes, John, *1:294-95*; 3:31
Ford, Stephen, *1:295*; 2:215, 246
Ford, Thomas, *1:295-96*
Foster, George, *1:296-97*
Fowke, John, *1:297-98*; 2:210
Fownes, George, *1:298-99*; 1:33; 3:2
Fox, George, *1:299-302*; 1:4, 25, 29, 36, 48,
49, 54, 59, 68, 74(2), 84, 93, 102, 107(2),
119, 120, 130, 144, 153, 174, 183, 201,
214, 228, 232, 253, 257, 269, 272, 273,
275, 285(2), 292; 2:2, 37, 74, 105, 107,
112, 117, 118, 122, 138, 145, 152, 157,
179, 216(2), 235, 256, 257, 271, 281; 3:1,
6, 7, 10, 15, 23, 24, 30, 64, 74, 81, 97, 105,
134, 160, 209, 210, 216, 226, 239, 245,
247, 252, 296, 314, 315, 319, 321, 325
Fox, George, the Younger, *1:302-3*
Fox, Margaret. See Fell, Margaret.
Franklin, William, *1:304*; 2:1; 3:101, 224
Frankyn, Robert, *1:304*
Freeman, Francis, *1:305*; 2:273
Freeze, James, *1:305-6*
Fry, John, *1:306*; :233; 2:60
Fuller, Nicholas, *1:306-7*; 3:282
Furly, Benjamin, *1:307-8*; 2:177; 3:26, 172,
217, 244

Gadbury, Mary, *2:1*; 1:1, 304; 3:101, 293
Gale, Theophilus, *2:1*; 2:183
Gargill, Anne, *2:1-2*
Garland, Augustine, *2:2-3*; 2:245; 3:96
Geare, Allan, *2:3*; 1:287
Gerard, Charles, first Baron Gerard of

Brandon, Viscount Brandon, first Earl
of Macclesfield, *2:4-5*
Gerard, Charles, second Baron Gerard of
Brandon, Viscount Brandon, second
Earl of Macclesfield, *2:5-6*; 2:4, 29
Gerard, Sir Gilbert, *2:6-7*; 1:44; 2:224
Gibbons, Sarah, *2:7*; 3:64, 295
Gibbs, John, *2:7-8*
Gifford, Andrew, *2:8-9*; 3:275
Gifford, John, *2:9*; 1:105
Gilbert, Thomas, *2:9-10*
Gildon, Charles, *2:10*
Gilpin, Richard, *2:10-11*
Gladman, John, *2:11*; 1:93; 2:198
Glasse, Thomas, *2:11-12*; 1:155, 163;
3:210, 273
Goffe, William, *2:12-13*; 1:25, 129, 215,
230, 264; 2:31, 37, 130, 249; 3:30, 45, 74,
183, 218, 306, 311
Goodenough, Richard, *2:13-14*; 1:31, 177;
2:29, 32, 106, 259, 265; 3:120, 275, 303
Goodgroom, Richard, *2:14-15*; 1:53
Goodwin, Arthur, *2:15*; 3:306
Goodwin, John (c.1593-1665), *2:15-17*;
1:60, 109, 116, 129, 283; 2:31, 47, 115,
161, 165, 166; 3:22, 55, 59, 168, 181, 226,
270, 273, 294, 345
Goodwin, John (c.1603-1674), *2:17-18*
Goodwin, Robert, *2:18-19*; 3:200
Goodwin, Thomas, *2:19-21*; 1:18, 78, 102,
109, 116, 215; 2:31, 75, 101, 109, 228, 233,
252, 267, 285; 3:83, 138, 163, 169, 178
Goodyear, Hugh, *2:21-22*
Gouge, Robert, 2:22
Gould, Nicholas, *2:22*
Gower, Thomas, *2:23*; 2:95; 3:241
Grantham, Thomas, *2:23-24*; 1:115; 3:33
Gratton, John, *2:25*; 2:256
Greenhill, William, *2:25-26*; 1:78, 99, 108,
140, 176; 2:31, 233; 3:28, 176, 183, 254
Greville, Robert, second Lord Brooke,
2:26-28; 1:82, 109, 238, 279, 286; 2:15, 48,
67, 70, 119, 186; 3:67, 90, 123, 138, 189,
206
Grey, Baron, of Groby. See Grey,
Thomas
Grey, Ford, third Baron Grey of Wark,
Earl of Tankerville, *2:28-29*; 2:4, 5, 14,
50; 3:119, 276
Grey, Thomas, Baron Grey of Groby,
2:30; 1:219; 2:37; 3:162, 186, 277
Griffith, George, *2:30-32*; 1:118, 156, 295;